THE
WESTERN GREEKS

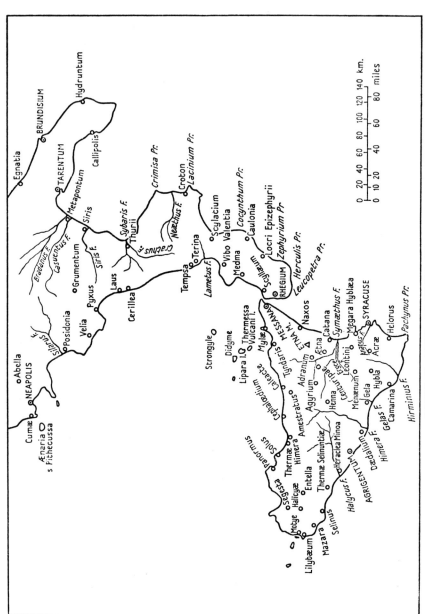

Cuma̱
Ænaria o
s Pithecussa

Abella
o
NEAPOLIS o

Egnatia
o

BRUNDISIUM

Hydruntum
o

Posidonia
o

TARENTUM
o
Metapontum o
Siris o

Grumentum
o

Pyxus o

Silarus F.

Callipolis

Velia o

Laus o

Bradanus F.
Casuentus F.
Siris F.

Sybaris F.

Thurii o

Crimisa Pr.

Cerillea o

Tempsa o

Crathis F.

Terina o

Neæthus F.

Croton
o

Lacinium Pr.

Scylacium
o

Lametus F.

Vibo Valentia
o
Medma o

Cocynthum Pr.

Caulonia
o

Locri Epizephyrii
o
Zephyrium Pr.

Herculis Pr.

Strongyle
o

Didyme
o

Scyllæum
o
RHEGIUM
o

Leucopetra Pr.

Lipara I. o
Thermessa
Vulcani I.
Mylæ o

MESSANA
M.

Naxos
o

Galeacte
o

Tyndaris
o

Adranum
o

ENNA M.

Cephalœdium
o

Amestratus
o

Agyrium
o

Cabana
o
Etna

Symæthus F.

Megara Hyblæa
o
SYRACUSE
o

Panormus o
Thermæ
Himera
o
Himera

Entella
o

Thermæ Selinuntiæ

Heraclea Minoa
o

Henna
o

Leontini
o

Acræ
o

Helorus
o

Centuripæ
iadi

Menænum
o

Amenus F.

Pachynus Pr.

Solus

Segesta
o
Halicyæ o

AGRIGENTUM
o

Hybla
o

Motye o

Selinus o

Dædalium F.
Himera F.
Gelas F.

Gela
o

Camarina
o

Hirminius F.

Lilybæum
o

Mazara o

Halycus F.

SICILY AND SOUTH ITALY

0   20   40   60   80   100 120 140 km.

0   10   20   40   60   80 miles

THE
WESTERN GREEKS

THE HISTORY OF SICILY AND SOUTH ITALY
FROM THE FOUNDATION OF THE
GREEK COLONIES TO
480 B.C.

BY

T. J. DUNBABIN

OXFORD
AT THE CLARENDON PRESS

Oxford University Press, Ely House, London W. I

GLASGOW NEW YORK TORONTO MELBOURNE WELLINGTON
CAPE TOWN SALISBURY IBADAN NAIROBI LUSAKA ADDIS ABABA
BOMBAY CALCUTTA MADRAS KARACHI LAHORE DACCA
KUALA LUMPUR HONG KONG TOKYO

FIRST PUBLISHED 1948
REPRINTED LITHOGRAPHICALLY IN GREAT BRITAIN
AT THE UNIVERSITY PRESS, OXFORD
BY VIVIAN RIDLER, PRINTER TO THE UNIVERSITY
1968

PREFACE

SICILY and south Italy together form the chief colonial region of the Greek world. Their coasts offered, more nearly than any other part of the Mediterranean, conditions similar to those of Greece; no strong and warlike race barred access; and so they were already dotted with colonies before less favoured regions began to be opened up. Here, as nowhere else outside the Aegean, were physical and social conditions favourable to reproduce the life of the city-state. The colonies equalled in population and power the cities of Old Greece, and made considerable contributions to Greek culture. They remained Greek long into the Roman domination, and the Greek spirit is even to-day not lost.

The title of Great Greece which was given to the south Italian colonies is extended by Strabo to include Sicily. Much would be lost by considering the two districts separately. They do not come into direct political relations until the fifth century; but they form an economic and cultural whole, so that a composite picture can be formed of life in the whole region. South Italy is less known and, in many respects, more interesting than Sicily; politically, economically, and artistically the Italian colonies reach independence of Old Greece earlier. Sicily has been more studied, and also there is more to be known, for the evidence is fuller.

Colonial history is threefold: relations with the mother country; development within the colonies; and relations with other races. The first is largely a matter of inference from archaeological evidence, for the literary sources record little. The second also can be only very briefly described, for lack of evidence; we have material for a full picture of Syracuse and some other colonies in the fifth and later centuries, but not of the period of growth. Among other races, the Phoenicians and Etruscans were the chief rivals of the Greeks in the West. The record of the relations between Greeks and Carthaginians is almost all one of wars, but the Greeks certainly had great influence on their adversaries, and had gain as well as loss from contact with them. The action of Greek culture on the Etruscans is too long a story to go into here: it is a subject as considerable as that of this book and, for the history of Italy and the world, perhaps of more moment. The hellenizing of

Campania and Apulia also lies beyond my present range. I have limited myself to the colonial region *par excellence*, the Great Greece in which the Greek element far outweighed the native, and omitted those regions where the Greeks were settlers among powerful races which attained some culture of their own.

Nowhere can the process of hellenization be followed so closely as in Sicily. The story has not before been told, and the evidence is complex and difficult to interpret. Though more is known of this than of any other colonial region, the literary evidence is meagre. It can be filled out from other sources, chiefly archaeological. Orsi's forty-five years of brilliant campaigning have produced an immense mass of material, some of which has direct bearing on history in the narrow sense of the word, all of which is relevant to a consideration of the circumstances of life and the colonial spirit. It cannot be expected that the archaeological evidence will always combine harmoniously with the literary history; but here is the attempt. The earlier stages only are dealt with here. By the fourth century the Sikels had lost their own culture, and the Romans found them as Greek as the inhabitants of the Greek colonies.

The question, how much the culture of the colonies owed to the native peoples of Italy and Sicily, has been much discussed in recent years. I am inclined to stress the purity of Greek culture in the colonial cities, and find little to suggest that the Greeks mixed much with Sikel or Italian peoples, or learnt much from them. It may be objected that I take too material a view. But, though there is little evidence of the spiritual content of colonial life, it appears to me that this evidence agrees with that of the fuller remains of material culture; and that, in spite of differences of circumstances, the colonials were not in important ways unlike the Greeks of Old Greece, and held strongly to the traditions of the mother country.

Differences of course there are. Colonial life was larger. Distances were greater than in Greece, and in few cases could the citizens see foreign territory from their city-walls. Material circumstances were easier, as most colonies had rich land and enjoyed the labour of subject races. As a result, life was less intense. The West was no place for fruitful political ideas. When the most progressive states of Greece were evolving democracy, the colonies acquiesced in tyrannies whose only justification lay in military necessities. The colonials were a

pleasure-loving people, sportsmen and athletes, and fond of
good cheer. The first impression they made on the Greeks of
Old Greece was in respect of these qualities. Otherwise they
excelled in practical sciences; the doctors of Kroton were the
first in Greece, some of the earliest big building and engineering
works were Sicilian; the practical art of rhetoric also came from
Sicily. Abstract thought and the higher arts first appear
transplanted from Ionia in Pythagoras and the Eleatic school,
the late archaic art of Lokroi and Pythagoras of Rhegion: all,
be it noted, in Italy, for Sicily has little to compare that is so
original and lively.

I have drawn much on the parallel to the relations between
colonies and mother country provided in Australia and New
Zealand. Here political independence is combined with almost
complete cultural dependence, on which the colonials pride
themselves. Difference in manner of life is due to difference
of material circumstances, and is not enough to destroy the
essential unity. This unity is the pride of most colonials; so
probably in antiquity. The economic life of the ancient colonies
also is illuminated by modern examples. They were, like
Australia until a few years ago, producers of raw materials,
with a few staples on which they grew rich, and importers of
manufactured goods. They brought most of their luxuries and
objects of art from the mother country. In the period under
study here, Corinth occupied the place as supplier of the rich
western market and, we may believe, as chief port of consign-
ment for corn and other exports, which Great Britain has held
with the Dominions. When Corinth's economic supremacy
was challenged, her cultural supremacy also weakened. The
first stages in the emergence of a specifically colonial spirit are
here studied. But it is long before any of the arts produced
work which had not Corinthian models.

Though so much of the material is archaeological and can be
discussed only by archaeological methods, I have tried to keep
before me the purpose of writing a history. Western art
deserves a fuller and more objective treatment than I have
given it, for my chapter on it uses it as a source-book for
history, not as a subject of study in its own right. Literature
also I have discussed only so far as it is evidence for political
history. Some other specialist subjects need to be gone into
more deeply than I, or others, have done.

Few books combine Sicily and south Italy, and none covers

the whole range of this work. In English, only Freeman's *History of Sicily* deals with the same subject; and it is over fifty years old. The only volume published of Pais's *Storia della Sicilia e della Magna Grecia* is almost as old. Since that time no history of Sicily has been written, though south Italy is covered by Ciaceri's *Storia della Magna Grecia*. Since Freeman wrote, a completely new picture of Sicily and south Italy has been revealed by the excavations of Paolo Orsi and his collaborators and successors. The flood of new discoveries has slackened, though not ceased, so this is a good time to incorporate them into a history of the colonies. The method is not new, for Freeman made use of such excavation as there had been before 1890; but scientific excavation had then barely begun. In other respects, Freeman's history stands the test of time, and his treatment of literary sources seldom needs to be departed from or added to substantially. His description of Sicilian sites, all of which he had seen, makes anything more of that kind unnecessary. Holm's older study is also valuable in both these respects. Lenormant has rendered the same service for the sites and country-side of south Italy. Randall-MacIver has given a brief up-to-date account of the Greek cities where most excavation has been done. For Sicily, Pace's *Arte e Civiltà della Sicilia Antica* offers a full-length integration of the results of half a century's archaeological research which, though from a different point of view, deals with many of the topics of art and culture which I study. More recently, Jean Bérard's *La colonisation de l'Italie méridionale et de la Sicile* deals with Sicily and south Italy together and, though formally limited to the origins, reaches far down into the early history of the colonies. I have not been able to make as much use of it as I should have liked, for the revision of my book was already well advanced when his came into my hands. The different purpose of the two works will be clear to any one who uses both; I am gratified to find how often a view which I had formed has been anticipated by Bérard. One other book deserves especial mention: Pareti's *Studi Siciliani ed Italioti* contains some acute and penetrating studies which are among the most stimulating pages written on the western colonies.

Much has been thought and said, though not written, in Oxford on the Western Greeks. Alan Blakeway introduced me to the subject, and many of his views will be recognized here. Mrs. Andrewes allowed me to work through his unpublished papers, from which I have sometimes quoted. Mr. R. H. Dundas and Professor H. T. Wade-Gery have constantly aided and encouraged me, and Mr. Dundas has added to my obligation by reading the proofs. Humfry Payne went through part of the archaeological material with me, and Professor J. D. Beazley has read part of the book. Mr. E. S. G. Robinson has always been willing to show me coins and talk of them; my errors in this field are my own. I was fortunate to have Orsi's guidance when I worked in Syracuse, and my obligations to other directors of Italian museums and excavations are innumerable. The chief of my other obligations are to the Derby Trustees, under whose auspices I began the work; to All Souls College, whose award of a Fellowship enabled me to continue it; to my wife, to whose patient support and unfailing encouragement its completion is largely due; and to the Delegates of the Clarendon Press for undertaking the book, and to their readers for much help with its form.

Most of the field-work was done as a Student of the British School at Rome in 1934 and 1935; and an early version of this book was in 1937 submitted to All Souls College for examination for Fellowship by thesis. Circumstances have since prevented me from spending the long periods in Italy necessary for revising it. I could have wished to go over the archaeological material again on the spot, and to comb the Italian periodicals, many of which are hard to come by in this country. But this would have involved an indefinite postponement which I am unwilling to incur. I have in the last two years revised and largely rewritten the book, so far as possible without revisiting Italy. The lack of illustration is also due to my inability to work over the material again on the spot, as many of the photographs needed to illustrate the more archaeological sections of the book are not available in England.

T. J. D.

ALL SOULS COLLEGE, OXFORD
Easter, 1948

CONTENTS

LIST OF MAPS AND PLANS

Map I is based on a map in Murray's Classical Atlas. The plans of Gela and Himera are based on Pareti, *Studi Siciliani ed Italioti*, Maps II and I; Megara on Pace, *Arte e Civiltà della Sicilia Antica*, i. 174; Kamarina on Pace, *Camarina*, pl. 1; Kaulonia on *MA*, xxiii, pl. 1; Kroton on *RM*, 1914, 144 (A. W. Byvanck); Lokroi on *RE*, xiii. 1305–6; Metapontion on *Guida del Touring Club Italiano, Italia Meridionale*, iii. 760; Poseidonia on Trendall, *Paestan Pottery*, 2, fig. 1; Taras on *JHS*, 1886, 4 (A. J. Evans); Selinus on Hulot and Fougères, *Sélinonte*, pl. 1; Akragas on D. Randall-MacIver, *Greek Cities in Italy and Sicily*, 207. My wife and sister, Miss M. I. Dunbabin, have given me much help with these plans. They have been redrawn by the draughtsmen of the Clarendon Press.

ABBREVIATIONS

AA	*Archäologischer Anzeiger.*
ABL	E. Haspels, *Attic Black-figured Lekythoi.*
ACSA	B. Pace, *Arte e Civiltà della Sicilia Antica.*
AFR	A. D. van Buren, *Archaic Fictile Revetments.*
AJA	*American Journal of Archaeology.*
AM	*Mitteilungen des deutschen archäologischen Instituts, Athenische Abteilung.*
Ann.	*Annuario della Reale Scuola archeologica di Atene.*
ARV	J. D. Beazley, *Attic Red-Figure Vase-Painters.*
ASCL	*Archivio storico per la Calabria e la Lucania.*
ASS	*Archivio storico Siciliano.*
AZ	*Archäologische Zeitung.*
BCH	*Bulletin de correspondance hellénique.*
BMC *BM Cat.* }	*British Museum Catalogue.*
Boll. d'Arte	*Bollettino d'Arte.*
BPI	*Bullettino di Paletnologia Italiana.*
Br.Br.	Brunn–Bruckmann, *Denkmäler griechischer und römischer Sculptur.*
BSA	*Annual of the British School at Athens.*
BSR	*Papers of the British School at Rome.*
Bull.Metr.Mus.	*Bulletin of the Metropolitan Museum of Art.*
CAH	*Cambridge Ancient History.*
CIL	*Corpus Inscriptionum Latinarum.*
CQ	*Classical Quarterly.*
CR	*Classical Review.*
CVA	*Corpus Vasorum Antiquorum.*
'Εφ. 'Αρχ.	*'Εφημερὶς 'Αρχαιολογική.*
FGH *FGrHist* }	*Fragmente der griechischen Historiker,* ed. F. Jacoby.
FHG	*Fragmenta Historicorum Graecorum,* ed. C. Müller.
FR	Furtwängler and Reichhold, *Griechische Vasenmalerei.*
GFR	E. D. van Buren, *Greek Fictile Revetments.*
GG	F. Lenormant, *La Grande-Grèce.*
GHI	M. N. Tod, *Greek Historical Inscriptions.*
Gött.Gel.Anz.	*Göttingische Gelehrte Anzeiger.*
Gött.Nachr.	*Göttingische Nachrichten.*
Gr.Ges.	*Griechische Geschichte.*
HN	B. V. Head, *Historia Numorum.*
IG	*Inscriptiones Graecae.*
JdI	*Jahrbuch des deutschen archäologischen Instituts.*

JHS	Journal of Hellenic Studies.
LAAA	Liverpool Annals of Archaeology and Anthropology.
MA	Monumenti antichi pubblicati per cura della Reale Accademia dei Lincei.
Mem.Acc.Linc.	Memorie della Reale Accademia dei Lincei.
Mem.Am.Acad.	Memoirs of the American Academy in Rome.
Mon. Piot	Monuments et Mémoires publiés par l'Académie des Inscriptions et Belles-Lettres: Fondation Piot.
NC	H. Payne, Necrocorinthia.
N Sc	Notizie degli Scavi di Antichità.
Num. Chron.	Numismatic Chronicle.
Ö Jh	Jahreshefte des Österreichischen archäologischen Institutes.
Op.Arch.	Opuscula Archaeologica.
PV	H. Payne, Protokorinthische Vasenmalerei.
QDAP	Quarterly of the Department of Antiquities in Palestine.
RA	Revue archéologique.
RE	Pauly–Wissowa–Kroll, Real-Encyclopädie.
REG	Revue des études grecques.
Rend.Acc.Linc.	Rendiconti della Reale Accademia dei Lincei.
Rev. épig.	Revue épigraphique.
RIASA	Rivista del R. Istituto d'Archeologia e Storia dell'Arte.
RIGI	Rivista Indo-greco-italica.
Riv.st.ant.	Rivista di storia antica.
RM	Mitteilungen des deutschen archäologischen Instituts, Römische Abteilung.
SB Bayr Akad	Sitzungsberichte der bayerischen Akademie der Wissenschaften.
SCE	Swedish Cyprus Expedition.
SE	Studi etruschi.
SEG	Supplementum Epigraphicum Graecum.
SIG	Dittenberger, Sylloge Inscriptionum Graecarum.
SMG	Atti e Memorie della Società Magna Grecia.
TAA	P. Orsi, Templum Apollinis Alaei.
VS	K. Friis Johansen, Les Vases sicyoniens.

NOTE ON NOMENCLATURE

THERE is no convenient ethnic, corresponding to Magna Graecia, which covers Sicily and south Italy. I have used 'western' and 'Western Greeks' wherever possible. Nor is there a term for the native peoples of Sicily and south Italy. In Sicily I speak generally of Sikels, using 'Sikan' only when it is used by an ancient authority. 'Siculan' is the archaeological term for the culture common to eastern and western Sicily, and 'Sikel' the corresponding ethnic.

CHAPTER I

THE FOUNDATION OF THE GREEK COLONIES

WHEN in the eighth century the Greeks began to send colonies to those western areas which later became known as Great Greece, these lands were not unknown. Both Sicily and south Italy had been included in the area of Mycenaean trade, though these contacts had long since been broken.[1] They were resumed in the early eighth century, when there is evidence both literary and archaeological that the western Mediterranean was at least occasionally visited by Greeks. The literary evidence, consisting of references in the *Odyssey* and the Hesiodic poems, is somewhat controversial. The archaeological evidence is that a few pieces of Greek pottery were imported to Italy in the early eighth century, and the quantity greatly increased in the generation before the foundation of the colonies (an epoch determined relatively by the archaeological content of the oldest graves and deposits from the colonial sites, without as yet having reference to absolute dates for the foundations).[2]

The earliest references in Greek literature to Sicily occur in the *Odyssey*,[3] and show it as a source of slaves, which might occasionally be visited by Greeks. It is possible to regard these references as a survival from the Mycenaean period, when many Mycenaean objects were imported to Sicily, but it is more likely that they reflect contemporary, early eighth-century, knowledge of Sicily. This is not the place to enter into a discussion of the date and composition of the *Odyssey*. One can, however, say with confidence that these passages are older than the foundation of the Greek colonies and illustrate a state of affairs when trading, in slaves and perhaps other commodities, took Greeks as far as Sicily.

At the time of the Mycenaean imports to Sicily the native sites were on the sea or easily accessible from it. Before the

[1] See my paper 'Minos and Daidalos in Sicily' (*BSR*, xvi. 1 ff.). For the possibility that at Taranto Greek contact may have been continuous between the Mycenaean period and the eighth century, see below, p. 28 f.

[2] Blakeway, 'Prolegomena to the Study of Greek Commerce with Italy, Sicily, and France in the Eighth and Seventh Centuries B.C.' (*BSA*, xxxiii. 170 ff.). Some archaeologists are inclined to give lower dates to certain of the vases described by Blakeway as pre-colonization imports from Greece. These dates may be accepted without thereby invalidating Blakeway's main thesis.

[3] ω 307, Σικανίη; ω 211 et al., Sikel slave; ν 383, Sikels associated with slave-trade.

ninth century the typical coast stations such as Thapsos and Plemmyrion had been abandoned and the centre of population moved to well-defended mountain sites.[1] This may have been caused by Greek slave-raids on the coast, such as are implied by the mention in the *Odyssey* of Sikel slaves. The coast was not indeed deserted, for the sites of Syracuse, Megara, Leontinoi, and, in south Italy, Lokroi, Taras, and Kyme were all occupied by native settlements when the Greeks arrived. The big towns and, presumably, the centres of power were, however, inland.[2]

In the Hesiodic corpus there is more precise knowledge of western geography: Etna, Ortygia,[3] and Cape Peloros[4] are named, a vague knowledge shown of Latium and Etruria,[5] and Ligurians (or Libyans) placed at the ends of the earth.[6] The interest is mythographical, not geographical. But though Peloros is named because of Orion's earthworks there, the fact that it is known implies that Greek ships already sailed north through the Straits of Messina; and the naming of Ortygia

---

[1] The Siculan II period (15th–9th centuries, according to Orsi's chronology) should be subdivided into two periods, that of the coast stations, the period of Mycenaean imports, and that of the mountain stations, of which Pantalica is typical. The criteria on which Siculan II pottery might be divided into earlier and later are: (i) introduction of new shapes (but shapes derived from Mycenaean models continue into Siculan III); (ii) the occasional use of glaze in the mountain stations (Orsi, *MA*, xxi. 339); (iii) the introduction at Pantalica of geometric decoration typical of Siculan III. Cf. G. Säflund, *Studi Etruschi*, xii. 45 ff.; Schachermeyr, *Etruskische Frühgeschichte*, 189; Åkerström, *Der Geometrische Stil in Italien*, 14 ff.

The Siculan periods, with their approximate chronology, are:

Period	Typical site	Main publication	Associations	Dates
Neolithic	Stentinello	*BPI*, 1890	—	*c.* 3000–2400
Siculan I	Castelluccio	*BPI*, 1892	Contact with Aegean and Crete	*c.* 2400–1400
Siculan II				
Coast	Thapsos	*MA*, vi	Mycenaean imports	*c.* 1400–1000
Mountain	Pantalica	*MA*, ix, xxi	—	*c.* 1000–800
Siculan III	Finocchito	*BPI*, 1897	Greek geometric imports	*c.* 800–650
Siculan IV	Licodia	*RM*, xiii	Corinthian imports	*c.* 650–500

For the date given for the beginning of Siculan I see Hawkes, *The Prehistoric Foundations of Europe*, 151 ff.

For the relations of Siculan III and IV see below, pp. 171 ff.

This is the sequence in eastern Sicily, all the 'typical' sites being in the neighbourhood of Syracuse, and is not immediately applicable to western Sicily, which had less contact with the civilizations of the Aegean and where development was slower.

[2] Five thousand rock-cut graves are still preserved at Pantalica, and thousands on other mountain sites of this period (*MA*, xxi. 391).

[3] *Ox. Pap.* xi. 1358, fr. 2. 26; Strabo 23. [4] Diod. iv. 85.

[5] *Theog.* 1011 ff.; Tyrrhenians, Strabo 23. [6] Strabo 300; *Ox. Pap.* 1358, fr. 2. 15.

implies that Syracuse was already visited. The period at which these poems were written is uncertain and may have been as late as the foundation of Syracuse. These references tell us nothing which could not be inferred from the distribution of Greek pottery, but give another and rarer sort of contemporary evidence, especially valuable for the contrast with the references in the *Odyssey*.

Protogeometric imports to Italy are so far known only at Taranto and at Coppa Nevigata on the Adriatic coast.[1] In Sicily there is a single vase, from Monteaperto near Agrigento, which may be derived from a Protogeometric original.[2] These isolated finds may in time be supplemented, but there is sufficient other material belonging to this period to show that the absence of Greek imports is real, and that Sicily and the Tyrrhenian Sea were beyond the range of the Greeks for some centuries.

It is in the early eighth century that Greek vases and, by implication, Greek traders begin to find their way again to these areas. The earliest and strongest contacts are with Etruria and Latium, not with the nearer shores of Italy and Sicily.[3] This indicates that so early as this date the interest of the Greeks was primarily commercial; the inhabitants of Etruria offered better markets than the barbarous peoples of south Italy and Sicily, and produced the metals which the Greeks needed. Some Greek potters indeed settled in Italian towns, and no doubt other Greeks also beside potters.[4]

The first Greek colony in Italy was also the most remote, at Kyme. This is the historical tradition;[5] it is also to be concluded from the archaeological evidence. Classes of vases which are unknown in the Sicilian colonies and are of types older than the oldest from Sicilian sites are found in the cemeteries of the Greek colony of Kyme. To anticipate the chronological discussion which follows: Kyme was founded about 750 B.C. or a little earlier, some twenty years before Naxos and Syracuse, the oldest colonies in Sicily.

At about the time of the foundation of Kyme Greek traders reached Sicily, and imported Greek vases which are older than any from the cemeteries of Syracuse are found on a Sikel site on the island of Ortygia and on half a dozen Sikel sites in the

---

[1] Blakeway, op. cit. 174 ff.   [2] Ibid. 189.
[3] Blakeway, *JRS*, 1934, 129 ff.; Schachermayr, *Etruskische Frühgeschichte*, 187 f.
[4] Blakeway, loc. cit.   [5] Strabo 243.

interior: Tremenzano, Finocchito, and Castelluccio behind Syracuse, Cava S. Aloè near Leontinoi, Ossini in the same neighbourhood, Mola above Taormina, Paternò on the southern slopes of Etna, and Monteaperto near Akragas.[1] At Gela also there are imports older than the foundation of the Greek colony, though not older than the foundation of Syracuse. It will be observed that there were Sikel sites on or near the sites of three at least of the oldest Greek colonies, Syracuse, Naxos, and Leontinoi. It is certain therefore that the Greeks had already a knowledge of the coasts of Sicily and its peoples before the first colonies were sent out. The volume of pre-colonization trade must not be over-estimated. It covers the space of a single generation only, and is not sufficient to imply regular trading-posts; single voyages are more likely. However, there was sufficient Greek pottery imported to influence the form and decoration of Sikel pottery.[2] On at least one Sikel site, at S. Aloè, there are vases in the local clay painted by Greeks:[3] proof, if the date and stylistic arguments proposed by Blakeway are accepted, as I think they must be, that some Greeks had settled among the Sikels before the foundation of the colonies.

The same conditions prevailed at Lokroi before the foundation of the Greek colony. Greek vases have been found in the native cemeteries, some of which are certainly imports from Greece, whereas others may have been manufactured in Italy.[4]

The origin of this Greek pottery is as yet uncertain. Many states are represented. There are many Cretan vases and fragments in the earliest finds from Kyme and on contemporary Etruscan sites; a few from Syracuse; also a number at Gela, where Cretan imports continue in the seventh century. Cycladic vases are found on Sikel and Italian sites, and there are many local vases which appear to imitate Cycladic models. These are rare after the eighth century. There are a few Cypriot vases or direct imitations thereof, and more extensive Cypriot influence may perhaps be traced in the development of the local geometric style of Siculan III. Corinth is represented, but only as one among many states, and that not the foremost. The Argolid also provided a few imports, and there may be some Argive influence in the local geometric styles. A few

---

[1] Blakeway, *BSA*, xxxiii. 180 ff.   [2] Blakeway's classes iii and iv, op. cit. 185 ff.
[3] Blakeway, op. cit. 185 ff., figs. 10 and 11 *a*.
[4] Orsi, *MA*, xxxi. 333 ff., pll. 15–16; Blakeway, op. cit. 176 ff.

parallels to Boiotian vases may be traced and are perhaps due to Euboian intermediaries. Parallels for some vases may be found in Rhodes and east Greece, but these are not striking enough to prove contact with these areas. The same is true of Laconia. Athens, which produced the finest vases in the late geometric as at most other periods of Greek art, did not join in the western trade to the same extent as these other cities. Two sherds from Syracuse and one vase from Veii are the only Attic found in the west before c. 620;[1] this is too little to establish direct contact. Attic models have been claimed for vases made in Etruria,[2] but the parallels are not close enough to compel acceptance of the thesis, in view of the absence of Attic there throughout the seventh century and the limited range of Protoattic.

The regions of Greece whose products we may trace in the west are thus Crete, the Cyclades, the north-east Peloponnese (Corinth and Argos), perhaps Cyprus. To these should no doubt be added Khalkis and Eretria, whose early pottery has not yet been identified.[3] It is possible that some of the pottery of uncertain fabric found on colonial sites, for which Cycladic parallels of a general nature are adduced, will one day be proved to have been made in Euboia. It is probable that much of the Cycladic pottery was taken to the west by Khalkidians or Eretrians. Eretrians are the more probable, as Eretria had an island empire,[4] and the disappearance of Cycladic pottery after the eighth century might be explained as a consequence of the crowding out of Eretria from western trade.[5]

Kyme is definitely stated to be the oldest of all the Greek colonies in Sicily and Italy.[6] The eleventh-century date given in Eusebius is certainly false;[7] in default of other evidence, the date is given, relatively to the foundation of Syracuse, by the finding in the earliest graves of Protocorinthian vases of an earlier type than any found at Syracuse. This suggests that an interval of about twenty years should be allowed between the two foundations, so that Kyme will be about 750 or a little earlier. The site was already known to Greeks, for Greek

---

[1] Åkerström, op. cit. 35; J. M. Cook, *BSA*, xxxv. 204, n. 5.
[2] Dohan, *Italic Tomb-Groups*, 60, 66, 72, 108.
[3] Gàbrici's view (*MA*, xxii. 318 ff.) that the Protocorinthian vases found at Kyme were of Khalkidian origin need not be discussed.
[4] Cf. *CAH*, iii. 621 ff.
[5] See Blakeway, *BSA*, xxxiii. 204 ff.   [6] Strabo 243.
[7] See below, p. 445.

geometric vases have been found in graves of the prehellenic settlement on what became the acropolis of the Greek colony.[1]

Kyme was not the first Greek settlement in the Bay of Naples, for it had been preceded by a settlement on the island of Ischia, in which Eretrians and Khalkidians shared.[2] This would naturally be not only the depot from which the Greek vases found in the prehellenic graves of Kyme were imported, but also a port of call for Greek ships on the way to Etruria. The site of the Greek colony on Ischia has been found, though not yet excavated, on Monte Vico, where there are said to be 'relatively abundant Greek geometric sherds of the eighth century'.[3] A native village on Ischia has yielded a L.H. III sherd[4] and two or three geometric fragments. This village was destroyed by volcanic action, which is brought by the excavator into relation with the eruption mentioned by Strabo (see below), and is dated by him c. 700. The chronology of the Greek settlement does not appear from the brief note thus far published, but the discovery, verifying the tradition preserved in Strabo and Livy, is of the utmost value in confirming the general value of that tradition.

The settlement on Ischia is said to have prospered, as the land was fertile and there were gold-mines; but the settlers first of all quarrelled among themselves and then deserted the island after earthquakes and an eruption.[5] Neither of these two events is brought into relation with the foundation of Kyme. Livy says that Kyme was founded from Ischia. It is likely that for some time the two establishments were inhabited together. The stasis among the Euboians of Ischia may plausibly be related to the quarrel between Khalkis and Eretria which caused the Lelantine War, for before this quarrel the two cities were friendly.[6] The Lelantine War is not earlier than the late eighth century; at the time of the foundation of Kyme, Khalkis and Eretria must still have been friendly, for they are both said to have taken part in it,[7] as in the establishment on Ischia. The Kymaians also joined in the colony, supplying one oecist;[8] these are said to be the citizens of Kyme in Aiolis.[9] This is commonly regarded as an invention of Ephoros who was a native of Aiolic Kyme, and corrected to Kyme in Euboia,

---

[1] *MA*, xxii, pl. 18. 7 and 9; Blakeway, 200.   [2] Strabo 247; Livy viii. 22.
[3] G. Büchner, *BPI*, i (1936–7), 65 ff.   [4] Id. 79, fig. 3.
[5] Strabo, l.c.; cf. von Duhn, *Italische Gräberkunde*, i. 554, 556.
[6] Strabo 448.   [7] Dion. Hal. vii. 3.
[8] Strabo 243.   [9] Ps.-Skymn. 238–9.

but there is no need for this rationalization.[1] It has been inferred, from the fact that the Romans called the Greeks Graeci and that the Kymaians were the first Greeks with whom they had official dealings, that the Graioi of eastern Boiotia took part in the colonization and gave their name to a division of the people.[2] The Kymaians gave the name of their city to the colony, but the Khalkidians, who provided the second oecist, were regarded as the founders,[3] and it came to be spoken of as a Khalkidian colony without qualification.[4] It was a combined effort of many cities of Euboia, no doubt under the joint direction of Khalkis and Eretria; if any Boiotians took part in it, they may have been subject to one or other city.[5] After the defeat of Eretria by Khalkis, the Eretrians dropped out.

The site of Kyme had many of the advantages of an island. The acropolis stands up boldly, and, though not high, is not commanded. Between it and the plain to the north extends a swampy lake which limits access from the landward. There are many better harbours in the Bay of Naples and even on Ischia, but for the purposes of early Greek shipping the long sandy beach, which was then probably nearer to the acropolis than now, was ideal.

Though the immensely fertile plains of Campania and the prolific volcanic soil of the Phlegraean Plains are near at hand, the immediate neighbourhood of Kyme is comparatively poor sandy soil, now given to vineyards. It is unlikely therefore that the colony was intended in the first place for the production of food, though, of course, it had to feed itself. Like the settlement on Ischia, it was intended for trade, with both the neighbouring peoples and the Etruscans. From the acropolis one looks north up the long curving beach, past the mouth of the Volturno, into the haze where appear the Auruncian hills, the Pontine islands, and, sometimes, Monte Circeo, the next great landmark on a coasting voyage north. So, most often, must the Kymaians have looked.

The staple of their trade was perhaps copper ore, whether mined in Campania[6] or brought from Elba. This view is sup-

---

[1] One Kymaian who returned from Aiolis to Boiotia about this time was Hesiod's father. Professor Wade-Gery suggests that others were recruited at Khalkis for the new colony.

[2] Bury, *JHS*, xv. 236 f. Cf. also the phratry of Eunostides at Neapolis, who may have derived their name from Eunostos the hero of Tanagra (Guarducci, *Mem. Ac. Linc.* viii (1938), 145; Bérard, *Colonisation*, 59).

[3] Strabo, l.c.   [4] Thuk. vi. 4.   [5] Cf. *CAH*, iii. 619 ff.

[6] Pliny, *NH*, xxxiv. 2; Diosc. v. 84; cf. Heurgon, *Capoue préromaine*, 20.

ported by the flourishing bronze industry of Kyme before and after the colonization.[1] The search for metals will explain why Kyme was the first colony founded in the west, and also why Etruria was reached by Greek trade earlier than nearer parts of Italy.

Citizens of many Greek states took part in the early trade with Kyme. Cretan and Cycladic vases of the eighth century are found there, as well as Corinthian, and perhaps there are other Greek fabrics not yet clearly distinguished. This distribution is essentially that of the pre-colonization period, not only on the site of Kyme but also in Etruria, and suggests that traders of many cities continued to visit Kyme; though, of course, it is possible that the Cycladic vases were brought by Khalkidians, and by no means certain that the Cretan vases came in Cretan ships. It is clear that in its first generation Kyme was open to receive the products of many Greek states, whereas in the next generation, and throughout the whole of the seventh century, its imports like those of the other western colonies were almost limited to Corinthian wares.

The oldest colony in Sicily was Naxos, founded in or about 734. It has not been excavated and little is known of it. Its founder was Theokles of Khalkis; in later sources he is called an Athenian,[2] probably because all Ionians were of Attic origin and Attic pride would not allow that their ancestors had had no part in the great colonial expansion. The settlers were Khalkidians and, Strabo says, other Ionians; from the name given to the colony it is reasonable to suppose that many of them came from the island of Naxos, as was stated by Hellanikos.[3] This is supported by the likeness of the types of the earliest coins of Sicilian Naxos (nearly two centuries after its foundation) with those of the island of Naxos, and by the common worship of Dionysos and Apollo.[4]

Naxos is, though not the nearest point of Sicily to Italy, that to which a ship sailing down the east coast would first be borne, for a current from Capo d'Armi, the ancient Leukopetra, reaches the Sicilian coast there.[5] It is a low promontory, the end of one of Etna's lava-flows; what its harbour was like in

[1] MA, xxii. 70 ff., 296 ff.
[2] Strabo 267; ps.-Skymn. 273-4.
[3] Ap. Steph. Byz. s.v. Χαλκίς (F 82 Jacoby).
[4] Cahn, Die Münzen der Sizilischen Stadt Naxos, 86 ff.
[5] Columba, Porti della Sicilia Antica, 321.

antiquity we do not know, but it had presumably at least good shelter. It is now a very fertile lemon-grove, and before the introduction of the lemon would no doubt have grown other crops. But there is not a large area of easily cultivable land, and, though the valley of the Alcantara immediately behind leads into the interior, there is no evidence that this way was used by Greek trade until a much later date. The purpose of the colony seems to be found in the fact that it is the first point of Sicily to be reached; a resting-place, not an end in itself, but a stage for further voyaging either in Sicily or north of the Straits. Naxos was always a small city, being surpassed by both Zankle and Leontinoi. The other Sikeliots (and not the Khalkidians only) recognized its primacy by sacrificing on the altar of Apollo Arkhegetes whenever they sailed on embassies.[1] But in itself it was not important.[2] It is not, however, plausible to argue that, because the Greeks founded their first colony in Sicily in the place first reached, they knew no more of Sicily. There were then no colonies in south Italy: why should they sail all along the deserted coast from the Iapygian promontory, to settle as soon as they touched Sicily? It is certain, not only from the imports of Greek pottery to many points in the east of Sicily, but also from the references in the *Odyssey*, that the Greeks already had some acquaintance with the east coast of Sicily; and it is clear, on archaeological grounds, that Greeks had long been visiting the richer markets of Etruria and had settled already at Kyme. Some of these difficulties can be avoided by pushing up the date of Naxos by about half a century and supposing it to be earlier than Kyme and the point of import of the earliest Greek vases found on Sikel sites;[3] but at the expense of preferring an uncertain tradition to a well-authenticated date. The view that the nearer must have been colonized before the more remote cannot be upheld without rewriting the history of Greek colonization, and is disproved by the abundant evidence that almost everywhere colonization was preceded by a long or a short period of trade, so that the country to be colonized must have been known to many sailors. Moreover, the excellence of the sites of many of the colonies would alone show that their

[1] Thuk. vi. 3.

[2] The strategic importance of Naxos is shown in the history of Athenian intervention in Sicily. If their allies had been situated in any other corner of the island the Athenians might have been unable to maintain communication with their base, perhaps even to reach it.

[3] Pareti, 310 ff.

founders must have carefully spied out the land before the colonists set out.[1]

Naxos should be considered, not alone, but in conjunction with Katane and Leontinoi. Within six years of the foundation of Naxos Theokles led a body of colonists south to Leontinoi, and shortly afterwards the Naxians also colonized Katane, under the leadership of Euarkhos. Theokles' objective must from the first have been the rich Laistrygonian plain, the home of wheat, and the site of Leontinoi, one of the richest Sikel sites of the period, which had already imported many Greek products. Leontinoi lay on the far side of the plain; it was seized first, and then (almost immediately afterwards, as appears in the working out of Thukydides' chronology) Katane was settled, on the north side of the plain and on the sea; at the southern foot of Etna, as Naxos lay near the northern slopes. This ensured that no other power should slip in between Naxos and Leontinoi and dispute with the Khalkidians the possession of the plain. It also gave them a better port than Leontinoi possessed, though the latter stood on a navigable river. The Khalkidians were successful, and for centuries their three colonies held together and possessed the richest land in Sicily.

The original settlers of Naxos must have been numerous to be able so soon to populate three cities; for it does not appear from Thukydides that they were reinforced. As well as these three colonies, Kyme, Zankle, and Rhegion in the west, and probably many of the northern colonies in the Khalkidike were founded from Euboia in a short space of time, at the most fifty years. We do not know how many colonists went to a new colony; probably no large number; but apparently whole families set out together;[2] and, however few citizens we suppose each city to have had originally, the total number of settlers of the Khalkidian colonies must have been a high proportion of the population of Khalkis at the time. We know that men from all over Euboia were brought together at Kyme,

[1] Ephoros' statement (ap. Strabo 267) that there was no trade before the colonization may be taken as disproved. With it falls to the ground the further statement that Theokles, the oecist, was first blown there, and seeing the goodness of the land and the nothingness of the inhabitants decided to raise men for a colony. Ephoros' account of the foundation of Naxos is full of points which other literary or archaeological evidence shows to be baseless. In contrast to Thukydides' account of the colonizations, it is full also of points on which we could not reasonably expect a Greek historian to be informed. So it may well be mainly invention.

[2] This is an inference from the fact that in no case are native women heard of (as in Cyrenaica) and that the colonies were later recognized as pure Greek. See below, pp. 184 ff.

that Messenians joined the Khalkidians at Rhegion, and suspect the presence of Naxians at Naxos. It is likely that the population of all the colonies was drawn from a mixed body of men, though the direction was supplied by Khalkis and, at Ischia and Kyme and many of the northern colonies, Eretria. Possibly both Khalkis and Eretria had a hegemony over their neighbours in Euboia, Boiotia, and the Cyclades[1] which would give them man-power to draw upon.

Two other Khalkidian colonies were founded at this period, one on either side of the Straits of Messina. No exact date is given for the foundation of Zankle or Rhegion. The foundation of Zankle may be inferred to be later than that of Naxos,[2] as the latter is described as the oldest colony in Sicily. It was first settled by pirates from Kyme; the line between piracy and trade was then, of course, not firmly drawn. It was later formed into a regular colony, with settlers from Khalkis and the rest of Euboia, and two oecists, Perieres of Kyme and Krataimenes of Khalkis.[3] The oecists were honoured annually with a banquet to which they were summoned by the magistrates; though their names were preserved, they were not called upon by name, but in a formula which Kallimakhos renders thus:[4]

ἵ]λαος ἡμετέρην ὅστις ἔδειμε [πόλ]ιν
ἐρ]χέσθω μετὰ δαῖτα . . . .

This annual commemoration of the foundation was, according to Kallimakhos, generally practised in the colonies and is of great historical importance, as it explains how the foundation legends and the founders' names were preserved and also perhaps how the era of the colony was reckoned.

There are no considerable remains of Zankle, but a deposit of objects, probably from a sanctuary, has been found on the north side of the northern arm of the harbour, the sickle to which the city owed its name. This included Protocorinthian and other early vases, going back to the eighth century. But this material is too scanty to throw light on the foundation or early history of the colony.[5]

---

[1] Andros was actively colonizing in the north both before and after the Lelantine War; some colonies are described as joint foundations of Andros and Khalkis (Plut. *QG* 30).

[2] Strabo 268 and ps.-Skymn. 283–6 make it a Naxian foundation. Thukydides clearly implies that it was not; and it is hard to see what ground these authors could have for their version. See Freeman, i. 585.

[3] Thuk. vi. 4. Later sources contaminate the account of the foundation with the later history of the city under its Samian and Messenian occupants. See below, pp. 396 ff.

[4] Kallimakhos, *Ox. Pap.* xvii, no. 2080 (Budé ed., p. 57).   [5] *N Sc*, 1929, 38 ff.

Zankle lived by and for its harbour. Other colonies, whether founded primarily for trade or agriculture, had enough land to live on. Zankle, as also Rhegion, lies on a narrow coastal strip at the foot of high mountains and must always have imported much of its food. The dependence on outside sources was reduced by a secondary foundation, that of Mylai on the north coast of Sicily, which was occupied a few years after Zankle. Under the year 717–716 Jerome has the entry *In Sicilia Chersonessus condita*, which is to be referred to Mylai. This site, at the base of a long hilly promontory twenty miles west of the Straits of Messina, secured the approaches to Zankle from the west and north-west; its strategical importance was shown in the campaign of 36 B.C. against Sextus Pompeius, and again in Garibaldi's march on the Straits. Also, it secured the possession of a fertile plain which here lies between the sea and the mountains, the best land in the neighbourhood of the Straits.

Rhegion is the complement of Zankle, and the history of the two towns is intertwined from the time of their foundation. The site has no value apart from its position on the Straits and must have been occupied to ensure that no other people should gain a foothold in the area of the Straits, passage through which was henceforth controlled by the Khalkidians. The Khalkidian settlers were, according to Antiokhos, summoned to the new colony by the Zanklaians, who provided the oecist Antimnestos.[1] The common version said that as a result of a poor season the Khalkidians vowed a tenth of their number to Apollo, who directed them from Delphi to Rhegion.[2] Famine in the mother city is a frequent element in foundation-stories, as no doubt it was in historical fact. But we may follow Antiokhos in believing that the colonization was planned at Khalkis and Zankle rather than at Delphi. With the Khalkidians were associated some Messenians, exiled from Messenia at the time of the First Messenian War, it is said because they wished to give satisfaction to Sparta. They also were said to have been directed by Delphi and were under the protection of Apollo. This may be accepted; Delphi, it would appear, introduced the Messenians to their Khalkidian fellow colonists.[3] The Messenians formed an important part in the colony.

[1] Ap. Strabo 257. Dion. Hal. (xix. 2) calls the oecist Artimedes, a Khalkidian.
[2] Strabo, l.c.; Diod. viii. 23. 2; Herakl. Pont. fr. 25 (*FHG*, ii. 219); Dion. Hal. xix. 2.
[3] Cf. Bérard, *Colonisation*, 114.

Though it was known as Khalkidian and spoke an Ionic dialect,[1] the Messenians formed the ruling class.[2] Anaxilas, the fifth-century tyrant of Rhegion, was of this Messenian stock and revived the Messenian connexion by inviting Messenian settlers to Rhegion and Zankle, which then took the name Messana which it still preserves.[3]

The First Messenian War gives a date, though not a very exact one, for the foundation of Rhegion. It was dated between 736 and 716, or thereabouts,[4] and as the Messenians left during its earlier stages, that would place the foundation of Rhegion c. 730, or in the early twenties at the latest. More important than the absolute date is its chronology relative to Taras, which was founded after the end of the First Messenian War. Rhegion was older than the other colonies of Magna Graecia and, after Kyme, the oldest colony in Italy.

Almost exactly contemporary with Naxos was the foundation of Syracuse, which is dated by Thukydides in the following year (c. 733). Syracuse has the best harbour on the east coast of Sicily, through which at all times most of the trade between Greece and Sicily appears to have passed. The island of Ortygia was at this time occupied by a Sikel settlement, with which Greeks had been trading for some years. The evidence of pre-colonization trade on the site itself is uncertain,[5] but it must have been the centre of distribution of pre-colonization imports found at Finocchito, Castelluccio, and Tremenzano, all reached naturally from Syracuse and from no other point on the coast. But there is not sufficient evidence to prove the existence of a

---

[1] Doric elements (see Collitz–Bechtel, iii. 2. 498) may have been introduced by later settlers, whether from Messenia or elsewhere, and are not necessarily original.

[2] Strabo 257: οἱ τῶν Ῥηγίνων ἡγεμόνες μέχρι Ἀναξίλα τοῦ Μεσσηνίων γένους ἀεὶ καθίσταντο.

[3] Seep. 396.   [4] Wade-Gery, CAH, iii. 537.

[5] The lowest strata below the Athenaion contained Greek geometric sherds mixed with Siculan. The stratification has been disturbed at many points, and the association of Greek geometric and Siculan is not always original. Elsewhere the strata are clearly distinguished and separated by a thin pavement. It does not appear from the publication in MA, xxv whether Greek sherds were found in the undisturbed Sikel strata, and the question whether any of the Greek geometric is to be dated before the foundation of the colony must be decided mainly on stylistic grounds. None of it appears to be much older than the oldest vases from the Greek cemeteries of Syracuse. But the Siculan imitations of Greek geometric (see below, p. 51) will be pre-colonization. There must therefore have been Greek imports to the Sikel town, whether any of them are preserved in the finds of the Athenaion or not. See Orsi, MA, xxv, esp. 735 ff.; Blakeway, BSA, xxxiii. 180 ff.; Åkerström, op. cit. 34–5. Åkerström, while regarding the so-called pre-colonization material from the Athenaion site (i.e. the Greek geometric sherds spoken of above) as substantially of the same date as the earliest vases from the cemeteries, does not exclude a short pre-colonization period.

permanent or semi-permanent settlement before the Corinthian colony was founded, likely as this is. It has been suggested that there was a Khalkidian settlement on the weak ground that certain place-names were common to Syracuse and Khalkis.[1] Though it is clear that Greeks visited the site before the colony was founded, there is reason to suppose that the early traders did not belong to any single Greek city. The earliest pottery from the site includes Cretan, Cycladic, Argive, Corinthian, and Attic.[2] So the archaeological evidence cannot be said to support the supposed Khalkidian settlement, which is better forgotten.

Syracuse was a Corinthian colony and its oecist Arkhias was probably one of the Bakkhiad rulers of Corinth.[3] As well as Corinthians, other Dorians are said to have taken part in the colony: Arkhias on his way west picked them up at the Zephyrian promontory, near the later site of Lokroi, where they had remained after parting company with the Megarians who were at the same time sailing west to found a colony.[4] Who these Dorians were is not stated. It is possible that some Argives joined the Corinthians. The relations of Argos and Corinth were at this time very close, and a number of Argive vases of the eighth century have been found at and near Syracuse, as at the Corinthian sanctuary of Perachora.[5] Argive vases are not common in the west, except on sites near Syracuse, and have not a wide general distribution,[6] so their presence at Syracuse is the more noteworthy. There is found a distinct class of vases of Argive style, many of which are thought to have been made at Syracuse; if this is so, the presence of Argives among the colonists is established; but the latest scholar to study them believes them all to be imports,[7] in which case they may have been brought by Corinthians. An Argive, Pollis, is said to have been king of Syracuse,[8] and if he

---

[1] Ortygia at Khalkis, Townley Schol. *Iliad* ix. 557; Arethusa at Khalkis, Strabo 449. This argument would apply with equal force to Aitolia, for in Nikander ap. Schol. Ap. Rhod. i. 419 the Sicilian Ortygia, and others, are said to be derived from an Aitolian Ortygia (and, incidentally, the Ortygia named in the Townley scholiast may have been near the Aitolian Khalkis); and there was a river Anapos in Akarnania (Thuk. ii. 82). See Holm, i. 113 ff.; cf. Hüttl, *Verfassungsgeschichte von Syrakus*, 29–30.

[2] Blakeway, op. cit. 183; Åkerström, loc. cit.

[3] He is described as a Herakleid, not in so many words as a Bakkhiad; but this seems a legitimate inference (Freeman, i. 572).

[4] Strabo 270; ps.-Skymn. 277–8.   [5] *Perachora*, i. 32.

[6] For detailed distribution see ibid., n. 2.

[7] P. E. Arias, *BCH*, 1936, 144 ff.

[8] Hippys of Rhegion ap. Athen. i. 31 *b*. See below, p. 93 f.

is historical he should be put at an early date and he or his ancestors thought of as coming from Argos to Syracuse at the time of the foundation; but the figure of Pollis is very shadowy. The presence of Argives among the colonists remains a mere conjecture.

Most of Arkhias' colonists came from the region of the Corinthia called Tenea.[1] This has been interpreted as indicating that the colony was predominantly agrarian in character.[2] This does not, however, follow. The Teneates left home no doubt because they found life increasingly difficult in their upland plain and hoped for better land overseas. But the Bakkhiad rulers who directed the colony will not have been moved solely by paternal care for their subjects. Their interest in trade is testified by ancient authorities as well as by the wide distribution of Protocorinthian vases. The colony, like all but a very few Greek colonies, had to be self-supporting in food, and so needed to have a majority of farmers and graziers. To relieve pressure of population at home may have been one purpose. But the main object of the rulers of Corinth can hardly have been other than to form a trading colony.

Of Arkhias a story was told to the effect that he had to leave Corinth after an unsavoury death in which he was involved.[3] It is interesting that such discreditable incidents should be remembered (or invented) about the founder of a colony who was awarded heroic honours. Whatever Arkhias' private reasons for leaving Corinth, the colony was an official venture of the Corinthian state, as is shown by the subsequent interest which Corinth took in it as in all her colonies. One other colonist is known by name: Aithiops, who was immortalized by Arkhilokhos as an example of improvidence, having parted with his lot on the voyage out for a honey-cake.[4] This story shows that the original lots of land ($\kappa\lambda\hat{\eta}\rho o\iota$) were not inalienable.

Together with Arkhias sailed another Herakleid, Khersikrates, who remained at Korkyra.[5] Synchronizations of this sort are suspect, and there is another story according to which Syracuse and Kroton were founded at the same time, which

---

[1] Strabo 380.   [2] A. Gwynn, *JHS*, 1918, 92–3.

[3] Plut. *Am. Narr.* 772; Diod. viii. 10; Schol. Ap. Rhod. iv. 1212.

[4] Arkhilokhos, fr. 145 Bergk, ap. Athen. 167 *d*. Freeman (i. 344) takes Clem. Alex. *Strom.* i. 21. 131 to indicate that Eumelos joined in the colonization. But Clement states only that Eumelos was contemporary with the foundation of Syracuse, not that he took part in it.

[5] Strabo 269.

involves chronological difficulties and seems unhistorical.[1] But the synchronization of Syracuse and Korkyra is factual and without romantic detail. There is no reason to doubt that the two colonies were founded at the same time and as part of the same scheme. Syracuse was the more important, and Korkyra was occupied to secure the route to Sicily. It had previously had an Eretrian settlement;[2] the Eretrians were driven out and settled on the mainland to the north, at Orikos.[3]

The occupation of Naxos by the Khalkidians and of Syracuse by the Corinthians were also regarded by the ancient historians, including Thukydides, as happening in two successive years. We may believe that this was, in fact, so, and that the two foundations were not unconnected. The Khalkidians took the best land in Sicily, the Syracusans the best harbour. The colonial voyages of Khalkidians, Corinthians, and Megarians took place very nearly at the same time. They may all have been in rivalry, racing for the best sites in Sicily. But there are indications that Khalkis and Corinth were not rivals. At the time of the war between the Greek states which accompanied the Lelantine War, Khalkis and Samos were allies;[4] at the same period, and perhaps on the same occasion, the Corinthians lent the Samians a shipwright to build the newly invented triremes.[5] The Corinthians expelled the Eretrians from Korkyra, but there is no evidence of conflict between Corinthians and Khalkidians; the Khalkidians of Leontinoi, for their part, quarrelled with the Megarian settlers, and Megara was in Greece the neighbour and enemy of Corinth.[6] It is likely therefore that Corinthians and Khalkidians had an agreement in colonizing Sicily, the Khalkidians to take the northern part of the east coast and the Leontine plain, the Corinthians to have Syracuse. Certainly Corinth reaped the benefit of trade not only with Syracuse but also with the Khalkidian colonies and the west generally. We cannot recognize any Khalkidian product as we can Corinthian vases, bronzes, and ivories, but if Khalkis had been so highly developed industrially as Corinth, and had had as great a share of the western trade, we should find some sign of it in the existing remains. The western export of such imperishable objects as have been preserved belonged

---

[1] See below, pp. 444 ff. [2] Plut. *QG* 11.
[3] This indicates that the Corinthians had at this time no interest in the mainland (Beaumont, *JHS*, 1936, 165).
[4] Herod. v. 99. [5] Thuk. i. 13.
[6] Hicks and Hill, *GHI*, no. 1.

from the end of the eighth century onwards to Corinth, in so complete a manner that we may reasonably infer that export of perishable objects also was confined to Corinth, who must have had a virtual monopoly of the western trade. This contrasts strongly with the period before the foundation of the colonies, when Corinthian is no more than one of many Greek pottery fabrics found in the west; indeed, before the foundation of Kyme, Corinth is less well represented than other centres. The change is working rapidly in the generation between the foundation of Kyme and that of Leontinoi; the vital point appears to be the foundation of Naxos and Syracuse. It is difficult to avoid the conclusion that those foundations were designed to have this effect, which was furthered by Corinthian action to secure Korkyra. Syracuse alone could not have assured this monopoly to the Corinthians, for the Khalkidian colonies, besides sharing in the effects of the monopoly, were so situated geographically that without them it could not have come into being. Seeing that Naxos and Syracuse were founded in successive years, it is reasonable to suppose that they were planned in execution of a mutual understanding. There must have been some *quid pro quo* for the Khalkidians to compensate for the suppression of free trade; we may find it in the help which they received from Corinth against the Eretrians. And there must have been something which Khalkis could supply but Corinth could not. What it was we do not know, but we must remember that Khalkis was at this time a well-established and populous power, Corinth a new power with a small territory.

Syracuse was from the first a great city, not limited to the island of Ortygia, but occupying also a considerable area on the mainland opposite.[1] In addition to the important trade in supplying Syracuse and the other Sicilian colonies with the products of their manufactures, possession of Syracuse also ensured to the Corinthians almost a monopoly of trade with the Sikels. The goods which Corinth exported are still in large part recognizable in the clay vases and bronzes from colonial sanctuaries and graves. In return, there can have been only one colonial product which was of sufficient value to pay for these goods: the import of corn to Greece must have already begun. Before the Pontos and Egypt were opened up, Sicily and south Italy would be the chief overseas source.

[1] See below, pp. 48 ff.

The success of this colonial venture and of wider trading in the west was one of the factors which transformed Corinth in a short space of time from a not very significant city to the leading state in Greece and the first to develop its trade and industries on a large scale.[1] For over a century Corinth controlled the whole colonial area economically, and in that time the colonies made Corinth what she was.

Only one other colony was planted on the east coast of Sicily, and that after much difficulty and many wanderings. Megara was Corinth's enemy in Old Greece; some time earlier she had lost the southern portion of her territory to Corinth,[2] and she was constantly pressed by further encroachments and reduced to doing some sort of homage;[3] but in the late eighth century she won a victory in a border quarrel, under the Olympic victor Orsippos.[4] A little earlier, probably soon after Arkhias sailed for Syracuse, the Megarians dispatched a colony to Sicily under Lamis. They came too late and, finding the land divided into 'spheres of influence', tried to settle on the edge of the Khalkidian sphere. Their first establishment was at Trotilon, which is now La Bruca, a narrow creek-like inlet on the north side of the promontory which divides the Gulf of Catania from the Bay of Megara. It has little hinterland, but was admirably situated for piracy, as ships could lie hid in the creek (which is not seen until near to, either by sea or on land), and, in particular, it lay across the Khalkidians' route to the mouth of the river of Leontinoi. It is probable but not certain that Leontinoi was already founded when they settled there. It is not known how long they stayed, but soon, on the Leontines' invitation, they removed to Leontinoi and shared in the colony there. The Leontines may have preferred to absorb them rather than leave them on their flanks and have been unable to expel them from Trotilon. In any case, the Leontines were in difficulties with the Sikels and needed help. The Megarians expelled the Sikels but were themselves driven out,[5] and established themselves at Thapsos. This is a small low barren island, joined to the mainland by an isthmus over which the waves sometimes break—again a site better suited for

---

[1] Payne, *Perachora*, i. 33 f.　　[2] Plut. *QG* 17. Cf. *Perachora*, i. 20 ff.
[3] Schol. Plato, *Euthyd.* 292; Schol. Ar. *Ran.* 442; Schol. Pind. *Nem.* vii. 155, *b*.
[4] Hicks and Hill, *GHI*, no. 1; Paus. i. 44. 1.
[5] Thuk. vi. 3; Polyaen. v. 5. For the relations of Greeks and Sikels at Leontinoi see below, p. 45 f.

piracy than agriculture, but this time at the Syracusans' expense. They remained there a short time only, perhaps six months,[1] and their leader Lamis died there. It is a remarkable coincidence that in the Siculan II cemetery of Thapsos which has yielded many Mycenaean vases one grave was used again in the late eighth century, when a Protocorinthian cup was buried in it.[2] Perhaps this is the grave of Lamis. Finally, they were invited to settle on the mainland opposite by the Sikel prince of Hybla[3] (located at Mellili, on the hill immediately behind Megara, where there are remains of all Sikel periods).[4] He gave them a place on the shore, where there is shelter and good water, and a little plain which stretches south to the edge of the plateau over which Syracuse later spread. Here they had land enough to live on, and room to use the sea; but they depended on the favour of the Sikels, and, even if they could expand at their expense, they would be checked by their more powerful neighbours Syracuse and Leontinoi. This happened. Megara remained a small and poor city, far outshone by her daughter city Selinus.

It has sometimes been asked why neither the Megarians nor any other Greeks occupied the site of Augusta, the ancient Xiphonia.[5] This peninsula, which occupies roughly the same position relative to the Bay of Megara as Ortygia does to the Great Harbour, has been since the thirteenth century A.D. the site of a flourishing town. Lack of water seems to be the reason why it was not occupied in antiquity; the water at the end of the peninsula is poor and scanty, and the inhabitants used to draw water with boats from the site of Megara.

How Syracuse regarded this establishment less than ten miles from her walls is not known. They must have maintained normal relations, for there is no natural boundary in the plain between Syracuse and Megara, and some boundary must early have been marked out. With the support of the local Sikels,

---

[1] Polyainos says that after their expulsion from Leontinoi they lived for six months at Trotilon. The simplest way of harmonizing this with Thuk. is to suppose that Polyainos has confused Trotilon and Thapsos, and written the former for the latter.

[2] *MA*, vi. 103 and pl. iv. 16; Arias, *BPI*, 1936–7, 62, fig. 4. The Greek deposit is separated by a metre of earth from the Sikel burial.

[3] His name Hyblon may be an eponymous formation of later date. No other Sikel name is known before the fifth century. [4] *BPI*, 1891, 53 ff.

[5] Freeman, i. 388–9. The supposed city of Tauromenium on the heights to the north of Augusta, overlooking this peninsula, has no foundation in fact (Pais, *Stor. Sic.* 592 ff.). Steph. Byz. s.v. is no doubt mistaken in speaking of a city of Xiphonia; he calls any geographical name a city.

Megara was probably strong enough to be respected by Syracuse during her early years.

All this colonizing activity in Sicily falls within a very short period, perhaps no more than a decade. One other colony was founded in the early period, but after a considerable interval of time. In 688 Cretans and Rhodians, under the leadership of Entimos and Antiphemos, founded the first Greek colony on the south coast of Sicily. Gela lay on a long sandy hill at the mouth of the river Gelas, from which it took its name, for the official name Lindioi soon dropped out of use. It lies above a shelving beach such as was used for drawing up ships, and commands a wide and rich plain, Vergil's *campi Geloi*. The site was already known to Greeks, for there are pre-colonization imports, Cretan among them, associated with Sikel pottery, below a sanctuary outside the walls at Bitalemi.[1]

After this there is another long interval before the Greeks moved into the west of Sicily, with the foundation of Himera in 648. This move brought them into contact, though not yet into conflict, with the Phoenicians who occupied the west end of the island. In all the colonization of eastern Sicily there is no word of Phoenicians.[2] There is no archaeological evidence that Phoenicians frequented the coast of Sicily before, or so soon as, the Greeks. Thukydides states that they had established themselves all round Sicily for the sake of trade, settling on promontories and small islands off the coast, but when the Greeks came in numbers withdrew to Motye, Soloeis, and Panormos.[3] The absence of archaeological material which might be due to their commerce makes it very difficult to accept this statement as it stands. The argument that because the settlements were only trading-stations therefore Phoenician remains need not be expected seems to misunderstand the nature of such settlements. In the first place, even a trading-station must have some degree of permanence and some semi-permanent inhabitants, some of whom would die and be buried there. If Thukydides' word ᾤκουν were to be pressed, it would imply something like a permanent settlement. There are not a great many places round the coast of Sicily which answer to Thukydides' description. Two on the east coast which do are

---

[1] Blakeway, op. cit. 183.
[2] A Phoenician pirate occurs in a late story about the foundation of Gela, Zenob. i. 54; see below, p. 327.   [3] vi. 2. 6.

Thapsos and Syracuse, that is, the Island. These have names which are not obviously Greek or Sikel, but for which plausible Phoenician etymologies have been proposed.[1] Both have been excavated, Thapsos thoroughly, the island of Syracuse considerably, and have yielded no trace of anything which could belong to a Phoenician settlement or have been brought by Phoenicians. At Thapsos there is a Sikel cemetery of the Second period, with many Mycenaean vases; this comes to an end in perhaps the eleventh century. The brief occupation by the Megarians before they finally settled at Megara has left its mark in a burial with Protocorinthian vases in a re-used tomb.[2] If this very shortlived settlement (perhaps of only six months)[3] has made a mark, surely a Phoenician settlement or trading-post, however transitory, should have left some casual burial or dropped object. In Syracuse the lowest stratum under the Athenaion is the remains of a Sikel settlement immediately preceding the Greek colonization. There are some pieces of Greek pottery among the Sikel, and some which appear to be local imitations of Greek geometric. There may have been Greeks living among the Sikels before the foundation of the colony; certainly there were Greeks trading with the Sikel inhabitants. If Phoenicians were also trading on any but the smallest scale, we should expect to find something of theirs, or at least something oriental such as they might have imported. There is no such object. This makes it extremely unlikely that Syracuse was one of the places from which they withdrew on the arrival of the Greeks. Syracuse is the natural harbour for an area the inhabitants of which were at this time among the richest and most advanced of Sicily. Thapsos is in the same area. No other coastal site of this period has been excavated, but nothing that can be ascribed to the Phoenicians has been found on the many inland sites.[4] We know what to expect of

---

[1] Holm, *Geschichte Siziliens*, i. 80 ff.; cf. Busolt, *Gr. Ges.* i. 373–4; Freeman, i. 243 ff., 559 ff., who is very cautious on the argument from names; for the extreme view, Movers, *Die Phönizier*, ii. 2. 324 ff.

[2] See above, p. 19. [3] Ibid.

[4] Blakeway suggested in an unpublished note that 'it is possible that it is to Phoenician elements that we owe the apparently Syro-Cypriot character of much of the painted Graeco-Siculan pottery of Licodia Eubea, Lentini, Finocchito during the III Siculan period'. But these elements lead to *Greek* Cyprus, not to Syria or Phoenicia; a number of Cypriot parallels for Siculan vases are recognized in his published work, and could be multiplied; and he rightly speaks of Phoenician influence as no more than a possibility (op. cit. 185, n. 2). An iron knife found at Atlit in Palestine is, its excavator suggests, of Sicilian type (C. N. Johns, *QDAP*, vi. 151, fig. 16 and pl. 39. 4; cf. pp. 136, 150). If he is correct, this will be an object brought back to Palestine by some Phoenician trader.

the Phoenicians from contemporary finds in Etruria, where objects of Syro-Phoenician manufacture and other oriental objects which would normally be carried by Phoenician traders are as common as Greek. In Sicily there is nothing of this sort, and only a few overseas objects cannot be confidently asserted to be Greek.[1]

It is improbable that the Phoenicians ever visited eastern Sicily in any but the most casual way, though it is possible that they came slave-raiding in the period when the *Odyssey* was composed, before the Greeks began to visit Sicily. Of their supposed trading activity hardly a trace can be recognized. Their settlements in western Sicily occupy the sort of site described by Thukydides, and it may be due to a mistaken inference of him or his source that their occupation is extended to the whole island. They settled at Motye, a small island at the extreme western point of Sicily, at least as early as the beginning of the seventh century, for from this date Motye imported considerable quantities of Protocorinthian vases. The cemeteries of Motye can give only a *terminus ante quem*; but taken in conjunction with the absence of Phoenician remains in eastern Sicily, they suggest that the Phoenicians arrived in Sicily only after the Greeks had settled the east coast, and were obliged to limit their activities to the west. Their African colonies were already in existence. Carthage was founded in 813 B.C., according to tradition,[2] and at least as early as the eighth century, to judge from the oldest material remains.[3] The other African colonies (Utica, Hadrumetum, and the two Hippos) and the Spanish colonies are said to be older, and even if the dates *c.* 1100 handed down or inferred for the earliest of them are grossly exaggerated, they should be older than any Greek colony in the west.[4] The Phoenicians will have moved from Africa to occupy the west end of Sicily.

Thus far we have had the guidance of Thukydides, who gives a connected account, with dates, of the foundation of the Sicilian colonies. Later authors add further details and dates, some of

---

[1] The main class is the scarabs and other porcelain or paste objects of Egyptian manufacture, or imitations of such. These are common in Greece from the eighth century and may have been brought west as well by Greek as by Phoenician or any other traders. Cf. below, p. 254, n. 3. [2] Dion. Hal. i. 74.

[3] D. B. Harden, *Iraq*, iv. 59 ff. For a lower dating of the earliest material from Motye and Carthage cf. Åkerström, op. cit. 162–4.

[4] Gsell, *Histoire de l'Afrique du Nord*, i. 359 ff.; Schulten, *Tartessos*, 16 ff.; Ashby, *CAH*, ii. 581.

which conflict with Thukydides, but in the main his authority prevailed.[1] The system introduced thus early into the history of Sicily may have suppressed variant origins and dates. However, the confidence with which Thukydides writes and the logical nature of his account indicate that he based himself on a sound historical tradition. The foundation of each colony appears as a marked event, celebrated annually in later times, and due in most cases to a single body of colonists.

It is otherwise with the south Italian colonies. Their origins are known only from later and less systematic historians, but the tradition appears in itself to have been very different. Unlike the Sicilian colonies, many of those in Italy claimed heroic origins in the era of the Trojan War. Some of them had mixed populations and may have had more than one foundation. There were other settlements which never received the form of a *polis*. It appears that, while colonization in Sicily was planned and directed by a few Greek states, there were in south Italy many colonial ventures which just grew.

In Italy there is little archaeological evidence except for the neighbourhood of Taras and Lokroi. But there can be no doubt that, like the farther west, it was in the earliest period open to the trade of any Greek city. This state of affairs perhaps continued during the period when the colonies were founded. They were open to the citizens of many Greek states in a way that the Sicilian colonies were not. Sicily was controlled by Corinth and Khalkis in agreement, which cornered the trade of Sicily and took the best sites for colonies. The south Italian colonies were founded for the most part by people from both sides of the Corinthian Gulf who were not themselves commercial. The sites which they chose show that they were more concerned with finding corn-land than with commercial possibilities. They could afford to be more receptive than the commercial colonizing powers.

The first of the colonies on the east coast of Italy, the coast which faces Greece, was founded a generation after Kyme, some fifteen years after Naxos. This coast was well known therefore to Greeks, and the sites of two colonies certainly, Lokroi and Taras, and probably of others, were occupied by native settlements with whom Greeks traded and among whom they settled. This rich land was less attractive to the first

---

[1] For a critical account of the traditions of the colonizations and a reasoned statement of their chronology see Appendix I.

traders and settlers than the farther shores of Etruria and Sicily, whose inhabitants had reached a higher degree of civilization.

When colonization began on this coast it was due not to any of the great trading centres but to the little cities of Akhaia, on the north coast of the Peloponnese. The first, and for long the greatest, of the Akhaian colonies was Sybaris. This was planted in the greatest and most fertile plain of the Ionian coast, at the mouth of two considerable rivers, the Sybaris and the Krathis. It had no natural port, and lies at the head of a gulf where ships bound for Sicily and the Straits of Messina would naturally stand off shore. It became an important point of call, being at one end of the shortest portage from Ionian to Tyrrhenian Sea, but commerce must originally have been secondary to agriculture.

The oecist was Is of Helike, the capital of the Akhaian federation, the date of foundation most probably 720.[1] The name Sybaris shared between city and river is that of a spring near Bura;[2] the other river, the Krathis, was named after the river which runs into the sea by Aigai in Akhaia.[3] Together with the Akhaians, some Troizenians took part in the colony, but the Akhaians were soon reinforced and drove out the Troizenians.[4] In doing so they broke an oath of some sort, the first of a series of impious acts for which the Sybarites were distinguished down to the last days of their existence. We are reminded of the dealings of Khalkidians and Megarians at Leontinoi. As there, so probably at Sybaris, the stronger party, at first unable to stand alone, could within a few years defy the religious sanction which protected the weaker party. It is not known with certainty where the Troizenians went, but it

---

[1] Strabo 263. On the correct form of the name Is see Byvanck, 77, n. 6; Pais, *Stor. Sic.*, 534, n. 3. There is a variant date 708, under which Eusebius puts the foundation of Sybaris as well as that of Kroton. But it appears from Antiokhos' account of the foundation of Kroton (ap. Strabo 262) that Sybaris was already founded, though not very firmly established. The variant which makes Sybaris and Kroton contemporary is probably due to a careless reading of Antiokhos or a work derived from him. The figure of 210 years between the foundation of Sybaris and its destruction in 510 (ps.-Skymn. 356–60) may well be the era of the city rather than a calculation of six generations of thirty-five years. See below, p. 448.

[2] Strabo 386. [3] Ibid.; Herod. i. 145; Paus. vii. 25. 11; viii. 15. 9.

[4] Arist. *Pol.* 1303ᵃ 29: ὅσοι ἤδη συνοίκους ἐδέξαντο ἢ ἐποίκους, οἱ πλεῖστοι διεστασίασαν· οἷον Τροιζηνίοις Ἀχαιοὶ συνῴκησαν Σύβαριν, εἶτα πλείους οἱ Ἀχαιοὶ γενόμενοι ἐξέβαλον τοὺς Τροιζηνίους (ὅθεν τὸ ἄγος συνέβη τοῖς Συβαρίταις). As Aristotle uses συνῴκησαν not ἐπ-, it may be inferred that Akhaians and Troizenians arrived together. It has been thought that Lokrians also joined in the colony, but the evidence is weak. See below, p. 37.

has been suggested that they went with the blessing and support of the Akhaians to Poseidonia,[1] which was a Sybarite colony[2] and was occupied as early as 700.[3]

Poseidonia lay near the mouth of the Sele (ancient Silaris) in a fair-sized plain, one of the largest on the west coast south of Naples, and tapped a rich and varied country-side. There were a number of places in the neighbourhood which in the seventh century imported Protocorinthian vases;[4] these must have reached them through Poseidonia. Though without natural defences and at the mercy of the inhabitants of the hills behind it, it is well situated for agriculture and trade. Also, it lies at the northern end of a land route which begins at Sybaris and traverses the inland valley of the Diano, a tributary of the Sele. This route passes Sala Consilina and other places where much archaic Greek material has been found, and was probably early used for through trade.[5] In the sixth century, after the Etruscan expansion into Campania, it was no doubt used for the famous commerce between Sybarites and Etruscans, and Poseidonia was important as the point of interchange, being the northernmost Sybarite post.[6] But there is no evidence to carry this intercourse back into the early seventh century when conditions were greatly different, or to suppose that Poseidonia was founded with an eye to this trade.

There may already have been Greek occupation of the site at the mouth of the Sele before the Sybarite colony was founded. The excavators of the Heraion have expressed the opinion that the earliest material found there dates back as far as c. 700.[7] Until study and publication of the finds are further advanced this must remain a provisional opinion; it is not out of the question that this site was occupied before 700 (Geometric vases are reported to have been found at a cemetery in the neighbourhood),[8] in which case it would antedate the arrival of the Sybarites. It has been suggested that the original

[1] Pais, *Stor. Sic.*, 533 ff. The direct evidence to the effect that the Troizenians went to Poseidonia is slight. There was a celebrated worship of Poseidon at Troizen, and the city is said once to have been called Poseidonia or Poseidonias (Strabo 373; Paus. ii. 30. 8). But there is no need to seek further for the origin of the name Poseidonia than the Poseidon of the federated Akhaians worshipped at Helike. There is no reason to identify the city of Steph. Byz.'s confused passage (s.v. Τροιζήν) ἔστι καὶ ἄλλη Τροιζὴν ἐν Μασσαλίᾳ τῆς Ἰταλίας with Poseidonia.

[2] Strabo 252; ps.-Skymn. 249.

[3] *N Sc*, 1937, 209.

[4] See below, p. 263.

[5] For this route see below, pp. 154, 207.

[6] See Randall-MacIver, *Greek Cities in Italy and Sicily*, 12.

[7] *N Sc*, 1937, 209.

[8] *JHS*, 1938, 251.

settlement was here, at the mouth of the river Sele.[1] This is likely enough, as Strabo says that the first settlement of the Sybarites was on the sea.[2] What cannot yet be determined, however, is whether this original settlement was that of the Sybarites, to be dated somewhere near 700, or whether it preceded the Sybarites, who were responsible only for the settlement on the site of Poseidonia. If indeed, as appears possible, the Sybarites found other Greeks established before them at the site of the Heraion, it might explain why they should ascribe a high antiquity to this temple, attributing its foundation to Jason. What is clear from the excavations is that the Heraion is as old as the early seventh century, and was always Greek; no trace of a preceding native cult has been found. Further progress of the excavations will illuminate this early period, as the sensational finds of metopes have revealed a new chapter of the colonial culture of the sixth century.

The first few years of Sybaris' existence will have been spent in consolidation and dealing with the Troizenians. A few years after its foundation (in 708 according to the Eusebian chronology)[3] Myskellos of Rhypes set out to found a colony, and inquired at Delphi whether he would not do better to settle at Sybaris than at Kroton.[4] Antiokhos, who is our authority for the story, clearly regarded Sybaris as not very firmly founded when Myskellos went on his visit of reconnaissance, so that admiring the site and the country he thought of bringing his own settlers there to reinforce or drive out their compatriots.

The part of Delphi in the foundation of Kroton is more fully stated than in the case of any other western colony. Myskellos, like so many other founders of colonies, was at Delphi on private business and was told to settle at Kroton; asking for further information, he was given sailing-directions; and coming back yet again after his voyage of reconnaissance to ask if he might not settle at Sybaris instead, he was told to take what the gods gave with good grace.[5] The Delphic connexion is further asserted on the earliest coins of Kroton, which have as

[1] Bérard, *Colonisation*, 236. I have not seen Bérard's paper, 'Les Origines historiques et légendaires de Posidonia à la lumière des récentes découvertes archéologiques', in *Mél. arch. hist.* 1940.

[2] Strabo 252. It can hardly be supposed that the first settlement was on the beach and was later moved inland to the present site, which is less than half a mile from the sea; such a move would be insignificant and purposeless.

[3] With which agrees the date 710/709 given in Dion. Hal. ii. 59.

[4] Strabo 262; Diod. viii. 17.

[5] Ll. cc.; Hippys ap. Zenob. iii. 42 (*FHG*, ii. 14).

emblem a tripod. That it is the Delphic tripod is made clear by a stater of the late fifth century on which Apollo is shown shooting the Python, with the tripod between; the obverse shows Herakles, with the inscription OSKSMTAM,[1] in reference to the legendary foundation by Herakles, who killed the eponymous hero Kroton or Lakinios and in expiation founded the temple of Hera on the Lakinian promontory.[2]

The city lay seven miles to the north of the Lakinian promontory. It had a harbour of sorts,[3] the only natural harbour between Taras and the Straits, and was therefore a port of call for ships before rounding the Lakinian promontory, the main feature on this coast. But it was only a port of call, not important for commerce. Behind Kroton rises the mass of the Sila mountains, cutting it off from the interior and the opposite coast. The slopes and foot-hills offer an extensive and fertile territory, not, however, comparable with Sybaris for riches. The growth of Kroton was slower than that of Sybaris; it was celebrated not for wealth and luxury but for its doctors and athletes. Thence arose a story that Myskellos and Arkhias both consulted Delphi at the same time, and were given the choice of wealth or health; Arkhias chose wealth, Myskellos health. This story is of the late sixth century or early fifth, the period of the fame of Kroton's doctors, not earlier, and the synchronization of Kroton and Syracuse which it states is a chronological crux not easily resolved.[4]

Except for a poor tradition which makes Kroton and Lokroi Spartan colonies before the First Messenian War,[5] the Akhaian origin of Kroton is universally admitted. The founder, Myskellos, came from Rhypes.[6] There are no definite indications of the presence of other elements, whether Akhaian or not, among the colonists.

A number of subsidiary foundations were due to the Krotoniates,[7] of which only one, Kaulonia, was of much importance at an early date. Kaulonia is commonly called a Krotoniate foundation.[8] But the name of its oecist, Typhon of Aigion,[9] is preserved, which indicates that it was an independent city; and this is confirmed by its sixth-century coinage.

---

[1] Head, *HN*², 97.
[2] Diod. iv. 24. 7; Serv. ad *Aen.* iii. 552; Ovid, *Met.* xv. 15 ff.   [3] Cf. Polyb. x. 1. 6.
[4] Strabo 269; cf. Parke, *History of the Delphic Oracle*, 71–2; and see below, pp. 444 ff.
[5] Paus. iii. 3. 1.   [6] Strabo 387.   [7] See below, pp. 159 ff.
[8] Ps.-Skymn. 318 ff.; Solinus, ii. 10; Steph. Byz. s.v. Αὐλών.
[9] Strabo 261; Paus. vi. 3. 12.

Its foundation will have been inspired by Kroton, to which it stood in the same relation as Metapontion to Sybaris. The town of Klete, named after the Amazon of that name, sacked by the Krotoniates, is identified with Kaulonia.[1] The story of Klete implies that Kaulonia was occupied by native peoples before the foundation of the Greek colony; and under some Hellenistic houses in the town was found Protocorinthian and some uncertain Geometric pottery of the early seventh century.[2] This probably antedates the colonization. There is no direct evidence of the date of this event, which may have been soon after that of Lokroi.[3] It has been regarded, for geographical reasons, as an Akhaian outpost against Lokroi; but there is no other evidence to support this view. Its position on the Punto di Stilo, the chief promontory between the Lakinian headland and the Zephyrian, is like that of Kroton and Lokroi, but much weaker; and though it had no harbour, the town may have rendered useful service to shipping rounding the point.

When Kroton was founded the finest site on the east coast of Italy was still occupied by Iapygians. On this open coast Taranto provides the only good harbour; the islands of St. Peter and St. Paul, the ancient Khoirades, shelter the outer harbour, from which a narrow channel leads to the quiet waters of the inner harbour. Taras thus resembles Syracuse with its double harbour. The acropolis is on a small promontory between the two harbours (the present eastern channel is an artificial creation of the Middle Ages), and, like Syracuse, Taras early spread to the mainland opposite. The harbour of Taras, again like Syracuse, had been a centre of Mycenaean trade and was well known to Greeks before its colonization.

Near the western point of the entrance to the Little Harbour is the prehistoric site of Scoglio del Tonno, where above a Bronze Age settlement of the type called 'Adriatic' or 'Apennine'[4] were found Late Mycenaean vases and a figurine, and Geometric and Protocorinthian vases. The stratification is confused, and the Protocorinthian sherds are reported to have been found mixed with the Mycenaean. Apparently there was no native pottery in this stratum, which would indicate

---

[1] Lyk. 1002 ff. and Schol.; cf. Bérard, *Colonisation*, 172, 382.
[2] *MA*, xxiii. 817, fig. 77.   [3] Bérard, op. cit. 173.
[4] Falsely described by the excavator, Quagliati, and frequently since, as a *terramara*. See Säflund, op. cit. *infra*.

that it was a settlement from overseas. Contact with the Aegean was not broken for long, if at all, between the Mycenaean imports of the late thirteenth century and the coming of the Greeks; there is Protogeometric and Geometric, including probably Laconian Geometric, as well as Protocorinthian.[1] Occupation of this site comes to an end about 700; it appears therefore that it ceased to be inhabited on the foundation of the colony.[2]

Another settlement on the site of Taranto, in the Borgo Nuovo, used painted pottery in the Early Iron Age, which is clearly the ancestor in shape and decoration of Apulian geometric pottery. Its relationship to Greek Protogeometric and Geometric is not certain; it is of local manufacture, but appears to owe something to Greek originals.[3] Little direct connexion can be traced, however, between this pottery and that of Scoglio del Tonno. These pots were found in a well, where they had probably been dumped by the Greeks when clearing a native settlement on the site of which they wished to build. They are to be regarded as the products of those Iapygians who preceded the Greeks in occupation of the site.[4]

The story of the foundation of Taras is told with abundant and untrustworthy detail,[5] but the main lines are clear. It was a Laconian colony, the only one sent out at this period from Sparta. After the First Messenian War there were a number of Laconians of whom the State wished to be rid. They were branded as base-born; we need not go into all the explanations offered of their name Partheniai. They are said to have gathered themselves together at Amyklai in revolt against the Spartans, whence it has been thought that they belonged to

[1] The material from this important site, dug by Q. Quagliati and described by him in *N Sc*, 1900, 411 ff., has never been adequately published. Some is included in *CVA Taranto*, ii; a good selection is published by G. Säflund in *Δράγμα M. P. Nilsson dedicatum*, 458 ff.; but he does not include any of the Greek geometric other than Protocorinthian. Quagliati, *Il Museo Nazionale di Taranto*, 11, speaks of geometric pottery from Laconia and the Cyclades, and Droop, *BSA*, xiii. 121, n. 1, mentions Laconian geometric sherds.

[2] Säflund, op. cit. 490, concludes: 'Die Siedlung auf Punta del Tonno kann die Koloniengründung nicht lang überdauert haben.' But nothing from this site is certainly later than the foundation of Taras; there is no developed Protocorinthian such as is found at Taras, and the latest material appears to belong to the eighth century.

[3] Mayer, *Apulien*, pll. 3–4; Blakeway, *BSA*, xxxiii. 175–6.

[4] So Mayer, op. cit. 1 ff.; Messerschmidt in von Duhn, *Italische Gräberkunde*, ii. 323–4. Säflund, op. cit. 489, calls the native 'Apennine' material from Scoglio del Tonno Iapygian; but the Borgo Nuovo material has a much better claim.

[5] Strabo 278–80; ps.-Skymn. 330 ff.; Paus. x. 10. 6–8; iii. 12, 5; Dion. Hal. xix. 1; Arist. *Pol.* 1306b 29; Justin, iii. 4.

the pre-Dorian population of Laconia, whose capital was at Amyklai. This hypothesis is supported by the worship at Taras of Apollo Hyakinthios,[1] the god of Amyklai. The Spartans agreed to send them out to a colony, and on Delphic advice Phalanthos, their leader, chose Taras as the site. There is a strong mythical element in the legends attaching to Phalanthos, who like Arion was saved from drowning by a dolphin,[2] and he has been commonly regarded as a faded god. But there is no reason to doubt the historical fact that the founder of the colony was a Spartan of that name, though he has been confused with Taras, the mythical eponym of the city. And we may believe that he was expelled from Taras and ended his days at Brentesion, the modern Brindisi;[3] but was remembered with divine honours at Taras.

The first settlement was perhaps at Satyrion, which is to be located at Leporano, a few miles east of Taranto, which like Scoglio del Tonno imported both Mycenaean and Protocorinthian vases.[4] Satyrion was named in the oracle to Phalanthos:

Σατύριόν τοι δῶκα Τάραντά τε πίονα δῆμον
οἰκῆσαι, καὶ πῆμα Ἰαπύγεσσι γενέσθαι.[5]

This oracle has as good a chance as any foundation-oracle to be genuine; whether it is so or not, it shows, as is implied also by the naming of the nymph Satyria as mother of Taras, that Satyrion was part of the original settlement. It has been suggested that the colonists settled at Satyrion while negotiating their lodgement with the Iapygians.[6] This is not unlikely, but it should be noted that Scoglio del Tonno would suit this purpose equally well; Laconian geometric pottery has been found there, and as it was nowhere else exported in the way of trade, it may well have been carried there by the first settlers. The pre-Laconian inhabitants of Taras are described by Antiokhos[7] as Cretans and Iapygians; the Iapygians will be the makers of the Borgo Nuovo painted pottery, the Cretans, descendants of the companions of Minos, the people of Scoglio del Tonno,

---

[1] Polyb. viii. 28. 2. [2] Paus. x. 13. 10.

[3] Strabo 282; Justin, iii. 4.

[4] *CVA Taranto*, ii, III A, pl. 2. 6–8; Johansen, *VS*, 101; there is also unpublished Protocorinthian of earlier date than the Late Protocorinthian mentioned by Johansen.

[5] Diod. Sic. viii. 21; cf. Parke, op. cit. 77–9. The silly story of Phalanthos and his wife Aithra, told to settle where he felt rain from a clear sky (Paus. x. 10. 6), is a good example of an unhistoric foundation-oracle.

[6] Wuilleumier, *Tarente*, 46.

[7] Ap. Strabo 279.

occupied since Mycenaean times by people from the Aegean (though not Cretans).[1]

The cults of Taras are almost exclusively Spartan.[2] Taras in its later history retained close and friendly relations with Sparta.[3] The dialect is Doric, though with noticeable pre-Dorian elements.[4] There is a considerable import of Laconian vases in the sixth century.[5] The late archaic art of Taras, the earliest distinguishable Tarentine art, is strongly influenced by Laconian.[6] Though we do not think of Sparta as a colonial power, her economic needs being satisfied and her man-power occupied by the conquest of Messenia, the Spartans found their colony of value, and kept up as close connexions as are attested between any mother city and colony. Economically, however, Taras was from the first included, like all the rest of the western colonial area, within the Corinthian sphere, and has yielded fine Protocorinthian vases.

The date is given by Eusebius as 706. This confirms, rather than is confirmed by, the current dating of the First Messenian War. It is supported by the date of the oldest vases from the cemeteries of Taras, which are of the first quarter of the seventh century.[7]

Taras had not been long founded when the Akhaians, under Sybarite leadership, decided to occupy the territory between Sybaris and Taras in order to forestall possible Tarentine expansion in this rich land.[8] It is surprising to find Sybaris and Taras already in collision in the first generation after their foundation, and the story has been regarded as a reflection of the hostility of Thuria and Taras over the foundation of Herakleia in 432.[9] But it is difficult to see why Antiokhos, who is quoted explicitly by Strabo, should refer the contemporary situation back into the seventh century, and his story is not impossible. It implies that the first expansion of both cities was along the sea, keeping close to their communications with Greece and casting eyes on the fertile plain. There is no natural barrier in the plain between Taras and Metapontion, which are distant about twenty-seven miles.

There were two sites in this plain which were occupied by

---

[1] See *BSR* xvi. 1 ff.   [2] Giannelli, *Culti e Miti della Magna Grecia*, 1 ff., 283 ff.
[3] Wuilleumier, op. cit. 43–4.
[4] Ibid. 659.   [5] Lane, *BSA*, xxxiv. 181.
[6] Ashmole, *Late Archaic and Early Classical Greek Sculpture in Sicily and South Italy*, 11.
[7] Johansen, *VS*, 89, 182, n. 2.
[8] Strabo 264–5.   [9] Byvanck, 72.

Greek colonies: Siris and Metapontion. The Akhaians occupied the site more distant from Sybaris, that of Metapontion. Antiokhos speaks of these two sites in language which might imply that they were already cities in existence (δυεῖν δὲ οὐσῶν πόλεων) at the time of the Sybarite proposal to colonize Metapontion; though he says that Metapontion, settled by Pylians after the Trojan War, was then deserted (ἐκλειφθέντα τὸν τόπον ἐποικῆσαι τῶν Ἀχαιῶν τινάς . . .). It may be that they were both native towns with Greek elements in them. The date of the foundation of Metapontion is uncertain,[1] but it may be assigned to the first quarter of the seventh century, as it was after Taras and before Siris. Early material has been found in recent excavations at Metapontion,[2] including a terra-cotta head which may be as old as the eighth century, and appears to have Boiotian affinities.[3] Though it is rash to argue from a brief preliminary publication, it appears as if occupation of Metapontion goes back farther than Taras—that is, that the site was already Greek before the Akhaians planted their colony.

It is generally called an Akhaian colony, but it is not recorded from which city or cities her settlers came. The oecist was, according to one version, Leukippos,[4] who appears on the coins of Metapontion in the fourth century.[5] The story, which relates how Leukippos gained possession of the land from the Tarentines by a quibble, is related of the same Leukippos in connexion with Kallipolis,[6] the modern Gallipoli on the Sallentine peninsula, and is more in place there; Leukippos was a Laconian hero, and the story was no doubt introduced to Metapontion during the Tarentine domination.[7] According to Ephoros the founder was Daulios, tyrant of Krisa;[8] but he is a legendary, not an historic figure, and this version offers an alternative for the legendary origin in the period of the Trojan Wars.[9] The commonly received account ascribed to Metapontion a foundation by Nestor and the Pylians. This is as old as Bakkhylides, who calls it a foundation of the Akhaians after the fall of Troy.[10]

[1] It is recorded in Eusebius under the year 773. This is meaningless as it stands; see below for a possible explanation.

[2] Briefly referred to in *AJA*, 1941, 471 ff. I have not seen the excavator's reports in *N Sc*, 1940, 51 ff.; *Le Arti*, iii (1940–1), 92 ff., cited in *AJA*.

[3] Ibid., figs. 20–1.

[4] Strabo 265.

[5] Head, *HN*², 78.

[6] Dion. Hal. xix. 3.

[7] Pais, *Stor. Sic.*, i. 220 ff.

[8] Ap. Strabo, l.c.

[9] See Bérard, *Colonisation*, 196–7.

[10] x. 120 ff.

The lack of precision about the oecist and the founders suggests that the origins of Metapontion were less certain than those of other cities. The cults also indicate a mixed origin. Elements have been traced with more or less probability to many Greek states.[1] Some of these depend on the rather delicate interpretation of late legends and can hardly be taken to establish the presence from early times of contingents from these states. The most interesting is the legend of Melanippe, who found refuge with Metabos or Metapontios, the eponym of Metapontion, and gave birth there to Boiotos and Aiolos.[2] Metabos' wife, supplanted by Melanippe (or Arne, according to some versions), is given many names, one of which is Siris, eponym of the neighbouring colony. This Boiotian legend appears to be located in Italy as early as Euripides, and it is most natural to suppose that it was brought there by Boiotians.[3]

The Eusebian date 773 for Metapontion and Pandosia (presumably the one named in the Herakleian Tables,[4] which lay near Siris, not the more famous inland town), though it cannot be accepted for the definitive foundation of Greek colonies, may yet have some foundation in fact. Many of the south Italian colonies were alleged to have heroic origins in the period of the Nostoi. In the neighbourhood of Taranto these tales are supported by the Mycenaean remains at Scoglio del Tonno and elsewhere in the Sallentine peninsula. Elsewhere in Magna Graecia there is no archaeological evidence of this sort. It would be bold therefore to assert that the reputed settlement of Metapontion by the Pylians, of Siris by Trojans, of Petelia and the neighbourhood by Philoktetes, of Lagaria by Epeios, has any basis in fact. But these connexions are better vouched for, and in themselves more plausible, than such mythical colonizations as that of Argyripa by Diomedes, of Skylletion by the Athenians under Menestheus, of Praeneste and other sites in Latium and on the west coast of Italy by companions

---

[1] Giannelli, op. cit. 62 ff., 291 ff.

[2] Strabo 265; Hygin. 186; Diod. Sic. iv. 67; Schol. Dion. Perieg. v. 461. In the two latter versions Arne, not Melanippe, is the mother of Boiotos and Aiolos. How far any of the extant versions preserves the story related by Euripides in the Μελανίππη Δεσμῶτις is doubtful. He is, however, quoted by Athen. 523d as authority for the name Siris, so must have located the action in Italy.

[3] This is not to say that Metapontion was mainly settled by Boiotians (as Giannelli, op. cit.). Nor is this supported by the supposed equation of the name Metabos-Metapontion with that of Mount Messapion in Boiotia. The name is found in many other parts of Greece and there is no need to look farther for a parallel than Messapia in Italy.

[4] IG, xiv. 645, l. 12 et al.; cf. Pais, op. cit. 224–5.

of Odysseus. These heroic colonizations are outside our present scope,[1] except to suggest the possibility that there were in some places on the east coast of south Italy settlements of Greeks made in the disturbed period after the Trojan War, which had not been entirely destroyed or absorbed by the natives at the time when Greeks again began to sail these waters.[2] If this probability is allowed, then Metapontion, Siris, and the neighbourhood of the Alaian promontory are the most probable situations for such settlements.

There is another less vague possibility to which the Eusebian date can be attached. The origin of the Metapontines, to judge from the variety of their cults, was mixed. It is possible that Boiotians and others came there, not with the Akhaians who gave Metapontion the definitive character of a colony in the early seventh century, but earlier; that they were already in possession, though not organized, when the Sybarites brought other Akhaians to found the colony.

The same thing is possible of Siris. The evidence for a pre-colonization occupation is as good, and as weak, as for Metapontion. Siris also had a heroic origin, ascribed this time to Trojans, on the quite unsubstantial ground that there was a statue there of Athena Ilias.[3] It is said also to have been a Rhodian colony.[3] It is tempting to associate this Rhodian origin with the record of Rhodian voyages in the far west, and as far as Spain, before the first Olympiad;[4] it may, however, have been later, and in the seventh century. But the better-attested version makes Siris Kolophonian.[5] The Kolophonians are said to have left after the capture of their city by the Lydians[6] (between c. 685, date of Gyges' accession, and c. 670, after which he was occupied with the Kimmerians). The city was called Polieion; this is probably the official name, Siris being the popular name taken from that of the river, which as at Gela ousted the other even on the coins. Siris, an Ionian wedge between the two most northerly Akhaian cities, prospered for over a century and reached a height of luxury second only to Sybaris. It has been regarded as an Akhaian city, another Sybarite foundation,[7] but this is stated by no ancient source. The case is founded entirely on the coins, which seem

---

[1] See *BSR*, xvi. 1 ff.
[3] Strabo 264.
[5] Strabo 264; Athen. 523*c*.
[7] Perret, *Siris*, esp. 212 ff.

[2] Cf. Myres, *CAH*, iii. 670 ff.
[4] Strabo 654.
[6] φεύγοντας τὴν Λυδῶν ἀρχήν, Strabo 264.

to date after the 'destruction' of the city at the hands of the Akhaians in the second half of the sixth century.[1]

One other town in the neighbourhood had a heroic origin, though it was never an independent Greek colony. The small town of Lagaria, which lay between Sybaris and Siris, was the foundation of Epeios and the Phokians returning from Troy, and the tools with which Epeios made the Wooden Horse were preserved there.[2] It was otherwise an obscure place famed only for its wine.

Another set of Greeks of different origin lived in the midst of the Akhaian cities, between Sybaris and Kroton. Sybaris on the Traeis is said to have been a Rhodian colony.[3] No more is known of its circumstances than of the Rhodian origin of Siris, recorded in the same passage. Its original name may well have been changed when the Sybarite remnant was expelled from Thuria and came there to live. Farther south, near the Alaian promontory (Cape Cirò), was a group of small towns centred on the famous sanctuary of Apollo Alaios, which were said to have had a Rhodian origin, this time certainly legendary. Makalla and Krimissa were ascribed to a Rhodian foundation under the leadership of Tlepolemos. With him was associated Philoktetes, whose bow was dedicated in the temple of Apollo.[4] The origin of these stories is discussed at more length below;[5] it may be here remarked that the persistent record of Rhodians in this area should have some foundation in fact, but these little towns were not Greek *poleis* nor properly established Greek colonies.

One colony remains to be considered: Lokroi Epizephyrioi, founded *c.* 673 according to Eusebius; this is approximately confirmed by the archaeological evidence, for the oldest vases from the Greek cemeteries of Lokroi are later in style than those of Syracuse, Megara, Taras, and Gela.[6] The site was already

[1] See below, p. 356 f.

[2] Strabo 263; Lyk. 930, 946 ff.; ps.-Arist. *de mir. ausc.* 108. The tools were later transferred (literally or on paper) to the better-known Metapontion; cf. Justin, xx. 2. 1; and Epeios is called founder of Metapontion (Vell. Pat. i. 1). On this and the phrase ἐγγὺς Μεταποντίου in *de mir. ausc.*, loc. cit., Bérard locates Lagaria between Siris and Metapontion (*Colonisation*, 351 ff.; *ASCL*, vi, 1936, 1 ff.). But it seems preferable to follow Strabo's statement that it was between Sybaris and Siris, though the common location at or near Trebisacce is not strongly based.　　　　　　　　　　　　　　　[3] Strabo 264.

[4] Ps.-Arist. *de mir. ausc.* 107; Lyk. 911 ff.　　　　　　　[5] See pp. 159 ff.

[6] Johansen, *VS*, 182. On the other hand, there are no seventh-century vases in the native graves which belong to the people driven out by the Greek settlers; which would imply that the colony was founded *c.* 700. This date is accordingly proposed by Oldfather, *RE*, xiii. 1311. It is supported by Strabo's statement that Lokroi was founded soon after

occupied by a number of native settlements which used Greek vases, some of them almost certainly made on the spot by Greek potters;[1] we have seen that at the time of the foundation of Syracuse, some sixty years earlier, Arkhias picked up some Greeks at the Zephyrian promontory. This was the site first occupied by the Lokrian colonists, who after three or four years moved to a hilly site above a beach a few miles north. This is not a compelling site, and the land of Lokroi though beautiful and well wooded is not rich. The reason for the choice of site was no doubt the existence of the Italian town.

The oecist was Euanthes. It was uncertain in antiquity which Lokrians were the founders. Ephoros said the Opuntians; the general view, as reported by Strabo, was the Ozolians from the Gulf of Krisa.[2] This is at first sight the most plausible, as Krisa on the Corinthian Gulf would be the natural point of embarkation for the west, but this argument is not decisive, for the eastern Lokris is a close neighbour of Khalkis. The cult of Aias and the late derivation from Naryka,[3] one of the towns of Opuntian Lokris, favour the Opuntian origin; the connexion with the Hundred Houses of Old Lokris is not decisive, as these belong as much to Opuntian as to Ozolian Lokris. It may be that both branches of the Lokrians were represented in the colony.

Vigorous polemic also raged over the question of the social class of the colonists. Aristotle described them as fugitive slaves, δραπετῶν, οἰκετῶν, μοιχῶν, ἀνδραποδιστῶν;[4] Timaios took him to task for this. They were thus calumniated in the same way as the Partheniai. Further, they were described as slaves of the Spartans, and their colonization brought into relation with the First Messenian War.[5] This is to be taken with the account which made Lokroi a Spartan colony of this period.[6] The story is in itself unlikely, and further suspect because of the parallelism with Taras. Though it has the authority of Aristotle, it appears that this is one case in which he was taken in by the slander of contemporary pamphleteers, and that Timaios is right in affirming that the Lokrians were of honest

Syracuse and Kroton, but no close chronological reasoning should be founded on this passage, which implies the synchronization of Syracuse and Kroton.
  [1] Blakeway, *BSA*, xxxiii. 176 ff.; Åkerström, op. cit. 37 ff.
  [2] Strabo 259; Polyb. xii. 5; ps.-Skymn. 316–17; cf. Oldfather, *RE*, xiii, s.v. 'Lokroi'.
  [3] Verg. *Aen*. iii. 399 and Serv. ad loc.; Ovid, *Met*. xv. 705; Pliny, *NH* xiv. 128.
  [4] Quoted by Polyb. xii. 8.
  [5] Polyb. xii. 6.   [6] Paus. iii. 3. 1.

and respectable origin. The connexion with the Old Lokrian aristocracy of the Hundred Houses[1] would alone prove this.[2]

It is stated that the Lokrians were aided in establishing themselves by Syracusans (and Tarentines, according to a plausible emendation).[3] This might be a confused reminiscence of the party picked up at the Zephyrian promontory by Arkhias; but Arkhias is not named and the story does not agree at any other point. Those scholars who explain all foundation-stories as a reflection into the distant past of fifth- and fourth-century history find a justification for this tale in the relations of Syracuse and Lokroi under Dionysios I. But this method, though applicable to some cults and legends which have been borrowed from one state by another for political purposes, is inadequate to explain away all early colonial history. It is best, therefore, to regard the tradition of Syracusan help as historical and to seek an explanation in seventh-century history. The Syracusans would have every interest in the extension of the Corinthian sphere of influence, which by the date of the foundation of Lokroi was well established. The site of Lokroi is not of great commercial importance, but as a port of call before crossing to Sicily the neighbourhood of the Zephyrian promontory would be of value. Ozolian Lokris also was in the Corinthian sphere, and it is therefore likely that Corinth inspired the Lokrian colony.[4]

The Lokrians were recognized as founders of one colony only, that which bore their name. They settled also in the region Abantis in Illyria, colonized by Euboians.[5] And to Lokrians are ascribed Nostoi-foundations at Sybaris[6] and among the Sallentines.[7] Their neighbours the Phokians are similarly 'founders' in the heroic period of Metapontion,[8] Lagaria,[9] and Temesa;[10] and they were said to have been one of the elements

[1] Polyb. xii. 5. 7.
[2] The arguments derived from the standing of women at Lokroi, from matriarchate and temple prostitution, are discussed below (pp. 183 ff.). They may have contributed to the origin of the story of servile origins, but cannot be used to support it. [3] Strabo 259.
[4] Cf. Oldfather, RE, xiii. 1317. The mythological connexions between Lokroi and Korkyra, which Oldfather emphasizes (op. cit. 1172; cf. Konon, 3), are further, though slight, evidence of the Corinthian interest in Lokroi.
[5] Paus. v. 22. 4; Beaumont, JHS, 1936, 164–5.
[6] Nikandr. ap. Ant. Lib. viii, fin.; Solin. ii. 9.
[7] Varro ap. Prob. ad Buc. vi. 31; Fest. 329. Cf. Oldfather, op. cit. 1173.
[8] Strabo 265; see above, p. 32.
[9] Strabo 263; Steph. Byz. s.v. Λαγαρία (quoting Strabo); Lyk. 930.
[10] Lyk. 1067 ff.; cf. the Portus Parthenius Phocensium (Pliny, NH, iii. 72; Solin. ii. 7) in the neighbourhood. See Bérard, Colonisation, 356 f.

in the formation of the Elymians in Sicily.[1] These settlements may have been pushed back into the period of the Trojan War by some systematizer of legend, and may belong in fact to the eighth or seventh century. Then, as also in Mycenaean times, the north side of the Gulf of Corinth had more political and commercial importance than in the classical period. It may well have contributed fairly extensively to the man-power, and thus incidentally to the cults and legends, of the Italian colonies. But Phokians and Lokrians seem, like the Akhaians, to have come west seeking somewhere to live, not to trade, and firmly established only one colony. If we ask to whose interest was the colonization of south Italy, carried out mainly by people from both sides of the Corinthian Gulf, we are irresistibly drawn to Corinth, whose commercial expansion was founded on trade with the west. The cities of Euboia drew for the man-power of their colonies on the Cyclades and perhaps Boiotia, and probably carried the Cycladic and Boiotian vases common in the west in the eighth century, rare after the Lelantine War distracted both Khalkidians and Eretrians from the western colonial area. So also, it appears, Corinth encouraged and directed the surplus population of Akhaia and Lokris to colonies in south Italy, trade with which remained for more than a century in Corinthian hands.

The Corinthian Gulf was the centre of colonization in another sense. It was part of the ritual of founding a colony that the founder should ask the blessing of the Pythian Apollo before setting out, and many verses which purport to be oracles given to the founders of colonies are extant. Some of these are clearly inventions of a later date; others may well be part of genuine oracles, which would be preserved piously together with other details of the foundation-saga.[2] In this class fall the oracles given to the founders of Kroton, Taras, and Rhegion, among others, all of which show an abundance of topographical detail. The priests of Apollo must have known a good deal about overseas conditions, which they can have learnt only from traders, Corinthian or Khalkidian. The copious finds of Corinthian geometric vases, which cover the whole of the eighth century, show the close connexions existing from a very early date between Corinth and Delphi. It is possible to see the hand of Corinth directing many colonies besides the two which she herself sent out in the eighth century; thus the Corinthian mono-

---

[1] Thuk. vi. 2. 3.   [2] Parke, *History of the Delphic Oracle*, 47 ff.

poly in western trade from the end of that century is more easily understood. One means by which this directing hand was exercised, it may be, was through Delphi. The oracle, by sending bands of emigrants and exiles from all over the Peloponnese and central Greece to the best sites in south Italy, ensured the rational development of that area and its Greek nature during the most brilliant period of its history. Delphi had its reward in the throngs of colonials, whose number and importance in the early sixth century are shown by the archaic treasuries[1] and in the history of the First Sacred War;[2] more profoundly, in the prestige gained in the cities of Old Greece, for it is in the period of the colonization that Delphi becomes of panhellenic importance.[3]

The other great sanctuary of Greece also owed much to the colonial expansion. Living in a rich land, the Eleans and Triphylians had no need of overseas ventures, nor were they driven out by over-mighty neighbours, like the Messenians. Accordingly there are no colonies from this part of the Peloponnese. It has been conjectured that Eleans joined in some of the western colonies; in particular, the legend of Alpheios and Arethusa has been explained as due to an Elean element at Syracuse.[4] But this legend, though as old as Pindar, may have arisen some time after the foundation of Syracuse. The early connexion of Syracuse and Olympia is witnessed by the appearance of a Syracusan victor in the middle of the seventh century.[5] Nor does the worship of Zeus Olympios or other deities venerated in Elis indicate the presence of Eleans in the colonies, being adequately explained by the importance of Olympia to the colonists.

Though not a colonizing region, Elis is one of the nearest parts of Greece to Italy and Sicily; and Olympia, situated in a

[1] For these see de La Coste-Messelière, *Au Musée de Delphes*, 29 ff.; and for other archaic dedications and records of visitors from the colonies Pomtow, *RE*, iv Suppl. 1189 ff., v Suppl. 61 ff., nos. 2, 21, 22, 23, 30, 34, 108, 133–6, 170, 200; Dittenberger, *SIG* i³, nos. 11, 12, 25.

[2] Strabo 418.

[3] Rhys Carpenter makes the interesting suggestion (*AJA*, 1945, 452 ff.) that the alphabet of Syracuse, as that of Megara Hyblaia and Lokroi Epizephyrioi, is derived not from Corinth but from Delphi. The material on which this is based is very scanty, for few of the Syracusan inscriptions are archaic, and the peculiarly Corinthian letter-forms are at Corinth given up by the late archaic period (cf. Payne, *NC*, 158 ff.).

[4] The further argument that members of the Iamid family joined in the colonization of Syracuse, founded on Pindar, *Ol*. vi. 6, is baseless. Agesias, a Stymphalian by birth, is there addressed as συνοικιστὴρ τᾶν κλεινᾶν Συρακοσσᾶν in his own right, having joined Gelon in founding the enlarged Syracuse, not in virtue of his ancestors, as the scholiasts took it.

[5] Paus. v. 8. 8; Euseb. ed. Schoene, i. 197.

country-side which with its broader and less rugged outlines resembles Italian rather than typically Greek scenery, early attracted colonial visitors. It has been suggested that the development of the Olympia from a local gathering, interesting only the people of the Peloponnese, to a panhellenic festival, was due in great part to the colonists of Magna Graecia, and that they, brought into daily dealings with the barbarian, were the first to develop the sense of a common Hellenic nationhood.

What sort of people did the Greeks find in Sicily and south Italy? There were a number of peoples to whom different names were given, and over whose origins and relationships the Greeks indulged in learned speculation: Sikels, Sikans, and Elymians in Sicily; Oinotrians, Opikians, Iapygians, and many other names in Italy. Two complexes of fact or theory in the ancient testimonies are worth following: that the Sikels of eastern Sicily had come there from Italy and had kin in many parts of central and south Italy; and that the Iapygians of Apulia or people related to them had a wide southern extension. These two statements are confirmed by modern research. On the other hand, the differentiation of Sikans and Sikels, to which peoples the ancient tradition ascribed widely different origins, is not supported. The names *Siculus* and *Sicanus* are obvious doublets, and the *Odyssey*, in which Sicily is first named in literature, calls it Σικανίη. Archaeologically the Sikans are not in the historical period distinguishable from the Sikels,[1] and the island presents a fairly homogeneous culture, more advanced in the south-east which lay open to Aegean influences. This culture develops without a break from the beginning of the Bronze Age, and does not reflect the arrival in Sicily of the Sikels, who were agreed in antiquity to have come at no very remote period[2] from Italy. Sikels were recorded in Bruttium, and particularly on the site of Lokroi;[3] this is confirmed by the similarity of grave-architecture and bronze ornaments. But the Siculan culture of prehellenic Lokroi and kindred sites in Bruttium is not older than the tenth century, at the earliest, so it appears that the Sikels moved from Sicily to Italy, not

[1] Cf. Orsi, *Atti della R. Acc. di Palermo*, xvii, 1932, 18 (quoted below, p. 140). For the other people whom the Greeks found in Sicily, the Elymians, see below, pp. 335 ff.

[2] Hellanikos and Philistos placed the coming of the Sikels before the Trojan War (Hell., F 79b Jacoby; Dion. Hal. i. 22), Thukydides 300 years before the founding of the Greek colonies (vi. 2. 5).

[3] Polyb. xii. 5–6; cf. Thuk. vi. 2. 4.

vice versa.[1] Tradition also placed Siculi in Latium.[2] An older generation of philologists held that the Sikel language belonged to the Latin rather than the Osco-Umbrian group of dialects, but this is now doubted and it is not even certain that Sikel was an Italic rather than an Illyrian dialect.[3] Its remains, four inscriptions, a few glosses, and a number of place-names,[4] are inadequate to form a judgement. None of the languages of south Italy at the time of the Greek colonization is known, the native peoples of this area having been swamped by the Lucanian and Bruttian invasions in the fourth century.

Many elements in Siculan culture are due to Aegean influence; the cutting of tholos-shaped graves and the use of the Aegean invention of the fibula, as well as the more easily communicable Mycenaean influence in Sicilian Late Bronze and Early Iron Age pottery. The introduction of the fibula in particular, implying a new dress, should be due to settlers rather than traders. It first appears in Sicily after the period of Mycenaean imports (fourteenth century),[5] and has been used as an argument for overseas immigration in the intermediate period.[6] Its introduction may be due, not to fourteenth-century Mycenaean trade, but to a Late Mycenaean settlement, such as is associated in Sicily with the name of Minos.[7]

The many tribal names recorded in south Italy do not necessarily indicate a greater racial variety than in Sicily. The name *Italia* was originally limited to the extreme southern end of the peninsula, south of the Isthmus of Catanzaro,[8] and is derived from an Italic stem cognate with *uitulus*.[9] From this 'most ancient Italy' the name spread in the fifth century to cover the modern Basilicata and Calabria, south of the line Metapontion–Laos.[10] This area was commonly known as Oinotria; it does not appear from any ancient evidence to what family of peoples the Oinotroi belonged. This is the main colonial area, though

[1] Whatmough, *The Foundations of Roman Italy*, 338 ff.
[2] Testimonia in Whatmough, *Prae-Italic Dialects*, ii. 431 f.
[3] Whatmough, *Foundations*, 364.
[4] Whatmough, *Prae-Italic Dialects*, ii, nos. 576–81.
[5] Blinkenberg, *Fibules grecques et orientales*, 39, says that it appears in Sicily at the same time as the imported Mycenaean vases. Though fibulas occur in the same cemeteries as Mycenaean vases (e.g. Cozzo del Pantano, *MA*, ii. 5 ff.), they do not occur in the same graves, and graves with fibulas appear to be later than graves with Mycenaean vases.
[6] Säflund, *Studi Etruschi*, xii. 54.
[7] See my paper quoted p. 1, n. 1.
[8] Antiokhos ap. Strabo 254–5; Arist. *Pol.* 1329[b] 11 ff.; Dion. Hal. i. 35.
[9] Whatmough, *Prae-Italic Dialects*, ii. 433; Hellanikos ap. Dion. Hal., loc. cit.
[10] Antiokhos ap. Strabo 254–5; cf. Steph. Byz. s.v. Βρέττος.

Kyme, Poseidonia, and Taras lay outside it. Archaeologically it is very little known, but the scattered remains of the Early Iron Age show considerable uniformity. According to the latest inquirer, a common culture obtained in the ninth and eighth centuries from Scoglio del Tonno near the site of Taras round the coast to Lokroi, Torre Galli on the west coast of Bruttium, Kyme, and Rome and its neighbourhood. This is an extension with certain differentiae of the so-called 'Apennine' culture of eastern Italy.[1] It is suggested that it is related to the fossa-culture of Etruria, and was brought to Italy by sea not long before the arrival of the Greeks.[2] This thesis cannot be taken as proved; what is certain is that the whole area from Kyme to Taras is at this time more closely connected with Sicily than with northern Italy. Taras was a Iapygian site,[3] and the Iapygians are shown by place-names and linguistic resemblances confirming the ancient tradition to be of an Illyrian stock.[4] It is likely that they crossed the Adriatic during the centuries of the Dark Ages which produced the great migrations of the eastern Mediterranean. As well as in Apulia, Iapygians are met with in the neighbourhood of Sybaris and Kroton.[5] People of Illyrian origin may have been still more widely spread, and the affinities of the Sikel and Illyrian languages should be remembered in this connexion. The apparent uniformity of the peoples of Sicily and south Italy might thus be explained by their having been recruited over many centuries from successive waves of immigrants from Illyria.

The inhabitants of both Sicily and south Italy at the time of the Greek colonization were of similar stock to the Greeks, speaking in the most general terms. They were of a Mediterranean base, more or less penetrated by northern elements derived immediately from the Balkan peninsula, and spoke an Indo-European language. They had absorbed a small amount of Aegean culture, and were fibula-wearers, that is, had learnt the new mode of dressing from the Aegean. They were considerable metal-workers, especially in bronze, the material of their most ambitious artistic efforts, some small figurines.[6] They showed much skill in the cutting of tombs in the native

---

[1] Säflund, *Studi Etruschi*, xii. 17 ff.; *Δρᾶγμα M. P. Nilsson dedicatum*, 458 ff.; cf. U. Rellini, *MA*, xxxiv. 129 ff.

[2] Säflund, *Studi Etruschi*, xii. 54.   [3] Strabo 279; cf. Mayer, *Apulien*, 1 ff.

[4] Helbig, *Hermes*, xi (1874), 257 ff.; Whatmough, *Prae-Italic Dialects*, ii. 258 ff.; Kretschmer, *Glotta*, xxx. 99 ff.; Wuilleumier, *Tarente*, 10 ff.

[5] Strabo 261, 262; ps.-Skylax, 14.   [6] *Ausonia*, viii (1913), 52 ff.

rock, but there is little evidence that they exercised skill or elaboration in their dwelling-places; the 'palace' of Pantalica, a rough stone building vaguely reminiscent of the Mycenaean megaron,[1] is without parallel in the prehellenic period. The size of some of their settlements, notably Pantalica, indicates that they had reached some degree of political and economic organization, but this hardly went beyond tribal groups of villages.[2] Of their religious and other ideas we are completely ignorant; they were illiterate, and little can be inferred about their beliefs from their burial customs and material remains, or from survivals in the classical period, when they had long been hellenized.[3]

The Greeks were no doubt more conscious of the differences than of the likenesses to themselves in these barbarous peoples, and took little note of their capability for civilization. Their first contacts were at least in part peaceful. Beside the slave-dealing passages of the *Odyssey* can be put the evidence that Greek traders dealt with native communities over a wide area of Italy in the eighth century, and that some of them settled in native towns and made pots there. When the era of official colonization began, however, the Greeks preferred the sword to peaceful penetration. At least half the Greek colonies were built on sites previously occupied by native towns, and it is likely that most were.[4] In every case of which we hear, the Greeks drove out the Sikels or Italians by force.

Of the foundation of Syracuse Thukydides says: Ἀρχίας . . . ᾤκισε, Σικελοὺς ἐξελάσας πρῶτον ἐκ τῆς νήσου.[5] There is no evidence of joint occupation by Sikels and Greeks. Below the Athenaion, where the first colonists raised an altar at the highest point of the island of Ortygia, are the remains of a Sikel village which imported a few Greek vases and produced imitations of them. This was abandoned before the debris of the Greek sanctuary began to collect; this goes back to the earliest years of the colony, for the oldest material from it is as old as the oldest graves of Syracuse.[6] The Sikels, therefore, must have ceased to

---

[1] See below, p. 95.

[2] For the culture of prehellenic Sicily see Pace, *ACSA*, i. 329 ff.

[3] In *ACSA*, iii. 453 ff. Pace attempts to isolate prehellenic elements in the religion of archaic and classical Sicily; but overvalues, I think, the Sikel contribution. For south Italy see Ciaceri, *Storia della Magna Grecia*, ii. 1 ff. See further below, pp. 176 ff.

[4] Selinus is an exception. No pre-colonization remains have been discovered in the extensive excavations there, and it appears to have been a virgin site.

[5] vi. 3. 2.

[6] *MA*, xxv. 743; and see pp. 13, 49.

occupy the site at about the time of the colonization. Furthermore, there are no Sikel remains of colonization date in the immediate neighbourhood of Syracuse, though the area was earlier thickly inhabited. More important and conclusive, there are no Sikel remains either in the votive deposits of the Athenaion or in the Greek cemeteries of Syracuse.

At Lokroi also the colonists were said to have driven out the Sikels, after being received by them and agreeing to share the land in common; they swore to abide by this agreement as long as they stood on the same earth and kept their heads on their shoulders, and avoided the consequence of their oath by putting earth in their shoes and heads of garlic on their shoulders, which they removed and expelled the Sikels at the first opportunity.[1] The story of the trick by which the colonists gained possession of the land is a commonplace which recurs at Metapontion and Kallipolis.[2] The site of Lokroi had been occupied by a number of native villages, and there are three prehellenic cemeteries on or near it. All these come to an end at or before the colonization. They contain Greek geometric vases, but of pre-colonization date, and there is no overlap with the Greek cemeteries. The expulsion of the Sikels is thus confirmed. Lokroi is the only colony said by any ancient authority to have taken over native Italian customs;[3] but the passage in question is highly tendentious and its statements are not confirmed but rather disproved by the archaeological evidence, which shows that Greeks and Sikels did not occupy Lokroi in common for any appreciable period of time.[4]

The Megarians had better relations with the Sikels, whose ruler invited them to settle and gave them the site for their colony. But it is likely that they soon rid themselves of their Sikel benefactors, for the Sikel Hybla disappears from history.[5] There is no indication that Greeks and Sikels lived side by side at Megara (it is noteworthy that there is no princess in the story of Hyblon, as in the parallel case of Massalia). Megara has been thoroughly excavated and neither the town nor the cemetery has yielded a single Siculan vase or bronze. Any

---

[1] Polyb. xii. 6.   [2] Strabo 265; Dion. Hal. xix. 3.

[3] Polyb., loc. cit. The passage is discussed below, pp. 183 ff.   [4] *MA*, xxxi. 339.

[5] This is the Greater Hybla (see Steph. Byz. s.v. ῞Υβλα; Paus. v. 23. 6, both quoted below, p. 144); but Hybla Geleatis on the slopes of Etna had greater fame. The bronze coins of the Roman period with the legend ΥΒΛΑΣ ΜΕΓΑΛΑΣ, ascribed by Head, *HN²*, 147–8, to Hybla Geleatis, must belong to that near Megara; but the latter is not heard of from the foundation of Megara until the Roman period (cf. Freeman, i. 512 ff.).

admixture of Sikel blood was so slight as not to affect the purely Greek culture.

The Khalkidians seem to have had a more tolerant policy towards the Sikels than the Syracusans. At Cocolonazzo di Mola, above Taormina, the Sikels continued to live after the foundation of Naxos, and used Greek pottery and bronze. The fourteen graves excavated are of the period of the colonization (second half of the eighth and early seventh centuries).[1] But the site remained Sikel until the end of the fifth century, when Dionysios destroyed Naxos and gave it to the surrounding Sikels.[2] For Naxos to prosper and indeed to continue to exist, its relations with these Sikels who held the hill-tops behind must have been good.

At Leontini also the Sikels continued for some time to live in close neighbourhood to the Greek city. The Sikel cemetery of S. Aloè[3] is less than a mile west of Lentini, and the Sikels probably inhabited the hill next to the west from the acropolis of Leontinoi, across a small valley. It was an important place when the Greeks arrived, and had for some time been receiving Greek imports.[4] But most of the graves are a little after the colonization, though within the eighth century. The imported pottery in them is the richest and most varied of that at any Sikel site of the period, and the native ware among the most interesting, much of it being very close to Greek models.

Thukydides' account of the colonization is simple: $\Lambda\epsilon o\nu\tau\acute{\iota}\nu o\upsilon s$ $\tau\epsilon$ $\pi o\lambda\acute{\epsilon}\mu\wp$ $\tau o\grave{\upsilon}s$ $\Sigma\iota\kappa\epsilon\lambda o\grave{\upsilon}s$ $\grave{\epsilon}\xi\epsilon\lambda\acute{a}\sigma a\nu\tau\epsilon s$ $o\grave{\iota}\kappa\acute{\iota}\zeta o\upsilon\sigma\iota.$[5] According to Polyainos[6] the two races made a contract to live together peaceably, which the Leontines avoided by bringing in Megarians to expel the Sikels. This is not inconsistent with Thukydides, if it is allowed that Thukydides has compressed into a single sentence two narrowly separated phases of the winning of the site. Polyainos' account is probably derived indirectly from the same source as Thukydides has abbreviated. The archaeological evidence suggests a period of about twenty years' joint occupation, which is longer than a natural interpretation of Thukydides and Polyainos would allow. On the received chronology, Megara was founded within two years of Leontini. It may be that the date given as that of the foundation of

---

[1] N Sc, 1919, 360 ff.

[2] Diod. xiv. 15. These Sikels were kindly disposed to Naxos in 425; Thuk. iv. 25. 9.

[3] RM, 1900, 62 ff.; N Sc, 1899, 278. Other Sikel graves at Rocca Ruccia east of Lentini, N Sc, 1887, 301 ff. (Cavallari); RM, 1898, 340 ff.

[4] Blakeway, 185 ff.; Åkerström, 20.   [5] vi. 3.   [6] v. 5.

Megara (728 B.C.) is in fact that of the Megarians' first arrival in Sicily and settlement at Trotilon. It will be seen that the archaeological evidence supports this view, for the oldest finds in the graves of Megara are appreciably younger than those of Syracuse and nearer in time to those of Taras and Gela, founded in 706 and 688.[1]

The Greeks were drawn to Leontinoi, which alone of all the original colonies was inland,[2] by the importance of the trade with the Sikel town there. At first it was a trading-post, founded by the oecist of Naxos, and open to other Greeks. Possession was guaranteed by an understanding with the Sikels, as the position of the Khalkidians at Naxos must have been. Within some twenty years, if this interpretation of the remains is right, the Greeks (Khalkidians and Megarians) were strong enough to expel the Sikels, and soon after the Khalkidians rid themselves of their fellow Greeks. The military value of the site made Greek or Sikel neighbours intolerable to the Khalkidians. It was equally strong against attack from north or south, and with Katane it secured possession of the most fertile plain in Sicily. The wealth of the Sikel graves, and the importance of the native pottery found in them, makes it clear that the Sikels were not subject to the Greeks. Their sudden end, late in the eighth century, supports the tradition of the expulsion of the Sikels. The only point on which the archaeological evidence disagrees with the literary is the period between the foundation and the expulsion. Considering the brevity of his account and the antiquity of the events, it is not unreasonable to suppose that Thukydides omitted to mention a period of about twenty years during which the Greeks and Sikels lived side by side. The important point is that this is the only colony in Sicily where the Greeks did not keep the natives at arm's length.

The strongest argument that Sikels and other native peoples were not admitted to the Greek colonies except perhaps as slaves lies in the cemeteries of the colonies. Thousands of archaic graves have been excavated in a dozen cities of Sicily and Italy. Not more than one or two of them contain objects which can be regarded as Sikel or Italian. The local geometric vases of Greek manufacture or inspiration common on native sites are not found in the colonies, with the rarest exceptions.

---

[1] See below, pp. 443, 455.
[2] The river was, however, navigable as far as Leontinoi: see below, p. 197.

The majority of the vases, bronzes, and other small objects of use or ornament were brought by the colonials from Greece, and there is very little indeed that would be out of place in Corinth. Archaic colonial culture was purely Greek. This is true of all classes of society, rich and poor, who were not so completely poverty-stricken as to be buried in bare earth without the customary grave-offerings. If there were Sikels or mixed breeds among the colonials, they were completely hellenized and did not in material things keep any trace of their origin. Intercourse between Greeks and natives went on in the interior of Sicily and Italy, in the little towns which kept their freedom or were subjugated by one or other Greek city; and the Greek trader remained a potent hellenizing force. In the colonies, however, the natives had no place. This change from the freer intercourse of the pre-colonial period, which continued in Etruria and elsewhere beyond the range of Greek colonization, took place at or very soon after the colonization, certainly within the eighth century. It is another proof that colonization was not a series of accidents but a deliberate policy.

CHAPTER II

THE GREEK CITIES

THE history of Sicily can be told as a connected story only from 510 onwards. Earlier, some parts are consecutive: the hellenization and enslavement of the Sikels; the development of colonial economic life; the relations of Greeks and Phoenicians from the foundation of Selinus to the battle of Himera. For south Italy the evidence is less, and less good, than for Sicily, but it is possible to give a continuous though very scrappy history from about 530. The internal development of the cities and their relations are most obscure. We have only a number of isolated facts which lack their setting. The literary authorities can be supplemented by the more complete archaeological record. Even so, there is only one city in the archaic period of which it is possible to give a coherent picture: Syracuse. The odds and ends related about the other cities will be dealt with in this chapter so far as any general meaning can be drawn from them, and the material remains discussed in their historical bearing in the broadest sense of the term. The continuous history from the late sixth century onwards, and special studies of the subjects named in the first part of this paragraph, follow in later chapters.

SYRACUSE

Syracuse was marked from its origin for rule among the cities of Sicily. Its great possession is its harbours, the broad sheet of the Great Harbour, shelving gently at the northern end, where ships could easily be drawn up, and the landlocked Little Harbour, suitable for dockyards. The harbour had already, before the arrival of the Greek settlers, been the centre from which first Late Mycenaean and later Greek geometric vases had reached the Sikels. It was later the feature which moved Gelon to transfer his seat there from Gela,[1] and was, we may believe, what attracted the Corinthians. The land of Syracuse, with its bare limestone hills and steep scarps, recalls in its purity of line and clarity of atmosphere the landscapes of Greece more than do the luxuriant country-sides common elsewhere in Sicily and Italy. Looking eastward from the rocks

[1] See below, p. 415 f.

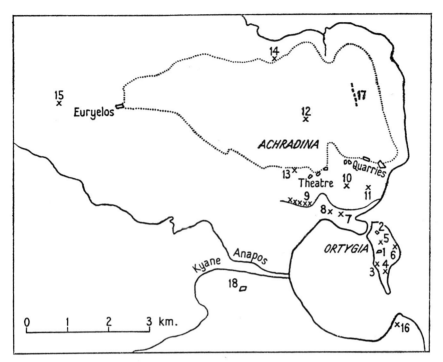

PRE-DEINOMENID SYRACUSE

1. Athenaion.	10. Ex-Spagna cemetery.
2. Apollonion.	11. S. Lucia cemetery.
3. Arethusa.	12. Ottone cemetery.
4. Piazza S. Giuseppe.	13. Grotticelli cemetery.
5. Sperduta.	14. Scala Greca.
6. Wells in Via Gelone.	15. Belvedere.
7. Agora.	16. Plemmyrion.
8. Piazzale Stazione.	17. Gelonian Wall.
9. Fusco cemetery.	18. Olympieion.

The line of cliffs round Epipolai is marked, and the 5-metre contour in the neighbourhood of the Isthmus.

by the Little Harbour, one feels that the sea is a path, not a barrier, and that this land is indeed Greek.

Syracuse is a double city. The acropolis occupied the island of Ortygia, the site of a Sikel settlement before the Greeks arrived. This, though now and from the second half of the sixth century joined to the mainland by a causeway,[1] was originally an island[2] cut off by a narrow channel joining the two harbours, and was always commonly known as Νᾶσος.[3] The mainland opposite is a low shore, stretching away to the south-west into the swamp Lysimeleia, fatal to the health of many of the attackers of Syracuse. Part or all of this swamp was no doubt the original Syrako from which the city took its name.[4] This low land slopes up gently to the north to the foot of the line of cliffs which forms the southern edge of Epipolai, now followed by the remains of the Dionysian walls and marked by the theatre and the great quarries which cut into the hillside. The island of Ortygia is large enough for a city, and until recent times contained the whole of modern Syracuse. But from the foundation of the Greek colony there was also a settlement on the mainland, on this low sloping land north of the harbours, later known as ἡ ἔξω πόλις or Achradina. The extension on top of the cliffs of Epipolai was due to Gelon, the walling of the whole of Epipolai, most of which can never have been built over, to Dionysios.

That Syracuse was from the first a double city is shown by its name, taken from the swamp Syrako on the mainland, whereas a city limited to the island might be expected to be called Ortygia;[5] and, more conclusively, by its early remains. The Sikel remains which precede the colonization are found only on the island of Ortygia. But the Syracusans occupied the mainland as early as they did Ortygia. To judge from the isolated finds belonging to the eighth and seventh centuries, the part on the mainland was then little less extensive and important than the island.

A. *Ortygia*

Athenaion (1 on plan): a few sherds are of types found on Sikel sites but not in the Greek cemeteries, and may belong to

---

[1] Ibykos, fr. 22; see below, p. 62.
[2] Thuk. vi. 3. 2: (ἡ νῆσος) ἐν ᾗ νῦν οὐκέτι περικλυζομένῃ ἡ πόλις ἡ ἐντός ἐστιν.
[3] Cf. Livy xxv. 24. 8.   [4] Steph. Byz. s.v. Συράκουσαι; ps.-Skymn. 281.
[5] Holm, *Geschichte Siziliens*, i. 125; see below.

the third quarter of the eighth century (*MA*, xxv, fig. 109; Blakeway, *BSA*, xxxiii. 181, fig. 7: Argive and Cycladic). The oldest Protocorinthian (*MA*, xxv, figs. 122, 140) is of about the same date. There are Siculan imitations of Greek geometric (ibid., figs. 97, 98, 99; Blakeway, op. cit., pl. 24, nos. 25–7) in the Sikel stratum, which is earlier than the expulsion of the Sikels which accompanied the foundation of the colony. The stratification is at many points confused, so that it is not possible to be certain whether the association of Greek geometric and Siculan is original; the Siculan imitations of Greek geometric must be older than the foundation.[1]

Sperduta (5 on plan): *N Sc*, 1925, 320–1; cf. *N Sc*, 1920, 310–11. Protocorinthian cup of the type of Johansen, *VS*, pl. 2, which should be a little earlier than the foundation; aryballos, *N Sc*, 1925, 320, fig. 76, a little later; all the material is of the first generation of the colony.

Piazza S. Giuseppe (4 on plan): *N Sc*, 1925, 317–19, figs. 72–5. Rhodian lebes, Argive (?) kraters, necks of large Protocorinthian oinochoai, and other Protocorinthian. Goes back possibly into the eighth century.

Wells on shore below Via Gelone (6 on plan): *N Sc*, 1889, 372 ff.; 1891, 377 ff. One has some Late Protocorinthian and rough ware belonging also to the seventh century.

The Apollonion and other sanctuaries were no doubt dedicated at the epoch of the colonization, but nothing of so early a date has been found.

B. *Mainland*

Piazzale Stazione (8 on plan): Attic sherd (*N Sc*, 1925, 316, fig. 69; recognized as Attic by Åkerström, *Der Geometrische Stil in Italien*, 35, and independently by J. M. Cook); from an 'imposing stone building'. Last quarter of eighth century.

Near the ancient Agora (7 on plan): houses, apparently more than one, and two wells (*N Sc*, 1891, 391–2). Protocorinthian kotylai and Late Protocorinthian pyxis; East Greek (fragment of large vase with rosette in metope, another with small concentric circles); &c. Early seventh century onward.

Piazza d'Armi Vecchia, south-west of Agora, in foundations of a house (*N Sc*, 1925, 319–20): Protocorinthian conical oinochoai, ibid., pl. 21; Rhodian bird-bowl; &c. Orsi speaks of 'beautiful and spacious houses of the seventh and sixth

[1] Cf. above p. 13, n. 4.

centuries, which denote easy circumstances and at the same time a high development in private architecture' (*N Sc*, 1925, 313).

Archaic street and large house, probably sixth century, north of the Agora.[1]

C. *The Fusco cemetery* (9 on plan)

The bulk of the earliest material from the Athenaion is exactly contemporary with the contents of the earliest graves from Fusco: a few pieces which may be a little older than Fusco have been mentioned. The amount of material from Fusco and the Athenaion which must belong to the first years of the colony makes the foundation of Syracuse one of the best-defined archaeological landmarks of the century. The age of the earliest graves makes it clear that as soon as the colony was founded the cemetery was laid out on the mainland; it is unlikely that some of the oldest graves have not been found. Its position is another argument that there was from the beginning a settlement on the mainland, or one would have expected the cemetery to be just opposite the island, not three-quarters of a mile away on the other side of the swamp Syrako. This does not imply that the settlement extended as far as the beginning of Fusco, which is on the first solid ground across the depression which was the swamp.[2]

The careful selection of a cemetery site well outside the city, which continued to be the main burial-ground for more than five centuries, implies a certain degree of town-planning. And the grouping of archaic remains near the classical Agora suggests that the Agora was laid out almost at once; it is situated just where the point of land opposite the island broadens. These generous plans (for the island is by no means too small for a town) allowed Syracuse to grow into one of the greatest of ancient cities. Even before its extension under Gelon, it was as large as any Sicilian city.

In the late seventh and sixth centuries there is further topographical evidence in the situation of the secondary cemeteries. The chief of them, the ex-Spagna, begins about 640, with Late Protocorinthian and contemporary Rhodian. To the east in a similar position is the S. Lucia cemetery.[3] I have seen nothing

---

[1] *N Sc*, 1909, 338–40; Fabricius, *Die Antike Syrakus*, 7, and fig. 17 (plan). None of these houses, discovered during building-operations, could be preserved.

[2] There were, however, later burials in Lysimeleia (*N Sc*, 1903, 428, 525).

[3] 'del sec. VI e forse VII', Orsi, *N Sc*, 1925, 178. See *N Sc*, 1893, 122 ff.; 1915, 188 ff.; the Corinthian vases, *N Sc*, 1893, 126.

from here earlier than 600. Orsi treats the two as parts of the
same cemetery,[1] and as belonging particularly to the mainland
quarter, his 'lower Achradina'. But there is no topographical
reason to regard Fusco as the cemetery of the island and the
northern cemetery as belonging to Achradina. The two are as
conveniently situated for either part of the city. Ex-Spagna
is of equal splendour and importance with Fusco, and grave I
is the most magnificent of all Syracusan graves. Certainly it is
not evidence of the growth of the mainland city in the middle
of the seventh century. If Orsi is right in supposing that the
greater part of it is still unexplored, it may be that it begins
earlier than the last half of the century. On the other hand,
there is no reason in the nature of the ground why it should be
just where it is, and it was probably placed at the edge of the
city as it was when it came into use, or at the boundary to
which it was anticipated that the city would grow. There is
no knowing when the wall of the ἔξω πόλις was built[2] or how
far inside the cemeteries its course lay. The opinion that it was
before 664[3] rests on the absurd ground that Achradina must
have been occupied before Akrai; but it is not unlikely that the
defence of the outer city was provided for in this early period,
perhaps on a large scale along the line indicated by the
cemeteries ex-Spagna and S. Lucia. A wall just inside these
cemeteries would leave outside a good deal of the level ground
of Achradina, but include an area on the mainland as large as
the island.[4]

[1] Loc. cit.: 'necropoli arcaica a S. Lucia . . . che probabilmente attaccava con quella
del predio Spagna'.   [2] Thuk. vi. 3. 2.
[3] Schubring, *Achradina*, 17, *Bewässerung*, 617; followed by Cavallari and Holm, 170 =
Lupus, 87; Holm, i. 126; Hüttl, 17.
[4] See the discussion of this archaeological evidence in Orsi, *N Sc*, 1925, and especially
pp. 312–14; Fabricius, 5–11: both concluding that the mainland settlement opposite the
island is very nearly as old as the colony. Orsi says: 'il quartiere di Acradina bassa . . .
risale alla metà del VII–VI [*sic*] secolo', i.e. to the beginning of the ex-Spagna cemetery.
I do not put that cemetery into such close relation with the mainland quarter of the city,
but the sporadic finds near the Agora carry that quarter back into the eighth century.
Fabricius is of opinion 'dass sehr bald nach der korinthischen Kolonisation Siedlungen auf
dem Festland gerade gegenüber der Insel angelegt worden sind'. Holm (*Geschichte Siziliens*, i.
125; cf. Freeman, i. 359) suggested that the plural form Συράκουσαι indicates a double city,
and that the daughters Ortygia and Syrakousa attributed to Arkhias (Plutarch, *Mor.* 773b)
are evidence of a city in two parts. This is very uncertain ground, but it is possible that the
name Syrakousa or Syrakousai was first used for the quarter on the mainland, near the
swamp Syrako, and Ortygia for the island. This is much more likely than Holm's view that
the twin to Ortygia was that which was later called Polikhna near the Olympieion. In the
Topografia (trans. Lupus, 66–7) he gives up this hypothesis and places Syrako and Syrakousai on the mainland just opposite the island, supposing the swamp to have been cleared
very early.

Freeman holds that there were in this period outposts holding
the three main roads out of Syracuse: Polichna to the south,
Temenites overlooking the western road, 'upper Achradina' on
the northern road.[1] 'Upper Achradina' is a misnomer. It is
clear that Achradina was the name of the quarter on the low
ground, generally called 'lower Achradina', and that the
quarries, including the so-called Gelonian wall, had no military
object.[2] Temenites also is Gelonian in both name and occupation. He also finds an indication of the growth of the city in
the monument to Lygdamis by the quarries.[3] It is not certain
that the dedication is contemporary with his victory (648),
far from certain that the quarries were there when the monument was set up.[4] The pre-Deinomenid buildings round the
Athenaion are of a soft stone, called *giuggiolena*, some of it said
to come from Plemmyrion,[5] some presumably from the latomia.
The greatest quarrying activity was under the Deinomenids;
at this period the stone of the Mellili quarries was available
and used for the temple of Athena, but the local stone must
have been used for the building of the new quarter. The
quarries would have very little military value, but they would
have hindered approach to a line of wall lying a little inside
them.

The Olympieion in its present form was built in the early
sixth century and was preceded by a seventh-century building,
whose terra-cotta revetments are simpler than any of those
which fit the existing temple.[6] This is likely to be at least as
old as the first Syracusan victory at Olympia; the earliest
known is that of Lygdamis in 648. It is very probable that
there was already a little village and a military post there
when the site was first dedicated.[7] It is a military point of some

---

[1] ii. 42 ff. The name Achradina, as pointed out by Haverfield (*CR* 1889, 110) does not occur
earlier than the fourth century. Thukydides does not use it, but speaks of ἡ ἔξω πόλις. But
the name belongs to the older mainland quarter, without Gelonian and later additions, and is
probably the original name (see Fabricius, 29; d'Orville, *Sicula*, i. 178 (1764), gives the wild-
pear etymology, not the misleading connexion with ἄκρον).

Fabricius, 21–5, discusses Achradina according to the ancient historians; 27–30, according
to the modern topographers; ibid. 13–14, the Gelonian wall. His qualification of this undis-
tinguished quarry as a 'Fata Morgana' is not unjustified. Orsi (*N Sc*, 1925, 314) had already
spoken of the 'leggendario muro di Gelone'. And Haverfield (*CR* 1889, 110–12) had shown
that Achradina lay entirely below Epipolai, and places pre-Dionysian Syracuse within
these limits.

[2] Lupus, 95, Freeman, ii. 43 and others; defending the south of the mythical Upper
Achradina.

[3] ii. 448; Paus. v. 8. 8.

[4] So Lupus, loc. cit.

[5] *MA*, xxv. 411; cf. 737.

[6] *MA*, xiii. 381 ff.; Van Buren, *AFR*, 74–7.

[7] Cf. Hüttl, 17.

importance, more as an encampment for an enemy attacking
Syracuse from the south than as a strong defensive position.

There is no archaeological support for the view that there
was an outpost on Epipolai. There is some Siculan III pottery
from Belvedere.[1] Probably this was a Sikel village subject
to Syracuse, in a somewhat similar position to the Sikels at
S. Aloè near Leontinoi and Mola above Naxos. On top of
Epipolai on the Catania road is the small cemetery of Predio
Ottone,[2] which goes back into the seventh century. It is clearly
the burying-place of a small group of inhabitants living outside
the city. There are some reasonably well-to-do graves, and the
contents are about the average for Syracuse, though there is
nothing really fine. There are other small suburban cemeteries
at the Scala Greca,[3] of the sixth to the third century; on
Plemmyrion[4] some graves of the mid-fifth century; and at
Belvedere[5] of the fourth century. These are all places where
one would expect to find a small population tilling the adjacent
fields, and also all points of some military importance. They
may well have been inhabited earlier than the fifth and fourth
centuries.

Comparisons with other Corinthian colonies, Korkyra and
Epidamnos, and with Dionysian foundations, Black Korkyra,
Tauromenion, the new Rhegion, make it highly probable that
Syracusan public life closely followed the Corinthian model.[6]
But in the number of tribes they appear to have had the Dorian
three, not the Corinthian eight. The three old-Dorian tribes
are found at Black Korkyra,[7] which presumably followed the
example of Syracuse.[8] This is to be explained if the foundation
of Syracuse is earlier than the introduction of the eight tribes
at Corinth, due presumably to Kypselos.

The constitution as established by Arkhias would naturally
be a close aristocracy like that of the Bakkhiads at Corinth.
The rulers of Syracuse down to the early fifth century formed
an aristocracy called the Gamoroi. We do not know the composition of this body, nor whether it was open to other families
than the Bakkhiads, as is on general grounds not unlikely. It

---

[1] From an illicit excavation made in 1931; including an amphora of Fusco style.
[2] Unpublished. Fabricius (p. 13) misinterprets it as an outlier of the Grotticelli cemetery,
which begins only in the fifth century.
[3] *N Sc*, 1897, 493 ff.   [4] Libertini, *Guida*, 77.
[5] Taracati cemetery, ibid. 57.
[6] Hüttl, *Verfassungsgeschichte von Syrakus*, 32–4, 43 ff.   [7] Dittenberger, *SIG.* i³. 141.
[8] Cic. *Verr.* ii. 2. 127 is not evidence that there were three tribes at Syracuse; cf. Hüttl, 33.

has been inferred, from analogies in Corinth and other Corinthian colonies, that there was a single prytanis and a court of
life members in whom power rested; and further that this was
the constitutional position of Pollis the Argive, recorded as an
early king of Syracuse.[1] If Pollis existed, he must belong to
this earliest period of the history of Syracuse; but he is named
only in connexion with a kind of vine, and it is doubtful whether
he is not a literary fiction.[2]

Before and after the fall of the Bakkhiads there are disturbances at Korkyra and Syracuse which suggest that political
life in the colonies was closely connected with that of the
mother city. Shortly before c. 664, Korkyra declared her
independence of Corinth, and successfully asserted it after a
sea-battle.[3] In c. 663 the Syracusans founded the colony of
Akrai; no oecist is named, which may be because the Syracusans did not call for one from Corinth as they were in duty
bound to do.[4] If so, they may have taken advantage of the
revolt of Korkyra to show their independence in this manner.
The Bakkhiads were overthrown c. 655: at the same period
there was a disturbance at Syracuse which led to the expulsion
of the clan or family of the Myletidai, who joined with the
Zanklaians in the foundation of Himera in c. 649.[5] The
Myletidai with their clients were a large enough element to
affect the dialect of Himera, and they may have been responsible for the situation of the colony so far to the west, on the
edge of Phoenician territory, instead of nearer Zankle.

Certainly the evidence of stasis at Syracuse, revolt of
Korkyra against Corinth and possibly strain on the relations
of Syracuse and Corinth, and fall of the ruling house at Corinth,
all within a few years, suggests that the fortunes of mother
state and colonies were closely connected: perhaps, that the
rulers of all were related. The Bakkhiads were allowed by
Kypselos to establish themselves in the Corinthian north-west;

---

[1] Hüttl, 43–7. At Korkyra, Apollonia, and Epidamnos the prytanis was the eponymous
magistrate. The Sicilian parallels are doubtful, and traces of the office at Syracuse (*Pyth.*
ii. 58; perhaps Hieron liked to be addressed by the republican title: Cic. *Verr.* ii. 4. 119,
prytanium) are not conclusive for the earliest period of the colony.

[2] See note on p. 93.　　　　　　　　　　　　　　　　[3] Thuk. i. 13. 4.

[4] Thuk. vi. 5. It may, however, be that Akrai was not properly a colony but a mere
outpost of Syracuse (it does not coin until the Roman period). See below, p. 109.

[5] Thuk. vi. 5. 1. See Freeman, i. 410 ff., ii. 24; Hüttl, 48; and below, p. 300. Strabo, 272, says
τὴν μὲν Ἱμέραν οἱ ἐν Μυλαῖς ἔκτισαν Ζαγκλαῖοι. The mention of Mylai may be a misunderstanding of the name Μυλητίδαι, or a coincidence, or it may be that the Myletidai took their
name from Mylai. It is unlikely that they gave their name to Mylai (as Freeman, i. 411–12).

there is no evidence that any of them came to Syracuse.¹ A few years after the expulsion of the Myletidai the Syracusans founded Kasmenai (c. 643), perhaps because there was still a body of Syracusan citizens who were safer away from the capital.²

In this period perhaps comes a stasis mentioned by Aristotle.³ This took place ἐν τοῖς ἀρχαίοις χρόνοις, which one would expect to be at least as early as the sixth century.⁴ Another argument against attaching it to the fall of the Gamoroi in the early fifth century is that τοὺς ἐν τῷ πολιτεύματι were drawn into the stasis. The πολίτευμα is not the citizen body but those administering the constitution.⁵ There is no mention of calling in the demos. Aristotle may stop before the conclusion, but it is remarkable that he does not mention the Gamoroi, if he is really describing their fall. A quarrel within the body of the oligarchs, such as might result in the expulsion of the family of the Myletidai, would affect τοὺς ἐν τῷ πολιτεύματι. Further, the νεανίσκοι who quarrelled were τῶν ἐν ταῖς ἀρχαῖς ὄντων; they could hardly be office-holders, but might be members of the ruling families in an aristocracy.

The result, μετέβαλε ἡ πολιτεία in Aristotle, τὴν ἀρίστην πολιτείαν ἀνέτρεψαν according to Plutarch, does not involve a change to a democracy. There were many forms of oligarchy. It has been suggested that the constitution changed from aristocracy to oligarchy, the wealthy non-noble landowners being admitted to the ruling class, and the commercial and industrial classes being allowed to acquire land, which became the only source of political privilege.⁶ This certainly goes beyond the evidence; but, assuming that the stasis described

---

¹ Korkyra, Nic. Dam., fr. 58, 7. Lenschau in RE Suppl. iv. 1018 suggests that others went to Sicily, but on very slight grounds.

² Thuk. vi. 5. 2. Cf. Holm, i. 148; Freeman, ii. 23–4. In this and the previous paragraph I am closely following Blakeway. For the dates of Akrai and Kasmenai see p. 449, of Himera, p. 445; for the fall of the Bakkhiads, CAH, iii. 764 f. I think that the dates are sufficiently reliable to draw these admittedly tentative conclusions.

³ Pol. 1303ᵇ 7 ff. Plutarch (Praec. reip. ger. 825c) tells the same story, with a different interest, but his source is probably indirectly Aristotle. The only point which he adds is the advice given by one of the elders to the boule which is thought of as trying the case; but no reliance can be placed on his use of the term.

⁴ The other cases of similar phrase in the Politics all apply to a date which is at the latest sixth century. 1285ᵇ 13, ἐπὶ τῶν ἀρχαίων χρόνων, of heroic kingship; 1310ᵇ 21, τὸ ἀρχαῖον, longer terms of office (e.g. ten-year archonships); 1285ᵃ 30, ἐν τοῖς ἀρχαίοις Ἕλλησιν, aesymnetes (a 7th–6th-century phase); 1305ᵃ 7, ἐπὶ τῶν ἀρχαίων, tyrants arose from demagogy plus strategia: below, τῶν ἀρχαίων τυράννων (this description applies to Peisistratos). But in Ath. Pol. 28. 5 Aristeides and Kimon are included among οἱ ἀρχαῖοι.

⁵ Newman, i. 243, and note on 1278ᵇ 10.   ⁶ Hüttl, 48–52.

by Aristotle and Plutarch belongs to the early archaic period, as it seems to do, this hypothesis makes sense. Aristotle is silent about τὰ μεγάλα, which were the real cause of the stasis. The conquests in the hill region had enriched the State with a good deal of fertile territory and slaves to work it. There may well have been dissension whether this was to go to the nobles, or whether the wealthy men who were not noble should be allowed to acquire it. This, and the political tension heightened by the fall of the oligarchy at Corinth, may be at the root of the troubles in the middle of the seventh century. At Corinth the excluded class was commercial and industrial, and the result of the change of government was a tyranny. Syracuse was economically less advanced and politically more conservative, and it was only the basis of the oligarchy which changed. There may have been a compromise, with the effect of including in the oligarchy those large landholders who were not noble. But it must be remembered that this is only hypothesis. There is no evidence of the nature of tenure in the sixth century, nor any indication that the Gamoroi were not descended from the nobles among the original colonists.

We hear little of the Gamoroi until their fall. They sit as a court of law to hear the impeachment of Agathokles, who was convicted of sacrilege in using for his own house stone intended for the temple of Athena.[1] The story is parallel to those about Phalaris and Theron, of the contractor of works who became tyrant,[2] and Agathokles' real offence was no doubt aiming at the tyranny.[3] The Gamoroi appear to have sat as a body and must have been few enough for them all to meet and manage the affairs of state, like the Bakkhiads in that respect. The date is quite uncertain, but should be in the seventh century or early sixth, when, I think, the temple of Athena which lasted until the time of Gelon was built.[4]

The only other mention of the Gamoroi is in the Parian marble, in connexion with Sappho's exile in Sicily.[5] The date is between 603–2 and 596–5; probably the date given as the *floruit* of Sappho and Alkaios (600 or 599, according to Eusebius),[6] as their exile was the most exactly datable event of both their lives. The Gamoroi are named apparently as an addition to the date supplied by the Athenian archon. But it

---

[1] Diod. viii. 11.   [2] Below, pp. 315, 413.
[3] Cf. Van Buren, *AFR*, 64.   [4] See below, pp. 60 ff.   [5] Ep. 36.
[6] 599, Eusebius, ed. Schoene, ii. 93; 600, Jerome, ed. Fotheringham, 175.

is unlikely that any event in their rule provided confirmation of the date; more probably there was a direct reference in Sappho to the Gamoroi.[1] The date is very nearly that of the foundation of Kamarina, but that was merely an ordinary act of expansion. Kamarina became an undutiful daughter; but there is not the same ground in Syracusan or Corinthian history as in the case of Akrai and Kasmenai for suggesting that the foundation was intended to relieve internal difficulties. This was the end of the territorial growth of Syracusan power for more than a century, and there was also no marked political development for most of the period. After the disturbances of the middle of the seventh century Syracuse became more stable. To welcome aristocratic exiles from Mitylene the government must have been stable and conservative, and there is no reason to suppose that there was a change in the form or spirit of the government when Sappho arrived. There was a period of material prosperity in the early decades of the sixth century, followed apparently by an unprogressive period. Through the whole of the sixth century we hear nothing of internal affairs and can infer little; the contrast with the seventh century suggests that there was in fact quiet.

The first quarter of the sixth century was one of the high points in the early history of Syracuse. With the foundation of Kamarina she gained control of the south-west to within a few miles of Gela. Megara was economically dependent on Syracuse, perhaps even politically.[2] The Apollonion[3]

---

[1] Jacoby, *Das Marmor Parium*, 100. This is not invalidated by Bowra's demonstration that Sappho was very young when she came to Sicily (*Greek Lyric Poetry*, 435; cf. 186-7). She may have written some autobiographical poem of the sort that Alkaios favoured; perhaps, as Jacoby suggests, in return for hospitality.

[2] The only indication of the political status of Megara is to be found in her support of Syracuse against revolted Kamarina in 552 (below, p. 106).

[3] Koldewey and Puchstein, 62; Cultrera, *RIASA*, ix (1942), 54 ff. I continue to call the temple the Apollonion; but although the inscription on the stylobate records a dedication to Apollo it is not certain that the temple was dedicated to him. It may have been the temple of Artemis recorded by Cicero (*Verr.* II. iv. 53. 118); so Cultrera, op. cit. 66, n. 2; C. Picard, *RA*, x, 1937, 115 f. The reading of the inscription is difficult; see *IG*, xiv. 1; *SEG*, iv. 1; G. Oliverio, *L'iscrizione dell' Apollonion di Siracusa* (Bergamo, 1933); E. Drerup, *Mnemosyne*, ii, 1935, 1 ff.; A. von Blumenthal, *RM*, l, 1935, 331-2; R. Vallois, *REG*, l, 1937, 99. I repeat Drerup's reading with von Blumenthal's supplements: κλεο[. . . .]ϵς : ϵποιϵσϵ το πϵλονι : ho κινιδϵ[.]α : τϵπιπ[ρ]ϵσ(σ)τυλϵια : κα[λ](λ)α ϝϵργα. Oliverio's reading is somewhat different. The proper name, read by von Blumenthal as Kleosimenes, is generally read Kleomenes, probably wrongly, as there appears to be space for more than three letters (but see Oliverio); van Buren, *AFR*, 77, suggests Kleosthenes. He was perhaps an official of the State charged with the building of the temple, as Agathokles was of an early Athenaion.

and the Olympieion[1] were built, and some building was done in the precinct of Athena. The temples of Apollo and Zeus were built on very similar plans, perhaps by the same architect, and show that Syracuse was in the forefront of the development of the Doric temple.[2]

Orsi declined, with all the material before him, to assign any of the terra-cotta or stone fragments on the Athenaion site to their buildings.[3] The foundations have now been covered up. Therefore it is impossible to use the site as a running commentary on the growth of Syracuse. So much may be said: the temenos is as old as the colony; the earliest thing in the sanctuary was the open-air ἐσχάρα; there are some seventh-century buildings,[4] but the fullest series of revetments[5] belongs to the early sixth century, when the temple was either completely refaced or, more probably, rebuilt. There are foundations of other small buildings of the οἶκος type, to which some of the architectural fragments in stone and terra-cotta will belong. The fourth, the second, and the first revetment from the temenos belong to the second quarter of the sixth century[6] and to three different small buildings. None of the revetments from the site appears to belong to the middle of the century: we have a full series of sixth-century Sicilian revetments and all these come early in it. Orsi's date for the building which is probably the pre-Deinomenid temple[7] is 'in the advanced sixth century'.[8] This is a date founded on the technique of building, and especially the excellence of the masonry, on which Orsi's opinion deserves great respect. On the other hand, the absence of any stone to be referred to the elevation[9] makes it extremely probable that the columns and superstructure were of wood. This is unlikely so late as the late sixth century; conservatism might replace an earlier building in the same materials, but it is difficult to believe that, after the noble buildings of the Apollonion and the Olympieion, Syracusans would go back to a timbered building for their other chief deity. Taken with the

---

[1] *MA*, xiii. 381 ff.; Koldewey and Puchstein, 66.

[2] Cf. Koldewey, op. cit. 60. For the date of the two temples see Robertson, *Greek and Roman Architecture*, 69, 324 (*c.* 575).

[3] *MA*, xxv. 683 ff.

[4] One of these should be the temple of whose building Agathokles was supervisor (see above, p. 58).

[5] *MA*, xxv. 644 ff., pll. xx–xxi; Van Buren, *AFR*, 65 ff.; Darsow, *Sizilische Dachterrakotten*, 23 (roof B).

[6] For the dating see below, pp. 272 ff.

[7] *MA*, xxv. 370 ff.; pll. v–vi.

[8] 'Nel secolo VI avanzato', ibid. 738.

[9] Ibid. 379.

difficulty that none of the revetments belongs to the date to which Orsi assigns the foundations, or to a later date, this suggests that the temple which the Deinomenids destroyed was at least as old as the early sixth century. At this period the authority of Corinth and her control of the west were at their height, and it is reasonable to suppose that Syracuse shared in her glory. It is likely that Syracuse had a considerable part in the import of Corinthian goods to the rest of Sicily also.[1] Towards the middle of the sixth century, however, the Corinthian hold on the west begins to slacken.[2] This economic movement, which led in time to the emancipation of the colonies, may have had as effect a setback in the position of Syracuse. There appears to have been a period about the middle of the century when the other cities moved forward while Syracuse was standing still. This was the time when Kamarina revolted, and though the Syracusans won the war, the fact of such a revolt shows that all was not well with Syracuse. The general aspect of the sixth-century graves indicates that Leontinoi and Gela rose to a considerable height of luxury in the second half of the century, but Syracuse lagged a little. There may be other reasons for the absence of jewellery and fine vases in the Syracusan graves, as such things are a matter of taste. Orsi finds one in the sterner Dorism of the Syracusans.[3] But the Geloans and Megarians were also Dorians. In the seventh century, moreover, there are exceedingly delicate Protocorinthian vases, some of the finest known coming from Syracusan cemeteries. In the second half of the sixth century there are no fine black-figure and early red-figure vases such as other Sicilian sites have yielded. The Fusco cemetery continued in use in the sixth century, and there was added to it the important ex-Spagna cemetery, which has some of the richest graves of the period c. 600. Considering the large number of sixth-century graves at Syracuse, one can conclude that there was less display of wealth there than at Gela and Leontinoi. Probably the riches of Syracuse were more concentrated in the hands of the Gamoroi; the wealth from the rich cornlands of Gela and Leontinoi was perhaps more equally distributed than the returns from the Syracusan lands, tilled by serfs. Also, the importance of Syracuse in the early period of its history depended largely on the trade-connexion with Corinth. In the sixth century Corinth's position was weakening and her

[1] See below, p. 227.   [2] See below, pp. 241 ff.   [3] *N Sc*, 1895, 114 f.

exclusive hold on trade with the western colonies passing away. The new influences were felt earlier in the Khalkidian cities and in the Rhodian group of the south coast. Attic black-figure vases are not imported in quantity to Syracuse before *c.* 530, about a quarter of a century after Corinthian has given way elsewhere to Attic.[1] Artistically, Syracuse was even more tied to Corinth, and only towards the end of the century are the revivifying East Greek influences felt. The middle of the century was everywhere in eastern Sicily a dull unproductive period, to judge from the scanty remains, but particularly so in Syracuse.

About 530, the date of the beginning of the coinage,[2] may be taken as the beginning of the Syracusan revival.[3] It is certainly wrong to associate the beginning of the coinage with the establishment of democracy,[4] for this would imply that the Gamoroi were driven out about 530 and languished for nearly half a century at Kasmenai before Gelon restored them in 485.[5] But it certainly marks a change of economic policy, and Syracuse soon regained the pre-eminent position in Sicily which she had held previously as a result of Corinthian friendship.

Though I do not agree with Orsi's view, which would date the rebuilding of the Athenaion at the end of the sixth century, the great altar,[6] replacing the last of a series of simple ἐσχάραι,[7] is probably of that date. A relief with Ionic volute and palmette, of the late sixth century, comes probably from the end of the great altar.[8] This is a large and important structure, and the style of the relief shows one of the earliest examples in Sicily of that wave of East Greek influence, due to Ionian immigration, which reaches the west in the late sixth century.[9]

At about the time of this inferred revival the mole was built which joins the island of Ortygia to the mainland. Ibykos wrote of the work in a way which suggests that it was new in his day; he probably visited Syracuse before he left the west for the court of Polykrates, i.e. before *c.* 525.[10] He also related the under-sea connexion of Alpheios and Arethusa, by which

[1] See below, p. 244; cf. B. L. Bailey, *JHS*, 1940, 69.

[2] Boehringer, *Die Münzen von Syrakus*, 6, 91.

[3] But Ashmole (p. 20, n. 2) finds the art of Syracusan coins of the late sixth and early fifth centuries still very backward.

[4] Hüttl, 51; cf. Weickert, *Gnomon*, 1933, 19 f.

[5] See below, pp. 400, 415.

[6] *MA*, xxv. 433 ff., 447 ff.

[7] Ibid. 391 ff.

[8] Ibid. 693 ff., pl. 23.

[9] See below, p. 297.

[10] Fr. 22; Schol. Pind. *Nem.* i. 1; Strabo 59; cf. Bowra, *Greek Lyric Poetry*, 253-4.

a phiale thrown into the river at Olympia reappeared at Syracuse.[1] A generation later the Homerid Kynaithos of Khios came to Syracuse and was the first to recite the Homeric poems there.[2] The date given for this event in the scholiast to Pindar, 69th Olympiad (504–500), is difficult, if it is supposed that the *Iliad* and *Odyssey* were previously unknown in Sicily; it is hard to think Stesikhoros ignorant of them. It has, therefore, been amended to give an earlier date (e.g. 49th Olympiad, 584–580),[3] but the date given in the manuscripts may be kept if it is taken to mean that regular public performances or contests, such as were instituted at Athens by the Peisistratids, were set up when Kynaithos came to Syracuse.[4] The scholiast says further that Kynaithos composed the Hymn to Apollo, and it has been concluded that he put it together for a western audience, more familiar with Delphi than Delos. Other poems in the Homeric Hymns and the Theognidean collection may have been composed, or collected, at or near Syracuse at the same period.[5] This is the beginning of the literary movement which made Hieron's court one of the most splendid of all time.

It was perhaps now that the wealth of Syracuse was contrasted with the health of Kroton in the story of the oracle given to the founders of the two cities.[6] The fame of Kroton's medical school belongs to the late sixth century, the age of Demokedes and Alkmaion; the great age of her athletic victories is the late sixth and early fifth centuries. The contrast would be pointless in the fifth century, when Kroton as the chief city of Magna Graecia might claim wealth as well as health; and a meaningless piece of antiquarianism at a later date, when her doctors had lost their pre-eminence. Pre-Deinomenid Syracuse, already as large as any Greek city, and possessed of a territory larger than any Greek state except Lakonia and, perhaps, Sybaris; the only Sicilian city to have completely subdued the Sikels in its territory; the proprietors of a race of serfs whose numbers became a proverb; the best and safest port in Sicily, the natural terminus for all shipping from Greece, and the natural distributing centre for the goods of her mother city, Corinth, whose commercial and artistic

---

[1] Fr. 23.

[2] Schol. Pind. *Nem.* ii. 1; cf. Wade-Gery in *Greek Poetry and Life*, 56 ff., esp. 71 ff.

[3] Dornseiff, *Die archaische Mythenerzählung*, 38 ff.

[4] Christ–Schmid, *Gesch. Gr. Lit.*[6] (1912), i. 75 f.   [5] Wade-Gery, loc. cit.

[6] Paus. v. 7. 3; Strabo 269; cf. Parke, *History of the Delphic Oracle*, 71–2. See further below, pp. 444 ff.

influence was until the second half of the sixth century predominant in Sicily: pre-Deinomenid Syracuse was already, surely, more than the equal of Gela and Leontinoi. Contemporary witness is borne by Hekataios, who called it πόλις Σικελίας μεγίστη.[1]

GELA

At Gela and Leontinoi, as at Syracuse, there were seventh-century disturbances which severely tried the constitution. At Gela, the party defeated in stasis seceded to the strong post of Maktorion[2] and prepared to make war on their rivals. Telines, Gelon's ancestor, restrained them by an appeal to their piety and brought them back to Gela.[3] The nature of the stasis is quite uncertain.[4] At such an early date it is most unlikely that there was a democratic party, and the combatants were probably two parties within the oligarchy, as at Syracuse. Telines is either Gelon's great-grandfather[5] or a remoter ancestor, so he can have flourished at the latest in the early sixth century. The fact that he is described as θηλυδρίης τε καὶ μαλακώτερος ἀνήρ does not exclude a very early date, for the Deinomenid house had certainly vivid traditions if not indeed archives. A date in the second half of the seventh century is most probable.

The cult of Demeter and Kore was already in the hands of the descendants of Deinomenes, who brought it from the Triopian headland.[6] It may have been private, but was of sufficient standing for the awe inspired by the holy objects to bring back the seceders without further hostilities. Telines' reward was the elevation of his family worship to a state cult, with privileges for the priest (ἐπ' ᾧ τε οἱ ἀπόγονοι αὐτοῦ ἱροφάνται

---

[1] Steph. Byz. s.v. Συράκουσαι, πόλις Σικελίας μεγίστη, ὡς Ἑκαταῖος Εὐρώπῃ. μεγίστη appears to be part of the quotation; it is unlikely that Stephanos would add such a detail. For Hekataios' date see Jacoby, *RE*, vii. 2670–1.

[2] The site is unknown; see below, p. 113.   [3] Herod. vii. 153.

[4] Pais (*Ancient Italy*, ch. xx) holds that the secession to Maktorion was exactly parallel to the secession of the Roman plebs to the Mons Sacer. I am not sure to what extent he supposes the traditional account of the secession at Rome to be modelled on the historical account of the secession at Gela and Syracuse.

[5] Gelon's father being Deinomenes, his grandfather Molossos (*Lind. Chron.* xxviii; *Lindos*, ii. 171 ff.). See the genealogical table on p. 483.

[6] Schol. Pind. *Pyth.* ii. 27b: Δεινομένους γὰρ υἱεῖς εἰσιν οἱ περὶ τὸν Ἱέρωνα τοῦ τὰ ἱερὰ ἐκ Τριοπίου τῆς Κύπρου εἰς Σικελίαν κομίσαντος. I take it that there is solid foundation for this note in spite of the obvious blunders of putting Triopion in Cyprus and confusing Deinomenes, father of Gelon, with Deinomenes, founder of the family (not named in Herodotos). Xenagoras made the same mistake (in *Lind. Chron.* xxviii), calling him Lindian whereas Telos was a Kamiran island.

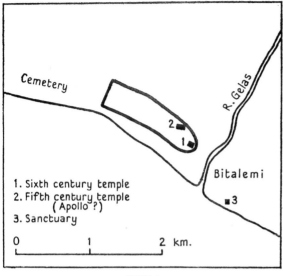

1. Sixth century temple
2. Fifth century temple
   (Apollo?)
3. Sanctuary

0   1   2 km.

GELA

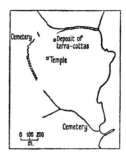

MEGARA HYBLAEA

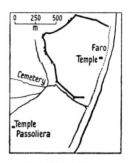

KAULONIA

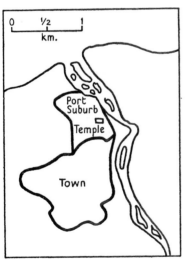

HIMERA

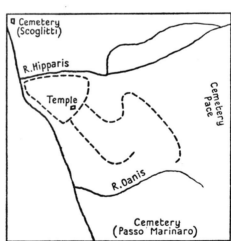

KAMARINA

F

τῶν θεῶν ἔσονται: state recognition). The priesthood passed to the eldest of the family, from Gelon to Hieron, then Thrasyboulos, passing over the younger generation. The honour attached to it was probably one reason for Gelon's popularity at Gela. This tantalizing story, which really says no more than that there was a stasis and secession at Gela, is the only recorded event in the internal history of the city before the tyranny of Kleandros (505 B.C.). The remains of the temple of Athena just outside the walls and of its seventh-century predecessor show that the city was reasonably prosperous, but it was clearly of the second rank. The richest graves are those of the fifth century, when it had settled down after its moment of glory to a peaceful provincial existence.

LEONTINOI

Similarly the one recorded piece of Leontine history, from its foundation to its subjection by Hippokrates, is the tyranny of Panaitios. This was in the last decade of the seventh century.[1] The previous constitution was an oligarchy, and Panaitios rose to power by championing the unprivileged.[2] Polyainos says that he was commander of the Leontine army against Megara, and sowed dissension between the poor men who formed the infantry and the rich cavalrymen. He seized power with the aid of a band of 600 light-armed and the cavalrymen's servants, who assisted him to disarm the rest of the army and put the knights to death.[3] As usual, the details of the coup in Polyainos are suspect, especially the trick by which he disarmed his opponents, and their massacre. But it does appear that Panaitios was one of the frequent cases of demagogy plus strategia: his prowess in the war with Megara gave him the personal support he needed, and he was able to discredit the cavalry owing to their part in the war. What was his real title, which Polyainos records as πολεμαρχῶν, is impossible to guess.

The important point about Panaitios is that he is the first of Sicilian tyrants. The ferment of discontent with the exclusiveness of the rich nobles was brought to a head sooner at Leon-

---

[1] 608, Vers. Arm. (Schoene, ii. 90) 'Panetius primus in Sicilia arripuit tyrannidem'; 615. Jerome (Fotheringham, 171).

[2] Pol. 1310^b 29 Παναίτιος δ᾽ ἐν Λεοντίνοις . . . ἐκ δημαγωγίας. Pol. 1316^a 34 καὶ εἰς τυραννίδα μεταβάλλει ἐξ ὀλιγαρχίας, ὥσπερ ἐν Σικελίᾳ σχεδὸν αἱ πλεῖσται τῶν ἀρχαίων, ἐν Λεοντίνοις εἰς τὴν Παναιτίου τυραννίδα. . . .

[3] Polyainos v. 47.

tinoi than elsewhere. Polyainos' picture of a rich cavalry and a poor half-armed mob of infantry, ready to support the selfish demagogue, is probably approximately true not only of Leontinoi but of all the Sicilian cities. The descendants of the original nobles owned the land and had all the political privilege: the others, poorer settlers and late-comers, were not in greatly better condition than the natives. They did not even provide the chief arm in war. But at Leontinoi they found a spokesman sooner than in any other city.

The wealth and progressiveness of Leontinoi in the sixth century is evident from other sources. There was a proverb ἀεὶ Λεοντῖνοι περὶ τοὺς κρατῆρας which should belong to the period of their independence: the first testimony to the Sicilian love of good cheer. It is brought into relation with Phalaris, quite unjustifiably.[1]

Though the Greek cemeteries at Leontinoi have often been sought, only small and isolated finds have been made. But they show greater riches than the other cities of Sicily in the sixth century. Gold ornaments are plentiful; there is some of the earliest and finest bronze-work; a few magnificent pieces of black-figure and severe red-figure pottery; and more archaic sculpture than from any other site, including a head in Catania which is to my mind the finest piece of sculpture in Sicily.[2] But the finds have not been enough to form any picture of life in Leontinoi. The hope of making a big discovery led Orsi there season after season, and had to be left unsatisfied. The riches and strength of the city in the sixth century are chiefly a matter of inference. Its history begins really with its first destruction. Leontinoi had possession of the largest and richest wheat-growing plain in Sicily, the *campi Leontini*, which was the source of riches in Roman times for Kentoripa, and is now the *piano di Catania*. This is the plain where wild grain still grew in Diodoros' time: ἔν τε γὰρ τῷ Λεοντίνῳ πεδίῳ καὶ κατὰ πολλοὺς ἄλλους τόπους τῆς Σικελίας μέχρι τοῦ νῦν φύεσθαι τοὺς ἀγρίους ὀνομαζομένους πυρούς;[3] which disputed with Eleusis to be the place where Demeter gave the gift of corn to man.

[1] See below, p. 319.
[2] NC., nos. 901, 1089A from Leontinoi. Orsi, 'Vasi di Leontini', in *RIASA*, 1930, 149 ff.; *RM*, 1900, 82 ff.; *N Sc*, 1884, 440 ff. Bronzes in Berlin, Winnefeld, *Winckelmanns Programm*, 1899. Marble torso, *MA*, xviii, 169–74, pl. VI; *N Sc*, 1904, 369; Langlotz, *Frühgriechische Bildhauerschulen*, pl. 64. Head in Catania, Libertini, *Cat. del Museo Biscari*, pl. 1–2. Walls, and the site in general, Orsi, *SMG*, 1930; Columba, 'Archeologia di Leontini', in *ASS*, 1891.
[3] Diod. v. 2.

There is no natural boundary in this plain, unless it be the river Symaithos, to divide the land of Leontinoi from the land of Katane. Probably there was none needed. When misfortunes fell upon them in the fifth century, the three Khalkidian cities had a feeling of unity and common consent, which may have kept them from warring in the days of their prosperity. Theokles was founder of both Naxos and Leontinoi. The three sites are in a way complementary: Naxos holds the approach from Greece, the first port of call on passing from Leukopetra; Katane and Leontinoi between them hold the *piano di Catania*, and neither is complete without the other. Kharondas legislated for other Khalkidian cities as well as Katane.[1] This suggests that the ties between the Khalkidian cities were stronger than those among the Dorian cities, that they formed a bloc and were inclined to act together. The Khalkidian colonists had a genius for closer union: in the Khalkidike no one town was of importance, but the whole people, τὸ Χαλκιδικόν, which transcended the local units. There, one of the first Greek experiments in federation was made. The Khalkidian cities of Sicily were certainly completely independent units, but they accepted the same laws and may have carried out a common foreign policy.

THE LAWGIVERS: LOKROI AND KATANE

None of the remains of Lokroi belong to the early period of the colony's existence. The prehellenic graves are discussed above;[2] the abundant and important finds of temples, sanctuary deposit, and graves from the second half of the sixth century onwards will be discussed below in another context.[3]

Within a very short time from the foundation a lawgiver, Zaleukos, arose in Lokroi.[4] The Eusebian figure *c.* 661[5] is the only direct evidence of his date. It is very early but not impossible. Lokroi was founded, according to Eusebius, in 673, and though the date cannot be insisted on, it was apparently the last of the Italian foundations, and in the seventh century.[6] Acceptance of the Eusebian date would imply that the Lok-

---

[1] Below, p. 75.   [2] p. 44.   [3] pp. 292 ff.

[4] Arist. *Pol.* 1274ᵃ 22; Aristotle ap. Schol. Pind. *Ol.* x. 17; Strabo 259 (= Ephoros fr. 139 Jacoby); ps.-Skymn. 314–15; Polyb. xii. 16; Demos. xxiv. 139; Aelian, *VH*, iii. 17. See Max Mühl, 'Die Gesetze des Zaleukos und Charondas', *Klio*, xxii. 105–24, 432–63; Arangio-Ruiz and Olivieri, *Inscr. Gr. Siciliae et infimae Italiae ad ius pertinentes*, 189 ff.

[5] Hieronymus, ed. Fotheringham, p. 165 (661 B.C.), Vers. Arm., ed. Schoene, ii. 86 (663 B.C.).   [6] Johansen, *VS*, 182; cf. above, p. 35.

rians, men of doubtful antecedents, got into difficulties before
the colony was very old and were fortunate in finding an able
man to rescue them. Demosthenes gives a vague chronological
indication when he says that the laws of Zaleukos stood for
more than 200 years with only one change, but it is not clear
whether he means that they had stood for 200 years when the
amendment was introduced or that they were 200 years old in
his day. According to Ephoros, Zaleukos was the first man to
give written laws, and he therefore belongs to the seventh
century, before Drakon. The codifiers made him the disciple
of Thales the Cretan and contemporary with Lykourgos.
Aristotle takes them to task for disregard of chronology, but
does not state the truth. Certainly Zaleukos' legislation was
well within the seventh century, and probably in the second
generation of the colony. There is no indication what sort of
trouble he was called upon to allay. But the disease was
probably of the same kind as the social disorders from which
many of the cities of Sicily suffered in the seventh century.
The tradition that he was a herd to whom Athena appeared in
a dream and dictated the laws, wherefore he was freed and
appointed nomothetes, is clearly fabulous, but not necessarily
hostile. It is romantic rather than detractive. Very probably
he claimed the inspiration of Athena, whose worship was
popular at Lokroi.[1] The 'shepherd' may be due to a misunderstanding of such a phrase as λαοῦ ποιμήν.[2] He was probably appointed with special powers to codify the laws, as
Drakon was at Athens; his position being akin to *aisymneteia*,
so far as his appointment was intended to put an end to civil
strife.

The tradition about his legislation is very poor. None of the
authorities goes back farther than the fourth century, and
Quellenkritik has not derived them from an earlier source.
Aristotle does not give the text of any of his laws. In the
Politics he names him as lawgiver, in the same breath as
Kharondas, with the implication that neither of them was also
a constitution-maker; and he rejects the list of successions
drawn up by persons unknown. He is quoted by the Scholiast
on Pindar for the legend that Zaleukos was a shepherd, but
again has nothing definite to say about his work. Ephoros
names him as the first giver of written laws, and says that he

---

[1] Cf. Giannelli, *Culti e Miti della Magna Grecia*, 243 ff.; Orsi, *N Sc*, 1911 Suppl., 62 ff.
[2] Oldfather, *RE*, xiii. 1939.

put together his code from the examination of the laws of
Crete, Sparta, and the Areopagos. The addition of the Areo-
pagite laws betrays the influence of Isokrates' *Areopagitikos* on
Ephoros.[1] The tradition of Cretan and Spartan influence means
no more than that these two communities were regarded as
models of eunomia.[2] The same idea was expressed by those
who made Zaleukos and Lykourgos fellow disciples of Thales:
all good laws were derived ultimately from Crete. But knowing
the tradition that Lokroi was the home of the first lawgiver,
these pre-Aristotelians who cared not for chronology made
Thales learn from Onomakritos, the legendary seer, said to be
a Lokrian resident in Crete.

Ephoros recorded that Zaleukos fixed the penalties for different offences by law, instead of leaving them to the chances of
the justices' feelings. As a step to the equality of rich and poor
before the law, this is hardly less important than the publication of the laws. It would vastly limit the power of the βασιλῆες
δωροφάγοι to interpret the laws in their own interests.[3] Ephoros
recorded also some unspecified ordinance about contracts. The
only other laws which rest on good authority are those to
which Polybios refers, that disputed property, including slaves,
should remain in the hands of the party from whom it was
seized until judgement was given; and the law of an eye for an
eye, which Demosthenes quotes. The enactment which ensured
the permanence of the laws is also given by Demosthenes and
Polybios, to the effect that any citizen who had an amendment
to propose should advocate it with his neck in a noose which
might be drawn on the spot if his proposed law was not carried.

This is the whole extent of Zaleukos' code about which any
confidence can be felt. Diodoros[4] gives a summary of his legislation, which he prefixes by saying that Zaleukos was ἀνὴρ εὐγενὴς
καὶ κατὰ παιδείαν τεθαυμασμένος, μαθητὴς δὲ Πυθαγόρου. He is
made a pupil of Pythagoras also by Diogenes Laertius (viii. 16),
Porphyrios (*Vit. Pyth.* 21), Iamblikhos (*Vit. Pyth.* 33, 130, 172),
and Seneca (ep. 90. 6),[5] and the same was said of Kharondas.
The Pythagoreans seem to have owed something to Zaleukos,
and to have agreed with him in the reverence paid to law.
They repaid their debt by enrolling him posthumously in their
ranks, and by producing a new edition of his laws. Diodoros

[1] Mühl, 112.   [2] Cf. Aelian, *VH* ii. 22, for the eunomia of the Lokrians.
[3] Cf. Bonner and Smith, *The Administration of Justice from Homer to Aristotle*, i. 67–82.
[4] xii. 20–1.   [5] References in Mühl, 458.

begins with a prooimion, which is certainly a forgery, because
Plato knows nothing of it.[1] Mühl points out the similarity
of its content to Stoic thought as expressed in Cicero,[2] and
Seneca's statement that Zaleukos and Kharondas were Pythagoreans derives from Poseidonios.[3] Poseidonios may be
Diodoros' immediate source for some of his account of the two
legislators, but it is equally possible that they both drew on
a common source, and in any case the responsibility for the
forgery lies with a nameless Pythagorean, probably of the third
century. The remainder of the legislation of Diodoros, after
the prooimion devoted to the worship of the gods, is concerned
with ethical precepts and sumptuary ordinances. The moral
tone of these suits a Pythagorean author better than a seventh-
century legislator, and though there is no *a priori* reason why
the sumptuary laws should belong to one period rather than
the other, the authority of Diodoros is so shaken by the demonstrated falsehood of his statements about Zaleukos' date and
about the prooimion that we can have no confidence that he
contains any part of Zaleukos' original legislation. Mühl's conclusion that 'Die Tradition bei Diodor bietet wohl im all-
gemeinen authentisches Gut, aber im angegebenen Zeitraum
kam neues, verfälschtes Material hinzu'[4] is not justified by
the evidence he quotes. There is no point of contact between
Diodoros and the older tradition, and so much of him as may
be assigned to a definite source comes not from a tradition
independent of Aristotle, Ephoros, and Demosthenes but from
a forgery of probably later date than these authorities. It is
likely that the rest of Diodoros comes from the same more
than suspect source. The Pythagorean forger doubtless used
genuine material, but we cannot assume that anything for
which he is authority is genuine.[5]

The law quoted by Aelian and Athenaios prescribing the
death penalty for drinking unmixed wine without a doctor's
order[6] has the same ethos as the laws in Diodoros, and doubtless comes from the same source. The story in Aelian how
Zaleukos was caught in the noose of his own law when his son
was to be blinded for adultery, and gave one of his own eyes
to save one of his son's,[7] belongs to another tradition: the

---

[1] *Laws*, 722e.   [2] *de nat. deor.* ii. 5. 13 ff.
[3] Mühl, 118 ff., 458.   [4] Mühl, 124.
[5] Cf. Oldfather, *RE*, xiii. 1323, 'einige gewiss alt sein können', but he does not say which.
[6] Aelian, *VH* ii. 37 ; Athen. 429a.   [7] Aelian, *VH* xiii. 24.

romantic personalia of Hellenistic times which preceded the development of the novel. Kharondas' death, killing himself with his sword because he had broken his own law against bearing arms in the assembly,[1] belongs to the same sort of romance. There is no more reason to suppose that this law is genuine than that the others are, but it may be so *per accidens*. Whether Zaleukos' proverbial reputation for severity[2] was based on the genuine laws or forgeries such as these cannot be certain, but the provision which controlled new legislation would alone justify it.

Zaleukos in no respect appears as a constitution-giver, and Aristotle excludes him from the class of lawgivers who were also makers of constitutions. But, of course, his work had its political side, like Solon's. A law of the Lokrians, without Zaleukos' name and not definitely ascribed to the Epizephyrian Lokrians, belongs probably to this side of his legislation. The Lokrians were forbidden to sell their estates unless in case of absolute necessity, and then had to keep their original kleroi.[3] This law would contribute to the stability of an aristocracy based on the possession of land. The constitution of Lokroi brought from the homeland remained an old-fashioned aristocracy. There was a council of a thousand,[4] deriving their nobility from the Hundred Houses of Opuntian Lokris, where a council of a thousand is also attested.[5] This is the ἀριστοκρατία οὐκ εὖ μεμειγμένη which was destroyed by Dionysios.[6] One of the higher magistrates, perhaps the supreme magistrate, was called κοσμόπολις.[7] The title may descend from Zaleukos; it would be an appropriate office for him to hold, and to be bequeathed for his successors to guard the fabric which he had set up. A supreme council of a thousand is also found at Rhegion[8] and Kroton.[9] At Rhegion, which used the laws of Kharondas, this council may have been introduced in imitation of the constitution of the neighbouring Lokroi, famed for its good laws. The thousand at Kroton may be post-Pythagoras and the result of Pythagorean imitation of Lokroi. There is no evidence that the laws of Lokroi were used in the sixth century in the Akhaian cities or that her constitution was imitated there so early. Lokroi held aloof from the alliance of

---

[1] Diod. xii. 19.   [2] Zenob. iv. 10.   [3] Arist. *Pol.* 1266[b] 18.
[4] Polyb. xii. 16.   [5] Tod, *GHI*, no. 24, l. 39.
[6] Arist. *Pol.* 1307[a] 38.   [7] Polyb. xii. 16.
[8] Herakleid. Pont. fr. 25; cf. Greenidge, *Greek Const. Hist.* 23.
[9] Iamb. *Vit. Pyth.* 35. 260.

south Italian cities witnessed by their coins,[1] and when she came into contact with Kroton the relations were not friendly. The influence of Lokrian good government and good laws in the Akhaian cities cannot be dated before the fifth century, the period of Pythagorean influence in Kroton and of the legislation of Thuria.[2]

At Katane, as at Lokroi, a lawgiver preserved the aristocracy.[3] Kharondas was said by some to be a pupil of Zaleukos. Aristotle rejects all this scheme on chronological grounds, but does not give the true chronology. Kharondas' laws agreed in general tone, and probably in many provisions, with Zaleukos'; so far the pupil tradition is justified.

The laws which can confidently be ascribed to Kharondas are laws of evidence (αἱ δίκαι τῶν ψευδομαρτυριῶν: Pol. 1274ᵇ 6) and perhaps something about contracts (Theophr. ap. Stob. Serm. 42). Another law laid down a large penalty for rich men who did not attend the law-courts, a small penalty for poor men, with the result that the rich men took a much more active interest in the administration of justice. Kharondas was occupied also with the position of the family (Pol. 1252ᵇ 14, ὁμοσιπύους); it is not stated with what intention.

The main body of 'laws of Kharondas' preserved by Diodoros[4] is suspect. They are the laws which Kharondas is said to have given for Thuria in the fifth century. They may be in part the original laws of Thuria, based on the laws of Zaleukos and Kharondas, but some of them, giving philosophical advice rather than laying down laws, cannot be older than the fourth century, and have a strong Pythagorean flavour. The remainder agree in many provisions with the laws of Zaleukos preserved from other sources. While there may be something of Kharondas as of Zaleukos preserved in Diodoros, the body of the laws as he gives it was certainly brought up to date in the fifth and fourth centuries. There is no single provision which can plausibly be ascribed to the archaic code of any western city.

Though the laws of Kharondas were not tied up with the constitution of Katane, for they could be adopted in other states,[5] they had a political direction. The result of the legisla-

---

[1] See below, pp. 355 ff.

[2] Ephoros ap. Strabo 260; Diod. xii. 12; Athen. 508a; ps.-Skymn. 346-7; cf. Suidas s.v. Ζάλευκος.

[3] Arist. Pol. 1274ᵃ 23, 30; 1274ᵇ 5; 1296ᵃ 21; 1297ᵃ 14 ff.; Plato, Repub. 599e; Aelian, VH iii. 17; Herakleides Pontikos, fr. 25.

[4] xii. 11-19.   [5] Cf. Gilbert, Griechische Staatsalterthümer, ii. 251.

tion was the same as at Lokroi, that the aristocracy was preserved without such disturbances as occurred in the other cities of Sicily, including Leontinoi.[1] Aristotle appears to include Kharondas in the judgement διαμαρτάνουσι πολλοὶ καὶ τῶν τὰς ἀριστοκρατικὰς βουλομένων ποιεῖν πολιτείας, and certainly regards his enactment about the law-courts as a σόφισμα πρὸς τὸν δῆμον.[2] Although not a constitution maker, no ancient lawgiver could avoid affecting the working of the constitution. Kharondas was thought to have, like Zaleukos, an aristocratic bias which one would expect in a lawgiver of the seventh century.

Kharondas' death on the breaking of his own law is parallel to Zaleukos' blinding and an exact doublet of the death of Diokles,[3] the Syracusan legislator of the last decade of the fifth century. It is not possible even to conclude that there was a law of Kharondas forbidding the wearing of arms in the ecclesia.[4] The exile of Kharondas from Katane to Rhegion[5] is an unjustifiable inference from the fact that his code was used there. In fact, nothing is known of Kharondas' circumstances except Aristotle's statement that he was ἐκ τῶν μέσων, but even that is something more solid than the conflicting legends about Zaleukos' origin.

The observance of the laws of Kharondas at Mazaka in Cappadocia,[6] their recital at Kos,[7] their singing at banquets at Athens[8] instead of skolia, are interesting evidence of the diffusion of his fame after the fifth century, but tell little about their nature. The 'laws' sung at Athens may have been versifications of the matter of Kharondas, or he may have cast them in that form to be more easily remembered. They were probably gnomic. There is no evidence that they had any influence on Athenian law; it is as an adjunct of the banquet that they are imported. It is striking how many of Sicily's contributions to the life of Greece were in the way of good cheer: the kottabos, earliest and most popular; later, delicacies of sea and land, and ways of cooking them; and a literary form derived from Epikharmos' Ἥβας Γάμος. This may sound strange company for Kharondas, but I wish to guard against attaching too much importance to the literary or ethical value of the

---

[1] Onomarkhos the tyrant of Katane, who kept lions as table companions (Aelian, NH v. 39), is probably a fourth-century eccentric.

[2] Pol. 1297ª 7, 21.

[3] Diod. xiii. 33. 2.

[4] As Mühl does, op. cit. 462.

[5] Aelian, VH iii. 17.

[6] Strabo 539.

[7] Herondas, Mim. ii. 48.

[8] Athen. 619b.

custom of singing him after dinner. The knowledge of Kharondas in Kos and Cappadocia may well derive from this Athenian
custom. In any case it is later than the Thuria–Pythagorean
contamination and implies very little about the genuine laws.

The constitution of Rhegion was an oligarchy of one
thousand, chosen from the aristocratic families according to
wealth.[1] These families were the Messenians who came west
after the First Messenian War. This mixed aristocratic-
oligarchic constitution resembles that of the Gamoroi at
Syracuse, who were probably an aristocracy of descent from
the original settlers into which a wealth-qualification was
introduced. The supreme body of the Gamoroi may have been
an assembly of comparable size. The constitution of Rhegion
also resembles that of Lokroi in having a council of a thousand,
and may have been assimilated to it.[2]

The Rhegines themselves used the laws of Kharondas,[3] but
produced a lawgiver for the Khalkidians of Thrace, Androdamas.[4] There is no evidence for the date, but a general
probability that Androdamas like Zaleukos and Kharondas
belonged to the seventh century. As Androdamas must have
reached Thrace by way of Khalkis, continued relations between
the Khalkidian colonies and Khalkis are proved. The movement of distinguished colonials back to the mother country,
and even, as in this case, on to another colonial region, may
have been more frequent than the evidence allows us to state.

SYBARIS

The only south Italian city about which there is much
information belonging to the archaic period is Sybaris. As it
was destroyed in 510 B.C., we may be confident that references
to it will be to an earlier period.[5] The site of the city is uncertain, and though a few isolated remains have been found, they

---

[1] *Pol.* 1316ᵃ 38: ἐξ ὀλιγαρχίας, ὥσπερ ... ἐν Ῥηγίῳ εἰς τὴν Ἀναξιλάου. Herakleides Pontikos,
fr. 25, § 4: πολιτείαν δὲ κατεστήσαντο ἀριστοκρατικήν. χίλιοι γὰρ πάντα διοικοῦσιν, αἱρετοὶ ἀπὸ
τιμημάτων. Strabo 257: οἱ τῶν Ῥηγίνων ἡγεμόνες μέχρι Ἀναξίλα τοῦ Μεσσηνίων γένους ἀεὶ
καθίσταντο. The ἡγεμόνες, the ruling houses, not a kingship as Freeman suggests (ii. 489); it
is not an exact word, and fits a body such as Herakleides' thousand better than a magistracy.

[2] Whibley, *Greek Oligarchies*, 135. He goes too far in speaking of a general tendency to
assimilate the constitutions of the western colonies.

[3] Herakleides, loc. cit.; cf. *Republic* 599e; Aelian, *VH* iii. 17.

[4] Arist. *Pol.* 1274ᵇ 23.

[5] It is possible that some of them will belong to the revived Sybaris of 453–448, or to
Sybaris on the Traeis. Alkisthenes, who dedicated a storied himation to Hera Lakinia, is
thought by Jacobsthal to have been a citizen of one of them (*JHS*, 1938, 205 ff.).

are without historical importance;[1] a rich harvest still lies buried under the stony bed of the Krathis. But there is a good deal of literary tradition of a sort, from which it is possible to form an idea of life in the last half-century of the city's existence, the period when the most luxurious of mortals came to woo Agariste: the great banquets and splendid public festivals; the elegant youth of the city; the costly wares of Ionia, the metal-work of Etruria, the rarities of the whole Greek world; the shaded streets, the well-tilled fields, the flourishing little inland towns; the care taken for health and comfort, the pride in wines and cuisine; the encouragement to foreign merchants, and the kindly contempt for anyone who had to travel.

Most of our information, preserved in Athenaios, comes from Timaios, who wrote not without a certain moral purpose. His source was perhaps a collection of anecdotes, the Συβαριτικοὶ λόγοι, which had a similar reputation to Æsop's fables and made very good after-dinner entertainment: Aristophanes quotes them in the *Wasps*, where Philokleon repeats two, which are hardly historical.[2] Epikharmos is a possible parallel source.[3] Kleitonymos wrote a work called Συβαριτικά, in at least two books, from which Plutarch draws a silly story.[4] Apart from this author of the Roman period, no one else is known to have dealt specially with Sybaris. For most of the authors who refer to it, Sybaris was a byword, to be used for moralizing or slightly scandalous purposes, and the original Συβαριτικοὶ λόγοι were not strictly historical. It is a delicate matter to draw history from such a tradition, but it is worth trying to discover what lies behind the gossip.

The reason why Sybaris made such an impression, which has endured in common language to this day, was simply, as the ancient authors state, her luxury. The colonials were set in a richer land than Greece, and their external circumstances were easier than those of the cities of Asia. Sybaris excelled all the western cities in the richness of her territory and the

---

[1] *N Sc*, 1879, 49, 77 ff., 122 ff., 156 ff., 245 ff.; 1880, 68, 152 ff.; plan *N Sc*, 1879, pl. v (Cavallari); *N Sc*, 1932, 130 ff.; E. Galli, 'Alla ricerca di Sibari', *SMG*, 1929 (Roman *villa rustica* and some sporadic sixth-century pieces). Unpublished, Crotone Museum (cf. *N Sc*, 1897, 356): stamped pithos-rims of Rhodian type (nos. 1288, 2400-3); terra-cotta head of the last quarter of the sixth century (no. 1282). Cosenza Museum, architectural terra-cottas (cf. Orsi, *MA*, xxix. 473 ff.; this museum has been inaccessible to me).

[2] *Wasps* 1258 ff., 1427 ff.; cf. Suidas s.v. Συβαριτικαῖς; Hesykhios s.v. Συβαριτικοὶ λόγοι. Aelian found one of his more pointless stories (*HV* xiv. 20) ἐν ἱστορίαις Συβαριτικαῖς; it made him laugh.

[3] Suidas, loc. cit.   [4] *Eth.* 310 (=*FHG*, iv, p. 366).

extent of her empire, and had also a flourishing through commerce. She was the greatest colonial city of the time, and in material circumstances probably the equal of any city of Greece. The ancient view was that Sybaris' extraordinary prosperity was due to the richness of her soil.[1] This was the first thing that the Greeks sought for in their colonies, and the chief resource of most of them. Varro says: 'In Italia in Subaritano dicunt etiam cum centesimo redire solitum.'[2] But Timaios records that they grew only sufficient corn for their own use: τῶν καρπῶν σχεδὸν ἁπάντων ὑπὸ τῶν πολιτῶν καταναλισκο-μένων.[3] The ancient population of the area must be considered. The figures of 100,000 and 300,000 are given for the number of Sybarites,[4] and the former at least may not be a gross exaggeration of the total number, though not of the inhabitants of the city or the army which it could put into the field. Strabo's figure of fifty stades for the circuit of the walls[5] is not unreasonable, for the city, lying between two rivers, may well have been long and narrow. The extant walls of Poseidonia have a circuit of about three miles; its mother city Sybaris is likely to have been quite four times as big. A citizen population of 100,000 would give a total population of about five times the number. The present population of the province of Cosenza, which corresponds fairly closely to the territory of Sybaris, is 530,000, and this population hardly succeeds in feeding itself.

There were sources of income which promised more to the Sybarites than the growth of corn for export. They grew a great deal of wine, and had a system of cellars and pipes for dealing with it in bulk and shipping it;[6] presumably from the hills along the coast south of Sybaris. The wine of Thurii is praised above all others of south Italy except that of the neighbouring Lagaria.[7] The wine of Cirò to the south has now a reputation higher than any other Calabrian wine. The plain was famed for stock-raising, horses, cattle, and sheep. The two rivers were credited with remarkable properties: the Krathis made the hair of all that washed in it, men and beasts,

---

[1] Diod. xii. 9: συνέβη ταύτην λαβεῖν ταχεῖαν αὔξησιν διὰ τὴν ἀρετὴν τῆς χώρας. . . . νεμόμενοι πολλὴν καὶ καρποφόρον χώραν μεγάλους ἐκτήσαντο πλούτους.

[2] RR, i. 44. 2.   [3] Ap. Athen. 519f.; FHG, i. 205.

[4] Ps.-Skymn. 341, 100,000: Strabo 263 and Diod. x. 23; xii. 9, 300,000.

[5] Loc. cit.   [6] Athen. 519d.

[7] Strabo 263; Pliny, NH xiv. 69. The grapes were not harvested until the first frosts: xiv. 39.

go white or yellow, besides other useful properties;[1] the Sybaris, on the other hand, made horses sneeze, so they were kept from drinking it.[2] A more symmetrical version says that it made cattle and sheep, and men too, go black.[3] Wool and hides are also important products; and honey and bees-wax,[4] and, though we have no statement definitely connecting them with Sybaris, timber and pitch from the Sila.[5] On the whole, the Sybarites produced sufficient foodstuffs and raw materials for their own use, but little for export: some wine, a little corn, probably some timber and hides. They imported Milesian woollens,[6] and the importers of purple had exemption from duty.[7] Like all other colonial cities, their painted pottery, metal-work, works of art, and luxury objects must have been nearly all imported from Greece. In the way of luxury imports there are κυνάρια Μελιταῖα.[8]

The purple-dyeing has just been mentioned, but it is never compared to the great Tarentine industry, and it does not appear that the murex was fished in Sybarite waters; probably it was imported from Taras. Sybaris had a certain industrial development, but noisy trades were not allowed within the city: πρῶτοι δὲ Συβαρῖται καὶ τὰς ποιούσας ψόφον τέχνας οὐκ ἐῶσιν ἐπιδημεῖν τῇ πόλει, οἷον χαλκέων καὶ τεκτόνων καὶ τῶν ὁμοίων:[9] these may have been only for their everyday needs.

The Sybarites were not themselves commercially minded. They had no harbours, and we do not hear of Sybarite marine or shipping. They were not travellers, and were proud of growing old on the bridges of their rivers.[10] The boast indicates a metropolitan frame of mind, most like the Parisian spirit; their city was important enough for foreigners to come to them and be laughed at. The chief frequenters of their markets were the Milesians, whose friendship for the Sybarites was famous.[11] Sybaris was the entrepôt for Milesian goods *en route* to Etruria, via the portage to Laos; Milesian ships presumably brought

---

[1] Strabo 263; Aelian, *HA* xii. 36; Pliny, *NH* xxxi. 13; Vitruvius viii. 3, 14 *et al.*
[2] Strabo, loc. cit.   [3] Pliny, loc. cit., quoting Theophrastos.
[4] Theokr. vii. 78–85: the bees which nourished Komatas shut in the chest.
[5] See Dion. Hal. xx. 15.   [6] Athen. 519*b*.   [7] Phylarkhos ap. Athen. 521*d*.
[8] Athen. 518*f*; from Malta, or from Melite in the Adriatic, as R. L. Beaumont has suggested (*JHS*, 1936, 188).   [9] Athen. 518*c*.
[10] Timaios ap. Athen. 519*e*: καταγελῶντες δὲ τῶν ἀποδημούντων ἐκ τῶν πατρίδων αὐτοὶ ἐσεμνύνοντο ἐπὶ τῷ γεγηρακέναι ἐπὶ ταῖς τῶν ποταμῶν γεφύραις. But note all the anecdotes about a Sybarite at Kroton, a Sybarite at Sparta (Athen. 518*d*), a Sybarite at Miletos (Diod. viii. 20): not that they have great historical value.
[11] Herod. vi. 21; Timaios ap. Athen. 519*b*.

the goods to Sybaris, and Etruscan ships carried them from Laos. We know that the Sybarites gave exemptions from tax to eel-sellers and hunters, and the importers and dyers of purple.[1] It is only those occupations which minister to more obvious luxuries which are named; we may conjecture that they had a reasoned system of exemptions, a sort of preferential tariff, from which the Milesians in particular benefited. It is not known when the Milesian connexion with Sybaris began. Attempts to carry it back to the period of the Lelantine War are unsubstantiated; probably it became increasingly important during the sixth century. It was most active at the fall of Sybaris, for which the Milesians went into public mourning.[2] The Samian merchants who were disturbed by a flight of partridges in the Siritis on their voyage to Sybaris were probably on their way to Thuria, not Sybaris.[3] For Rhodian merchants, leaving aside the supposed Rhodian origin of Sybaris on the Traeis,[4] there is the evidence in the *Lindian Chronicle* of a journey made by Amphinomos and his sons to Sybaris.[5]

The roads near Sybaris were probably better kept than most Greek roads. It was possible to travel on them in some degree of comfort, though slowly.[6] Where they left the city they were shaded.[7] It has been frequently pointed out that most of the luxuries for which the Sybarites are reproached are simply the first steps towards a reasonably comfortable and convenient manner of life. In this respect they were the forerunners of the Romans. Shade-trees are a luxury which would be welcomed in these days in the south. The exclusion from the city of noisy trades, and crowing cocks, 'would now be regarded simply as good police regulations'.[8] But it is more than that: it is one of the earliest examples of functional town-planning. The Sybarites invented the Turkish bath; indeed this is the oldest reference to public baths.[9]

---

[1] Phylarkhos ap. Athen. 521c.   [2] Herod. vi. 21.

[3] Athen. 656c (Hegesander's reminiscences); Ponelle, *Mélanges d'archéologie et d'histoire*, 1907, 256.

[4] Strabo 264.

[5] Ep. xxvi; *Lindos*, ii. 171. See below, p. 237.

[6] But it was more comfortable to go to Kroton by sea; Athen. 521a, a rich Sybarite chartered a special ship to take him and his horse to Kroton. (Kaibel suspects that this dull story is an interpolation in Athenaios, but the interpolator must have found it somewhere.)

[7] Timaios ap. Athen. 519c.   [8] Lenormant, *GG* i. 288.

[9] Athen. 519e. They arranged that the water should not be too hot by fettering the attendants (518b); this is still the Homeric arrangement by which water was poured by hand onto the bather (κ 358–63).

The unhealthy site of the city, in a hollow between two rivers, was noted in antiquity:

ἡ δὲ πόλις αὐτῶν ἐν κοιλῷ κειμένη τοῦ μὲν θέρους ἕωθέν τε καὶ πρὸς ἑσπέραν ψῦχος ὑπερβάλλον ἔχει, τὸ δὲ μέσον τῆς ἡμέρας καῦμα ἀνύποιστον· ὥστε τοὺς πλείστους αὐτῶν ὑπειληφέναι πρὸς ὑγίειαν διαφέρειν τοὺς πότους. ὅθεν καὶ ῥηθῆναι ὅτι τὸν βουλόμενον ἐν Συβάρει μὴ πρὸ μοίρας ἀποθανεῖν οὔτε δυόμενον οὔτε ἀνίσχοντα τὸν ἥλιον ὁρᾶν δεῖ.[1]

This is the simple rule of health adopted in the last century in the malarial parts of Italy, of which the plain of Sybaris was one of the worst. It has been suggested that it was already malarial in the sixth century.[2] Malaria was not endemic either in Italy or Greece, but was introduced in historic times by the arrival of infected bodies. It is possible that the luxury of Sybaris and Siris partly reflects precautions against malaria, partly the slackening of energy and loosening of moral standards in a region suddenly attacked by the disease. But the evidence is too slight to say so confidently. There is only one passage which points at all definitely to malaria, and it does not demand this explanation. The unhealthiness of the site is one of the reasons why the Krotoniates did not occupy it; and cultivation must have been less intense, and drainage and health precautions less well cared for, in the sixty years after the fall of Sybaris, giving the disease, supposing it to be established, a chance of spreading.

There are a great number of tales about Sybarite banquets. Aristophanes is the earliest witness to Sybarite good cheer.[3] They were the first in the field later occupied so brilliantly by the Syracusans and Tarentines, the founders of that art of dining which gave vicarious pleasure to the hungry audiences of the Middle Comedy and the comfortable raconteurs of the Empire. They gave prizes for the most successful providers of banquets, and for the best cooks;[4] and protected the inventors of new dishes by a year's exclusive use of the recipe.[5] Fisher-

---

[1] Athen. 519f. In summer the *jeunesse dorée* avoided the heat and unhealthiness by taking the waters at the baths of the Nymphs by the Lousias, a river noted for its white waters and black fish (Aelian, *HA* x. 38), probably one of the little streams running into the sea south of Sybaris. Cf. Schol. Theokr. vii. 78–85 (= *FHG*, ii. 372, 6); Λύκος φησὶ τῆς Θουρίας ὄρος Θάλαμον, ὑφ' ὃ ἄντρον τῶν Νυμφῶν· καλοῦσι δὲ αὐτὰς Ἀλουσίας οἱ ἐπιχώριοι ἀπὸ τοῦ παραρρέοντος Ἀλουσίου ποταμοῦ: and Theokr. vii. 130–57.

[2] Jones, *Malaria and Greek History*, 30–1.

[3] *Daitaleis* (fr. 216) Συρακοσίων τράπεζαν Συβαρίτιδάς τ' εὐωχίας. συβαρίζειν, in *Peace* 344, should probably read συβριάζειν (Meineke, 56).

[4] Athen. 519e.

[5] Athen. 521c.

men and hunters are especially mentioned in the later versions of Smindyrides' train at the wooing of Agariste.[1] They invited their womenfolk to their great banquets and sacrifices,[2] giving them a year's notice to prepare their dresses: a point of female emancipation in which they compare with the Etruscans. Their public festivals must have been most magnificent, when their cavalry, over 5,000 strong, went in procession, with saffron robes over their breast-plates,[3] and winding up with magnificent dinners and a display of feminine modes. The final touch at their banquets was provided by the cavalry horses who were trained to dance to the flute.[4]

The voluptuousness of the Sybarites is summed up in the person of Smindyrides son of Hippokrates.[5] He is one of the few Sybarites whose name we know. At the wedding of Agariste he and the son of Amyris of Siris were the only representatives of the western Greeks. He is already in Herodotos Σμινδυρίδης ... ὃς ἐπὶ πλεῖστον δὴ χλιδῆς εἷς ἀνὴρ ἀπίκετο, but Herodotos missed a great opportunity to tell some tall stories recorded by later writers. He travelled with a kitchen of a thousand, at the lowest figure.[6] He arrived from Sybaris in his own ship, and entertained not only the other suitors but Kleisthenes himself.[7] He complained that his bed of roses gave him blisters.[8] But it is a nameless Sybarite who replied to a companion who complained of a rupture caused by watching labourers at work in the field: 'My dear fellow, it hurts my side even to hear you speak of it.'[9] It is rather unjustifiable to conclude from this anecdote that the tillers of the soil were wretched native serfs. If there is anything to be drawn from the story, it is that, however comfortable they liked to be, the Sybarites did oversee the labourers on whose toil their income depended; and they did drive out into the country, both no doubt for a summer holiday and to watch the harvest come in. There must have been slaves enough at Sybaris; there is a story of a Sybarite at Kroton wondering why they did not have slaves to dig the athletes' pit in the palaestra.[10] The impiety

---

[1] Athen. 273 b–c; 541c (Timaios); Aelian, VH xii. 24.

[2] Athen. 521c. Another custom which they are credited with introducing was more suited to bachelor parties (Athen. 519e: πρῶτοι δὲ καὶ ἀμίδας ἐξεῦρον, ἃς εἰσέφερον εἰς τὰ συμπόσια).

[3] Athen. 519c.

[4] Aristotle, Constitution of Sybaris, ap. Athen. 520c.

[5] Herod. vi. 127; Diod. viii. 19; Athen. 273b–c, 511c, 541b; Aelian, VH ix. 24; xii. 24.

[6] Timaios ap. Athen. 541b: also 273b, probably from Khamaileon.

[7] Diod. viii. 19.

[8] Aelian, VH ix. 24.

[9] Tim. ap. Athen. 518d.

[10] Ibid.

which fulfilled the oracle about their fall was concerned with the punishment of a slave.[1]

The anecdote-mongers loved to contrast Sybarite cheer with the hard living of the Spartan *phiditia*, with a glance at Spartan courage and Sybarite softness. 'I understand the secret of Sparta: men should be willing to die a thousand times rather than eat this dinner.'[2] Similarly they contrasted the athletes of Kroton with the voluptuaries of Sybaris. Only one Sybarite victory at Olympia is recorded: in 616, when the boys' boxing event was first competed for, Philytas won.[3] This falls in the period of Sybarite expansion. It should have been already a place of sóme athletic, and therefore probably military, note, to win an event which had just been inserted in the programme. Sybaris had her Treasury at Olympia; this was one of the earlier treasuries, probably of the first half of the sixth century, but its remains are negligible.[4] They also made rich dedications at Delphi, which included four gold tiaras (στλεγγίδια) which were stolen by Onomarkhos of Phokis.[5] But the panhellenic period of Sybaris' activity, or more properly speaking the colonial period, passed away early. These offerings were made at a time when, like the other colonial cities, Sybaris looked up to the mother country as the source of her culture, before she became metropolitan and tried to organize a great power in the west which would yield in no respect to the mainland or Eastern Greeks. Then she left Olympia, which was at this time rather a Krotoniate preserve, and set about creating her own sacred games, with big prizes, to be held at the same time as the Olympia.[6] Thus she incurred grave warnings from Delphi, and a reputation for impiety.

By the middle of the sixth century the Sybarite power extended over all the valleys of the Krathis and Sybaris and the coastlands of this region on both sides of the peninsula. Some of this territory was occupied by Greek towns, colonies of Sybaris, like Laos and . . ?MA,[7] and no doubt others, which soon after the middle of the century began to coin for themselves with Sybarite types. These had internal independence up to the point of coining, a freedom from interference seldom conceded by imperial powers, but shared the policy and no

---

[1] Athen. 520b.
[2] Athen. 138d; 518e.
[3] Paus. v. 8. 9; Philostratos 268. 12–14.
[4] *Olympia*, iii. 25, fig. 22.
[5] Theopompos ap. Athen. 605a. Cf. Xen. *Anab.* i. 2. 10, στλεγγίδες χρυσαῖ as prizes in games.
[6] Athen. 522a.
[7] See below, p. 356.

doubt the constitutional changes of Sybaris. To the north was
Poseidonia, a Sybarite colony, whose territory was not conti-
guous. It appears to have been independent, but with proper
filial sentiments. The interior of the country was occupied by
the native Italian peoples, living in small towns in complete
dependence on Sybaris and probably becoming quite hellenized.
One of them, Pandosia, coins in the subsequent period with
the Sybarite type of a bull, representing the river Krathis.

Sybaris was liberal with the citizenship.[1] We need not
suppose that Italians were admitted to citizen rights; it is
more likely that Greeks, not Akhaians or descendants of
the original settlers, were welcomed. The Ionian connexions
of Sybaris must have been kept up by many visits of Milesian,
Rhodian, and other traders, some of whom will have settled
permanently. There is a certain Ionian flavour about Sybarite
culture which would be explained by their presence.

Sybaris is said, surely wrongly, to have used the laws of
Zaleukos.[2] Diodoros somewhat anachronistically says that
Kharondas legislated for Thuria.[3] Probably the laws of Thuria
were compiled from various western codes, including that of
Zaleukos, and this state of affairs was erroneously carried back
from Thuria to Sybaris, so that Sybaris was said to have used
Zaleukos' laws.[4] In fact, nothing is known of the constitution
of Sybaris. Just before her fall she was ruled by a tyrant
Telys, who gained power by raising discontented elements
against the aristocracy.[5] He is once called βασιλεύς,[6] but this
is clearly a complimentary misuse of the title.

KROTON AND KAULONIA

The material remains of archaic Kroton are scanty. The city
was a large one, but the exact trace of its walls is uncertain.[7]
The temple of Hera Lakinia, which lay on the Lakinian promontory six miles from Kroton, has been excavated, but the
excavation was not repaying, either in architectural remains
or in offerings.[8] The only important finds are the terra-cotta
revetments of the temple, the fifth-century revetment being

---

[1] Diod. xii. 9.   [2] Ps.-Skymnos 346–7.   [3] Diod. xii. 11–19.
[4] See above, pp. 70 ff.; and cf. Bentley, *Dissertation on the Epistles of Phalaris*, 274 ff.
[5] Herod. v. 44; Diod. xii. 9.   [6] Herod. loc. cit.
[7] Byvanck attempts to follow it in *RM*, 1914, 145 ff. Cf. plan on p. 84.
[8] *AJA*, iii (1887), 181; *VIII Report of American Institute of Archaeology* (1887), 42 ff.;
N Sc, 1911 Suppl., 77 ff.

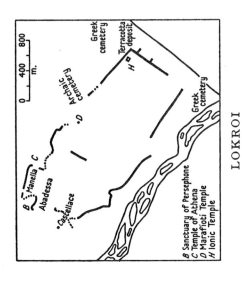

METAPONTION

Foundations of houses

N

0   500   1,000   1,500
km.

1 Temple "Tavole Paladine"
2 Temple of Apollo Lykeios
3 Agora (?)

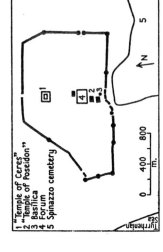

LOKROI

0   400   800
m.

Greek cemetery

Archaic cemetery

Terracotta deposit.

B Manella *C*
Abadessa
Castellace

Greek cemetery

B Sanctuary of Persephone
C Temple of Athena
D Marafioti Temple
H Ionic Temple

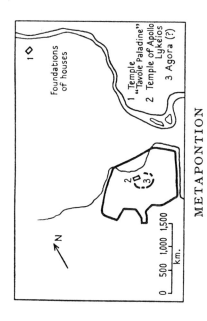

KROTON

0   400   800
m.

R. Esaro

KROTON

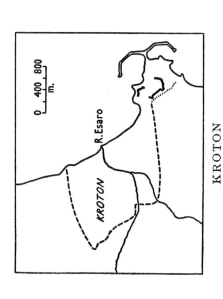

POSEIDONIA

N

0   400   800
m.

Tyrrhenian Sea

1 "Temple of Ceres"
2 "Temple of Poseidon"
3 Basilica
4 Forum
5 Spinazzo cemetery

among the finest from south Italy.[1] There have been many small finds within the ancient city, and some of the objects are of great interest;[2] among them is a dedication made by Phayllos, holder of the long-jump record, to Zeus Meilikhios.[3] But there is not enough material to compare with the remains of Taras, Lokroi, and the Sicilian cities, or to form a view of the artistic and commercial relations of Kroton.

The lack is in part remedied by the extensive excavations at another Akhaian city, Kaulonia, which lay within the Kroton-iate orbit. Apart from geometric sherds of the early seventh century, which are probably pre-colonization material brought to a native predecessor,[4] the earliest finds are of the early sixth century, and there is little older than the middle of that century. The territory of Kaulonia is neither extensive nor rich, and it was a small town, with an area of about 110 acres,[5] and a population of about 10,000 only could be accommodated within the walls. In fortifying it, the builders not only took advantage of the ground but adopted an unusual building technique.[6] There is no building-stone, so they used squared blocks very sparingly for the corners of towers, the faces of gates, and such crucial points. Elsewhere they used loose stones from the rivers, with a cement of earth, often strengthened with lime. The wall is up to 18 feet thick on level ground. This technique of building is known on inland sites of Sicily, but is nowhere else used for city walls. The considerable remains still standing are a tribute to the skill and resourceful-ness of the Kauloniates.

There are many remains of houses on the acropolis and in the lower town, but these are all very late;[7] a sewer, running down to the sea, is older than the houses whose foundations are built over it, and yielded a red-figure lekythos.[8] Wells were used, and probably supplemented by the use of river water.[9] The cemeteries have been explored, but produced only very poor material from the late sixth century onwards.[10] The chief remains, apart from the walls, are those of the temple by the

[1] *N Sc*, 1911 Suppl., 111 ff.; Van Buren, *AFR*, 12 ff.

[2] F. von Duhn, *N Sc*, 1879, 227 ff.; 1897, 343 ff.; R. Lucente, *N Sc*, 1932, 364 ff.

[3] In Reggio Museum, unpublished. For Phayllos see Herod. viii. 47; Paus. x. 9. 2; Preger, *Inscr. metr.* 142; *IG*, i². 655; Tod, *GHI*, no. 21; *Fouilles de Delphes*, iii. 1. 1 f.; *RE*, Suppl. iv, 1204; E. N. Gardiner, *JHS*, xxiv. 70 ff.; and below, p. 375.

[4] See above, p. 28.   [5] *MA*, xxiii. 773; 46·75 hectares.

[6] Ibid. 776: 'una ammirabile tecnica muraria del ciottolo'.

[7] Ibid. 806 ff.   [8] Ibid. 815.

[9] Ibid. 880.   [10] Ibid. 906 ff.

sea. The foundations are of a sandstone which must have been brought some distance, the elevation of limestone, probably Syracusan,[1] the tiles of Parian marble, and some sculpture in Pentelic.[2] There is also a deposit of architectural terra-cottas on the Passoliera hill,[3] and a little sanctuary on the Faro.[4] The site has been especially prolific in arulae. Nothing is older than the middle of the sixth century, except one Early Corinthian alabastron.[5] The great period is the early fifth, when the temple was built. The import of stone from such a distance shows the desire of the builders to make it as splendid as they could. The main part of the Passoliera deposit belongs also to the early fifth century.[6] The copious and handsome coinage helps to prove that Kaulonia reached a high degree of prosperity at this period.

METAPONTION

A certain amount is known of the city organization of Metapontion;[7] not datable, but certainly Greek, as the town was abandoned by the beginning of the Christian era. Lacava describes the houses as 'isolated houses, looking out on the street, all with a single story';[8] stone foundations, the material of which is not found nearer than the middle course of the Bradano, are inferred to have had brick walls on them. He found no trace of a system of water-supply or of sewers, but there are still to be seen wells, tile-lined, with stone upper works, into which the water filtered through the sand, thus purifying itself.[9] The wall and ditch, the emplacement of agora and theatre, the temple of Apollo Lykeios,[10] are normal. The port and port-suburb were outside, and the other great temple, now called the Tavole Paladine, three miles away, with a little village surrounding it. At a number of other points within a radius of five miles remains of houses or villages have been found;[11] some are to be regarded as suburbs, the more distant ones would naturally house little groups of farm-labourers.

The archaeological content of Metapontion consists chiefly of the splendid revetments of the temple of Apollo.[12] The cemeteries have given, except for sporadic material, nothing

---

[1] MA, xxiii. 831 ff.
[2] Ibid., figs. 126–7.
[3] MA, xxix. 409 ff.
[4] MA, xxiii. 779 ff.
[5] Ibid., fig. 135; cf. Payne, NC, fig. 20e.
[6] Van Buren, p. 10.
[7] Plan, Lacava, Metaponto, 64.
[8] Ibid. 92.
[9] Ibid. 68, 101.
[10] See the inscription, IG, xiv. 647.
[1] Lacava, op. cit. 91.
[12] Van Buren, AFR, 38 ff., pl. 5.

earlier than the fourth century.[1] Important finds at Metapontion since Lacava's excavations have been frequently rumoured, but little has been officially reported; one find is a torso of the Chiot school of the end of the sixth century, in Potenza Museum. Excavation has recently been resumed near the temple of Apollo, with important results, but only brief preliminary accounts are yet available.[2]

Metapontion was a small city whose many unusual cults may reflect an obscure and mixed origin.[3] It had no wide-reaching commercial relations, but its citizens grew rich from its horse-raising plains[4] and cornland. They took as emblem of the city an ear of barley, dedicating it in gold at Delphi[5] and putting it on their coins. The coinage is abundant in the late archaic period, when also the temple of the Tavole Paladine was built.[6] The plain, swelling and rising towards the bare hills of the Basilicata, is to-day a desolation which has barely begun to be reclaimed by the modern agricultural methods of the *bonifica*; in antiquity it was a worthy object of strife, and the Metapontines had to maintain themselves against both Tarantines and the native Oinotrians.[7]

TARAS

In the development of the modern town and naval base extensive remains of the ancient Taras were found, but not recorded, and almost nothing can now be said about the organization of the city.[8] It compares with Syracuse in lying on an island or peninsula,[9] with a very much larger landward expansion. The acropolis, slightly larger now than in antiquity, was capable sixty years ago of containing the whole population of Taranto, then 34,000. It is not certain how early the city spread from the acropolis to the eastern extension on the mainland (Borgo Orientale).[10] The only building of the archaic

---

[1] Cf. *JHS*, 1939, 219–20.   [2] *AJA*, 1941, 471 ff.; cf. *JHS*, 1939, 220.

[3] See Giannelli, *Culti e miti della Magna Grecia*, 62 ff., 291 ff.

[4] Bakkh. x. 30, πορτιτρόφ[ον πεδίον]; 114, ἱπποτρόφον πόλιν.   [5] Strabo 264.

[6] Robertson, *Greek and Roman Architecture*, 75, 326 (*c.* 520); Koldewey and Puchstein put it a little later (op. cit. 36 ff.).   [7] Strabo 265.

[8] There is little in Wuilleumier's important book on Taras which relates to the archaic period of its existence. See *Tarente*, 239 ff.

[9] The acropolis, now an island, was in antiquity a peninsula; the channel on its eastern side connecting the Mare Grande and Mare Piccolo was cut in 1480.

[10] See Messerschmidt, *Italische Gräberkunde*, ii. 324–5. The oldest finds, according to Messerschmidt, are not limited to the acropolis but are widely spread, Protocorinthian vases having been found at the Arsenal and at Vaccarella, on the shore of the Great Harbour,

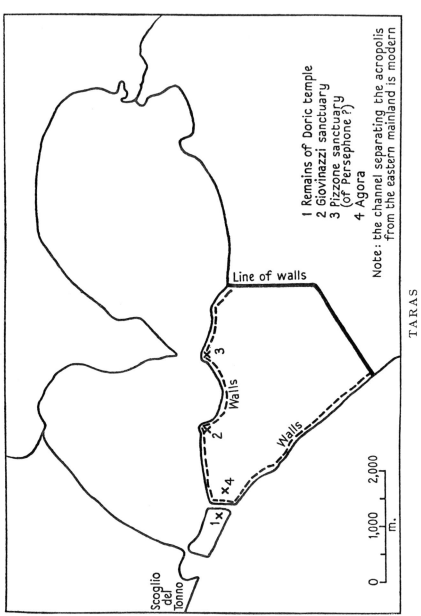

Scoglio del Tonno

1 ✕

✕ 4

2 ✕

Walls

3 ✕

Walls

Line of walls

Walls

1 Remains of Doric temple
2 Giovinazzi sanctuary
3 Pizzone sanctuary
  (of Persephone ?)
4 Agora

Note: the channel separating the acropolis
from the eastern mainland is modern

0   1,000   2,000
         m.

TARAS

period which survives is the pair of Doric columns from a
temple on the acropolis, which is about contemporary with the
Apollonion and Olympieion of Syracuse.[1] Many sanctuaries
lay in the new town, where large deposits of terra-cottas have
been found. One, in the locality Giovinazzi on the south shore
of the inner harbour, is said to have yielded 30,000 terra-cottas,
the earliest being of the sixth century.[2] Another, at Pizzone
farther east, identified as a sanctuary of Demeter and Persephone, goes back to the seventh century.[3] Both these are
within the walls, but lay outside the city when they were first
dedicated. None of the house-remains in the Borgo Orientale
can be definitely dated to the archaic period, but the manner
of their recording leaves everything to be desired. The wall
and ditch were discovered,[4] but few traces now remain. It is
impossible to date the wall, but it should belong to the years
around 400,[5] the period of the city's greatest power and
prosperity, that in which Dionysios fortified the enlarged
Syracuse, with which Taras can compare in area. Its area is
calculated as over two square miles.[6] There was also a suburb on the western side of the entrance to the Little Harbour,
where the railway station now is; Lenormant saw a piece of
wall which may have defended this.[7]

The Tarantines, like the Spartans, buried within the walls.[8]
There is no certain case of a burial within the acropolis; the
earlier excavators reported that some of the discoveries in the
Città Vecchia were from tombs,[9] but were possibly mistaken.
The Protocorinthian vases found on the site have come mainly
from the Via d'Aquino, in the westernmost part of the Borgo
Orientale, so the oldest cemetery was presumably there, just

among other places. Messerschmidt therefore regards the original town as an agglomeration
of settlements. Most of these vases presumably come from graves (there is an extensive
cemetery at Vaccarella), and are not prima facie evidence for the extension of the inhabited
area, though it is likely that each of the cemeteries adjoined a suburb or quarter of the town.

[1] Koldewey and Puchstein, 55; Robertson, op. cit. 71, 324; Wuilleumier, op. cit. 253.
[2] Wuilleumier, op. cit. 399 ff.
[3] Id. 396 ff.   [4] N Sc, 1881, 390 ff.; cf. Lenormant, GG, i. 104.
[5] Mr. D. F. Allen, who has studied the fortifications of south Italy and Sicily, is of the
opinion that the wall is not older than the middle of the fifth century; so also Oehler, RE,
iv A. 2307; cf. Wuilleumier, op. cit. 242 (end of 5th cent.). Mr. Allen agrees with me that
before the late sixth century the city lay within the walls of the acropolis.
[6] 560 hectares, according to Wuilleumier, op. cit. 246.   [7] GG, i. 108.
[8] Polyb. viii. 28; Livy, xxv. 9, 10. Messerschmidt, loc. cit., regards this as a custom
adopted from the Iapygians; unnecessarily, as it is recorded at Sparta, alone of Greek
cities (Plut. Lyc. 27; cf. BSA, xiii. 155 ff.). See further below, p. 186.
[9] N Sc, 1881, 415.

outside the early limits of the city. But there were also early graves in other areas within the ancient city. The later tombs are grouped in several regions of the city, and casual finds show that there were also scattered burials outside the larger cemeteries. It is probable that when the city was extended the cemeteries, which were now brought within its bounds, continued to be used; so large an area as was included within the walls cannot have been closely settled.[1]

The exploration of the cemeteries has yielded many fine vases, one of the best of Late Protocorinthian vases, and a number of interesting Corinthian and black-figure Attic. Taras was certainly reasonably prosperous. She already had a bronze industry in the sixth century, though this is best established in the fourth century.[2] Most of her art, and indeed most of the material remains of the city, belong to this later period. Sixth-century Taras was a comparatively small city. Its relations with the Iapygians and Messapians imply that it was not yet the great power it became in the fifth and succeeding centuries.[3] In 473 an Iapygian army of 20,000 terrified the Tarantines and inflicted a defeat which was the greatest disaster known to Herodotos.[4] Athenaios' stories of Tarantine and Iapygian luxury[5] belong to the period of their greatest prosperity, from the middle of the fifth century onwards.

Considerable information about the objects of Tarantine commerce may be derived from the terra-cotta moulds for cakes, which are crowded with symbols.[6] Many of them refer to natural products, wool, oil and wine, corn, and various kinds of sea-life, including the famous murex. These all occur also in subordinate positions on the coins of Taras. Though this evidence is all later than the archaic period, and most of the literary references to Tarantine products are of the Roman period,[7] there can be little doubt that these were always the chief source of the city's livelihood. The riches of the sea and harbour were, then as now, most important. The democracy set up after 473 is characterized by Aristotle as one of fishermen.[8]

After the mass of rather fabulous stories about Parthenioi and Phalanthos, there is no definite information about Taras

[1] Cf. Wuilleumier, op. cit. 250.   [2] See below, pp. 290 ff.
[3] See below, pp. 146 ff., and Messerschmidt, op. cit. 323.
[4] Herod. vii. 170; Diod. xi. 52.   [5] Athen. 522–3.
[6] W. B. McDaniel, *AJA*, 1924, 24 ff.; A. J. Evans, *JHS*, 1886, 44 ff.
[7] McDaniel, loc. cit.   [8] *Pol.* 1291^b 23.

until the late sixth century. It appears to have stood somewhat apart from the main current of life of the Italian colonies. Unlike most of the others it was not a great athletic city, for only one victory of the archaic period is recorded.[1] It had some economic if not political relations with them, for its coinage, beginning in the second half of the sixth century, is on the same standard.[2] Some of the early coins have the reverse type the incuse of the obverse, like the Akhaian cities, but most have not. This suggests that relations were spasmodic, certainly not close and continuous.

The Laconian connexion was long kept up. Figured Laconian pottery is found in the west only at Taras and in Etruria.[3] This contrasts with the distribution of the small aryballoi and black kraters which are found on most sites. The latter was utility ware; the fine vases, mainly bowls, may have been brought to Taras by settlers from Laconia. Three of the finest bowls were in one grave (285), which suggests that its use was a matter of personal preference. All these vases are of the sixth century, which is also when Laconian export to Etruria, which may have passed through Tarantine hands, was most active. One of the latest of Laconian vases to be exported is the Kyrene cup found at Taras.[4] Laconian influence continues into the fifth century, the style of the late archaic coins and terra-cottas being essentially Laconian.[5]

The cults of Taras are almost exclusively Laconian. The hero who rode on a dolphin, whether identified with the eponymous Taras or the oecist Phalanthos, is also found in Laconia;[6] he perhaps belonged to the pre-Dorian population which formed a considerable part of the population of Taras.[7] The Tarantines began to spin a myth about Phalanthos. Another local development on a Spartan basis is the cult of Apollo Hyakinthios;[8] Hyakinthos is not known to have been identified with Apollo at Amyklai, the centre of the cult.

The Atreidai and the Agamemnonidai had cults at Taras,[9] and Menelaos was said to have come there on his wanderings.[10]

---

[1] Anokhos won the stadion and diaulos at Olympia in 520 (Euseb. ed. Schoene, i. 201; Paus. vi. 14. 11).　　　　　　　　　　　　　　　[2] See below, pp. 356 ff.

[3] E. A. Lane, BSA, xxxiv. 181; see below, p. 240.

[4] Ibid. 153; FR, iii. 212, fig. 102.

[5] Ashmole, 11.　　　　　　　　　　　　　　　[6] Cf. Herod. i. 24.

[7] Giannelli, Culti e miti della Magna Grecia, 1 ff.; where bibliography.

[8] Polyb. viii. 28. 2; Giannelli, ibid. 18 ff.

[9] Ps.-Aristotle, de mir. ausc. 106; Giannelli, 38 ff.

[10] Lykophron 852 ff.; Giannelli, loc. cit.

This is probably a late development under Spartan influence. Agamemnon and his children were not localized in Sparta until the sixth century. The only authority for their worship at Taras names in the same breath the Tydeids, the Aiakids, and Laertiads, who belonged to countries not especially connected with Taras or Sparta, so that the Atreids also may have come to Taras with the Homeric poems, without especial Spartan interest.[1] However, Akhilles is also named as having a separate worship; his cult is especially Laconian,[2] and his worship and that of the Atreids at any rate probably came from Sparta.

The Dioskouroi also were brought from Sparta to Taras, probably at a later date than the foundation. They had a flourishing cult, and hundreds of pinakes representing them have been found.[3] But none of these are older than the fourth century, and the Dioskouroi also appear on gold coins of the late fourth century.[4] It is possible that the cult was introduced, or became popular, only at the time of the Tarantine appeal to the Spartan king Akrotatos in 329 B.C.[5] At the same period Herakles replaces Poseidon in the Tarantine mythology as the father of Taras or Phalanthos,[6] and appears on the coins.[7] But the Tarantines were already interested in Herakles when they named their colony in the Siritis Herakleia, in 432. So the Spartan influence which increased the importance of Herakles was at least as old as the fifth century.

None of the cults of Taras are of native Italian origin. The only ones not brought from Laconia are those of Zeus Olympios and Zeus Kataibates, which suggest Eleian influence.[8] This is not peculiar to Taras and reflects the panhellenic value of the Olympic Games. The strength of the Laconian connexion is well brought out by Giannelli when he says that the cults of an Athenian cleruchy do not show greater homogeneity.[9]

[1] So Wernicke, *RE*, i. 722.

[2] Wide, *Lakonische Kulte*, 232 ff.

[3] Petersen, *RM*, 1900, 3 ff.; Giannelli, 32 ff.

[4] *BM Cat. Italy*, 160, no. 5; Head, *HN²*, 57.

[5] So Evans, *Horsemen of Tarentum*, 16; Petersen, loc. cit.

[6] Serv. *ad Aen.* iii. 551: and Interp. Serv., quoted by Giannelli, 38, n. 2. Giannelli (38 ff.) rightly dates this variant to the second half of the fourth century, on the evidence of the coins.

[7] *BM Cat. Italy*, 162, nos. 10–15; Head, *HN²*, 57; Evans, *Horsemen*, 53 ff.

[8] Cf. Giannelli, 22.

[9] Op. cit. 286: 'Se avessimo studiato . . . una delle tante cleruchie che Atene disseminò per il suo vasto impero marittimo, non credo vi avremmo potuto riscontrare omogeneità maggiore di quella che ci presentano i culti praticati a Taranto e gli dei ed eroi ivi onorati.'

At the end of the sixth century Taras was ruled by a king Aristophilides who, to judge from Herodotos' account of his action in freeing Demokedes from the Persians,[1] was no figurehead; he was apparently a king after the Spartan model. Nowhere else in the west is kingship definitely established.[2] Aristophilides had few successors, for the state of affairs before the introduction of democracy after 473 is described by Aristotle as πολιτεία.[3] The change may have been due to the political activity of the Pythagoreans. The ephorate, though not directly attested at Taras, occurs at its colony Herakleia;[4] so the presence of this element also of the Spartan constitution may be inferred.

The Tarentines had also a special friendship with the Knidians.[5] The Knidians were among the most active of the east Greeks in the west, and especially in the Adriatic.[6] There are few remains of East Greek art and commerce in Taras or its immediate neighbourhood, but the Rhodian penetration of Iapygia[7] cannot have been entirely without effect on Taras.

NOTE: POLLIS KING OF SYRACUSE

Pollis rests on less good authority than is usually thought: Hippys ap. Athen. i. 31b; Pollux vi. 16; Aelian, VH xii. 31; Etym. Magn. s.v. Βίβλινος οἶνος: see Holm, i. 346; Freeman, ii. 431 ff.; Hüttl, 44–6. The chief authority, Hippys of Rhegion, is shown by Jacoby (RE, viii. 1927 ff.) to be not an author of the early fifth century but a forgery of the third (Pythagoreischer Schwindel-autor). Aristotle is quoted by Pollux, without his naming the work: some of Pollux's other quotations from Aristotle are from works falsely ascribed. All that is known of Pollis is that he imported a celebrated vine from Thrace to Sicily (or, as Hippys said, perhaps through local pride, from Italy), and the wine, known in Thrace as Βίβλινος οἶνος, was in Sicily called Πόλλιος. The Βίβλινος οἶνος is as old as Hesiod (WD 589), but the Sicilian wine is not vouched for earlier than Aristotle. It is remarkable that Epikharmos, writing in Syracuse of Βίβλινος οἶνος, does not mention its transference to Sicily by Pollis. Both Athenaios and the Etym. Magn. quote him in the same context, and if he had gone on to speak of Pollis or Πόλλιος, they could not fail to have quoted him. The story must therefore be later than Epikharmos. On the other hand, Pollis, if he existed at all and was king of Syracuse, must have been earlier than Gelon, for we know the tyrants from Gelon onwards who might have been called king. Then Epikharmos might have been expected to mention him, if he were a real person whose name was perpetuated in the wine. Only the Etym. Magn. calls Pollis tyrant, and that of Sikyon, which has

[1] Herod. iii. 136.
[2] See below, p. 385.
[3] Pol. 1303a 6.
[4] IG, xiv. 645a, ll. 1, 95; cf. Wuilleumier, op. cit. 176.
[5] Herod. iii. 138.
[6] Beaumont, JHS, 1936, 173 ff.
[7] Ibid. 172 f., 192 f.; see also below, p. 237.

obviously been written by a slip for Syracuse; the better tradition calls him king. Aelian calls him an ἐγχώριος βασιλεύς; but surely not a Sikel. Hippys calls him an Argive—Πόλλιν τὸν Ἀργεῖον, ὃς ἐβασίλευσε Συρακοσίων—and this unlikely detail is the main reason disposing one to accept him. But Pollux distinguished Polis the Argive from Pollis king of Syracuse, for whom he quotes Aristotle's authority; and it is quite likely that Hippys has confused the two names. Pollis is a not unusual Dorian name (Hüttl, 45, n. 10).

The constitutional position of Pollis, supposing him to have been a pre-Gelonian king, is difficult to explain. Freeman (ii. 9 ff., 433) supposes a revival of heroic kingship at Syracuse, though it had recently come to an end at Corinth. This is in itself unlikely, and Arkhias is nowhere called king. Hüttl suggests that he was prytanis, but the evidence for this title at Syracuse is slender (see above, pp. 56 ff.), and it is not proved that the prytanis of Corinth was called basileus (as Busolt, i. 631): Diod. vii. 9. 3 does not describe an annual magistracy, and vii. 9. 6 says only that the prytanis took the position, not the title, of king; and though Nic. Dam. fr. 58. 6 calls the Bakkhiad ruler overthrown by Kypselos βασιλεύς, he also says that Kypselos was appointed βασιλεύς by the people, so no reliance can be placed on his use of the term. The comparison with kingship at Argos (Herod. vii. 149) is hardly relevant, for though it is possible that Argives joined in the colonization of Syracuse (see p. 14; cf. *Perachora*, i. 32; Busolt, i. 389, n. 3; Hüttl, 44), the constitutional and other connexions between Syracuse and Corinth indicate that the colony should have followed the Corinthian, not the Argive, model for the head of the State.

Considering the weakness of the tradition and in particular the silence of Epikharmos, stronger than most arguments from silence in that he is quoted for the parent wine and not, in the same context, for the descendant, it seems most probable that Pollis king of Syracuse is an etymological fiction, invented in the fourth or third century to explain the name given in Sicily to the wine of the type elsewhere called Βίβλινος.

The name Pollis has been read in the *Lindian Chronicle* (ep. xxxi, *Lindos* ii. 175), but the dedicator in question is demonstrably not Pollis king of Syracuse, and probably belongs to some other city. The date is the late sixth century, after Amasis' offering (*c.* 540) and the Akragantine capture of Minoa (probably after 510; see below, p. 353) and immediately before Artaphrenes' offering (490). We should surely hear of a tyrant of Syracuse in the late sixth century, and know moreover that Syracuse was then ruled by the Gamoroi. It is impossible to place a tyrant (or rather two tyrants, for -λις the dedicator is uncle of a tyrant) either just before or just after the fall of the Gamoroi. All the other Sicilian offerings to Athena Lindia are Geloan or Akragantine, and it would be possible to restore in the passage in question

[. . . λις Ἱπποκράτ]ευς θίας τοῦ τυραννεύσαντος ἐν
[Γέλαι ξύλινα ἀγάλμ]α[τ]α, &c.

This is exactly the same length as Blinkenberg's supplement, and involves no more grammatical difficulties. Sosilas, father of the dedicator, has a Rhodian name (Hüttl, 45, n. 10).

CHAPTER III

THE EXPANSION OF THE SICILIAN COLONIES

SYRACUSE

SYRACUSE was marked out by Nature for rule over the whole south-western corner of Sicily; but its growth was slow. To the north its territory was limited by Megara, which is only twelve miles away; there is no natural boundary between them, but Syracuse had probably little territory in this direction, and that poor, as the best part of the plain is near Megara. To the south is a fertile coast-plain of varying width; inland a tangled limestone hill-country, not inaccessible yet easy to defend against invasion, which rises to 3,000 feet at Monte Lauro. For two generations after the foundation of Syracuse these hills remained in native hands. The chief Sikel towns were at Pantalica, fifteen miles west of Syracuse above the middle course of the Anapos, and Finocchito, about the same distance south-west of Syracuse. Other smaller Sikel places of this period are Noto Vecchio and Tremenzano in the same direction as Finocchito.

Pantalica is a flat-topped hill protected by 100-foot cliffs which cut off all approach except by a narrow neck to the west. Inside is an area of nearly one square mile, large enough to offer refuge to all the inhabitants of this country-side. The only building remains are the foundations of the 'palace', a building 120 by 35 feet, built of large roughly-squared stones in the Cyclopean manner, consisting of a walled court, in which were found moulds for bronze working and fragments of bronze axes, together with Siculan II sherds, and a corridor leading out of the court, on to which four square rooms open. The plan has been compared by Orsi with that of the Mycenaean palace, the court corresponding to a megaron. This is the best built of Sikel buildings, in which it is reasonable to see the influence of Greek models and perhaps the hand of Greek workmen.[1] Outside, the cliffs are honeycombed with tombs rising tier above tier in the most inaccessible positions in the cliff-face. The thousands of graves show that there was an extensive population. The strength of the place and the importance of the palace make it likely that Pantalica was the capital of all the Sikels in the hill-region. Its greatest period is roughly between the

[1] *MA*, ix. 75 ff.

SICILY

TYRRHENIAN SEA

IONIAN SEA

RHEGION
MYLAI
ZANKLE
TINDARIS
Patti
Cocolonazzo di Mola
?KALLIPOLIS
Randazzo
TAUROMENION
NAXOS
KALE AKTE
Acircale
S.Maria Licodia
INESSA-AITNA
Paternò
KATANE
HYBLA
HADRANON
ΔETNA
Mendolito
S.Mauro
R.SYMAITHOS
?PIAKOS
LEONTINOI
Agnone
TROTILON
?XUTHIA
EUBOIA
Hommello
MEGARA
THAPSOS
Belvedere
SYRACUSE
PLEMMYRION
AMESTRATOS
Troina
AGYRION
KENTORIPA
ENNA
R.Pergusa
M.Judica
Scordia
Militello
Mineo
Palikè
Grammichele
Florida
Vizzini
AKRAI
Milocca
Cassibile
Melilli
HELORON
Vindicari
?INA
CAPE PAKHYNOS
Gangi
Nicosia
Ajimena
Serra
Orlando
Piano de Casazzi
?Kallagirone
S.Mauro
Pantalica
Buscemi
S.Casale
Finocchito
Castelluccio
Tretenzano
Ragusa
Magazzinazzi
Ispica
Spaccaforno
Scicli
Burgio
NEETON
HYBLA HERAIA
SOLOEIS
Cefalù
HIMERA
THERMAE
R.HIMERAS
Castronovo
Caltanisetta
S.Cataldo
R.HINERAS
S.Angelo di Muraro
Mussomeli
Vassalagi
Canicatti
Ravanusa
Naro
Butera
GELA
Nisseni
Dessueri
R.Mazzarino
M.Bubbonia
R.GELAS
Giarrantana
Biscari
?AKRILLAI
Vittoria
Comiso
Modica
KAMARINA
Chiaramonte Gulfi
Vicari
Parco
PANORMOS
ENTELLA
S.Margherita Belice
Sambuca
Caltabellotta
AKRAGAS
HERAKLEIA MINOA
THERMAE SELINUNTIAE
SELINUS
MAZARA
SEGESTA
ERYX
Salemi
HALIKYAI
Salaparuta
Partanna
MOTYE
LILYBAION

x Sikel } in VIth Century
o Greek }
Ancient names in capitals

0 10 20 30 40 km.
0   10   20 miles

tenth and eighth centuries, after the abandonment of the coast stations of the Siculan II period.[1] There are no imports of Greek pottery during this period, but bronze fibulas and gold came in small quantities from Greece.[2] There is some material of the period of the foundation of Syracuse,[3] and probably Pantalica continued to be the great stronghold of the Sikels at this time. There is nothing to be dated later than Syracuse (except a sporadic Protocorinthian kotyle of the early seventh century).[4]

Finocchito has a similar but much less strong position above the Heloros. It also is approached by a narrow neck from the west, defended not by cliffs but by steep banks. Its graves belong to a later period than Pantalica, most of them being of the second half of the eighth century. They show more signs of luxury and imports from overseas, which include pottery of the period immediately before the foundation of Syracuse,[5] scarabs, and ivory plaques from fibulas.[6] Most of the graves are later than the foundation of Syracuse, but there is less Greek pottery of this period than of the preceding. It appears therefore that relations between Syracuse and the Sikels became strained as soon as the colonists felt themselves established. Probably occupation ceased early in the seventh century, the date of the latest graves,[7] a short time before the foundation of Akrai. There is not enough ground for a precise date, but it is plausible to suppose that Finocchito was destroyed as one of the earlier steps in the conquest of the hills which was completed by the foundation of Akrai.[8] Perhaps Pantalica also was taken at this period. It must have fallen before the way to Akrai was safe, for it lies across the communications of Akrai with Syracuse, commanding the Anapos gorge.[9] Neither site is directly commanded from Akrai.

It is unlikely that the wall which defended Finocchito is as old as the seventh century. The plan, with a large and a small semicircular bastion,[10] shows the influence of Greek military

---

[1] See above, p. 2, n. 1.   [2] *MA*, xxi, pl. 7. 36; ibid. 339; ix. 101-2.

[3] Säflund, *Studi Etruschi*, xii. 45 ff.; Åkerström, *Der Geometrische Stil in Italien*, 15.

[4] Syracuse Museum, from an unauthorized excavation; type of Johansen, *VS*, pl. 17. 4.

[5] Blakeway, 189-91; cf. Åkerström, op. cit. 17 ff.   [6] *BPI*, 1894, 42; pl. 4. 11.

[7] The latest contains a Middle Protocorinthian kotyle (700-675); ibid., pl. 4. 3; Johansen, 89.   [8] Cf. *BPI*, 1897, 187.

[9] The road ran not up the gorge of the Anapos, which below Pantalica is difficult and passable only in the bed of the stream, but up the ridge on the opposite side from Pantalica, where traces of the ancient road have been discovered. Pantalica is less than a mile from the line of this road, and could not have been left by the Syracusans in hostile hands.

[10] *BPI*, 1897, 179 ff. and pl. 8; Pace, *ACSA*, i. 351-2, figs. 142-3.

architecture of a later date. The construction in irregular unshaped blocks gives no indication of date, and there is no pottery within the town to establish the period of occupation. No other Sikel site of this period is fortified; the later works at Mendolito and Monte Bubbonia are both after the arrival of the Greeks.[1] Though there are no remains at Finocchito of any but the Siculan III period, it is possible that it was used as a place of refuge at a much later date, perhaps in the early Byzantine period. The fortification of Pantalica is analogous. There the narrow neck on the west, the only side unprotected by cliffs, was defended by a ditch, the plan of which appears to be derived from Euryalos.[2] Pantalica was at the time of this fortification almost certainly not inhabited, but sporadic finds show that it was used as a place of refuge in the classical period.[3]

Nothing replaces these big Sikel places, and the inhabitants were presumably dispersed. Smaller sites show more continuity. The Tremenzano cemetery, of the same period as Finocchito, replaced the Siculan II site of Castelluccio (Cava della Signora) on the other side of the valley from it. It comes to an end about the same time as Finocchito, and may also have been captured early in the seventh century; but as only fifteen graves were excavated, such conclusions are more than ordinarily dangerous. Just above Tremenzano is a small group of earth graves,[4] of Greek type, not Sikel, and in one of them a Middle Corinthian oinochoe.[5] At Castelluccio are two sixth-century houses, probably Greek;[6] Siculan houses with stone foundations are limited to the 'palaces' of Pantalica, Monte Bubbonia, and San Mauro. It is possible that these two houses also were the habitations of Sikel chiefs, but this is unlikely in a district which was then in complete Syracusan control. Near the houses are rock-cut tombs of Greek type. Houses and tombs should belong to Greeks who had settled among their Sikel subjects.

Orsi regarded the sixth-century remains of Castelluccio and Tremenzano as those of hellenized Sikels. The form and con-

---

[1] Cf. below, pp. 132, 119. Though the neolithic settlements of Stentinello and Megara and the early Siculan I site at Branco Grande near Camarina had ditches (references in Pace, op. cit. 349–51), Siculan II and III sites were defended only by their natural strength.

[2] *BPI*, 1889, 167; *MA*, ix. 85 ff. [3] *MA*, xxi. 344.

[4] *N Sc*, 1891, 353–4. [5] *NC*, no. 1097; late, i.e. towards 575.

[6] *N Sc*, 1891, 351–3. The date is uncertain, depending on Orsi's not very detailed account of the material found in them.

tents of the Tremenzano graves are quite Greek; his opinion rests therefore not on interpretation of the objects but on his general views about the population of the area. In the absence of definitely Siculan material of the sixth century from this district, and indeed the whole of the Syracusan territory, we must conclude either that the Sikels were so completely hellenized as to be indistinguishable from Greeks, or so badly treated by the Syracusans as to leave no material remains. Against the first supposition there is no reason why the Sikels of this area should progress so much more rapidly than their free neighbours at Licodia or Ragusa;[1] and the paucity of any sort of remains of the archaic period supports the view that most of the conquered territory was populated by serfs, with only a few Greeks living in the country-side.

The centre of all this hill-country of the extreme south-east of Sicily is Akrai. It is naturally very strong, rising steeply on three sides and joined only by a narrow neck to a lower ridge, on which the town of Palazzolo now stands. On top is a level area large enough for a fair-sized town. A thousand feet below are the upland valleys of the Anapos and Heloros, and on the Syracuse side are good fruit-gardens. It is one of the most favoured spots in the hill district, and had always a reasonable prosperity, witness the graves which have enriched the Museo Judica in Palazzolo and Palermo Museum with Corinthian vases, and the little theatre and plentiful third-century inscriptions. But its importance in early times was military. It commands the valleys of the Anapos and Heloros and all the hills between, a triangle of country based on the coast between Syracuse and Pakhynos. To the north-west Monte Lauro, the central knot of this system, shuts out the view, but in every other direction it looks out over flat-topped limestone ridges and deep valleys, and all the hill towns are visible as far as Chiaramonte Gulfi and Ragusa. If anything was moving in this corner of the hills, it could be seen and controlled from Akrai. Due east, the Great Harbour and Plemmyrion are in sight. Ortygia is just hidden, but in clear weather it would be possible to signal direct with Plemmyrion.

Akrai was a considerable Sikel centre. The hill-side of Pinnita opposite is honeycombed with tombs.[2] There are

---

[1] See below, pp. 126, 107.

[2] There are also Greek tombs cut in the rock of Pinnita which have produced Corinthian pottery (*N Sc*, 1889, 387–8).

Siculan III vases of the seventh century in the Museo Judica at Palazzolo, probably but not certainly from this cemetery.[1] But as it has not been regularly excavated it is not certain whether the Sikel town was still flourishing when the Greek colony was founded. At Buscemi to the north across the deep valley of the Anapos there are also Siculan graves, said by Orsi to belong to the third period, but 'completely despoiled *ab antiquo*'.[2] It is quite likely that the Sikels remained in both places as tillers of the soil in subjection to the Greeks who had occupied the strongest point in the neighbourhood.

The date of Akrai is given by Thukydides as *c.* 664–3 B.C.[3] The site has yielded many Corinthian vases, but no Protocorinthian. The earliest known to me are Transitional (Palermo 2475, 2478 = *NC*, nos. 75 A, 75 B). On the archaeological evidence alone the foundation would be dated *c.* 640–625, at least a quarter of a century too late. Though it has not been scientifically excavated, Akrai has been well explored and is better known than most inland sites. This illustrates the need for caution when the archaeological evidence, incomplete at best, is our only source. Even the best of my dates for the occupation of inland sites are lower limits, and on the analogy of Akrai may well rise by a quarter of a century.

Even higher than Akrai on the windy heights of Monte Lauro was the little town now called Monte Casale.[4] It lies on a long open ridge in a less strong position than Akrai, which it complements by covering the upper valley of the Hyrminos, the third large river of the south-east. It is not a favourable spot for an agricultural settlement, and the remains indicate that it was chiefly military. The lower courses of the wall, with towers, were excavated; a cross-wall cut the town in half at its narrowest point. At the top of the town was a small temple, without columns, and in a *favissa* was a heap of hundreds of iron lance-heads. There were also more peaceful weapons, sickles and pick-axes, but the lance-heads are far more numerous. A few bronze vessels, large nails, and flat pieces of bronze folded over into the shape of short spear-blades almost complete the list of dedications at this strange sanctuary. The

---

[1] e.g. no. 2355. cf. *RM*, 1898, 358, fig. 73; no. 2353, pithos, cf. *RM*, 1900, 71, fig. 14 for decoration; no. 2350, oinochoe, decoration as *RM*, 1909, 81, fig. 12.

[2] *N Sc*, 1899, 452. [3] For this date see below, p. 450.

[4] Excavated by Orsi in 1922 and 1927-8-9-31; unpublished, except for a brief note in *BPI*, 1928, 75 ff. Material in Syracuse Museum and Museo Judica, Palazzalo. I am grateful to Prof. R. Carta for much information.

temple wall is built of rough stones presenting an external face, held together by a sort of earth cement (*tajo*).[1] The upper courses, which are part of a rebuilding, are isodomic.

A large part of the town was excavated, and provides some of the best evidence for archaic house-plans.[2] It was long and narrow, about 7 furlongs by 2½ (1·37 × 0·45 km.). The streets all ran up its length and were about 10 feet wide (3·10–3·20 m.). There were no cross streets, but narrow lanes between the houses, which were small, grouped round a courtyard and presenting a blank wall to the street. A hall, with a hearth in the middle, and three or four rooms opening off one side, is frequent. Such houses and narrow streets are well adapted to a little hill-town. The contents of the houses are agricultural implements, as before; lumps of iron and lead to be worked; bronze fittings and fastenings; and loom-weights, both the common terra-cotta cones and pierced pebbles. There are some arms, including a dagger and knives. There are domestic utensils of bronze, a spoon, a grater, a strainer; and rough porous pottery made on the spot. There is little painted pottery, which agrees in character and quality with that in the graves. So do the few terra-cotta statuettes, bronze ornaments, and little pieces of glass and amber.

The commonest burial method differs from that at Syracuse and every other city of Sicily. The body was placed in the rock-cut grave and burnt there, grave-furniture and all, and the remains covered with earth. This rite is common in the seventh and early sixth centuries at Ialysos among other places, but is rare in the Rhodian colonies of Sicily.

The earliest material that I have seen is Early Corinthian pottery, from the houses.[3] This takes the first settlement back at least to the end of the seventh century; it may be that the earliest part of the temple is older, but its roughness and simplicity need not be an indication of early date. Until the definitive publication appears it is not possible to give a more precise date than between the foundation of Akrai and 600, not necessarily much before the later date.[4] There is more sixth-century material than fifth, as on many Sicilian sites. The town was still existing in the fourth century, but the sixth-

[1] Orsi, *Templum Apollinis Alaei*, 76.   [2] Orsi, *N Sc*, 1925, 313.
[3] Conical oinochoe, cf. *NC*, no. 758; kotyle, of the type *NC*, no. 201; both these vases are late in the Early Corinthian period, i.e. towards 600.
[4] Pace, *ACSA*, i. 183, calls it a Greek city of the seventh century B.C.

century remains are the most interesting and there is more passably good pottery of that period. The site then still had value against incompletely subjugated Sikels.

The name of this town is not known. It may have been Kasmenai, the site of which has never been satisfactorily settled. Monte Casale fulfils the conditions of being a purely Greek town and of being at least as old as the seventh century, though none of the finds are as old as 643, the date of the foundation of Kasmenai.[1] I shall return to the question in discussing the exile of the Gamoroi to Kasmenai.

Another small town was at Chiaramonte Gulfi, at the highest point of the ridge which runs from Monte Lauro down towards Kamarina. There is here a Siculan II cemetery contemporary with those of Thapsos and Plemmyrion. The next material is of about the middle of the sixth century, and from this time onward everything is Greek.[2] Giarratana, between Chiaramonte Gulfi and Akrai, has Siculan III–IV graves and an early deposit of bronzes including a Greek situla-handle;[3] these remains fail to establish how long it remained Sikel. One of these small towns, perhaps that at Chiaramonte Gulfi, was Akrillai, where Marcellus defeated Hippokrates, who was moving to the west of the island, and drove him back to Akrai.[4]

The first Syracusan step to the south was probably Heloron,[5] though nothing older than the sixth century has been found there. The earliest graves are nearly a mile outside the walls,[6] and it is possible that older cemeteries nearer the town have not been found. It is a disappointing site: the chief remains

---

[1] The suggestion is made by Pace, loc. cit. For other suggested sites see below, p. 103.

[2] Syracuse Mus. inv. no. 41496, Ionian banded kylix. The only Corinthian vases are a kothon and a small skyphos, *NC*, no. 1517, both after 550.

[3] *BPI*, 1900, 267 ff.; Peet, *Stone and Bronze Ages in Italy*, 465. The eighth-century date proposed in *BPI*, 1900, 283 is rightly lowered, by implication, in *BPI*, 1927, 45.

[4] Livy xxiv. 35; Plut. *Marcellus*, 18; Steph. Byz. s.v. Orsi, *Riv. st. ant.* v. 45, makes the identification; Pace, *Camarina*, 117–18, claims to find the name surviving in the hill of Piano Grillo.

[5] So Hackforth, *CAH*, iv. 363. Pace, *ACSA*, i. 181, takes the absence of early remains at Heloron and in the country between there and Cape Pakhynos to show that the Syracusan expansion was for two centuries westward only, not southward. He thinks that Kamarina was reached from Syracuse by an overland route via Akrai. But though there is no documentation of Greek settlement south of Syracuse in the seventh or first half of the sixth century, there is no evidence of the survival of Sikels. The region is archaeologically not rich. When once the Syracusans held the hills which command the coastal plain, it would be surprising if they did not occupy its good land.

[6] *NSc*, 1899, 241–4. Orsi does not give details of the contents of the graves, which I have not seen.

are the walls, a small theatre, now hardly recognizable, and a temple *in antis*. It is not possible to form any idea of the development or degree of refinement of the little town, which must have had some importance. It is in one of the richest agricultural areas in all Sicily,[1] which finds from the adjacent country-side show was well populated in the fifth century.[2]

Another secondary colony on this coast was perhaps Ina, on the Gulf of Vindicari, which offers good shelter to ships sailing south from Syracuse.[3]

At Neeton there is a lacuna between Siculan III of the eighth century, without Greek imports,[4] and Greek graves of the third century. The earliest mention of the town in history is in 263 (Diod. xxiii. 6). So it is impossible to say whether the Sikels were displaced by Greeks or remained in subjection to the Syracusans and gradually became hellenized.[5]

Kasmenai is usually placed in the extreme south-eastern corner of Sicily, but no important Greek remains have been found in this area. Spaccaforno, at the mouth of the Cava d'Ispica with its considerable Sikel population, has a poor Greek cemetery of the sixth century; it has the best claim, topographical and archaeological, of any site in this area.[6] Near Burgio, between Spaccaforno and Pachino, was found a head of Pentelic marble in low relief, of *c.* 400.[7] This might have come from Kasmenai or from any other little Greek settlement. Scicli, which has also been suggested, was certainly Sikel, as a small group of Sikel graves has been found there which produced two Corinthian kothons with a Siculan IV amphora and oinochoai.[8] Another proposed site is Comisò, at and

---

[1] Cf. *Aen.* iii. 698: *praepingue solum stagnantis Helori*. The sugar-cane was successfully cultivated at Avola in this area after it had been given up everywhere else in Sicily (Smyth, *Sicily*, 177).

[2] Rock tombs in the Tellaro valley, by the railway bridge (*N Sc*, 1891, 348); from Bimisca, between Noto and Pachino, a column-krater by the Orpheus painter, *c.* 440 B.C. (*N Sc*, 1915, 211, fig. 20; Beazley, *ARV*, 703, no. 2).

[3] Pace suggests that Ἶνα should be read for Ἔννα in Stephanos' notice of the Syracusan colony sent to Enna in 663 (*ACSA*, i. 184; cf. below, pp. 106, 136. Ina is otherwise hardly known (Cic. *Verr.* iii. 103; Ptol. iii. 4. 15), but one is not justified in concluding from this lack of history that the attempt at colonization failed.

[4] Unless the two amphoras mentioned, *RM*, 1898, 338, whose decoration has perished.

[5] Pace, *ACSA*, i. 197, goes beyond the evidence available to me in speaking of it as a Sikel city 'influenzata di civiltà ellenica, ma libera dal dominio politico del popolo sopravvenuto'.

[6] Freeman, ii. 25 ff.; Orsi, *N Sc*, 1912, 360-1.

[7] Orsi, *N Sc*, 1905, 428; Pace, *ACSA*, ii. 68, fig. 71.

[8] *RM*, 1898, 339-40, figs. 55 and 57. There is also a b.f. amphora from Scicli, *CVA Siracusa*, i, iii H, pl. 3. 4.

near which are traces of Greek settlement; the most important remains are Roman, and it is probable that there were outlying villages dependent on Kamarina, one of which, at Comisò, became a centre of population after the destruction of Kamarina. Another village or small town in this neighbourhood may have been at Vittoria, where a grave containing three early-fifth-century Attic lekythoi has been found.[1]

There was still one attractive site on the coast between Syracusan territory and Geloan. The valley of the Ippari, and the gentle hills between it and the Dirillo, are all good land, now charmingly set with fruit-trees.[2] Kamarina, like Gela, but on a smaller scale, is the outlet of a rich land whose other access to the sea is blocked by sand-hills. The channel between the lake and the sea formed a port, and remains of quays have been found flanking it.[3] The marsh into which the river spread defended the city effectively on one side, though it was very unhealthy. Low sandy cliffs are presented to the sea, and to the east the flat-topped hill is succeeded by rolling country. It was an easy site to fortify. The first circuit of wall included all the area between the Hipparis and the Oanis, with a perimeter of about three miles.[4] The acropolis has an area of about 22 acres,[5] large enough if only a small military or trading-post had been intended, but the wall which separates it from the rest of the city belongs to one of the rebuildings of the town.

The foundation of Kamarina is about 135 years after Syracuse. Eusebius and the Scholiast to Pindar agree with the Thukydidean date. Forty-six years later it is destroyed, in the 57th Olympiad. The combination of these dates gives 598–7 for the foundation, 552–1 for the first destruction.[6]

---

[1] Syracuse Mus. 43.051–3; Haspels, *ABL*, 112; two by the Diosphos painter, the third from his workshop.

[2] In ancient times heavily wooded; see Pindar, *Ol.* v. 11 ff.

[3] Columba, *I Porti della Sicilia Antica*, 351. The quays, Orsi, *N Sc*, 1907, 484; Pace, *Camarina*, 91 ff.; Fazello (v. 230) says that stones from the river-mouth were carried off to Terranova (now Gela) between 1544 and 1554. In the sixteenth century ships of war could lie in the canal and water without disembarking (Camiliano, cited by Columba, loc. cit.).

[4] Schubring, *Camarina*, *ASS*, vi. 45 (I know only the Italian translation); Orsi, *MA*, ix. 209; Pace, *Camarina*, 68 ff. Much of the wall had disappeared between Schubring's visit in 1864 and Orsi's in 1896.

[5] Schubring, loc. cit. (45 hectares).

[6] Thuk. vi. 5; Eusebius, ed. Schoene, ii. 92 (599 B.C.), ed. Fotheringham, 175 (601 B.C.); Schol. Pind. *Ol.* v. 16: κτίζεται μὲν γὰρ ἡ Καμάρινα μέ 'Ολυμπιάδι [600–596]· ἐπικρατησάντων δὲ Συρακουσίων πορθεῖται τῇ νζ' 'Ολυμπιάδι [552–548]; ps.-Skymn. 294–6. See Pareti, 35–6; Pace, *Camarina*, 33.

There are traces of a Siculan IV predecessor of Kamarina at Pianoresti, two miles north-east of the town.[1] Orsi suggests that there was a Geloan post in the seventh century, and that the name is Cretan, comparing Καμάρα in Crete and Kamiros in Rhodes.[2] But there is no evidence that Kamarina was inhabited by Greeks before the Syracusan foundation. The only graves which belong to the first period of its existence (598–552) are a small group at Dieci Salme on the sand-hills to the north-east.[3] All but one of these are miserably poor; that one contained a collection of twenty-three Corinthian kothons, black Attic cups with reserved zone, and other vases, including two bucchero kantharoi. The earliest of the kothons are Early Corinthian (as *NC*, no. 722), but the burial is not before 550, and the older vases appear to be part of a collection buried with its owner, not an earlier deposit. There is no reason to suppose that these vases came to Kamarina before 600.

The oecists of Kamarina are named. Daskon is surely a Syracusan, taking his name from the point of land in the Great Harbour; Menekolos presumably a Corinthian (compare the action of the Korkyraians in founding Epidamnos with one oecist from Corinth). Thukydides does not name the oecists of Akrai and Kasmenai, perhaps because there were none recorded. It seems that Kamarina had more independence than the other Syracusan foundations, which were less than autonomous cities. Kamarina was a much bigger and more important place, with a self-sufficient territory. It was seventy miles from Syracuse, too far for complete control, and the direct way was through territory not immediately Syracusan but belonging to the friendly Sikels. Perhaps Kamarina was subject to no more than such control as Corinth exercised over her north-western colonies and Potidaia, and asserted over Korkyra. Whatever this control was, in the second generation the Kamarinaians found it irksome and fought a war of independence.[4] They had on their side Sikels and 'other allies'.

---

[1] Pace, op. cit. 23, 32.

[2] *Ausonia*, i. 11. Pais, *Storia di Sicilia*, 616, favours the Cretan origin of the name. In the text of the same book, p. 113, he proposes an Italic origin, comparing Cameria in Latium. So also Pace, op. cit. 26.

[3] *N Sc*, 1912, 370–2; Pace, op. cit. 100. See Payne, *NC*, 25. None of the Corinthian vases in the Biscari Collection in Catania is known to have been found at Kamarina.

[4] Thuk. vi. 5; Philistos ap. Dion. Hal. ad Pomp. 5. 5 (Muller, *FHG*, i, fr. 8): Συρακούσιοι δὲ παραλαβόντες Μεγαρεῖς καὶ Ἐνναίους, Καμαριναῖοι δὲ Σικελοὺς καὶ τοὺς ἄλλους συμμάχους, πλὴν Γελῴων, ἀθροίσαντες· Γελῷοι δὲ Συρακουσίοις οὐκ ἔφασαν πολεμήσειν· Συρακούσιοι δὲ πυνθανόμενοι Καμαριναίους τὸν Ὕρμινον διαβάντας . . . .

The Sikels would be those of Ragusa and Modica. The 'other allies' must have been Greeks, the inhabitants of the small Greek towns belonging to Syracuse;[1] they were not the Geloans, who were neutral, and none of the other Greek cities could have taken part in an advance on Syracuse along the south coast. The Syracusans were supported by Megara and, if the reading in Dionysios is correct, by Enna.[2] It is very difficult to see how Enna could support Syracuse in the south-east of the island; Pais reads ΚΑΙ ΚΑΣΜΕΝΑΙΟΥΣ for ΚΑΙ ΕΝΝΑΙΟΥΣ, not a difficult emendation and perhaps correct.[3] The Kamarinaians felt that the Sikels of the Syracusan overlordship were sufficiently near to them to make common cause, as the demos of Syracuse did half a century later. This is the first time we hear of Greeks fighting side by side with Sikels against other Greeks.

The Syracusans moved against the Kamarinaians when they heard that they had crossed the Hyrminos, the Fiume di Ragusa. It is generally taken that this was the boundary between Syracuse and Kamarina. But Hybla Heraia lay on this river and belonged to neither. The immediate territories of the two Greek cities did not touch, and the importance of the Hyrminos was not as a political but as a natural boundary. Though Dionysios' quotation breaks off without giving the course of the war, Thukydides says that Kamarina was destroyed, and it used to be inferred that the site lay waste until Hippokrates refounded it after the battle of the Heloros. But all the evidence shows that it was prospering in the last half of the century. In 528 Parmenides of Kamarina was victor in the foot-race at Olympia.[4] This does not prove that his city was in existence; he may have been in exile. But it is unlikely that he was holding to the memory of a city destroyed, physically or politically, twenty-five years earlier. Graves of the second half of the century are more numerous than of the period before or after, and have produced some fine vases.[5]

---

[1] Pace, op. cit. 36.

[2] Stephanus of Byzantium says that Enna was a Syracusan colony, founded in 663. The date, that of Akrai, is unlikely, but the statement should not be rejected out of hand. But this passage of Philistos is poor support. For the foundation of a colony, even an inland one, it is not essential that its lands should march with those of the mother country, but it could hardly, in this case, give military support. See below, p. 136.

[3] *Storia di Sicilia*, 236, 560-4. I do not follow him when he proposes ΑΚΡΕΙΣ for ΜΕΓΑΡΕΙΣ.   [4] Eusebius (Schoene, i. 201).

[5] In Syracuse Museum (e.g. no. 26857) and Catania (Libertini, *Catalogo del Museo Biscari*, nos. 664, 666, 668, 679, 680, 681, 682, 688; also terra-cottas of the second half of the sixth century, nos. 930-2, 934). See Pace, op. cit. 37, 100 ff.

The Dieci Salme graves are to be regarded as part of an extensive cemetery which covers the whole of the sixth century,
without a break corresponding to the 'destruction' of 552.[1]
From the combined evidence of the graves for the material
circumstances and Parmenides' victory for the political conditions, it appears that the city was not only existing but
flourishing. Thukydides' ἀναστάτων may imply that the original
Kamarinaians were exiled, but does not necessarily mean that
the city was destroyed. Presumably it remained politically
closely attached to Syracuse; but it must have retained some
measure of independent existence.[2] The Sikel allies of Kamarina
continued, so far as we can tell, as they were before.

The foundation of Kamarina marks the end of Syracusan
expansion, which was followed by a period of consolidation
during the sixth century. Her territories now marched with
Greek neighbours, Megara, Leontinoi, and Gela, except for a
short stretch where they abutted on the free Sikels of Licodia
Eubea and Vizzini.[3] These were perhaps felt to belong within
the sphere of influence of Leontini or Gela. Everything to the
east and south of Monte Lauro was under Syracusan control,
direct or indirect, and the territory of Kamarina extended to
the west as far as the Dirillo. This is an area of about 1,500
square miles, larger than any state of old Greece except
Laconia.

The Sikels had not all been subdued, and at least one town
inside these boundaries had some degree of independence.
Ragusa, where the Herajan Hybla is placed,[4] had a flourishing
Sikel settlement of the Third period, with some Greek imports
of the early seventh century. At several points on the outskirts
of Ragusa Inferiore, in the narrow valley of the Hyrminos and
the cliffs on its west side, Sikel tombs have been found, though
not in good condition. On the hill-top above at Contrada
Pendente, about a mile from the lower town, is a sixth-century
cemetery, mainly Greek but with some Siculan pottery. The
form of the graves is Greek, though with some affinity to the

---

[1] So Pace: his opinion on this point is especially valuable, as he was brought up at
Camarina.

[2] Another argument for Kamarina's continued existence after 552 is that Hippokrates
destroyed it, it seems, on his march to Syracuse. See Pareti, *Studi Siciliani,* 37 ff.; and
below, pp. 399 ff.

[3] See below, pp. 126 ff.

[4] Freeman, i. 162–4. This is the least of the three Hyblas (Steph. Byz. s.v., quoted p. 144);
Paus. v. 23 does not mention it.

shapes at Licodia (itself somewhat hellenized).[1] Of twenty-two graves in the main group, six have Siculan with Late Corinthian and Attic vases, four have only Greek pottery. The others are empty, or nearly so. None is entirely or even mainly Siculan in content. The earliest (no. 1) has more than one burial, the oldest being of the first quarter of the sixth century. No. 15 includes, as well as black-figured vases of the end of the century, some fragments of sculpture and inscriptions which have probably been swept in at a later date but belong to the same period. The sculptures are in local stone[2] and as good as any other Syracusan work. The muzzle of a horse and the hind-quarters of a running animal, with tail lying straight up the back, show a considerable study of anatomy, applied without exaggeration. The alphabet of the inscriptions agrees with the Syracusan. They are too fragmentary to throw any light on the status of the inhabitants.

Archaic inscriptions are very rare in Sicily, and sculptural remains almost as rare. This little body of Greeks was by no means backward. But this is the only clearly Greek cemetery in the Syracusan sphere of influence in which more than one or two Siculan objects have been found.[3] This Siculan pottery may have come from Sikels living among the Greeks or from exchange with the Sikel town below. There is no close parallel on either hypothesis. Whichever is the case, this little settlement is not military but commercial, and appears to have belonged to Syracusans who grew rich from trade with the independent Sikels. Nothing suggests that the Sikels were subject to any form of control from this post on the hill above them. The latest of the graves are of the end of the sixth or beginning of the fifth century. This perhaps indicates that the Sikels expelled the Greek sojourners during the Sikel Wars of Hippokrates.[4] His death at Hybla has been thought to have been in an attempt to avenge them; but it is not certain that it was this Hybla where Hippokrates died.[5] Certainly this was the only place within the Syracusan sphere where the Sikels had not already been reduced to subjection.

The country to the south-east of Ragusa also remained Sikel, but without any great centre. There was a town at Modica

---

[1] See below, p. 126.
[2] N Sc, 1899, 407–9, figs. 5–7. Orsi speaks of ancient quarries, loc. cit. 415.
[3] See below for similar conditions at Grammichele and Caltagirone (pp. 122, 114).
[4] Orsi, loc. cit. 418.   [5] Herod. vii. 155. See below, p. 403.

where unpublished excavations have produced some interesting Siculan III vases of the first half of the seventh century and Protocorinthian imports.[1] But there is nothing to show what happened to it after this date. Scicli, six miles downstream from Modica, was Sikel in the sixth century.[2] On the plateau above Modica is a small fifth-century cemetery belonging probably to an agricultural estate. There was another house or farm at Magazzinazzi, about five miles south-west of Ragusa. The Cava d'Ispica, running south-east from Modica, is a Sikel necropolis some miles long. Such graves as have been examined contain plain pottery of the fifth and later centuries. They are rather poor graves, grouped haphazard, belonging to a population scattered through small villages and farms. The type of rock-cut tomb is Sikel. There is nothing clearly Greek except an Ionic pilaster capital, which is so rude that it may well be the work of a Sikel imitating a Greek model.[3]

The whole area of Modica and Ispica is thin limestone country, suited to a poor and industrious race of peasants. It is full of unimportant remains, mainly of the Roman and Byzantine periods.[4] The allegiance of these peasants in the sixth century is uncertain. From the fifth century onwards they must have tilled the soil for Syracusan masters, but earlier they may have remained free, perhaps attached to Hybla. The troubles of Syracuse with Kamarina are more easily understood if there was still a body of unsubdued Sikels across the direct line of communication between the two cities. Between the east coast and Kamarina there is no evidence of sixth-century Greek settlement except the little trading-post at Ragusa.

There are no coins of Akrai older than the third century, and none at all of Kasmenai. In the sixth century these places had, it appears, less independence than the secondary colonies in Italy, which issued coins derived in type from the mother city.[5] Considering the change of status brought about by the tyrants in the smaller cities of Sicily, it is not licit to infer the con-

---

[1] The best is a cup, Syracuse Mus. 45825, like Johansen, *VS*, pl. 19. 1.

[2] Above, p. 103.

[3] *N Sc*, 1905, 437, fig. 22.

[4] Cf. Orsi, *N Sc*, 1915, 213: 'l'*ager motykanus* . . . già in epoca greca, ma sopra tutto nella romana e bizantina, era fittamente costellato di piccoli villaggi e di fattorie', and *N Sc*, 1905, 436: 'come la sicula Motyka rispecchia oggi nel tipo fisico di buona parte dei suoi abitanti, e di quelli delle circostanti montagne, la sopravvivenza della razza sicula, non mai obliterata, così penso che attraverso tutti i secoli la populazione ispicana rimanesse in gran maggioranza sicula, con insignificanti infiltrazioni di Greci, Romani, Bizantini, ed Arabi'.

[5] Cf. p. 158.

stitutional position of Akrai in the sixth century from evidence belonging to the fifth and later centuries. But we hear of no movements of population at Akrai, and considering its military importance it is likely to have been continuously inhabited. Probably it was part of the Syracusan state, without autonomy, and the other towns of Syracusan territory, such as Neeton and Heloron,[1] which receive independent existence in the third century, had the same status. They are likely to have had some local self-government, as a measure of decentralization of this territory, which was as large as any Greek state; but this is only a guess. The foundation of Akrai and Kasmenai is mentioned by Thukydides, but not that of other Greek towns. This need only mean that the circumstances of the foundation were different, not that these two towns had a position privileged above the others. Most of these little places, like the *oppidum tenue sane* of Bidis,[2] would be settlements of a few hundred Greeks, small men, engaged in agriculture and garrison duty. The towns were purely Greek, and if there were Sikels living in them, their remains and their burial customs had become indistinguishable from the Greek. The Sikels no doubt lived outside the walls, like the demos at Megara Nisaia.[3] At dozens of points, especially in the fertile zone between Syracuse and Cape Pakhynos, single graves or small groups have been found in the fields. Some of these have been mentioned; they are for the most part Greek. Others are bare burials, or miserably poor, and are probably the graves of Sikel serfs. Sometimes a number of poor graves are grouped round one richer one, the cemetery of a large farming establishment with a Greek owner or manager and probably Sikel labourers. There are very few positive traces of the Sikels, except in the places where they maintained their independence into the sixth and fifth centuries. On many sites we can only say that there is a Sikel settlement which lasts until some date in the seventh century, and no remains of the subsequent period. In these cases we may infer that the Sikels were enslaved as the Greeks advanced, and remained to till the fields for their conquerors. Their enslavement accounts for the absence of any sign of independent culture, and also for the

---

[1] Ὅπερ ἦν πάλαι Συρακοσίων φρούριον, Aelian, *NA* xii. 30.

[2] *Verr.* II. ii. 22. 53; placed by Pace (*Camarina,* 118) on the Dirillo near Biscari. There is from Biscari a seated terra-cotta statuette of the late sixth century (Mus. Biscari, no. 935).   [3] Theognis 56.

absence of anything Greek on sites which had been flourishing Sikel centres.

These Sikels were presumably the Killyrioi, 'slaves' of the Syracusans. It is nowhere stated that the Killyrioi were Sikels, but in no other way could the presence of a large body of slaves, more numerous than the citizens, be explained. This is supported by the analogy of other conquered races with whom Aristotle compares them, especially the Maryandines of Herakleia. The Helots and the Penestai, also quoted by Aristotle in the *Constitution of Syracuse*, were conquered races tilling the soil. Perhaps the Killyrioi, like these races, were not the property of the men whose lands they worked, but belonged collectively to the whole body of Gamoroi. Though Herodotos calls them δοῦλοι, they need not have been personal slaves, but, in Eustathius' words, μὴ γόνῳ δοῦλοι, ἀλλὰ πολέμῳ. But all that is really known of them is that they joined the demos in driving out the Gamoroi.[1]

There is no evidence in the Syracusan sector of an intermediate state between independence and serfdom, though in the sphere of influence of the less acquisitive Khalkidians and Geloans some such suzerainty is possible. In 415 the Syracusans were receiving tribute from their Sikel subjects;[2] but as this is after the revolt of Duketios and the great expansion of Syracusan rule, there is no reason to suppose that tribute was exacted in the early fifth century, or from Sikels living in the original Syracusan lands.[3]

[1] Herod. vii. 155; Photius s.v. Καλλικύριοι and Κιλλικύριοι (identical entries); Hesykhios s.v. Κιλλικύριοι; Suidas s.v. Καλλικύριοι, quoting Timaios (*FHG* i, p. 204) and Aristotle (fr. 544 Rose); Eust. *Il. B.* 584; Zenobius iv. 54, Καλλικυρίων πλείους (in alphabetical order under κι-). See Freeman, ii, appx. ii; Hüttl, 38–40. The later references add little to Herodotos. The form and etymology of the name are uncertain. There is not more manuscript authority in Herodotos for Κυλλύριοι than for Κιλλύριοι. The Καλλι- and Κιλλικύριοι variants, one or other of which is sometimes accepted, are attempts to provide a Greek etymology. The name, which is generally taken to be that of an enslaved Sikel tribe, may in fact be Greek, the form Κιλλύριοι being perhaps derived from the Doric κίλλος = ὄνος (Pollux vii. 56). It would then be an abusive name like that of the serfs at Epidauros and elsewhere. An alternative etymology (Ceci, *Rend. Lincei*, 1932, 51, cited by Pace, *ACSA*, i. 179, n. 6) explains κυλλύριοι as 'skin-wearers', comparing the Latin *culleus*, which also has a Greek origin.

[2] Thuk. vi. 20. 4.

[3] Orsi was of opinion that the Sikels of the mountain area were not reduced to the status of κιλλύριοι, but were ὑπήκοοι, payers of tribute: 'Di questo stato di cose e prova non dubbia la assoluta mancanza di reliquie greche sull' altipiano, mentre vi si riconoscono in più punti avanzi siculi, dove puri, dove con tinta ellenizante....' But these remains are of the period before the Syracusan conquest. The paucity of Sikel remains of the second half of the seventh and of the sixth century suggests strongly that the Sikels of the hills were enslaved and had no material culture.

The Syracusan territory at the end of the sixth century had a patchwork appearance. Military colonies at Akrai and Monte Casale, probably with Sikel villages to work their land; Greek farmers in a walled town at Heloron, and in other little country towns; Greek farmers dotting the open country-side in the more fertile parts (though the evidence for most of these is fifth-century and later); Sikel serfs scattered on big estates over the same area; Sikels round Modica and Ispica who kept their nationality and appear to have been free peasants; one free Sikel town, Hybla, with a Greek trading-post outside it. Large landholders, small landholders, serfs, lived side by side, and trouble was to come when the serfs had been so far assimilated that the smallholders felt that they could make common cause. And there was still an unabsorbed remnant of Sikels, peaceful and on good terms with the Greeks at ordinary times, but a possible rallying-point for their enslaved fellows.

GELA

The Geloan advance began under their oecist, that is, in the early seventh century, at the same time as the Syracusan advance. Antiphemos sacked the Sikan fortress of Omphake and carried off to Gela a Daedalic statue.[1] This may have been an object imported in the pre-colonization period, or may have been 'planted' to establish the Cretan claim to the territory. In any case, there was in Gela in a later century (it was lost in Pausanias' time) a statue associated with the founder's wars. As Omphake is Sikan it should be west of the river Gelas, the boundary between Sikel and Sikan. This is country less well explored archaeologically than the hinterland of Syracuse, and there is no site with which it may be plausibly identified.[2] Dessueri, the chief Siculan site of the Geloan territory, comes to an end at least a century before the foundation of Gela.[3]

The Scholiast on Pindar, Ol. ii. 8 explains that the phrase καμόντες οἳ πολλὰ θύμῳ suits Gela, but not Akragas, and it appears that there was a tradition of early Sikan wars of the

---

[1] Paus. viii. 46. 2; ix. 40. 4.

[2] Omphake is placed at Dessueri by Schubring, Rh. Mus. xxviii. 121–2; Giuliano, Riv. st. ant. xi. 132. For another location see p. 116.

[3] There is Siculan III pottery in one grave only (MA, xxi. 379), and one iron fibula (ibid.). The only imported pottery is some Corinthian in two earlier graves to which it does not belong (ibid. 382, 387, graves 42 and 71).

Geloans.¹ The Sikels appear to have been a fairly peaceable people. Their sites, though naturally strong, were not fortified, and they seldom buried weapons in their graves. None of the cities on the east coast had difficulties that we know of in establishing themselves, and at Megara and Leontinoi the Sikels welcomed the Greek settlers to their country. The Sikans may have been tougher fighting-men, for the Akragantines also had Sikan wars.

Another unknown place taken by the Geloans is Ariaiton. At some time in the seventh century they dedicated to Athena of Lindos a krater as part of the spoils of Ariaiton.² This is after the dedication by the Phaselites under their founder (soon after 690?), before Phalaris (c. 572–556). Probably it is part of the first conquest, though if Antiphemos had commanded the Geloans his name would have been given. With the natives hostile, the Geloans could have no rest until they controlled the hills which surround their plain in a semicircle. At some time in the seventh century they founded Maktorion,³ which was perhaps at Niscemi or Butera; both sites stand up boldly about ten miles from the ramparts of Gela. Mazzarino, which is suggested as the site by the resemblance of the name, is too far away: Maktorion should have been near Gela, as part of the population seceded there in the seventh century.⁴

The central point in the Heraian hills behind Gela is Caltagirone, which stands at the head of the valley of the Gelas, at the head also of the Fiume di Caltagirone, above the pass which is the lowest and most direct way from the plain of Gela to the plain of Leontinoi. It was a rich and important Sikel town in the second period, and almost alone of inland sites has imports

---

¹ Σ. Pind. Ol. ii. 16b: τὸ καμόντες ἔφη προσήκειν μᾶλλον ἀκούειν ἐπὶ τῶν τὴν Γέλαν ἐκτικότων, ἀλλ᾽ οὐ τὴν Ἀκράγαντα. οἱ μὲν γὰρ ἀπὸ τοῦ ῥᾴστου συνῳκίσθησαν, οἱ δὲ χαλεπῶς καὶ μόλις. Ἀντίφημος γὰρ ὁ Ῥόδιος καὶ Ἔντιμος ὁ Κρής, οἱ τὴν εἰς Γέλαν στείλαντες ἀποικίαν, πρῶτον μὲν περὶ τὴν συναγωγὴν ἔκαμον οὐ μετρίως, συναθροίζοντες τοὺς ἐκ Πελοποννήσου καὶ Ῥόδου καὶ Κρήτης, εἶτα περὶ τὸν διάπλουν, εἶτα περὶ τὸν κατοικισμόν, καὶ πάλιν διαγωνισάμενοι πρὸς τοὺς Σικάνους. Σ. 15d: . . . μόγις καὶ ταπεινῶς διέζων, ἐπὶ φυλακῇ τῆς πόλεως μισθαρνοῦντες. Σ. 70g (Ambr.): . . . μαχεσαμένων Σικελιώταις περὶ τοῦ χωρίου.

² Lind. Chron. xxv (Lindos, ii. 171): Γελῶιοι κρατῆρα μέγα[ν] ὃς ταύταν εἶχε τὰν ἐπιγραφάν· Γελῶιοι τᾶ[ι] Ἀθαναίαι τᾶι Πατρώιαι ἀκροθίνιον ἐξ Ἀριαίτου. . . . Reinach, Rev. épig. i. 103, takes Ariaites as a person.

³ Steph. Byz. s.v. Μακτώριον· πόλις Σικελίας· Φίλιστος πρώτῳ, ἣν ἔκτισε μόνην. Müller (FHG, i, Philistos fr. 4) suggests that μόνην conceals the founder's name. One manuscript reads Μόνων (see Meineke's edition).

⁴ Herod. vii. 153; Freeman, i. 409; ii. 103; above, p. 64. Mingazzini (MA, xxxvi. 690 ff.) suggests that Maktorion was at Ravanusa (see below, p. 138), but this also seems too far away from Gela.

from the Aegean in the Bronze Age. Imports in the third (Finocchito) period are frequent.[1] The Montagna cemetery, which consists of groups of burials scattered over a whole hillside, where habitation and graves were side by side,[2] comes down only to the beginning of the seventh century. The neighbouring site of Bersaglio, inhabited throughout prehistoric times, also comes to an end at this period.[3] The next document of Caltagirone is the cemetery of S. Luigi, on the slope of the hill on which the present town stands, between the pass and the summit. The town to which it belonged was probably on the present site,[4] rather than on the lower ground to the east, as Orsi suggested.[5] There is some sporadic Siculan, including a fine amphora.[6] Of the eleven graves regularly excavated, only two, both of the fifth century, have each a single Siculan vase. There is no doubt that the persons buried in these graves were Greeks. The graves are covered with tiles *a cappuccina* or are clay sarcophagi, both particularly Geloan types. Cremation was practised,[7] though not certainly before the fourth century; it is unknown in Siculan cemeteries. The plain pottery recalls that of Gela, where perhaps it was made.[8] There can be no doubt that there was a small settlement of Geloans, perhaps an outpost of S. Mauro,[9] who acquired a few Siculan vases from their neighbours. The cemetery goes back hardly earlier than 550; there are a few Late Corinthian vases.[10] The Attic pottery is poor, but not worse than on other inland sites. There are half a dozen East Greek kylikes with reserved lip and handle zone, and some glass and silver.

[1] Rocca Alta 73, Protocorinthian kylix (Johansen, *VS*, 89); do. 59, kylix, Protocorinthian shape, painted red, perhaps a Sicilian imitation (*N Sc*, 1904, 92, fig. 52); do. 41, Siculan imitation of Greek geometric (ibid. 90, fig. 49; cf. *MA*, xxv, figs. 98 and 97). Rocca Bassa, Protocorinthian fragments (*N Sc*, 1904, 93). Orsi (ibid. 98) thinks that these have nothing to do with the Sikel burials, but have penetrated accidentally. I see no reason to follow him in this. His ground is a doubt whether the cemeteries lasted as late as the seventh centuries, and whether the Siculan III vases are genuinely burial deposits. The poverty of most of the Rocca graves is due to their despoilment.

[2] Ibid. 69.   [3] *BPI*, 1928, 82 ff.

[4] Libertini, *MA*, xxviii. 126.   [5] *N Sc*, 1904, 138.

[6] Ibid. 133, fig. 55. Other Siculan amphoras (as *RM*, 1898, 350 ff., fig. 64, 67) in the Liceo of Caltagirone are not certainly from S. Luigi. It is very probable that some of them come from the Montagna; see ibid. 344, where Orsi mentions oinochoai and paterai in the Liceo.

[7] *N Sc*, 1904, 138, 140.

[8] The kylikes mentioned below; the paterai, op. cit., fig. 58, cf. Bitalemi, *MA*, xvii, fig. 498; plain oinochoai, also as at Bitalemi; 'Samian' lekythos with six rings at neck, in Liceo.   [9] Orsi, op. cit. 141; Libertini, op. cit. 122. For S. Mauro see below.

[10] Kothon, stamnos (*N Sc*, 1904, 133) and banded cup in grave 21; two miniature kotylai in Liceo (exact provenience uncertain).

Whether the Montagna hill-side continued to be inhabited is uncertain. Though there are no remains later than the early seventh century, it is possible that the Sikels continued to live there, and that one purpose of the settlement at S. Luigi was to trade with them. But the gap of over a century between the latest Siculan graves and the earliest Greek makes it impossible to say when, or under what circumstances, the Greeks arrived.

Three miles south of Caltagirone, on a lower spur of the same system of hills, is S. Mauro. This site commands even more closely the route from Gela up the Maroglio into the Heraian hills and over to the plain of Leontinoi. It is not a single hill but a semicircle of low summits open to the south, up which climbs the modern road.[1] It has remains of the first three Siculan periods.[2] The central and strongest hill, a long narrow platform which narrows so that it is nearly divided into two, was the Sikel site. On it is a two-roomed building, in plan like the 'palaces' of Pantalica and Monte Bubbonia,[3] but much smaller. Beneath the foundations are scanty Siculan I–III remains, above which is a stratum of red earth, the result of a fire. The village was burnt early in the third Siculan period (ninth century), but continued on the same site. Above the fire stratum are some Siculan III sherds. The foundations of the 'palace' reach in places down to this stratum. The building is very rough. The foundations depend for solidity on breadth, not depth; the walls are roughly faced, and filled up with small stones; additional strength is given where needed by widening the wall.[4] At each end is an extension of the side-walls to form a sort of porch. There is no need to ascribe this extremely rude building to Greek architects. It was certainly not occupied by Greeks. The only Greek remains are an inscribed bronze tablet which is discussed below[5] and some architectural terra-cottas from the surface.[6] These are probably strays having nothing to do with the palace, but it is possible that the terra-cottas were added to it at some date after its construction. The other end of the hill has slight remains of habitation, and so have the slopes beneath the palace. Here are some house-foundations, hand-mills, and water-jars. The pottery is mainly Siculan, but there are fragments of Greek sub-geometric pottery[7] which are

[1] Plan and panoramas, *MA*, xx, pll. 1–3. [2] Ibid. 739.
[3] See above, p. 95, and below, p. 119.
[4] Plan, op. cit., pl. 4. [5] p. 128.
[6] Van Buren, *AFR*, 49.
[7] *MA*, xx. 751, fig. 11, no. 4, from the palace; fig. 12, perhaps nos. 3 and 5.

evidence of trade in the period just before and just after the foundation of Gela.

None of the pottery on this hill is later than the early seventh century except a group from a well-built house on the slopes which obviously belonged to one of the Greek settlers of the sixth century. The bronze tablet found under the palace does not date it, for it had an earth floor through which the metal could penetrate. Apart from the tablet and the architectural terra-cottas, which also have probably nothing to do with the building, this hill is like any other Siculan III site, with a few Greek imports among a larger quantity of Siculan pottery, and one solid building among barely discernible hut-foundations.[1] It was a small place, and the palace no magnificent building, the abode of a little princeling and his people. Nothing shows whether they were in close relation with the larger settlement of Caltagirone.

The evidence of the pottery suggests strongly that the palace and the site were abandoned by the Sikels early in the seventh century; they were not necessarily driven out with violence. The fire of which trace is found at several points on the hill happened at least a century before the Greeks arrived, and the culture was the same after it as before. The earliest remains of the Greek city are of the early sixth century (600–575).[2] The Greeks may, however, have arrived at any time after the first quarter of the seventh century. Orsi is of opinion that this city was Omphake;[3] but Omphake, being Sikan, was probably to the west of Gela. There were other places taken by the Geloans in the seventh century, and there is no reason why S. Mauro should be any of those of which we happen to hear by name.

Though the site has considerable military value, commanding the upper part of the Geloan plain and the route into the hills, the Greek town was not fortified. The houses were scattered in small groups over the tops and slopes of the several

---

[1] I am not confident that the wall (op. cit. 746, fig. 8) is part of the Sikel foundations, or that it is ancient.

[2] Middle Corinthian vases, NC, no. 871, MA, xx, 817, fig. 72 (sporadic), end of Middle period; ibid., fig. 71, shape as NC, fig. 140, near to no. 843. Stone relief of same period, MA, xx. 825 ff., pl. 9; NC, 124; Pais, Ancient Italy, ch. xii; Della Seta, Italia Antica, fig. 131; Pace, ACSA, ii. 16, fig. 14.

[3] MA, xx. 849–50. Pais (loc. cit.) suggests that S. Mauro was Galaria. But there is too little evidence for even probable identification of these 'anonymous cities' of the Heraian hills. None of them has given an inscription naming itself, and the topographical indications in ancient authors are of the vaguest.

hills, their position being governed chiefly by the scanty supply of wells. The house whose ground-plan is best preserved measured 10·10 × 5·70 m., and consisted of two rooms opening off a large court, with what appears to be the foot of a staircase leading up between the rooms to an upper story.[1] In a corner of the courtyard against the house wall is a little walled-off enclosure with two water-jars. Other houses on the south slope of the acropolis,[2] all of whose contents are of the sixth century, are built in the same style as this one, with walls of picked stone held together by an earth cement. Near one of these was found a fragment of a pithos of a type otherwise found only at Gela.[3] Orsi calls it 'a poor mountain village, with isolated groups of houses, and without luxury in building'[4] and allows a population of about 4,000. It is not a military post like Monte Casale, but a settlement of poor farmers. They were certainly Geloans. As well as the pithos fragment already mentioned, other pithoi used for burial are Geloan in both shape and use.[5] Ἐγχυτρισμός of infants was practised as at Gela. The tombs *a cappuccina* are especially Geloan. These similarities are due partly to the lack of good stone as at Gela. The most interesting grave, which contained gold and silver ornaments and a bronze flask, is a sarcophagus of imported stone with a lid of local stone. Twenty-two of the first fifty-eight graves excavated were cremations, but this high percentage was due perhaps not to religious reasons but to the plentiful supply of wood.[6]

There is nothing except the inscribed bronze tablet that is particularly associated with the Khalkidian colonies.[7] All the pottery is either of the dominant Corinthian and Attic or

[1] Op. cit., fig. 61.

[2] Plans, op. cit., figs. 59, 10. The latter is regarded by Orsi as belonging to a Greek settler in the Sikan town. But the style of the building and the contents of a deposit just outside and almost certainly connected (Corinthian krater and Lakonian krater fragments; the pithos fragment mentioned in the text; gorgoneion and head of terra-cotta statuette, both of the late sixth century) show that it belongs to the Greek town of the sixth century, not to its Sikel predecessor.

[3] Op. cit. 751; cf. *MA*, xvii, pl. V. 3.

[4] Op. cit. 799.   [5] Op. cit., figs. 14, 15, 16.

[6] About 300 graves have since been excavated but not published in detail. In *N Sc*, 1915, 225–6, they are said to be 'circa 300 sepolcri poverissimi, per lo più a cappuccina od in nuda terra, con frequentissimi ἐγχυτρισμοί infantili in anfore od in giarre' with Corinthian and black-figure, grey alabastra and glass. The contents, in Syracuse Museum, exactly confirm the sixth-century date. There is a ring-aryballos (cf. *NC*, 313) and an alabastron (as *NC*, 285), both dated *c*. 600. Nothing in the cemetery is later than 500. Orsi, loc. cit., says: 'tutto accenna al VI secolo e ad una popolazione prettamente greca.'

[7] *Pace* Orsi, *MA*, xx. 760, 775, 830.

paralleled at Gela. The inscription, which has Ionic forms and Khalkidian lettering,[1] was perhaps carried in antiquity from some town on the Leontinoi side of the pass, and cannot have anything to do with the building in whose ruins it was found, which had ceased to be used a century before.

There are fragments of Siculan amphoras from a house,[2] and Siculan III pottery in grave 20, alone of all the graves.[3] Orsi thought of a Sikel slave buried over his master; but though the slave might be able to get Siculan pottery from his free relations, it is unlikely that his masters would be so tender as to bury it with him. It is more probable that we have isolated examples of infiltration of wares used by the neighbours of the Greek outpost. There is more Siculan in the S. Luigi cemetery at Caltagirone, as at Ragusa, where there were Sikels in close neighbourhood with the Greeks. But S. Mauro is very nearly pure of admixture. The wonder is not that a few Siculan pieces should be found in a Greek town in the midst of the Sikels, but that the Greeks while trading with Sikels should have guarded their own cultural integrity so jealously. Even if they had no use for Siculan wares, one might expect more pieces to come to the Greek towns by accident of intercourse. Even when Greeks lived on the edge of a Sikel town, there is very little evidence of two-way traffic which might suggest that the two races lived together in close contact.

The chief remains of S. Mauro are the terra-cottas of the sanctuary.[4] No other remains have been found of the building. The stones of the foundation have doubtless been carried away for building, and the terra-cottas were also disturbed, and many important pieces lost before the excavation began. But no recognizable pieces of column or capital have been found, and the upper structure was no doubt of wood, to which the terra-cotta revetments were nailed.[5] The terra-cottas were probably not made on the spot. Some of the slabs have a numeral painted or scratched on the back, as directions from the maker to the builder who set them up.[6] It is generally agreed that they came from Gela.[7] Parallels at Syracuse are

---

[1] Comparetti ap. Orsi, op. cit. 843.   [2] Op. cit. 805.   [3] Op. cit. 759.
[4] MA, xx. 778 ff., pll. v–vii; Van Buren, AFR, 49 ff.   [5] Orsi, op. cit. 777.
[6] Ibid., 779, fig. 42. Cf. the directions on the back of the terra-cotta revetments found at Kalydon (Poulsen and Rhomaios, Erster Vorläufiger Bericht über die Dänisch-Griechischen Ausgrabungen von Kalydon, 23–6; Payne, NC, 249, 258; Rhomaios, 'Αρχ. Εφ. 1937, 300 ff.).
[7] Orsi, op. cit. 797: 'Il tempietto . . . sorse per opera di operai gelesi, e con terracotte gelesi.' Mrs. Van Buren is a little less certain (AFR, 53).

as close and as numerous as those with the Treasury of the Geloans and the archaic temple at Gela.[1] There is not a Geloan style of painting terra-cotta revetments distinguishable from the Syracusan style. The case for the Geloan origin of the S. Mauro revetments rests less on exact parallels than on the probability that they would come from a known centre of export, which was also the city from which the inhabitants came.

The main revetment is one of the richest and most varied, later than that of the Treasury of the Geloans and the first type in the temenos of Athena at Syracuse, to which it is most like. These both belong to the first half of the sixth century, so that a date about the middle of the century is possible for the S. Mauro revetment.[2] The sculptural fragments in terra-cotta (*MA* xx. 790 ff., figs. 51–5 and pl. VII. 2: Van Buren, *AFR*, 51, 153, 159) are so miserably scanty that it is hazardous to attempt to reconstruct the composition and put the groups in place in the building.

There is no temple deposit to assist in the chronology and we must fall back on the cemeteries, which cover the whole sixth century and extend very little into the fifth. The temple was burnt down.[3] It is natural to relate this to the sudden end of the cemetery, and infer that the town was destroyed and the Greeks driven out. Orsi connects this with Duketios.[4] But there are no red-figure vases on the site, and not the latest, fifth-century, black-figure. It is more reasonable therefore to connect it with Hippokrates' Sikel Wars. The Sikel town of Monte Bubbonia, in a strong position above one of the headwaters of the Gelas, came to an end at the end of the sixth century.[5] It is tempting to put the two together and suppose that the destruction of the one was followed by the destruction of the other.

Monte Bubbonia is a hill with steep sides everywhere but at the east, where the highest part is closed by a wall of picked stones. Inside this acropolis is the 'palace', measuring 50×7.50 m., of similar plan to that at Pantalica. The building is partly rough, partly of squared stones like Greek masonry.

---

[1] So also Van Buren, 79: 'at one time Syracusan influence predominated at the smaller city' (S. Mauro).
[2] See below, pp. 272 ff.
[3] Orsi, op. cit. 777.
[4] Ibid. 846.
[5] See below, p. 379.

It had terra-cotta revetments[1] with a simple meander. At
the foot of the hill, to the north, was a similar building
(68·30 × c. 30 m.) with large rooms round a courtyard, some of
them storerooms. This Orsi calls the 'winter palace'. The
summit of the hill had in places stone foundations of houses,
and the whole soil was covered with fragments of plain water-
jars, tiles, and lava millstones; so was the winter palace. The
painted pottery, both from the town and the cemetery[2] on the
slope to the north-east, is in about equal proportions Greek
and Siculan. There is nothing earlier than the sixth century,
the last phase of Siculan IV, some Corinthian, and rather more
Attic black-figure and black glaze vases. All the graves were
used several times. The terra-cottas are all of types represented at Gela.[3] There is also a little gold and some silver
ornaments. Most of the bronzes are Greek, and there are paste
beads and worked bone from the Greek colonies.

There is no evidence to take the occupation of the site back
earlier than the beginning of the sixth century. The exploration, especially of the cemetery, is far from complete, and it
may be that traces of earlier habitation (except Siculan I
pottery which was found under the palace) have vanished. But
it is not inconceivable that this site overhanging the plains of
Gela was seized by the Sikels during the Geloan advance, as a
counter-stroke to the Geloan attacks on Omphake and Ariaiton.
In any case, Greeks and Sikels must have reached a *modus
vivendi*. For the Greeks, a hostile power on this strong site
commanding the upper part of their plain would have been
intolerable. Moreover, the material culture was half-Greek.
The palace was built in part by Greek craftsmen,[4] and had a
decoration of painted tiles in the Greek manner such as is found
on no other Sikel site. The pottery and other grave-furniture
is in quantity more Greek than Sikel, and the Siculan pottery
is less important and less original than at contemporary Sikel
sites. Even within the houses Greek vases were used as much
as Siculan. Most of the town had only its natural defences and
was waterless. The winter palace, though it had a 'robust sur-

---

[1] Kalypter with simple meander, Van Buren, kal. 2, p. 135; gorgoneion antefix, ant. 3,
p. 137, dated early sixth century.

[2] Thirty-five graves were explored, but most of them were nearly ruined by the plough
and the pottery was in very bad condition.

[3] Including a Siren vase, like *MA*, xvii, fig. 544, a provincial imitation of a Rhodian type.

[4] *MA*, xx. 744, 'l'influenza e la direzione se non anche la mano di operai greci'; cf. Van
Buren, 45.

rounding wall', would be untenable except in time of peace. The little Sikel community had made its peace with the Geloans, with whom it lived in unusually close relations, enjoying some degree of comfort. We cannot say whether there were Greeks living at Monte Bubbonia, but it is possible. For the Geloans the chief disadvantage must have been that the wealth of the cornlands in this part of the plain went not into their granaries, but to the native prince, who built his palace with some magnificence and had at the foot of the hill another building which was at least in part a storehouse. The palace was burnt about the end of the sixth century, when the rulers of Gela put an end to these peaceful relations.[1]

LEONTINOI

The Khalkidian cities have not been favourable ground for the excavator, and nothing of the seventh century has been found at Leontinoi. In the absence of a complete series of objects from a large excavation, which should make the local specialities as well known as those of Syracuse, Megara, and Gela, there is no means of determining what objects found on inland sites are specifically Khalkidian. But the northern edge of the Heraian hills and the valley of the Fiume di Caltagirone are naturally reached from Leontinoi and from no other part of the coast. As the culture of this part of the country in the sixth century lacks some of the characteristics of sites in the territory of Syracuse or Gela, we are justified in assuming that it was hellenized from Leontinoi. As there are signs that at Naxos and Leontinoi the Khalkidians entered into friendly relations with the Sikels, so it appears that the inhabitants of the country under Leontine influence received more tolerant treatment than other natives.

Within ten miles of Leontinoi is Scordia, at the foot of a peaked hill rising out of the little plain now partly filled by the lake of Lentini, in a commanding situation. A Siculan III–IV cemetery has been excavated in part, giving Siculan vases and some Attic of the last quarter of the sixth century. Probably the site was still Sikel as late as the end of the sixth century, though further investigation is needed before the point can be proved. The top of the hill, called S. Basile or Casale, was fortified in the fifth century, and an immense reservoir provided water. This may well be the fort of Brikinniai, which the

[1] *N Sc*, 1907, 498. See below, p. 379.

Leontines held in 424.[1] It will have been fortified, and probably first seized by Greeks, during the wars of the fifth century which began with Hippokrates. There is a cemetery of the Hellenistic period; the chief grave is that of a Sikel chieftain of the late fourth century who was still barbarian enough to be buried with weapons. Considering the changes of population in this area in the fifth and fourth centuries, continuity of Sikel occupation here is unlikely, even if there were not reason to suppose that the site had been held by Greeks in the fifth century.

A site of similar nature farther north, on a strong hill called Monte Judica, had some hundred or so houses in little groups, each group with a cistern. The hill was not walled, but the weakest points of the ascent were barred. There were few sherds, which range from Siculo-Greek of the eighth or seventh century to Attic of the fifth century; an obol of Rhegion of the early fifth century was found.[2] The important Sikel town of Morgantina was in this area,[3] but there is no reason to identify Monte Judica with this or any other known place.

Not far to the south of Scordia, in the Val d'Ossini, is another Sikel site[4] which continues after the colonization. It is a small cliff-sided plateau joined to the mountains by a narrow neck 'like a little Pantalica'.[5] The graves have Siculan II–III vases and Greek vases covering the period from the middle of the eighth to the early seventh century.[6] There is more distinction about the Greek vases here than on most inland sites. They include a Rhodian plate (*RM* 1909, 83, fig. 16)[7] and a grey bucchero aryballos (cf. Johansen, 175). The flourishing nature of the Sikel town here and the continuance of Sikels in so important a stronghold as S. Basile contrast with the disappearance of all trace of them within comparable distance of Syracuse.

Intimate relations between the two races are shown at Grammichele, on the shelf which looks over the valley of the Fiume di Caltagirone and, more widely, over the plain of Leontinoi. There had been a number of small Sikel villages grouped loosely together within a few square miles. The cemetery of

---

[1] Thuk. v. 4. The identification is suggested by Orsi, *N Sc*, 1899, 276–7; Freeman, iii. 71.
[2] *N Sc*, 1907, 489 ff.   [3] Diod. xi. 78; cf. Freeman, i. 153.
[4] This site is known indifferently as Ossini and Militello.   [5] *RM*, 1909, 74.
[6] A round Corinthian aryballos, decorated with bands (Syracuse Mus. no. 22989; not mentioned by Orsi), is of the early sixth century. This is a century later than any of the other material and is apparently sporadic.   [7] See p. 474.

Molino della Badia was 'almost completely free from infiltration of Greek objects'.[1] Pottery is scarce, bronze very frequent, some of it Greek,[2] and an ivory comb is Greek.[3] This cemetery belongs to the earliest period of contact, the eighth century or early seventh. At Madonna del Piano is another Siculan II–III cemetery which has not been excavated.

A number of scattered graves at Pojo dell' Acqua belong to the Siculan IV period (seventh–sixth centuries). They lie on the slope of the hill, which was crowned by the sanctuary and had Greek graves at its foot. It would be natural to suppose that the Sikel graves were all older than the Greek occupation, among whose remains they are interspersed. But some of the pottery seems to be of the sixth century rather than the seventh, and it may be that Greeks and Sikels lived together and buried their dead in separate cemeteries. Other graves have Siculan IV vases and many more imports, Late Corinthian and Attic. Four out of forty-six are cremations, and are more probably those of Greeks than of Sikels who had assimilated the Greek rite. The other graves are of Greek types: pithoi, a cappuccina, monolith sarcophagi, and earth graves.[4] The presence of Siculan pottery in these Greek graves implies very close relations between the Sikel inhabitants and the Greek settlers.

The Greek settlement is at least as old as the late seventh century. The earliest remains are architectural terra-cottas from two sanctuaries, on the sites Madonna del Piano and Pojo dell' Acqua. The antefix from the Madonna del Piano favissa is dated to the seventh century.[5] The raking cornice from Pojo dell' Acqua belongs to the seventh or early sixth century.[6] The older of the two seated statues from the site should be put early in the sixth century.[7] Statue and revetments are difficult to date for lack of parallels, and because they are very provincial, simplicity and crudity indicating not a very early

---

[1] MA, xviii. 122.

[2] BPI, 1905, 122, fig. 26, wheel pendant, cf. Finocchito, BPI, 1897, 178, pl. vii, fig. 18; Fusco 250, N Sc, 1895, 140; Megara 660, unpublished. P. 118, spiral ἕλικες like examples in silver from Megara.

[3] BPI, 1905, 119, fig. 23.   [4] N Sc, 1920, 336–7.

[5] Van Buren, 137, ant. 1; MA, xviii. 146, fig. 7.

[6] Van Buren, 96, r. cor. 1, fig. 20; MA, vii. 261, fig. 44. Mrs. Van Buren and Darsow (Sizilische Dachterrakotten, 99) date it to the early sixth century. The nearest parallel is from the Athenaion at Syracuse (Van Buren, 85, lat. sim. 1, fig. 1), which belongs, I think, to the seventh century; so perhaps also the Grammichele piece. See below, p. 272.

[7] MA, vii, pl. 3; Van Buren, JHS, 1921, 205, says that it 'cannot be dated later than the middle of the sixth century'.

date but inexperience. But allowing that local workmen may have copied models which had gone out of date in the great cities, both sanctuaries must begin at the latest about 600.

The pottery cannot confirm this date. The Pojo dell' Acqua sanctuary produced little pottery; no Corinthian is mentioned in the publication,[1] but there is exhibited in Syracuse a Late Corinthian pyxis of the type *NC*, no. 1298. Madonna del Piano has no Corinthian but a good many small black-figure vases.[2] The earliest vases from the Pojo dell' Acqua cemetery are Late Corinthian.[3] None of the terra-cotta statuettes is so old as the beginning of the sixth century.[4] The cemetery has not been completely excavated, and the whole site is poor in pottery. But from the vases and terra-cottas we should conclude that the Greeks arrived in the second quarter of the sixth century. The revetment fragments alone carry their arrival back to the seventh century. This is another warning of the caution necessary in those cases where there is no check on the vases. The dates given for the arrival of the Greeks on other inland sites are strictly dates *ante quem*.

The Madonna del Piano deposit is a *favissa*, with no sign of the building. At Pojo dell' Acqua the terra-cotta revetments are the only architectural remains. Probably there was a little wooden building which has disappeared without trace. The other remains are equally scanty. Nothing on the acropolis hill is as old as the fifth century; there are a few house-walls, within one of which was a deposit of bronzes belonging to an ancient foundry.[5] It is impossible to be precise about the relations between Greeks and Sikels. The remains of the two sanctuaries are almost entirely Greek, though their extremely rude provincial character has caused a few of the terra-cottas to be taken for Sikel work.[6] Only in the cemeteries and in some pieces of the foundry deposit is there evidence that Sikels and Greeks were there at the same time. There are many more Greek than Siculan objects, but Siculan industry was already in a fatal decline in the sixth century. There may have been as many Greeks as Sikels living there then. The Greeks apparently did not occupy a special quarter, for groups of Greek and Sikel graves are juxtaposed. We do not know which race had political predominance, but it is clear that the Greeks came as peaceful

---

[1] See *MA*, vii. 261, black-glaze vases.
[3] *MA*, vii. 270.
[5] *BPI*, 1900, 276 ff.

[2] *MA*, xviii. 155–62.
[4] See ibid., figs. 31 and 32.
[6] See below, p. 174.

settlers, not as conquerors. They may not have all been Khalkidians, though Leontinoi is the city most conveniently placed
for intercourse. But the pithos burials of the Greek cemetery
of Madonna del Piano 'recall the Greek types of Gela and
S. Mauro'.[1] This may be because the light soil was suitable for
that sort of burial, or because some of the settlers were of
Geloan origin.[2]

The Sikel cemetery of Favara, about six miles from the site
of Grammichele, covers the sixth and early fifth centuries. It
is contemporary with the Greek settlement at Grammichele,
and the Siculan vases are very similar and in the last stages of
desiccation.[3]

Not far from Grammichele in the direction of Leontinoi was
Menai, Duketios' birthplace. It was only a small town before
his time,[4] not so important for instance as Morgantina, which
lay in this tangle of hills.[5] The existing remains of Menai are
all of later date, except two bronze lance-heads, said to be
from an early deposit, and a late black-figure skyphos.[6] The
Palikoi and their lake, and the great Sikel cult there, are not heard
of earlier than Ducetius and have no archaeological content.

Another town near the lake of the Palikoi was Eryke, which
lay ninety stades distant from the Geloan boundary.[7] This
would naturally be at the pass of Caltagirone. Eryke was
probably above the lake of the Palikoi on the west of the Fiume
di Caltagirone, the other side being occupied by Menai.[8] The

---

[1] *MA*, xviii. 126.

[2] Cf. Orsi's conclusions (ibid. 168): 'We have here a city ἀτείχιστος, unwalled, probably
rather a complex, an aggregate, of Sikel quarters, one near the other, to be placed in the
tenth to sixth centuries, on which at the beginning of the sixth was superposed the vigorous
Greek civilisation, apparently accompanied in the course of the century by an invasion, we
do not know whether violent or peaceful, of Greek racial elements, probably Khalkidians,
of Catanian and Leontine origin.'

[3] Amphora as *RM*, 1898, 340, fig. 55, but rougher; another as *MA*, vii. 265, fig. 48 *bis*.
An early Corinthian kothon, as *NC*, no. 722; Corinthian kotylai and aryballoi, Attic kylikes
and lekythoi.   [4] *BPI*, 1900, 275.

[5] Cf. Diod. xi. 78. 7: Ducetius' fame grew after his capture of the πόλιν ἀξιόλογον Μοργαν-
τῖναν. Pais, *Ancient Italy*, 138 ff., places it at Grammichele. But it lay on the borders of
Kamarina, Leontinoi, and Syracuse (Thuk. iv. 65), and Grammichele is too far north.
Perhaps Morgantina was at Licodia (Pace, *ACSA*, i. 203; *Camarina*, 50). Echetla is generally
placed at Grammichele (Orsi, *MA*, xviii. 167, doubtfully).

[6] Catania, Mus. Biscari, no. 655; Libertini, pl. LXIX.

[7] Kallias, fr. 1 (*FHG*, ii. 382), ap. Macrobius v. 19. 25: ἡ δὲ 'Ερύκη τῆς μὲν Γελῴας ὅσον
ἐνενήκοντα στάδια διέστηκεν. ἐπιεικῶς δὲ χερρός ἐστιν τό τ' ὄρος καὶ ἡ τὸ παλαιὸν Σικελῶν
γεγενημένη πόλις, ὑφ' ᾗ καὶ τοὺς Δείλλους καλουμένους εἶναι συμβέβηκεν.

[8] Pais, *Ancient Italy*, 137. On the name Eryke, cf. ibid., ch. ix. The river Eryke, named
only in Duris ap. Steph. Byz. s.v. 'Ακράγαντες, may be either the Fiume di Caltagirone or the
Margherita.

state of our knowledge of the ancient topography of Sicily is aptly summarized in an early Italian commentator's note on Eryke: 'De eius situ, ortu, et obitu non constat. Falso queritur de natura sua genus humanum, quod mortale sit, quandoquidem urbes et regna moriuntur.'[1]

Another site in this area, S. Cataldo, about ten miles north of Caltagirone, has produced a deposit of bronzes belonging to the seventh and sixth centuries, many of them Greek, including three vases. This deposit is comparable to the more interesting and important one at Mendolito.[2] In the immediate neighbourhood of S. Cataldo is a fortified Greek post at Piano dei Casazzi, which is probably due to Hippokrates, certainly to be brought into relation with the troubles of the fifth century.[3] This has absolutely nothing Sikel, and one can hardly doubt that the Sikels of S. Cataldo were suppressed and their territory held down by force.

The chief site of Orsi's Fourth Siculan period is Licodia at the head of the Dirillo, and just below the pass which is, next to that of Caltagirone, the most important route from Gela and Kamarina to Leontinoi. Neither of these are passes in the true sense of the word. The highest point in the south-east of Sicily, Monte Lauro, is just over 3,000 feet high and has a road over the top of it. The towns lie now, as then, on top of the long ridges, which are not infertile. But the valleys, and the nicks in the hills between them, are the natural means of communication, and Licodia occupies a strong position where the ground falls to the Dirillo.

The extent of the cemetery, which Orsi estimates at 200 acres,[4] shows that this was a considerable city. There are also two small outlying cemeteries. The type of grave is a rock-cut chamber with a funeral couch. Others are shafts, up to 10 feet deep, with a niche on either side. Intermediate forms show that the latter is only a simplification of the former. There is much Greek influence in the development of these forms from the common chamber tomb of the Siculan III period.[5] The contents date from the second quarter of the sixth century[6] to

---

[1] De Pinedo in Steph. Byz. s.v. Ἐρύκη.

[2] See below, p. 133.

[3] See below, p. 380.

[4] ¾ sq. km., *RM*, 1898, 308.   [5] Ibid. 326.

[6] Quatrefoil aryballos, as *NC*, no. 1263, in grave 2 (to be added to Ure's list, *Aryballoi and Figurines*, 102); unfigured Late Corinthian, Ure, op. cit. 91. Siana cup, *RM*, 1909, 68, fig. 6.

the late fifth century. The small vases, lekythoi, kylikes, kotylai, small askoi, are Greek, and most graves have an Attic lamp. The larger vases, hydriai, amphoras, oinochoai, and paterai, are Siculan. This is not without exception, but there is a good deal of regularity in the deposits. In quantity Siculan and Attic are about equal. Few of the Attic vases are even second rate, and most of them are unfigured. The metal, bronze fibulas, silver rings, buttons, &c., is all Greek.

Two miles south of Licodia is the cemetery of Scifazzo, which belonged probably to a small separate village. The form of grave is the same as at Licodia, and the contents very similar, but the cemetery is, on the whole, earlier. Grave 3, with Middle Corinthian ring-aryballos and kylikes, and grave 10, with kotylai of the type *NC*, no. 928 and other Middle Corinthian, belong to the first quarter of the sixth century. The latter has sixteen skeletons; such mass burials, common in the second Siculan period, are rare so late.

The two cemeteries give the clearest picture of a free Sikel town in the sixth and fifth centuries, becoming gradually more completely Greek in outward appearance. None of the graves is without Siculan pottery, and the proportion is fairly constant.[1] But the importance of the Siculan vases decreases. The sixth-century graves have some handsomely shaped hydriai, though their decoration is extremely limited. By the late sixth century the painted Siculan vases disappear, and only plain jugs and deep saucer-like vases (*scodelloni*) are made. There are also certain Attic vases which are found much more frequently here and on other Sikel sites than in the Greek cities,[2] e.g. the reserved-band kylikes of the type *RM*, 1898, fig. 52. These were cheap productions especially suited for the barbarian market. The lamps in tombs are also a Sikel speciality.[3]

Though it is not absolutely proved that there were Greek settlers at Licodia, it is hard to believe that there were not. The Greek influence on the form of grave indicates very close

---

[1] 6 Siculan vases, 9 Greek, in Scifazzo 3 (first quarter 6th cent.).

30 „ „ 15 „ in Scifazzo 10 (first half 6th cent.; perhaps not all contemporary).

11 „ „ 8 „ in Licodia 1 (late 6th cent.; two skeletons).

2 „ „ 6 „ in Licodia 13 (early 5th cent.).

3 „ „ 4 „ in Licodia 9 (*c.* 450).

These are the graves whose contents are most completely preserved.

[2] Cf. Orsi, *RM*, 1909, 70.

[3] For lamps in graves cf. F. Messerschmidt, *AA*, 1933, 328 ff.

contact, the Sikel borrowings being by this time not only material but affecting also their religion. Their everyday life was becoming more Greek. The only relic of their art, a gravestone,[1] though rough work and certainly Sikel, is based directly on Greek models.

It is rather unprofitable to guess what this or any other of these unknown cities was called. The topographical indications in ancient authors are too vague and apply to a period after the profound changes of the fifth century. In a very small area in the Heraian hills there are half a dozen excavated sites, and another unexcavated Sikel necropolis at Vizzini,[2] and three or four ancient names to fit them. The one thing certain is that in spite of the local pride which has affixed Eubea to the name Licodia, this was not that Leontine post or any Greek town. Euboia is still unidentified, but probably lay farther to the east, in the hills south of Leontinoi in the direction of Syracuse. Its people, like the Megarians, were carried off by Gelon to Syracuse,[3] so it was perhaps neighbouring on Syracusan and Megarian territory. Another χώρα τῆς Λεοντίνης was Xuthia,[4] which has been placed near Sortino, where the Leontine, Megarian, and Syracusan territories met. It has no history.

Probably from an undiscovered Khalkidian colony in the Heraian hills came the inscribed bronze tablet found in the 'palace' of S. Mauro.[5] This cannot belong to the Sikel town of S. Mauro, and its Ionic forms and Khalkidian alphabet make it most unlikely that it belonged to the Geloan town there. It was probably carried over from some place on the Leontine side of the hills.[6] Its date is the late sixth century. The only intelligible part of the inscription contains a homicide law; a fine of three talents is provided, and fines of two talents and one stater for this or other offences. The figure 400 which occurs twice is perhaps not a sum of money but a boule or a court of law. It is distressing to be able to do no more with this important document, but its very fragmentary state, and our inability to supplement it from other sources, make its interpretation almost impossible. It is, however, the only

[1] *N Sc*, 1902, 222, fig. 5; Libertini, *Guida*, fig. 34 r.

[2] From Vizzini comes one of the small group of Sikel bronze figures, illustrated in Pace, *ACSA*, ii. 157, fig. 147.   [3] Herod. vii. 156.

[4] Diod. v. 8; Philistos (fr. 19 Müller) ap. Steph. Byz. s.v.

[5] *MA*, xx. 831 ff.; Pace, *ACSA*, iii. 255 ff., fig. 49; V. Arangio-Ruiz and A. Olivieri, *Inscriptiones Graecae Siciliae et infimae Italiae ad ius pertinentes*, 171 ff. See above, p. 115.

[6] Orsi, *MA*, xx. 845.

archaic inscription which throws any light on the public life of the colonies, and if, as appears, it consists of a set of provisions for cases of homicide, it is part of a milder code of laws than the literary tradition about Kharondas[1] would lead us to expect in a Khalkidian city.

KATANE

The Heraian hills have been so thoroughly explored by Orsi that it is possible to form a fairly complete picture of the position of the Sikels at the end of the sixth century, just before the first of the wars that lost them their independence: a central nucleus of unsubdued Sikels who probably owed allegiance to none of the Greek cities; among them, Greek settlers who had come from all sides, a half-Greek city at Grammichele, a Greek quarter on the outskirts of the Sikel town of Caltagirone, small Greek posts for agriculture and trade rather than military purposes. Military outposts are found in this period only in the territory of Syracuse, where the Sikels had been reduced to serfdom. The Geloans and Leontines appear to have had good relations with their Sikel neighbours, but the Leontines alone were tolerant enough to mix with them more than was needed for commercial purposes. Nothing speaks certainly of admixture of blood, but at Grammichele and Licodia it is fairly clear that Greeks and Sikels were living in the same town.

The Sikels of the Heraian hills, having Greeks on three sides, were in a favourable situation to receive the benefits of civilization, and in time to suffer complete subjection. The land of the other main groups of Sikels, in the centre around Enna, and to the north on the slopes of Etna, is archaeologically less thoroughly known. But there is a group of excavated sites in the hinterland of Katane which were as well placed as the towns of the Heraian hills for intercourse with the Greeks. These northern Sikels were at least as important as the southern. The policy of Katane was as liberal as that of the other Khalkidians, to judge from the support they received from the Sikels during the Athenian invasion.[2]

Immediately behind Katane the Sikels maintained themselves at Paternò. One tomb which was in use for about a century (c. 575–475) has been published. There were about 100 skeletons; such large-scale burial in a single grave had already been given up in most Sikel places. Arms are buried, which is

---

[1] See above, p. 74.   [2] Thuk. vi. 62, 86; vii. 32, 57.

unusual so late as the sixth century and offers a presumption of barbarism. The pottery begins with Late Corinthian (aryballoi as *NC*, no. 1294) and plain black and red cups. The Siculan is limited to amphoras with linear decoration and a plain askos. Terra-cottas are Greek, including a Siren vase and a bird vase which has parallels from Rhodes.[1] There is also a crude imitation in the local grey clay of the East Greek type of Siren vase.[2] Other material in Syracuse Museum from Paternò confirms the evidence of this tomb, but the sixth and fifth centuries are less well represented than the fourth and later. The quantity of Siculan pottery is very small, but the appearance of the town is the usual one of a Sikel place becoming hellenized by slow degrees, replacing the native pottery by cheap wares from Greece. The terra-cottas and such vases as have the slightest artistic value are Greek. During the fifth century the plain Siculan pottery disappears completely. Small jugs with an orange-red glaze, resembling the pottery produced in great quantity at Randazzo,[3] on the other side of Etna, are probably local ware of the second half of the fifth century.

Paternò was probably Hybla Geleatis.[4] This identification is not proved by the dedication to Venus Victrix Hyblensis found at Paternò,[5] for this might have been made in a neighbouring town to the great goddess of Hybla. There are two sites, those of Paternò and S. Maria di Licodia, which fit the position of Hybla on the slopes of Etna, between Katane and Kentoripa, and at a later date in the territory of Katane. There are also two ancient towns known to have lain in this area: the second is Inessa-Aitna, which is stated by different authorities to have been twelve miles or eighty stades on the road to Kentoripa.[6] This agrees exactly with the distance from Catania to Paternò. But Paternò does not show traces of the violent changes of population which Aitna suffered with the expulsion of the Sikel inhabitants and resettlement as a Greek colony. The chequered history of Aitna could hardly fail to be reflected in its cemeteries. The remains of Paternò, though scanty and

---

[1] Cf. Ialysos, xxxvi. 30–41 (Maiuri, *Ann.* vi–vii. 300, fig. 195).

[2] *RM*, 1909, 87–8, fig. 17. [3] See below, p. 134 f.

[4] Thuk. vi. 94; vi. 62, ῞Υβλα ἡ Γελεᾶτις; Paus. v. 23. 6; Steph. Byz. s.v. See 'Note on Γελεᾶτις and Γαλεῶται' on p. 144. [5] *CIL*, x. 7013.

[6] *Itin. Ant.*, ed. Cuntz, p. 13; Strabo 268. Pareti, 332, n. 2, gives conflicting modern estimates of the Touring Club Italiano for the distance from Catania to Paternò: ten or twelve miles according to the exact starting-point and route. Pace in his discussion of the *Itineraries* (*ACSA*, i. 443) disregards the distances given, as the manuscript tradition is so bad that no conclusions may safely be drawn.

insufficient to illustrate the progress of hellenization, suit a sacred place of the Sikels which was still barbarian at the end of the fifth century but was already considerably hellenized. It is therefore difficult to accept the identification of Aitna with Paternò which the *Itinerary* suggests. S. Maria di Licodia, which has not been excavated,[1] is about three miles beyond Paternò, a good deal more than eighty stades from Catania, but I do not think the figures sufficiently certain to exclude the identification of this site with Aitna. It is unlikely that either Hybla or Aitna is on some undiscovered site, for, though there has been little scientific excavation, the southern slopes of Etna are too well known for an important place to have lain completely hidden. The common view which places Hybla at Paternò and Inessa-Aitna at S. Maria di Licodia is probably correct. But the difficulty of reaching certainty about these two sites, although much more is known about them than about most places in the interior of Sicily, shows that in dealing with most of the excavated sites it is hardly worth discussing conjectures for the ancient name.[2]

It is particularly unfortunate that it is not possible to be certain of the identification of Paternò with Hybla, because Hybla is one of the most important of Sikel places. It was probably this Hybla at which Hippokrates died,[3] and which alone of the Sikel towns declined to join Duketios.[4] The Hyblaians are the only Sikel people known to have made a dedication in Greece, a statue of Zeus at Olympia.[5] Their goddess, known only as the Hyblaian goddess, but later identified with Aphrodite, was honoured not only by the Sikel people but also by the Greeks of Sicily.[6] Her priests were interpreters of visions; the Galeotai consulted by Dionysios' mother, and by Dionysios himself, were probably these priests of Hybla

---

[1] The only antiquities I know are a bird vase with Cypriote affinities (*RM*, 1909, 88, fig. 18, *r*) and a gorgoneion antefix (Van Buren, 144, ant. 35). Only the latter has any relevance to the state of the town in the fifth century, and a single object can establish nothing.

[2] Cf. Pace, *ACSA*, i. 426 ff., on the difficulty of identifying sites named in the *Itineraries*.

[3] See below, p. 404.   [4] Diod. xi. 88. 6.   [5] Paus. v. 23. 6.

[6] Philistos ap. Paus. loc. cit. (fr. 49 Müller). Philistos says that the Hyblaians were pious above all the *barbarians* of Sicily; he does not say their activity was limited to the barbarians. Pausanias speaks of the fame of the goddess παρὰ Σικελιωτῶν. It is not certain that Philistos is his authority, much less that Philistos used the word Σικελιῶται. But though by Pausanias' time it was used of all the inhabitants of Sicily, whether their origin was Greek or barbarian, it is probable that in this case, where he quotes in the next sentence τῶν ἐν Σικελίᾳ βαρβάρων from Philistos, he is using Σικελιῶται with the proper antithesis between Greek and barbarian.

Geleatis.[1] The temple whose fifth-century revetment has been found at Paternò[2] belonged in all probability to this goddess who attracted the worship of the Greeks.

Terra-cotta revetments of this period are rare and unimportant in the Greek cities of Sicily, and there are few examples of the developed style in which polychromy is given up and the design is in relief picked out in black on white. Being in a small town, and in a fashion which was already being given up in the great cities, the Paternò revetment may be later than the revetment of the Olympieion of Syracuse, to which it is close.[3] The sima, with palmette and lotus in relief, is of a type not known elsewhere in Sicily but common in Magna Graecia, though it is not very close to any example there.[4] Terra-cotta revetments were given up in Sicily before the general adoption of this Ionic type from south Italy. It seems that the small town at Paternò, not able to pay for the most progressive artists, decorated its temple in a fashion already out of date in the big cities, probably by the hands of artists who found their livelihood slipping from them in their own cities. This is quite in place in a Sikel town which, though it has made considerable progress in hellenization, is still regarded by the Syracusans as barbarian. It would not be expected in Aitna, the city of Hieron's Peloponnesian settlers.

Farther west on the rich slopes of Etna another cult survived the absorption of the Sikels. The worship of Hadranos, the fire-god identified with Hephaistos, and the temple in the sacred grove guarded by a thousand hounds who knew how to distinguish friend from enemy,[5] were famous all over Sicily from the fourth century onwards. The town of Hadranon was founded by Dionysios. Its Sikel predecessor lay in the valley of the Symaithos below, at Mendolito. While only cemeteries have been excavated on most Sikel sites, here the cemetery has not been found, but part of the town, houses built of lava blocks, which show 'a development of singular decorative architectural forms applied to the native lava',[6] and a rough city wall of piled stones. In one of the houses, within a pithos, was a deposit of bronze weighing nearly a ton. This was a

---

[1] See 'Note on Γελεᾶτις and Γαλεῶται' on p. 144.

[2] Van Buren, lateral sima 40 (p. 94), dated to the second half of the fifth century; geison 33 (p. 110), to the end of the sixth century, probably by a slip for fifth century.

[3] Van Buren 111, geison 39.

[4] Darsow, *Sizilische Dachterrakotten*, 27, regards it as an import from south Italy.

[5] Aelian, *NA* xi. 3.   [6] *N Sc*, 1909, 387.

smith's hoard, to be melted down and used again, and consisted of fragments of plain vases, lances, and pieces in relief for attachment to dress and perhaps to wooden objects. Fibulas are few. There are also large lumps of unworked bronze and some lumps of iron. The most interesting pieces are bronze belts and buckles with simple patterns in relief, for the most part linear or in groups of dots, but rising once to a crude schematization of a face.[1] None of these pieces can be asserted to be Greek, and few of them show a close imitation of Greek work. There can be little doubt that they are nearly all the product of local workshops, in which Greek influence on the decoration is felt from the seventh century onwards, but does not alter the Sikel character of the work.[2]

Greek influence is seen most clearly in the barbarous copies of architectural terra-cottas, chief of which is a lion's head in red clay full of volcanic matter, without modelling except for the deep-set eyes and flame-like hair.[3] A flat fragment decorated with stamped concentric circles with two dots between each may have served an architectural purpose. The decoration is that of a stamped pithos, but this fragment is not curved, and so cannot have been part of a pithos. Orsi speaks of rough sculpture in lava from this site, showing a corruption of archaic Greek motives,[4] but I do not know the pieces to which he refers.

The bronze statuette called the ephebos of Adernò,[5] which has had a certain renown in discussions of west Greek sculpture, is not relevant to the Sikel town, as it was certainly not locally made. Equally important in themselves, and as indications of the progress of Mendolito in the fifth century, are two inscriptions on the rims of otherwise plain pithoi. These are two of the four known Sikel inscriptions, the others being on an askos in Carlsruhe from Kentoripa and on a bronze statuette in Catania, probably found in the province of Catania.[6] People who were writing their own language in Greek letters and setting their own artists to copy Greek architectural and sculptural forms were proceeding towards a genuine Greco-Siculan

[1] *Ausonia*, viii. 55, fig. 4, illustrates a few of these belts, and a bronze statuette from Mendolito wearing one (fig. 3); cf. Pace, *ACSA*, i. 164, fig. 81.

[2] Orsi speaks (*N Sc*, 1909, 387) of Greek influence from the seventh or possibly the eighth century on the local pottery. I have seen nothing older than the seventh century, and no imported Greek pottery older than the last quarter of the sixth century; but I have not had access to all the material.

[3] Darsow, *Sizilische Dachterrakotten*, 12.   [4] *N Sc*, 1912, 415.

[5] *Ausonia*, viii. 44 ff., pl. 2; Pace, *ACSA*, ii. 59, fig. 62.

[6] Whatmough, *Prae-Italic Dialects*, ii. 441 ff.

culture to which both sides should contribute—not, as had already happened in the Heraian hills and finally happened all over Sicily, an absorption of the Sikel by the Greek.[1]

Kentoripa was a place of some degree of riches in archaic times, though little earlier than the Hellenistic period has survived. The inscribed askos has just been mentioned; its alphabet, derived from the Khalkidian, differs from it in the form of lambda (Γ for L).[2] The Grotta dell' Acqua tomb, which contained many skeletons, from the early seventh century (*RM* 1909, 97, fig. 26, scarab, fibulas of ivory and amber) to the middle of the sixth (Late Corinthian kotyle, red-and-black-banded kylix, ibid. 98), has Greek imports more varied and numerous than most Sikel sites, including ivories (ibid., fig. 23) and worked amber as well as the objects already mentioned. The Mammana collection, made in Centuripe and now in Syracuse Museum, contains a few sixth-century objects.[3] In Palermo is some late sixth-century material which adds nothing to the picture of prosperity obtained from the Grotta dell' Acqua tomb.

On the western side of Etna, at a height of over 2,000 feet, was a small town at S. Anastasia near Randazzo. Everything about this place, pottery, terra-cottas, and burial methods,[4] is Greek. The earliest pottery is Late Corinthian: kotylai and miniature oinochoai, stamnoi, pyxides, hydriai, and a kothon, all decorated entirely with lines and dots. The kotylai, which are most numerous, are exactly like those at Lokroi.[5] It is very unlikely that any of them are other than Corinthian, but they

[1] It is unfortunately impossible to be as full as I should like on this important and interesting site. Only short notes on Orsi's explorations have been published (see Bibliography), and most of the material is no longer accessible. For the plan of the town and the architectural details these notes are the only evidence, as the site has been partly covered up again, partly overgrown. The bronzes have never been adequately studied, and it is possible to see only a small selection of them. The collection of antiquities made by Petronio Russo has been neglected since his death, and I could obtain no information about it at Adranò. Some of it is illustrated by G. Paternò Castello, *Nicosia etc. (Italia Artistica*, no. 34), on p. 130: the illustration shows only Greek vases, the earliest being b.f. of the end of the sixth century. Russo's own book, *Adernò* (Catania, 1911), is a typical piece of Sicilian erudition, abounding in learned conjecture about the Cyclopes. Mendolito and Dionysios' foundation of Hadranon would well repay further exploration on the sites and in the magazines of Syracuse Museum.

[2] Libertini, *Centuripe*, 8; *CAH*, iv. 436; Whatmough, *Prae-Italic Dialects*, ii. 444. Sikel alphabet, ibid. 541.

[3] Terra-cotta of Rhodian type (Libertini, op. cit. 101). A Protocorinthian kotyle, and a lakaina, exhibited with the collection in Syracuse, are not certainly from Centuripe.

[4] Of the graves published in 1907, four are cremations, sixty-six tile sarcophagi; cf. Rizzo, *RM*, 1900, 238, tombs *a cappuccina*.   [5] For which cf. below p. 262.

all belong to the latest phase, in the second half of the sixth or even in the fifth century.[1] A terra-cotta antefix (Van Buren, 138) is of the late sixth century. Though it is unlikely that there is any local imitation of Corinthian, pottery was manufactured, small bright red oinochoai, rarely with black bands, being the commonest shape. Small plates, with one or two handles, and stamnoi, are also frequent, with the same orange-red glaze. Most of these adopt Attic shapes of the late fifth century. One curious hydria, clay a light red, paint a dull black washed to brown for the lines, with three running figures in black silhouette, is among the rare and incompetent western imitations of Attic black-figure.

The Greek settlement is associated by Rizzo with the movement of population caused by Hieron's settlement of Aitna.[2] But subsequent investigations have carried the beginning back for about half a century before his date of c. 475, and it cannot be related to any event preserved in the literary history; it is simply another document of the Greek advance, which was intensified towards the end of the sixth century. The proposed identification as Tissa, *perparva ac tenuis civitas*[3] (Rizzo, p. 239, very doubtfully) or Trinakia (Van Buren, p. 82) are mere guesses. The very existence of Trinakia is doubtful, and its bit of recorded history (Diod. xii. 29) is rightly referred to Piakos.[4]

CENTRAL AND WESTERN SICILY

The material remains of the rest of Sicily do not permit of any such detailed picture of the process of hellenization as has been given for the Heraian hills and the region of Etna. The main reason for this is that the exploration of these regions has not yet been as thorough and methodical as that of eastern and south-eastern Sicily. But apart from this accident, the nature of the country and the distance from the Greek cities made

[1] Attic: lekythoi of Ure's shape H; alabastron by the Diosphos painter (Haspels, *ABL*, 237, no. 107). The Lakonian krater, Mingazzini, *I Vasi Castellani*, 186, no. 36, is contemporary.

[2] *RM*, 1900, 248: 'I pochi esemplari di vasi attici a f.n. ci dicono che siamo nell' ultima fase di questo stile già declinante . . . non possiamo assegnare come *terminus a quo* della necropoli che il primo quarto del v secolo av. Cr., accostandosi, forse, un po' di più alla metà di esso.' But the material from subsequent excavations carries it back to the sixth century.

[3] *Verr.* II. iii. 38. 86; cf. Sil. Ital. xiv. 267.

[4] Pais, *Ancient Italy*, ch. xi. Piakos is placed by S. Mirone (*Demareteion*, ii. 17 ff.) at S. Maria li Plachi, north of Catania. He mentions Roman remains at many points in the neighbourhood.

central and western Sicily less open to Greek penetration. The native peoples were less advanced; the Greeks had less reason to go among them for trade or conquest. A few sites near the south coast which have recently been excavated, in the westward extension of Geloan territory and behind Akragas, illustrate the difference: Palma, Ravanusa, S. Angelo Muxaro, Mussomeli. Elsewhere, in the inland parts of western Sicily, on the north coast and in the mountains behind it, and in the very centre of the island, remains older than the fifth century are so slight that they cannot be called illuminating. There are in these areas interesting sites which may be expected with the progress of excavation to give material for comparison with better-known regions. But it is already clear that hellenization proceeded more slowly in the west, and that the natives did not develop so fast either by their own efforts or through Greek influence. This is not due to the different capacities of Sikel and Sikan, peoples who are not distinguishable archaeologically, but to geographical reasons.

At Enna there is a small collection which I have not seen, of which Orsi mentions 'a few Corinthian vases and some black Attic of local provenience . . . documentation of Greek Enna of the sixth century'.[1] I am informed that there is not enough material to support Stephanus' supposed Syracusan colony, or to throw light on the process of hellenization. At Conventazzo on the Lago di Pergusa, scene of the rape of Persephone, was a Sikel town with ordinary Siculan IV pottery of the sixth century and a few Greek imports beginning c. 550:[3] a poor place with no essential differences from the Licodia type.

The remains of Serra Orlando near Aidone, and especially the farm-implements,[4] are very informative for the condition of the interior in the fourth and third centuries, when it appears that the little town was inhabited by men of uncertain descent but Greek customs, who went out to till the neighbouring fields and brought their implements home with them. The likeness to the modern system of agriculture extends to the shape of hoe and ploughshare. Two black-figure lekythoi and

---

[1] *N Sc*, 1931, 375. There is in Syracuse Museum a Corinthian kothon of the type of *NC*, fig. 135, said to be from Enna; in Oxford, a Late Corinthian aryballos (ibid., no. 1273).

[2] Ἔννα, πόλις Σικελίας, κτίσμα Συρακοσίων, μετὰ ὁ΄ ἔτη Συρακουσῶν. The date is that of Akrai. For Pace's suggestion that Ἔννα is a mistake for Ἴνα see above, p. 103.

[3] Corinthian kothon; Lakonian black krater, Mingazzini, *I Vasi Castellani*, 186, no. 39; unfigured Attic from last quarter of the sixth century. Other material in Enna Museum, *RM*, 1898, 345–6.   [4] Illustrated by Pace, *ACSA*, i, figs. 161–2.

a seated terra-cotta statuette of the last quarter of the sixth century are the earliest objects from this site, but throw no light on the origin of the town. There is nothing Sikel, but a few Greek things of the late sixth and early fifth centuries are not enough, without an account of the circumstances of their discovery, to establish that the place was Greek at that date.

At Alimena, twenty miles north of Enna at the foot of the Madonie mountains 3,000 feet above sea-level, there is an ancient town with 'Cyclopean' walls and an extensive but poor Greek cemetery. Such material as I have seen dates from the late sixth century onwards and has nothing Sikel.[1] If this were indeed a Greek settlement, in one of the poorest and most mountainous parts of Sicily, and most remote from any Greek colony,[2] it supports the view that Enna, the capital of the district, was Greek. But so little is known of this part of the country that it is rash to form any opinion on its circumstances.

I give a brief summary of the earliest Greek material from other sites in the centre of Sicily.

Gangi: in Palermo, unpublished: Late Corinthian kothons and black-figure oinochoai of the early fifth century; plain oinochoai and 'saucers'. No distinctively Siculan pottery.

Troina: negro's head vase, Catania, Museo Biscari, no. 869, Libertini, pl. xcix. The 'Cyclopean' wall (G. Paternò-Castello, *Nicosia etc., Italia Artistica*, no. 34, p. 97) is no doubt later.

Nicosia: Paternò-Castello, op. cit. 10, mentions *vasi greco-siculi* among other antiquities found there. At or near Nicosia was perhaps Engyon, mythically a Cretan foundation, celebrated for its temple of the Mothers.[3]

Geloan expansion to the east and north-east was limited by other Greek communities. To the west they had a free field, and their occupation of the central part of the south coast was as intensive as that of the hill-country nearer to them. Akragas, which became an independent colony in 580 B.C., was already occupied by Geloans as a trading-post, probably in the late seventh century.[4] Other intermediate points were Geloan at

[1] Marconi, *N Sc*, 1928, 510 n.: 'le testimonianze archeologiche risalgono in parte maggiore al periodo ellenico (o, diremo meglio, ellenizzante); ma trovai quantità notevole di frammenti ceramici preistorici, del II e III periodo siculo'.

[2] The nearest Greek colony is Himera, from which, however, the mountains cut it off except by difficult and devious routes.

[3] Diod. iv. 79–80. Engyon is frequently placed at Gangi (e.g. by Freeman, i. 146), but that is too far from Agyrion whence stone for its temple was brought.

[4] See below, pp. 305 ff.

the same period. The chief of them is Palma di Montechiaro, near the coast about fifteen miles east of Akragas. A number of points in the neighbourhood of Palma were occupied before the middle of the sixth century, some of them at the beginning of the century or perhaps even in the seventh.[1] The most interesting is a small country sanctuary near a sulphureous spring, among whose not very precious offerings were three wooden statues which have been preserved by the action of the sulphur. These are most valuable as the oldest Greek wooden sculpture extant[2] and also as pieces of archaic sculpture whose Sicilian origin cannot be questioned. The oldest of them is a little earlier than the middle of the sixth century, which is also the date of the earliest terra-cottas and vases.[3]

Palma was probably the Daedalium named in the *Itinerary*[4] as the stage between Akragas and Phintias (Licata). The name of Daidalos is associated with the territorial advance of both Gela and Akragas.[5] Daedalium might belong geographically to either, but it is now certain that this area was visited by Greeks before the foundation of Akragas, and so it may confidently be called Geloan. The castle of Palma and the hill Castellazzo above the sea control the road from Akragas to Licata and there is also passable shelter, which was important on the harbourless south coast of Sicily. Though Palma did not develop into an independent colony as Akragas did, its early importance may be judged by considering the evidence of Greek penetration into the country behind.

A Greek town at Ravanusa is at least as old as the seventh century, though there is little material older than the foundation of Akragas.[6] Its sixth-century graves are of a type known

---

[1] From the town of Palma a Middle Corinthian alabastron (*BPI*, 1928, 61; cf. *NC*, 303, group B). At Piano della Città a fortified site occupied by Greeks in the sixth century. At Castellazzo, on a hill above the sea, a Greek site with some sixth-century material, but more of the fifth and fourth centuries.

[2] See G. M. A. Richter, *Kouroi*, 14, n. 11.

[3] Caputo dates the bad Late Corinthian pottery (*MA*, xxxvii. 619–20, figs. 24–5) too early in suggesting a seventh-century date.

[4] p. 13, ed. Cuntz. Caputo's suggestion (ibid. 683) that the sacred spring was called Gelonium stagnum (Solinus, v. 21–2) is not contradicted by this conjecture of the name of the town.   [5] See p. 318.

[6] Corinthian vases (*MA*, xxxvi. 672, fig. 30c (Late Corinthian kotyle) and p. 667; Attic, Siana cup, late (ibid., figs. 26–7). A Protocorinthian cup of the early seventh century (ibid. 685, fig. 40) was found casually; this is about 100 years older than any of the material found in the excavations. Mingazzini (ibid. 687 ff.) suggests that this town was founded about 580 by Geloans and passed from Gela to Akragas at the time of Phalaris (a fragment of pithos-rim, ibid. 683, fig. 38, is Akragantine). See below, p. 317.

elsewhere only at Gela.[1] There was probably a small Greek post at Canicatti, where Corinthian and Attic black-figure vases have been found.[2] Corinthian vases are said to have been found in the construction of the railway from Canicatti to Licata.[3] The site at Naro in the same neighbourhood has nothing Greek older than the end of the sixth century. At Monte Sabbucina near Caltanisetta on a Siculan III site is a siren vase, a Geloan imitation of a Rhodian type,[4] and a lydion, such as are found more frequently at Gela than other Sicilian sites. There is also a fragment of pithos rim, with Nike and chariot, which is Akragantine.[5] Both Geloans and Akragantines, therefore, were trading with these Sikels in the sixth century. Another site near Caltanisetta, at Gibil-Gabib, has extensive Greek cemeteries, nothing in which, however, is older than the fifth century.[6] Vassalagi, near S. Cataldo in the same district, is the site of 'an unknown Sikel town, hellenized in the fifth century', according to Orsi; the Greek cemetery begins probably in the fourth century.

This territory could be reached from the coast either from Gela or more naturally from Palma or Licata. Licata, the ancient Eknomos at the mouth of the southern Himeras, is better situated than Palma for trade with Ravanusa and Caltanisetta, and was probably used for the purpose. It has produced few remains of antiquity, but these include some late sixth-century terra-cottas.[7] The literary evidence associates Eknomos with Phalaris and names a φρούριον Φαλάριδος there, but gives some ground for supposing that there was already a Greek post before Phalaris.[8]

There are two excavated sites in the country behind Akragas. S. Angelo Muxaro, on the Platani, the ancient Halykos, is Sikel until the early fifth century. The tholos tombs, the largest in Sicily, were in use from the eighth century, if not

[1] Marconi, N Sc, 1930, 413.
[2] Coll. de Angelis, Agrigento (I thank Mr. D. F. Allen for drawings of these vases). The earliest is a Late Protocorinthian kotyle of the type NC, no. 191, fig. 9 c, which continues until the last quarter of the seventh century.
[3] N Sc, 1879, 231. Some of the material was sent to the Museo Preistorico in Rome, but I have not traced it there. At Passarelli near Campobello in the same locality were found graves with 'geometric' vases, whose nature and date is uncertain (ibid. 233).
[4] Syracuse Museum, unpublished; cf. M A, xvii, figs. 23, 544 (both Rhodian).
[5] Cf. Marconi, Agrigento, 201 ff., figs. 137–9.
[6] Salinas, N Sc, 1884, 446, corrects the reference in N Sc, 1881, 251 to Corinthian vases.
[7] Palermo Museum, unpublished; cf. Mingazzini, M A, xxxvi. 687, n. 1.
[8] See below, p. 317.

earlier, to the early fifth. Only towards the end of that period are there a few Greek imports. There are no Protocorinthian or Early Corinthian vases. That is, the Greek imports begin about the date of the foundation of Akragas.[1] The commonest vases are tall oinochoai with a bright orange-red varnish, whose shape, and especially the trefoil mouth, is derived from Corinthian examples. Long-stemmed vases with basin-like top (*fruttiere*), derived from a Siculan II type of south-eastern Sicily, especially common at Cassibile, are almost as frequent. 'Saucers' and amphoras of Siculan shape are rather rare.

It is not possible to say how long the Siculan pottery continued, as the contents of the tombs cannot be separated into the individual deposits which will have accompanied each burial. But the small quantity and comparative poverty of the Greek imports suggest that they did not supplant the local industry, and the profusion of oinochoai, which are nearest in shape to Early Corinthian models, but tend to become taller and thinner, makes it probable that they lasted for some time after 600.[2] The latest deposit, black-glaze kotyle, oinochoe, &c., of the early fifth century, was at the feet of one skeleton. The latest material in the other tombs is lekythoi of the same date. Down to that period, therefore, the Sikel chiefs kept up their ancestral rites and customs, and show small signs of intercourse with their Greek neighbours.[3]

S. Angelo Muxaro, occupying a strong position above the Platani near the Akragas–Himera road, would be an effective bar to Akragantine expansion northwards. It also commands some of the best corn-land in the district. Mussomeli, higher up the Platani and commanding the same route from the slopes of a peak with sides like a glass-house, shows little trace of

---

[1] Oinochoe from grave 6, Middle Corinthian, shape as *NC*, fig. 10 G; short rays at foot, body black, goat on shoulder; dot rosette as on *NC*, no. 1073, and incised rosette with petals indented. Late Corinthian stamnos in grave 4.

[2] Some of these may be made by Greek hands (cf. pp. 171 ff., 264, below); e.g. Orsi, op. cit. *infra*, figs. 6 and 9. Orsi looks for parallels in Crete, and, though he does not find them, fig. 9 might be a seventh-century Cretan vase.

[3] Orsi, 'La Necropoli di S. Angelo Muxaro' (*Atti della R. Acc. di Palermo*, xvii, 1932). Other material in Giudice Coll. in Agrigento and in Palermo, from Giudice Coll. This is in the main Siculan II. Following Orsi, I have called the inhabitants Sikels, not Sikans. Cf. op. cit. 18: 'Ho sempre parlato e di proposito di Siculi e non di Sicani. Il tipo dei sepolcri ed il rito di seppellimento a masse od a famiglie, cogli arti lunghi ancora, per quanto debolmente, piegati, sono caratteristiche ostinatamente conservate dalle gente primitive. Ebbene: esse sono comuni a tutta la Sicilia di quà e di là delle due Imeri. I corredi e le suppellettili sono cose accessorie; ma anche essi, salvo lievi ed accidentali variazioni di tinte, sono comuni alle due regioni.'

Greek influence in the Third Siculan period.[1] It has some of the most remarkable examples of native art in Sicily, including an oinochoe with the only known painting of the human figure in Siculan pottery. The filiation of this work is uncertain, but it must owe a good deal to the imagination of the painter. The shape is influenced, perhaps at second hand, by Protocorinthian oinochoai. The village has been excavated and has yielded only one fragment of an uncertain Greek fabric, and quantities of fragments of large vases incised with chevrons, wavy lines, hatched triangles, and concentric circles. This is akin to the ware of the period of transition from Siculan II to III on eastern sites. The Greek influence is less than in the east, and the pottery is probably later, but more traditional, than in regions which came into contact with the Greeks. The cemetery has produced almost purely Siculan III pottery, both incised and painted. A 'mysterious edifice' contained Greek ivories (Syracuse Mus. 45242–6), a disk with cable-pattern and dots being exactly paralleled at the Athenaion of Syracuse. Another interesting object found at Mussomeli is a bronze axe with a Corinthian *beta* inscribed on it, part of a hoard of bronze.[2]

It is difficult to say how long this independent Sikel town lasted. There are only casual Greek imports, none certainly later than the early sixth century. The place can hardly have maintained its independence after the Akragantines reached across to Himera, but it is not known how long before Theron that contact was established.[3]

S. Angelo Muxaro and Mussomeli are the first two native sites in western Sicily to be thoroughly explored. Comparison between the material and that of south-eastern sites shows that the culture of the two regions was beyond question the same. There is no archaeological reflection of the division of Sikel and Sikan, and though identity of culture does not prove identity of race, the common burial customs as well as the similarity between the pottery makes it probable that they were closely related. But the natives of western and eastern Sicily reacted differently to Greek culture. The Sikels of the Heraian hills, hemmed in on every side by Greeks who were ready to exploit or enslave them, had lost their independent culture at a time

---

[1] Gàbrici, 'Polizzello, abitato preistorico presso Mussomeli' (*Atti della R. Acc. di Palermo*, 1925). Unpublished material in Syracuse Museum.

[2] *AA*, 1926, 333–4; for the hoard see *BPI*, 1925, 155; Ebert, *Reallex. d. Vorgesch.* ii. 371, no. 38.

[3] See below, p. 420.

when that of S. Angelo Muxaro was at its height. The eastern Sikels of the Heraian hills and Etna absorbed Greek customs and Greek art sooner than their western relatives. They could be regarded as hellenized when the chieftains of S. Angelo Muxaro were still guarding their independence. But some of the most striking examples of Sikel art come from the west, though this end of the island has been so much less thoroughly explored. The most elaborate and finest painted Siculan vases are a few from S. Angelo Muxaro, the most original from Mussomeli. The eastern Sikels were swamped, those of the west were able to absorb what they received of Greek example and held much more firmly to their traditions. It is not possible in the present state of our knowledge to carry out the comparison in detail. But the vigour and tenacity shown on the western sites are in marked contrast to the melancholy spectacle of Licodia Eubea, where a decadent Sikel culture is replaced by a third-rate Greek.

The north coast between Mylai and Himera was almost untouched until the fifth century was well advanced. It is a mountainous coast with only small patches of good land, and the Madonie mountains, rising to over 6,000 feet, cut it off from the rest of Sicily. But it is surprising to find sites which afterwards prospered at Tyndaris, Halaisa, Haluntion, Kale Akte remaining neglected. The neighbourhood of Tyndaris has some Greek imports in the early fifth century;[1] an enigmatical piece of sculpture from Mistretta[2] favours the view that there was some Phoenician influence on this coast. The Sikel fortress of Cephaloedium has a rare instance of a building which is Greek but does not conform to normal standards; on a rock behind the town a rude megalithic shelter over a spring was embellished with a spring-house, in a rough pseudo-polygonal style, with finished doorways whose mouldings are clearly due to Greek workmen. The shelter is pre-Greek; the building in front of it was first put up in the late sixth century, if not later.[3] The walls of Cefalù, which join the acropolis to the harbour, are certainly later (fourth century), like most walls on Sikel sites. Cefalù is near Himera. Another strong post near Himera, at Castellaccio on the side of Monte S. Calogero, about equidistant from Himera and Thermae (Termini), was fortified by the Greeks probably in the sixth century. There are Siculan IV

---

[1] B.f. lekythoi from Patti in Palermo Museum.
[2] Pace, *ACSA*, ii. 115, fig. 108.　　　　[3] *N Sc*, 1929, 273 ff.

and Greek sherds here, in a cave; which indicates that it was a place of refuge for Sikels. Elsewhere on the mountain Sikel occupation is continuous before and after the foundation of Himera.[1] The hellenized village of the sixth century and later is a poor one. At some uncertain date it was moved down to a lower point on the hill, where there are exclusively Greek remains.[2]

The degree of hellenization of Segesta can be judged by the fact that it had marriage rights with Selinus in the late fifth century,[3] and from the whole account of Segesta in Thukydides' narrative of the Sicilian expedition one would hardly gather, except when he specifically insists on it, that it was not a Greek city. The unfinished temple belongs to this period. Unfortunately it is not possible to follow the stages of hellenization from the archaeological record. There is Siculan II material, and Siculan III–IV in a grotto under the theatre, access to which was left when the theatre was built, thus demonstrating continuity of worship.[4] Apart from these scanty remains, excavation has revealed nothing older than the fourth century.

The other main site of the Elymians,[5] Eryx, lay in the Carthaginian corner and may best be considered with the Phoenician cities. The rest of the Elymian territory is as little known in the archaic period as Segesta; and western Sicily is, with the north coast, the least explored part of Sicily. There are Siculan III vases, with nothing Greek, from Sambuca; Attic lekythoi of the early fifth century from Vicari and Contessa Entellina, near Entella, which was more probably Sikan than Elymian;[6] plain pottery akin to that of Motye from Partanna, Salemi, Milocca, and other western sites.[7] The pieces of Punic shape at Salemi are of the fourth and third centuries. Partanna is almost directly inland from Selinus: the scantiness of Greek objects in this part of the country suggests that Selinus was concerned only with the road across to Segesta, not with the native peoples in the way.[8]

---

[1] *N Sc*, 1936, 462 ff.; Mauceri, *Sopra una acropoli pelasgica esistente nei dintorni di Termini Imerese* (1896); *MA*, xviii. 426 ff.

[2] Ibid. 473.

[3] Thuk. vi. 6. 2.

[4] *N Sc*, 1929, 295 ff.

[5] For the Elymians see further below, pp. 335 ff.

[6] Cf. Freeman, i. 122; Elymian according to late sources (cited by Bérard, *Colonisation*, 378).

[7] All in Palermo Museum, unpublished.

[8] For relations between Selinus and the Phoenicians see below, pp. 334 ff., 352 f.

NOTE ON ΓΕΛΕΑΤΙΣ AND ΓΑΛΕΩΤΑΙ

Thuk. vi. 62. 5: Ὕβλα ἡ Γελεᾶτις.

Paus. v. 23. 6: αἱ δὲ ἦσαν ἐν Σικελίᾳ πόλεις αἱ Ὕβλαι, ⟨ἡ μὲν⟩ Γερεᾶτις ἐπίκλησιν, τὴν δὲ—ὥσπερ γε καὶ ⟨ἦν⟩—ἐκάλουν Μείζονα. ἔχουσι δὲ καὶ κατ' ἐμὲ ἔτι τὰ ὀνόματα, ἐν τῇ Καταναίᾳ δὲ ἡ μὲν ἔρημος ἐς ἅπαν, ἡ δὲ κώμη τε Καταναίων ἡ Γερεᾶτις καὶ ἱερόν σφισιν Ὑβλαίας ἐστὶ θεοῦ, παρὰ Σικελιωτῶν ἔχον τιμάς. παρὰ τούτων δὲ κομισθῆναι τὸ ἄγαλμα ἐς Ὀλυμπίαν ἡγοῦμαι· τεράτων γὰρ σφᾶς καὶ ἐνυπνίων Φίλιστος ὁ Ἀρχομενίδου φησὶν ἐξηγητὰς εἶναι καὶ μάλιστα εὐσεβείᾳ τῶν ἐν Σικελίᾳ βαρβάρων προσκεῖσθαι.

Steph. Byz. s.v. Ὕβλα: Ὕβλαι τρεῖς πόλεις Σικελίας. ἡ μείζων ἧς οἱ πολῖται Ὑβλαῖοι ⟨Μεγαρεῖς⟩, ἡ μικρὰ ἧς οἱ πολῖται Ὑβλαῖοι Γαλεῶται [Μεγαρεῖς], ἡ δὲ ἐλάττων Ἡραία (MS. Ἥρα) καλεῖται. ἐστὶ καὶ πόλις Ἰταλίας. ἡ δὲ ⟨μείζων⟩ Ὕβλα ἀπὸ Ὕβλωνος (MS. τὴν δὲ Ὕβλαν ἀπὸ Ὕβλου) τοῦ βασιλέως, διὰ ⟨δὲ⟩ τὸ πολλὰς Ὕβλας καλεῖσθαι τῶν Σικελῶν πόλεων τοὺς ἐνοικοῦντας ἐκάλουν Μεγαρέας· μία δὲ τῶν Ὑβλῶν Στύελλα (MS. Τιέλλα) καλεῖται, ὡς Φίλιστος τετάρτῳ Σικελικῶν. The emendations are Schubring's.

Cic. de Div. i. 20. 39 (=FHG, ed. Müller, Philistos fr. 47): 'Dionysi mater eius qui Syracosiorum tyrannus fuit, ut scriptum apud Philistum est doctum hominem et diligentem et aequalem temporum illorum, cum praegnans hunc ipsum Dionysium alvo contineret, somniavit se peperisse satyriscum. huic interpretes portentorum, qui galeotae tum in Sicilia nominabantur, responderunt, ut ait Philistus, eum quem illa peperisset clarissimum Graeciae diuturna cum fortuna fore.'

Aelian, VH xii. 46. . . . ἔφασαν οὖν οἱ Γαλεῶται πρὸς τὸν Διονύσιον ἐρόμενον ὑπὲρ τούτων, ὅτι ταῦτα μοναρχίαν δηλοῖ.

Steph. Byz. s.v. Γαλεῶται· ἔθνος ἐν Σικελίᾳ ἢ ἐν τῇ Ἀττικῇ ἀπὸ Γαλεώτου υἱοῦ Ἀπόλλωνος καὶ Θεμιστοῦς. . . . τινὲς δὲ ὅτι Γαλεῶται μάντεων εἶδος Σικελῶν. γαλεός δὲ καὶ ὁ ἀσκαλαβώτης . . . καὶ Ἄρχιππος Ἰχθύσιν·

τί λέγεις συ; μάντεις εἰσὶ γὰρ θαλάττιοι;
— γαλεοί γε πάντων μάντεων σοφώτατοι.

Hesychius: γαλεοί· μάντεις. οὗτοι κατὰ τὴν Σικελίαν ᾤκησαν. καὶ γένος τι, ὡς φησι Φανόδημος καὶ Ῥίνθων Ταραντῖνος.
Γαλεώτης· ὁ ἀσκαλαβώτης. καὶ ἰχθῦς. καὶ ζῶον χερσαῖον.

See Pareti, Studi Siciliani, 331 ff. (I Galeotai, Megara Iblea, ed Ibla Geleatide); Ziegler, RE, ix. 25 ff., s.v. Hybla; Freeman, i. 512 ff.

The true form of the epithet of Hybla is Γελεᾶτις as in Thuk. vi. 62. 5. Pausanias' Γερεᾶτις (v. 23. 6) is presumably due to faulty manuscript transmission. It is absurd to quote it as having Philistos' authority (Pareti, 342) or to regard it as an earlier form changed in honour of Gelon (Ciaceri, Studi Storici, ii. 174). By etymology the name may be connected with the Sikel root of Γέλας (Ziegler, RE, ix. 26), but it is not even certain that it is Sikel.

Stephen in his corrupt and confused note calls the citizens Ὑβλαῖοι Γαλεῶται. This may be regarded as a confusion with the Γαλεῶται of Philistos ap. Cicero, de Div. i. 20. 39 (= fr. 47 Müller), and Aelian, VH xii. 46, and does not certainly prove that the Γαλεῶται were associated with Hybla Geleatis. But this association is likely on grounds other than etymological. According to Philistos ap. Cicero, the Galeotai in Sicily interpreted a portentous vision of Dionysios' mother. According to Aelian, Dionysios himself consulted the

Galeotai. Aelian's authority is also Philistos, as the same story is told by Cicero, *de Div.* i. 33, without mention of the Galeotai, but naming Philistos as authority (fr. 48 Müller). Philistos is therefore authority for the consultations of Dionysios' mother and of Dionysios with the Galeotai. It is possible that the two references are to the same passage of Philistos: it is a strain on coincidence to allow no connexion whatever between them (Pareti, 341). The scene is not specified further than Sicily. Cicero speaks of the Galeotai as Sicilians, but not as a 'γένος di μάντεις di tal nome, diffuso anche tra i Sicelioti non appartenenti a una sola città, e consultabile specialmente a Siracusa', as Pareti, loc. cit.; cf. Ziegler, loc. cit. *supra*: 'waren die Γαλεῶται keine Bevölkerung einer bestimmten Stadt, sondern ein in Sizilien verbreitetes γένος oder εἶδος μάντεων'. If the fame of the goddess of Hybla was spread among the Sicilians, as Pausanias says, probably on the authority of Philistos, the seers of Hybla could be consulted at Hybla by people from all over Sicily. Though Cicero and Aelian do not associate the Galeotai with Hybla, the chief reason is the vagueness with which they both write.

The ethnic of Γελεᾶτις would be Γελεᾶται, of which Γελεῶται is a possible variant. The form Γαλεῶται need be only an error for this latter. It is in no good author except Cicero, and a might have been substituted for ε in the transliteration into Latin. The alternative derivation of Γαλεῶται from γαλεοί is not certain. Γαλεῶται might be a by-form of Γελεᾶται or Γελεῶται to bring it into line with prophetic γαλεοί. Hesykhios gives γαλεοί as the name of the seers of Sicily, and a fragment of Arkhippos' *Fishes* names the γαλεοί, the fish, as the wisest of seers. It is not too outrageous to see in Arkhippos only a pun on γαλεοί and Γαλεῶται or Γελεῶται, and the γαλεοί of Hesykhios may have no other authority than Arkhippos. If the pun on γαλεοί were sufficiently successful it might influence the spelling of Γελεῶται.

One cannot be certain about the etymology of Γαλεῶται and Γελεᾶτις or even whether they are Greek or Sikel. But it is rather perverse, considering the identity of functions of the Γαλεῶται and the priests of Ὕβλα Γελεᾶτις, and the fact that Philistos is quoted for both, to deny all connexion between the two. It may be taken as probable, though by no means demonstrated, that the Galeotai consulted by Dionysios and his mother were the priests of the goddess of Hybla. If this is so, it is one of the most important cases of Sicilian Greeks adopting Sikel worship.

Steph. Byz. s.v. Γαλεῶται calls them an ἔθνος ἐν Σικελίᾳ. It is not an exact use of the word, but agrees with Philistos ap. Pausanias, where the whole people are apparently gifted with the extraordinary powers. Hesykhios s.v. Γαλεοί speaks of a γένος of γαλεοί, not necessarily either the seers or Sicilians. His authorities are Phanodemos the Atthidographer and Rhinthon of Taras. Phanodemos' reference was presumably to the ἔθνος of Γαλεῶται in Attica whom Stephen names as an alternative to the Sicilians. But nothing suggests that they also had divinatory powers and their only relevance is in suggesting that the name is Greek.

CHAPTER IV

THE EXPANSION OF THE ITALIAN COLONIES

TARAS

TARAS seems as late as the sixth century to have been a small though prosperous city. Its territory was limited to the low land immediately round the Mar Piccolo.[1] Finds, for the most part casual, of Late Corinthian and black-figure vases have been made at Massafra, Gravinola, Monteiasi, Faggiano, San Giorgio, and Leporano, all within fifteen miles of Taranto.[2] There is no native Apulian pottery in this group, and the small towns or villages to which the finds belong will have been inhabited by Greeks. Some of them had reasonably good painted vases; in particular some of the finest pieces in Taranto Museum come from Leporano, which was, unlike the other little towns, a settlement on the sea to which the Greeks had come even earlier than to Taranto. There are said to be inhabited sites round the Mar Piccolo, near Capo S. Vito, and at other points nearer to Taranto than this little ring of towns;[3] the remains are of the Roman period, so far as can be judged, but possibly represent Greek villages. We should think of this sheltered plain as fairly thickly settled with Greek villages and perhaps isolated farms.

Greek imports to Messapia before 500 are very few. At Brindisi there is Protocorinthian pottery which may be connected

---

[1] Cf. Wuilleumier, *Tarente*, 51.

[2] Leporano from 8th century (see Bibliography).

Gravinola	„	600–575 (Middle Cor.; Quagliati, *Il Museo Nazionale di Taranto*, 23; band-cups, Ure, 'Εφ. 'Αρχ. 1915, 118, n. 4, 120, n. 1).
Faggiano	„	575–550 (Late Cor.).
Massafra	„	550–525 (b.f. in Lecce; *CVA Lecce*, i, III F, pl. 1. 1–2; III He, pl. 3. 1–2).
Monteiasi	„	550–525.
San Giorgio	„	525–500 (Quagliati, op. cit. 23; lekythos by Beldam painter, Haspels *ABL*, 268, no. 32).

I cannot give full details of this material because most of it is unpublished, and when I last visited Taranto in 1935 much of it was inaccessible in the overcrowded magazines of the museum. This was already being remedied at the time by the extension of the museum and the improvement of the display. The Director, Dr. Ciro Drago, gave me much assistance and information, so that my list of localities, though probably incomplete, is not inaccurate. Messerschmidt gives a full list of native sites in von Duhn–Messerschmidt, *Italische Gräberkunde*, ii.

[3] Viola, *N Sc*, 1881, 420; tombs and fragments of terra-cotta and plaster scattered over the surface.

SOUTH ITALY

with the settlement there of exiles from Taras.[1] At Ceglie Messapica, between Brindisi and Taranto, there is Late Corinthian pottery with Messapian. At Egnazia on the coast there are black-figure vases and architectural terra-cottas of the late sixth century.[2] At Rudiae, black-figure lekythoi and terracottas probably Tarentine of c. 500.[3] Imports to this area become frequent only in the second half of the fifth century. It is surprising that this, the nearest part of Italy to Greece, should be passed over, while there are on the coast to the north many more sixth-century imports, and apparently also Greek settlers in the sixth century.[4] This should indicate that the Greek imports to Messapia, unlike those to Peucetia and Daunia, came via Taras and became important only when the Tarentines spread themselves over this part of the country.

Beyond the low hills which separate the Gulf of Taranto from the rest of Apulia is a zone at present sterile, the Murge. North of this, in the ancient Peucetia, Greek imports of the sixth century are in a great minority to the native fabrics.[5] It is likely that they came through the Adriatic ports at Bari and Noicattaro rather than through Taras.[6] Taras had probably commercial as well as warlike relations with the Iapygians and Peucetians, but before the fifth century these were unimportant. These peoples preserved their own culture into the fourth and third centuries, considerably influenced by Greek examples.[7] They were closely related to the inhabitants of Illyria,[8] and hence akin to the Greeks. They were not altogether uncultured, and in time became rich and given to luxurious living.[9] But they were also very useful warriors.

There is little reason to suppose that the Tarentines had

---

[1] Johansen, VS, 89 ff. Cf. CVA Goluchow, pl. 6. 1 (Beazley, Vases in Poland, 1); Munich, Sieveking-Hackl, no. 264, pl. 6, for Protocorinthian vases from Apulia.

[2] Quagliati, op. cit. 17. Messerschmidt, op. cit. 322, carries it back to c. 600: I do not know on what evidence.

[3] In Lecce Museum.

[4] Cf. Jatta, 'La Collezione Jatta e l'ellenizzamento della Peucezia', (Iapygia, iii), 14; Mayer, Apulien, 267 ff.; Beaumont, JHS, 1936, 172 ff.

[5] Gervasio, Bronzi arcaici e ceramica geometrica nel Museo di Bari (1921); Quagliati, op. cit. 14 ff., 25; Jatta, op. cit. 3 ff., 241 ff.; Beaumont, JHS, 1936, 192–3.

[6] Jatta, op. cit. 278 f.; cf. Messerschmidt, Italische Gräberkunde, ii. 305.

[7] M. Mayer, Apulien, passim.

[8] Ibid., esp. 326 ff.; Schulze, de Hecataei fragmentis quae ad Italiam meridionalem spectant, 14–15; Krahe, Balkanillyrische geographische Namen, 103 ff.; Messerschmidt, op. cit. 266 ff.

[9] Athen. 522f; the best evidence of their wealth is the size of the offerings made by the Tarentines from a tithe of the spoils.

wide relations with either Iapygians or Messapians before the beginning of the fifth century. The wars of that period presumably had predecessors of which we know nothing; but the archaeological evidence suggests that Tarentine interest was not great. Their policy changed at some time about the turn of the century, and in the first quarter of the fifth century they won great victories over all their barbarian neighbours. They dedicated at Delphi a monument consisting of bronze horses and captive women, the work of Ageladas of Argos, for their victory over the Messapians;[1] and another monument with many figures, by Onatas of Aigina and an uncertain collaborator, for a victory over the Peucetians in which Opis king of the Iapyges, ally of the Peucetians, was killed in battle.[2] The dates are uncertain. The inscriptions of both monuments are dated on epigraphical grounds in the first quarter of the fifth century, and both the artists were at work during this period. As Ageladas was older than Onatas, there is some likelihood that the victory over the Messapians was earlier than that over the Peucetians and Iapygians;[3] Taras struck first west, then north. At some point in these wars took place the sack of the Iapygian town Karbina, recorded by Athenaios;[4] but there is no evidence of date, and the position of Karbina is uncertain.[5]

War between Taras and the Iapygians continued for some time, and was finally fought out in a big campaign c. 473. The Iapygians were at the head of a confederation of native peoples; the Tarentines were helped by Rhegines, sent by Mikythos. In a great battle the Tarentines were defeated, and the slaughter was greater than was suffered by Greeks in any battle in Herodotos' time; the Rhegines' loss was 3,000, the Tarentines' uncounted.[6] This defeat was followed at Taras by a change of constitution which introduced a moderate democracy.[7] It probably took a generation for Taras to recover. After the middle of the fifth century it is a great and rich city, and its

---

[1] Paus. x. 10. 6; *Fouilles de Delphes*, iii. 1. 73 ff.; Dittenberger, *SIG*, i, no. 21; Pomtow, *RE*, Suppl. iv. 1240.

[2] Paus. x. 13. 10; Dittenberger, i. 40; Pomtow, op. cit. 1409.

[3] The latter is dated by Pomtow ap. Dittenberger, loc. cit. c. 470–460, i.e. after the great defeat of the Tarentines. In *RE*, loc. cit., he inclines to an earlier date, c. 480. Onatas may quite well have been active at the earlier date, though his *floruit* is in the generation after the Persian Wars.   [4] 522e.

[5] It is otherwise named only in the *Itineraries*; see v. Geisau, *RE*, x. 1930.

[6] Herod. vii. 170; Diod. xi. 52 (gives the date, and the information that the Iapygians pursued the fleeing Rhegines as far as their city).   [7] Arist. *Pol*, 1303[a]3.

influence over Iapygians and Messapians is wider than it had been at any earlier period. But there is no evidence that the intensive hellenization was accompanied by political control; the Messapians certainly were independent under their king, with whom Athens made a treaty.[1] It may well be that the Tarentines found peaceful penetration more effective than victory in war.

METAPONTION

The territory of Metapontion also was confined to the plain and the neighbouring low hills visible from the city walls. Beyond a range of five miles from the city there is no sign of Greek towns or villages.[2] The valleys of the rivers Bradano and Basento stretch up like long fingers into the heart of southern Italy, but there is little evidence of Metapontine penetration up them.

Pisticci, only fifteen miles inland, above the right bank of the Basento, has late fifth-century red-figure vases, Attic and Italian, in the same graves as the local geometric pottery. The earliest material from Pisticci goes back to the late sixth century, without details as to its associations.[3] This place was certainly native all through the fifth century, though it had considerable intercourse with its Greek neighbours. It rather bars the way to expansion farther up the valley, and the sites of Lucania, including Croccia Cognato, Vaglio, Pomarico Vecchio,[4] Grottole, Anzi,[5] show little that is Greek, or remotely influenced by Greek work, older than the fourth century. The Garaguso cemetery, below Croccia Cognato, has reserved-band kotylai; local imitations of this shape, and of Corinthian

[1] Thuk. vii. 33. 4.

[2] For suburban settlements see Lacava, *Metaponto*, 91. For the limit of Metapontine territory, Lacava, 9; Mayer, *Apulien*, 226.

[3] Unpublished in Potenza Museum.

1862, black trilobate oinochoe, Late Corinthian shape; reserved foot and line where neck joins shoulder;
  linear kothon, Late Corinthian II.

1860, kylix, reserved bands at lip, and handle level;
  b.f. lekythos with quadriga
  lekythos with black palmettes
  handleless cup, quadriga between palmettes, dot-branch } early fifth century.
  above; very careless

[4] Dinos-stand by the Antiphon painter (*c.* 480) from Pomarico, Berlin 2325, *FR*, pl. 162. 1; *ARV*, 230, no. 1.

[5] Skyphos by Epiktetos in Naples, *ARV*, 50, no. 71; column-krater by the Agrigento painter, *ARV*, 378, no. 5. Both without contexts.

kotylai; terra-cottas of the late sixth century.[1] From a shrine belonging to the same town comes a small alabaster figure of a seated goddess, to be connected with a group of late archaic Tarentine works, probably as an Italian imitation.[2] This important place was certainly native then and later. So also was Matera, where Greek vases and imitations of the same types as at Garaguso are found in graves with local pottery;[3] in the fourth century, on the other hand, nearly all the material is Greek. At Gravina there is Attic black-figure of the late sixth century; this was presumably a native site, being farther up the Bradano valley than Matera. These two places might be reached as well from Taras as Metapontion. At Montescaglioso, which lies between Matera and Metapontion, there is little Greek earlier than c. 400.[4]

Finds of a number of isolated archaic objects have been made on sites of the Basilicata. The best known is the horseman of Grumentum, made in the first half of the sixth century in one of the south Italian colonies, probably Taras.[5] Another archaic rider from Grumentum is Forman Coll. no. 54, pl. 2 (Jantzen, p. 26, no. 6). Some other bronzes are:

Louvre 172, from Acerenza (Jantzen, p. 5, no. 47);
B.M. 219 and 317, from Anzi;[6]
B.M. 270, from Armento (Jantzen, p. 5, no. 44).

From S. Mauro Forte comes a terra-cotta pyramid bearing an inscription in Akhaian letters of the sixth century.[7] This site has no other sixth-century Greek material of this period, and in the fourth century was like any other of the native sites.

Bronzes and single objects like this pyramid pass from hand to hand more easily than pots. Greek and Roman bronzes have often been found in places where there is no evidence of direct

---

[1] Potenza Museum, unpublished.
[2] Cf. Langlotz, *Frühgriechische Bildhauerschulen*, 186 n. 5.
[3] *N Sc*, 1935, 107 ff., 380 ff.; 1936, 84 ff.
[4] Material in Taranto Museum; column-krater, Taranto 7482, near Orchard painter, *ARV*, 349.
[5] B.M., 1904, 7-3. 1; Jantzen, *Bronzewerkstätten in Grossgriechenland und Sizilien*, 26, no. 5. Cf. Lamb, *Greek and Roman Bronzes*, pl. 39b; Payne, *Archaic Marble Sculpture*, 7, n. 4. See below, p. 290.
[6] Cf. also B.M. 265, leg of a colossal statue of the middle of the fifth century, said to be probably from Anzi or Potenza.
[7] *IG*, xiv. 652; Lacava, 112; *N Sc*, 1882, 119. Giannelli, *Culti e Miti*, 96, n. 3, gives Pisticci as provenience, probably in error (but see Mayer in *RE*, xv. 1334). See also Roehl, xv. 5; Roberts, *Introduction to Greek Epigraphy*, 302; Rouse, *Greek Votive Offerings*, 61-2, fig. 7; Furtwängler in Roscher, i. 2137, suggests that the pyramid was a cult symbol.

contact with the barbarians, much less of civilizing influence. The absence of pots may be in part explained by the lack of regular excavation, as there are a few fine vases from sites in the Basilicata; less valuable pieces may not have been preserved or recorded. But though the Basilicata has hardly been intensively explored, there is material from a great number of sites, gathered almost entirely by the hand of Vittorio de Cicco and now in Potenza Museum. Most of it is of the fourth and third centuries, but there is evidence of continuity on a sufficient number of sites to ensure that conditions were not completely changed by the Lucanian invasion, and to give force to the cumulative argument from the scantiness of Greek material of the fifth and sixth centuries.

Lucanian geometric pottery, which continues from the sixth to the fourth century, shows definite Greek influence, chiefly in shapes.[1] But this is limited, and the closest relations of this pottery are with Apulian fabrics. It covers a large area, open to Greek influence on the west, in the Val di Diano,[2] as well as on the east; but there can be no doubt that Metapontion was the main source. The extent of the influence has, however, been exaggerated by Mayer, the only scholar to give a general account of this pottery. There is no good ground for his view that some pieces may be of Metapontine manufacture;[3] the pieces on which he relies come from somewhere in the region of Metapontion, not necessarily from Metapontion itself, and the absence of similar material from excavations there, although there are a few pots which were locally made, is against this hypothesis. Certainly Corinthian and perhaps other Greek vases were available for imitation on native sites, and shapes and a few decorative elements were occasionally adopted. There was therefore some Metapontine trade with the country behind, but it was probably not extensive and had little effect in spreading Greek culture. The Basilicata is not an attractive or fertile country, though it was perhaps less barren and treeless in antiquity. It is now one of the poorest regions of Italy. The Greeks very reasonably stayed in their rich plain and left the windy barren mountains to their own people.

There is even less evidence of Greek penetration of the country behind Siris before the fifth century. It was as little attractive for Greek settlement as the country behind Meta-

[1] Mayer, *Apulien*, ch. xii.
[2] See below, p. 154 f.
[3] Loc. cit. 231–2, 237.

pontion. As the περίοικοι of Siris are spoken of,[1] it is possible
that she, like Sybaris, ruled over the native peoples of the Siris
and Akiris valleys; but this rule is not likely to have extended
far inland. Native places of the Lucanian type[2] at S. Arcangelo
and Gallichio above the upper course of the Agri (Akiris) are
innocent of Greek influence. The course of the Sinni (Siris) is
archaeologically *terra incognita*; this region has been as little
explored and excavated as any part of Italy. Its neglect has
been due to its backward condition, and the same conditions
probably obtained in antiquity. The joint coins of Siris and
Pyxus in the second half of the sixth century[3] have been used
as evidence of an overland trade-route between them at this
time. But it is a long route through country which appears on
present evidence to have been untouched, and it is possible
that another explanation should be sought of the joint coinage.[4]

SYBARIS

South of Monte Pollino the nature of the country completely
changes. The peninsula narrows at the Sybaris–Laos isthmus,
south of which all parts of the interior are fairly accessible
from the coast. The geological basis is different, and instead
of the desolate clay and limestone of the Basilicata there are
old mountains, in part intrusive, and fertile valleys. The foot-
hills round the upper course of the Crati are among the
pleasantest parts of Italy. At the mouth of the now united
stream formed by the Crati, the Esaro, and the Coscile is
Sybaris. All the country watered by these rivers came within
the control of Sybaris, a little empire larger than that of any
other colony (the present province of Cosenza, whose boundaries
nearly coincide with those inferred for the Sybarite empire, has
an area of *c.* 2,500 sq. m.; compare Syracuse at the end of the
sixth century, including Kamarina, *c.* 1,500 sq. m.).

It is not possible to follow the stages of Sybarite territorial
expansion. The written evidence is very scanty and without
mark of time. The area has not been well explored archaeologically, and the few archaic remains can only supplement
other evidence, which consists of a passage of Strabo and one

---

[1] Athen. 523*d*.

[2] Using the word in a geographical sense, without opening the question of their race.

[3] Head, *HN*[2], 83; cf. below, p. 356. Pyxus lay at the mouth of the Busento, on the right
bank, 2 km. west of Policastro; it has no remains.

[4] Cf. Perret, *Siris*, 256 ff.

of Herodotos, several names of cities drawn by Stephanos from Hekataios, and the coins of Sybaris and others which share their types. But it is possible to form an outline of the Sybarite territory in the last fifty years of the city's existence. From c. 570 Sybaris was at its height of luxury and power; ἡ δὲ Σύβαρις ἤκμαζε τοῦτον τὸν χρόνον μάλιστα.[1] Probably its territorial expansion had then reached its full development, except for the addition of Siris. The period of growth is roughly the seventh century.

The most distant colony of Sybaris is Poseidonia. There was never a continuous stretch of territory under Greek control between Sybaris and Poseidonia, which was reached in the first place by sea, for the oldest settlement was on the beach.[2] But there was also an overland route via Campo Tenese and the Val di Diano,[3] where sixth-century Greek imports have been found at Sala Consilina, Atena Lucana, and elsewhere. At Sala there are some 'Protocorinthian' kotylai[4] and imitations thereof; no certain Corinthian;[5] a little black-figure.[6] The local geometric pottery, of a style common also in the eastern part of Lucania, is somewhat indebted to Corinthian shapes (including a lekythos of Corinthian shape)[7] and is much more frequent than the imported vases. There are Greek bronze vessels of the sixth century (N Sc. 1897, 164–5, figs. 8–14), silver fibulae, and amber. The bronzes are fine, the vases relatively few and poor, but others may have been found and not preserved. The Greek influence on the local manufacture would suggest this. This was certainly a rich little community, well supplied with luxuries by Greek traders. It is uncertain how far back the connexion goes; most of the Greek objects are of the second half of the sixth century, some probably as old as the seventh. Atena has nothing that is sixth-century Greek, but there and at Oliveto Citra there is Greek influence in the shapes of the native pottery of the fifth and fourth century. The natives were not thoroughly hellenized; they adopted Greek shapes and motives, but their pottery kept its individuality; the Greek

---

[1] Herod. vi. 127.

[2] Strabo 252.

[3] See below, pp. 204 ff., for a full discussion of this route.

[4] As NC, fig. 9a. It is not certain whether these were manufactured at Corinth or in the west; cf. p. 263 for a possible provincial fabric at Poseidonia.

[5] Though some is recorded in N Sc, 1896, 173.

[6] CVA Petit Palais, pl. 3, nos. 2–9.

[7] Tongues on the shoulder of N Sc, 1897, 168 ff., fig. 18 (= CVA Petit Palais, pl. 1. 2) and 21; chequers, ibid., fig. 20.

elements are less strong at Atena and at Oliveto, where the material is also of later date (fifth century). Perhaps contact ceased after the fall of Sybaris.

This is all outside the area controlled by Sybaris, within which Laos, on the Tyrrhenian coast opposite Sybaris, was the chief of her colonies. It was the only one, apart from Poseidonia, to issue its own coins;[1] but these are probably to be dated after the fall of Sybaris, when the remnant took refuge in Laos and Skidros.[2] Skidros was probably also on the Tyrrhenian coast, though none of the sites suggested is convincing.[3] Kerilloi, the modern Cirella a little south of Laos, was probably another Sybarite colony.[4] The name, though first recorded in the Roman period, is Greek. The importance of these places, especially Laos, for the through traffic of goods for Etruria is discussed below.[5] They were of no other economic value, for this coast is mountainous and barren, no place for a 'subsistence colony' of the smallest size. The limestone mountains behind Laos are particularly barren, and it lies in a poor little plain, now covered with detritus and brushwood, at the mouth of the Lao.[6]

The possession of the Sybaris–Laos isthmus formed a baseline for advance against the natives. The four ἔθνη τῶν πλησίον and twenty-five subject towns over which Sybaris ruled[7] were all in the ancient Oinotria, corresponding to the later Lucania and the north of Bruttium. The towns recorded in the fragments of Hekataios[8] will be among these twenty-five. Nine are given in Stephen of Byzantium with the formula πόλις Οἰνώτρων ἐν μεσογεία, ὡς Ἑκαταῖος Εὐρώπῃ. Six other entries have the same formula without the citation of Hekataios. These probably come from him also. If they were from a source later than the fifth century, the region would be described not as Oinotria but as Lucania. Hekataios, a Milesian, had opportunities of knowing about the interior of this part of Italy from the Milesian merchants who traded with Sybaris. Not all the towns are in the territory of Sybaris, but the majority of those identi-

[1] *BM Cat. Italy*, 235; Head, *HN²*, 73.
[2] Herod. vi. 21.　　　　　　　　　　　　　　[3] See below, p. 204.
[4] Strabo 255; Galli, *Per la Sibaritide*, 134 ff.　　　[5] pp. 206 ff.
[6] On the right bank of the Lao, near the mouth, at 'Foresta' (see Galli, *SMG*, 1928, 151 ff.).
[7] Strabo 263. The 'πόλεις' of this passage and of Hekataios ap. Steph. Byz. (see below) are of course not to be dignified with the name of cities; cf. Caspari, *JHS*, xxx. 240–1.
[8] Frs. 64–71 Jacoby; cf. B. Schulze, *de Hecataei Milesii fragmentis quae ad Italiam meridionalem spectant*, Leipzig, 1912.

fied are, and probably a high proportion of the others. The identifications depend entirely on linguistic grounds, and are at best uncertain.

The towns for which Hekataios is expressly cited are:

Fr. 68. Kossa: *Cosam in agro Thurino*, Caes. *BC* iii. 22, where Milo was killed: Cassano, on the hills north of Sybaris (Schulze, 107) or rather at the foot of the hill, where there are Roman remains near the railway station Sibari (Lenormant, *GG*, i. 228; *CIL*, x. p. 18).

Fr. 71. Ninaia: S. Donato di Ninea (Schulze, 116) on the hills which separate the Crati basin from the Tyrrhenian Sea.

Fr. 64. Arinthe: Rende (Schulze 94) on the river Arente, a western affluent of the Crati (*JHS*, xxx. 241; Tropea, *R. Stor. ant.* i. 4. 146; Pais, *Italia Antica*, 19).

Fr. 67*b*. Menekine: Mendicino (Schulze, 111), in the extreme south of the Crati basin, rather than the vicum Mendicoleum of the *Itineraries*, between Forum Popilii and Nerulum.

Fr. 67*a*. Ixias: may be near Menekine, as they are named together by Hekataios (ἐν δὲ ᾽Ιξιὰς πόλις, ἐν δὲ Μενεκίνη πόλις).

Fr. 69. Kyterion: Cutro, south-west of Kroton (Schulze, 113).

Frs. 65, 66, 70. Artemision, Erimon, Malanios: unidentified. Barrio placed Artemision at S. Agata (see below); the identifications of Malanios (Maleventum, Pais; Magliano, Lenormant, *GG*, i. 230; Maida, Barrio) are all certainly wrong, Maleventum (Benevento) and Maida being outside Oinotria, Magliano being derived from a *fundus Manlianus*.

In Stephanos, without express quotation:

Brystakia: Umbriatico or Briatico near the Lipuda (see below, p. 161). Briatico on the south side of the Golfo di S. Eufemia is not in the land of the Oinotroi but in the 'most ancient Italy' (Schulze, 98).

Siberine: S. Severina, above the middle course of the Neto (Lenormant, *GG*, i. 428).

Drys, Patykos, Pyxis, Sestion: unidentified.

Pyxis may be Pyxus (Πυξόες adj. on coins), although Pyxus is not ἐν μεσογαίᾳ; Stephanos may have misapplied a formula. Patykos is traditionally Paola.

Three of these sites, Umbriatico, Cutro, and S. Severina, are in Krotoniate territory, the others in the Krathis valley. Artemision is a difficulty. There is no evidence of the cult of Artemis at either Sybaris or Kroton, and the Doric form quoted by Stephanos from Philistos[1] is also unaccountable in a region where there were no Doric colonies. Few of the other names lend themselves to. etymologizing, and none has an obviously Italic sound. As has been pointed out, Hekataios calls them

---

[1] Fr. 53 Müller.

Oinotrian in an ethnographical and geographical, not a political, sense.[1]

One of the subject towns of Sybaris will be at S. Agata, where an inscribed bronze double-axe[2] was found; this is on the headwaters of the Esaro, a tributary of the Sybaris (Coscile) and on the road to Belvedere by the lowest pass through the mountains that fence off the Tyrrhenian Sea (744 m.).[3] Remains of another little town are at Malvito,[4] in the lower valley of the Crati; the period is uncertain. Sixth-century remains come from other places in the neighbourhood of Sybaris, including Tarsia[5] and S. Lorenzo del Vallo.[6] Slight remains of another small place, probably not Greek, have recently been excavated at Francavilla Marittima, a few miles north of Sybaris.[7] The suburban regions of Sybaris were probably thickly inhabited. Some of Cavallari's excavations in the suburban area were successful, and finds are occasionally made in the vicinity of Terranova di Sibari and Spezzano Albanese. There are some bronzes from Rossano,[8] and also two black-figure lekythoi of the late sixth or early fifth century. It is not certain that Rossano was occupied before the fall of Sybaris,[9] though it is a likely place for a village of farmers. It seems to have received some of the Sybarites after the destruction of the city, and was perhaps a predecessor of the new Sybaris on the Traeis.[10]

Pandosia on the Akheron, the most favoured site for which is on the upper course of the Moccone,[11] an eastern tributary of the Crati, will be another of these subject towns. It issued coins in the middle of the fifth century, when this territory had passed from Sybaris to Kroton,[12] and was thus the first inland town of south Italy to coin, at the same period as the earliest inland towns of Sicily. It had some importance in the fourth

---

[1] Schulze, op. cit. 79 ff.; Jacoby, *FGH*, i, p. 334.

[2] *BM Bronzes*, 252; *IG*, xiv. 643.   [3] See below, p. 203 f.

[4] Davies, *Roman Mines in Europe*, 74.

[5] Pesce, *Boll. d'arte*, 1935, 228 ff.; *N Sc*, 1897, 357, figs. 14–15; Courby, *Les Vases grecs à reliefs*, fig. 21. Two pieces of pithos-rim, with Herakles and centaurs, in Crotone Museum.

[6] Pesce, *Boll. d'Arte*, 1935, 228 ff. I thank Cav. Raffaele Lucente for information about this piece.

[7] *N Sc*, 1936, 77 ff.   [8] *Boll. d'Arte*, 1919–20, 95–101.

[9] The Iron Age settlement, *N Sc*, 1934, 459 ff., is probably but not certainly pre-Greek.

[10] See below, p. 365.

[11] Lenormant, i. 442 ff. Galli, *Per la Sibaritide*, 73–91, suggests a site near Mendicino, where there was a Casale Pantosa in the time of Frederick II; and identifies the Akheron with either the Caronte or the Campagnano.

[12] *BM Cat. Italy*, 370.

century, when Alexander the Molossian died under its walls,[1] and was always of more mark than the little places we have been considering.

The names of unknown towns which issued coins in the sixth century begin with Ami . . . or Asi . . .[2] and Pal . . . and Mol . . . .[3] Nothing else is known of these towns, and as they do not appear in subsequent history or coin after the sixth century, they may have shared the fate of Sybaris, whose colonies or subject cities they perhaps were, for Poseidonia and Laos also coin before her destruction.

Another town which had some independence was Lagaria, where Epeios was fabled to have dedicated the tools with which the Wooden Horse was made.[4] It is otherwise famed only for its wine.[5] It was probably a small colony of Phokians who brought with them the legend of Epeios, and by the middle of the sixth century, at or before the conquest of Siris, became subject to Sybaris.[6] It has been placed at Trebisacce, on the road between Sybaris and Siris, but there is no ground for giving it an exact site.[7]

It is certain that Sybaris conquered a larger territory in a shorter time than any other city of south Italy or Sicily. Even Syracuse's conquests were more gradual. The Oinotroi appear to have been a peaceable folk, ready to receive civilization, but the Sybarites must have been conciliatory as well as valorous to reduce them. Nothing is known of the treatment they received. Sybaris was free with the citizenship, but this would hardly extend to admitting Italians. The πόλεις Οἰνώτρων are surely native towns, but the names are in many cases Greek, in no case certainly Italian. If any trust may be put in the suggested identifications, most of them are on the foot-hills in places well fitted for forts controlling the valleys, less well sited for overland traffic from sea to sea. Rende and Mendicino do not easily connect with the Tyrrhenian Sea over the high passes to Paola and Fiumefreddo,[8] and S. Donato di Ninea,

---

[1] Strabo 256; Livy viii. 24.

[2] Head, *HN*[2], 70. Pais restores Aminaioi and places the issuing city on the Traeis; without evidence (*Rendiconti dei Lincei*, 1907, 8 ff.). Aminaia and the Aminaioi are difficult to locate, and known chiefly for their vines. Hesykhios, s.v. Ἀμιναῖον, equates Aminaia with Peucetia, for which Bérard, *Colonisation*, 416 ff., reads Πικεντία, placing it thus in the neighbourhood of Poseidonia; perhaps rightly.

[3] Head, *HN*[2], 83. [4] Strabo 263; Lykophron 930.

[5] Strabo, l.c.; Pliny, *NH* xiv. 69.

[6] Giannelli, *Culti e Miti della Magna Grecia*, 74 ff.

[7] Lenormant, *GG*, i. 219. [8] See below, p. 203.

though almost on the exact line between Sybaris and Laos, has impassable mountains behind it. It is possible that these native towns were used by the Sybarites as garrison posts, and some of them may have been founded for this purpose.

KROTON

Between Sybaris and Kroton lay a group of small towns whose origin and history is obscure. Their foundation was credited to Philoktetes, who dedicated the bow of Herakles in the temple of Apollo Alaios near Krimissa, and lay buried near Krimissa[1] or Makalla.[2] Most of the sources[3] are late and contradictory in detail, and this legend is neither more nor less credible than other heroic foundations in Italy. It is probable, however, that this region received settlers from Greece, who never formed a colony but were in time absorbed by Kroton. There were also Lindian settlers;[4] with this compare the Rhodian settlement at Sybaris on the Traeis.[5]

The chief of these towns was Krimissa, called βραχύπτολις by Lykophron (911). The Κρίμισσα ἄκρα[6] must be the Punto d'Alice, where is the temple of Apollo Alaios. The town lay either near Cirò Superiore, where there are some unimportant remains,[7] or between here and Cirò Marina, where a deposit of terra-cottas has recently been found.[8] At the mouth of the Lipuda, where Lenormant puts it, there are late ruins.[9] Makalla[10] and Khone are names only; the former, we are told, was 120 stades from Kroton.[11] The latter gave its name to or took it from the people, the Khones, who have many affinities in Illyria and Epeiros.[12] Probably there was no concentration of population in one city, but a number of small settlements. The bronze coin with the legend OMON[OIA] and K]PIMIΣΣAIΩN[13]

[1] Ps.-Arist. de mir. ausc. 107.　　　　　　　　　　[2] Lykophron 927–8.
[3] See Fiehn in RE, xix. 2507; Giannelli, Culti e Miti della Magna Grecia, ch. viii; Strabo 254, Lykophron 911 ff., ps.-Arist. de mir. ausc. 107, are the chief sources.
[4] Lykophron 923; ps.-Arist., l.c.　　　[5] Strabo 654.　　　　　[6] Ibid. 254.
[7] N Sc, 1921, 490–2; Templum Apollinis Alaei, 17, 180.
[8] Crotone Museum, cases 7–8.　　　　　　　[9] TAA, 180; La Grande-Grèce, i. 378.
[10] For the form of the name cf. Κρόταλλα, named by Hekataios as a πόλις Ἰταλίας (i.e., Italy within the isthmus of Catanzaro); fr. 85 Jacoby.
[11] Ps.-Arist. de mir. ausc. 107. Bérard, Colonisation, 363, suggests that it was the same as Petelia (see below); the distance of 120 stades from Kroton agrees, and the two are never named together.
[12] Schulze, de Hecataei Milesii fragmentis quae ad Italiam meridionalem spectant, 14–16; cf. Krahe, Balkanillyrische geographische Namen, 48, 105.
[13] Num. Chron. 1931, 87.

may refer to the co-operation of a number of villages of the Krimissaioi.

There are ancient remains at Cariati and Pietrapaola, between Rossano and the Punta d'Alice, which have not yet been much explored.[1] The chief site of the area is the temple of Apollo Alaios in the sand-dunes near Punta d'Alice, below Cirò, which has been excavated by Orsi. Very little of the content of the temple is earlier than the second quarter of the fifth century, when it was rebuilt.[2] There is one Protocorinthian kylix (fig. 91), and scattered sixth-century material: bronzes (pp. 112, 116), marble (p. 126), terra-cottas (fig. 81). These are insufficient to throw light on the origin of the temple or the people who worshipped there. Its great period is that of Krotoniate supremacy, and the oldest coins found there are of Kroton.[3] Among the offerings are rude statuettes of the nude male type, certainly made by Italian workmen with only a vague general indebtedness to Greek art.[4] The population was probably mixed and the Italian peoples admitted to an equality with the Greeks. But some of the evidence may belong to a date after the Lucano-Brettian invasion, which here broke through to the sea.[5]

On *a priori* grounds, a union between Greeks and Italians is more likely here than anywhere else. The legends and cults of the region are all Greek,[6] and so are nearly all the offerings at the temple. But there is no good tradition of the founding or refounding of the cities, and no single one was important enough to absorb the others. Their legendary origins, like the *nostoi*-legends of Metapontion, Siris, and Lagaria, may reflect settlement by small groups of Greeks before the definitive foundation of a colony. Definitive colonization did not take place at any of the cities of Philoktetes, and their pure Greek feeling is therefore likely to have been weaker. The native peoples, too, were not entirely barbarian. They, like the Iapyges, have Illyrian affinities in their toponymy and were probably immigrant, and more nearly related to the Greeks than the neighbouring Oinotroi. The confusion between the names of a native people and a town thought to be Greek suggests that they had in part fused.

[1] *N Sc*, 1900, 604; Lenormant, *GG*, i. 372 (Khone?): *N Sc*, 1900, 605; 1901, 27.
[2] *Templum Apollinis Alaei*, 67.   [3] Ibid. 132–3.
[4] Ibid. 90, fig. 51, silver (probably fifth century, not sixth); 99 ff., pll. XI–XII, bronze.
[5] Strabo 254; Diod. xii. 22.
[6] Giannelli, loc. cit.

Petelia also is fabled to have been founded by Philoktetes.[1] It became an important town in the fourth century, when the Lucanians made it a metropolis,[2] and is famous for its siege by Hannibal. There is one Middle Corinthian ring-aryballos[3] and a few sixth-century terra-cottas,[4] and an interesting fifth-century *defixio* has been found there,[5] as well as the more celebrated Orphic tablets. At Verzino behind Petelia were found two fine bronze buckles.[6] Lenormant speaks doubtfully of 'filons de minerai argentifère avec des traces d'exploitation antique' in this region.[7] Brystakia, named by Stephanos of Byzantium as an Oinotrian city, is doubtfully identified with Umbriatico, which is in this district. At Belvedere di Spinello, above the Neto, were found some terra-cottas,[8] the oldest, a bust with polos, of the late sixth century. The question of early Greek towns at S. Severina, on the other side of the Neto from Belvedere, and Cutro has already been discussed.[9] But in spite of these signs of penetration up the Neto and the other rivers of the Sila, that mountain mass effectively checked Krotoniate expansion inland by cutting them off from the valley of the Krathis. The Sila, though not difficult to traverse in summer, could never serve for more than pasture and timber. Kroton's chief expansion before 510 was down the coast, by the foundation of subordinate colonies such as Kaulonia and Terina.

Terina lay on the sea at the western end of the Isthmus of Catanzaro; its exact site is uncertain, but it was probably near S. Eufemia Vecchia.[10] The river Terina is possibly the unimportant Torrente dei Bagni;[11] the larger rivers of this region, the

[1] Strabo 254; Serv. *Aen.* iii. 402; Solinus, ii. 10. For the exact site see Lenormant, *GG*, i. 383–4.

[2] Strabo, loc. cit.

[3] Crotone Museum, no. 1786 (the provenience is not absolutely above suspicion; see Norman Douglas, *Old Calabria*, 224, confirmed by recent inquiry among the illiterate).

[4] Museo Civico, Reggio.

[5] Arangio-Ruiz and Olivieri, *Inscriptiones Graecae Siciliae et infimae Italiae ad ius spectantes*, 147 ff.

[6] Von Duhn, *N Sc*, 1897, 356: 'due fermagli di cintura d'un lavoro squisito, coperti d'una patina mirabile; gli uncini fissati alla cerniera mediante belle volute ioniche, finiscono in testa di cavallo; il margine è traforato per fissarvi il cuoio.' They have apparently not passed to the Crotone Museum with the rest of the Collezione Albani.

[7] *GG*, ii. 15.

[8] Crotone Museum, nos. 1269–78.

[9] See above, p. 156.

[10] Lenormant, *GG*, iii. 95 ff., quotes a *vetus civitas* named in Robert Guiscard's charter to the abbey of S. Eufemia. Cf. also Regling, *Terina*, 4; H. Philipp, *RE*, v A, 726–7; *N Sc*, 1921, 470.

[11] Philipp, loc. cit.

M

Savuto and Amato, are the ancient Okynaros and Lametos.[1] The Siren Ligeia was buried on an island named Terina in this sea, which is now islandless.[2] An ancient site farther up the coast, on a hill above the mouth of the Savuto, west of Nocera Terinese, is probably Temesa.[3] Another town in this neighbourhood was Lametinoi, named by Hekataios as a town of Italy, that is, the 'most ancient Italy' south of the Lametine and Skylletian gulfs. It or the river Lametos gave its name to the gulf, and it perhaps lay at the mouth of the river.[4] Near the railway station of Curinga, on the southern edge of the plain of S. Eufemia, was found a hoard of silver coins, mainly archaic, which was deposited c. 470.[5]

Terina is said to have been a Krotoniate foundation,[6] and must have been founded before c. 480, when its coinage begins;[7] perhaps some time before. The early state of Temesa is unknown, but there is some ground for associating it with Sybaris.[8] In the early fifth century it appears to have been dependent on Kroton, for one of the alliance coins of Kroton is ascribed to Temesa.[9] Lametinoi also should be a Krotoniate colony, like the neighbouring Terina.

The territory under direct Krotoniate control ends at the Punto di Staletti behind Skylletion. This is a considerable barrier to land communication.[10] The antiquity of Skylletion is not known; passing over its legendary Athenian origin,[11] the earliest documents are terra-cottas of the second (?) quarter of the fifth century.[12] Beyond this point lies Kaulonia, an Akhaian colony founded on the initiative of Kroton, which though independent fell within the Krotoniate sphere.[13] It may be inferred from the omission of any mention of it in connexion

[1] The Okynaros is by Philipp regarded as the same as the Terina, and by Regling identified with the Torrente dei Bagni; but Lykophron's description (v. 1009) will only fit a larger river. Lykophron's geography is not so precise that we must insist on placing Terina on the Okynaros; cf. the confusion of rivers in 911 ff.

[2] Lykophron 726 ff.

[3] Orsi, *Templum Apollinis Alaei*, 181, n. 1; Philipp, *RE*, v A, 459–60. Nukeria (Steph. Byz. s.v.; Head, *HN²*, 105), a neighbour of Terina which has given its name to Nocera Terinese, was probably of later birth. This area is full enough of archaic towns.

[4] Lenormant, iii. 103; Hekataios, fr. 80 Jacoby; Schulze, op. cit. 75; Lykophron 1085.

[5] *N Sc*, 1916, 186; Noe, *Bibliography of Greek Coin-hoards*, 85.

[6] Steph. Byz. s.v. Τέριυα; Pliny, *NH* iii. 72; Strabo 256; ps.-Skymn. 306.

[7] Regling, op. cit.   [8] See below, p. 203.

[9] Head, *HN²*, 112. For its later conquest by the Lokrians see Pais, *Ancient Italy*, 39 ff.

[10] See below, p. 210.   [11] Strabo 261.

[12] Crotone Museum, 1289–90; 1290, seated Samo-Milesian type, archaizing.

[13] See above, p. 27.

with the battle of the Sagra, and the fact that the battle was fought on the boundary of Kaulonia and Lokroi, that it was then under Krotoniate suzerainty.[1]

LOKROI

Lokroi was in a very favourable position for a landward extension. The Ionian coast here is not infertile, but there is better land in the plain on the Tyrrhenian Sea between the rivers Metauros and Mesma, and easy routes lead straight across to it. On the eastern side the present distribution of population in four towns each of about 10,000 inhabitants fits the nature of the country better than a closer concentration, and Lokroi is by no means the natural site for the chief town of the region. Probably, therefore, there were other centres of population on the Ionian Sea. But the chief Lokrian colonies were on the other side. Medma and Hipponion are certainly Lokrian; less certainly Metauron.

The chief remains of Medma are from the *favissa* of a sanctuary probably of Persephone. The terra-cottas from the lower stratum are of the sixth century,[2] the earliest being some time before the middle of the century. The repertory is the same as at Lokroi, and the likeness to Lokrian terra-cottas leaves no doubt that the same models were copied. This is less marked in the sixth than in the fifth century, but the oldest Medma statuette is compared by Orsi to unpublished examples at Lokroi;[3] and a type of mask at Medma[4] is elsewhere known only at Lokroi, being a local variant of the common Rhodian type.

There is very little pottery, the earliest being Late Corinthian.[5] Nothing from the cemetery[6] is earlier than the end of the fifth century, except sporadic pieces, including a Protocorinthian aryballos,[7] which is the only object from the site older than the sixth century. The Greek colony was founded at least as early as the second quarter of the sixth century, the date of the oldest material from the temple whose *favissa* has

---

[1] See below, p. 358 f.

[2] *N Sc*, 1913 Suppl., 63, 70 ff.; cf. Giannelli, 251–5, who thinks that the same goddesses were worshipped as at Lokroi: Athena and Persephone.

[3] *N Sc*, 1913 Suppl., fig. 92; cf. p. 83.   [4] Ibid., figs. 79, 80.

[5] Ibid. 136.   [6] *N Sc*, 1917, 37–58.

[7] Ibid. 55: 'una lekythos protocor., cuoriforme, molto guasta del fuoco, ed un aryballos corinzio-italico con pessime fig. di opliti.' I have not seen either of these; the latter is probably Corinthian, not Italo-Corinthian.

been explored. There is some reason to believe that the Lokrian expansion to the west coast was as early as the seventh century,[1] but there is as yet no archaeological support for this.

The beginnings of Hipponion are not clear. There is said to be Corinthian pottery from the Belvedere temple.[2] Almost all the remains, the walls, the Ionic temple, probably the little Doric temple, are of the late fifth century.[3] There is therefore no archaeological evidence for close connexion between Hipponion and Lokroi before this date. In the Collezione Capialbi at Vibo Valentia there are bronze mirror-handles; an ephebos standing on a tortoise, the volutes above his head ending in snakes' heads, who is fairly near to *N Sc*, 1913 Suppl., fig. 49, may be Lokrian; an Aphrodite mirror of the late sixth century is probably Corinthian, but it is noteworthy that archaic mirror-handles are found elsewhere at Lokroi alone of south Italian sites. Few of the terra-cottas are older than the fifth century, but many of the fifth-century pieces are imported from Lokroi, and almost all the others are of types familiar at Lokroi and Medma. Pinakes also were brought from Lokroi to Hipponion.[4]

The literary tradition is unanimous that Hipponion and Medma were Lokrian foundations.[5] Traces of sixth-century Lokrian influence are few, but little of the material is older than the fifth century. There is no good reason to doubt that both cities were Lokrian from their foundation in the sixth century, or perhaps even in the seventh.[6]

Medma is named from a spring, probably a native name and a local pre-Greek worship. Hipponion is the Greek version of a native name which survives as ᄃEIᄁ on Brettian coins[7] and Vibo in the Roman period. It does not follow that there was a native element in either town before the Brettian invasion. Place-names survive (as at Zankle and Gela) when

[1] See Oldfather, *RE*, xiii. 1308 and p. 168 below.

[2] *N Sc*, 1921, 481, 'bombylioi ed aryballoi cor.' A little Late Corinthian and many black-figure lekythoi, in the Collezione Capialbi at Vibo Valentia.

[3] *N Sc*, 1921, 473–85; Crispo, *SMG*, 1928, 55 ff.

[4] *RIGI*, 1926, 126, n. 2; and in Coll. Capialbi. The Coll. Cordopatri now in the Museo Civico at Reggio, made chiefly at Hipponion but in part perhaps at Medma, also has terra-cottas certainly manufactured at Lokroi.

[5] Thuk. v. 5; Strabo 256; ps.-Skymn. 307–8.

[6] Crispo, *SMG*, 1928, 58–61, holds that Lokroi is a late comer, winning control in the late sixth century over cities already established. The archaeological evidence cannot be said to support this view. His reference to the Lokrian poets as falsifiers of history is unhappy, as there is no myth or legend associated with either Hipponion or Medma, as there is with Temesa.   [7] Head, *HN*², 100.

nothing else of the original inhabitants is left. It is needless to say that the remains of Medma and Hipponion in the sixth and fifth centuries are purely Greek.

The relation of these posts to the city of Lokroi is indicated in a third-century inscription: Δήμαρχος Φιλώτα Λοκρὸς ἐκ τῶν Ἐπιζεφυρίων Ἱππωνιεύς.[1] This is not direct evidence for the fifth century, for it is after the colonial war of 423 when Hipponion and Medma revolted from Lokroi;[2] but it is likely that this double nationality, or rather this local qualification of Lokrian nationality, is older than that event. It is suggested above[3] that the secondary foundations of Syracuse had a similar separate existence within the Syracusan state.

The native town of Torre Galli, on the breezy height of a promontory which runs out to Capo Vaticano, shows no signs of intercourse with Greeks earlier than the late seventh century. There are none of the pre-colonization and early colonization imports which are found in the native cemeteries at Lokroi. The Greek imports are almost entirely Corinthian. In most cases they are found in graves with no native pottery:

238 (*MA*, xxxi, fig. 109). Corinthian only.
288 (ibid., fig. 123). Corinthian; Ionian krateriskos with graffito; silver rings.
300 Late Corinthian aryballos, and 'Ionian' kylix.
309 Corinthian; 'Ionian' kylix.
334 Entirely Late Corinthian.

Grave 328 has 'Ionian' kylikes, an imitation of an Attic lamp, and no other local pottery.

256 has, besides Corinthian, a wheel-made aryballos of local clay, quite Greek in shape, and a stamnos developed in shape and technique from the local ware.

281: Corinthian aryballos and kotyle; jug of local clay and Greek shape; in the local ware (kyathoi, cups, and jugs) the clay is more refined and the technique better than usual (fibulae, including bone-and-wood fibula, and a local oinochoe are from an earlier burial).

Imitations in the local clay and technique of Greek shapes are found in graves 301 (amphora, kotylai) and 302 (amphora). An oinochoe in grave 248 imitates the Late Protocorinthian shape. A kyathos (the most distinctive native shape) in grave 321 shows the distant influence of a Corinthian oinochoe (*MA*, xxxi, pl. 1. 21).

---

[1] *Fouilles de Delphes*, iii. 1, no. 176.   [2] Thuk. v. 5. 3.   [3] p. 110.

The earliest Corinthian vases are in grave 251,[1] with native cups, and a fragment which may belong to a hydria. This is the only case in which the ordinary native ware is associated with Corinthian. The local pottery in graves 256 and 281 may well have been made by Greeks. It is in a different class from native imitations of Corinthian shapes in graves 301, 302, 248, and others. The rite changes also in the later graves. 288, 7 and others are no longer exactly orientated. Tiles of Greek manufacture replace the rough stone lining in grave 288. There are eight cases of cremation:

278. Three ossuaries, contents all Greek.
289. 'Refined' amphora, containing Corinthian aryballos, and lance-head; native amphora adjacent.
295. No pottery: arms and fibula.
139. Cremated and uncremated body in same grave (the cremated bones are laid in open grave: no ossuary).
281, 300. 'Open' cremations.
300 is the only grave with the remains of a wooden coffin or couch. All the other bodies were laid on a couch of herbs.[2] See p. 165 for its contents.

Cremation was practised in no other cemetery of any native race of south Italy or Sicily. There is a very strong probability, therefore, that these were actually the graves of Greeks.[3] There is not the long and deep-reaching intercourse at Torre Galli that there had been at Licodia and other Sicilian towns before their inhabitants modified their burial rites in accordance with Greek practice. It is only in the last quarter of the seventh century that the first Greek vases appear.[4] Some of the silver ornaments, and the bone-and-wood fibula in grave 281, may be older, but they are of less value than pottery in establishing actual intercourse. Probably the late seventh century was the date of the first contacts, and of the Lokrian foundation of Hipponion, from which Torre Galli is about ten miles distant. But before the middle of the sixth century the native element is on the point of disappearing. The change of rite is the most important point; the production of pottery which apart from its clay might be Greek, and the absence of any local pottery in

[1] Late Protocorinthian or Transitional aryballos; six alabastra, cf. *NC*, fig. 121 B; two aryballoi.
[2] Cf. *MA*, xxxi. 149.
[3] Ibid. 152, 'Elementi greci infiltratisi per ragioni varie nella tribù indigena.'
[4] It is not safe to date the intercourse to the third quarter on the strength of the one Late Protocorinthian aryballos in grave 251, along with Early Corinthian alabastra. It might have continued in use until they also were current.

many of the sixth-century graves, combine to make it probable that these were Greek graves.[1] In the sixth century Greek elements are in every respect stronger than native. The period since the first contact is hardly long enough for the native to have absorbed the Greek culture. It seems more like a peaceful infiltration than a conquest, though of course the Lokrians must have exercised control of the little place. There are points which suggest mixed marriages. The arms in the cremation burials 289, 295 are not according to Greek custom, and the native amphora adjacent to the ossuary of 289 might be the deposit of a relative. The rare case of a cremated and an uncremated body in the same grave (139) might be explained in the same way. At least, it is likely that the Greeks living among the Sikels of Torre Galli were less insistent on race distinctions than the Sicilian Greeks.

The latest graves of Torre Galli are after the middle of the sixth century; grave 328 is perhaps towards the end of the century. This does not mean that the settlement came to an end then. The latest graves were being excavated when work stopped, and if it had been possible to continue in the same direction more might have been found. But the site was more suited for a settlement of Italians, herdsmen and woodmen, than for a village of Greek farmers. It is on a defensible height about four miles from the sea, a position more adapted for defence than offence, and very much exposed to the weather. The Greeks would have preferred either a place on the coast or a commanding position like Hipponion. Perhaps with the growth of Greek control in the course of the sixth century the little town was removed.

Sporadic finds from Nicotera are said to be comparable with the Torre Galli material. The only Greek object is a fragment of a gorgoneion like a fragment from Medma.[2] This indicates that the Greek occupation is as old as the late sixth century, and it appears that so late as this the natives were hardly touched by the neighbourhood of Greeks at Medma, five miles away. Not too much stress should be laid on this, as there is very little material, and that not from a regular excavation.

Other Calabrian sites such as Oppido Mamertino[3] which

[1] Cf. Orsi, op. cit. 149: 'la zona delle tombe ellenizzanti, se non sono già elleniche', and 359: 'nelle tombe grecizzanti vi è un indizio, se non della convivenza, certo di un accordo tra indigeni e greci conquistatori.'

[2] N Sc, 1928, 481, fig. 5.

[3] Some material in Antiquarium at Reggio.

might supplement the evidence of Torre Galli are almost unexplored. It is unsafe to base on the excavation of a single site a survey of the whole Lokrian territory. But so far as the evidence goes, it appears that the people of the extreme south, who may on both historical and archaeological[1] grounds be called Sikels, were brought less early into contact with the Greeks, by way of commerce or conquest, than the people of Sicily. Their own culture is less developed, and in spite of the neighbourhood of Greek towns and the probable presence of Greeks they do not absorb Greek culture to the same extent as the Sicilians. Greek and Sikel live side by side, but there is not much material which shows the effect of Greek influence on the Sikels. Torre Galli ceases soon after the middle of the sixth century, after no long period of intercourse with Greeks. There is little material of this period from Medma and Hipponion, so the relation of Greeks and Italians when these towns developed is not clear.

The remains of Metauron by Gioia Tauro at the mouth of the river Petrace, the ancient Metauros, consist chiefly of terracotta revetments, the oldest of which is a fine female head of the early sixth century.[2] The deposit in Contrada Monacelli is 'entirely homogeneous, and betrays no signs of even partial restoration later than the sixth century'.[3] The metope fragment from S. Maria is also sixth century. Mrs. Van Buren quotes parallels from the earlier Marazà temple at Lokroi for the Monacelli group. The excellence of these terra-cottas is the more remarkable in view of the insignificance of the town of Metauron, which is heard of only as a claimant for the honour of giving birth to Stesikhoros. They show what fine work Lokrian or Rhegine artists could do even in a secondary town and before their great art begins.

Metauron is said to be a Lokrian colony:[4] another tradition makes it Zanklaian.[5] The evidence for either is bad; it was said to be Stesikhoros' birthplace, and may therefore be thought to have been Khalkidian. On the other hand, Stephanos calls it a Sicilian city, presumably because Stesikhoros' birthplace would be expected to be in Sicily. Stesikhoros was closely con-

---

[1] *MA*, xxxi. 326.

[2] Van Buren, antefix 53, p. 148; Richter *Sculpture and Sculptors*, fig. 157.

[3] Van Buren, 43.

[4] Steph. Byz., Μάταυρος, πόλις Σικελίας, Λοκρῶν κτίσμα. τὸ ἐθνικὸν Ματαυρῖνος. Στησίχορος Εὐφήμου παῖς Ματαυρῖνος γένος, ὁ τῶν μελῶν ποιητής.

[5] Solinus, ii. 11, *Metaurum a Zanclensibus*; Mela, ii. 68.

nected with Lokroi, and probably composed some of his poems there. He may have been born at the *Lokrian* town of Metauron, and his parents have migrated to Himera soon after its foundation. The probable date of his birth is *c.* 630.[1] There is no evidence of Lokrian occupation of the western side of the peninsula as early as this.[2] But Medma and Hipponion may have been founded in the seventh century, although their earliest remains are of the sixth; those of Metauron are of the same date.

If Metauron was ever Khalkidian it probably became Lokrian at an early period. But there is no other evidence for a Khalkidian extension up the coast,[3] and no record of ill-feeling between Rhegion and Lokroi earlier than the quarrel which Hieron composed.[1] The περιοικίδες πόλεις of Rhegion are known only from Strabo and may belong to a period later than the archaic, when Rhegion maintained its importance while the other cities of south Italy declined.[5] Rhegion had no hinterland but a mountain, and probably no land interests before Mikythos. The country, a fringe round the edge of Aspromonte, was not rich in antiquity (before the introduction of citrus fruits), but offers many sites for sea-coast settlements.

---

[1] Bowra, *Greek Lyric Poetry*, 77 ff.

[2] Oldfather's view (*RE*, xiii. 1308) 'die Lokrer haben daher die Berge wohl schon früh im VII. Jahrhundert überschritten', rests only on the evidence of Stesikhoros and his brothers Helianax and Mamertios or Mamerkos.

[3] See above (p. 164, n. 6) for Crispo's view that the port of Hipponion also was originally Khalkidian.

[4] *Pyth.* ii. 18 and Schol. Giannelli, *La Magna Grecia da Pitagora a Pirro*, 43 ff., regards the relation of Lokroi and Rhegion as one of constant enmity. But the only sixth-century reference shows them allied at the battle of the Sagra (Strabo 261). I can draw no conclusions about the political relations of Rhegion and Lokroi from the habits of the cicadas of each. Those of Lokroi were the most musical of their kind, those on the Rhegine side of the river Halex were silent. Timaios (ap. Strabo 260; cf. Aelian, *NH*, v. 9; Konon 5) associated this with the rivalry of Eunomos of Lokroi and Ariston of Rhegion at the kitharodes' contest at the Pythia. Aelian contrasts the friendship of the men of Rhegion and Lokroi, extending to the right to cross and work the fields in the territory of the other state, but gives no note of time. Solinus (ii. 40) gives a different reason, the annoyance which Herakles felt when his sleep was disturbed by the Rhegine cicadas. A saying of Stesikhoros warning the Lokrians to mind their behaviour for fear their grasshoppers should sing on the ground (Arist. *Rhet.* ii. 21. 8; iii. 11. 6) obviously refers to this rivalry, the danger being that the Rhegines would invade the Lokrian territory and cut down the trees. The date is uncertain, and also the ascription to Stesikhoros, the poet of Himera of the early sixth century (cf. Vurtheim, *Stesichoros' Fragmente und Biographie*, 80); the wisecrack is put also into the mouth of Dionysios of Syracuse (Demetrios 99). Cf. further Wilamowitz-Moellendorff, *Sappho und Simonides*, 233 ff.

[5] Most of the ancient remains in the territory of Rhegion, for which see Putortì, 'L'Antico Territorio di Reggio Calabria', *Historia*, iii. 89 ff., and local historians there quoted, are of Roman date.

One such is Skyllaion, fortified by Anaxilas as a naval base.[1] Another is by Leukopetra, at Contrada Grufo, where there are 'traces of a sanctuary of the two goddesses';[2] and in the Museo Civico at Reggio there is material from the neighbouring Saline.

[1] Strabo 257.

[2] N Sc, 1931, 662; see *Rivista Storica Calabrese*, xii, 1904, 227 ff., and *Italia Antichissima*, v–vi. 261 ff. The inscription quoted in the last-named is published with erroneous provenience, N Sc, 1909, 324.

CHAPTER V

NATIVE ELEMENTS IN THE CULTURE OF SICILY AND SOUTH ITALY

THE history of independent Sikel culture is one of decline from the time when contact with Greeks became continuous. It is best followed in the pottery, which in the Siculan II period (Late Bronze and Early Iron Age)[1] had a good deal of vigour and originality. The traditions of this period, in part formed by Mycenaean contact, had a long life. At the beginning of the Siculan III period (eighth century) painted decoration is introduced, and soon displaces the incised linear design of Siculan II.[2] The earlier Siculan III painted vases are better than the later. Figure decoration, animal or human, is rare. The early vases with figures found on Sikel sites[3] are probably Greek, not Siculan. On later vases, such as those from S. Angelo Muxaro and Mussomeli mentioned above,[4] figures occur occasionally but not often enough to establish characteristics which might distinguish a school or style of vase-painting. Pattern is commonly limited to geometric designs, of which as a rule the more elaborate are all early, later decoration being limited to very simple sub-geometric motives.

Many of the earlier vases found on Sikel sites (S. Aloè near Leontinoi, Finocchito, Tremenzano), dating just before and just after the foundation of the Greek colonies, are very close imitations of Greek models, and it is not always easy to distinguish Greek imports from the local product. At Tremenzano indeed there is hardly anything that is not either Greek import or close imitation of Greek work, and Orsi says that, considering only the content of the graves without their form or situation, it would be difficult to distinguish them from Greek.[5] Other vases are sufficiently Greek in general appearance and details to indicate that they may have been made by Greek potters for Sikel customers. As none of this graecizing Siculan is found in the Greek colonies, it is unlikely that it was made there for

---

[1] See the table of periods above, p. 2, n. 1.
[2] Orsi, *RM*, 1898, 305 ff.; Åkerström, *Der Geometrische Stil in Italien*, 14 ff.
[3] Ibid., pl. 3. 5; 4. 2; Blakeway, *BSA*, xxxiii. 186–7, figs. 10–11.
[4] pp. 139 ff.
[5] *BPI*, 1892, 93: 'Il dubbio sulla pertinenza etnica dei sepolcri di Tremenzano, che a taluno potrebbero sembrare greci anzi che siculi, si toglie con argomenti sopratutto d'indole topografica'; below, 'rito esclusivamente siculo'.

the Sikel market, as Orsi suggested.[1] It is more probable that some Greek potters took up their abode in Sikel towns, and that their example supplemented the efforts of Sikel potters to imitate vases imported from Greece.

At Lokroi also Greek vases imported to the Italian predecessor of the Greek colony were imitated there, presumably by Greek potters.[2] But this does not continue beyond the foundation of the colony, and nowhere in the colonial area of Italy is there known a local fabric of mixed antecedents such as grew up in Sicily and in Etruria, Latium, and Apulia. It is with these that we must compare the vases of the Siculan IV period. This is differentiated from Siculan III (which overlaps in date the foundation of the Greek colonies) by being later and by its association with Corinthian vases, rather than by any marked internal development. In shapes and decoration Siculan geometric is near its Greek originals and shows little development, so that individual pieces must be dated mainly by their association with Greek vases. Many of the shapes are derived from Greek models (amphora, oinochoe; in the course of the seventh century is added the hydria), and the decorative elements also are largely selected from the repertory of Greek geometric and sub-geometric vase-painting, of Corinth, the Cyclades, and other centres. It is possible that Greek potters not only assisted in the early stages of Siculan geometric and helped to establish the style, but continued to exercise their craft for Sikel patrons through the seventh and sixth centuries and made many of the larger vases. The artistic poverty, coupled with technical competence, of Siculan IV might be explained if the vases were made by provincial Greeks for the Sikel market.

Side by side with this painted pottery the types derived from Siculan II continue. The incised linear designs give way to painting, and as the decoration is usually so simple it is not easy to say whether a painted design is derived from Greek geometric or from Siculan II. Plain ware in some of the shapes used in Siculan II, particularly the saucer (*scodellone*), continues as long as Siculan pottery exists. But in the more careful productions elements drawn from imitation of Greek geometric are more important than pure Siculan survivals. This is in contrast to Apulian geometric, in which local elements of form

---

[1] *MA*, xxxi. 339. See below, p. 264.
[2] Ibid. 333 ff., pl. 15–16; Åkerström, op. cit. 37 ff.

and decoration continue until the fourth century and have some influence on the shapes of south Italian red-figure. In both shape and decoration Siculan geometric is nearer its Greek models and has less continuity with its predecessors than Apulian geometric.

The Sikels were skilful workers in bronze, and the import of metals which are not found in Sicily must have played a considerable part in their economy. There was a bronze-foundry adjoining the 'palace' of Pantalica, the biggest and most elaborate building of the prehellenic period, which was used for the manufacture of arms.[1] A number of hoards of bronze weapons, pins, and ornaments, together with rough lumps of metal, have been found at Sikel sites of the interior[2] and were no doubt smiths' stores. These deserve fuller study than they have yet received. Some of the objects have close parallels in Etruria and central Italy, the most probable source of metal for Sicily. Other objects, particularly a number of plain bronze vases, look Greek. The chronology of these hoards is ill established; some appear to antedate the Greek colonization, others come down into the sixth century. Most of the metal objects (bronze fibulas and ornaments) in Siculan III graves are of the same types as those of southern and central Italy,[3] but already some objects are Greek; for instance, bronze beads found on many Sikel sites have exact parallels at Syracuse, which is the most likely place for their manufacture.[4] Sixth-century Sikel graves lack the abundance of bronze objects found in earlier graves and most of what there is is Greek. The Sikel bronze-working craft, like the manufacture of pottery, died out early in face of Greek competition.

Of any Sikel art, as distinct from craft, there are only the scantiest remains. There are known a few bronze figurines of Sikel workmanship, which are thoroughly barbarian, almost without style, but with some fidelity of representation.[5] I cannot judge their technical competence; artistically they are grossly incompetent. The occasional fragments of stone sculpture are, more definitely than these bronzes, crude imitation of Greek work. Though the Sikels were good stone-cutters and their soft limestone is easy to work, they appear not to have

[1] *MA*, ix. 77 ff.; cf. p. 95.
[2] *BPI*, 1900, 164 ff., 267 ff.; 1927, 35 ff.
[3] Cf. Åkerström, op. cit. 28 ff.
[4] *MA*, xxv. 578, fig. 164. Cf. also above, p. 123, n. 2.
[5] Orsi, *Ausonia*, 1913, 52 ff.; Pace, *ACSA*, i. 164–5, figs. 81–2; ii. 156–7, figs. 145–7.

made sculpture in the round, or represented the human form, before they learnt it from the Greeks (a few Bronze Age terra-cotta figurines are copies of a common Mycenaean type). It is not surprising, therefore, that those few works which can be claimed as Sikel are imitations of Greek work or completely without style. The most interesting were found at Grammi-chele, where, more definitely than on any other site, Sikel and Greek are shown to have lived together in the sixth century.[1] They are an amorphous terra-cotta statue of a seated goddess[2] and a terra-cotta bust, crude but vigorous with its gross features, drooping eyelid, and twisted mouth.[3] The case for a Sikel origin is not proved beyond doubt, as the other objects from the sanctuary where this was found are all Greek; but of the bust especially it is easy to believe that it was the work of a Sikel, and not very hellenized at that.[4]

It has been suggested that certain works of sculpture from the Greek colonies show an 'Italian' spirit of realism which is due to the Sikels and is seen also in the bronzes and terra-cottas just cited.[5] These works are few and cannot be held to show either clear marks of Sikel workmanship or influence of Sikel style. It is held, however, that whether they are actually from the hand of Sikel workmen or not, they express a spirit which is un-Greek and may be assigned to the Sikel element in a culture and society formed by a fusion of Greek and Sikel. Most of the sculptures in question are not un-Greek in execution and would not be unthinkable in a context in Greece; for instance, the staring bust from Selinus which Marconi takes as his text in the article cited.[6] Others are un-Greek in the sense of being completely without style and untouched by the canons of any art. Among these the most noteworthy are a series of stelai from Selinus, dedicated to Meilikhios, an associate of Malophoros, the great goddess of the suburban sanctuary west of the city.[7] Some of these are aniconic; others have two heads side by side on a single rough-hewn base.[8] A small number of the latest examples (late fifth century) follow the conventions

[1] See above, pp. 122 ff.

[2] MA, vii, pl. 3; Van Buren, JHS, 1921, 204, fig. 1; Pace, ACSA, ii. 153–4, figs. 142–3.

[3] MA, vii. 219, fig. 8; Pace, op. cit. 159, fig. 149.

[4] For other Sikel sculptures see above, p. 133.

[5] Marconi, 'L'Anticlassico nell' Arte di Selinunte', Dedalo, xi. 395 ff.; Pace, ACSA, ii. 151 ff.

[6] Op. cit. 397, fig.; MA, xxxii, pl. 47. 6; Jenkins, BSA, xxxii, pl. 13. 4 ('under exclusively Argive influence').   [7] See below, p. 280.

[8] MA, xxxii, pl. 27–9; Pace, ACSA, ii. 161, fig. 151; iii. 476–7, figs. 113–14.

of Greek art; others, including some shown by their inscriptions to be archaic, indicate the features in a summary though vigorous manner which owes nothing to artistic training or convention. There is no close parallel for these works, either in Greece or Italy; a general comparison is provided by the sculpture of the great sanctuary at Capua,[1] which is of much later date. They are clearly not the work of artists of the Selinuntine or any other school, or indeed of craftsmen of any sort, and therefore elude classification. The suggestion has been made that their sculptors were Sikels;[2] against it is the evidence of the inscriptions, recording dedications in good Doric by persons with Greek names.[3] Moreover the cult, like that of Malophoros, is Greek, having been brought to Selinus from Megara Nisaia.[4] What is needed is an explanation why the artists who wrought the offerings dedicated in the main sanctuary of the Malophoros were not employed in this subsidiary sanctuary of Meilikhios. It must be sought, not in the field of the history of art, but in some religious peculiarity of the cult.[5] That there is Sikel influence in the form of artistic expression is not to be entirely excluded, but if so it must have been exercised indirectly, as part of a general Sikel contribution to colonial religion and spirit, as there are no direct proofs of the participation of people of Sikel descent in the cult.

In south Italy, although there has been less extensive excavation than in Sicily, there are clearer signs of the emergence of a mixed Italo-Greek art and culture, best seen in the votive offerings of the temple of Apollo Alaios at Cirò. These include a number of bronze statuettes which, though imitating a common Greek type, are to be ascribed to non-Greek artists.[6] With them have been compared a few bronzes from other south Italian sites of the interior; more important, an attempt has been made to trace the same spirit in major works such as the acrolithic statue from Cirò, and in bronzes and terra-cottas of

---

[1] Adriani, *Cataloghi illustrati del Museo Campano*: I, *Sculture in tufo.*

[2] Von Dühn, *Gnomon*, 1929, 532.

[3] *MA*, xxxii. 381 ff. Cf. Gàbrici's judgement, ibid. 176: 'Non v'è ragione di far luogo alla ipotesi, che le divinità, alle quali rendevasi onore in un angolo del santuario subordinatamente alla dea maggiore, la Malophoros, fossero divinità indigene, e come tali venerate con sacerdoti indigeni e rappresentate con la ingenua espressione di un' arte locale. Le iscrizioni rinvenute essendo greche nei caratteri e nel contenuto, rimuovono ogni dubbio su questo punto.'

[4] Hanell, *Megarische Studien*, 175 ff.

[5] Cf. C. Picard, *Rev. Phil.* 1933, 341 ff.

[6] Orsi, *Templum Apollinis Alaei*, pll. x–xii.

Lokroi and Medma.[1] As for the acrolith,[2] there is no case for regarding it as in any way non-Greek, though it has a quality not found in contemporary works from Old Greece. Its artist arose in a 'colonial' ambit which he further helped to develop; a distinctive school of art is distinguishable at an earlier date in south Italy than in Sicily.[3] How far this art is due to the non-Greek element in the population is difficult to assess. The supposed Italic elements have been related to Etruscan and Roman art; but the number of works in question is as yet too small to give a definite judgement on this point. In default of this direct evidence, the answer depends on one's view on other questions, the numerical weight of the non-Greek population in the colonies and the degree of their contribution in other cultural and social activities. These questions will now be discussed.

In material culture the Sikels had little to contribute to a Sicilian civilization. Other, more profound, borrowings by Greeks from Sikels in matters of religious spirit and outlook on life are difficult to determine. The supposed religious influences are the most important and among the hardest to estimate, as Sikel religion is known to us only in a Greek dress. It is impossible to trace a connexion between the primitive beliefs inferred from the material remains of the prehellenic period and the cults of Hybla, Hadranos, and the Palikoi which attracted the attention of the Greeks when the Sikels had become fully hellenized,[4] though of course a connexion must have existed.

These all appear to be divinities of the powers of Nature: Hadranos and the Palikoi deities of the volcanic soil of Sicily, like the obscure deity worshipped near the sulphur springs of Palma Montechiaro,[5] Hybla a nature-goddess, in Roman times identified with Venus.[6] Cults of this sort were very wide-spread in Sicily, whether under the Sikel form of one of these deities or the Greek form of Demeter and Kore, or the anonymous form of nymphs or river-gods. It may be that the worship of the nymphs, of minor deities of lake and wood and sacred source, is more true to native Sicilian practice than that of hellenized gods such as Hadranos, who was assimilated to Hephaistos. The nymphs, or kindred beings such as the

[1] Marconi, 'Italicità nell' Arte della Magna Grecia', *Historia*, ix. 574 ff.
[2] Orsi, op. cit. 135 ff.   [3] See below, pp. 288 ff.
[4] For Hybla see above, p. 131; for Hadranos, p. 132; this cult became of importance to the Greeks at the time of the Dionysian foundation of Hadranon.
[5] *MA*, xxxvii. 585 ff.; see above, p. 130.   [6] *CIL*, x. 7013.

Meteres of Engyon, were commonly worshipped in small country sanctuaries and, in the Greek cities, in suburban shrines.[1] They appear as elements of popular religion, whereas the official religion of most states, whether Greek or Sikel in origin, is Olympic. This is best observed on the coins: when, from the fifth century onwards, the Sikel towns begin to coin, their commonest types represent Greek gods, with Greek attributes; an example is the Demeter on the earliest coins of Enna.[2] Heads conventionally identified as nymphs,[3] and river-gods, also occur frequently on the coins of Sikel towns. It must be remarked that none of this evidence for Sikel religion is earlier than the middle of the fifth century, by which time the Sikels were, on the evidence of their material remains, almost completely hellenized. Further, the religious ideas ascribed to the Sikels, the worship of divinities of springs and rivers, of goddesses of growth, of powers of Nature such as are especially in evidence in a volcanic land, are in no way alien to Greece. It is not therefore possible often to determine what in the religion of Sicily is of surely local origin, what Greek. In general, the form of religious representation, in art or legend, is Greek, even when the content, the basic religious conception, may be native to Sicily.

It is frequently held that many of the cults of the Greek colonies were derived from the religion of the peoples whom they supplanted. These cults, so far as known to us from literary sources, coins, and inscriptions, were almost entirely Greek, and in most cases demonstrably brought from the mother city. It is not necessary to go through the whole inventory of colonial cults, but it will be enough to mention the best-known and most striking cases.[4] The cults of Syracuse, well known from a wealth of reference mainly of late date, are all clearly of Greek origin, though it is noteworthy that the great goddesses of Corinth, Hera and Aphrodite, were not among the most venerated deities of her colony.[5] These were Athena and Artemis, Apollo and Zeus Olympios, all of whom had temples in the archaic period; Poseidon also had Isthmian

---

[1] Pace, *ACSA*, iii. 481 ff.

[2] Head, *HN²*, 137; *BM Cat. Sicily*, 58.

[3] Fifth-century examples: Abakainon (Head, op. cit. 118); Nakona (ibid. 159); Segesta (ibid. 165).

[4] Ciaceri, *Culti e miti nella storia dell' antica Sicilia*; Pace, *ACSA*, iii. 533 ff.; Giannelli, *Culti e miti della Magna Grecia*.

[5] At Akrai, however, they had a common priesthood (*IG*, xiv. 208).

Games celebrated in his honour, as at Corinth.[1] Syracuse was
called by Pindar δέμνιον Ἀρτέμιδος;[2] most of the terra-cottas
found there are not of the types associated elsewhere with
Demeter and Kore, which are the commonest on most western
sites, but are Artemis-types; they come especially from the
suburban Artemisia of Scala Greca and Belvedere.[3] The worship of Demeter and Kore was, it appears, introduced by Gelon,
who built them a temple.[4] It took firm hold, the rape of
Persephone was localized near the spring Kyane,[5] and it is
likely that from Syracuse it spread to the Sikels.[6]

The cults of Selinus are well known, primarily from the fifth-
century inscription which gives thanks for victory to the gods
of the city, and especially to Zeus.[7] The cult best known from
the remains is that of Malophoros and Pasikrateia, chthonic
deities identified with Demeter and Persephone, with whom
was associated in the same sanctuary Meilikhios. Demeter
Malophoros and Zeus Meilikhios are attested at Megara Nisaia,[8]
and there can be no doubt that these, which, a priori, are the
most likely of Selinuntine cults to have incorporated local
elements, are derived from the mother country. The same can
be said more or less conclusively for most of the cults of
Selinus.[9] Similarly the Rhodian founders of Gela brought with
them the cults of Apollo Lindios and Athena Lindia; a family
among the settlers, the Deinomenids, brought the sacred
symbols of Demeter and Persephone from the Triopian headland, and long kept them in a private priesthood; the oecist,
Antiphemos, received heroic honours; and the river-god, Gelas,
was worshipped and figured on the coins. The last is the only
cult known at Gela which may, but need not, have had a Sikel
origin. At Akragas again, the cults of Athena and of Zeus
Polieus or Atabyrios are Rhodian; theirs are the early temples
on the acropolis. There is no direct evidence of the cult of
Apollo, except the existence of a month Karneios.[10] Akragas

---

[1] Schol. Pind. Ol. xiii, 158; cf. IG, xiv. 7. The worship of Poseidon from an early date
in the history of the colony is also implied in the story of the cup thrown into the sea by
travellers when they sailed out of sight of the city (Athen. 462b).

[2] Pind. Nem. i. 3. On the question whether the temple commonly called the Apollonion
is not rather the famous temple of Artemis mentioned by Cicero (Verr. II. iv. 53. 118), see
above, p. 59, n. 3. The cult of Apollo is attested early in any case by the inscription on this
temple and the existence of a month Karneios (Plut. Nic. 28).

[3] N Sc, 1900, 353 ff.; 1915, 192–3.   [4] Diod. xi. 26. 7.

[5] Diod. iv. 23. 4.   [6] See below, p. 180.   [7] IG, xiv. 268.

[8] Paus. i. 44. 3; JHS, xviii. 1898, 332; Hanell, Megarische Studien, 175 ff.

[9] See Pareti, Studi Siciliani, 227 ff.; Hanell, op. cit. 163 ff.   [10] IG, xiv. 952.

was especially Φερσεφόνας ἕδος,[1] and two of the small archaic sanctuaries excavated in the lower town are believed to belong to Demeter and Kore. It is mere guess-work to assign names to the other sanctuaries and temples of Akragas, with the exception of the colossal Olympieion. The cults of the other Sicilian colonies are less well known, especially in the archaic period, but so far as known derive from Old Greece. It is the same story in the south Italian cities, whose cults have been methodically analysed by Giannelli. With a few exceptions which will be discussed shortly, they lead back to the mother country, whether to local cults brought by the colonists or to panhellenic cults such as those of Pythian Apollo and Olympian Zeus. This is most marked in the case of Taras, whose cults are known in considerable detail and can in most cases be conclusively shown to be of Laconian origin.[2]

It has been held that many of the cults of the Greek colonies, though outwardly assimilated to the observance and belief of the mother country, so that they were directed by name and epithet to the deities whom the Greeks knew, were originally taken over from the Sikels and Italians. The strongest case is made out for the worship of Demeter and Kore in Sicily and of a goddess identified as Hera or Aphrodite in the Italian colonies, and our examination may be limited to these two. The cult of Demeter and Kore was widespread throughout Sicily among both Sikels and Greeks, so that it could be said 'insulam Siciliam totam esse Cereri et Liberae consecratam'.[3] This is as old as Pindar's time; he relates how Zeus gave the island to Persephone:

> σπεῖρέ νυν ἀγλαΐαν τινὰ νάσῳ,
> τὰν Ὀλύμπου δεσπότας
> Ζεὺς ἔδωκεν Φερσεφόνᾳ, κατένευ-
> σέν τέ οἱ χαίταις, ἀριστεύοισαν εὐκάρπου χθονὸς
> Σικελίαν πίειραν ὀρθώσειν κορυφαῖς πολίων
> ἀφνεαῖς.[4]

Pindar is of course speaking of Greek Sicily, for he had no interest in the half-barbarous Sikels. We can trace the stages of the extension of the cult, for Pindar probably saw it happen and himself assisted with the words just quoted. They come from a Syracusan ode addressed to Khromios the kinsman of

---

[1] Pind. Pyth. xii. 2. Cf. Schol. Ol. ii. 15d, 70h, where also Akragas is specified.
[2] Giannelli, op. cit. 1 ff.; cf. above, p. 91 f.
[3] Cic. Verr. II. iv. 48. 106.   [4] Nem. i. 13.

Hieron, the origin of whose power was in the priesthood of the goddesses. The cult originated in the private mysteries of Telines of Gela,[1] was no doubt taken to Akragas, Φερσεφόνας ἔδος, from Gela, and was brought to Syracuse by Telines' descendant Gelon, who built a temple there to Demeter and Kore.[2] From Syracuse it was carried to Hieron's foundation of Aitna on the site of Katane; with Hieron's priesthood of Demeter and Kore was associated that of Zeus Aitnaios, who is also named in juxtaposition with Persephone in the ode to Khromios.[3] Their family cult was, we may believe, used as an instrument of policy by the Deinomenids, and its extension among the Sikels may have gone together with the extension of Syracusan political influence. Its popularity may be due to an affinity with the religious ideas of the Sikels, and it must in many places have absorbed or replaced the worship of some kindred divinity of the Sikels; but this does not imply that its content was in any respect non-Greek. In Cicero's time the centre of the cult was at Enna,[4] as it already was for Kallimakhos.[5] The cult of Demeter at Enna is witnessed by the earliest coins, which belong to the middle of the fifth century;[6] Enna had already then long been open to Greek influences and had perhaps received a Syracusan colony.[7] The introduction of the cult of Demeter, or rather the identification of the divinity worshipped as Demeter, may therefore be due to that Syracusan influence which was also responsible for the introduction of coinage and Greek coin-types. The rape of Persephone is not located at Enna earlier than Roman times.[8] Pindar does not refer to it, and Bakkhylides, writing in Sicily of the rape of Persephone, places it not in Sicily but in Crete.[9] So the location of the rape in Sicily must have taken place after the time of Pindar and Bakkhylides, and the port of entry of the story was surely Syracuse. The rape was also located at Syracuse, near the fountain of Kyane;[10] this version may be as old as the early fourth century, for it is likely that Karkinos, who wrote at Syracuse, related it.[11] Another version placed the

---

[1] Herod. vii. 153.   [2] Diod. xi. 26. 7.

[3] Pind. *Ol.* vi. 95–6. Perhaps the mention of a temple of Demeter and Kore at or on Aitna, said by Diod., loc. cit., to have been planned but not built by Gelon, refers in a confused way to a temple of the two goddesses built at Aitne-Katane by Hieron.

[4] *Verr.* II. iv. 106 ff.   [5] *Hymn.* vi. 30; *Iamb.* v. 7 (ed. Budé).

[6] *BM Cat. Sicily*, p. 58; Head, *HN²*, 137.   [7] See above, p. 136.

[8] Cic. *Verr.*, loc. cit.; Lactantius, *Div. Inst.* 2. 4 (events of 133 B.C.); Livy xxiv. 39. 8 (events of 214 B.C.); Ovid, *Fast.* iv. 419 ff.; *Met.* v. 346 ff.   [9] Fr. 64 Bergk.

[10] Diod. iv. 23. 4; v. 4. 1.   [11] Ap. Diod., loc. cit.; cf. Freeman, i. 533.

event near Hipponion,[1] in another area of Syracusan influence. From Syracuse also it must have been transferred to Enna. The proof is in the mention of Arethusa in one of Ovid's versions of the story;[2] she is out of place at Enna and implies the logical priority of the version which placed the rape of Persephone near Syracuse. In Ovid's other narrative also Kyane plays a prominent part, though here the transition from Enna to Syracuse is more skilfully managed.[3] The reason why Enna was regarded as the scene of the rape will have been the neighbourhood of Lake Pergus, the most considerable lake in Sicily; the growth of the story belongs as much to the history of Hellenistic poetry as to Sicilian religion.

At many places the Greeks worshipped on Sikel sites. Sometimes, as at the Athenaion of Syracuse, the Greek sanctuary is underlaid by part of a Sikel village, and there is no indication that the site was sacred to the Sikels. Elsewhere, as at Akragas, it appears that a sacred site of the Sikels was occupied by a Greek sanctuary. The clearest case is that of the little sanctuary in a cave just outside the walls, below the church of S. Biagio.[4] Further, the sanctuaries outside the walls of the colonies may well have had native predecessors, which might account for their location. These in Sicily include the Olympieion of Syracuse and the suburban sanctuary at Bitalemi near Gela (the latter going back as early as the foundation of Gela if not indeed earlier),[5] in Italy the celebrated shrines of Hera Lakinia near Kroton and Hera Argeia near Poseidonia. Many but not all of these shrines belong to goddesses who are on other grounds thought to owe something to Sikel or Italian predecessors. At those of Gela and Akragas Demeter and Kore are thought to have been worshipped, at Kroton and Poseidonia Hera has been regarded as a Greek translation of an Italian deity.[6] Except at Akragas and, more doubtfully, at Gela, excavation has yielded no evidence of the supposed prehellenic forerunner of the Greek sanctuary. There may be other explanations of the choice of a site outside the walls; as at Naxos, where the altar of Apollo Arkhegetes, one of the most

---

[1] Strabo 256.   [2] *Fast.* iv. 423.
[3] *Met.* v. 407 ff.
[4] Marconi, *Agrigento*, 24 ff.; *RIASA*, i. 31 ff.; see below, pp. 307 ff. Siculan sherds were also found under the 'Temple of Aesculapius' (*Agrigento*, 92), but appear to be fortuitous and not to prove continuity of worship on the site.
[5] Cf. Blakeway, *BSA*, xxxiii. 183.
[6] Ciaceri, *Storia della Magna Grecia*, ii. 20 ff.

Greek of deities,[1] lay outside the city, presumably where the Khalkidian colonists first touched land, so the Heraion of Poseidonia may have occupied the first emplacement of the colonists.[2] The Lakinian promontory, where the Heraion of Kroton lay, was an object of much greater mark to Greek sailors than it could ever have been to landsmen.

It is likely enough that in many cases worship continued on the same spot, and the Greeks replaced the old cult by that of the member of their pantheon who seemed most appropriate. They would naturally placate the gods of their new land and of the people whom they had driven out. This does not, however, prove that there was any native element in the population of the colonies or in the content of their religion. That religion appears in externals, in details of cult and legend, completely Greek.[3] The gods of the Greek colonies are Greek, in many cases traceable directly to the mother city of the colony. There are, of course, variations of colonial religious ideas and observances from those of Old Greece; particularly in the pre-disposition to chthonic cults with a mystery element, from which Orphism and Pythagoreanism developed. But these do not establish the presence of non-Greek elements, for in the different social and cultural atmosphere of the colonies such variations would inevitably occur in the course of centuries, and need not be due to the interaction of Greek and Italian.

A few minor cults in some of the Italian colonies may have been taken over from the Italian peoples. One is that of Diomedes, to whom honours were paid at Taras, Metapontion, and Thuria.[4] The centre of this cult is in Apulia, and it is properly regarded as that of a native hero identified with the Akhaian leader,[5] though its extension over the whole Adriatic may be due to Greeks. The southward extension to the Greek colonies is not early nor much vouched for, and was evidently unimportant. This makes it likely that it was derived from Apulia, not brought by the colonists from Greece.[6]

[1] Brought from Khalkis; cf. Cahn, *Die Münzen der Sizilischen Stadt Naxos*, 91.

[2] See above, p. 25.

[3] A purely Greek legend of local origin is the story of the birth of Pan in the Sybaritis (Aelian, *HA* vi. 42; Theokr. v. 14, and Schol.).

[4] References in Beaumont, *JHS*, 1936, 194.

[5] Ibid. 195. *Contra*, Giannelli, op. cit. 52 ff., regards it as introduced to Apulia through the Rhodians of Elpiai. As there is no evidence connecting Diomedes with Rhodes, this is not a satisfactory origin, though Rhodians and other East Greeks may have helped to spread the cult.

[6] Giannelli, loc. cit., regards it as a Troizenian contribution to the cults of Sybaris.

Kalkhas, like Diomedes, was venerated among the Daunians on Monte Gargano;[1] and also, if Lykophron's words may be taken at their face value, at Siris, where he was buried (his grave was shown also at Klaros, near the mother city of the Sirites, Kolophon; hence it was doubted whether the grave at Siris was that of the seer or of a homonym).[2] The cult and oracle on Monte Gargano is best regarded as that of a native deity, sometimes called Kalkhos, not Kalkhas, who was identified with the seer. The Kalkhas of Siris may be equivalent with this Daunian hero, taken over by the Greeks from the Iapygian Khones, or may have been introduced by the Kolophonians. But it must be noted that the naming of Kalkhas in his own name is too simple for Lykophron's style and may well conceal a reference to some other heroic personage; and there is no other testimony to Kalkhas at Siris.[3] This is therefore a weak text on which to argue the question of Italian influences.

Metapontion and Siris are, *a priori*, the colonies where borrowing from the Italians is most likely, for the tradition of the origins of these cities is most confused.[4] Metapontion has a wide range of unusual cults which may reflect a mixed origin, but except for Diomedes they are all Greek.[5] The legend of Melanippe and Metabos, which has been used to establish the intermarriage of the early colonists with native women,[6] is Boeotian.[7]

At Lokroi it is clearly stated by an ancient source that there was a partial fusion between Greeks and natives, and that the Greek colonists took over a number of customs from the Sikels. Unfortunately these statements are made in the course of a violent polemic about the origin of the Lokrians, which makes it difficult to take them at their face value. Polybios says of the colonists πλείω τῶν Σικελικῶν ἐθῶν παραλαβόντες, διὰ τὸ μηδὲν αὐτοῖς πάτριον ὑπάρχειν, and explains so the matriarchal system and especially the custom of choosing a girl not a boy as φιαληφόρος.[8]

Diomedes was honoured at Troizen (Paus. ii. 32. 1). But the cult is attributed to Thuria, not Sybaris (Polemon ap. Schol. Pind. *Nem.* x. 12), and there is no good reason to suppose that it had been originally Sybarite.

[1] References in Beaumont, op. cit. 196.

[2] Lyk. 978 ff. and Schol.; Giannelli, op. cit. 108 ff.; Perret, *Siris*, 101 ff.

[3] Perret, op. cit. 111 ff. This was already the view of Holzinger, *Lykophrons Alexandra*, on l. 980.

[4] See above, pp. 33 ff.   [5] Giannelli, op. cit. 62 ff.

[6] Ciaceri, *Storia della Magna Grecia*, ii. 9.

[7] Giannelli, op. cit. 87 ff.; which see for bibliography.   [8] xii. 5. 9.

The archaeological evidence does not support the view that there were Sikel elements in the culture of Lokroi. For more than half a century before the foundation of the colony the Sikels living on the site imported a few Greek vases and manufactured others in imitation.[1] There is no Protocorinthian in the native graves, and no geometric pottery of any sort in the graves of Greek Lokroi. The native cemeteries come to an end about the end of the eighth century;[2] the Eusebian date for the foundation of the colony, c. 673, is about that of the earliest pottery from the Greek cemetery.[3] This strongly favours the view that the Sikels were expelled as soon as the colony was founded; as is natural, for their villages on the hills above the Greek town would have been dangerous to the colonists. Polyainos records the trick by which the Lokrians gained a footing and swore a misleading oath φυλάξειν τὴν πολιτείαν as long as they kept their heads on their shoulders and trod the same ground.[4] The same sort of quibble is said to have been used at Metapontion,[5] and the device by which the Leontines drove out the Sikels without breaking their oath is similar.[6] Polybios has the same story about the Lokrians,[7] concluding μετ' οὐ πολὺ καιροῦ παραπεσόντος ἐκβαλεῖν τοὺς Σικελοὺς ἐκ τῆς χώρας. None of these tales is very convincing, but the ancient tradition accords with the archaeological evidence to the effect that the Sikels were driven out when the colony was founded.

I am not competent to pursue the inquiry whether matriarchy is more natural to primitive Italian or Greek custom. But Polybios' general presumption that the Lokrians would have no traditions of their own is unfounded. A little earlier he derives the favoured position of women from the high descent of the women of the original settlement. It is not a priori impossible that some customs in a Greek colony should be derived from the natives by way of intermarriage with their women. But at Lokroi the pure Greek blood of the women is stressed, and the Lokrian aristocracy was clearly proud of its descent. It is unlikely that any custom connected with the

---

[1] Orsi, MA, xxxi. 211 ff.; Blakeway, BSA, xxxiii. 176 ff.; Åkerström, 37 ff.

[2] Blakeway, loc. cit.; Oldfather, RE, xiii. 1310, 'die Eingeborenen um 700 v. Chr. ausgerottet oder geknechtet worden sind'. Åkerström, in accordance with his tendency to lower all dates, brings them down into the seventh century.

[3] Johansen, VS, 182.   [4] vi. 22.

[5] Suidas s.v. Φοινίκων συνθῆκαι. ἐδεήθησαν τῶν ἐπιχωρίων δέξασθαι αὐτοὺς νύκτα καὶ ἡμέραν.

[6] Polyainos v. 5; see above, pp. 45 ff.   [7] xii. 6.

honour shown to women, or with the importance of descent in the female line, would derive from the Sikels. In general such other Lokrian customs as can be traced are derived mainly from Lokris,[1] and the Lokrian aristocracy was descended from the Hundred Houses of Lokris.[2] The custom of temple prostitution is derived from the east through Greece, though not through Lokris; it has little if any relation with the matriarchal elements.

The mixed nature of the founders of Lokroi, ἀποικίαν . . . δραπετῶν, οἰκετῶν, μοιχῶν, ἀνδραποδιστῶν,[3] is exaggerated for the purpose of polemic. Polybios is making a point against Timaios, and seems to have overreached both the evidence and the probability. Apart from his statement there is no evidence that the Lokrians were less pure Greek than any other colonials. To say that they were contradicts the implication of his own statement that the Lokrians drove out the Sikels after a short period of uneasy joint occupation, and is also contrary to the archaeological evidence. There is no archaeological evidence at Lokroi, as there is at Leontinoi, that the two races lived side by side for any length of time. And there is nothing in the remains of Greek Lokroi which faintly suggests a non-hellenic element in their culture.

The favoured position of women has been used as an argument that there was intermarriage between Greeks and Italians.[4] Elsewhere than at Lokroi this female predominance is uncertain; but if it were true, it would imply that the women were of pure Greek descent rather than that the Greeks looked up to their women because they were more truly representative of the Italian tradition. The admission of women to the Pythagorean brotherhoods is of very doubtful relevance. The fact that a goddess was the chief divinity of most of the cities is also beside the point, unless Athens and Argos are also unhellenic. The Italian women, like the Massaliot women,[5] are said not to have drunk wine, the αἴτιον being a dull story that

---

[1] Cf. Giannelli, *Culti e Miti*, 231, 'una serie di contatti notevoli e singolari coi culti praticati dai Locresi Opunzi'. I cannot follow him when he supposes them to be due to the influence of the colony on the backward mother country.

[2] See above, p. 72.   [3] Polyb. xii. 8.

[4] Ciaceri, *Storia della Magna Grecia*, ii. 1 ff. So also Giannelli, op. cit., ch. xii, esp. 240–1; regarding as native customs the privileged position of women, the sacred prostitution, and 'il carattere lussurioso della vita della città'. He may be right in thinking the Lokrian Persephone a native goddess assimilated by the Greeks. But it does not follow that there was anything Sikel about the manner of her worship.

[5] Athen. 429*a*.

Herakles asked for a drink when he passed by Kroton, and the housewife, having secretly consumed the bottle of wine, told her husband to give him water.[1] The reason is possibly that some of the colonists took native wives, as at Massalia; at part-Carian Miletos also the women drank water.[2] This slight evidence for the inferior position of women is more in favour of a mixed origin than all the evidence for female predominance.

It has been suggested that the Tarentine custom of burying within the walls was adopted from the Iapygians.[3] As this was also a custom at Sparta,[4] it may equally well be derived thence, and the absence of any other indication in the material remains of Iapygian admixture among the Greeks of Taras favours the latter view.

Failing substantial proofs of Italian influence on the Greek colonies, certain arguments from probability may be admitted. The mother cities of all the colonies except Taras and Rhegion were the unimportant communities on both sides of the Corinthian Gulf, which so declined in the course of the seventh and sixth centuries that relations between colony and metropolis could be only sentimental. Many of the colonies also were composed of a mixture of men from many states of Greece, and had confused traditions of more than one foundation. This might dispose them to hold less strongly to the traditions of their mother country (though there is no evidence that this was so at Lokroi) and might also dispose them more readily to intermarry with the natives. It is possible also that when the definitive colonization of Metapontion and Siris was effected there were on the sites considerable numbers of Greeks, or a small mixed community. In this way some native blood and native customs might have been introduced. Naturally there is only presumptive evidence of the most intangible sort, except for Polybios' controversial statement about Lokroi. A mixture of blood is more likely than an Italian element in colonial customs, for the native people had little to contribute to Greek civilization. But the Iapygians and the related Khones were more akin to the Greeks than the other peoples of Italy

---

[1] Alkimos the Sikeliot ap. Athen. 441a.

[2] Modern analogy does not favour this view. The women of Anogeia in Crete at this day do not drink wine, or, if they do, they drink it behind the door, like the Krotoniate housewife. The Anogeians are very jealous of their traditions and pure Greek descent, and still tend not to intermarry much with other Cretans.

[3] Messerschmidt, *Italische Gräberkunde*, ii. 324.

[4] Plut. *Lyc.* 27. See above, p. 89.

and Sicily, and perhaps more receptive. A cultural fusion, in which the Iapygian element was dominant, took place by the fourth century in Apulia and Calabria. This suggests that something of the sort may earlier have taken place farther south, in the hinterland of Metapontion and Siris, Sybaris and Kroton. Sybaris was liberal with the citizenship,[1] though probably to other Greeks, not Italians. The Oinotrians were regarded by the Greeks as somewhat civilized,[2] and so might have absorbed Greek culture more readily than the Sikels of Italy or Sicily. There may have been a mixed population in the inland towns of the Sybarite empire, whose names are Greek,[3] but whose inhabitants must have been mainly Oinotrian. The rapid growth of Sybarite influence over so large an area, which contrasts with the slow expansion of the Sicilian and most of the other Italian colonies, suggests that the Oinotrians were tractable.

The country-side was then in the late archaic period inhabited by a population which had a leaven of Greek culture and blood. At Torre Galli it is almost certain that there were Greeks living among the Sikels.[4] It is less likely that the Greeks admitted any such admixture in their cities. There is no direct evidence of such a thing, and only the most tenuous arguments for it. The Italic names of Velia, Laos, Hipponion or Vibo do not prove an Italic element in the population of the Greek colonies there. The reassertion of the Italic forms, Velia outliving Elea, Lavinium, Vibo, and Paestum replacing Laos, Hipponion, and Poseidonia, is due to invasion and capture, not to the continuance of pre-Greek elements. The remains of these cities, so far as they have been excavated, and of the larger cities, are purely Greek. We should expect little else. In the temple of Apollo Alaios, which belonged to a people which was mainly Italian or at any rate not Greek, there are few offerings which are not of Greek workmanship.

The cemeteries and sanctuaries of Taras, Lokroi, Rhegion, and such minor sites as have been excavated show that life in the colonies was completely Greek in its material aspects. No clear signs of native Italian influence can be seen in archaic Lokroi or Metapontion, where, if anywhere, it might be

---

[1] Diod. xii. 9. 2.

[2] Syssitia were native to Italy (i.e. probably Italy south of the line Laos–Metapontion) and were associated with the change from nomadism to agriculture: Arist. *Pol.* 1329^b 5 ff.

[3] See above, pp. 155 ff.

[4] See above, pp. 165 ff.

expected. The very few remains of Italian art of the early archaic period are, like that of Sicily, of Corinthian origin. Sybaris and Siris, the most prosperous cities of south Italy, the two represented at the wooing of Agariste,[1] may have had an independent art. But they are archaeologically almost unknown, and the cities which have been excavated are, like those of eastern Sicily, poor in art, but strongly Peloponnesian in what has survived. The earliest school of art in south Italy is largely the work of a body of immigrants from the eastern Aegean. Only when the fifth century is well advanced is it possible to distinguish a local element in the art of Lokroi and other south Italian cities.[2] Then it is surely more natural to attribute it to the Italian Greeks, modified by their environment, than to the survival of an Italian population which had lain dormant for two centuries.

The south Italian colonies appear at the vital period of their development, the turn of the archaic and classical periods, more original and independent than the Sicilians. Economically, they break loose earlier from dependence on Corinth;[3] artistically, they develop an art of their own which is fresher and more beautiful than anything which grew on Sicilian soil; in religion and, we may suspect, in social life, they brought forth new ideas which influenced the development of both Greece and Rome. The causes of this greater originality are to be sought mainly in the different circumstances of their development; partly in causes which lie outside Italy, and in the immigration from Ionia of men of genius; perhaps also in part to a certain admixture of Italian blood. Farther than this vague and general statement it is hardly possible to go in an attempt to trace what elements of colonial culture may be due to the native peoples. There is, however, direct negative evidence in the absence of clearly traceable links between Italian and colonial culture, whereas most colonial customs are seen to be directly derived from Greece. It must be remembered that there is extremely little evidence of the development of the native peoples in south Italy before the fifth century. The temple of Apollo Alaios is the only excavated site of importance. In any case, the Lucanian invasion at the end of that century enslaved the original inhabitants and cut short any possibility of the growth of a mixed culture. Such a culture grew up, outside Etruria, only on the fringes of Greek coloniza-

---

[1] Herod. vi. 127.   [2] See below, pp. 289 ff.   [3] See below, pp. 241 ff.

tion in Apulia and Campania. In Sicily also it failed to develop, though at the beginning of the fifth century there were signs that the Sikels might produce a half-Greek culture of their own.

The chief proved contribution of Sikels and Italians to colonial culture is linguistic. The place-names of native origin include those of a number of Greek colonies, Gela and Zankle, perhaps Katane,[1] and, in Italy, Taras and Metapontion. It may be remarked that the use of a Sikel name for a site taken over by Greeks from Sikels does not prove very much. The example of the British in North America and Australia shows that words and names and legends can be taken over from the native populations without miscegenation or profound cultural influence.

The languages of the native peoples of Sicily and south Italy are known mainly from words taken over into Greek or recorded by Greek and Latin grammarians and lexicographers. The few inscriptions in Sikel and other native languages are so slight and difficult to interpret that they give little information about these languages.[2] The glosses are complicated by the confusion of Σικελοί and Σικελιῶται in late Greek authors and the use in Latin of *Siculi* to represent both, so that many Greek dialect words used by the Sikeliots are quoted as Sikel.[3] Among these is apparently the word λάταξ,[4] used in the specifically Sicilian game of *kottabos*. There remains a number of words cited from the Syracusan comic poets, Epikharmos and Sophron, which from their likeness to Latin or Oscan words may confidently be regarded as Sikel. These indicate that the common language of Syracuse had adopted many Sikel words, especially those of weights and measures (*nummus*, *litra*, *onkia*; cf. μοῖτον = *mutuum*), food (τέλλις, a shell-fish) and names of domestic objects (πατάνιον or βατάνιον = dish; cf. κάτινος = dish or purse, not in the comedians), and common slang (κάρκαρον = *carcer*; σύφαρ, 'skin of milk', as a term of abuse; γέρρα = αἰδοῖα, probably from Epikharmos).[5] Other Sikel glosses, though not quoted from the comedians, are of the same categories and perhaps came from them, as the comedians were the chief source of information about Sicilian dialect.

---

[1] Whatmough, *Prae-Italic Dialects*, ii. 477 ff. De Sanctis ap. Orsi, *MA*, xxiii. 690, suggests that the endings in Kaulonia, Ἀκραγαντῖνοι Ταραντῖνοι, &c., are taken over from Italic peoples. Cf. Conway, *Italic Dialects*, 47.

[2] See above, p. 133.

[3] Whatmough, op. cit. ii. 471.   [4] Cf. p. 220, n. 4.

[5] Whatmough, op. cit. ii. 449 ff.

Italiot dialect is less well known than Sikeliot, but many Tarentine dialect-words are recorded in the lexicographers,[1] and may be derived from Messapian.

Of the Sikel words taken over into Greek, the most important are those relating to weights and measures.[2] The three words νοῦμμος or νόμος, λίτρα, and οὐγκία or ὀγκία are cited as occurring in Epikharmos and Sophron, and also in Aristotle.[3] The hypothesis that they are borrowed from Latin is therefore ruled out by the early date at which they are attested. Their appearance in similar forms in both Sikel and Latin must indicate either that the Latin and Sikel languages were akin or more probably that the Latins learnt their weights and measures from the Sikels.[4] The Sikel measures were also adopted by the Greek colonists of both Sicily and south Italy. The standard on which the Greek cities coined was, from the early fifth century onward, adapted to include silver equivalents of the bronze weight, the λίτρα.[5] This was an anomalous introduction into the system of division of drachma and obol, the litra being one-fifth of a Syracusan or Attic drachma. Many of the higher denominations were reckoned in litras, thus: dekalitron = didrachm; pentekontalitron = decadrachm (the Demareteion).[6] At Taras the stater was called νόμος.[7] The use of these terms by the Greeks shows that the Italic system, based on the pound of bronze, which found another expression in the *aes grave* of Rome and central Italy, must have been already well developed during the early period of Greek intercourse with Sikels and Italians. The skill of the Sikels in bronze-working and the many Sikel hoards of bronze[8] come to mind, though the hoards contain no weights or anything which can be interpreted as currency. The Sikels therefore had a fairly well-developed commercial system, since the Greeks found it worth while to take over their weights and bronze standard and their names for them. This is one of the few respects in which Sikel or Italic influence on the Greeks is clearly traceable. It is of great importance in itself, and should be a warning

---

[1] Whatmough, *Prae-Italic Dialects*, ii. 428 ff.   [2] Ibid. 456, 459–60.

[3] νοῦμμος, Epikharmos ap. Pollux ix. 79; λίτρα, Epikharmos and Sophron, Kaibel, *Com. Gr. Fr.*, pp. 144, 149, 160, 166; οὐγκία or ὀγκία Aristotle ap. Pollux iv. 174.

[4] Cf. Whatmough, op. cit. ii. 457–8.

[5] Pollux iv. 174–5; Head, *HN²*, 115; Hill, *Greek and Roman Coins*, 42; *Coins of Ancient Sicily*, 42.

[6] Pollux iv. 174; Diod. xi. 26. 3.

[7] Ἰταλικὸς νόμος, Arist. ap. Pollux ix. 80; *Fouilles de Delphes*, III. v. 49; cf. Head, *HN²*, 54, 67; K. Regling, *Klio*, vi. 504 ff.   [8] See above, p. 173.

against drawing sweeping conclusions from the fields of art and literature in which the Greeks had nothing to learn.

If they had been allowed to develop as they were beginning to in the fifth century, the Sikels might have produced a half-Greek culture like that of the Italian peoples neighbouring on Greek colonies. They were beginning to write their own language, in an alphabet derived from Khalkidian.[1] The earliest coins of Sikel towns are in the second quarter of the fifth century. These are of course Greek work, and it is not always possible to say which places in the interior were still Sikel, which Greek, towns. But Morgantina, one of the first places in the interior to coin, was certainly Sikel.[2] Galaria is less certain.[3] By this time Sikels like Duketios could be received into Greek society; the rulers at any rate were fairly thoroughly hellenized. The development of a Siculo-Greek culture was, however, checked by the defeat of Duketios and the extension of Syracusan power over all eastern Sicily. The native elements were frozen, the Sikels assimilated to the Greeks, and only a provincial flavour distinguished Sicilians, Greek or Sikel in origin, by the time that the Romans came in contact with them. The rapid hellenizing of the Sikels in the first half of the fifth century, no less than the series of Sikel Wars begun by Hippokrates, made Duketios' national rising possible. But too many Sikels were already completely won over and had become Greek subjects. If Duketios' object was to preserve the Sikel character of native life, he was too late. The remains of Mendolito in particular illustrate what the Sikels might have done; there is some evidence that they were learning from the Greeks without forgetting their own traditions. But in Duketios' own country, the more hellenized region of the Heraian hills, Sikel culture had, to judge from the material remains, already died out by the fifth century, killed by political pressure and the impact of Greek culture.

Sicily was more thoroughly and permanently hellenized than south Italy,[4] and by the Roman period there was no distinction

---

[1] See above, p. 134; Whatmough, op. cit. ii. 441 ff.
[2] See above, p. 125; *BM Cat. Sicily*, 114; Head, *HN*², 157.
[3] *BM Cat. Sicily*, 64; Head, *HN*², 139.
[4] This is true from the point of view of an inquirer like Strabo of the Roman period, when many of the Greek colonies in Italy had lost their Greek customs and spoke Latin. But Greek has been more persistent to our own day in south Italy, where it is still spoken in small enclaves (see Rohlfs, *Griechen und Romanen in Unteritalien* and *Scavi Linguistici nella Magna Grecia*), whereas it has long since died out in Sicily.

between Sikel and Sikeliot. The Sikels became almost completely Greek in material civilization, used Greek names, spoke Greek instead of their own language. This assimilation was already far advanced in the fifth century. By 500 Greeks had penetrated most of eastern Sicily and occupied many of the best sites (see map, p. 96). In most cases the Greeks kept the Sikels at arm's length in the beginning even when they lived in Sikel territory. Grammichele is the only certain example of a town which before the fifth century was inhabited jointly by the two races.

The Sikels were, in the Greek view, a poor, hard-working race of serfs or labourers.[1] The little men who went out to till their fields did not, as Orsi points out, differ much from the industrious peasantry of Cicero's time and of the present day. There is no trace of Sikel in the population of the Greek towns, nor evidence of such intermarriage as is known to have happened at Kyrene,[2] for example, and we never hear of half-caste Greek and Sikel, though on general grounds some intermarriage is likely enough. The citizen bodies of the colonies were as pure Greek as those of Old Greece. In the thousands of graves which have been excavated at Syracuse, Megara, Gela, and other sites of Sicily and south Italy, there is only a handful of objects which can be ascribed to native industry or art, and very few indeed which would be out of place in a city of Greece proper. Probably the Sikels were not allowed to live in the Greek cities, but lived in the fields or had quarters outside the towns. At the most, an occasional bare grave among the thousands at Megara and Gela may be that of a Sikel slave. Some few probably came as slaves to Athens, among them perhaps the painter of black-figure vases Sikelos and the potter Sikanos. Sikon was a common slave-name, and also a citizen-name at Athens as early as the fifth century.[3] But most of the enslaved Sikels remained to till the fields for their Greek masters. The Sikel, free or slave, was a good butt for the quicker-witted

---

[1] ὁ Σικελὸς τὴν θάλατταν was known as a variant of the proverb ὁ Κρὴς τὴν θάλατταν. Alkman's reference (fr. 115 Bergk) was doubtless to the better-known Cretan version. The substitution of the Sikel has some kinship with the mocking references of Epikharmos, when the Sikel was becoming a sort of imitation Greek. The explanation τὶς Σικελὸς ἐμπορευόμενος καὶ ναυαγήσας, εἶτα ἐκπεσών, ἐπὶ πέτρας καθήμενος, ὡς γαληνιῶσαν εἶδε τὴν θάλατταν, οἶδά φησιν ἃ βούλει, βούλει γὰρ καὶ αὐτόν με λαβοῦσα καταποντίσαι· ἐγὼ δὲ νῆσον οἰκῶν ἐκ παιδὸς οἶδα τὰ σὰ σοφίσματα (Schol. Aristid. iii. 490: Bergk, loc. cit.) is obviously pragmatical. The original point was that the Sikel, like the Cretan, was an islander who never went to sea.　　　　　　　　　　　　　　[2] Herod. iv. 164. 4; 186; Pind. Pyth. ix. 105 ff.

[3] See note on the names Sikelos, Sikanos, Sikon, on p. 193.

Greek. Epikharmos, whom unkind posterity charged with being himself a Sikan, could get a ready laugh by introducing a Sikel into his comedies. But nowhere did the Sikeliot owe much to the Sikel, or receive him to any degree of intimacy. This holds, with the slightest of exceptions, for the first two and a half centuries after the first colonization. Afterwards the distinction between Greek and Sikel was blurred, the Sikel adopted Greek names and was taken for a Greek. But so long as the Sikel remained Sikel the Greek regarded him as an inferior being and was proud of his own descent. The change is beginning when Greek and Sikel fight side by side in the Kamarinaian War of Independence, and when the demos of Syracuse calls on the aid of the Killyrioi. But the final struggle of Sikel and Greek, and the fullness of co-operation which succeeded it, lie outside our present range.

NOTE: THE NAMES SIKELOS, SIKANOS, SIKON

Sikelos, vase-painter: Beazley, *AJA*, 1943, 445–6; Hoppin, *BFV*, 324; K. Peters, *Studien zu den panathenäischen Preisamphoren* (Berlin, 1942), 47 ff.

Sikanos, potter: Beazley, *ARV*, 43, no. 9; Hoppin, *RFV*, ii. 409; Ada Bruhn, *Oltos*, 70.

Both active late sixth century.

Sikon was a common slave-name, used by Aristophanes and vase-painters as the first name which came to hand (*Eccles.* 867; Adria, r.f. fragment, Schöne, *Antichità del Museo Bocchi*, pl. 1; a Paestan kalyx-krater gives the name to a phlyax, A. D. Trendall, *JHS*, 1935, 48, pl. 6B). But it could be respectable, for it was borne by one of the Erekhtheid tribe who fell in 459–458 (*IG*, i². 929, l. 59). It is given also to a young Athenian on a b.f. hydria by Psiax (*FR*, iii. 231, pl. 154. 2; Beazley, *ARV*, 10, no. 20); and is borne by a Cypriote who made a dedication at Naukratis (*BSA*, v. 32). It thus became a common name, not limited to men of Sicilian origin.

Sikanos also could be a respectable name, being that of one of the Syracusan generals in 415 (Thuk. vi. 73; vii. 46, 50, 70) and of an Athenian citizen (*IG*, i². 960, l. 8; late fifth century). The name Sikelos is not otherwise known, to my knowledge; Schol. Theokr. vii. 40*a* explains Sikelidas as a patronymic, son of Sikelos, probably wrongly.

Though the names Sikelos, Sikanos, and Sikon have their origin no doubt as slave-names, they do not necessarily imply slave origin or even Sicilian blood. Similarly Siculus, a *cognomen* in the *gens Cloelia* (Q. Cloelius Siculus, consul in 497 (Dion. Hal. v. 59. 1); T. Cloelius Siculus, triumuir ad coloniam Ardeam deducendam in 442, according to Livy's chronology (iv. 11. 5); Q. Cloelius Siculus, censor in 378 (Livy vi. 31. 2)) is probably a name given in compliment. If the tradition is sound, it carries back before the first otherwise proved contact between Sicily and Rome, the dispatch of corn in the late fifth century (see below, p. 216).

CHAPTER VI

COMMUNICATIONS

THE regular route to the west from any Greek port lay up the coast to Korkyra, across to the Iapygian promontory, and down the coast to Italy.[1] Most of our information is about ships of war, which had less provision for eating and sleeping on board than merchant ships.[2] The advantageous situation of Korkyra for τῆς τε Ἰταλίας καὶ Σικελίας παράπλου is insisted on especially from a naval point of view: ὥστε μήτε ἐκεῖθεν ναυτικὸν ἐᾶσαι Πελοποννησίοις ἐπελθεῖν τό τε ἐνθένδε πρὸς τἀκεῖ παραπέμψαι.[3] This route was taken by the theoroi sailing from Sicily who sacrificed on the altar of Apollo Arkhegetes at Naxos before taking their departure;[4] for if they had taken the direct route across the Ionian Sea they would not have come up to Naxos. It was taken by the *Salaminia*, accompanying Alkibiades under arrest, but he gave them the slip at Thuria, and crossed direct to Kyllene ἐπὶ πλοίου φορτηγικοῦ.[5] The direct crossing was frequently made, as is implied by the name Σικελικὸν πέλαγος[6] for the lower part of the Ionian Sea. The two alternatives are put in Thuk. vi. 13, where the boundaries between Sicily and Athens are said to be τῷ τε Ἰονίῳ κόλπῳ παρὰ γῆν ἤν τις πλέῃ, καὶ τῷ Σικελικῷ διὰ πελάγους. The direct route appears to be that taken by merchant ships, the coasting route by ships of war

---

[1] Thuk. v. 4, 5; vi. 30; vii. 26, 33, &c. R. L. Beaumont infers from the fact that the Corinthians expelled the Euboians from Korkyra, but not from Orikos, (1) that their interest was not in the mainland opposite Korkyra, but in the way to Syracuse; (2) that the route to Sicily, even in the eighth century, was straight across from Korkyra, not up to the Akrokeraunian promontory, whence is the shortest crossing (cf. *JHS*, 1936, 165). But the sea farther north, opposite Lissos, was called τὸν Ἰόνιον πόρον (Diod. xv. 13), which Dionysios' colony of Lissos was perhaps intended to guard against pirates; and the sea-way from Greece to Sicily in Roman times is via Aulona and Sasena to Otranto, thence from Cape Leuka to the Lakinian promontory, and so from headland to headland (*Itin. Rom.*, ed. Cuntz, 76 ff.).

[2] Cf. A. W. Gomme, *JHS*, 1933, 16 ff.; *Essays in Greek History and Literature*, 190.

[3] Thuk. i. 36; cf. i. 44; cf. Cornford, *Thucydides Mythistoricus*, 41 ff.

[4] Thuk. vi. 3. Cf. Strabo 418 on the importance of the commerce up the Corinthian Gulf: εὐτυχήσαντες γὰρ οἱ Κρισαῖοι διὰ τὰ ἐκ τῆς Σικελίας καὶ τῆς Ἰταλίας τέλη, πικρῶς ἐτηλώνουν τοὺς ἐπὶ τὸ ἱερὸν ἀφικνουμένους. This is a movement of persons, not goods. But the sanctuaries of Olympia and Delphi, which most attracted western Greeks to Greece, lay near the main trade-route which supplied the colonies.

[5] Thuk. vi. 61; 88. 9.

[6] Thuk. iv. 53: (ἡ Λακωνικὴ) πᾶσα γὰρ ἀνέχει πρὸς τὸ Σικελικὸν καὶ Κρητικὸν πέλαγος; cf. vi. 13, quoted below; Strabo 123 (reaches up to the Iapygian promontory and mouth of the Ionian Sea (Ἰόνιος κόλπος) which is part of the Adriatic); cf. id. 323, 334, 335; Ziegler, *RE*, ii A. 2470 ff.

and official travellers. In clear weather there would be no long interval between the disappearance of the Kephallenian mountains and the first sight of Etna. A well-found ship could cover the 250-odd miles[1] from Zakynthos to the Straits or Syracuse in two days or a little more, sailing at five to six knots.[2] The ship in which Zenothemis and his principal Hegestratos neglected to load wheat sailed direct from Syracuse across the Ionian Sea, and when they were two or three days out Hegestratos tried to scuttle the ship, but he was drowned, and it came safe to Kephallenia.[3] They must have been nearly across in three days, and apparently making for the mouth of the Corinthian Gulf. In spite of holding the Gulf of Corinth and Korkyra the Athenians could not prevent corn crossing from Sicily to the Peloponnese, presumably direct to the harbours of Elis.[4] This is in time of war, and we cannot be certain that this was the regular way; some of the Peloponnesian troopships bringing relief to Syracuse crossed direct.[5] Some came via Kyrene, Neapolis Carthaginensium, and Selinus,[6] no more a commercial route than the way from England to Egypt round the Cape of Good Hope.

From the African coast to Sicily the shortest crossing was two days and a night.[7] This agrees exactly with conditions in the last century, when 50-ton luggers (*schifaggi*) with a crew of four men and a boy crossed from Marsala to Tunis via Pantellaria in two days and a night.[8] The Greek γαῦλοι were probably not greatly different from these ships.

The coasts of Sicily have a bad reputation.[9] Smyth spends some time minimizing the dangers of the Straits, where there are no more wrecks than on any other equally frequented

[1] Two hundred and fifty-five miles from Syracuse, 244 from Taormina (Naxos) to Zante; 352 from Taormina to Cape Matapan (Smyth, *Sicily and Its Islands*, Appx., xviii).

[2] Köster, *Das antike Seewesen*, 177–81.

[3] Demos. xxxii. 8.

[4] Thuk. iii. 86. 4.

[5] Thuk. vii. 17.

[6] Thuk. vii. 50.

[7] Thuk. vii. 50. 2; Νέαν πόλιν Καρχηδονιακὸν ἐμπόριον, ὅθενπερ Σικελία ἐλάχιστον δυοῖν ἡμερῶν καὶ νυκτὸς πλοῦν ἀπέχει.

[8] Columba, *Porti della Sicilia Antica*, 239, speaking of conditions in his youth. The distance is 112 miles; the crossing, from Cape Granitola to Cape Bon, 80 miles in a direct line. If it was calm they sailed towards Girgenti to pick up the wind. Smyth's evidence of sailing-ship days is the best commentary on ancient conditions. He was on the Sicily station for many years, including the period of British protectorate, and prepared the Admiralty chart. Columba has much valuable evidence derived from the portuolans, whose ships were probably of the same type as Greek shipping.

[9] Ibid. 241; Smyth, op. cit. 195, 223; Appx., xx, xxv.

stretch of coast,[1] but one of his ships was turned completely round in the whirlpool of Charybdis. The same thing is said to have happened to a 12,000-ton liner. In spite of these discomforts of navigation the Straits are not particularly dangerous, but it can be a long business for a ship to tack through against wind and current. There is good anchorage at Acqua Ladrone and at the Faro Point[2] for ships waiting to come through from the Tyrrhenian Sea, but they may have to wait days together. This stretch between Milazzo and Faro is 'the most dangerous lee-shore in the Mediterranean'.[3] Such conditions of course were all to the profit of the Zanklaians.

Of all the good harbours of Sicily[4] only Syracuse and Messina were in Greek hands, and their possession became of primary importance when the Sikeliots began to build up a fleet. Otherwise the Greeks neglected a number of passable ports. The Akragantines used the beach and mouth of their river in preference to Porto Empedocle, for commercial purposes at least. South of Syracuse there are good anchorages at Vindicari and Marzamemi.[5] This is now a rather desolate country-side, but considering the nature of the ancient roads preserved near Syracuse, these ports were probably used to ship produce. Between Syracuse and the Heloros mouth was a Naustathmos.[6] The coast immediately west of Cape Pakhynos has sanded up fairly recently. Marza, Pozzallo, Sampieri, Marzarelli, Scalambri used all to be small ports, from which crossings were made in the sixteenth century to Malta.[7] Some of them still have Scali for the export of wine. Cape Pakhynos could be a serious obstacle, the prevalent north and east winds making it difficult to round. Bomilcar found this in 212 B.C.[8] But there was anchorage on both sides, and Porto Palo, probably the ancient Portus Odysseae, gives shelter.

Naxos and Katane have both been so altered by lava-flows that nothing is known of their harbours.[9] Neither of them

---

[1] pp. 108 ff. Thuk. iv. 24 is very reasonable: διὰ στενότητα δὲ καὶ ἐκ μεγάλων πελαγῶν, τοῦ τε Τυρσηνικοῦ καὶ τοῦ Σικελικοῦ, ἐσπίπτουσα ἡ θάλασσα ἐς αὐτὸ καὶ ῥοώδης οὖσα εἰκότως χαλεπὴ ἐνομίσθη.

[2] Smyth, Appx., viii, xi.   [3] Id., Appx., viii.

[4] Catalogue in Lehmann-Hartleben, *Die antiken Hafenanlagen*, and id., pp. 60, 84 ff. (Syracuse). The harbour of Augusta was apparently not regularly used (see p. 19), though the point provides shelter for the beach at Megara.   [5] Smyth, Appx., xvii.

[6] Pliny iii. 8. 89.   [7] Columba, 239.   [8] Livy xxv. 27.

[9] Katane: cf. Columba, 324; Livy, xxvii. 8. 19. Columba's opinion that Catania had not really a true port but only a mediocre anchorage consisting chiefly of the present *porto vecchio* is unfounded, for the lava of 1669 has run into the sea and altered the coastline.

could alone provide for the Athenian fleet during the winter of 415–414,[1] but that was probably because of commissariat difficulties. Leontinoi, though lying inland, was reached by a river which was still navigable in the Norman period, before its waters were diverted into the lake of Lentini.[2] There was also a sheltered beach at the south end of the Plaia di Catania, and a useful little port at La Bruca (Trotilon), in the mouth of a small stream, where the Megarians had attempted to settle on their first arrival in Sicily.

There is not a single harbour on the south coast,[3] but several tolerable summer anchorages: Gela, Licata, Palma, Girgenti. Boats could be taken into the mouth of the Fiume Salso, and the mouth of the river Salemi, at Mazzara, 'forms a very convenient haven for small craft'.[4] This was a type of harbour very suitable for Greek commerce. Mazara was a Selinuntine ἐμπόριον,[5] a subsidiary port of export for Africa. Selinus had a small harbour on each side of the acropolis, and that on the east was artificially enlarged and lined with quays and warehouses.[6] This port appears to have had separate defences. At Gela the beach was used, as it is to-day, and perhaps the river-mouth, in spite of the sailing-directions contained in the phrase *verticibus non adeunde Gela*.[7] At Kamarina also the beach and the river-mouth were used. The channel between the lake and the sea was artificially widened and deepened, to drain the lake and also to provide for shipping. The remains of the quays, to which the ships lay bow-on and swung down-stream with the current, are still to be seen.[8] The river-mouth and adjacent beach were similarly used at Himera.[9]

Metapontion[10] and Sybaris[11] each had an artificial port consisting of a basin, cut or enlarged from a natural hollow, with a channel to the sea and a canal from the river filling it and keeping the entrance open. Most of the other Italian towns,

[1] Thuk. vi. 74, 88.   [2] Ps.-Skylax 13; Pace, *ACSA*, i. 171, n. 3.

[3] Smyth, Appx., xix.

[4] Cf. Schubring, *Gött. Nachr.* 1865, 416 ff.; Lehmann-Hartleben, op. cit. 268; Columba, 252, 'un porto-canale naturale'.

[5] Diod. xiii. 82.   [6] Columba, 250–2; Hulot and Fougères, *Sélinonte*, 154 ff.

[7] Ovid, *Fast.* iv. 470.

[8] Pace, *Camarina*, 91 ff.; Lehmann-Hartleben, op. cit. 81, n. 1.

[9] Columba, 283–4.

[10] Lacava, *Metaponto*, 94: it is uncertain whether the canal was artificial, and whether there was a natural depression which was enlarged for the port. Lacava's excavations were not successful, but he quotes oral testimony that remains of the quays and buildings adjoining had been seen. A large building lying between the port and the walls was partly excavated by Lacava.   [11] Lenormant, *GG*, i. 158, 274–5.

except Taras, probably used beaches or river-mouths.[1] Lenormant says that the modern moles of the port of Crotone rest in part on the submarine foundations of the moles of the Greek port.[2] This must be taken with reserve; his reconstruction of the port as a horseshoe, with two rounded side-jetties, divided into two basins by a central jetty, is a flight of fancy. The mole is built of ancient blocks, chiefly from the temple of Hera, and this may be the basis of Lenormant's tale of ancient foundations. Crotone is the best natural harbour between Taranto and the straits. Other possible points of loading, e.g. Rossano, Cariati, Kaulonia, are of no great importance. Pliny's 'amnes navigabiles Carcinus, Crotalus, Semirus, Arogas, Thagines',[3] between the Isthmus of Catanzaro and the Lakinian promontory, are torrents from the Sila which cannot have been very navigable, but their mouths may once have been useful. This coast has sunk since antiquity[4] and the sand-bars across the mouths of the rivers are probably fairly recent. The mouth of the Sinni is now foul with sunken rocks and shoal, but it was probably the port of Siris and later of Herakleia.[5] The sunken rocks which make part of the coast dangerous (especially from Spartivento to Stilo Point, and round Capo Rizzuto and Capo Colonne) were possibly above sea-level in antiquity. Pliny is witness that there were islands off the Lakinian promontory.[6] Now there is only a shoal; it is difficult to believe that five islands have quite disappeared, and it may be that Pliny's geography went wrong. But there are now no islands between the S. Pietro and S. Paolo (the Khoirades) off Taranto and the Straits.

The ports on the Tyrrhenian coast are of importance either as ports of call on a voyage from the Straits to Etruria or as terminal points for the land routes across from the Ionian Sea considered below. The chief port is Porto S. Venere, the port of Hipponion. North of this there is a beach most of the way until a few miles north of Paola; somewhere on the big gulf of S. Eufemia, where Italy is at its narrowest from sea to sea, was

[1] Petersen, RM, 1890, 165, thought that Lokroi had a port like Metapontion and Sybaris. It is a small slight depression (just south of Casella 381 on the railway) less than 50 by 100 ft., and it would be difficult to keep a mouth open to the sea through the sand-dunes. Lokroi, unlike the other towns, lay on the beach. The port-quarter was separate from the rest of the town (Livy xxiv. i).   [2] GG, ii. 196.   [3] NH iii. 10. 96.

[4] Fr. Genovese, La Malaria in provincia di Reggio Calabria, 18; cf. ASCL, ii. 127. The Tyrrhenian coast is rising: see Fischer, Mittelmeerbilder, Neue Folge, 225.

[5] The river was navigable in the Middle Ages: see Galli, N Sc, 1934, 472.

[6] Loc. cit.

Terina. North of Paola the coast is rocky, and shelter important. The little island of Cirella (Kerilloi) would provide shelter
for boats in any weather. The promontory of Scalea (Laos) is
shelter from the north and north-west. North of Scalea, the
rocky Dino island gives good shelter. Scalea, Cirella, Diamante
might all be small ports. The Gulf of Policastro is dangerous
for small boats in a south-west wind, but has good ports at
Sapri and Policastro. Sapri is a small but very sheltered cove
at the head of the gulf. Pyxus, near Policastro, had also a very
sheltered little port at the mouth of the Busento. Velia had
a small but adequate harbour, Poseidonia a long beach; and
so on to the Bay of Naples and Kyme.

A beach shelving fairly steeply was perfectly satisfactory for
ancient merchant vessels, which could lie in and load over the
stern or be drawn up on the beach. Both operations can be
seen on the Sicilian coast at the present day, two-masted ships
of about 50 tons being drawn up for the winter at Gela, for
instance. But in the late sixth century, if no earlier, the advantage of lying in to a quay was felt, and at the same time the
development of navies made a good sheltered dock essential.
The results of the ownership of Syracuse and Zankle are discussed below.[1] Syracuse is the only city of Sicily known to
have possessed any fleet worth mentioning. We hear of five
Geloan ships,[2] two Selinuntine,[3] ten Rhegine ships,[4] ten Lokrian,[5] ten Thurian.[6] Of course these are not the whole force of
these towns, but they indicate on what a small scale naval
power, outside Syracuse, was. It is striking that ships or naval
action of Akragas are never heard of. The Spartan programme
at the outbreak of the Peloponnesian War of 200 ships from
Italy and Sicily[7] left out of account the ability as well as
the willingness of their allies there. The Syracusan fleet was
allowed to decline during the democracy. The fleet built up by
Gelon[8] was used in the civil wars after Hieron's death.[9] Many
of the ships were lost and the pick of the crews were no doubt
among the exiled mercenaries. Syracuse once again became
predominantly a land power. Although Hermokrates could
propose that the whole Sicilian fleet should take two months' provisions and meet the Athenians ἐς Τάραντα καὶ ἄκραν Ἰαπυγίαν,[10]
sea-power was their weakest point. After they had had a year's

---

[1] p. 425. [2] Thuk. vii. 33. 1. [3] Id. viii. 26. 1. [4] Id. iii. 88.
[5] Id. iv. 1. [6] Id. viii. 35. 1. [7] Id. ii. 7. 2.
[8] See pp. 415, 419. [9] Diod. xi. 68. [10] Thuk. vi. 34. 4.

warning in which to strengthen and equip their fleet they could man only eighty ships,[1] which were no match for sixty Athenian ships. Nikias numbered πολλαὶ δὲ τριήρεις καὶ ὄχλος ὁ πληρώσων αὐτάς among the dangers of the Sicilian expedition,[2] but the Syracusans made no move to prevent the Athenians entering the Great Harbour and blockading them.

LAND ROUTES

Many stretches of ancient roads are preserved in Sicily, especially near Syracuse. That leading north towards Megara, down the Scala Greca, is one of the best known of Greek roads. It consists of parallel ruts in the soft rock, up to a foot deep; on the plain there are many series of ruts, showing that from time to time a new course was taken. In earth or mud the ruts would doubtless be deeper. A model cart in terra-cotta in Syracuse Museum has an exiguous body between tall four-spoked wheels and a central pole for a horse on either side.[3] Neither the vehicle nor the roads inspire any confidence in the efficiency of rural transport; nor does Diodoros' account of the difficulty of transporting stone from Agyrion to Engyon.[4] Most traffic between the Greek colonies, all of which lay on or near the sea, was probably sea-borne, the roads serving mainly for transporting country products to the nearest town or point on the coast.

In Roman times Sicily was covered by a network of roads, some of which served needs brought into existence by the Roman administration, while others no doubt correspond with those in use in Greek times. An able study by Pace of the *Itineraries*, with reference also to medieval geographers and the modern *trazzere*, has elucidated their course.[5] Apart from those along the north and east coasts, the following may have served the Greek penetration of Sicily: the road from Katane inland to Akragas, which probably followed roughly the line of the railway, perhaps passing the considerable site of Vassalagi;[6] the route from Katane to Aitna, Kentoripa, Agyrion, Enna, and thence to Thermai (or Himera), which in Roman times did not follow the valley of the Dittaino, cultivated but, as now, not inhabited, but went from hill-town to hill-town; and the inland route from Akragas to

[1] Thuk. vii. 21. [2] Id. vi. 20. 4.
[3] Fabricius, *Das antike Syrakus*, fig. 19; owing to the difficulty of rendering the framework in terra-cotta it is uncertain how the body was built or suspended. The vehicle at Lokroi (*N Sc*, 1912, Suppl., fig. 15) is a chariot, not a cart.
[4] Diod. iv. 80. [5] *ACSA*, i. 425 ff. [6] See p. 139.

Syracuse,[1] by which the Syracusans would reach Akrai, Kamarina, and other of their smaller posts. The natural lines of penetration into central Sicily, the Chrysas (Dittaino) leading from the plain of Leontinoi to Enna, the southern Himeras leading up to Caltanisetta, the Halykos (Platani) which leads directly from Akragas to Himera, are clearly marked, and some of them are followed by these Roman roads. But most of Sicily presents few difficulties, and either the hill-tops or the valleys may be followed. Etna and the Madonie mountains on the north coast are the only difficult regions.

It is very different in south Italy. Most of Sicily, with the exceptions just named, is a tertiary deposit of soft level-topped hills; Calabria is geologically a very old region which stood as an island in the secondary period. The mountains which rise straight from the sea to 6,000 feet in Monte Pollino, the Sila, and Aspromonte,[2] are serious barriers to communication, and offered safe refuge to malcontents. The inhabitants have from the days of the Bruttians to this a reputation for backwardness and often incivility. The nature of the country had a great deal to do with the early growth and the fall of the cities of Magna Graecia. Present conditions or those of a few decades ago are relevant to ancient communications. In spite of modern road-engineering, there is yet no road along the whole length of either the Tyrrhenian or the Ionian coast,[3] and the number of places at which the peninsula can be crossed may be counted.

---

[1] The inland route from Akragas to Syracuse probably coincided for most of the way with the route *per maritima loca*. Pace (*ACSA*, i. 439 ff.), gives it as Favara–Naro–Ravanusa–Butera–Niscemi–Ragusa, that is, an entirely inland route. This is longer and much less convenient than the coast route via Phintias and Gela; it identifies Calvisiana in the inland route as Niscemi, in the coast route as the mouth of the Dirillo (site of Gela); and incidentally contradicts Pace's statement on p. 437 that there was no crossing of the Himeras in the neighbourhood of Ravanusa. It seems more likely that the two routes coincided as far as Hybla Heraia (Ragusa). Only one intermediate stage is named on the 'inland route' between Akragas and Hybla, which would be explained if thus far the stages were the same as on the coast route. Hybla on the former, Heraeum on the latter, would then represent the same place, Hybla Heraia. But if the second route nowhere diverged from the coast, as it apparently did not round Cape Pakhynos (the station Apollo is placed by Pace at Porto Palo), Heraeum would be some unknown site, and the point of bifurcation would be Kamarina. It is argued that because a gate of Akrai was called the Selinuntine the road which left by it avoided Gela, and was older than the foundation of Akragas. Neither of these follows; the reason for the name will be that at the time when it was given Selinus was recognized as the terminus of the road. The Dover road is so called, although it runs through Rochester and Canterbury.

[2] Dolcedorme 2,271 m.; Botte Donato 1,929 m.; Montalto 1,956 m. Heights and distances, and much other information, from the *Guida del Touring Club Italiano, Italia Meridionale*, vol. iii.

[3] This was true in 1936. Both works have since been put actively in hand.

As the Greeks were not great engineers, the mule-tracks of the last century are probably fair representatives of the ancient roads, considering that the same geographical conditions controlled them. There is this difference, that Magna Graecia was more prosperous, and almost certainly more populous, than modern Calabria, and that transverse communications were far more important then than now. But these considerations affect the volume of the traffic, not the lines along which it must have flowed.

In two places the Calabrian peninsula narrows between the Tyrrhenian and Ionian seas: opposite Sybaris, and between Catanzaro and S. Eufemia. These routes became important as by-passes for traffic from Greece to Etruria, avoiding the straits. The most important crossings are those which began from Sybaris. The easiest, though the longest, is up the Crati and down the Savuto to Terina. The Crati valley as far as Cosenza is a highroad. Thence it is a very easy climb to Pian del Lago, at a height of 627 m., a level shelf of about a mile in width, with the Apennines on one hand and the Sila on the other. The shelf continues as far as Rogliano, above the Savuto, into which there is a sharp drop (Rogliano 641 m., bridge over Savuto, 287 m.). There has been an old road down the Savuto, crossing and recrossing, with one isolated bridge. The river cuts through the Apennines, but without a gorge; it would be possible to go down the river-bed, or, if the river was high, along the rounded sides of the mountain, which recede a little from the river, so that the summits north and south of it are lower than the rest of the chain. It is a considerable stream, fed by the snows of the Sila and not always easy to ford, but there would be little difficulty in following the right bank as far as the old bridge and crossing there.

The total distance from Sybaris to the other sea is about 113 km. (70 miles). It is a fairly easy route, through gentler country and over a lower pass than the northern routes, but it has the disadvantage of being longer and of leading to a point much farther south, whereas through traffic was northward bound. In these circumstances it was probably little used for goods in transit to Etruria, but it led straight to Temesa and the only copper-mines of Greek Italy. It has been suggested[1] that this was the earliest route by which the ores of Temesa were exported. The kinship of the Hero of Temesa

[1] Ponelle, *Mélanges d'archéologie et d'histoire*, 1907, 253 ff.

to the Sybaris at Delphi suggests a connexion between Sybaris and Temesa. Sybaris appeared in the picture of Euthymos and the Hero recorded by Pausanias.[1]

The road down the Savuto is not now used, because of the desolation of that part of the coast to which it leads. The coin-hoard of S. Stefano di Rogliano,[2] found near the highest point, suggests that it was used in the early fifth century. Only nineteen coins were recovered of a total of about 300, so no conclusions can be drawn from the composition of the hoard. They were all of the incuse reverse types of Metapontion, Sybaris, Kroton, Kaulonia, and Poseidonia.

The crossings north of the Savuto to Amantea, Fiumefreddo, Paola, Fuscaldo, Cetraro, are all possible, but grow in difficulty as they go northward. All of them give a hard scramble up hills, once well wooded, to a height of nearly 1,000 m. (990 m. on the road from Cosenza to Amantea; 950 m., Passo di Crocetta, between Cosenza and Paola). There is a very steep descent to the Tyrrhenian Sea, the summit of the Apennine chain being in this stretch only about four miles from the sea. These and other bridle-paths are of only local interest. They have the same disadvantages as the Savuto route and more difficulties.

More important is the route up the Esaro to the Passo dello Scalone (744 m.) and Belvedere. This is the most direct route from sea to sea. The Esaro valley, a tributary of the Coscile (Sybaris), points almost due west from Sybaris. The upper valley is impracticable, the valley rising steeply and the river carrying a good deal of water; a deep gorge, with very steep sides, wide circles bitten out of the sides, and a few cliffy places. It is heavily wooded, with some fine oaks whose preservation, in the melancholy state of Calabrian forestry, is a testimony to the difficulty of access. But there is an easy way up the ridge to the north and over the open shoulders of the hills to the upland valley in which S. Agata all' Esaro stands. The scenery here is quite alpine, especially after recent snow. Above S. Agata the valley narrows again and is very steep-sided. Both banks rise in places to 200-foot cliffs, and the only way, without engineering a track, would be up the river-bed. The river being snow-fed would be impassable in spring. The pass is a real pass, with a great mountain of rock towering to the north, and the

---

[1] vi. 6. 11: νεανίσκος Σύβαρις καὶ Κάλαβρός τε ποταμός; a curious anticipation of the shift which in Byzantine times transferred the name Calabria to the ancient Brettian region.

[2] N Sc, 1932, 383; Noe, Bibliography of Greek Coin Hoards², 240 (buried c. 470).

descent to the sea is steep, but through open country and presenting no difficulties.

This route is followed in part by the Strada statale no. 87 from Castrovillari to Belvedere. A road would be impossible without modern engineering methods, but a track could go over the shoulders to avoid the valley below S. Agata, and then up the river-bed. The distance is approximately 60 km. (40 miles) in all; the length of the modern road is not a guide. This route though difficult is of the same kind as the better-known Campo Tenese route, and has the advantage of being shorter and crossing by a lower pass.[1] The inscribed bronze double-axe found at S. Agata,[2] one of the few Greek inscriptions of south Italy, suggests that the route was used. Perhaps Skidros lay at the end of it, on the square mile of level ground at the mouth of the Sanginete, an affluent of which runs down from the Passo dello Scalone. There is no shelter there, but a little beach. The sites found for Skidros at Sapri[3] and Papasidero[4] are unsatisfactory, resting on nothing but the similarity of name. My suggestion, though supported by no ancient remains, is geographically possible and would explain the importance of Skidros as an alternative to Laos.[5]

North of the Passo dello Scalone the mountains, whose summits to the south are between 1,000 and 1,500 m., rise in a solid mass to 1,986 m. at Cozzo Pellegrino, and effectively cut off the plain of Sybaris from the narrow Tyrrhenian seaboard. North of Sybaris, Monte Pollino and its outliers divide Calabria from the Basilicata. Between them is the pass of Campo Tenese.[6] The ascent up the Coscile is easy enough. The road to Castrovillari runs past Cassano over gentle hills; the gorge of the Coscile between Morano and Castrovillari is easily avoided by crossing a low ridge; the climb from the level of Morano to the pass is steep, but up an open valley.[7] The

---

[1] I have described this route in full because I do not know that anyone has called attention to it before. Ponelle does not so much as mention it. I followed it and the two other main routes in the last week of March 1935, in severe weather, with snow-storms.

[2] See p. 157.

[3] Philipp, *RE*, iii A, 521; Lenormant, *GG*, i. 259. Galli suggests Piarelli near Monte Paleocastro, S. of Sapri and 4 km. from the sea; a highly improbable site (*Per la Sibaritide*, 121).

[4] Byvanck, *De Magnae Graeciae Historia Antiquissima*, 109.

[5] It is made independently by Bérard, *Colonisation*, 159–60.

[6] Ponelle describes this road, op. cit. 267 ff.; he is better on the Sybaris side of the pass than on the descent.

[7] This part of the road, though it looks easy enough to the occasional traveller, has the sinister name of La Dirupata.

highest point of the road is 1,030 m., at Le Teste; the Campo Tenese, a level boulder-strewn plain once filled by a lake, is at 967 or 950 m. according to different calculations. Campo Tenese is not free from snow in winter and is a resort (though not a satisfactory one) of the neighbouring townsfolk in the new-found Italian passion for winter sports. So far the route is followed by a light railway. The difficulties begin on the western side. The Fiume di Campo Tenese falls in a tremendous gorge to the Lao. The most direct way to the sea is along the left bank, across the shoulders high above the stream, to a point opposite Mormanno. A slight rise leads to the valley of another tributary of the Lao, the Torrente S. Nocáio, which falls very steeply and rockily to Papasidero. The mule-track from Scalea to Mormanno follows this valley, the motor-road winding over the hills to the north. This route is rough going, but not really difficult. Below Papasidero the Lao plunges into a rocky cauldron, and then runs between steep hills.[1] It is a biggish stream, one of the largest flowing into the Tyrrhenian Sea south of the Sele, and it would often be impossible to follow the river-bed. A road over the foot-hills at a lower level than the modern road, which has many viaducts over side-valleys, would be possible. There is a path at this level for some way up the river, but it ceases before reaching Papasidero.

An alternative route, avoiding the steep descent of the Torrente S. Nocáio, leads along a shelf on the right bank of the Fiume di Campo Tenese, past Mormanno, to the Lao, just above Laino. This is the route followed by the main road and railway.[2] I have not seen the valley of the Lao between Laino and Papasidero, but imagine it not to be difficult. The river falls little (278 m. at Laino, 219 m. at Papasidero: the drop below Papasidero is much sharper). A path is marked on the map of the Touring Club Italiano at a little height above the river. The length of the direct route is about 75 km., and the Laino deviation would add between 10 and 15 km. The distance by the modern road is about 100 km.[3]

[1] Cf. Fischer, *Mittelmeerbilder, Neue Folge*, 236, on the 'wild zerrissenes Gebiet'.

[2] An alternative descent from Campo Tenese to the Lao via Rotonda to the east of the modern road was followed by Keppel Craven (*Tour through the Southern Provinces of Naples*, 349).

[3] There is no road all the way, and this calculation is based on the railway between Spezzano Albanese station and Sibari. Galli (*SMG*, 1929, 151 ff.) holds that the Sybaris–Laos route was in use before the arrival of the Greeks. But the evidence which he adduces

This route is rough rather than really difficult, except for the little gorge below Papasidero. But it would need a good deal of engineering to make it passable for wheeled traffic. Barone Lucifero of Crotone naïvely remarks[1] that the Sybarites cannot really have used it considering that the Greeks were not engineers. His remarks call attention to the nature of the country traversed, which has been too facilely assumed to be a broad highway. All the traffic must have crossed on muleback. This must have been a serious drawback considering the delicate nature of some of the goods in transit. The advantages that the Sybarite portages had for goods from Ionia and Greece to Etruria was the saving of time. The journey across could be made comfortably in three days, the sea-voyage would certainly be much longer and might be a matter of weeks if the winds were not favourable. But the time element was not of great importance in Greek navigation, and if it was, the Straits could be reached in as short a time as Sybaris by making the direct crossing instead of the coasting voyage. The disadvantages were double transhipment and a rough carriage over mountain tracks. The importance of the *loi des isthmes* has been monstrously exaggerated, and in the sixth century, as at every subsequent period of history, sea-carriage was cheaper than land. Geographical position alone cannot explain the importance of through traffic to Sybaris. The reason for its development is probably political. The Straits could be barred by the Khalkidian cities. Zankle was first founded as a pirates' resort. When the Zanklaians became respectable they may have carried on the same business more delicately by imposing tolls. They could easily prevent the ships of any power from passing the Straits. Relations between Greek sea-power, including Rhegion's Phokaian friends, and Etruscan sea-power became progressively worse until Anaxilas in the early fifth century fortified Skyllaion to bar the Etruscans from access to

proves only that there was a common culture in the area extending across the peninsula. The similarity of ninth- and eighth-century material from Tortora, Laino, Cassano, with that of Torre Mordillo proves that there was intercourse between the natives of these places. But this has no relevance to the date at which the Sybarites first used the route *for through traffic*. Galli's study of material from Laino shows very little between the eighth and the late fourth century; nothing to support his view that Laino was at all periods a 'station' on the overland route. So far as it goes it favours the view that the main route came straight down from Campo Tenese to Papasidero, avoiding the detour by Laino. Laino would be as easily reached from Herakleia, up the Sinni, as over the Campo Tenese.

[1] Introduction to Italian translation of Lenormant, *La Grande-Grèce*.

the Straits. The war was carried on largely by privateers operating against merchant ships. The ships which carried the trade between the Sybarite ports and Etruria must have been Etruscan. It is no wonder that they preferred the friendly Sybarites as intermediaries to the dangers of the Lower Tyrrhenian. On the other hand the Milesians, and probably many other states, found this route more secure, and perhaps cheaper, than the Straits because Sybaris was less intransigent than Rhegion. There is nothing to say how much earlier than 510 the route was used. But Sybaris' Greek correspondents were, so far as is known, mainly Ionians, and the wave of Ionian influence which sweeps over Etruria in the last half of the sixth century, replacing the earlier Corinthian, suggests that the chief importance of the Sybarite portages as an international trade-route belongs to that period. They did not replace the route by the Straits, which was more active than ever, but they provided a useful supplement for those who had not the favour of the masters of the Straits.

The land-route to Poseidonia, across the Campo Tenese and then north via Laino, Lauria, Lagonegro, and down the Tanagro to the Sele, was probably less used than the sea-route from Laos. It is the Via Popilia, the main road from Rome to Rhegion, but is not an easy route. There is a good deal of mountaineering and some places which call for engineering. It passes through the high-lying and fertile Vallo di Diano, where sixth-century Greek imports have been found at Sala Consilina, Atena Lucana, and other places.[1] These may have come north from Sybaris or inland from Poseidonia. But the rather casual nature of the hellenization suggests that this route was not used intensively.

The other crossings are much less important. The coins of Siris and Pyxus indicate an association of these two cities.[2] The way between them, up the Siris (Sinni), across the valley of Lagonegro, and down to the sea near Policastro,[3] is not difficult, but it is much longer (c. 170 km. = 105 miles) than the

---

[1] See above, p. 154.

[2] See below, pp. 356 ff., Perret, *Siris*, 247 ff., argues that as these coins have Sybarite type and are to be regarded as 'imperial' coinage of Sybaris, not as independent coins of Siris and Pyxus, they are not evidence of an alliance or connexion between the two cities. But there must have been some reason for the Sybarites to associate them on a single coin.

[3] Pyxus is placed at the mouth of the Busento, on the right bank, 2 km. west of Policastro; but there are no remains. See Strabo 253; Byvanck, 106; Ciaceri, *Storia della Magna Grecia*, i. 273–5; Ponelle, loc. cit. 270 ff., on the portage.

Sybarite routes, and not more advantageously placed. The nature of the country changes north of Monte Pollino, and it is possible to ascend the valleys of the Sinni, the Agri, or the Basento, cross the hills by a number of paths at heights between 800 and 1,000 m., and come down to the Gulf of Policastro or down the Vallo di Diano to the Sele. The chief discomfort of these regions is not rock but mud. But these roads were at the mercy of the native peoples, who were not so effectively controlled as those of the Sybarite empire. The archaeological evidence of the region round Potenza and of the Vallo di Diano,[1] the only parts of this area at all well explored, shows that little progress towards hellenization had been made before the Lucanian invasion. The routes north of the Siris–Pyxus route were therefore probably little used, either for through traffic or for exploitation of the country. These include the way up the Basento to the Sele, which is the easiest and the most obvious of the roads through the Basilicata, leading straight from Metapontion to Poseidonia[2] (219 km. by railway from Salerno to Metaponto). Even the Siris–Pyxus route could compete with the Sybarite routes only if it had some political recommendation to outweigh the disadvantages of its length and uncertainty. Siris, as an Ionian city, might be favoured by Ionians of Asia Minor and Etruria. This is, however, less important than the desire on the one part to share in the riches which the overland trade brought Sybaris, on the other to avoid any danger of a monopoly.

The easiest crossing, between Catanzaro and S. Eufemia where the peninsula narrows to 35 km. (20 miles) and may be crossed in a day[3] (the highest point is only 250 m.), was in the hands of Kroton. Skylletion commanded the eastern end, and though it had a bad name for shipwrecks[4] (not borne out by the *Admiralty Pilot*), the beach to the north could be used, as it was by Hannibal during his Bruttian retreat. At the other end was Terina, a Krotoniate colony whose exact position is uncertain. The importance of Tiriolo, on a height above the pass and commanding also the road northward into the Sila, is not earlier than the fourth century. There is no clear evidence for the use of this route,[5] but it can hardly fail to have been

[1] Mayer, *Apulien*, 236; see above, pp. 152, 154.
[2] Mayer, op. cit. 225; Wuilleumier, *Tarente*, 227.
[3] One hundred and sixty stades, Strabo 255; half a day's journey, Arist. *Pol.* 1329ᵇ 13.
[4] *Aen.* iii. 553, *nauifragum Scylaceum*.
[5] Lyk. 1071 appears to refer to it, calling Temesa Κροτωνιᾶτιν ἀντίπορθμον αὔλακα.

used. Its disadvantage from the Krotoniate point of view was that its eastern end was a long way from the city. The mass of the Sila immediately behind prevented Kroton from developing a land empire so early as Sybaris. So the political incentive to use this crossing was less strong than in the case of Sybaris and Siris. It is possible that rivalry over these trade-routes played a part in the wars of the late sixth century between Sybaris and Siris, Sybaris and Kroton; but the view that sees Sybaris and Kroton as the representatives in south Italy of rival trade leagues in the Aegean rests on very slender grounds.

South of this isthmus there is a long ridge joining Aspromonte to the rather confused mountains of Serra S. Bruno which pen Kaulonia in. These mountains do not rise above 1,420 m. (M. Pecoraro), and there are paths all over them but no easy ones. Behind Lokroi there is a comparatively low level-topped ridge which can be crossed almost anywhere. The main routes are directly up from Lokroi to La Lenza di Gerace (950 m.) and down the Petrace (ancient Metauros) to the site of Metauron or else to Medma across the tilted plain which runs up from the sea to Cittanova and Polistena; and from Gioiosa Marina over the Piano della Limina[1] (805 m.) and down a tributary of the Mesima to Medma. Both are now crossed by main roads, and a light railway is being built across the latter. From Gerace Marina to Gioia Tauro (Lokroi to Metauros) is 53 km. by road, less by path; from Gioiosa Marina to Rosarno (Medma) 50 km.: both a long day's journey, even avoiding the serpentines of the modern road. These two routes have an obvious importance in leading direct from Lokroi to the Lokrian colonies, and from Medma north to Hipponion, up the river Mesima. But they can hardly have mattered as through routes. As regards the time factor, they have the worst of both worlds, the sea-voyage being shorter by a few miles only than the way through the Straits and the delays and dangers of transhipment being added. They are not easy enough crossings to compare with the shorter and better-placed way across the Isthmus of Catanzaro. As Rhegion and Lokroi were allied about 530, when the search for alternative routes was at its height, there was no reason to prefer the Lokrian portages to the voyage through the Straits or the more northerly crossing.

There was still in 1935 no road along the Ionian Sea south of

---

[1] The Piano della Limina is a quaternary terrace filling a former strait between Cinquefronde and Mammola (see Fischer, *Mittelmeerbilder, Neue Folge*, 223).

Soverato (between Skylletion and Kaulonia).[1] North of Skylletion there is no serious barrier to intercourse, and the natural boundaries, though real, are not difficult to cross. But the Punto di Staletti immediately below Skylletion is a formidable barrier, with broken cliffs over which the path must climb several hundred feet. Skylletion lay perhaps on the rising ground on the right bank of the Torrente Grande, where it would command the approaches to both the road over the cliffs and the possible circuit over the mountain of Staletti, an important strategic position, though the approach from the north would be more difficult than the crossing of the mountain from the south. Below this point, every few miles a torrent runs straight down from the mountains and covers up to a quarter of a mile's width with stones through which the stream takes a violent and changing course. The difficulty of crossing one of these torrent beds was perhaps the cause of the Krotoniate defeat on the Sagra.[2] South of Lokroi, the Zephyrian promontory (Capo Bruzzano) is again a bold projection over which the road has to climb, and from there round to Leukopetra the wild hills and torrents make communication difficult. Leukopetra, though less difficult than Capo Staletti and Capo Bruzzano, is a bold point. Cape Spartivento, like the famed Kokynthian promontory (Punta di Stilo), is of more importance from the sea than on land, as it simply marks a change of direction of the coast.

Communications by land up the Tyrrhenian coast are difficult, and become intensely so from Scalea all the way to Sapri, where the mountains rise straight out of the sea with cliffs and rocky headlands. The modern road can be carried along only with tunnelling.[3] There was little reason in Greek times for traffic up this coast, for the colonies of Sybaris, Kroton, and Lokroi would communicate with their capital cities rather than with each other. As in Sicily coast-wise communications were probably more by sea than by land. The contrast between local and inter-colonial traffic happens to be pointed in the Sybarite stories; the roads near the city received some care, but the natural way to go to Kroton was by sea.[4]

[1] Cf. Keppel Craven, *Tour through the Southern Provinces of Naples* (1821), 256.

[2] See below, p. 359. Torrents of this kind became very familiar to the Eighth Army in its advance up the east coast of Italy.

[3] Keppel Craven, op. cit., 339, remarks the complete absence of land communications along the coast between Amantea and the Gulf of Policastro.

[4] See above, p. 79, n. 6.

CHAPTER VII

AGRICULTURE

THE first line of colonial economics was wheat. Almost every city had its own plain, larger and more fertile than the territory of most states in Greece. The choice of sites shows that the intentions of the colonists were both commercial and agricultural, but a port could be more easily dispensed with than a good plain. The Khalkidians colonized Naxos, the first port of call on the coasting voyage to Sicily, and then by founding Leontinoi and Katane secured the whole of the richest corn-land in the island. Syracuse, though first and foremost a port, controlled a large and fertile territory, and the immediate neighbourhood of the city is good land. The rich cities of Gela, Selinus, and Kamarina are all placed in unhealthy sites with poor ports, while the better harbours of Porto Empedocle and Licata were occupied at first only by little posts.

In Italy, where the colonies were not founded by the great commercial and industrial powers, the importance of good cornland is even clearer. The oldest of the Akhaian colonies is Sybaris, in the richest plain, and the sites of Siris and Metapontion have little recommendation except their plough-lands. Taras and Kroton have both good land and a harbour in a favourable position for trade. It was only Lokroi, the last of the direct foundations, which had to accept a site not indeed infertile but not well suited for corn-growing.

The only exceptions to the rule that whatever else it had a colony must have a fertile territory are Zankle and Rhegion. The circumstances of their foundation differ from those of all the other colonies. The impulse to colonize Zankle was given by the Khalkidians of Kyme, a colony founded for commerce. Zankle in turn founded Rhegion to secure control of the Straits. While Zankle and Rhegion were in agreement they had complete control of all the traffic which passed through for Etruria and elsewhere in the western Mediterranean. They lived to a greater extent even than Syracuse on commerce. But within a short time of the foundation the Zanklaians made a settlement at Mylai, which remained a part of the Zanklaian state. It had two objects: to secure the northward approach to the Straits,[1] and to grow, on the best plain of the north coast of

---

[1] Cf. Columba, *I porti della Sicilia Antica*, 311–12. The strategic importance of Milazzo

Sicily, the food which the mountains behind Zankle and Rhegion could not supply.

Sicily was the birth-place of wheat. The worship of Demeter and Kore was one of the most popular in every part of the island, and though originally chthonic became especially associated with agriculture. Legend, recorded first in Cicero, made Sicily the birth-place of both the goddesses, and placed the gift of corn to man in Sicily instead of the Eleusinian plain.[1] In Syracuse Demeter was worshipped under the title of Sito, the discoverer of wheat.[2] The corn-wreath on the head of Persephone on a bronze coin of Tyndaris also testifies to the association.[3] Nearly every state of Sicily and south Italy has at some time an ear or a grain of wheat among the accessory symbols on its coins. Metapontion declared its dependence on agriculture by the adoption of the ear of barley as its coin-type,[4] and by the dedication of the χρυσοῦν θέρος at Delphi.[5] The earliest coins of Morgantina, of the middle of the fifth century, have a similar type,[6] expressing the same dependence. The frame of three or four grains of wheat on the coins of Leontinoi,[7] the corn-wreath or grain regular with the human-headed bull of Gela in the late fifth century,[8] are the most notable instances among dozens of other coins which indicate the importance of agriculture. The earliest coins of Enna and Abakainon, both among the earliest Sikel towns to coin (c. 450), also have an ear or grain of corn.[9]

In the plain of Leontinoi, the fabled Laistrygonian plain, wheat is said to have grown wild.[10] This land compared with the richest parts of the Roman world, producing a proverbial hundred-fold.[11] Cicero writes it down to tenfold at the best;[12]

for the command of the Straits is shown in the Naulokhos campaign and in its defence against Garibaldi.

[1] *Verr.* II. iv. 48. 106.   [2] Athen. 109a.

[3] Head, *HN²*, 189; *BM Cat. Sicily*, 235.

[4] Head, *HN²*, 75; *BM Cat. Italy*, 238 ff.; Noe, *Coinage of Metapontum*. Barley, not wheat; cf. Noe, op. cit. i. 28.

[5] Strabo 264. Mayer, *RE*, xv. 1339, suggests that it was a repeated offering. For an actual χρυσοῦν θέρος said to have been found near Syracuse see Wolters, *Festschrift Loeb*, III ff.

[6] *BM Cat. Sicily*, 114; Head, *HN²*, 157.

[7] *BM Cat. Sicily*, 89 ff.; Head, *HN²*, 148-9.   [8] *BM Cat. Sicily*, 72; Head, 141-2.

[9] Enna, *BM Cat. Sicily*, 58; Head, 137; Abakainon, *BM Cat. Sicily*, 1; Head, *HN²*, 118.

[10] Smyth speaks of wild flax and wheat growing in the plain of Catania, then poorly cultivated and marshy in many places (p. 156).

[11] Pliny, *NH* xviii. 95: 'cum centesimo quidem et Leontini Siciliae campi fundunt . . .'; cf. Varro, *de re r.* 1. 44. 2: 'in Italia in Subaritano dicunt etiam cum centesimo redire solitum'.

[12] *Verr.* II. iii. 47. 112.

his figures of 30,000 iugera, on which 1 medimnus per iugerum was sown,[1] give a maximum yield of 300,000 medimni from 30,000 iugera. This is equivalent to about 24 bushels per acre, which would be a fair yield to-day, and better than the same land now gives.[2] Cicero's object is to minimize the total crop of the Leontines and thereby exaggerate the exaction of tithe. He allows 36,000 medimni as a fair tithe,[3] so that it is possible that the total crop is underestimated. The amount finally taken was nearly 90,000 medimni.[4]

A small farm, 50 iugera of the ager Murgentinus, gave something near a hundredfold if the figures are correct. Seven hundred medimni were demanded as tithe, and 1,000 finally exacted.[5] If this was no more than two tithes, a total yield of 5,000 medimni would, on Cicero's allowance of 1 medimnus sown per iugerum, be one-hundredfold. This figure, however, equivalent to nearly 50 bushels per acre taken as tithe, and at least 200 bushels per acre yield, is too much for the most fertile land under good management. But the discrepancy between Cicero's tenfold and Varro's hundredfold is to be explained thus: that Cicero's figure is the average over a large area, and his interest leads him to underestimate; Varro's is the maximum, with a trifle of exaggeration, that a single ear could produce.

I quote these figures to show the ancient reputation of this piece of ground, and because they are the basis for our most reliable estimate of the yield of ancient agriculture.[6] In general, of course, Greek conditions are not to be illustrated by the facts and figures of Cicero, 400 years later when Sicily had long been administered as the granary of the Roman people. Our evidence for Greek conditions is slight and vague. Orsi's survey of the country-side near Gela shows that it was dotted with small poor villages of agricultural workers,[7] and large farmhouses on which the labourers of an estate lived, with a more magnificent house for the owner. Similar establishments have been found near Kamarina and Selinus and at many points over the lower part of the Syracusan territory. Small groups

[1] Ibid. 49. 116.
[2] Thirty bushels per acre is an average yield in England, a little less in Italy; Sicily is below the average.
[3] 46. 110.   [4] 49. 116.   [5] II. iii. 23. 56.
[6] See the discussion in Jardé, *Les Céréales dans l'antiquité grecque*, 58 ff.; Scramuzza, *Economic Survey of Ancient Rome*, iii. 253 ff.
[7] *MA*, xvii. 731 ff.

of graves in open country belong to such small villages or large estates. It may be presumed that the processes of pressing oil, making wine, threshing, were carried on within the four walls of these large farm-yards. But none of these establishments has been fully excavated.

The shipment of wheat from Sicily to Greece is not attested before the fifth century, nor should we expect it to be. But almost from their foundation the colonies must have assisted to feed the mother country. The abundant imports of all kinds of pottery, bronze work, jewellery, and all sorts of perishable industrial products which may be inferred, are in part carried by successive settlers, but most are due to ordinary commercial transactions. Sicily and south Italy have no metals to speak of, and no monopoly such as Kyrene enjoyed of silphium. They must have paid for their imports chiefly with slaves and foodstuffs, especially wheat, which was the mainstay of their agriculture and the food of which Greece had most need. The riches it brought them are not surprising when we consider how Canada has prospered on the export of wheat. In the early period, before the Euxine was effectively colonized and before Egypt was open to the Greeks, the west must have been of paramount importance. Corinth owed a great part of her prosperity to her control of all western trade, which gave her an expanding market for her goods and in return a source of food. By the fifth century the Greek west had fallen into third place as a supplier of wheat to Greece. But the population of the colonies had increased enormously and they now consumed a larger proportion of their own produce. Sybaris is known before its fall to have reached the point of absorbing all its own production.[1] But Sybaris was the most advanced economically of all the colonies, with probably the largest population within her boundaries, and had already begun to turn from agriculture to other forms of production.

In 480, when the Persians controlled Egypt and the Dardanelles, Sicily at once became of importance. Gelon's offer to provide corn for the Greek army[2] was possible in circumstances which would not allow him to think of military assistance. For how long he could feed the whole Greek army, at the same time keeping his own army in the field, is an unprofitable question. But Sicily and Italy were the only

---

[1] Athen. 519f; see above, p. 77.
[2] Herod. vii. 158 σῖτόν τε ἁπάσῃ τῇ Ἑλλήνων στρατιῇ . . .; Diod. x. 33 σιταρκῆσαι.

sources from which in the years 480–479 the Greek combatants could expect to supply their deficiencies.

The export surplus available is impossible to estimate, because even if conjectures of the area under plough, the yield, and the consumption per head are made, estimates of the population of the colonies are ill founded, and no estimate of the rural population is possible. Beloch's figures[1] for Syracuse after the fall of the Deinomenids, which I repeat with the utmost reserve, are a crop of 2,000,000 medimni, a total population of 250,000, consuming 1,750,000 medimni, and a surplus for export of 250,000 medimni. Syracuse had the largest, but not the most fertile, territory of any Sicilian state,[2] and had a much larger population than any other city. The amount available for export from the whole of Gelon's empire will multiply many times this conjectural figure for Syracuse.

The earliest Athenian preoccupations with the west had the same motives as the Corinthian trade monopoly, the wish to widen the market for their goods and to secure an important source of corn. The break with Corinth about 460, when Athens determined to seize the Gulf of Corinth and the Greek end of the western trade, coming at the same time as the Egyptian expedition, suggests that Athens was attempting to get control of all the overseas supplies of corn to Greece. But the Sicilian corn-trade could not be controlled by seizing the entrance to the Gulf of Corinth, or by Athenian ships supplanting Corinthian in the carriage westward of Athenian goods. One of the motives which led the Athenians to interfere in Sicily during the Archidamian War was the desire to prevent shipments of corn to the Peloponnese.[3] Direct sailings across the Ionian Sea could be checked only in Sicily, control of Korkyra and the approaches of the Corinthian Gulf being insufficient. The occupation of Kythera and Pylos blockaded Laconia more effectively, but to cut the Peloponnesians off completely the Athenians needed to control the ports of export. Their system of alliances in Sicily was quite inadequate for this purpose. Nothing less than the success of the Syracusan expedition could have achieved it.

---

[1] *Gr. Ges.* ii. 1. 120 ff.

[2] The prosperity of Syracusan agriculture is shown by the proverb Συρακουσίων δεκάτη; see the story in Pliny, *NH* xvii. 30, 'at in Syracusano agro aduena cultor elapidato solo perdidit fruges luto, donec regessit lapides'. But it is not less fertile for the necessity to plough between the stones, like some of the flint-strewn soils of the Chilterns.

[3] Thuk. iii. 86. 4.

Though export in the fifth century was evidently regular, the volume may not have been great. Nikias had no expectation of being able to live on the country, and insisted on the importance of taking supplies of wheat and barley, and keeping communications open so that further supplies might follow.[1] But this reflects the weakness of the Athenian allies in Sicily, and has little relevance to the size of the exportable surplus of Sicily in time of peace.

Also in the late fifth century occasional export from Syracuse to Rome begins. The accounts of Livy iv. 25. 4 (433) and iv. 52. 6 (410) are doublets, and the reference to Sicilian corn in 491 (Dion. Hal. vii. 1; Livy ii. 34. 3) is generally suspected to be a reflection backwards of the later state of affairs. But in the second half of the fifth century at least Syracuse was sending corn regularly to Greece and occasionally to Rome. In the fourth century the arrival of Sicilian wheat at Athens reduced the prices[2] by competing with Egyptian wheat whose harvest was earlier. Demosthenes' speech against Zenothemis is concerned with the fate of a shipment from Syracuse on a Massaliot ship.[3] Spring wheat from Sicily was acclimatized in Akhaia in the fourth century, if not earlier.[4]

It is striking that Italian wheat is not heard of, even in the sixth book of Thukydides, nor is the coin evidence, apart from the type of Metapontion, so extensive as in Sicily.[5] The cultivation of the great plains may in the last part of the fifth century have already begun to be affected by malaria. The luxurious habits of Sybaris and Siris, particularly the custom of avoiding the setting and the rising sun, have been regarded as empirical precautions against malaria.[6] This may sound far-fetched, but a good deal of the apolaustics of Sybaris are simply misunderstandings of this sort. On the other hand, Thuria would hardly have prospered as it did if the plain of Sybaris was malarial. Sixty years of comparative neglect and the diversion of the river would have encouraged the mosquito, but without the introduction of the infection by a human subject the mosquito cannot carry the disease. There is little ground for conjecture as to the date of its introduction. The danger to health from

---

[1] Thuk. vi. 22.
[2] Demos. lvi. 1285.
[3] Demos. xxxii.
[4] Theophr. *HP* viii. 4. 4.
[5] The coins of Metapontion are the only ones in the fifth century; later Kroton (Head, *HN*², 96 ff.; *BM Cat. Italy*, 349 ff.), Herakleia, Paestum, and the Lucani (Head, *HN*², 73, 82, 70) have a grain or ear. Seventeen Sicilian cities have a similar symbol at one time or another.
[6] Jones, *Malaria and Greek History*, 30–1.

the choked streams of Selinus[1] and the immovable lake of Kamarina,[2] both of which were drained in the fifth century, may have been malaria; so also the pestilence which destroyed Himilco's army camped in the swamps of Lysemeleia. But we have no medical details, and there are other forms of disease which come from living on the edge of a swamp. Selinus and Kamarina were both deserted in the middle of the third century, and malaria may have aided Carthaginian ravages in making them unfit to live in. But the geographers of the Roman period give less ground for suspecting that malaria was endemic in Sicily than they do for south Italy.

Other natural products[3] beside wheat were exported to Athens. The Pseudo-Xenophontic Ἀθ. Πολ. speaks of ὅ τι ⟨τ'⟩ ἐν Σικελίᾳ ἡδὺ ἢ ἐν Ἰταλίᾳ in the first place of the benefits which come to Athens from control of the sea.[4] Hermippos includes in his list of Athenian imports ἐκ δ' αὖ Ἰταλίας χόνδρον καὶ πλευρὰ βόεια and αἱ δὲ Συράκουσαι σῦς καὶ τυρὸν παρέχουσιν.[5] Sicilian swine had already been imported to Samos by Polykrates when he sought out the best livestock of the Greek world.[6] Sicilian cheese was famous; other references are in Aristophanes[7] and Antiphanes,[8] and the Σικελίας αὔχημα τροφαλίς of Philemon in his Σικελικός:[9]

ἐγὼ πρότερον μὲν ᾠόμην τὴν Σικελίαν
ἐν τοῦτ' ἀπότακτον αὐτὸ τοὺς τυροὺς ποιεῖν
καλούς.

What animal's milk was used for the celebrated cheese is unknown.

Sicily is in general πολύμαλος (Pind. Ol. i. 12) and especially Akragas (Pyth. xii. 2, ὄχθαις ἐπὶ μηλοβότου . . . Ἀκράγαντος). The first specific reference to Sicilian woollens is in Philemon;[10] the famous Tarentine woollens[11] are not heard of in the sixth or fifth centuries, but may, as also the purple-dyeing industry, have developed so early. On the other hand, the fine woollens

---

[1] Diog. Laert. viii. 70; Head, HN², 167 ff.
[2] Serv. ad Aen. iii. 701; Suidas s.vv. Μὴ κίνει Καμάριναν; Sil. Ital. xiv. 198.
[3] For a full list of the natural products of Sicily see Scramuzza, op. cit. 269 ff.
[4] ii. 7.
[5] Ap. Athen. 27e. For pressed beef from Sicily cf. Euboulos ap. Athen. 396a.
[6] Athen. 540d.   [7] Wasps, 838, 896.
[8] Τυρὸς Σικελικός ap. Athen. 27d.   [9] Ap. Athen. 658a.
[10] Loc. cit. supra. Alexander wore a Sicilian shirt (Plut. Alex. 32. 8). For Sicilian weaving cf. Cic. Verr. II. ii. 2. 5, and references in Scramuzza, op. cit. 288 ff.
[11] References in Wuilleumier, Tarente, 219 ff.

of Miletos were imported to Sybaris.¹ Twenty thousand talents of raw wool is among the cargo which the *Syrakosia* is said to have carried from Syracuse to Alexandria.²

The plains, especially of Gela, and the territory of Syracuse were great horse-raising lands. The Sicilian aristocracy was as fond of horse-racing as the great families of Old Greece, and the greatest racehorse of antiquity was Hieron's Pherenikos. The Sicilian cities were always strong in cavalry.

The chief development of pasture, especially in south Italy, was in the Roman period; but Italia, the name originally of the extreme south below the Isthmus of Catanzaro, is confidently derived from a word equivalent to *vitulus*.³ Of Sicily also Strabo says: 'Ρωμαῖοι κατακτησάμενοι τά τε ὄρη καὶ τῶν πεδίων τὰ πλεῖστα ἱπποφορβοῖς καὶ βουκόλοις καὶ ποιμέσι παρέδοσαν and οὐχ οἱ καρποὶ μόνον, ἀλλὰ καὶ βοσκήματα καὶ δέρματα καὶ ἔρια καὶ τὰ τοιαῦτα.⁴ But, apart from the hill-pastures, most of the plain and low hill of Sicily and south Italy was nearly as well suited for stock-raising as for agriculture. The development of the bucolic in Sicily is perhaps as old as Stesikhoros, certainly a good deal older than Theokritos. Theokritos' most vivid scenes, those which he places in the country of Kroton and Sybaris, might go back to the sixth century; not that he intended that they should be dated then or at any other moment of time.

The timber of south Italy also attracted the Athenians westward, as they were coming to depend on more and more distant and uncertain supplies. During the expedition they prepared a stock ἐν τῇ Καυλωνιάτιδι,⁵ for replacement of their fleet at Syracuse, or possibly to send back to Athens. It appears from the speech put into Alkibiades' mouth at Sparta that the Athenians intended to use the timber of south Italy to build a fleet which could blockade the Peloponnese.⁶ The timber for Hieron's ship *Syrakosia* was from Etna, but a tree large enough for the mainmast could be found only in the Brettian forests.⁷ To-day there is almost no timber in Sicily, but Smyth speaks of timber conveyed a century ago from Etna down the Alcantara.⁸ There is a certain amount still shipped from the ports of

---

¹ Athen. 519b. See p. 78. ² Moschion ap. Athen. 209a.
³ Conway, *The Italic Dialects*, i. 48.
⁴ 273. Hides, cf. Cic. *Verr.* II. ii. 2. 5; Roman army supplied from Sicily during the Social War. ⁵ Thuk. vii. 25. 2. ⁶ Thuk. vi. 90. 3.
⁷ Athen. 206 ff. Cf. Diod. xiv. 42. 4–5; timber for Dionysios' fleet from Etna and from Italy. ⁸ Op. cit. 130.

Calabria, but the forests of the Sila and Aspromonte have been terribly destroyed in the last century and indeed until a few years ago.[1] The forests of the Sila and Aspromonte were famous also for another ship-building material: pitch, Virgil's *Narycia pix*.[2] It is curious that Brettian pitch is passed over in the *Syrakosia* in favour of pitch from the Rhône; there is a touch of fancy in the fittings from Italy and Sicily, rope from Spain, hemp and pitch from the Rhône, and so on, searching as far afield as possible for embellishment.

Fishing played an important part in the life of other cities than Taras. Most of the seas and rivers of Sicily were famous for their fish, and the Sicilian cooks for their preparation.[3] The tunny was taken in Italian and Sicilian waters, as well as in the northern part of the Mediterranean, where the Celts and Ligurians and the Massaliots took him with hooks instead of nets. Kephaloidion, Tyndaris, Hipponion were the centres for the tunny-fishing in the southern Tyrrhenian.[4] The squid was a delicacy then as now.[5] There was probably a large export of fish to Greece. Athens is known to have imported salt fish from the Pontos, and to have lived very largely on fish. But there is no direct evidence of export from Sicily until the third century, when 10,000 jars of salt fish were included in the cargo of the *Syrakosia*.[6]

It would be a long story to go through all the fish of Sicily:[7] eels of the Straits, thought better than those of Kopais,[8] and

---

[1] Norman Douglas, *Old Calabria*, passim; Fischer, *Mittelmeerbilder, Neue Folge*, 237.

[2] *Georgics* ii. 438; Columella x. 386; Pliny, *NH* xiv. 127–8, 135; Dion. Hal. xx. 15; Strabo 261: τὴν δ' ὑπὲρ τῶν πόλεων τούτων μεσόγαιαν Βρέττιοι κατέχουσιν· καὶ πόλις ἐνταῦθα Μαμέρτιον καὶ ὁ δρυμὸς ὁ φέρων τὴν ἀρίστην πίτταν τὴν Βρεττίαν, ὃν Σίλαν καλοῦσιν, εὔδενδρός τε καὶ εὔυδρος, μῆκος ἑπτακοσίων σταδίων. The cities are Lokroi and Rhegion; but he seems to refer to the Sila, not Aspromonte, to judge from the distances given.

[3] Cf. the complaint of Arkhestratos of Gela (ap. Athen. 311b):

μηδὲ προσέλθῃ σοί ποτε τοὔψον τοῦτο ποιοῦντι
μήτε Συρακόσιος μηθεὶς μήτ' Ἰταλιώτης.
οὐ γὰρ ἐπίστανται χρηστῶς σκευαζέμεν ἰχθῦς,
ἀλλὰ διαφθείρουσι κακῶς τυροῦντες ἅπαντα
ὄξει τε ῥαίνοντες ὑγρῷ καὶ σιλφίου ἅλμῃ . . .

Freeman, ii. 397 ff., collects the references to the Συρακοσίων τράπεζα.

[4] Arkhestratos ap. Athen. 302a; cf. Athen. 116f, 399d, Sicilian tunnies; 4c, the paunch of the tunnies of Pakhynos, an especial delicacy; Aelian, *NA* xiii. 16; xv. 6, quoting Sophron, ἡδὺν Θυννοθήραν. Cf. the Campanian krater from Lipari, in Cefalù, Pace, *ACSA*, iii. 345, fig. 72.

[5] Athen. 4b, 341a.

[6] Athen. 209a.

[7] See Scramuzza, op. cit. 283 ff., for full list.

[8] Arkhestratos, ap. Athen. 298e: cf. Smyth, *Sicily and its Islands*, 106, for eels of Peloros.

lampreys, sword-fish, and mussels of Peloros and the Straits[1] are mentioned even more often than those of other coasts, suggesting that fishing was particularly important for the citizens of Rhegion and Messana.

Though most of the references to this luxury of the table come from the Middle Comedy, it is full-blown by the time of Epikharmos, who set the example of a Gargantuan dinner in the "Ηβας Γάμος.[2] Sybaris was already famous for good cheer before Syracuse.[3] The kottabos, a Sikeliot sport accompanying the banquet, attracted the attention of poets as early as Alkaios and Anakreon.[4]

The only wines from Magna Graecia mentioned in Galen's list of the wines of Italy[5] are the Rhegine, like the dry Surrentine but smoother, and not lasting so well; the Buxentine raisin wine; Tarentine, which like others of the neighbourhood was weak but pleasant, a quality it has to-day; and the Mamertine. But this is at a period when war and mismanagement had reduced the south of Italy to economic ruin. At a far earlier time Sybaris had exported wine,[6] and the wines of Thuria and the neighbouring Lagaria are praised.[7] Naxos, in Sicily, proclaimed her dependence on the vine by putting it on her first coins: reverse, head of Dionysos, obverse, bunch of grapes.[8] The vine was the only plant growing in antiquity that was really suited for the steep terraces along the coast between Naxos and Messana. The unknown town of south Italy whose name begins with Mer . . . or Ser . . . also had a bunch of grapes on its coins, treated with more realism and less fine stylization than on the coins of Naxos.[9] The earliest coins of Galaria, one

---

[1] Arkhestratos ap. Athen. 313a, 314f; Kharmos of Syracuse ap. Athen. 4c; Athen. 311f, 341a, fish from the Straits.

[2] Com. Graec. Frag. Kaibel, I. i. fr. 41 ff.   [3] See esp. Ar. Daitaleis, fr. 216.

[4] Alkaios fr. 43 Bergk, ap. Athen. 668d; Anakreon fr. 53 ap. Athen. 427d; cf. Athen. 479d–e, 665b–666c. It is by no means, however, a contribution of the Sikels to Greek civilization:

τούτην πρώτων εὑρόντων Σικελῶν, ὡς Κριτίας φησὶν ὁ Καλλαίσχρου ἐν τοῖς Ἐλεγείοις διὰ τούτων·
κότταβος ἐκ Σικελῆς ἐστι χθονὸς ἐκπρεπὲς ἔργον,
ὃν σκοπὸν ἐς λατάγων τόξα καθιστάμεθα—

where Athenaios has written Σικελῶν from Kritias' Σικελῆς χθονὸς (cf. ἦλθον μὲν γὰρ ἔγωγε καὶ εἰς Σικελήν ποτε γαῖαν, Theognis 783, and Epikrates ap. Athen. 59f). Anakreon wrote Σικελὸν κότταβον ἀγκύλῃ δαίζων, without necessarily using the adjective in a strictly ethnographic sense: Σικελιώτην would not have fitted his verse (Σικελόν is Grotefend's emendation for Σικελικόν). The special vocabulary of the game is dialectal Greek, not borrowed from the Sikel language (as Freeman, i. 490): λατάγη Σικελικὸν ὄνομα, Dikaiarkhos ap. Athen. 666b; cf. λάταξ, Thessalian and Rhodian, Kleitarkhos, ibid.

[5] Ap. Athen. i. 26e.   [6] See above, p. 77.

[7] Strabo 263.   [8] BM Cat. Sicily, 118.   [9] BM Cat. Italy, 395.

of the first Sikel places to coin, have the type, similar to the reverse of Mer . . . , of Dionysos standing holding a kantharos.[1] Inykon was famous for its wine,[2] and the Mamertine and Murgentine were named varieties.[3] The export of wine to Carthage was one source of wealth to Akragas.[4] This, with the wine of Pollis,[5] completes the tale of Sicilian wines.

Olive-oil was exported in quantity from Akragas to Carthage,[4] and perhaps also from Selinus. Pliny's statement that no crop but wheat would succeed in Africa[6] is not true of his own time, when oil was exported from Africa to Ostia,[7] and should refer to this period, when oil and wine were imported from Sicily. He names both: 'Cereri totum natura concessit, oleum ac vinum non inuidit tantum, satisque gloriae in messibus fuit.' Much of Sicily and south Italy is especially well suited for the olive, and the fine trees of Corigliano to-day had their ancient parallels in the celebrated olives of Thuria.[8] Of lesser products, the honey of Hybla is the most famous. The saffron also was better than the best in Italy.[9]

Though they belong to a period later than that which we are considering, Tarentine acclimatizations are among the most permanent services of the Italian Greeks to civilization. Though not extraordinarily fertile, the land round the Great Harbour of Taranto faces due south and is protected from land winds by a line of low hills. Its mild climate makes it a pleasant place to winter, as Horace knew.[10] The cypress was introduced to Italy by the Tarentines, and spread northward not long before Cato's time.[11] He wrote a long diatribe against the difficulties of the tree and its uselessness. Pliny doubted whether the almond was cultivated in Italy in Cato's time, as he called it Graeca;[12] but Cato may have meant that it was a tree of Magna Graecia. There were two varieties called Tarentina, which suggests that it also reached central Italy from Tarentum. It is now one of the chief crops of Sicily and south Italy, but Athenaios does not mention Sicilian almonds in his dissertation;

[1] BM Cat. Sicily, 64.   [2] Steph. Byz. s.v.
[3] Pliny, NH xiv, 35 and 66.
[4] Diod. xiii. 81. 4–5. For the vineyards and fruit-gardens of Akragas see also Diod. xi. 25. 5.
[5] See above, p. 93 f. For fuller references to Sicilian wines see Scramuzza, op. cit. 269 ff.
[6] NH xv. 8.   [7] CAH, x. 410.
[8] Amphis ap. Athen. 30b, 67b.
[9] Strabo 273.   [10] Odes, ii. 6. 17–18.
[11] Pliny, NH xvi. 141: 'huic patria insula Creta, quamquam Cato Tarentinam eam appellat, credo, quod primum eo venerit.'
[12] NH xv. 90.

those of the island of Naxos were the best, and several other islands are named as growing them.[1] On the Sikel site of Torre Galli in Bruttium wild almonds were found, but curiously enough they were used not as food but as fuel. Tarentum was the home of one of the best varieties of chestnuts, Neapolis in Campania being the other.[2] The pears of Tarentum, a very late fruit, were also a named variety,[3] and so were the extra-sweet figs.[4] A small-leaved myrtle was called Tarentina by the Roman landscape-gardeners.[5] Cato also named the Sallentine olive, suitable for a warm rich soil[6]—the oil of this region, and that of Bari to the north, is to-day among the best in Italy. That so many fruits and trees were called Tarentine by the Romans does not prove that they were introduced to Italy by the Tarentines, but only that they were made known to the Romans by the Tarentines. As Taras was the greatest power of Magna Graecia in the fourth and third centuries, and the first with which the Romans came into close contact, it is natural that anything from the south of Italy should be called Tarentine. But there are so many more Tarentine varieties than, for example, Campanian, that it is likely that they were actually introduced from Greece or the east by the Tarentines. There was a Brettian pear,[7] and the double-cropping apples of Consentia were famous,[8] but these are little to compare to the number of Tarentine varieties.

Some parts of Sicily must in ancient times, as now, have been beautiful with fruit-trees; but as most of our evidence is of the Roman period when Sicily was given over entirely to wheat, we do not hear much of other branches of agriculture or horti-culture. In the time of Agathokles the country round Palermo was called a garden, because it was full of cultivated trees.[9] Some plants typical of the Sicilian scene to-day were already growing in ancient times. The wild parsley was so abundant that it gave its name to Selinus and appears on its coins. The dwarf-palm is on the coins of Kamarina, and also of Motye and

---

[1] Athen. ii. 52–4.
[2] *NH* xv. 94.
[3] Ibid. 54–6, 61.
[4] Ibid. 72.
[5] Ibid. 122; cf. xvii. 62.
[6] Ibid. 20; cf. Horace, *Odes* ii. 6. 15–16.
[7] *NH* xv. 54–6.
[8] Varro, *RR* i. 7. 6 = Pliny, *NH* xvi. 115.
[9] Kallias ap. Athen. 542a.

Segesta.[1] An edible cactus, which from Theophrastos' description closely resembled the prickly pear, the *fico d'India* so
common a feature of the Sicilian landscape, grew in Sicily
only, not in Greece.[2] Epikharmos, like the present Sicilians,
ranked it among edible plants.[3] Other specialities were the
silver beet, called Siculum by the Greeks,[4] and the rushes of
Panormos.[5]

The colonial region had few other natural resources besides
fields, pastures, forests, and seas. Sulphur, which now plays
so large a part in the economic life of Sicily, was mined in
Roman times, but not certainly in Greek.[6] Salt is spoken of in
connexion with the Lacus Cocanicus, between Kamarina and
Cape Pakhynos;[7] the salt-lagoons of the south and east coasts
are now of some importance. The metals of Sicily and south
Italy are almost negligible. There are traces of copper near
Temesa,[8] which, however, is not to be identified with the
Homeric $T\epsilon\mu\acute{\epsilon}\sigma\eta$.[9] There is silver in the territory of Sybaris, but
no evidence that it was worked before the sixteenth century.[10]
There is also silver in the province of Messina near the Fiume
di Nisi, and some of the mines may be ancient,[11] but it is unlikely
that they were worked in the archaic period. The iron near
Serra S. Bruno was almost certainly not worked in antiquity.
There is a story of a merchant in the time of Dionysios who
was able to corner all the iron in Sicily.[12]

[1] Pace, *Camarina*, 15 n.   [2] *Hist. Plant.* vi. 4. 10.
[3] Ap. Athen. 70*f*.
[4] Theophr. ap. Athen. 369*f*; cf. Pliny, *NH* xix. 132.
[5] Ibid. xvi. 172.   [6] Pace, *ACSA*, i. 393 ff.
[7] Pliny, *NH* xxxi. 79.
[8] Orsi, *N Sc*, 1916, 359; cf. Davies, *Roman Mines in Europe*, 73 ff.
[9] Strabo 255-6.
[10] I thank Mr. O. Davies for this information.
[11] Davies, op. cit. 75; cf. Dioscurides, v. 102, ἐν Σικελίᾳ ἀργυρῖτις.
[12] Arist. *Pol.* 1259ᵃ 23.

735–600 : Overwhelming Corinthian predominance.
735–700, some Argive and Cycladic in Sicily.
690–650, Cretan at Gela.
Small amount of East Greek, of Rhodian and perhaps other fabrics.
640–580, Rhodian at Syracuse and Gela, and at Selinus.
Faience and paste scarabs, &c., from Egypt.

600–550 : *c.* 590, Attic begins at Taras.
Attic begins at Rhegion.
580–570, Attic begins in Sicily.
Rhodian plain pottery at Gela.
Rhodian and Samo-Milesian terra-cottas.
Plain Ionian on all sites.
Laconian on many sites, especially at Taras.
Etruscan bucchero at Selinus and Syracuse.

550–480 : Attic predominance.
Some Corinthian after 550, especially at Syracuse.
Silver coins from Corinth.
East Greek plain pottery and terra-cottas.
Island marble.
Phoenician glass.

CHAPTER VIII

COMMERCE

THE chief evidence for the commercial relations of the western Greeks with the motherland is in the material from the great excavations. Only the sites which have been completely explored are really valuable. But where a whole temple deposit or a whole cemetery has been excavated, it is possible to argue from the relative proportions of different classes among many thousands of objects. Some dozen cities have yielded enough material to form a basis for such arguments. A brief conspectus of them, with the nature of the site and approximate dates, is given below.

City	Nature of site	Date	Main publications
Kyme	Graves	8th–5th cent.	MA, xxii
Syracuse	Graves	8th–3rd cent. (no good 5th-cent. graves)	N Sc, 1893, 1895, 1925
	Temple deposit, Athenaion	8th cent.–c. 480	MA, xxv
Megara	Graves	c. 700–485	MA, i
	Town and sanctuary	,,	,,
Gela	Graves	7th–4th cent.	MA, xvii
	Temple deposit, Bitalemi	c. 700–500	,,
Taras	Graves	7th–3rd cent.	..
	Temple deposit, Giovinazzi	6th–3rd cent.	..
Poseidonia	Temple deposit	700–400?	N Sc, 1937
Metapontion	Temple deposits	c. 700–5th cent.	..
Lokroi	Graves	6th–4th cent.; few 7th-cent. graves	N Sc, 1911 Suppl., 1913 Suppl.
	Temple deposit	c. 550–400	N Sc, 1911 Suppl.
Rhegion	Temple deposit	6th–3rd cent.	..
Selinus	Temple deposit, Malophoros	c. 625–500	MA, xxxii
	Temples, Akropolis	c. 600–400	MA, xxxv
	Graves	End 7th cent.–6th cent.	..
Akragas	Temple deposits	6th–5th cent.	Marconi, Agrigento Arcaica
Kamarina	Graves	c. 600–5th cent.	MA, ix, xiv
	Temple deposit	6th–5th cent.	,,

Other sites of secondary importance both in these and in other cities must be taken into account, but the more general arguments can only be founded on these big excavations. There are serious gaps in the list. Sybaris is an unknown quantity. The Khalkidian cities of Sicily have given little material; there are not inconsiderable finds from Katane and Leontinoi, but not enough to compare with the great mass from other Sicilian cities.

Commerce other than in pottery and metals is difficult to trace because of the perishable nature of the objects. In effect, we have to base most of our arguments on pottery, because it was used universally, because it is indestructible, and because it is easier to assign fragments of pottery to their place of origin than bronze- or metal-work. Many if not most of the other objects preserved in graves and sanctuaries will have come from the same sources as the pottery. This includes the jewellery of gold, silver, and bronze, the small bronzes, pins, fibulas, and vases or fragments from vases, and the ivories. Most of the objects in these materials found in Sicily, and to a less extent in south Italy, are of classes and types well represented at Corinth. There are a certain proportion of types which appear to be peculiar to the west, and to have been taken over from the native peoples of Italy.[1]

Each of the excavated sites has its own peculiarities, due to the nature of the site, cemetery or sanctuary, and the local conditions of preservation, as well as to genuine local preferences. But on the whole the imported material found all over Sicily and south Italy is remarkably uniform. There is an absolute predominance of Corinthian pottery. From the last quarter of the eighth century to the middle of the sixth any pottery other than Corinthian is a notable rarity. In the late eighth and early seventh centuries there are still a few other fabrics imported, some Cretan to Gela, a little Rhodian, a few pieces of Argive and Cycladic. From the middle of the seventh century the Rhodian increases, without, however, reaching noteworthy proportions, and there are a few pieces of other East Greek fabrics. There is plain pottery of Rhodian, and perhaps also Samian, types; a little Laconian, especially at Taras. These extend into the sixth century, when there are also some unimportant East Greek vases, and figurines from Rhodes and other East Greek cities, and also strong East Greek influence in the local terra-cottas. In the sixth century Attic vases appear beside Corinthian, and in the second half of the century replace them in absolute predominance. All the pieces of other fabrics than Corinthian and Attic may be listed and enumerated, while the dominant industries are represented by hundreds of vases on every site.

The predominance is more complete than in other parts of the Greek world because there was no local style of vase-

[1] See below, pp. 265 ff.

painting, and because Corinth, being much more favourably situated geographically than other industrial centres, could control the trade with the west. The causes of the establishment of Corinthian predominance are to be sought partly in the politics of Old Greece.[1] In its continuation for more than a century there is no reason to look for other than natural economic causes.[2] There was only one Corinthian colony in the west, and Syracuse has as many foreign imports as Megara or Gela. It is unnecessary to speak of commercial treaties safeguarding Corinthian trade, or to invoke special filial sentiment urging the Syracusans to buy Corinthian goods. Neither hypothesis explains why the Geloans should have so preferred Corinthian to Rhodian vases, for Syracuse was not yet able to impose her choice on her neighbours. Corinth was the chief industrial state in Greece. Her fine wares were more beautiful and delicate than any other fabric, her ordinary goods turned out on a larger scale and without doubt cheaper. Any other city (except Sparta) which wished to send goods to the west had a very much longer journey than Corinth, and had either to break bulk at the Isthmus and forward in Corinthian ships, or to ship round Malea. It is probable that many of the objects from the islands and Asia Minor which are found in the west came in cargoes made up at Corinth. While she was on good terms with Korkyra, Corinth had another important advantage. The joint intervention to save Syracuse from Hippokrates[3] suggests that there were times when the traditional enmity was at rest. In any case, political differences seem not to have always interfered with the westward passage of Corinthian goods. No doubt the harbour dues and provisioning of ships were too important for the Korkyraians always to allow politics to upset trade.

Most of the fine vases were imported for their own sake, but many pieces also for their contents. Most of the countless Corinthian aryballoi have no artistic merit to recommend them and their decoration is often only a perfunctory covering of the surface of a receptacle. They were no doubt exported from Corinth filled with perfumes and fine oils. The continued import of aryballoi in the second half of the sixth century, when other Corinthian shapes had been supplanted by Attic, implies that this Corinthian industry was still supreme. These

---

[1] Blakeway, *BSA*, xxxiii. 203 ff. See above, p. 16.
[2] As Orsi, *N Sc*, 1925, 311–12. [3] See below, p. 401.

wretched things are in a way better evidence for ancient commerce than fine vases, because it is not safe to infer that the cities which produced and exported vases were the only great industrial powers of Greece. But we have, for lack of other evidence, to argue from the finds of pottery, and to a less extent of bronzes and terra-cottas. In the particular instance of trade between Greece and the western colonies the Corinthian monopoly in pottery is so overwhelming that it is unlikely that any city could have effectively competed with Corinth in the products of other industries.

The mass of this trade was, no doubt, in Corinthian hands. It stands to reason that most of the trade in Corinthian products would travel in Corinthian ships. Colonial-owned ships are not heard of before the fourth century, although both Sicily and south Italy had forests of pine and fir for shipbuilding. Until the beginning of the fifth century none of the colonies had any fleet to speak of, and while they had no fleet they probably had little merchant marine. Arion returned from Taras in a Corinthian ship, though there were evidently others to choose from.[1] A Rhodian merchant, Amphinomos, sailed in his own ship to Sybaris.[2] As the sixth century drew on, the number of Ionians, led by the Phokaians and Rhodians, who sailed the western seas increased. But still Corinthian trade and shipping were predominant.

The chief of the non-Corinthian fabrics, and the one which speaks most conclusively of commercial relations, is Rhodian. The complete list is given in Appendix II A. Here we may briefly analyse the finds from Syracuse and Gela. They are mostly from temple deposits, few from datable graves, and some of the pieces are not easy to date even approximately.[3] But only a small handful belongs to the first half of the seventh century: four fragments from Gela (nos. 1, 12, 15, 16 on the list in Appendix II A), and about ten from Syracuse. (Nos. 30–2 should be of the late eighth century, before the unrestricted competition of the precolonization period had completely given way to the Corinthian dominance; nos. 33 and 35 are *c.* 650, perhaps after rather than before; nos. 26, 27–9, 48, and 49 are all dated by their associations to the first half of the seventh century.) This extremely scanty material is too little to be

[1] Herod. i. 24
[2] *Lind. Chron.* xxvi (*Lindos*, ii. 171).
[3] On the chronology see note on p. 472.

interpreted as evidence of regular commercial relations. In the second half of the century the quantity increases. All the remaining pieces, about twenty from Gela and the same number from Syracuse, are of the second half of the seventh century or early sixth. The pieces from Selinus are of the last quarter of the seventh century and the early sixth,[1] and the fragments from Rhegion and Militello belong to the same period. All the graves containing Rhodian are of this period. Fusco 29 has also Late Protocorinthian (650–40); Borgo 374 (Gela) and ex-Spagna 72 have Transitional (640–25); Borgo 132 is dated 625–600, ex-Spagna 1 a little before 600. Ex-Spagna 113 and Megara 820 descend towards the middle of the sixth century. More than half of the Rhodian vases found in Sicily thus fall between 640 and 580.

This period of little more than half a century which covers nearly all the Rhodian vases in the west coincides almost exactly with the Kypselid rule in Corinth.[2] The period of greatest intensity, the last quarter of the century, is the first part of Periander's reign. At this time Early Corinthian appears in the Milesian colonies, previously a Rhodian preserve, and at Naukratis.[3] There is also a considerable increase in the imports of Corinthian to Rhodes, and a Corinthian influence on Rhodian pottery. On the other hand, the development from Proto-corinthian to Corinthian is in part due to new oriental influences. There is no need to enlarge on the increasingly close relations of the Corinthian tyrants with Ionia and Lydia, but it should be noted that these relations, political, artistic, and commercial, begin with Kypselos, that is, exactly when Rhodian vases first come to Sicily in any quantity. This suggests that their appearance is due to the friendly relations between Corinth and the East Greek cities and the less exclusive policy of Kypselos and Periander, which permitted friendly powers to compete in markets which had previously been practically closed. The complete absence of Kamiran from Corinth and Perachora and the remarkably small amount of East Greek there belonging to the period under discussion does not

[1] Cf. Rumpf, *JdI*, 1933, 62.

[2] I believe that the traditional chronology of the Kypselids, in spite of recent attacks, is sufficiently well established to permit the association of historical and archaeological facts in this manner. The argument in no way depends on these associations, which on the contrary may be brought as an argument (though not a very strong one) in favour of the traditional chronology.

[3] Payne, *NC*, 25.

invalidate this hypothesis, for the Rhodians could not hope profitably to send to Corinth. But this fact makes it almost certain that the Rhodian in Sicily was shipped direct, not via the Isthmus. The absence of Rhodian from Taras and other south Italian sites, except Rhegion, strongly supports this.

The old view that the Rhodian vases were imported direct to Gela, and that some few pieces found their way thence to Syracuse, must be given up. It depended on the absence of Rhodian from the cemeteries of Fusco and Megara, and was upset by the fairly copious discoveries in the Athenaion and the ex-Spagna cemetery. On these two sites, and in scattered finds of the last twenty years at Syracuse, the proportion of Kamiran and allied fabrics is almost exactly the same as in the Geloan graves and sanctuaries. On the whole, there is very nearly the same quantity at Syracuse as at Gela, and it covers the same period. The sites are sufficiently alike in other respects, and in the quantity of material, for this comparison to be a fair one. Moreover, there are less than half a dozen pieces of Rhodian at Gela belonging to the first half-century of the colony; this shows that its later presence is not due to sentimental attachment of the colonists to the land of their birth. The Cretan pottery at Gela, which lasts for barely half a century and is not paralleled in other Sicilian cities, may be so explained.[1] But the Rhodian connexion gathers strength with the years. There is little evidence of it in the first half-century of the colony's existence, and its most striking manifestations fall in the sixth century. The Geloan buried in grave 132, with good Rhodian and unimportant Corinthian

[1] To the Cretan imports to Gela named in *Necrocorinthia*, 5, n. 1, add *MA*, xvii, fig. 155, and figs. 110–12, from one grave; and the following fragments of large vases of uncertain shape from the Tempio Arcaico (unpublished: see *MA*, xix. 89; *N Sc*, 1907, 38 f.):

1. Concentric circles, cf. *MA*, xvii, fig. 412.

2 and 3. Concentric circles, with parallel lines above, cf. *CVA Oxford*, ii, IIa, pl. 2. 18.

4. Fragment of a hatched meander (?) turning back at an acute angle; below, dots.

5 and 6. Simple meander.

7. False meander.

8. Hindquarters of bull (?).

For Cretan at Kyme see *NC*, 5, n. 1; Blakeway, *BSA*, xxxiii. 202; *JRS*, 1935, 130, 143–4. The fragment at Syracuse, *N Sc*, 1925, 318, fig. 72, which Blakeway suggests is Cretan (*BSA*, xxxiii. 182, no. 30) belongs rather to an East Greek fabric (cf. below, Appendix II A, no. 49).

Though Cretan imports to Sicily are limited to Gela, there is definite Cretan influence in Siculan pottery. For instance, the shape of the Siculan III hydria such as *RM*, 1898, 314 ff., figs. 16–18, is derived from Late Cretan (e.g. *Thera*, ii, fig. 427; *Tanis*, ii, pl. 32. 5; cf. Fölzer, *Die Hydria*, 44). An oinochoe at S. Angelo Muxaro (*Att. R. Acc. Palermo*, xvii, fig. 9) shows the influence of orientalizing Cretan in the tongues at its base (cf. above, p. 140, n. 2).

For terra-cottas of Cretan style found in the western colonies see below, p. 267, n. 3.

vases,[1] may have had a sentimental attachment to the land of his descent, or may even have been a settler who came from Rhodes in the generation after the foundation of Gela. But no such explanation fits the whole body of Rhodian pottery at Gela, and by implication the similar body at Syracuse and Selinus.

Geloan commerce in the seventh century is, apart from the Cretan connexion, in no way different from Syracusan. Megara is, in respect of pottery, a shadow of the Fusco cemetery at Syracuse. It looks as if Syracuse, the chief port and the one Corinthian colony, was the distributing centre for the south-east of Sicily. Either cargoes of similar composition came from Corinth, or possibly cargoes were broken up at Syracuse.[2]

There is no difference of quality between the Rhodian and Corinthian imports. The Rhodian is, of course, nearly limited to the oinochoai, bowls, and plates in which this fabric specializes, but there are Corinthian examples of all these forms. On the whole, the Rhodian is neither better nor worse than the average Corinthian with which it is associated. There are therefore no aesthetic reasons and, as we have seen, no sentimental reasons for the presence of the Rhodian, which can be due only to commercial competition. This competition was not very serious, and soon after the end of the seventh century Kamiran and the allied East Greek orientalizing fabrics disappeared altogether from the western markets.

So far I have spoken only of Rhodian, covering Rhodian geometric, bird-bowl fabric, and Kamiran. Other East Greek orientalizing fabrics are very scantily represented.[3] There is one group of fragments, of a pale-brown clay with flaky white slip and exceedingly delicate drawing in brown paint, which

---

[1] *MA*, xvii. 89 ff.

[2] In his latest discussion of the subject (*N Sc*, 1925, 311), which supersedes opinions expressed before all the material now available was known, Orsi says: 'Che la corrente industriale rodia fosse più intensa che in passato non si credesse, emerse anche dalle scoperte fatte nel temenos dell' Athenaion, che ricevono ora conferma ed amplificazione in quelle del predio Spagna. Se le relazioni commerciali fra Rodi e Siracusa fossero nei sec. VII–VI dirette od indirette per il tramite di Gela non risulta chiaro, essendo la storia siracusana di quei secolo oscurissima. Certo con Gela intercessero, per ragioni di vicinanza territoriale, anche rapporti politici.... Così si spiega la presenza di un certo numero di ceramiche rodie. ... Del resto Siracusa, le quale col suo porto, il più bello del Mediterraneo occidentale, formava la testa di tutte le linee di navigazione provenienti dalla Grecia, accoglieva le merci più disparate per natura ed origine; infatto la rada di Gela, essendo per quasi metà dell' anno impraticabile, è possibile che una parte almeno dell' importazione rodia avvenisse per la via di Siracusa.'

[3] See Appendix II b.

has parallels in technique in the finds of the recent excavation of the Heraion at Samos,[1] and may be Samian or Milesian. There are two Chiot fragments at Selinus; a Fikellura amphoriskos at Syracuse, another from near Taranto. This small tale of oddments shows that it is possible to speak definitely of Rhodian commerce in the seventh century rather than use the general term 'East Greek', and that there is very little omitted in saying that these fabrics cease to be imported very early in the sixth century. In any case the few scraps of other East Greek fabrics and of Cycladic do not establish direct relations between the places of their manufacture and the colonies.

There are also vases and other objects, not certainly Rhodian but due to the same current of trade. Among these are grey bucchero vases, most of them alabastra which often attain a great length.[2] All this grey bucchero was not certainly manufactured in the same place. The finest piece, the patera with plastic heads in ex-Spagna[1] at Syracuse, has a strongly Rhodian look.[3] The ridged, round aryballoi may also be Rhodian;[4] so perhaps also the alabastra.[5] Some of the largest of the latter are, however, not grey all through, but yellow in section, and the clay appears to be Samian. Others may belong to the Aiolian area where grey bucchero has been shown to be at home;[6] but there is little typical of that fabric in the west.[7] Whether made in Rhodes, Samos, or Lesbos, these vases were not necessarily exported direct thence to Sicily. They are simply solid undecorated vases with the function of a bottle, and must have been sought for the sake of their contents; and they may not have been filled where they were made, but exported in bulk and filled with the product of Corinthian or Rhodian industry. They cover the period of the Rhodian imports in Sicily, and continue into the second half of the sixth century.[8] As they are rare at Corinth and Perachora, and also at Taras, they may have come by the Rhodian current of trade rather than the Corinthian.

[1] Cf. Technau, AM, 1929, 22 ff., and especially Beil. xiv. 4.

[2] See BSR xvi. 19 ff. for list.

[3] N Sc, 1925, 179, fig. 2.   [4] This was Payne's opinion.

[5] As is suggested by K. M. T. Atkinson, BSR, xiv. 124 ff.

[6] W. Lamb, JHS, 1932, 1 ff.; BSA, xxxii. 51 ff.

[7] N Sc, 1925, 180, fig. 4, and perhaps also fig. 3, belong either to that group or to the 'Phokaian' fabric studied by Jacobsthal and Neuffer in Gallia Graeca, 16 ff.

[8] Atkinson, loc. cit., dates them in the second half of the seventh century. I have shown in BSR, cit., that, though they begin then, they are found more frequently in sixth-century graves.

Various kinds of plain vases and terra-cottas will be spoken of shortly. I shall discuss first another class of object perhaps brought to Sicily in Rhodian ships. Small faience vases, figurines, paste beads, scarabs, and cones are fairly common. The place of their manufacture is uncertain. Most of them will be Egyptian or Naukratite, but some may have come from the Phoenician coast. Some of the scarabs are certainly of the eighth century,[1] and the majority are found with Protocorinthian vases; but they are found occasionally in graves as late as the middle of the sixth century.[2] One group, consisting of faience aryballoi, pyxides, animal vases (women, monkeys, hedgehogs), many of Greek shapes, has a limited range of distribution, being found in Rhodes and the Greek islands, the great sanctuaries of Greece (Argive Heraion, Olympia, Ephesos), Etruria and Sicily, Carthage, Emporion in Spain, and seldom outside these areas. In Sicily they are found at Syracuse, Megara, Gela, and a single example at Selinus.[3] Those from Syracusan graves belong to the first half of the seventh century, and the round aryballoi of Corinthian shape, common on other sites, appear to be lacking; the plastic vase from Selinus must be later than the middle of the seventh century. These vases have been studied recently by von Bissing, who concludes that they were manufactured in Rhodes, the workshops being started probably by Egyptians about 700 and long keeping up close relations with Egypt.[4] The range of these vases is contrasted with the much wider range of Egyptian or egyptianizing scarabs, amulets, &c., and whether manufactured in Rhodes or not, they were certainly distributed from Rhodes. Another class of pointed vases of glazed clay has almost the same range of distribution (north Syria and central Anatolia being added), and though the case for Rhodian manufacture is less strong than for the faience vases, Rhodes will

[1] Scarabs are found in the prehellenic graves of Kyme (MA, xxii. 114, fig. 54; cf. 110, fig. 51, faience pendant) and in a grave at Finocchito (BPI, 1894, 42, 69) of early colonization date. At Syracuse they are found in Fusco 308, 204, and 30, which are all among the earliest graves and are to be assigned to the eighth or early seventh century.

[2] e.g. Fusco 551; Gela, Borgo 60; Megara 762; Syracuse, ex-Spagna 115. The last two are probably later than 550. A faience statuette at Megara is in a grave of the first half of the sixth century (grave 784, unpublished).

[3] Syracuse: aryballoi of Protocorinthian shape, N Sc, 1893, 473; 1895, 123, fig. 4; figurines, ibid. 143; MA, xxv. 584, fig. 174. Megara, grave 816; and see MA, i. 882, n. 1; N Sc, 1893, 473, n. 2. Gela, MA, xvii. 719, fig. 552. Selinus, MA, xxxii. 378, fig. 176. Orsi speaks also of faience vases from graves at Selinus (N Sc, 1893, 473, n. 2).

[4] Von Bissing, 'Zeit und Herkunft der in Cerveteri gefundenen Gefässe aus ägyptischer Fayence und glaziertem Ton' (SB Bayr. Akad. 1941, ii).

have been the centre of their distribution also.[1] They are less well represented in Sicily. One example was found in Syracuse, and another is in the museum there.[2]

That Rhodes is a distributing centre for all these objects, whether made in Rhodes or Egypt, is shown by the thousands found there. Those found in Sicily might have been imported by way of Corinth, for such objects are very common at Perachora.[3] It is likely that those in Sicily older than the middle of the seventh century may have come via Corinth, as there is little Rhodian pottery of that date in the west. The more numerous later examples may as well have come direct from Rhodes.[4] There are more of them at Syracuse and Megara than at Gela, but it has already been shown that Rhodian merchants did not especially favour Gela. There are few at Taras, and those with datable contexts belong to the sixth century;[5] this agrees with the distribution of Rhodian pottery.

Also from oriental sources, Egyptian or Asiatic, are the glass alabastra and amphoriskoi and alabaster alabastra which are found in the west in the sixth and fifth centuries. As these are found in small quantities all over the Greek world, their presence need not be due to direct relations with the countries which produced them; no doubt they were distributed from Athens.[6] Some of the glass, as earlier some of the faience and paste, may have been made in Phoenicia or exported by Phoenicians. It is possible that it reached Sicily via Carthage, for in the fifth century, at least, Carthaginians lived at Selinus

[1] Von Bissing, op. cit. 98 ff. These rather coarse vases are clearly distinguishable from faience, though often treated together with it. Their most accessible illustration is in Blinkenberg, *Lindos*, i, pl. 44, nos. 953–6. H. R. Hall suggests (*JHS*, 1928, 66) that they are Mesopotamian, and von Bissing does not reject this view. As Hall and von Bissing point out, their absence from Phoenicia and Syria (except the northern border-land, Senjirli and Deve Hüyük) is against the common view that they are Phoenician.

[2] *N Sc*, 1903, 527, fig. 10; Syracuse Mus. no. 25145 (von Bissing, op. cit. 104).

[3] To be published in *Perachora*, ii; cf. *Perachora*, i. 34, 118.

[4] Von Bissing (op. cit. 97–8) favours the view that those in the western Mediterranean were shipped via Aigina and Corinth rather than direct from Rhodes. So far as his argument depends on the absence of Rhodian vases from Etruria and Italy in general, the preceding pages will show that it is not conclusive.

[5] The most important are aryballoi in tomb III, S. Francesco di Paola; tomb II, Vaccarella; and tomb LXIV, with Corinthian amphoriskos, four-leaved lotus aryballos (add to Ure's list, *Aryballoi and Figurines*, 101), and Laconian black aryballos. There are also figurines of a lion and a man, and a ram's head in blue faience, without exact contexts. Scarabs are very rare.

[6] So Fossing, *Glass Vessels before Glass-blowing*, 51 ff., who regards the glass found in Sicily and south Italy as Egyptian.

and Syracuse, and trade between Akragas and Carthage is recorded.[1] But there is not enough earlier material, Phoenician or Asiatic, to postulate a direct connexion in the seventh or sixth century between Phoenicia and the Greek colonies, and nothing else suggests the presence of Phoenician traders. There are many faience objects at Motye, including an alabastron which has a very close parallel at Syracuse;[2] and they do not fall off there in the sixth century as Greek pottery does.[3] This favours the view that they came via Carthage. On the other hand, there are few at Selinus and Akragas, though imports to Syracuse and Megara continue later than the foundation of these colonies. Corinth, Rhodes, Carthage may all have acted as intermediaries in bringing these Phoenician and Egyptian objects to Sicily, but on the whole the Rhodian hypothesis is the more probable, particularly as certain classes of egyptianizing objects appear to be of Rhodian manufacture.

Certain kinds of plain or simply decorated Rhodian pottery[4] are almost limited to Gela, in contrast to the painted Kamiran ware, which is not commoner at Gela than at Syracuse. This suggests a special connexion between Gela and Rhodes, which becomes a certainty when local imitations of forms current at Rhodes are also considered. The distinctive pink clay proclaims some pieces found at Gela to be Rhodian, and the decoration of others is exactly paralleled in Rhodes. Both classes are almost without parallel in the rest of Sicily. They are more numerous in the first half of the sixth century than in the seventh. Therefore they cannot have been brought by the same current of trade as the Kamiran ware, which disappears from Sicily early in the sixth century. They have a different distribution from the Rhodian terra-cottas which are imported and imitated all through the sixth century,[5] and are spread also over most of the Greek world. This plain pottery, which unlike the ordinary objects of Rhodian commerce is almost limited to Gela, probably came by channels not exclusively commercial. It is ordinary household ware, while the painted ware was more often an object of display.[6] It may have

---

[1] Diod. xiii. 81 ; cf. below, p. 254, n. 3. On the other hand, Vercoutter, *Objets égyptiens de Carthage*, 355–6, shows good reason to believe that many of the Egyptian objects at Carthage came there through Greek intermediaries.

[2] Whitaker, *Motya*, frontispiece; Syracuse, *N Sc*, 1893, 472.   [3] See below, p. 327.

[4] Appendix II C.   [5] Appendix II E.

[6] Certainly plates and many bowls, which have been pierced for hanging on a wall. Cups and jugs were intended to be beautiful as well as useful.

been brought by immigrants from Rhodes, who continued after their arrival to make the same sort of pot in the local clay.

The agreement of the burial methods of Gela and the Geloan country-side with those of Rhodes, in many details as well as in general feeling, proves that the population of Gela remained Rhodian throughout the archaic period. The custom of burying infants, and occasionally older children, in pithoi, the shape and decoration of the pithoi, and such coincidences as the cutting out of the side of a pithos to let a baby's corpse in, at both Gela and Ialysos, are peculiar to Rhodes and Gela.[1] The close parallels between the two more than a century after the foundation of Gela are more than would be expected if the Rhodians of Gela had during that period developed without further close contact. Further, the pithoi used in the early seventh century are Cretan in type and some at least in manufacture.[2] This makes it almost certain, on the argument from burial customs alone, that the Rhodian element at Gela was reinforced during the last half of the seventh century at the time when the Cretan connexion weakened.

There is evidence other than archaeological for the connexion of Gela and Rhodes in the period immediately after the foundation. The offering of the Geloans to Athena Lindia on the conquest of Ariaiton belongs to the first half of the seventh century.[3] The importance of the cults of Athena and Apollo, who was presumably Apollo Lindios,[4] indicates that they are probably as old as the colony. No altar or trace of sacrifice with fire was found in the archaic temple at Gela, probably that of Athena;[5] compare the ἄπυρα ἱερά at Lindos.[6] The rites which Telines' ancestor brought with him from the Triopian headland are Dorian, though not Rhodian, and he himself came from the Kamiran island of Telos.[7] But the archaeological evidence is silent about any especially close connexion during the first half of the seventh century. The striking parallels in both pottery and burial methods leave little doubt that during the second half of the century the Rhodian nature

[1] Burial methods in general, Gela, *MA*, xvii. 237; cf. *Ann.* vi–vii, 333 ff. Enchytrismoi, Gela, op. cit. 242 ff.; Ialysos, *Ann.* loc. cit.; Kamiros, *Clara Rhodos*, iv. 16; Vroulia, *Vroulia*, 35 ff. Pithos burials with opening in side to let in a baby's corpse, Gela, Borgo 278 *bis*, op. cit. 141, fig. 104; exact parallels in Ialysos LXXXV, *Ann.* vi–vii, 329, fig. 220; Ialysos V, ibid. 265; Kamiros CCXI, *Clara Rhodos*, iv. 366, fig. 412.

[2] See *NC*, 5, n. 1. [3] *Lind. Chron.* xxv; *Lindos*, ii. 171.

[4] Diod. xiii. 108. [5] *MA*, xxv. 738.

[6] Pindar, *Ol.* vii. 39 ff.; Blinkenberg, *L'Image d'Athéna Lindia*, 7, 11.

[7] Herod. vii. 153.

of Gela was asserted by the arrival of new colonists. This subsidiary migration continued until the foundation of Akragas, if not longer. The association of Rhodes in that foundation is more than common politeness on the part of the Geloans, for the Rhodian element in men and in religion and culture was very strong. Probably the moving force was Rhodian.[1] This might explain why Akragas rapidly outgrew Gela and soon became unwilling to acquiesce in a subordinate position (if I am right in inferring that Phalaris fought a war of independence against Gela).[2] The foundation of Akragas may have its part in larger schemes, including the Rhodian–Knidian attempt at Lilybaion. Strong Rhodian and East Greek influence is present in the sixth-century art of Selinus as well as Gela and Akragas.[3]

This Rhodian immigration is not to be too closely associated with the purely commercial expansion which brought Rhodian painted vases to Gela as well as to Syracuse and Etruria. In the second half of the seventh century Rhodians took second place to the Corinthians in Sicily and to the Phokaians in the far west. It was possibly at this period, and not before the first Olympiad, that they voyaged to Spain, founded Rhode, and colonized the Balearic Islands.[4] The cities of Philoktetes were said to have been founded by Rhodians under Tlepolemos,[5] and a Rhodian origin asserted for Siris and Sybaris on the Traeis.[6] It is uncertain how much value to give to these stories, and to what date to assign them. The Rhodian origin of Elpiai[7] and Rhodian activity in the Adriatic in the sixth century are better attested.[8] At least one Rhodian ship made a voyage to Sybaris before the middle of the sixth century. Amphinomos and his sons made a dedication to the Lindian Athena on saving a cargo from Sybaris from shipwreck.[9]

Not all the plain vases of Appendix II c are certainly Rhodian or of Rhodian derivation. One form especially, the so-called Samian lekythos, is as common at Samos as at Rhodes.

---

[1] See below, p. 311.
[2] See below, p. 317.
[3] See below, p. 239.
[4] Strabo 654; cf. p. 340.
[5] Lykophron 923; ps.-Arist. de mir. ausc. 107. See Giannelli, *Culti e Miti della Magna Grecia*, ch. viii.
[6] Strabo 264.
[7] Id. 654; Lykophron 1126 ff. Cf. Mayer, *Apulien*, 205–6, 382 ff.
[8] See R. L. Beaumont, *JHS*, 1936, 172 ff., 192 f.
[9] *Lindos*, ii. 171 = *Lind. Chron.* xxvi: Ἀμφίνομος καὶ τοὶ υἱοὶ βοῦν ξύλιναν καὶ μόσχον, ἐφ᾽ ὧν ἐπεγέγραπτο· Ἀμφίνομος καὶ παῖδες ἀπ᾽ εὐρυχόρου Συβάρειος ναὸς σωθείσας τάνδ᾽ ἀνέθεν δεκάταν. This entry comes before Phalaris' dedication, i.e. before 571–555, and may be of any date in the half-century c. 625–575.

Others are found at Samos and may be common East Greek. The evidence of the distinctive pinkish Rhodian clay of many of the Geloan examples, the pithos forms which are not paralleled elsewhere, and the historical connexion between Gela and Rhodes, make it likely that the common East Greek forms reached Gela from Rhodes; but other states may have contributed. The presence of Samo–Milesian as well as Rhodian terra-cottas supports this. Rhodes seems to have had close commercial and artistic relations with Miletos and Samos, and probably Lesbos, so that it would be easy for the products of these states to be brought to Sicily by Rhodians.

The plain red-ground vases of Appendix II D are products of the Ionian κοινή. They are found on almost every site in the west, especially on native sites in Sicily and Apulia where other Greek pottery is rare. What recommended them to the native peoples was probably that, being of simple decoration, they were correspondingly cheap. They made more appeal to the semi-hellenized barbarian who wanted some Greek vases than to the Greek who had not only more taste but more money. This applies especially to the commonest form, the cup, which was only a funerary vase *per accidens*. The plain Ionian cup might be a substitute for the more expensive Attic. Many of the plain cups described as of Ionian type are probably Attic, made for this sort of trade. Those which are certainly East Greek cannot be further specified; they may have been manufactured at a number of cities. The individual East Greek fabrics of the sixth century are represented in Sicily and south Italy by only a very small number of pieces which may be regarded as sporadic. There are three main routes by any or all of which this pottery may have reached the west. It may have been brought from Corinth, for just such unimportant East Greek is found at Perachora; from Rhodes; or by those Ionians who are known to have made voyages to the west, Phokaians and Milesians, or perhaps by Khalkidians. In the last case, the absence of the better East Greek fabrics which are found in Etruria but not in Sicily or south Italy would be difficult to explain. The quantity of plain Ionian at and near Taranto and in Apulia may reflect Rhodian or Ionian voyages to the Italian shore of the Adriatic.[1] Its presence elsewhere does not call for

---

[1] As there is no Kamiran and little other East Greek material at or near Taranto, these voyages may have begun in the sixth century only, but the argument has all the dangers of an argument from silence.

explanation, but is a part of the Mediterranean-wide fabric of Greek commerce. Its importance to the west is not in itself but as a small sign of the growing emancipation from Corinth. Taken with the literary evidence of voyages from Ionia to the far west it shows how new influences could reach the colonies, whose relations with Greece throughout the seventh century had been almost confined to Corinth. The pottery was not certainly brought by Ionians, but even if it was brought by Corinthians, it shows that other more important products of an art and industry other than Corinth's might be current in the colonies.

The imports of Rhodian terra-cottas and their influence on the local product[1] can be best studied at Selinus, where there is the fullest series and the best chronological evidence. The East Greek terra-cottas, like the Peloponnesian, appear at the end of the seventh century (few of the Selinuntine terra-cottas are of the first years of the colony) and the period of greatest import is before c. 580.[2] Gàbrici states that this is confirmed by the graves, the oldest of which have Ionian terra-cottas.[3] I have hesitated to use the evidence of the Selinus graves, because many of them have been used for several burials at dates not sufficiently far apart to be certain to which deposit the terra-cottas belong; I have quoted two in which figurine alabastra are definitely associated with Late Corinthian vases.[4] But most of the Rhodian imports to Selinus are of the first quarter of the sixth century, the period just before and including the foundation of Akragas and the expedition of Pentathlos.[5] At Akragas also the Rhodian influence is strongest during the earliest years of the colony.[6]

There is no certain evidence of the import of matrices from Rhodes and Ionia. Sicilian copies of East Greek types are easily distinguishable from their originals by the clay, absence of paint, and inferior modelling and less precise outline. At both Akragas and Selinus there is an East Greek influence in the development of the local style,[7] whose main descent is Pelopon-

---

[1] See Appendix II E.

[2] *MA*, xxxii, 298: 'le terrecotte di fabricazione ionica furono abbondanti nello strato *c* e sotto all' altare, vale a dire nello strato formatosi dopo la costruzione del primo megaron. In questo e negli strati superiori . . . le terrecotte figurate ioniche scomparvero a poco a poco di fronte alla preponderanza sempre più crescente della industria coroplastica locale.'

[3] *MA*, xxxii. 299.   [4] Below, Appendix II E.

[5] See below, pp. 310 ff., 328 ff.   [6] *Agrigento*, 175, imports; 173–5, 217, style.

[7] *MA*, xxxii. 226. To take some Selinuntine examples: ibid., pll. 63, 55 show development of East Greek type under Peloponnesian influence; style and some details are

nesian. The feeling of sixth-century Selinuntine terra-cottas of the common types is Peloponnesian, that of Akragantine is akin, though the import of East Greek originals there was stronger, after the first quarter of the century.[1] At Selinus there are a few later imports,[2] but they do not compare in quantity with the imports of the early sixth century. This is partly because Selinus had developed her own art and industry, partly because reproductions of the Peloponnesian types were preferred. Imports from the Peloponnese decrease at the same time as East Greek, but the development of Peloponnesian types continues.

Apart from the Rhodian and other East Greek, no other non-Corinthian commerce of the seventh and early sixth centuries has left any mark in the western colonies. Attic vases were little exported before the late seventh century, and two fragments at Syracuse are the only certain examples in the west.[3] The only other fabric which comes into question is Laconian. There is a special connexion with the Laconian colony of Taras which imported Laconian vases, terra-cottas, and bronzes in small quantities. Most of them are of the first half of the sixth century, and few pieces (apparently no vases) belong to the seventh century.[4] There is also a certain amount of Laconian in Etruria, with which we are not concerned. In Sicily, imports are almost limited to plain vases: black kraters, black amphoriskoi with reserved bands on shoulder and foot, black aryballoi with very simple decoration, and plain lakainai.[5] The same classes of Laconian vases as are imported to Sicily are found also at Perachora. There can be little doubt that the pieces in Sicily came via Corinth, and consequently do not prove commercial relations between Sicily and Laconia.

A minor but not unimportant article of trade at this time

Peloponnesian, scheme East Greek (op. cit. 257 ff.); pl. 47. 5 shows East Greek details in head of Peloponnesian style. See also below, p. 288.

[1] Marconi's opinion (*Agrigento*, 217), that as the Rhodian strain weakens in the course of the sixth century nothing takes its place, underrates the importance of the Peloponnesian influence. The truth is, however, that it praises most of the ordinary types too highly to speak of style.

[2] *MA*, xxxii, pll. 45. 8; 46. 2; perhaps 46. 1 and 4.

[3] *N Sc*, 1895, 189; 1925, 316, fig. 69; Åkerström, *Der geometrische Stil in Italien*, 35, figs. 8–9.

[4] E. A. Lane, *BSA*, xxxiv. 181; Dugas, *RA*, xx, 1912, ii. 88 ff. There are other Laconian fragments found in and near Taranto: Taranto Mus., case 49, bottom (labelled 1957; but inventory entry does not correspond), fragments of two cups, and a foot of the same shape as the Zeus cup Lane, pl. 37*b*; black jug, from tomb in Via d'Aquino (1910), like *Artemis Orthia*, fig. 62. Another cup, *N Sc*, 1936, 119, fig. 8. See also p. 234, n. 5.

[5] See Lane, op. cit. 182, 189; Mingazzini, *I Vasi Castellani*, 186; Payne, *NC*, 204.

was marble. Six marble lamps, or fragments of lamps, were found at Selinus and two at Syracuse.[1] One of the lamps, decorated with a head of the late dedalic style, is among the oldest objects found at Selinus. The others are not much later, and the whole series falls in the late seventh century and first half of the sixth. These were certainly imported, and were no doubt manufactured in some island which quarried marble. Beazley suggests Paros. Parian marble, in larger pieces than these lamps, continued to be imported to Sicily at a much later date. There is no marble in the territory of the western colonies, and little hard limestone suitable for sculpture. As a result, when the colonies became rich and wished to vie with the cities of the motherland in dedications to the gods, they had to bring marble from Greece, either in the form of statues or as blocks ready for working.[2] Most of the late archaic sculpture in Sicily is of Greek marble, mainly Parian. Marble was also brought from Greece for tiles for many of the great temples built in this and the succeeding periods.[3] The marble roof of the temple of Hera Lakinia was famous in antiquity,[4] and the temple was also adorned with sculpture in Parian marble.[5] In the second century A.D. a cargo of Luna marble, worked and unworked, was wrecked off the Lakinian promontory;[6] then also the Krotoniates wishing to honour Hera imported what was to the taste of the time the finest available stone.

From c. 580 the political and commercial relations between Corinth and Athens became very close.[7] This had profound effects in the west. In the last quarter of the seventh century Attic pottery appears in small quantities in Etruria. The earliest pieces are large vases, amphoras and hydriai, such as were rather rare in seventh-century Corinthian, and cups. Their fine finish and artistic excellence would command a place for them beside the corresponding Corinthian. But without the goodwill of Corinthian merchants they could hardly have found their way to Italy at all. Most of the Attic pottery in

---

[1] *MA*, xxxii. 162 ff., pl. 23. 1–2; *N Sc*, 1925, 207, fig. 45; Beazley, *JHS*, 1940, 22 ff., pl. 6.

[2] Whether stone or statues was imported is here irrelevant; see p. 286 for discussion of this important question.

[3] See list in Orsi, *Templum Apollinis Alaei*, 59, n. 1.

[4] Livy xlii. 3; Val. Max. i. 1. 20; cf. *N Sc*, 1911 Suppl., 97 ff., fig. 77; Lenormant, *GG*, ii. 229.

[5] *N Sc*, 1897, 344, fig. 1; 1911 Suppl., 102, fig. 79.

[6] *N Sc*, 1911 Suppl., 118 ff.

[7] This section is based largely on unpublished material of Blakeway's.

the west was probably carried in Corinthian ships.[1] The Corinthians had during most of the seventh century a hold on the Etruscan markets no less strong than their hold on south Italy and Sicily, but Etruria was opened to other traders sooner than Sicily, by the frequent voyages of Phokaians and other Ionians from the last thirty years of the seventh century onwards. Rhegion was friendly to the Phokaians: Sybaris was an intermediary between Miletos and Etruria. Either from the Straits or from the Sybarite ports on the Tyrrhenian Sea Etruscan ships might have picked up, as well as pottery of the various Ionian fabrics, some Attic which had been carried west by Ionians. Athenian interests in the east were developing at this period, and they must have had friendly relations with Miletos in order to export Attic pottery to the Pontos; this export begins in the late seventh century. Attic vases appear in Etruria earlier than in Sicily, and at a period from which very little Attic has been found at Corinth. The earliest Attic in Etruria is c. 620–610;[2] at Taras about 600; in Sicily c. 580–570.[3] The oldest Attic at Perachora, except a few casual pieces of Protoattic which cannot establish regular commerce, is c. 590–580. Both at Perachora and in Sicily corinthianizing Attic, of the Comast and C groups and kindred styles, is much better represented than other Attic of the first half of the sixth century. The development of this corinthianizing style shows that the close relations of Corinth and Attica, at their closest about 580, began before the end of the seventh century. There is therefore no difficulty in the suggestion that the earliest Attic vases in the west were carried in Corinthian ships; this is, of course, not proved, Ionian merchants being a possible alternative, but there is no direct support for the latter view. The Corinthians, seeing that Attic vases had gained a footing and were better than Corinthian, had the foresight not to attempt to suppress them but to reap a profit from them. It is reasonably certain that some Corinthian potters transferred to Athens, and there was a long period of mutual influence during which relations were very close. Political relations between Athens and Corinth during the century 580–480 were singularly happy. As the expansion of Attic exports to the west, where they succeeded in driving out Corinthian, did not interfere with political or industrial relations, it must have had Corinthian

[1] Cf. B. Bailey, *JHS*, 1940, 60 ff.
[2] *AA*, 1923-4, 46, fig. 1, by the Nessos painter, from Caere.   [3] See Appendix III.

favour. This would be possible if the Attic pottery was carried west from the isthmus in Corinthian ships. This would, indeed, be the most natural route from Athens to the west, being shorter than an all-sea route round Malea. The importance which Athens attached to the accession of Megara, in her attempt after 460 to cut Corinth out of the control of the Corinthian Gulf, suggests that she wished to develop the Megara–Pegai route as an alternative, temporary and much inferior to the Isthmus route.

The early Attic in Sicily agrees fairly closely with that at Perachora.[1] Comast cups, which have strong Corinthian affinities, are the earliest vases found in quantity in either place. At Perachora, as in Sicily, other pieces older than $c.$ 550 are far fewer than Corinthian, and the definite establishment of Attic predominance is at Corinth, as in Sicily, in the second half of the century. Tyrrhenian amphoras and allied forms, so common in Etruria, are absent both in Sicily and at Perachora. The agreement is sufficiently strong to support the view that the Attic black-figure in the west came via Corinth in Corinthian ships, and that the reason for the change from Corinthian to Attic is to be sought in Corinthian policy rather than in the circumstances of the colonies. The Attic imports to Taras, as to Etruria, begin earlier and are more plentiful in the first half of the century than the imports to Sicily, and may have been brought by other intermediaries.

In the first half of the century most of the Attic imports are fine large vases, and the quantity of second- and third-rate Corinthian is undiminished. 580 is about the date when Attic first arrived in any quantity on the western market, but it is not till about 550 that it supplants Corinthian. Aryballoi did not give way to Attic lekythoi till well after the middle of the century, lekythoi not being frequent before 530. Many of the earliest are good large vases. Aryballoi were imported less for their artistic merits than for their contents, and so long as these came from Corinth, it was cheaper to bottle them in the mass-produced Corinthian article. But in time the demand for the new Attic vases in place of the old-fashioned Corinthian nullified this advantage, and probably other industries beside the manufacture of pottery passed from Corinth to Athens.

Export of Corinthian to Sicily, mainly aryballoi, kotylai, and

[1] Cf. Payne, *NC*, 184, for Attic imports at Corinth; they begin early in the sixth century, and become common towards the middle.

other small vases, continued later than to any part of Greece except the Argolid and Boiotia.[1] A few cinquefoil and sixfoil aryballoi are found on Sicilian sites. There are none in Etruria, very few in Rhodes, none elsewhere except Delos, Boiotia, and the Argolid. Flat-bottomed aryballoi of Ure's group iv. 1 (= NC, no. 1294), are limited to Sicily; Kyme and Caere; Delos and south Russia; the greatest number come from Gela, Akragas, and Megara. Isolated exports, especially of miniature kotylai, continued into the fifth century; those in a grave at Kamarina are probably as late as the refounding of the city in 460.[2] The main stream of Corinthian export dried up rapidly after 550. Before that date Attic vases triumphed completely in Etruria, and at Rhegion and Taras; at Gela, Selinus, and Megara from that date onwards. At Syracuse, however, there is not much Attic older than c. 530.[3] Close relations between Syracuse and Corinth were kept up much longer and were stronger and more fruitful than those between any other colony and its metropolis.[4] At this period they were probably reinforced by the presence in Syracuse of Corinthian merchants, who controlled the commerce of Syracuse while they were gradually losing that of the rest of Sicily. Filial piety and business interest led the Syracusans to buy Corinthian vases for a short time after they had lost ground everywhere else.[5] Even at Megara, whose imports were in most respects exactly like those of Syracuse, there are many more Attic vases and fewer Corinthian of the period 550–525. But in the last third of the century Attic vases, and by implication other products of Athenian industry, have a supremacy in the west as complete as that of Corinth had been a century earlier. One result of the lack of rivals was that Athens sent, as Corinth had done, a very cheap pottery, well made and fired, but ornamented with the most careless and tasteless drawing. There are many good vases of this period from Taras and other centres of Magna Graecia, but

---

[1] See lists in Ure, *Aryballoi and Figurines*, Appendix. By way of caution against pressing too far the distribution of single types, I point out that all flat-bottomed aryballoi of his group iv. 2 (Middle Cor. = NC, no. 644) are from western sites, with the addition of Thera and Thebes. The distribution of Middle Corinthian in general does not warrant the inferences which might be drawn from the absences from this list. But the combined weight of all the Late Corinthian II distributions, the most striking of which are mentioned above, shows that Corinthian export shrank to Boiotia and Sicily before it disappeared.

[2] Grave 453 (*MA*, xiv. 876, 939). For the date of these kotylai cf. *NC*, 334.

[3] Cf. Bailey, *JHS*, 1940, 69–70.

[4] Ashmole (p. 19) stresses the Corinthian style of the early coinage of Syracuse.

[5] Cf. Orsi, *MA*, xxv. 744.

very few from Sicily. Some of the best finds from Sicily are now in museums outside Italy, often with no certain indication of origin; but very few good black-figure vases are known to have been found in Sicily, and early red-figure is rare indeed.[1] At Megara, destroyed in 483 or 482, there are scores of graves of the last half-century of the city's existence and no single piece of red-figure. Megara was a poor place, but the richer cities are hardly in better case. This cannot be due entirely to chance or the wholesale depredations of the rich cemeteries of Akragas and Gela. Rather than poverty the Sicilian Greeks are to be accused of indifference and lack of taste. The period before the last decade of the sixth century was in many ways a dead one, and the Sicilian cities were lagging behind those of south Italy.

The date at which the colonial coinages begin agrees strikingly with that of the change from Corinthian pottery.[2] It is impossible to be positive about the precise date of the first coins, but the order is reasonably established. In Sicily the earliest are Selinus and Himera, in the early sixth century, followed by Zankle.[3] Rhegion and Naxos begin to coin about the middle of the century;[4] Syracuse and Akragas, c. 530;[5] Gela and

[1] Gela: lekythoi by Gales painter, Boston 13.195 and Syracuse 26967, *ARV*, 30–1, nos. 1 and 2.
    Cup made by potter Kakhrylion, Syracuse 21190, *MA*, xvii. 458; *ARV*, p. 82.
    Cup fr. by Pithos painter, Syracuse 19820, *ARV*, 116, no. 11.
    Cup in manner of Pithos painter, Kassel, *ARV*, 117, no. 7.
    Cup related to Panaitian group, Oxford 302, *CVA*, pl. 1. 9; *ARV*, p. 212.
    Akragas: rhyton, manner of Euthymides, *Boll. d'Arte*, xxv. 64 ff.; *ARV*, 27, no. 2.
    Cup by Epiktetos, *ARV*, 48, no. 39.
    Selinus: cup frr. in manner of Epeleios painter, *ARV*, 109, nos. 2, 3; 111, no. 32.
    Cup frr. by painter of Berlin 2268, *ARV*, 114, no. 16 (*MA*, xxxii, pl. 95. 3); no. 17.
    Monte Casale: frr. of neck-amphora by Euthymides, Syracuse 49305, *ARV*, 25, no. 6.
    Rhegion: cup frr. by Epiktetos, *Ausonia*, vii. 173; *ARV*, 46, no. 17.
    Taras: cup fr. by Bonn painter, *Dedalo*, ii. 624; *ARV*, 225, no. 2.
    Stand, perhaps by Ambrosios painter, Amsterdam inv. 2237, *CVA*, III i B, pl. 8. 5; *ARV*, p. 73.
    Fr. in Oxford, of late sixth century, *CVA*, i. pl. 49. 15; *ARV*, p. 936.
    Lokroi: Six lekythos, Berlin 2241.
The earliest painters represented in any quantity in the western colonies are Myson, the Berlin painter, the Kleophrades painter. For the almost complete absence of early r.f. from Selinus cf. *MA*, xxxii. 329. The small quantity at Gela contrasts with the number of good vases of the period 480–450; contrast also the amount of good early r.f. at (e.g.) Adria.
I thank Dr. R. J. Hopper for assistance with this note.
[2] Cf. Cahn, *Die Münzen der Sizilischen Stadt Naxos*, 39.
[3] J. G. Milne, *Num. Chron.* 1938, 36 ff.; Cahn, op. cit. 78. Milne gives slightly different absolute dates, but almost the same order, for the Sicilian cities as those here given; cf. his review of Cahn's book, *JHS*, 1944, 107–8.   [4] Cahn, op. cit. 29 ff.
[5] Syracuse, Boehringer, *Die Münzen von Syrakus*, 91; Akragas, Milne, loc. cit.

Leontinoi, at the end of the sixth century.[1] The first cities of Magna Graecia to coin are Taras and the Akhaian cities, Sybaris, Metapontion, and Kroton, the date in the first half of the sixth century.[2] On the evidence of the imports of Attic vases (incomplete, as there is no evidence for the Akhaian cities of Italy nor the Khalkidian colonies in Sicily) the first of these cities to break away from Corinthian domination is Taras, followed closely by Rhegion, at a longer interval by Gela, Selinus, and Akragas, Syracuse being the last. Sybaris must have early attained economic independence, and neither her relations nor those of Zankle and Himera were in the first half of the sixth century limited to Corinth.

One result of dealing with other than Corinthian merchants would be that barter would no longer be so easy. In the seventh century, it would appear, all trade was in Corinthian hands, and transactions must have been simple: manufactured goods for food. In the sixth century traders from many cities of Ionia might be offering their goods in western markets and bidding for the products of the soil. The Corinthians themselves were becoming intermediaries of Athenian trade, selling Attic vases and perhaps carrying back corn intended for Athens. It is no coincidence that within a short period of the opening of wider relations the colonies found it necessary to issue their own coinage, and the first to do so were those who had the widest relations. That the coinage of the colonies was first issued for large-scale overseas transactions, not for local use, is shown by the fact that it is all in large denominations.[3] Small coins were not used until the fifth century, the date varying from place to place.

The standards of weight on which the colonies coin might be expected to throw light on their commercial relations. But this subject is extremely obscure and difficult. The earliest Sicilian cities to coin, Selinus, Himera, Zankle, and Naxos, use a drachma of approximately 89·5 gr. (5·80 gm.). Those of Himera are the heaviest, Zankle and Naxos falling slightly below this standard.[4] This fits with no system current in Greece. Attempts have been made to relate it to the Aiginetan, the Euboic, the Corinthian, the Korkyraian standard. It seems

---

[1] Gela, Cahn, op. cit. 37; Leontinoi, Boehringer, op. cit. 79 ff.; cf. Agnes E. Brett, *AJA*, 1930, 514–15.

[2] Vlasto, Τάρας Οἰκιστής, 31; Wuilleumier, *Tarente*, 52, 198–9; Noe, *Coinage of Metapontum*, i. 50.

[3] Boehringer, op. cit. 29, 167; Cahn, op. cit. 22.   [4] Cahn, op. cit. 74 ff.

safer to regard it as a local standard, not in use east of the
Adriatic.[1] It might be thought to show a relation to the bronze
λίτρα standard,[2] but this is not clear. What is certain is that
the standard was adopted with a view to easy interchange with
the main currencies in use in Greece, into which it can be con-
verted by a short sum in multiplication. The Attic standard
was introduced by Syracuse when she began to coin c. 530, and
in the fifth century was universally adopted.

The south Italian cities in the archaic period coined to a
standard weight of 128·5 gr. (8·32 gm.), but most coins fall well
below this weight. Taras, Sybaris, and Metapontion have the
highest averages, Kroton and Kaulonia fall lower.[3] This is the
Corinthian standard, adopted as will be seen because the silver
came from Corinth. All these cities coin in a remarkable fabric
in which the reverse is incuse and repeats the type of the
obverse. This fabric is adopted regularly by the Akhaian
cities, of which Sybaris appears from the slightly higher weight
to have set the standard;[4] and also for some issues of Taras,
Rhegion, and Zankle. The incuse coins of Taras are apparently
contemporary with the normal double-typed issues and are of
slightly lower weight, being intended for interchange with the
Akhaian cities.[5] Those of Zankle are not the earliest of that
city, as has been thought, but the fabric was adopted for a
specific issue, for a reason which escapes us.[6] Rhegion goes
with Zankle, and it is possible that the incuse coins of Rhegion
were struck at Zankle.[7] Throughout its coinage Rhegion goes
with Zankle–Messana and the Sicilian cities, not with the Italian
colonies. No coins of other Italian cities have been found at
Rhegion, though coins of many Sicilian cities and of Athens
have been;[8] and coins of Rhegion are found on many Sicilian
sites, but rarely elsewhere in Italy.

The coinage of the Italian cities was on the Corinthian standard. That of the earliest Sicilian cities to coin was not on the
Corinthian standard, though it was easily interchangeable with
it.[9] Their coinage was in another way modelled on that of

---

[1] Cahn, op. cit. 77–8.
[2] As suggested by Milne, *JHS*, 1944, 108.
[3] Regling, *Klio*, vi. 512 ff.
[4] See below, pp. 356 ff.
[5] Ibid. 524.
[6] Milne, *Num. Chron.* 1938, 36 ff.
[7] Ibid. 39.
[8] Noe, *Bibliography of Greek Coin-Hoards*[2], 225–6.
[9] Gardner, *History of Ancient Coinage*, 213 ff., regards the stater of Himera and Zankle
as a Corinthian didrachm. Three of these staters approximately equal two Corinthian
pegasi.

Corinth, from which the fabric is imitated.[1] Archaic Corinthian coins are found in Sicily and south Italy more commonly than those of any other city of Greece. In the sixth century Corinth probably controlled the chief source of silver for Greece. Corinth is therefore the most likely place from which silver could be brought to the colonies, as the supplies of Sicily and Italy are negligible.[2] That much of the silver was brought from Corinth is proved by the frequency with which archaic coins of Corinth were over-struck in colonial mints. This occurs most frequently at Metapontion, which had a very copious archaic coinage, and also in other Italian cities.[3] The flat-spreading fabric of these coins has been explained as caused by striking on a coin already once used or on a block cut and left blank for striking.

In the late seventh century with the opening up of Spain a new source of silver was available to the Greek world. The nearest Greek cities to Spain are Himera and Selinus, the first of the western colonies to coin. They will have used Spanish silver.[4] The standard of Himera is followed by Zankle and Naxos, whose coins are slightly lighter (2-5 per cent.), which indicates that these two cities got their silver from Himera. How much farther Spanish silver was distributed in the west there is no evidence. Other colonies also may have got their silver from the producing areas without the intermediary of Corinth or any other city of Greece, but there is positive evidence that much of their silver was obtained from Corinth. It is obvious therefore that the beginning of colonial coinage, though accompanying an economic breakaway from Corinth, was not entirely to the detriment of Corinthian interests, which were advanced by supplying silver to the colonies.

The colonies would pay for their silver chiefly in corn. This may explain the copiousness of the early coinage of Metapontion, a small city but entirely devoted to corn, as they recognized by putting an ear of barley on their coins.[5] It also offers a better explanation of the absence of coinage of Lokroi before the fourth century than the usual one that the laws of Zaleukos, like the laws of Lykourgos, forbade it. There are sumptuary

---

[1] Cahn, op. cit. 18 ff.   [2] See above, p. 223.

[3] Noe, *Coinage of Metapontum*, i. 14, 53, and see catalogue; Taras, Vlasto, *Τάρας Οἰκιστής*, 227, n. 108.

[4] Milne, op. cit. 45 ff.; Cahn, op. cit. 78.

[5] The Metapontines also dedicated a great quantity of silver in their Treasury at Olympia (Polemon ap. Athen. 479*f*).

laws handed down under the name of Zaleukos, but nothing which might prohibit the coinage of silver, and the special circumstances which led the Spartans to retain their currency of iron bars could not be repeated elsewhere. But the Lokrians, though not poor, had little wheat-land. They must have lived on their produce and may have been unable to acquire sufficient silver to issue their own coins.

There must have been many causes, political as well as economic, which determined the several cities to issue their own coins, and we possess only fragments of the evidence. From this it appears that the coinage is a decisive step in the emancipation of the colonies, which was followed in time by their cultural emancipation. This began in the last quarter of the seventh century, when commercial and personal relations ceased to be strictly limited to Corinth. It grew when Attic vases began to replace Corinthian. Even if Attic vases were carried in Corinthian ships and sold by Corinthian merchants, the colonies were no longer flooded by Corinthian goods. Their outlook might therefore become less single-minded. It would not be surprising if a feeling of their economic value should grow up, a sort of economic nationalism which should seek by all means to throw off their previous excessive dependence on Corinth. Issuing their own coins, and insisting on payment in silver for the goods which Corinth must import, would be one of the most effective ways of doing so. The cities of south-eastern Sicily, being more conservative than those of the north-west and the Italian cities, were slower to adopt the new economics. Syracuse did not coin until she had had long opportunity of watching its effects in other cities, and until it was quite evident that Corinthian industry had fallen from its predominant position. The middle of the century was a period of stagnation and set-back for Syracuse;[1] when she coined after 530, the copiousness of her coinage and, after a little interval, its artistic merit are signs of her prosperity.

I do not wish to over-emphasize the extent of the break-away from Corinth. Even after the change to Attic vases, the Corinthian merchants still probably controlled the trade. Most of the silver for the coinage probably came from Corinth. Attic coins are not found anywhere in the west until the last years of the sixth century,[2] when Athens had already begun to take a

[1] See above, pp. 61 ff.
[2] The earliest hoard to contain coins of Athens is the famous Taranto hoard (Babelon,

direct interest in Italy. Down to the Persian Wars, probably, Corinth continued to hold the lion's share of western trade. But there was now room for others beside her, and she no longer dealt exclusively in her own products. There need nowhere have been a conscious change of policy, or any antagonism to Corinth; but the result of coming into contact with other com‑ merce than Corinthian, and other art, was that the colonies began to develop an independent spirit.

Other cities, whose products cannot be traced in the sur‑ viving material remains, will have been interested in western trade. Among them was Sikyon, who may for a short period in the early sixth century have challenged the Corinthian monopoly at the very time that it was beginning to break down.[1] About half of Agariste's wooers came from west of the Corinthian Gulf.[2] The Sacred War had an effect on western trade; one of the pretexts was the toll which the Krisaians were levying on visitors to Delphi from Sicily and Italy.[3] In the eighth and seventh centuries many small places on both sides of the Corinthian Gulf had had an interest in the west and had founded colonies or provided men for them,[4] but it appears that in the course of the seventh century all these interests were taken up by Corinth. Kleisthenes may have designed to challenge this Corinthian monopoly. His fleet in the Corinthian Gulf[5] could easily have challenged Corinthian shipping, and the presence of so many colonials at Agariste's wooing suggests that he had relations with prominent men at the other end of the trade route, particularly in the north-west, a special Corin‑ thian preserve, and at Sybaris and Siris, the richest cities of Italy.

In the second half of the sixth century Khalkidian vases as well as Attic appear in quantity in the west, and their distribu‑ tion elucidates the commercial relations of the Khalkidian cities of the Straits, though their presence is not necessarily a proof of direct contact with Khalkis. Otherwise we cannot speak with confidence of the commerce of Khalkis, as the mother city has not been excavated and its products are not easily recognizable. Khalkidian bronzes are only a name, though Alkaios' mention

---

Revue Numismatique, 1912, 1 ff.; Noe, *Bibliography of Greek Coin Hoards²*, 275). Fifth-century hoards such as those of Leonforte (Noe, op. cit. 164) and Licata (ibid. 165–6) contain a few coins of Athens and much larger numbers of Corinthian Pegasi.

[1] R. L. Beaumont, *JHS*, 1936, 167.
[2] Herod. vi. 127.   [3] Strabo 418.
[4] See above, p. 37 f.   [5] See Schol. Pind. *Nem.* ix, *init.*

of Χαλκίδικαι σπάθαι[1] is evidence of their sixth-century date. Khalkis and Corinth had worked hand in glove since the period immediately after the foundation of the oldest colonies,[2] and the Khalkidian colonies, no less than others, were subject to the Corinthian monopoly. They shook it off at an earlier date than some other colonies, perhaps because of their consciousness of different origin, but probably far more because they were favourably situated for intercourse with the Ionians who visited the western Mediterranean.

Almost all the known Khalkidian vases have been found in the west. Of a total of 293,[3] the provenience of 245 is known: 129 at Rhegion,[4] 7 at Lokroi,[5] 5 at Taras, 1 at Ruvo, 2 at Kyme, 1 each at Capua, Suessula, Nola, 3 at Sala Consilina,[6] 2 at Selinus, 1 at Leontini, 6 (?) at Katane,[7] 1 at Massalia, 2 at Emporion; the others from Etruria (mainly Caere and Vulci). In short, two main areas: Rhegion, with the neighbouring towns of Lokroi and Katane; and Etruria, with outliers at Taras, Selinus, Massalia, and Spain, and in the neighbourhood of Kyme. The Etruscan distribution is not remarkable;[8] that in the Greek colonies is, though the picture may be changed by further finds. It is remarkable that Syracuse, Gela, and Megara,[9] which have been so extensively excavated, have yielded none.

The extensive find in the temple-deposit of Griso-Laboccetta at Rhegion, where Khalkidian stood to contemporary Attic vases in the proportion of 1 : 3,[10] makes it clear that Rhegion and Khalkis were in close commercial relations or that there was some especial reason for the import of Khalkidian vases. All the other Khalkidian vases could easily have been distributed from Rhegion, those in Massalia, Spain, and Etruria by the agency of the Phokaian friends of Rhegion, the few in Italian and Sicilian colonies by land or sea routes. Its absence from Syracuse should mean that the Khalkidian colonies at this

[1] Fr. 119 Lobel.

[2] Blakeway, *BSA*, xxxiii. 202 ff.

[3] Rumpf, *Chalkidische Vasen*, 43; with the pieces added by Smith, *The Origin of Chalcidian Ware*.

[4] As Rumpf points out, the number of vases will be smaller, as many of the fragments may be from the same vase.

[5] It may be that when all the material from Lokroi is accessible there will be found to be additional pieces which Rumpf did not see.

[6] See Rumpf, *Ph W*, 1934, 688. Now published in *CVA Petit Palais*, pl. 2, nos. 11–14.

[7] Catania Museum, unpublished, from recent excavations in Catania.

[8] Rumpf, *Chalkidische Vasen*, 43.

[9] One piece of the associated Memnon group was found at Megara.

[10] Rumpf, loc. cit. Nowhere else is Khalkidian other than a small minority beside Attic.

time had few relations with the rest of Sicily; their coins also suggest that they had more community with the other south Italian cities than with Sicily. It follows that direct connexions at this time between Khalkis and any other city than Rhegion are not established.[1]

Trade with barbarian neighbours and the wider Greek world was considerable. The interest of the Khalkidian cities, especially Himera, Zankle, and Rhegion, in the Phokaian voyages to Tartessos, Massalia, and in the Tyrrhenian has been discussed. In general the position of the Sicilian cities would be that of intermediaries. Harbour-dues and the provisioning of ships bound on long voyages would be a great part of the profit which they might expect, for there is no evidence of their direct participation. Also the export of stores from these, the nearest Greek cities, might reach considerable proportions. We cannot go beyond these conjectures based on geographical position in estimating the services which the Khalkidian cities may have rendered to the Greeks exploiting the far west. But the prosperity indicated by their early coinage, especially Himera's, suggests that they shared the profits of that exploitation.

Surviving imports from Etruria to Sicily consist almost

---

[1] The question of the place of origin of Khalkidian ware has been reopened by H. R. W. Smith (*The Origin of Chalcidian Ware*). His case for an Etruscan origin is weakened by T. Dohrn's demonstration that the object in Philadelphia by means of which he attached Khalkidian to Etruscan models (op. cit., pl. 9) is Etruscan and by the hand of a painter (the Ivy painter) who has little relation to Khalkidian (*Die schwarzfigurigen etruskischen Vasen*, 10). The argument from distribution is also weak, as the distribution of Khalkidian vases differs markedly from that of Etruscan vases, both Italo-Corinthian (see *NC*, 208–9, and below, p. 253) and bucchero (see p. 253, and works there quoted). No Khalkidian has been found at Syracuse or Carthage, where Etruscan bucchero kantharoi are found in fair numbers; no Etruscan vases, except a single Italo-Corinthian aryballos, in any of the south Italian colonies. It is likely, as Smith suggests, that bucchero kantharoi were carried to Sicily, Carthage, and Sardinia by Caeretan Greeks; it is therefore unlikely that the same men distributed Khalkidian vases to Rhegion, Lokroi, and Taras, but *not* to Syracuse or Carthage. The distribution in mutually exclusive fields suggests that the two classes were carried by trade rivals. If there were a case for believing that Khalkidian vases were not made at Khalkis (the strongest argument is the absence of Khalkidian from sites near Khalkis, such as Eretria, Delos, Rhitsona, Thebes, where it might be expected), then Rhegion would be a strong claimant (as suggested by Putortì, *N Sc*, 1924, 102, n., quoting a verbal opinion of Langlotz). But the argument from distribution, though opposed to Smith's suggestion of a Caeretan origin, need indicate only that Rhegion was a centre of distribution, not of manufacture. Until Khalkis has been excavated, the question cannot be regarded as conclusively settled. Dohrn tells me, however, that he has found sherds at Eretria which are closely allied to Rumpf's pseudo-Khalkidian groups and to the Eretrian vases now in Athens. I owe much in this discussion to Dohrn's knowledge and kindness. Langlotz has now re-stated his case for Rhegion: *Antike und Abendland*, ii. 117, n. 11.

entirely of bucchero kantharoi. These are fairly numerous at Syracuse, Megara, and Selinus, rare elsewhere.[1] Those at Syracuse and Megara must have come via the Straits of Messina, though it is curious that none has been found at Rhegion. Those at Selinus will have been carried either on ships *en route* to Carthage, or perhaps via Carthage. Bucchero of all sorts and Italo-Corinthian vases are plentiful in Carthage,[2] and it is also probable that much of the Corinthian there came via Etruria.[3] As Selinus was in close touch with Carthage it is possible that she got her bucchero thence. Syracuse and Selinus, the most active ports of Sicily, are those which would most readily receive Etruscan imports. Other bucchero, with the exception of kantharoi, was not to Greek taste. Etruscan imitations of Corinthian could not compete with the real thing; there are a few Italo-Corinthian vases at Katane, Rhegion, and Kroton,[4] but these do not indicate regular import. Etruscan pottery is not typical of Etruscan industry to the same extent that Greek pottery is of Greek industry. Metal-work was more important. There is no Etruscan bronze work found in Sicily and south Italy, nor can Etruscan influence be traced in the style of south Italian bronzes. Export of Etruscan metal-work to Greece, abundantly attested in literary sources,[5] is poorly documented in the surviving remains by a single Vulci tripod on the Acropolis,[6] but supported by the influence of Etruscan metal-forms on the Nikosthenic amphora.[7] Etruria would be

[1] In *N Sc*, 1925, 181, n. 2 Orsi enumerates those in Syracuse Museum: 45 from Syracuse, 18 from Megara, 2 from Gela (see *MA*, xvii. 253–4, 644–8, where he discusses the absence of bucchero from Gela). For Selinus see K. M. T. Atkinson, *BSR*, xiv. 116 ff.; one in Castelvetrano has the unpublished graffito ◁ ꓥ Ꮙo Ꮙ⅄M. None at Kamarina or Akragas. For exports from Etruria cf. Jacobsthal, *Gallia Graeca*, 42 ff.; H. R. W. Smith, *Origin of Chalcidian*, 107–8; G. Karo, Ἀρχ. Ἐφ. 1937, 316 ff. Bucchero kantharoi are found in quantity at Perachora and in Rhodes (*Clara Rhodos*, iii, fig. 6; cf. Jacobsthal, *Gött. Gel. Anz.* 1933, 4). Most of the bucchero exported from Etruria to Sicily and elsewhere belongs to the sixth century, but at least two kantharoi at Syracuse are in graves of the middle of the seventh century (grave 84, *NSc*, 1893, 470; grave 276, *N Sc*, 1895, 143).

The suggestion that some bucchero kantharoi are of Sicilian manufacture (Ducati, *Storia della Ceramica Greca*, i. 101, n. 4; cf. Atkinson, op. cit. 118) need hardly be considered, seeing that those found in Sicily are identical with other sixth-century bucchero.

[2] Gauckler, *RA*, xli (1902), 373 ff.; *AA*, 1903, 23 (Petersen), 91 (Schulten).

[3] Cf. *NC*, 188.

[4] Rhegion, aryballos, *NC*, 209; Kroton, alabastron, Crotone Mus. no. 1788, from the Albani collection, which was formed entirely within the limits of modern Calabria. Katane, Catania Museum (according to a letter from T. Dohrn).   [5] Cited by Karo, op. cit. 320.

[6] *MA*, vii. 277 ff. Add a Triton from Dodona, Carapanos, *Dodone*, pl. 13. 2; cf. Dohrn, *Die schwarzfigurigen etruskischen Vasen*, 104.

[7] Loeschke, *AZ*, 1881, 37; Gallatin, *AJA*, 1926, 76 ff.; Beazley, *JHS*, 1929, 41; Karo, op. cit., 319.

the natural source for base metals, including iron and copper. Most of the metals were probably exported refined but unworked.[1] Metals, and perhaps slaves, would be the chief Etruscan exports to Sicily and south Italy. The return traffic would be chiefly entrepôt trade, all the imports from Greece passing either through the Straits or over one of the south Italian landroutes. There is little that can be suggested in the way of direct imports originating in the colonies, but the through trade would bring them profits. In the late fifth century certainly corn was occasionally sent from Sicily to Rome, but the mention of Sicilian corn in the time of Coriolanus is probably a reflection of this later intercourse.[2]

It is difficult to assess the extent of trade with Carthage. An estimate must depend on how much of the Greek pottery found at Carthage came there through the nearest Greek colonies, and whether the Phoenician and Etruscan objects found in Sicily were re-exported there from Carthage.[3] Certainly there were commercial and personal relations even after the long series of wars between Greek and Phoenician had begun. The literary evidence belongs all to the fifth and later centuries; but it may be supposed that similar relations existed earlier.[4] Throughout the seventh century Corinthian vases are plentiful at Carthage and Motye, and they continue to be imported in the sixth century.[5] Malta, which throughout this period was Phoenician, receives Corinthian vases from c. 675 onwards.[6] These might as well be brought from Syracuse as from Car-

[1] For import of bronze from Etruria to Sicily see Orsi, *BPI*, 1900, 280 ff.

[2] See above, p. 216.

[3] In *Les Objets égyptiens et égyptisants du mobilier funéraire carthaginois*, 355-6, J. Vercoutter shows good reason to believe that most of the Egyptian objects at Carthage came there immediately from the Greek cities of Sicily. He limits this intercourse to the late seventh and sixth centuries, because he holds, following R. M. Cook, *JHS*, 1937, 227 ff., that Greek commerce with Egypt did not open until the end of the seventh century. But the abundant finds of Egyptian and egyptianizing objects of the seventh century at Rhodes, Perachora, and elsewhere in Greece, the proof of the establishment of Egyptians at Rhodes as early as 700 (von Bissing, *Zeit und Herkunft der in Cerveteri gefundenen Gefässe*, 81), and the quantity of Egyptian objects of the late eighth and seventh centuries in the Greek colonies (see above, p. 233) combine to make it possible that throughout the seventh century the Greeks (of Rhodes and Corinth) may have been responsible for the transport of the Egyptian objects found in the west, in Etruria, Sicily, and Carthage alike. This does not exclude the probability that the earliest Egyptian objects found in Greece and the west were carried by Phoenicians, or the possibility that Phoenicians and Carthaginians shared in the later traffic. But Vercoutter's hypothesis (op. cit. 354) of direct intercourse between Carthage and Egypt in the seventh century is not required by the absence of Greek objects in Egypt at that date, given the quantity of Egyptian objects found on Greek sites.

[4] Cf. S. Gsell, *Histoire ancienne de l'Afrique du Nord*, iv. 151-2.

[5] Carthage: *NC*, 187-8. Motye: see p. 327, below.   [6] Johansen, *VS*, 88.

thage. The same is true of Kossyra (Pantellaria), where a few Greek vases have been found.[1]

Little can be said about intercolonial trade, because it is difficult to recognize local manufactures. The colonies must all have produced the same staples, foodstuffs and raw materials, and probably worked them up for their own needs. Industrial products were imported to all alike from Greece. The chief surviving products of local manufacture are terra-cottas, with which each city seems in the main to have supplied itself. Most of the terra-cottas in all Sicilian cities are alike in general type and in some details, but this is not necessarily due to interchange between the cities. The common Sicilian element is greater than the local peculiarities, and is derived from close copying of the current Peloponnesian and East Greek models. The types developed locally do not in the archaic period spread to other cities. Even Selinus, the most inventive of the colonies, where there is abundance of original types, had no influence on her neighbours. In the sixth and early fifth centuries, when they were still in the main primary producers closely bound to Old Greece, commercial intercourse between the colonies was mainly limited to re-export from the larger centres to second-class towns. Political and religious intercourse, depending on the application of ideas deriving their force from the common environment of all colonies, was more important in this period than commercial intercourse.

Many of the sixth- and fifth-century terra-cottas at Kamarina came from Gela. Gela was the centre of a flourishing industry, which supplied the small Greek and Sikel towns of the interior, and made the revetments for the Treasury of the Geloans at Olympia.[2] Kamarina has a very poor sandy clay, much inferior to that of Gela. As Kamarina was from time to time under Geloan protection, the Kamarinaians naturally took Geloan terra-cottas in preference to their own inferior products. Similarly Kroton appears to have supplied architectural terra-cottas for the temples of Kaulonia and the Alaian promontory,[3] both of which were at the time of their building in territory subject to Kroton. At Megara a deposit of terra-cottas was found on the beach by the port. It is homogeneous, and almost certainly is a cargo which had just been unloaded when the

---

[1] *MA*, ix. 523, and figs. 56 and 69. Material in Syracuse Museum.
[2] See below, pp. 269 ff.
[3] Orsi, *Templum Apollinis Alaei*, 65.

city was destroyed. The clay agrees with that of Syracusan terra-cottas, though the predominant type is not found at Syracuse. Many of the terra-cottas found in the ditch of the town-wall of Megara, dumped there from a sanctuary, are of the same clay as this cargo. It seems that a large part of Megara's terra-cottas came from the neighbouring Syracuse, whose workshops turned out special types for the Megarian market.[1] Akragantine pithoi were occasionally exported to Selinus and Motye,[2] either for their own sake or for their contents. Lokroi had at the end of the sixth and in the fifth century a flourishing school of art, producing many special types, but they seldom travelled farther than the dependent colonies of Medma and Hipponion. There is part of a Lokrian pinax at Selinus.[3] One important terra-cotta at Kamarina is Lokrian;[4] another of the same type at Selinus is of the same clay, and is certainly not Selinuntine.[5] This type has a considerable vogue in Sicily, especially at Selinus, but it may have been developed both there and at Lokroi from imitation of imported sculpture. Lokrian exports in the second half of the fifth century are more frequent,[6] but there is little evidence of contemporary influence when the Lokrian artists were at their best. Tarentine terra-cotta figurines and antefixes of the second half of the fifth century are widely exported, even to Sicily.[7]

It must be remembered that, though there are many local types of Selinuntine terra-cottas, none of them is a copy of the metopes. Europa on the bull is found in terra-cottas only at Selinus, but the type is not the same as that of the well-known early metope. As terra-cottas are the chief artistic remains of other cities, we should not expect to find the influence of Selinuntine sculpture in them. In architecture, there are traces of Selinuntine influence on Akragas: at least one invention of

[1] MA, i. 913 ff.

[2] Selinus, Marconi, Agrigento, 209; Motye, Whitaker, Motya, fig. 103.

[3] MA, xxxii. 374, pl. 78. 6.

[4] MA, xiv. 869, fig. 74. Orsi says 'la creta chiara, biancastra, pulverulenta e non compatta non è camarinese, e forse nemmeno siceliota'. Lokrian terra-cotta from Taranto: Bull. Metr. Mus. 1922, 113, fig. 1; cf. N Sc, 1913 Suppl., 98, from Medma. See Ashmole, 20, n. 1.

[5] MA, xxxii, pl. LXVIII. 6.

[6] Mirror-handles, probably Lokrian, at Kroton (Mus. no. 1766), Taras (Jantzen, Bronzewerkstatten in Grossgriechenland und Sizilien, 4, no. 38), Rhegion (Mus. Civico); cf. p. 292. Pinakes at Kroton (Mus. nos. 2019–23), Herakleia (Crotone, nos. 2024–5), Taras (Il Museo Nazionale di Taranto, figs. on p. 44) are of a form adopted from Lokroi.

[7] Cf. Orsi, Templum Apollinis Alaei, 68 ff.; Darsow, Sizilische Dachterrakotten, 27; Wuilleumier, Tarente, 228, 422, 427. Import to Taras from Kaulonia: ibid. 432.

Selinuntine architecture was copied at Akragas,[1] and the stone sima of the temple of Herakles there was painted with lotus and palmette between lions' heads, in the same style as temple C at Selinus.[2]

In the early fifth century there was an export of building-stone from Syracuse. The finest stone near Syracuse, the 'pietra di Melilli' from the quarries behind Megara, was not available till the Deinomenid period, when it was used for the new temple of Athena. It was exported to Kaulonia, where the foundations of the temple built in the decade 470–460 are said to be of Syracusan stone.[3] Sarcophagi of the late sixth century at Katane are said to be of Syracusan limestone,[4] and at a much later date Syracusan stone was used in the theatre of Katane.[5]

Sicily is not rich in good stone. The chief effect was the use of terra-cotta in architecture and sculpture. But when stone had to be used it must often have been brought long distances. There is none on the south coast or in the flat-topped clayey hills inland. Diodoros' vivid description of the carriage of stone from Agyrion to Engyon to build the temple of the Mothers[6] illustrates the stonelessness of many Sicilian towns and the obstacles which bad roads put in the way of land transport. The stone of Akrai was similarly used in neighbouring towns which had no stone, or no good stone, as well as in Syracuse. From some place in the Heraian hills stone was carried to S. Mauro.[7] There is no building-stone near Gela and Kamarina, and both towns probably brought it by sea to build their walls and temples. The remains of Gela were not enough to build its successor Terranova in the thirteenth century A.D., and Kamarina also was despoiled.[8]

In south Italy also the available stone is either very soft friable limestone or hard intrusive rock, difficult to work and not attractive to Greek masons. The Syracusan stone was of a much higher quality, and was preferred when they wished to build the most splendid temples possible. In the access of

---

[1] *MA*, xxxv. 238–40. The angle of the pediment of temple C at Selinus is imitated in temple F and the temple of Herakles at Akragas.

[2] *MA*, xxxv. 227–8. Compare pll. LIX–LXI, LXIII (Akragas) with pll. XXIV–XXV (Selinus); pl. LXII (cf. *N Sc*, 1925, 448 ff.) with pll. XXI–XXII (Selinus). Cf. also Marconi, *Himera*, pl. at p. 70.

[3] *MA*, xxiii. 837 ff.; 'pietra di Siracusa' was used also at Rhegion (*N Sc*, 1886, 63).

[4] *N Sc*, 1918, 68–70.   [5] *N Sc*, 1885, 148 (Salinas).

[6] iv. 80.   [7] *MA*, xx. 795.

[8] Fazello, *de rebus Siculis decades*, i. 230.

prosperity which came to all cities in the early fifth century, they were able to get the best stone from Syracuse, and, at Kaulonia at least, the cost of sea-borne stone would not be much greater than of poorer stone from distant Italian quarries. Elsewhere in south Italy stone was brought from the neighbourhood of Taranto, where there is abundance of soft, easily worked limestone. The temple of Apollo Alaios was rebuilt in the second quarter of the fifth century with this stone.[1] Stone was also brought from Apulia to Herakleia, the successor of Siris.[2]

[1] Orsi, *Templum Apollinis Alaei*, 20 ff.
[2] E. Bracco, *N Sc*, 1934, 470.

CHAPTER IX

ART AND INDUSTRY

COLONIAL industry, before the fifth century at least, was
unimportant. Sybaris, the most advanced of the colonial
cities, is the only one known to have engaged in 'heavy'
industries, which may have been of only local importance.[1]
The evidence concerning the other cities is extremely slight,
but it is probable that the population was almost entirely
occupied in agriculture and commerce. Considering the profound change which the early fifth century brought to all cities
of Sicily and south Italy, we have no right to carry back to
an earlier age fifth-century and later references to industry in
these areas. In any case these references are few. The chariots
of Sicily were famous for their victories at Olympia and Delphi,
but their manufacture is not the mark of an industrial country.[2]
Sicilian beds and cushions were well known in Athens at the
end of the fifth century, and Sicilian furniture long remained
famous.[3] Syracusan skyphoi are praised by Athenaios next to
Boiotian and Rhodian, in a timeless reference.[4] The material
is unspecified; perhaps silver. But the best of the furniture
and precious vessels which Verres stole from Sicilian owners
was imported from Greece. Though Cicero alludes in general
terms to Sicilian work of that sort, he does not mention a single
Sicilian piece.[5]

There was no manufacture of the typical Greek product,
painted pottery, on any but the smallest scale. The reverse
has sometimes been stated,[6] and it has been thought that a
high proportion of the Protocorinthian and Corinthian vases
found in Sicily were made there. This opinion depends in part
on the naïve view that pottery is likely to have been made
where it is found, and on Orsi's suggestion, made when he

---

[1] See above, p. 78.

[2] Pindar, fr. 95 Bowra (106 Schroeder); cf. Kritias ap. Athen. 28*b*.

[3] Euboulos fr. 121 Kock (ap. Athen. 47*f*):

$$\Theta\grave{\epsilon}s \ \dot{\epsilon}\pi\tau\acute{\alpha}\kappa\lambda\iota\nu o\nu\text{---}\dot{\epsilon}\pi\tau\acute{\alpha}\kappa\lambda\iota\nu os \ o\dot{\upsilon}\tau o\sigma\acute{\iota}.$$
$$\text{---}\kappa\alpha\grave{\iota} \ \pi\acute{\epsilon}\nu\tau\epsilon \ \kappa\lambda\acute{\iota}\nu\alpha s \ \Sigma\iota\kappa\epsilon\lambda\iota\kappa\acute{\alpha}s\text{---}\lambda\acute{\epsilon}\gamma' \ \ddot{\alpha}\lambda\lambda o \ \tau\iota.$$
$$\text{---}\Sigma\iota\kappa\epsilon\lambda\iota\kappa\grave{\alpha} \ \pi\rho o\sigma\kappa\epsilon\phi\acute{\alpha}\lambda\alpha\iota\alpha \ \pi\acute{\epsilon}\nu\tau\epsilon.$$

Pliny, *NH* xvi. 225; Aelian, *VH* xii. 29.

[4] Athen. 500*b*. Cf. Σικελικὰ βατάνια, Euboulos ap. Athen. 28*c*; Alexis, ibid. 169*d*.

[5] *Verr.* II. iv. 21. 46: 'Credo tum cum Sicilia florebat opibus et copiis magna artificia
fuisse in ea insula.' See Scramuzza, op. cit. 285 ff., for further references.

[6] Pace, *ACSA,* ii. 462, and literature there quoted.

began to excavate the cemeteries of Syracuse, that a number of vases of the Protocorinthian style, then less well known than now and not yet localized, might be of local origin.[1] It is true that suitable clay occurs in the immediate neighbourhood of Syracuse as well as elsewhere in Sicily, and was used for figurines and architectural terra-cottas. But no criterion of technique or style has ever been proposed to differentiate the supposed Sicilian imitations from Corinthian originals. The criterion evidently, though not expressly, used is one of style: the ordinary vases of poor style must be local, because such things would not be exported all the way to Sicily. This argument is used equally of Protocorinthian and Corinthian vases. It will be easier to consider those of the Corinthian style first, because the poorer works of this series have been more thoroughly studied and are more easily accessible in publications.

No group of vases by the same painter, or from the same workshop, has an exclusively western range, although the finds from Sicily and Etruria are so large a part of the total of Corinthian vases. When vases of the same style are found in the islands, in south Russia, in Corinth and most parts of the Greek mainland, as well as in Sicily, it is clear that the examples in Sicily must have the same origin as the others; that that is Corinth is made certain by the discovery of damaged and misfired pieces in the Corinthian Kerameikos. The same argument holds for the styleless vases of no artistic merit which are so common in the west. The lists of degenerate aryballoi in the appendix to Ure's *Aryballoi and Figurines*,[2] and the proveniences of small kotylai in *Necrocorinthia*,[3] show that identical vases have been found over almost the whole Greek world, and can have been made only in Corinth. It applies also to Protocorinthian vases, whose distribution is nearly as wide. A very full series has been found, though not yet published, at the Corinthian sanctuary of Perachora, and no class of Protocorinthian vase found in Sicily is without a parallel there. To go more deeply into the question of style, other imitations, such as Italo-Corinthian, are easily distinguished from genuine Corinthian. This is true also of small groups, such as Boiotian imitations.[4] A local fabric which is to be ascribed to Corinthian

---

[1] See especially *N Sc*, 1893, 450.
[2] pp. 90 ff.; see also Blinkenberg, *Lindos*, i. 623 ff.
[3] p. 334; cf. p. 183.   [4] *NC*, 202 ff.; A. D. and P. N. Ure, *AA*, 1933, 8 ff.

colonists has now been found in Ithaka, and is clearly distinguishable by its style as well as on grounds of technique.[1] The Corinthian style (including also Protocorinthian) in spite of variations has at every period of its development a unity which does not allow us to detach any considerable body of vases and assign them to another centre of manufacture,[2] even if other considerations were not against this.

The same is true of clay and technique. Corinthian clay may vary considerably from the familiar greenish colour, according to the degree of refinement and the baking, and the clay of every vase found in Sicily has a parallel at Corinth or Perachora.[3] Therefore vases which on technical grounds alone *might* have been made in Syracuse may equally well have been made in Corinth. As the finds in the two places have the same range, there is a strong presumption that the two series were made in the same place. This becomes a certainty when the style of decoration is also considered.

The conclusion to be drawn from the number of ordinary little vases, both Protocorinthian and Corinthian, in Sicily is that they were extremely cheap. Corinth had such natural advantages and was able to produce on so large a scale that she could export her mass-produced goods to Sicily, as well as to nearer markets, more cheaply than they could be manufactured there. This supremacy lasted long after the export of fine painted vases had passed from Corinth to Athens. The mass of even the poorest and latest vases, the wretched aryballoi and miniature kotylai, was imported to Sicily.

This does not mean that absolutely no vases were made in the colonies, but that manufacture of anything but coarse unpainted pottery was of no artistic or economic importance. A few figured olpai are of Sicilian manufacture; Payne allows Palermo 153, from Gela, and Louvre C. A. 1695,[4] to which perhaps Palermo 156, from Gela, is to be added. Lane has distinguished a few south Italian imitations of unfigured Laconian vases.[5] There are isolated imitations of Attic black

---

[1] An account of the Ithakan style will be given by M. Robertson in publishing the vases found at Aetos in Ithaka; cf. *JHS*, 1933, 283; *BSA*, xxxix. 17.

[2] The group of Geometric vases detached by Weinberg and tentatively assigned to Aigina (*AJA*, 1941, 30 ff.) is not here in question. No members of it have been found west of the Adriatic.

[3] Cf. Payne, *NC*, 264 ff.; *Perachora*, i. 53.

[4] *NC*, 205.

[5] *BSA*, xxxiv. 186. Cf. below, p. 290, n. 5.

figure, all wretchedly bad. Most of them are south Italian.[1] There may have been occasional manufacture of this sort, and also of unfigured vases, at Syracuse; but its productions have not yet been clearly recognized.

On the Manella hill at Lokroi, above the sanctuary of Persephone, a fused mass of half a dozen miniature kotylai was found which went wrong in firing.[2] This is the clearest possible proof that some pottery was manufactured at Lokroi. But the frequent and authoritative statements[3] that the mass of the degenerate Late Corinthian vases found at Lokroi is of local manufacture are not justified. Orsi asserts that the clay is the same as the clay of the Lokrian terra-cottas. The Lokrian clay, sandy, with frequent gleams of mica, is very easily recognizable. But the clay in which the deposits were buried is also full of this micaceous sand, which has adhered to the surface of the sherds buried in it and is with difficulty completely removed by washing. Of the few sherds which I have been able to examine two only are of this composition through and through. Though it has not been possible to see anything like the 14,000 kotylai excavated, Payne has examined a representative collection of sherds in which a very small proportion, and none with figures, is of the local clay. There can be no doubt that the great mass of Late Corinthian pottery dedicated to Persephone was imported from Corinth. The local manufacture merely supplemented the supply of the poorer kinds of articles. The conclusion is that these vases could be shipped from Corinth to Lokroi more cheaply than they could be manufactured at

[1] Italian black-figure:
Reggio Calabria (?), from Kaulonia, neck-amphora, *MA*, xxiii. 925, fig. 164; cf. Jacobsthal, *Ornamente*, 113, n;
Reggio Calabria (?), from Lokroi, lekythos, *N Sc*, 1913 Suppl. 21, fig. 22;
Munich, Sieveking-Hackl, i, pl. 33, no. 834, amphora from 'Italy' with Akhaian alphabet;
Taranto, from Metapontion, vase with inscription, *N Sc*, 1885, 607;
Berlin, Antiquarium F 2137, column-krater 'unbestimmter unteritalischen Gattung' (Furtwängler);
Bari, krater, Dohrn, *Die sf. etruskischen Vasen*, 130, Abschnitt E (Dohrn now thinks this vase south Italian, not Etruscan);
—and other insignificant vases. Cf. Rumpf, *Chalkidische Vasen*, 44; Dohrn, *Studi Etruschi*, xii. 279 ff.; Ure, *Sixth and Fifth Century Pottery*, 74, n. 3, 77. See Dohrn's judgement, op. cit. 280: 'Es ist ausserdem bezeichnend, dass in der griechischen Kolonien Unteritaliens und Siziliens die lokalen Nachbildungen sowohl zahlenmässig wie gattungsmässig weit zurückstehen hinter denen Etruriens. . . . Im Gebiet der griechischen Kolonien ist es nie zu der Entwicklung eines nennenswerten, eigenen schwarzfigurigen Malstils gekommen.'
For Sicilian black-figure cf. p. 135.
[2] I thank Mr. D. F. Allen for this information.
[3] e.g. Orsi, *Boll. d'Arte*, 1909, 473; Rumpf, loc. cit.

Lokroi. This import continued until the end of the sixth century, as the types at Lokroi are identical with the Late Corinthian vases buried at Rhitsona in graves of that period.

There was perhaps a local variant of Corinthian at Poseidonia. Grave VI of the Spinazzo cemetery contained a kotyle, an amphoriskos, and a cinquefoil aryballos, all of a reddish-brown clay with brown varnish. A small proportion of the pottery of Corinthian style from the excavation of the Heraion in progress is of the same reddish or orange-red clay, which is the same as the clay of the local terra-cottas and agrees very nearly with the clay of Paestan red-figure. In Salerno Museum are other pieces of this fabric from Eboli, Battipaglia, and other sites in the immediate neighbourhood of Poseidonia.[1]

The Kymaian vases of Protocorinthian style are better known.[2] Most of these are early, and so pure in style that they are to be distinguished only by their clay, and may pass for genuine in photographs. There are similarly vases of pure Protocorinthian style made at Falerii and in Etruria.[3] The closeness of the imitations shows that the potters were Corinthians. It may be deduced that their object was to produce Corinthian vases to supplement supplies from Corinth, which might be irregular owing to the remoteness of this part of Italy. Poseidonia and Kyme were the most distant of the Italian colonies, and Corinthian economic domination was perhaps less complete there than in Magna Graecia and Sicily. Also, the closer neighbourhood of the Etruscans may have been more stimulating than that of barbarians.

These unimportant oddments are the only vases whose colonial origin is certain. It may be that the same causes which at Kyme produced imitations of Protocorinthian produced other shortlived fabrics in Sicily also. But as the lesser fabrics of Greece proper become better known, the number of vases which cannot be assigned to one or the other of them shrinks. The so-called Fusco kraters from Syracuse used to be thought local: P. E. Arias's recent study of them has shown convincingly that they are some Argive, some Cycladic.[4] I know only one considerable vase at Syracuse which has not found a home, and may therefore be local; the stamnos *N Sc*, 1925, pl. 12. Pos-

---

[1] Johansen, *VS*, 89, speaks of 'des poteries locales en partie imitées des types sicyoniens' at Suessula, Capua, Valle del Sarno.

[2] See Blakeway, *JRS*, 1935, 145; Payne, *PV*, 21, on pl. 4. 1.

[3] Blakeway, op. cit. 132 ff.

[4] *BCH*, 1936, 144 ff.

sibly imports of Cretan to Gela were eked out by imitations. In *Necrocorinthia* Payne has left open the question whether a number of situlas and other large vases were Cretan or Geloan;[1] in my opinion the probabilities are in favour of Cretan. One vase is certainly Geloan, for its decoration has Siculan II parallels which are earlier than it.[2]

Other vases found on Sikel sites appear to be of local clay, but Greek in form and decoration.[3] There are a few geometric vases of this sort, but they are much less common than imitations more or less faithful of Greek vases by Sikel hands. In the seventh and sixth centuries the Siculan fabric survives as a backward sub-geometric style (Siculan IV).[4] As far as shape is concerned, many Siculan vases, amphoras, hydriai, oinochoai might be Greek vases, and it may be that some Greek potters took part in the local manufacture on Sikel sites.[5] The very simple decoration, however, unlike that of any contemporary Greek fabric, makes it impossible to be certain how large a proportion is to be assigned to Greek potters and painters. If it is allowed that some of the more Greek-looking of Siculan IV vases were made by Greeks, it appears that the potters will have lived in the Sikel towns, or at least worked exclusively for the Sikel market; for none of these vases is found in the Greek colonies,[6] only one or two even in the small Greek inland posts in contact with the Sikels. The reason why pots should be made by Greeks for Sikels, but not for use in their own cities, will be partly economic, because problems of transport and supply made Greek vases more expensive inland than on the coast, partly because the Sikels had grown used to sub-geometric vases which were no longer made in Corinth or any other centre of Greek industry. A clear case of Greek potters at work in native Italian settlements is at Torre Galli in Calabria, where there are what can only be called Greek vases made in the local clay.[7] The clay is unmistakable and the wretched native potters cannot be held capable of successfully imitating a Greek vase. So Greek shape and style must be due

---

[1] p. 5, n. 1.

[2] *MA*, xvii, pl. 5, right.

[3] See Blakeway, *BSA*, xxxiii. 184 ff. ('local Geometric pottery painted by Greek craftsmen').

[4] See Åkerström, *Der Geometrische Stil in Italien*, 23 ff.

[5] Cf. above, pp. 171 ff.

[6] Such rare Siculan pottery as is found in the colonies is not painted; e.g. Selinus, *MA*, xxxii, pl. 78. 10 (cf. ibid. 344).

[7] *MA*, xxxi. 190.

to the presence of Greeks, which is inferred also from the burial customs.

Pottery may be taken as typical of other industries whose products have perished. Of other minor arts, only one was certainly practised extensively in the archaic period, the manufacture of terra-cotta figurines. Though there are imports from the Peloponnese and East Greece, the great majority of small terra-cottas were made where they were dedicated. Differences in clay indicate that though there was a uniform style throughout Sicily and south Italy, each town or large sanctuary manufactured for its own use. Thus there was a factory adjacent to the sanctuary of the goddesses at Akragas where two deposits of moulds extending from the sixth century to the third have been found.[1] These include some attractive works, the finest of which are two late archaic plaques, one figuring a gorgon, the other Herakles and Eurystheus. They are further important as providing the clearest case of a factory on the spot, just outside the sanctuary for which it supplied votive offerings. This sanctuary was in the archaic period before the great temples were built, and probably after, one of the busiest centres of the religious life of Akragas. Export from a centre of manufacture to the neighbouring towns was also fairly common.[2] The same is true of larger works and architectural terra-cottas. The stylistic affiliations of archaic terra-cottas will be discussed later: so much for them as evidence of colonial industry.

It is not so easy to discuss bronzes and other metal-work, because they have received less study than pottery, and there is little agreement about centres of manufacture. One class of bronzes has been the subject of a very thorough study: Blinkenberg is of the opinion that Greek fibulas are not found in Italy and Sicily, and that 'Italic' types are found in the graves and sanctuaries of the Greek colonies.[3] This categorical statement needs some modification. The common 'boat' and 'leech' fibulas, both plain and decorated with amber and ivory, are found on many Greek sites, and there is good reason to regard them as Corinthian.[4] So probably are the ivory disk-fibulas common on both sides of the Ionian Sea, which are also called

[1] Rizzo, *RM*, 1897, 253 ff.; I. Marconi, *N Sc*, 1930, 73 ff.; P. Marconi, *Agrigento Arcaica*, 50 f.

[2] See above, p. 255.

[3] *Les Fibules grecs et orientales*, 25 f.

[4] Payne, *Perachora*, i. 168, 170.

Sicilian or Italian by Blinkenberg.[1] These types cover most
of the fibulas found in the colonies; this is true especially of
Syracuse.[2] There are a number of Italian fibulas found in
Greece, notably at Olympia,[3] but it may be doubted whether
any of them are of specifically Sicilian types. The finding of
fibulas at the great sanctuaries of Greece proves, of course, the
presence of visitors from Italy who wore them, not commerce
between the colonies and the mainland.

Other bronzes of everyday use show a general and sometimes
close similarity to those at Perachora. For instance, the dress-
pins found at Syracuse have parallels at Perachora, and the
same types are common in both places.[4]

The archaic bronze figures and vases in Sicily were most if
not all imported. Only isolated figures of the archaic period
have been found, nearly all of poor quality. There is an inclina-
tion to regard the poorer pieces as local works made where they
were found. But there was provincial work in mainland Greece,
and we know that vases of the poorest artistic quality were
exported from Greece; why not then also bronzes? In any
case, no *group* of bronzes with any firm connexion with Sicily
can be put together earlier than that which forms round the
Adernò libation-pourer. Some of the poor earlier pieces may
be Sicilian, but there are no works of better quality from which
the characteristics, or even the existence, of a Sicilian style
may be deduced. Considering how much digging has been done,
it is fair to conclude that there was no important school of
bronze-working in Sicily in the sixth or fifth century.[5] South
Italy is a different matter, which will be considered later. To

---

[1] Op. cit., 262 ff.

[2] See, for instance, the statistics for the Fusco cemetery at Syracuse; out of 63 fibulas,
31 were of the ivory-and-amber type, 23 'boats', and only 2 of the typical Italian 'serpeg-
gianti' (*N Sc*, 1895, 115).

[3] Blinkenberg, op. cit. 197 ff.; Karo, 'Εφ. 'Αρχ. 1937, 317.

[4] *Perachora*, i. 172 ff.; especially type B of Payne's classification.

[5] U. Jantzen, *Bronzewerkstätten in Grossgriechenland und Sizilien*, 54 ff., discusses the
question fully. He gives a Sicilian origin to only small groups or single works only, and
cannot differentiate a Sicilian style or styles. Let us take the mirror-handles as an example.
One of the archaic period has been found in Sicily (Palermo Mus., from Akragas; Jantzen,
pl. 22. 89–90). Jantzen, p. 58, compares it with figures found at Lokroi, but rightly declines
to assign it to the same fabric. Now one swallow does not make a summer, and one mirror-
handle found in Sicily, even if made there, does not make a school or workshop. (The fifth-
century mirror-handle from Ravanusa, Syracuse 29179, Jantzen, pl. 22. 91, is perhaps
Corinthian.) In general, Jantzen places too much weight on the criterion of provenience,
or reported provenience. This is especially dangerous when it concerns pieces bought in the
market or coming from old Italian collections. It is no argument for a *Sicilian* origin that
a bronze was possibly or even probably found in south Italy (ibid. 60).

anticipate my conclusions, there were artists working in bronze in the late archaic period in the Italian colonies, but the industry did not assume importance until the second half of the fifth century.

For about a century after the foundation of Syracuse there is no colonial art of which we can speak. The absence of sculpture and other large works of art may be explained by chance of discovery, as the period is remote and their number would be few. But there are no remains of buildings with any architectural pretensions older than the late seventh century. There are none of the so-called minor arts, no bronze vases or gold jewellery such as the Etruscans were making, no pottery or terra-cottas. This cannot be explained by poverty or backwardness, for the state of affairs continues long after the colonists were well established, and the graves show prosperity if not great riches. It may have been due partly to choice, the colonists preferring things brought from the mother country, but more to economic conditions. During most of this period the hold of Corinth on the western markets was complete. The Corinthians could keep other traders from the west, and presumably could market their goods so cheaply that it was not worth while to attempt to compete with them by local manufacture. We need not suspect any but unconscious economic pressure, but must recognize that political circumstances did not encourage any state action to combat the monopoly; the Corinthian merchants were surely on the best of terms with the colonial oligarchies.

As there is a little Cretan commerce in the seventh century,[1] so some of the earliest works of art known to us are Cretan. A statue ascribed to Daidalos was said to have been captured by the Geloans soon after 690.[2] Other Cretan works were imported to the colonies,[3] and there is a considerable Cretan influence in some early western terra-cottas, though it may have been exercised indirectly, through the art of the Peloponnese, Sparta, or Corinth. These terra-cottas are associated with a

---

[1] See above, p. 230.

[2] Paus. viii. 46. 2. See above, p. 112.

[3] Terra-cottas: relief at Taranto, Langlotz, *Antike Plastik*, 113 ff. (third quarter of seventh century); figurine in Coll. Santangelo, Naples, probably from Magna Graecia, Jenkins, *BSA*, xxxiii. 66, n. 7; *Dedalica*, 60, n. 1; *RM*, 1891, 253 ff. (same date); figurine in Berlin, from Taranto, Jenkins, *Dedalica*, 54, pl. VII. 5 (last quarter). The Cretan influence in the wall-paintings of the Tomba Campana at Veii (cf. Rumpf, *Die Wandmalereien in Veii*, 37 ff.) and imports and influence of Cretan metal-work in Etruria (Kunze, *Kretische Bronzereliefs*, 270) are relevant.

group of sculptures in soft limestone which are loosely called dedalic,[1] though they do not show the same style as the Cretan and Peloponnesian works to which the term is now conventionally applied. They belong to the early sixth century and perhaps also the late seventh. One of them, the Laianello head,[2] is a work of distinction. The 'dedalic' terra-cottas are among the earliest in Sicily. It is noteworthy that a large number of them were found at Selinus, the youngest of the Sicilian colonies. There are neither imported nor local pieces older than the last quarter of the seventh century. This is precisely the period when the output at Corinth became copious. Protocorinthian figurines are individual, most Corinthian examples are of a few types and carelessly made.[3] There can be little doubt that these cheap figurines were exported to Sicily and imitated there. Many early terra-cottas found at Selinus were imported from the Peloponnese.[4] Technical methods are common to Corinth and the west.[5]

From this time forward Sicilian art is a province of Corinthian art. Payne is able in treating Corinthian sculpture to illustrate it by means of a number of colonial works. The earliest is the Syracuse gorgon, which is fully in place in the series of Corinthian gorgons.[6] A later example is a limestone relief from S. Mauro, which is purely Corinthian in style.[7] The most characteristic Sicilian art is the decoration of temples by painted terra-cotta sculptures and revetments.[8] These are in

[1] Orsi, 'Daedalica Siciliae', in *Mon. Piot*, xxii. 131 ff.; Pace, *ACSA*, ii. 3 ff.; P. E. Arias, 'Daedalica Siciliae', in *Annuario della R. Scuola Normale di Pisa*, ser. ii, vol. vi. 129 ff. For the terra-cottas, see also Gàbrici, 'Daedalica Selinuntia', in *Atti della R. Accademia di Napoli*, v, 1924, 3 ff.; *MA*, xxxii. 205 ff. and pl. 37. 1–11; Kekulé, *Die Terrakotten von Sicilien*, fig. 1 (= Pace, op. cit., figs. 7–8); *MA*, xvii, figs. 532, 534; *Bollettino d'Arte*, 1907, iii. 8, fig. 3.
[2] In Syracuse, from Syracuse: *Mon. Piot*, xxii, pl. 14 and fig. 2.
[3] See R. J. H. Jenkins, *Perachora*, i. 194.
[4] e.g. *MA*, xxxii, pl. 37. 7; 41. 7; 43. 1, 7; cf. pp. 206, 209, 220, 300.
[5] Jenkins, op. cit. 195.
[6] *MA*, xxv, pl. 16; Pace, *ACSA*, ii, pl. 5; Payne, *NC*, fig. 23 E; P. Montuoro, *Mem. Acc. Linc.* 1925, 282 ff.; compared with the Corfu gorgon by Hill, *Corinth IV*, i. 7. The purpose of this relief is uncertain. Mrs. Van Buren's view that it was a corner-akroterion is certainly wrong (*AFR*, 158). Darsow suggests a metope or, more probably, an antepagmentum (*Sizilische Dachterrakotten*, 56). It is earlier than any of the architectural terra-cottas from the Athenaion, and it would hardly have been so well preserved if it had been on a building the rest of whose terra-cottas have not been preserved even in small fragments. Mrs. Van Buren's earlier suggestion that it was an independent offering is the most likely (*JHS*, 1921, 209).
[7] *MA*, xx, pl. 9; Pais, *Ancient Italy*, ch. xii. Schaal, *Griechische Vasen aus Frankfurter Sammlungen*, 29, fig. 12, uses it to illustrate 'die Einheitlichkeit des korinthischen Stils'. Cf. Payne, *NC*, 124, 214, 218.
[8] See Van Buren, *Archaic Fictile Revetments of Sicily and Magna Graecia*; Darsow,

a form invented by Corinthians or Sikyonians,[1] and Corinthian in the elements of their style.[2]

The earliest architectural terra-cottas found in Sicily are in form and style exactly like those current in Greece in the seventh century; both the Laconian[3] style and the Corinthian[4] are represented, but only in small fragments. There soon developed a style which, while it has parallels in the Corinthian sphere of western Greece, is sufficiently distinct to be called Sicilian. The earliest examples of this[5] may be considered as developments of the still earlier pieces in Corinthian style. The most fully preserved Sicilian revetments are from the Athenaion at Syracuse, where three groups are well represented and a number of others in fragments (*MA*, xxv, pll. 18, 20-1, 22); Gela, archaic temple, unpublished; S. Mauro (*MA*, xx, pll. 5-7); Selinus, temple C (*MA*, xxxv, pll. 17-35); and the Treasury of the Geloans at Olympia (*Olympia*, ii. 53 ff.).[6]

The main elements of the 'Sicilian' style are the Doric leaf and the double-cable pattern. Both are found in the revetments of the early sixth century from Corfu, Kalydon, and Troizen.[7] The cable is present already in the seventh century at Thermon.[8] The temples at Corfu, Kalydon, and Thermon were built probably by Corinthians, certainly under exclusively Corinthian influence; Troizen is a near neighbour of Corinth. So, though this style has not been found at Corinth, there is no doubt that it is Corinthian.[9] There are no western examples

---

Sizilische Dachterrakotten. Darsow's recent synthesis of the Sicilian material is admirable on the technical side. As this is complicated and not easy to put briefly, I shall simply refer to Darsow for technical questions.

[1] Pliny, *NH* xxxv. 151-2; cf. Hill, *Corinth IV*, i. 5 ff.; Payne, *NC*, 248 ff.

[2] Cf. Orsi, *MA*, xxv. 687; Payne, loc. cit.; Demangel, *La Frise ionique*, 135; Dörpfeld, *AM*, 1914, 168 (Corfu).

[3] Darsow, op. cit. 61 (Gela only; *MA*, xxxv, pl. 36. 1, from Selinus is rightly rejected); Van Buren, *AFR*, 151-2, disk acroteria nos. 1-5.

[4] At Grammichele (Van Buren, op. cit., fig. 20) and Syracuse (ibid., fig. 1); cf. Darsow, 61 ff.

[5] Selinus, *MA*, xxxv, pl. 45; Gela, Van Buren, fig. 31; S. Mauro, ibid., fig. 24 (see Darsow, 39 ff.). By ignoring the fact that these are in decoration intermediate between those cited in the last note and the full 'Sicilian' revetments Darsow overemphasizes the independence of the latter.

[6] For a female head from the Treasury of the Geloans see *JdI*, 1937, *Olympiabericht*, pll. 26-7.

[7] Corfu, *NC*, fig. 108B; *AM*, 1914, 167, fig. 4; Van Buren, *Greek Fictile Revetments*, figs. 61-3. Kalydon, *NC*, fig. 108A. Troizen, van Buren, *GFR*, fig. 145.

[8] Van Buren, *GFR*, figs. 141-2; cf. Darsow, 83 ff.

[9] Darsow, 77 ff., prefers the hypothesis of direct intercourse between western Greece and Sicily. This is plausible in the case of Korkyra, less so for relatively obscure sites in Aitolia and Akarnania, and ignores the essentially Corinthian nature of the latter group. Considering

exactly like the Troizen and Kalydon revetments—tongue-pattern above double-cable pattern with eyes and simple palmettes. But the Syracusan–Geloan version with Doric leaf, chequers, double-cable pattern, with rosettes in the eyes and palmettes between in the space between the cables, though more developed, is clearly derived from it. The decorative elements are all Corinthian, the effective combination may justly be called Sicilian. Nothing in Greece compares with the gaiety and richness of the western group, including the Treasury of the Geloans. The many technical differences between Sicilian and Corinthian roofs, both in the shape of the tiles and the way they are put together,[1] show the originality, within the general system learnt from Corinth, of the Sicilian architects.

The Sicilian style is equally at home in Syracuse and Gela and in the region of the Heraian hills. Variants are not sufficient to establish the existence of local schools. The revetments of Selinus, the best preserved of which belongs to temple C, are decorated in a very similar style, and variations may be due simply to a slightly later date. They show also technical differences, however, which correspond with the modification at Selinus of canonical architectural forms. At Akragas both the Syracusan–Geloan and the Selinuntine varieties of the Sicilian style are found. In south Italy it is certainly used at Rhegion.[2] The most archaic sima from the temple of Hera Lakinia, of the early sixth century, is of the same general type, though it has no exact parallels in Sicily.[3] A later piece from Kroton which I have not seen[4] should be closely associated with the Sicilian group. The pieces from Sybaris or its neighbourhood, preserved in Cosenza, which also I have not seen, should, from Orsi's description,[5] be of this style, and the geison with cable-pattern

---

the strength of Corinthian ties everywhere in the west, it is much more likely that dependence on Corinth accounts for all the likenesses between the two sides of the Ionian Sea.

[1] Id., 29 ff. Darsow partly obscures their unity by confining the term 'Corinthian' to seventh-century examples found at or near Corinth, which are put together on a simpler system represented in Sicily only in the early buildings which are ascribed to the seventh century. If it is allowed that the Corinthian style of the first half of the sixth century is represented by Corfu and Kalydon, the development of the Sicilian forms from those of the seventh century, and their place within the Corinthian sphere, are clearer.

[2] N Sc, 1922, 172, fig. 21; Putortì, L'Italia Antichissima, i; cf. M A, xxv. 649; xxix. 459. Compare with M A, xxv, pl. XVIII and fig. 229.

[3] Van Buren, AFR, fig. 5.

[4] Ibid. III, no. 38; N Sc, 1897, 345.

[5] M A, xxix. 474. Mrs. Van Buren does not know them.

close to the Sicilian type. Of the Lokrian terra-cottas,[1] only
MA, xxix, fig. 30 has close parallels in Sicily; and the combination of elements is different.[2] The closest parallels are,
interestingly, not with Syracuse but with Selinus;[3] this may
be chronological, but may also be taken to illustrate a community of spirit. Most of the Lokrian revetments, those from
Kaulonia, and, indeed, all the typical south Italian architectural
terra-cottas, have a different system of decoration from the
Sicilian.[4] The finest of them belong to the fifth century, and to
a period when terra-cotta revetments were used in Sicily only
for small buildings. But there are sixth-century examples from
south Italy which do not conform to the Sicilian pattern,[5]
though they are too scanty to be said to represent a different
system.

In Greece the Sicilian style is found in the Treasury of the
Geloans at Olympia and at Delphi.[6] The terra-cottas of the
Treasury of the Geloans are shown by clay as well as style to
be Sicilian. Those at Delphi will belong to the treasury of
some colonial city, perhaps the Syracusans, and will also have
been imported ready-made from Sicily.

This style developed probably at Syracuse, because its
decorative elements are all Corinthian. But, considering how
completely all colonies were dependent on Corinthian commerce, it is possible that Corinthian influence might give rise
to a new development in any of them. The view that Gela was
the fountain-head of the style[7] is no more than possible. It is
not supported by the supposed Rhodian influence which, if it
exists at all, is insignificant.[8] The revetments of the Treasury

---

[1] Most of the material is unpublished and inaccessible. Mrs. Van Buren's account is confused.

[2] Cf. Van Buren, *AFR*, 29.

[3] Cf. Orsi, *MA*, xxix. 467 (comparing fig. 32 with Dörpfeld, *Winckelsmannsprogramm*, 1881, pl. IV. 3); Van Buren, loc. cit.

[4] Cf. Orsi, *MA*, xxix. 457, on the differences between south Italian and Sicilian revetments, within the 'fondo comune che si esplica nelle sagome e nel repertorio ornamentale', explained by a chronological difference. In *MA*, xxix, Orsi gives a conspectus of all the south Italian material.

[5] e.g. Caulonia, *MA*, xxiii, figs. 48–9.   [6] Darsow, 27.

[7] Cf., for example, Randall-MacIver, *Greek Cities in Italy and Sicily*, 181, who suggests that the terra-cottas of Syracuse and of temple C at Selinus were made at Gela.

[8] Van Buren, *GFR*, 67; *AFR*, 80 ('Gela must have been strongly influenced by Rhodian art forms and technique'). Rhodian influence in a few unrelated details is suggested; for instance, the form of the cable on the Apollonion at Syracuse (Van Buren, *AFR*, 78; Carta in *MA*, xxv. 663, fig. 237) which has as good parallels on Fikellura amphoras much later in date (e.g. Jacobsthal, *Ornamente*, pl. 20a) as on Rhodian oinochoai. Mrs. Hill, *Corinth IV*, i. 7, derives the cable-patterns and square-calyxed lotus and palmette band from oriental,

of the Geloans and of the Geloan colony of S. Mauro have closer parallels at Syracuse than at Gela.

As the chronology of the chief Sicilian revetments is by no means settled, it is necessary to discuss it at some length. There is no external evidence for dating any of the buildings to which they belong, except temple C at Selinus, but some of the comparable revetments outside Sicily may be dated. As the Sicilian revetments may be arranged in a sequence by the development of the decorative elements, these fixed points will give the limits of the style.[1] Support for the dating is given by comparisons with vase-painting, though it is difficult to draw binding parallels.

7th century

Syracuse, *MA*, xxv, fig. 243 (Van Buren, fig. 1).
Grammichele, Van Buren, fig. 20.
Megara A, Van Buren, figs. 21, 33.
Syracuse, Apollonion, Van Buren, fig. 32.

Thermon, Van Buren, *GFR*, figs. 141–2.

First quarter of 6th century

Syracuse, *MA*, xxv, fig. 240.

Selinus, *MA*, xxxv, pl. XLV.
Gela, Van Buren, fig. 31.

S. Mauro, Van Buren, fig. 24.

Corfu, Gorgon temple (*Korkyra*, i. 97 ff.).
Kalydon, *NC*, fig. 108A.
Troizen, Van Buren, *GFR*, fig. 145.

and specifically Rhodian, origins; but wherever the motives came from, their use in Sicily is derived immediately from Corinth. Darsow deals faithfully with the supposed Rhodian influence on pp. 96 ff. Contrast the East Greek style of some Etruscan architectural terracottas (Demangel, *La Frise ionique, passim*).

[1] Darsow allows about the same period for this development, but dates all his roofs consistently later: the earliest in the Sicilian style, and the Corfu revetment, in the middle of the sixth century; S. Mauro, *c.* 530; Selinus C in the last quarter, the Treasury of the Geloans at the end of the sixth century. As his is the only consistent scheme of chronology at present in the field, his arguments deserve closer examination than space will allow here. I hope to give them this examination elsewhere. They are based on a lowering of dates of all the comparative material from Greece and on a misdating of the Ak-Alan terra-cottas after 560, following Koch (*RM*, 1915, 22), whereas they must go back to the beginning of the sixth century (cf. Kjellberg, *Larisa*, ii. 144 ff.). With them goes Darsow's *terminus post quem* for the earliest of his roofs of 'Sicilian' style (pp. 84. 107 ff.). At the lower end, the low date for the Treasury of the Geloans is also proposed by Hampe and Jantzen (*JdI*, 1937, *Olympiabericht*, 97, n. 1), on the style of a head (ibid., pll. 26–7) thought to be from an akroterion of this building. It may be suggested that this akroterion is part of a repair, and that at the same time the corner-piece of the revetment with circumscribed rosettes (*Ol.* ii, pl. 117 = Van Buren, *GFR*, fig. 118), on which Darsow relies for his late date, is also a replacement. This suggestion needs to be controlled by a new examination of the material at Olympia. But if the lotus and palmette band on the sima of the Treasury of the Geloans is as late as *c.* 500, that amounts to saying that we have no sound grounds for dating these Sicilian revetments, as all the parallels imply a date over fifty years earlier.

Second quarter of 6th century
  Syracuse, *MA*, xxv, pl. XXII.
  „   *MA*, xxv, pll. XX–XXI.
  „   *MA*, xxv, pl. XVIII.
  S. Mauro, *MA*, xx, pll. V–VII.   Treasury of the Geloans.

Third quarter of 6th century
  Selinus C.   *Corinth IV*, i, fig. 17.

The Thermon revetment is dated in the third quarter of the seventh century by the heads in relief which form a part of it. The Gorgon temple at Corfu belongs to the first quarter of the sixth century; the pediments are dated *c.* 580, the terra-cottas will be of about that date and, as the sculptured decoration was regularly the last part of the temple to be completed, will not be later.[1] The Kalydon and Troizen revetments are about contemporary with this, so are the earliest examples of the Sicilian style. The more complete and typical Sicilian examples are all later, but not by much. To take the three groups from the Athenaion of Syracuse first: *MA*, xxv, pl. XVIII may be dated by the form of the lotus-chain. The closest parallel for this is the Aigina bowl of the Nessos painter,[2] and, among Corinthian vases, it is most like Transitional and Early Corinthian works; it has a lightness and delicacy which disappear before the end of the seventh century, and is, indeed, typically Protocorinthian.[3] It can hardly belong to so early a period, if the date for the Corfu temple is right, but, even allowing for colonial conservatism, cannot be drawn too low into the sixth century. This is, to judge from the form of the leaf-pattern, the latest of the Athenaion groups. Plates XX–XXI and XXII are very closely associated and probably not much earlier than pl. XVIII. The former has many points of likeness with the Corfu revetment, but should be later than it.

The S. Mauro revetment goes very closely with the Athenaion group; the form of the leaf and the inset palmettes suggest a date a little later than pl. XVIII: the more developed shape of the spouts agrees with this. The astragalos moulding, repeated in temple C at Selinus, is the first step towards making the

---

[1] The first quarter of the sixth century is Payne's date (*NC*, 259) and Buschor's (*Die Tondächer der Akropolis*, ii. 71); Weickert (*Archaische Architektur*, 23), suggests *c.* 600. Darsow's date in the middle of the sixth century (pp. 108 ff.) is untenable if the terra-cottas are the original revetment of the Gorgon temple, ill supported on other grounds. See further K. A. Rhomaios, *Korkyra*, i. 121 ff. (*c.* 600–590).
[2] *CVA Berlin*, i, pl. 46.   [3] Cf. also Orsi, *MA*, xxv. 641.

decoration in relief as well as painting. Later again is the Treasury of the Geloans. All these have so much in common that they should not cover a long period of time. They may be placed within the second quarter of the sixth century, or may, indeed, be earlier, as the lotus-chain of *MA*, xxv, pl. XVIII suggests.

The revetment of temple C at Selinus differs in detail from these. On the whole it is simpler; the eyes of the cable are filled with dots, not rosettes; the leaf-pattern is not embellished, and the torus is decorated with simple vertical bands. On the other hand, the lotus and palmette chain is more advanced than anything at Syracuse, and is the finest in Sicily.[1] Lions' heads are used for the first time in Sicily.[2] Temple C was building from about 570, the date which its plan and proportions suggest for the foundations, to 530, the date of the metopes. The revetment should belong to the middle of the century; this date agrees with the history of the building, the stylistic development of the revetment, and the parallels for the lotus and palmette chain. The whole development of the style will then fall within the first half of the sixth century, before the earliest examples of the Megarian Treasury type.[3]

The style of the Megarian Treasury has no representatives in Sicily.[4] During the period of its currency in Greece the older style was continued in Sicily in unimportant works; for instance, the replacement of the terra-cottas of the Olympieion of Syracuse.[5] The second half of the sixth century was in many respects a backward period in Sicily, and none of the existing temples was begun then. Small buildings in many places were covered with roofs of a simpler type, characterized by antefixes most often in the form of gorgoneia; both the system of roofing and the style of the gorgoneia have parallels in the Corinthian sphere.[6] This style continued well into the fifth century, the

[1] *MA*, xxxv. 183 ff., fig. 44; 238 ff. Gàbrici, op. cit. 243, sees 'una filiazione da originali ionici' in the lotus and palmette band. In contrast to south Italian lotus and palmette bands, this was certainly derived immediately from Corinth; cf. Payne, *NC*, 251.

[2] *MA*, xxxv. 246. They are found earlier in south Italy (Medma and Metauron; cf. Van Buren, *AFR*, 125, nos. 1–2). Their use is Corinthian; cf. Troizen, Van Buren, *GFR*, fig. 146; and see Darsow, 89.

[3] *Corinth IV*, i, fig. 17, pl. iv; perhaps from the temple of Apollo, dated *c.* 540 (see S. Weinberg, *Hesperia*, viii. 191 ff.).

[4] Mrs. Van Buren points out resemblances on temple C at Selinus (*AFR*, 56–61), which is the latest of the big Sicilian revetments and near in time to the introduction of the Megarian Treasury style.

[5] *MA*, xiii. 369 ff.; cf. Van Buren, *AFR*, 74 ff.

[6] Darsow, 61, 99 ff.

most notable instance being in the temenos of the temple built at Himera after 480 B.C., where it was used on a number of small buildings.[1] These show Campanian influence, and other fifth-century revetments follow south Italian models.[2] Finally, before the end of the fifth century, architectural terra-cottas are imported to Sicily from south Italy.[3]

The area covered by tiles was much restricted in the fifth century and was frequently limited to the roof and antefixes, the vertical members which in the sixth century had been most highly decorated being eliminated. This may be well seen in the roofs of the great temples at Akragas.[4]

Terra-cotta sculpture also has an especial extension in Sicily, though no such important works have been found there as in Etruria. Certainly pedimental sculpture, such as the gorgoneion of temple C at Selinus,[5] and probably metopes were in terra-cotta, but with few exceptions they are too fragmentary to judge the style. The finely decorated fragments from the Athenaion of Syracuse (*MA*, xxv, pl. 17), and the unpublished horse from the archaic temple at Gela, all parts of akroteria, give an idea of the brilliance and vigour of this work. Many other scraps show how widely this terra-cotta sculpture was used. This is largely due to the lack of good carving-stone; but there is no need to apologize for it by calling it a second-best. It also is essentially Corinthian. The gorgoneion and the full figure of the gorgon were very popular in Sicily,[6] for temple decoration and for lesser purposes, but the finest examples are of Corinthian type.[7] In the second half of the sixth century a type which may be called Sicilian differentiates itself by development from the Corinthian.[8] The scheme of horse and rider as central akroterion common in Sicily[9] was perhaps

[1] Marconi, *Himera*, 127 ff.; cf. also Darsow, 94 f., for Campanian influence.

[2] e.g. the sixth type at the Olympieion of Syracuse (Van Buren, 76) resembles the second revetment of Kaulonia, omitting the lotus and palmette band; the later types have double meander on the geison, are in black and white instead of polychrome, and are mainly or entirely in relief. They differ from contemporary south Italian revetments in not adopting the lotus and palmette.

[3] Darsow, 27.

[4] Marconi, *Agrigento*, 153 ff.

[5] See also Darsow, 57–8, for groups.

[6] See Montuoro, *Mem. Acc. Linc.* 1925, 282 ff.

[7] See Payne's cautious judgements, *NC*, 251: Selinus gorgoneion 'may be of Corinthian type'; Gela, 'at any rate related to the Peloponnesian–Corinthian tradition'.

[8] Cf. Darsow, 52; non-architectural examples, *MA*, xvii. 563 ff., figs. 381–2 (Gela); *MA*, xxxii, pl. 30. 2 (Selinus).

[9] Van Buren, 152–3, central akroteria nos. 6–11; Orsi, *MA*, xxv. 741. See *Dedalo*, vi. 358.

repeated at Halai in Lokris in a set of terra-cottas made probably at Corinth.[1]

In considering sculpture in stone after the early works already discussed we are almost limited to the Selinus metopes. The oldest of these, those of a little temple on the acropolis,[2] are of the early sixth century, and almost as old as any Sicilian sculpture. They represent Apollo and Artemis with their mother, Europa on the Bull, Herakles and the river-god Akheloos,[3] and a Sphinx.[4] They are strongly Peloponnesian in style. Exact parallels are difficult to find, because so little of similar date and purpose has survived in Greece; but comparison with Corinthian vases can put them in their place.[5]

The metopes of temple C are more specifically Selinuntine in their heavy simple forms and stern features; they are still closely attached to the Peloponnesian current of art, but exact Corinthian parallels can no longer be quoted for them. This is partly because they are not as advanced as contemporary Peloponnesian art in the great centres. They have frequently been dated too high, and, within the third quarter of the sixth century, their date is still a matter of uncertainty.[6] But the Perseus metope, for instance, shows a clumsiness of construction and a baldness of outline less advanced than the Corfu pediments.

The continuance of development of Selinuntine sculpture, from dedalic origins to the metopes of E, may be exaggerated. There is rather a series of bounds, the Peloponnesian influence being renewed throughout the sixth and early fifth centuries.

[1] H. Goldman, *Hesperia*, ix (1940), 448 ff.; Van Buren, *GFR*, 41, 177; cf. Payne, *NC*, 239.

[2] For the building see Gàbrici, *MA*, xxxv. 206 ff.

[3] For the subject see Payne, *NC*, 130.

[4] *MA*, i. 957 ff.; Gàbrici, 'Daedalica Selinuntia' (see above, page 268, n. 1); Pace, *ACSA*, ii, figs. 11–13.

[5] Payne (*NC*, 313) compares with the Apollo and Artemis metope the Middle Corinthian cup *NC*, no. 1056, Gräf 425, pl. 25 (*c.* 580–570). The Akheloos metope Payne dates by implication to the first quarter of the sixth century (*NC*, 126), and for the composition compares (ibid. 130) the cup *NC*, no. 986 (pl. 34. 6) and the treatment of the Herakles and Nemean lion scene on the Argive–Corinthian plaque, Gervasio, *Bronzi*, pl. 17. The Europa metope is more definitely Corinthian in feeling; the stylization of the dewlap is a regular Corinthian characteristic (Payne, *NC*, 70, n. 4, comparing pl. 9. 1, &c.). The forehead curls of the bull are in a style of hairdressing which had otherwise gone out by the end of the seventh century (Poulson, *Der Orient*, 156; Löwy, *ÖJ*, 1911, 15–16).

[6] Langlotz's date 520–510 (*Zeitbestimmung*, 37) is, I think, too low, for the complete set of metopes at least. Richter, *Sculpture and Sculptors*, 29, dates them *c.* 550–540; cf. Ashmole, *Greek Sculpture in Sicily and South Italy*, 26, n. 4. A date *c.* 540–530 seems preferable; cf. C. Picard, *Manuel d'archéologie grecque: La Sculpture*, ii. 912–13, and P. de La Coste-Messelière there cited.

The closeness in style of the metopes of E to Olympia makes this clear. Moreover, no direct development can account for the advance from the archaism of C to the fine work of F, the sculptors of which drew their inspiration rather from contemporary artists in Greece. It would perhaps be more exact to speak of a community of spirit in all Selinuntine sculpture than of a continuous school.[1] The rude figures of the Kekropes metope recur in the Gigantomachy scenes. The dispassionate Athena of the Perseus metope is akin to the cruel Artemis who sets her hounds on Aktaion. In the female heads especially there is an *air de famille* ;[2] no grace, but something hard, setting itself against feeling. This feature, found also in some Selinuntine terra-cottas, it is perhaps not too fanciful to regard as the effect of the struggle against the Phoenicians.

Most of the terra-cottas also are derived from Peloponnesian art, often with a considerable time-lag. But in a small group of important terra-cottas there may be distinguished an often brutal realism and a revolt from the proportions of Greek art.[3] The most striking piece is the mask, *MA*, xxxii, pl. XLVII. 6[4] (Marconi, op. cit., 397); a most vivid head, with great staring eyes, rather summary indication of facial planes, but most vigorous; not a comfortable thing. The great eyes are the chief common feature of this group, and are seen also in the marble female heads of E.[5] These works, spread over the late sixth and early fifth centuries, show one of the first attempts to break away from the idealism of Greek art. There is no beauty, nor yet engaging ugliness. The same refusal to idealize introduces the ferocity of the metopes of F and of the Aktaion metope; in these terra-cottas it produces a rather forced realism, not an external naturalism but an attempt to render the naked spirit. Whether

---

[1] Cf. Pace, *Arte ed Artisti*, 531–4. While insisting that 'una fondamentale unità di stile lega tutte queste sculture, sempre gravi e quasi rigide' and that 'la selvaggia espressione ed il verismo di alcuni particolari, sono caratteri che mancano fuori della Sicilia al pari di talune peculiarità di esecuzione', he rightly distinguishes the 'aria di provincia'. In *ACSA*, ii. 74 ff., he has somewhat changed his position. Amelung, *JdI*, 1920, 55–6, holds that 'die Bildung der Augen, insbesondere die Zeichnung der Lider mit dèm abwärts gezogenen inneren Augenwinkel' distinguishes Selinuntine sculpture, from C to E. He illustrates (fig. 3) a single head from C (*Br. Br.* 292). He puts together a group of late Selinuntine sculpture: heads in Hanover (esp. close to E), Vienna (next generation), Dresden.

[2] See the remarks of Fougères in Hulot and Fougères, *Sélinonte*, 285 ff.

[3] Marconi, 'L'Anticlassico nell' arte di Selinunte', *Dedalo*, xi. 395 ff. Something the same is seen in the stelai *MA*, xxxii. 174 ff.: heads with features indicated in a few lines, not portraits, but the more careful of them have the same force as these terra-cottas.

[4] Jenkins, *BSA*, xxxii. 29 'under exclusively Argive influence', *c.* 590–560. I see nothing specifically Argive: his date is certainly too early.   [5] Marconi, op. cit. 410–11.

one likes this or no, it is the most original contribution of the colonial West to Greek art. The Selinuntines, earlier than any other western Greeks, had something of their own to add to the intelligent adaptation of imported motives. This is of immense importance in considering how far Sicily and south Italy were simply colonial. It is largely by the accident of discoveries that the best archaic art in Sicily comes from Selinus, but it is not accident that a specifically Sicilian spirit is first manifested at Selinus.

Some works elsewhere than at Selinus are not in the direct Peloponnesian tradition, because they are almost styleless. The elder goddess from Grammichele[1] is the earliest example, a naïve work with no merits of observation or appreciation. Some of the Selinus terra-cottas have this lumpishness, and some at Megara. It would be unkind to dwell on them as typically Sicilian, but they do point the Peloponnesian and Corinthian character of any work earlier than the late sixth century which has any pretensions to art. Most of the small terra-cottas of the sixth and early fifth centuries from Syracuse, Megara, Gela, Akragas,[2] are ordinary repetitions of standard types, without artistic interest. The terra-cottas of Selinus are certainly the most interesting in Sicily, both in the sixth century and the fifth. The free-standing figures and architectural sculpture are miserably reduced, but there are many interesting fragments which might be the decoration of votive ναΐσκοι or independent offerings.[3] Many of the small terra-cottas are of types unrepresented elsewhere.[4] Few of these are older than the late sixth century, and the common types derived from Peloponnesian and East Greek art are only slightly modified by an occasional introduction of the local spirit. Of most of these Gàbrici's judgement will serve: they are 'struck from tired matrices; with changed proportions, and often of poor execution, without red paint and without modelling on the back'.[5]

---

[1] MA, vii, pl. III; Deonna, Les Statues de terre cuite, 45 ff.; Van Buren, JHS, 1921, 204, fig. 1.

[2] For Akragas cf. Marconi, Agrigento, 176: 'non si tratta di tipi speciali, peculiari . . . documenti di una corrente artistica assai generale in cui manca una particolarizzazione di scuole e di tendenze'. Few of the great terra-cottas of Akragas, for which see Marconi, 'Plastica Agrigentina' (Dedalo, ix. 579 ff., 643), are archaic.

[3] MA, xxxii. 181 ff.

[4] See MA, xxxii. 301. See the sphinx pl. LV. 8; and the types with arms raised under the dress, giving the effect of wings (pll. LVI. 2; LX. 2; LVII. 6; LVIII. 5; LXIII. 2, &c.).

[5] Ibid. 210 (speaking of the imitations of Rhodian; hence the reference to colour: otherwise holds of the commoner Peloponnesian types).

Though there is activity both architectural and sculptural in Selinus in the middle of the sixth century, it agrees with the remains of the eastern cities in showing the backward condition of Sicily. At Selinus there was more originality, and the weakening of Corinthian influence allowed the growth of a specifically Selinuntine art, based on Peloponnesian art of a generation earlier. The revival in the last years of the sixth century and the beginning of the fifth, due to new influences from the Peloponnese and Ionia, is more marked at Selinus than elsewhere in Sicily, because Selinus had already some name as a city of art. Nowhere else in Sicily are there such good parallels to the terra-cottas of Lokroi and Medma.

Elsewhere than at Selinus we must, in default of sixth-century sculpture, judge from terra-cotta figurines and arulae. The latter are, as the name says, terra-cotta trapezoids in the shape of small altars.[1] The form is completely western; it is one of the few borrowings from Italy in the art of mainland Greece.[2] The use is uncertain, so it is unprofitable to speculate on their religious or other significance. They are mould-made, the best being well modelled and retouched by hand, but most of them carelessly cast from tired moulds.

The style is, in almost all cases, Corinthian or a broken-down copy of Corinthian. East Greek influence is not general, and may almost be disregarded.[3] Some arulae, like the notable one from S. Lorenzo del Vallo near Sybaris,[4] are very near Corinthian work in detail and feeling. In others it is possible to see 'Italian realism'; for instance, in a fine arula from Akragas,[5] which has accentuated the solidity of form and firmness of line, and has a touch of ferocity peculiarly Sicilian. This is decorated with a lion attacking a bull, which is the commonest motive in arulae; another interesting one is from the Sikel town at Paternò, by the hand of an artist who had seen a bull, but had obviously never seen a lion.[6] The arulae at Selinus are more

---

[1] E. D. Van Buren, *Mem. Am. Acad.* ii. 15 ff.; P. Wuilleumier, *Mél. arch. hist.* xlvi. 43 ff.; unpublished dissertation of Elisabeth Jastrow: cf. *A A*, 1920, 102–4; *Opuscula Archaeologica*, ii. 1 ff.; *AJA*, 1946, 67 ff.

[2] There is one arula at Perachora, one at Corinth, *AJA*, 1932, 512 ff.; one from Skione, Robinson, *CVA Baltimore*, pl. 48, also Corinthian (Payne ap. Beazley, *JHS*, 1934, 90). Another has recently been found at Corinth; see O. Broneer, *Hesperia*, xvi. 214 ff.

[3] It may perhaps be seen in Kekulé, *Terrakotten von Sicilien*, figs. on p. 47; Pace, *Arte ed Artisti*, 513, fig. 17.

[4] Crotone Mus., 2049. Pesce, *Boll. d'Arte*, 1935, 228 ff., emphasizes the Corinthian style. For some details (intricated lotus), cf. *MA*, xxxii, fig. 101, from Selinus.

[5] *Dedalo*, 1929, 591; Marconi, *Agrigento*, 195, fig. 132.   [6] Syracuse Mus., unpublished.

elaborate and original than others in Sicily; the heads and half-figures of *MA*, xxxii, pll. 30. 1; 31. 4; 43 can well stand beside the metopes. It is, however, easy to overestimate the originality of arulae, and terra-cottas generally, elsewhere than at Selinus.

The sculpture of the Heraion of Poseidonia[1] will, with the Selinus sculptures, form the best text-book of archaic sculpture in the west. There are at least three small buildings of the sixth century with sculptured decoration. But until publication is more advanced, it is premature to do more than call attention to the main features of the sculptures. These are a lively interest in the story related, an extreme simplification of modelling and drawing, both of which are crude for their period—the metopes resemble nothing so much as outlines cut out with a quick firm hand and stuck on to a flat surface—and an extreme degree of archaic conservatism. The last feature they share with the Selinus sculptures.

Study of western architecture, like sculpture, must begin with Selinus, where there is a range of buildings from the small square *oikoi* of the seventh century to the colossal temple of Apollo finished in the middle of the fifth century. For the first half-century of their existence the Selinuntines were content with little temples.[2] At least five little buildings on the acropolis, destroyed when temples C and D were built, belong to this period. They were all of the *oikos* type, of extremely simple architecture, four walls and external decoration of painted terra-cotta slabs. The terra-cottas are all that remain of some, but the foundations of the 'megaron' are still visible.[3] At the same time there was activity in the sanctuary of Malophoros outside the city, where worship began almost as soon as the colony was founded. The original *oikos* was replaced by another unpretentious building, the 'first megaron'.[4]

The simple geison without mutuli of this megaron, the chief 'pre-Doric' example of Selinuntine architecture,[5] is paralleled in two other little buildings on the same site.[6] Gàbrici, their publisher, compares the Tholos of Delphi, the Treasury X, and

[1] *N Sc*, 1937, 339 ff.; *AJA*, 1942, 437–8.

[2] Gàbrici, 'Per la storia dell' architettura dorica in Sicilia', in *MA*, xxxv.

[3] Pace, *MA*, xxviii. 237–43.

[4] Gàbrici, *MA*, xxxii. 66 ff.; cf. Koldewey and Puchstein, 82.

[5] *MA*, xxxii. 50: 'la sagoma arcaicissima di questo geison . . . contiene in sè gli elementi della decorazione del geison e della sima dei tempi dorici con terrecotte dipinte.'

[6] *MA*, xxxv. 141 ff., the predecessor of the first megaron.

the Bouleuterion at Olympia.[1] The architects of these little buildings were a long way behind the times. Many of the so-called 'pre-Doric' features are survivals from the seventh century, the formative period of Doric architecture in the Peloponnese. There are few parallels in the Peloponnese, and the main value of the remains at Selinus is that they provide our chief information about the development of the canonical style. The abnormalities in the small Selinuntine buildings are not due to local inventiveness but to the survival in stone in the sixth century of types developed for wood-construction, which had already been replaced in Greece.[2]

In the course of the sixth century these little buildings were all replaced.[3] The second megaron of the Malophoros is to be dated c. 580; temple C on the acropolis c. 570–560;[4] the 'Tempio delle piccole metope' and the 'Little temple with polychrome terra-cottas like those of C',[5] are of the second quarter of the century, and with the construction of D, and the demolition of the last of the original little temples of the acropolis to make the terrace of D[6] (soon after 550), the reconstruction was complete. After this follow rapidly the great temples of the eastern hill.[7] This is a period of intense activity, at its height in the late sixth century and early fifth.

C is the most complete of sixth-century temples, no other temple having yielded so many different decorative elements —metopes, terra-cotta revetments and gorgoneion in the pediment, lions' heads masking the water-spouts. The elevation can be reconstructed with few controversial points.[8] The treatment of the angle of the pediment is unique, the raking cornice being cut away diagonally so as to disappear gradually behind the horizontal sima. Both plan and decoration of the temple are in their main lines faithful to Peloponnesian and Corinthian examples. There are traces of archaism in both plan and execution more than would be expected in a contemporary building in Greece. There are also signs of inventiveness in the application to technical problems and in the ability with which

---

[1] Ibid. 149.

[2] Gàbrici, *MA*, xxxv. 236; cf. 230: 'Talchè l'architettura primitiva dei paesi greci di Occidente, nei quali persistettero più a lungo che nella Grecia i procedimenti tecnici e i caratteri tipologici, propri della costruzione in legno.'

[3] Hulot and Fougères, *Sélinonte*, 146–7.

[4] Cf. Robertson, *Greek and Roman Architecture*, Appendix I: Dinsmoor in Anderson and Spiers, 193.

[5] Gàbrici, op. cit. 199 ff. [6] Ibid. 241.

[7] Koldewey and Puchstein, 79 ff. [8] Gàbrici, op. cit. 233–4, pl. xv.

so many decorative elements were combined. Like most temples, it took a long time in building, forty years being a reasonable time to allow from the laying of the first stone to the completion of the decoration.[1] A similar period is covered by the building of the archaic temple of Apollo at Delphi, whose foundations were probably laid soon after the fire of 548, but whose pediments were not finished until after 510.

Of Selinuntine architecture in general, as well as of temple C, it is possible to say that it is Doric and Peloponnesian in origin, with its own especial imprint.[2] It is in some respects more original than that of Syracuse, for the archaic temples at Syracuse appear nearer to the main line of development in Greece. Perhaps this is because Selinus was in less close touch with Corinth, perhaps because she had her own schools of art and craftsmanship. The Selinuntine temples of both sixth and fifth centuries are akin in certain details of plan, e.g. the tripartite cella,[3] and in some constructional methods. Indeed, such continued building activity could not fail to produce a local school of architects and craftsmen.

There are other early, not yet canonical, Doric temples in the west, notably those of Apollo (or Artemis) and of Olympian Zeus at Syracuse,[4] which are of importance in the development of Doric architecture. Other well-preserved temples of the sixth century have survived at Poseidonia (those called the Basilica and the temple of Ceres) and at Metapontion, as well as foundations and fragments of elevations elsewhere. A number of details of plan or construction are common to many of these western buildings. For instance, the arrangement of cella with two parts, cella proper and adyton, without pronaos, is found at Selinus in temple C, in the two early Syracusan temples and, outside Italy and Sicily, in the very early

[1] Cf. above, pp. 274, 276.

[2] Cf. Gàbrici's conclusions, *MA*, xxxv. 248: 'che i Greci colonizzatori recarono seco un patrimonio di cognizioni architettoniche legate ad una tradizione di origine remota in Grecia, e questo patrimonio utilizzarono con ingegnosa versatilità, riuscendo ad espressioni, che al tempo della massima indipendenza e creazione artistica delle colonie de Occidente, cioè prima della fine del secolo VI, avevano assunto fisionomia lor propria'; ibid. 229, 'una fisionomia sua propria e un indirizzo alquanto divergente e indipendente'. He insists on the origin from the 'purissimo seme dell' arte primitiva ellenica', disproving the old view which is concisely expressed by Pace (*Arte ed Artisti*, 480), 'i templi di Selinunte danno dunque prova dell' imporsi della forma dorica su di un substrato più antico dovuto ad influenze diverse'. The older substratum is only an earlier stage of the development of the Doric style, equally at home in the Peloponnese.

[3] Koldewey and Puchstein, 79; cf. further below.

[4] See above, p. 60.

Apollonion of Kyrene.[1] This feature, being found in Kyrene, is presumably one common also to the Doric of mainland Greece which has happened to be preserved only in the colonies, no doubt because it was retained there after it had been given up in Greece.[2] The same explanation may apply to other uncanonical features of colonial Doric, for instance the Ionic treatment of some capitals[3] and the *entasis* of columns at Poseidonia and Metapontion.[4] Some of these minor differences may, however, be due to colonial innovation. The relation of western to mainland Greek architecture in the archaic period is brought out clearly in Miss Shoe's study of mouldings. Her conclusions are that there are no new types in the west, and that, while following the same general development, western mouldings show a considerable time-lag. She allows that there are new combinations of types, and in particular the mixture of Doric and Ionic mouldings in a single building occurs earlier and to a far greater extent than in Greece. Finally, 'Western Greek mouldings have a local, provincial character of their own, definitely distinguished from those of Greece proper, yet based on them and following them in general development. The interest of the West is, however, not primarily in refinement, but in the creation of bigger and more novel forms.'[5] These conclusions drawn from a detailed study of the mouldings may be applied to western architecture in general. The claim which has been made that the colonies played an important part in the development of Doric architecture[6] fails on a consideration of relative chronology. It appears that, while many early features are well preserved in western buildings, these are not all of very early date, and owing to the conservative character of colonial art present many features which were already out of date in mainland Greece. This is not to deny the merits of western architects. The architects of temple C, in the treatment of the angle of the raking cornice of the pediment, for instance, were thinking out their problems anew and getting to the heart of large-scale building in stone. The builders of the Olympieion of Akragas with its enormous telamons, to take only one fifth-century building, were bold in design and construction beyond any other architects of the

[1] Robertson, 71 ; Dinsmoor in Anderson and Spiers, 77 ff. ; Weickert, *Typen der archaischen Architektur*, 107 f. ; for the Apollonion of Syracuse, Cultrera, *RIASA*, ix (1942), 56.

[2] Cf. Weickert, loc. cit.   [3] I. Kelly, *AJA*, 1941, 95 f.

[4] Robertson, 116.   [5] *AJA*, 1940, 112.

[6] Pace, *ACSA*, ii. 211 ff.

time. The colossal size of the Apollonion of Selinus, begun in the middle of the sixth century,[1] shows that this boldness was not lacking at an earlier period. Indeed, no one who to-day visits the ruins of Poseidonia, of Selinus, and Akragas can question the importance of the colonies in the development of ancient architecture. But the claim to have had an important share in the origination of Doric architecture must be rejected.

Throughout the sixth century, as well as the great temples and often side by side with them, simple little sanctuaries on a rectangular ground plan without columns continued to be built and decorated with painted terra-cotta slabs. The small buildings at Selinus, some of which have been described, are typical of these little *oikoi*. Others at Akragas are discussed below.[2] Many of them were of wood, as may be inferred from the absence of stones to be referred to their superstructures; for instance, the buildings at San Mauro and Grammichele whose terra-cottas have been preserved.[3] It is likely that even at Syracuse, where there is abundance of good building-stone, the Athenaion was rebuilt in wood in the sixth century.[4]

There is less difference, in architecture and art, between Corinth and her colonies Syracuse and Korkyra than between Corinth and her Peloponnesian neighbours. This implies that the cultural dependence of the colonies, not only Syracuse but also Gela, on Corinth was as close as their economic dependence. It is possible that some of the work was done by craftsmen from Corinth, as is probably true of the Corfu pediments.[5] What one finds at Korkyra one would expect to find at Syracuse, but what is preserved could equally well be regarded as the work of Sicilians brought up in the Corinthian tradition. Certainly the specifically Corinthian art of the west for nearly two centuries after the foundation of Syracuse, and the very close parallels between western and mainland Greeks, imply a connexion kept up over most of that time by constant interchange of men and ideas. The colonies do not simply develop on lines parallel to Corinth, but the Corinthian influence was constantly reinforced. The use of terra-cotta revetments, for instance, is not as old as the foundation of Syracuse,[6] and must have been introduced to Sicily by subsequent immigrants from Corinth. The strength of Corinthian influence in the seventh

[1] Robertson, 85, 325.
[2] pp. 313, 324.
[3] See above, pp. 118, 124.
[4] See above, p. 60.
[5] *NC*, 240.
[6] Payne, *Perachora*, i. 114 ff.

and early sixth century, when it is first possible to speak of colonial art, suggests that at this period, roughly the reign of Periander, Corinthians were especially active in the west. There is not enough material to form a judgement on the artistic capabilities of the colonials.[1] But Selinus stands out from the other cities of Sicily (that is to say, Syracuse and Gela, the only ones excavated to a comparable extent) by the greater variety and originality of its work; and though extremely little has survived from the Italian cities before the last part of the sixth century, there are signs that they also had something of their own to contribute to the interpretation of the Corinthian traditions. Syracuse and Gela, on the other hand, are more purely Corinthian. I should explain this by consideration of the economic circumstances of the different groups. The eastern cities of Sicily, and especially Syracuse, were more tightly bound to Corinth, and had less to do with other Greeks or barbarians. The result was that they were less open to new influences than, say, Sybaris or Selinus and, more important, it was to their interest to be as Corinthian as they could. Sicily therefore remained in a colonial state of mind longer than south Italy, and with the weakening of Corinthian influence in the course of the sixth century, Sicily, especially eastern Sicily, was left more and more behind the times.

This colonial dependence continues in Sicily down to the end of the archaic period, well into the fifth century. With the increasing wealth of the colonies in the late sixth century, rich dedications begin to be made at Olympia and Delphi, one of the earliest being the chariot dedicated at Olympia by Pantares the Geloan after his victory in 512 or 508[2] (an offering which had its precedent in that of another colonial, Kleosthenes of Epidamnos).[3] About the same time marble was brought to Sicily and south Italy, to satisfy a taste for greater luxury and better work than could be carried out in the local stone. Most if not all of the archaic marble sculpture in the western colonies

---

[1] Cf. Orsi, *MA*, xxv. 743: 'Siracusa non ebbe nè durante il suo massimo prosperare e quanto meno prima una scuola di scultori con indirizzo autonomo; essa era direttamente tributario dell' estero, ed attingevano all' indirizzo delle scuole forestiere i suoi scarsi scultori, nissuno dei quali assurto a gran fama. Appena a Selinunte . . . è il caso di parlare di una scuola locale di anonimi maestri . . .'; ibid. 411 'una impressione di povertà, quasi di miseria, della Siracusa predinomenidica in fatto di scultura decorativa'; not, however, peculiar to Syracuse. Cf. *Templum Apollonis Alaei*, 167: 'Ad una vera autonomia dell' arte siceliota non ho mai prestato fede, sebbene io non posso negare certe affermazioni, certi aspetti di carattere locale, e limitati, se mai, almeno sin qui, alla sola Selinunte.'

[2] *Olympia*, v. 241 ff. For the date see below, p. 378.   [3] Paus. vi. 10. 6.

was imported ready carved from Greece or Ionia.[1] There are Attic works, such as the Grammichele torso[2] and the Girgenti kouros;[3] Chiot, Nike at Syracuse;[4] perhaps Samian, the Leontinoi torso,[5] to which a head in Catania[6] belongs; and other East Greek works now in Syracuse.[7] This extensive import of finished works is to be explained partly on economic grounds. There is no marble in Sicily or south Italy, and it would be easier to import statues than blocks of marble.[8] But this is a symptom only, not the cause of the provinciality which outlasted the archaic period.

None of the imported East Greek sculpture in Sicily is closely connected with works of the late archaic and early classical period at Lokroi, which show a style whose chief ingredient is a later wave of East Greek influence. Sicilian sculpture of any sort shows little of this influence at first hand; it is still related to the Peloponnesian school, and continues to show archaism in detail well into the classical period.[9] This may be seen in a work whose Sicilian origin is unquestioned, the bronze kouros from Selinus.[10] The earliest group with a Sicilian style, elsewhere than at Selinus, consists of a number of terra-cottas and small bronzes, the chief of which is the libation-pourer from Adernò.[11] These have been brought into relationship with Pythagoras of Rhegion, but the connexion is problematical. Pythagoras' style is unknown,[12] and has been sought in almost every West Greek work of this period. The best guide is in the terra-cottas of Rhegion, and more particularly of the neighbouring Lokroi and Medma;[13] the Cirò statue also is probably to be related.[14] The Delphi charioteer has often been thought to be by a

---

[1] Cf. Langlotz, *Frühgriechische Bildhauerschulen*, 72. E. Homann-Wedeking discusses the question in *AM*, lx–lxi. 215, n. 5, and in a further study not yet published. He gives more credit to local sculptors. Langlotz's most recent opinion (*RM*, 1943, 208) is that the Girgenti kouros may be Sicilian, but if so it is the only Sicilian marble figure of the early fifth century, other works in marble being probably Cycladic.

[2] Richter, *Kouroi*, pl. 126, no. 152. For the ascription to Attica cf. Wedeking, op. cit. 201.

[3] Ibid., pl. 124, no. 149; *RM*, 1943, pll. 15–18.

[4] *MA*, xxv. pl. 15.

[5] Richter, op. cit., pl. 125, no. 150; Langlotz, op. cit., pl. 64*a*.

[6] Libertini, *Il Museo Biscari*, pll. 1–2; Richter, op. cit., pl. 127, no. 151.

[7] Langlotz, op. cit., pl. 64*c*; Orsi, *Antike Plastik*, 168 ff.

[8] Cf. Ashmole, 5.   [9] Cf. id., 12 f., 25 f.

[10] Marconi, *Opere d'arte*, fasc. i.

[11] Orsi, *Ausonia*, viii. 44 ff.

[12] On Pythagoras see Pliny, *NH* xxxiv. 59–60; Lechat, *Pythagoras de Rhégion* (1905); Hyde, *Olympic Victor Monuments*, 178 ff.

[13] Von Duhn, *Ausonia*, viii. 35 ff.

[14] Orsi, *Templum Apollinis Alaei*, 162 ff.

western artist, sometimes by Pythagoras himself,[1] but there are no good grounds for this view.

None of the other offerings of the Deinomenids was by a western artist. Gelon's Nike and tripod at Delphi were by Bion of Miletos, his chariot at Olympia by Glaukias of Aigina, Hieron's by Onatas of Aigina, the boys of the same group by Kalamis. Phormis of Syracuse employed Dionysios of Argos and Simon of Aigina. The Akragantine dedication for their victory over Motye had statues by Kalamis.[2] The tyrants and their dependants engaged the services of the best artists of the leading centres of Greece, just as they commissioned the best poets of all Greece to celebrate their victories. There was no thought of economic nationalism.

The complete lack of literary references to Sicilian artists is not really serious.[3] Other schools, including the contemporary Lokrian, are completely anonymous. The fact is that there is no body of existing works, large or small, which might establish the characteristics of a school of archaic art in Sicily. It is otherwise in the Italian colonies, as will be seen. The only western school known on literary authority is that of Rhegion, which began with Klearkhos, master of Pythagoras and pupil of Dipoinos and Skyllis or of Eukheiros of Corinth;[4] that is, deriving from Crete or the Peloponnese. Pythagoras of Rhegion, the earliest artist in the western colonial region who was considered by the ancients to be of the first rank, was by birth a Samian.

From the middle of the fifth century a school, common to all Sicily with local variations, can be found in the great busts of Akragas and other fine terra-cottas, the most attractive of which is an antefix with the youthful laurel-crowned head of Herakles.[5] The impulse which created this school came largely from the import of Ionian and Attic works, and perhaps from

---

[1] Von Duhn, loc. cit. R. Hampe has recently, following a suggestion of Homolle, convincingly associated with the charioteer a block from a base bearing the artist's signature of Sotadas of Thespiai (text to *Br. Br.*, pll. 786–90).

[2] Pace, *ACSA*, iii. 723 ff.; *Arte ed Artisti*, 615 ff., summarizes the Sicilian offerings in the sanctuaries of Greece. The wooden gorgon with stone face dedicated by Deinomenes father of Gelon at Lindos (*Lind. Chron.* xxviii) was presumably Sicilian.

[3] Pace, *Arte ed Artisti*, 536 ff.

[4] Paus. iii. 17. 6; vi. 4. 4. Another Rhegine artist is the painter Sillax (named by Epikharmos and Simonides, and therefore of archaic date; Athen. 210*b*).

[5] Marconi, *Agrigento*, 199, fig. 135. The likeness with the Delphi charioteer is less close than Marconi makes out; look at the heavy chin (partly obscured in the photograph), the fleshy cheek, the different proportions of the forehead.

the migration to Sicily of Ionian artists. This East Greek influence can be traced at Akragas from the late sixth century onward,[1] but is not so strongly marked as at Selinus, where we can be confident that Ionian artists were working on the spot.[2] The remains of Sicilian art, great and small, indicate that the immigrant element was here less prominent than in south Italy and Etruria. Immigrant artists can be traced most clearly in the coins. The first Sicilian city to show East Greek influence in its coins is Naxos, whose coinage begins about 530 and is vastly different in quality from contemporary issues of other Sicilian cities.[3] Down to the early fifth century most of these have little artistic merit. There is then a sudden flowering, and the most brilliant artist at work in this period, the man who cut the dies for the earliest coins of Gelon at Leontinoi and Syracuse,[4] was probably a foreigner. The earlier coinage of Syracuse, from its beginning about 530, is in a style reminiscent of Corinth.[5] There are no such close parallels between the coins of Syracuse and Corinth as would indicate that Corinthian artists were at work. Rather, the Syracusan die-cutters appear to have been trained in Corinthian forms, and their whole artistic feeling was in the Corinthian heritage. With the issues which may be ascribed to Gelon's rule new styles are introduced, and the artists of the new dies may be traced at work also in Gela and Leontinoi.[6] The output of the Syracusan mint is greatly increased at this period, and as there are no close connexions in style and technique with the earlier issues of Syracuse or any Sicilian city, it is likely that die-cutters were invited to Sicily by the tyrants, as we know that other settlers were. In the varied and beautiful types of the 'eighties and 'seventies many artists are at work, whose power and technical skill suggest that they had been trained in some more advanced centre of art than we know of in the west at this time. In one

[1] See N. Breitenstein, *Acta Archaeologica*, xvi. 115.
[2] For copies of East Greek terra-cottas at Akragas see Marconi, op. cit., 217; Breitenstein, op. cit. 125, figs. 11–22. At Selinus, *MA*, xxxii, pl. 39. 7; at Gela, *MA*, xvii. 709, fig. 535. The existence of these copies does not, of course, involve the immigration of artists. This is inferred from the creation of such Selinuntine types as *MA*, xxxii, pll. 45. 7; 51; 52. 3. Cf. Gàbrici, ibid. 225 ff., and above, p. 240.
[3] Cahn, *Die Münzen der Sizilischen Stadt Naxos*, 40–1.
[4] Boehringer, *Die Münzen von Syrakus*, 80 f.
[5] Ashmole, 19. Cahn finds East Greek influence in the early coins of Syracuse as well as Naxos (loc. cit.; cf. *Trans. Int. Num. Conf.*, 38). But this is less apparent than the marked Peloponnesian style of the coins.
[6] Boehringer, loc. cit.; for the chronological question, Ashmole, op. cit., 20.

case, that of the Samians who coined for Rhegion and Messana after 493, with Samian types,[1] it is certain that immigrant artists were at work in a western mint. But the Samians cannot be traced at work or their influence followed outside these two cities.

Elsewhere this degree of certainty is not easily attained. We may be sure, however, that Ionian artists migrated to Etruria and to south Italy during the late sixth and early fifth centuries, for the extent and quality of East Greek influence at this time cannot be explained solely by import and imitation of works of art. We know of large bodies of settlers who left Ionia, the Phokaians who colonized Elea, the Samians who came on the invitation of Skythes and occupied Zankle-Messana, the followers of Dionysios of Phokaia. These will have been a cross-section of a Greek community, with artists and craftsmen among them; and there will have been others not recorded in history. The first efflux from Ionia began with the Persian conquest c. 540, when the Phokaians and Teians left their homes, the second and probably the larger after the failure of the Ionian revolt, when the Ionians as a body debated migration to Sardinia. It is this second wave which was most felt in Sicily, but in Italy Ionian artistic influence is observable in the second half of the sixth century, especially at Lokroi.

The art of south Italy before the middle of the sixth century is hardly known. Some pieces already mentioned[2] suggest the same dependence before that date on Corinth as is observable in eastern Sicily. In the second half of the century the coinage of the south Italian cities begins, and many of the coins are of extremely fine design and execution. The broad spreading fabric in which the reverse type is that of the obverse incuse is peculiar to these cities. It is to be explained partly by the need for striking on a coin already used or on a blank supplied ready-cut to the mint, partly by the need for a broad surface on which to develop an ambitious design (which, as the coin was to contain a given weight of silver, meant that it would be thinner than most archaic coins). Partial parallels for style and fabric can be found in Corinth, which is the probable source of the silver.[3] The incuse coins display a bold inventiveness and independence, especially visible in the early types of the secondary city of Kaulonia.

The oldest material to be assigned with any confidence to a

---

[1] See below, pp. 388 ff.   [2] See pp. 270, 279.   [3] See above, pp. 247 ff.

south Italian manufacture is a group of small bronzes associated by Jantzen with Taras.[1] I do not think that it is possible in the present state of our studies to say with certainty that these were all made in the same place. Two or even three towns may have had closely similar styles founded in the same traditions; for instance, the horseman found at Grumentum must have reached that place immediately from Metapontion, and may well have been made there. However, it is reasonable to agree that the main branch of the style was Tarentine. This being allowed, it is interesting to find that the earliest members of the group are provincial Corinthian. This is seen most clearly in the horseman from Grumentum, B.M. 1904. 7–3. 1, which belongs to the early sixth century.[2] In the second half of the sixth century Laconian influence becomes stronger. The position is complicated by a doubt whether certain pieces are rightly described as Tarentine, and are not in fact Laconian.[3] Dependence on Laconian art is seen also in the coins of Taras and Tarentine terra-cottas of this period,[4] and is substantiated by the imports of Laconian vases, which continue until the late sixth century.[5]

[1] U. Jantzen, *Bronzewerkstätten in Grossgriechenland und Sizilien*, 26 ff. As pointed out by Ashmole, *Gnomon*, 1939, 424 ff., many of the bronzes associated by Jantzen with Taras have little connexion with any bronzes certainly found in the area, and appear to belong to other styles and fabrics; thus Jantzen's no. 8 is Corinthian (so also nos. 25 and 26, from Amandola; cf. Payne, *NC*, 352–3); no. 18 is Etruscan; nos. 13, 14, 34 differ in date and style from others in the list, and there is no reason to associate them with Taras. Nos. 1–6, 9, and 10 may be recognized as an early group, all, so far as their provenience is known, from Taras or some neighbouring part of Apulia or Lucania. No. 23 also was found at Taras, and nos. 16 and 27 may, on account of their likeness to Laconian bronzes, perhaps be thought of as the products of a provincial factory at Taras. These dozen bronzes, though only a third of Jantzen's list, have more unity of style and give a clearer picture of the archaic production of this part of Italy. There is no clear stylistic connexion with the bronzes of the later fifth century found at Taras, nos. 35, 36, and p. 44, n. 1.

[2] Walters, *Select Bronzes*, pl. 1; Lamb, *Greek and Roman Bronzes*, pl. 39b. The horse is rightly compared by Jantzen with horses on Middle Corinthian vases; *NC*, fig. 18F is even closer than pll. 32 and 34, which he quotes. Laconian works such as the riders from Dodona and Trebenishte, which are indeed later in date, offer only the most general parallels.

[3] The bronze protome in Munich, *Festschrift Loeb*, pl. 12, found at Taranto, appears to be Laconian; cf. R. J. H. Jenkins, *BSA*, xxxiii, 66, n. 6; Payne, *Archaic Marble Sculpture from the Acropolis*, 5, n. 3. The Nike London 495 (Jantzen, no. 4) may also be Laconian. For a cautious criticism of Jantzen's archaic Tarentine group, suggesting that some members of it may have been made in Corinth or Sparta, others at Metapontion or elsewhere in Italy, see Wuilleumier, *Tarente*, 311 ff. Another important group of archaic bronzes, the vases with tongue-pattern, is ascribed to Taras by Neugebauer (*RM*, 1923–4, 341 ff.). This view is not supported by the evidence of proveniences or by stylistic comparisons with Tarentine works, and is not generally followed (cf. *NC*, 215 ff.).

[4] Ashmole, 11 ff. For the Laconian style of the coins cf. also Vlasto, Τάρας Οἰκιστής, 26.

[5] The latest is the Kyrene cup, *FR*, iii. 212, which is to be dated *c.* 510, and is the last good Laconian vase we possess (E. A. Lane, *BSA*, xxxiv. 153). It has been suggested that it

There is some late archaic marble sculpture from Taras. A kore in Parian marble may be imported from somewhere in the Ionian area.[1] Wuilleumier mentions another fragment of a late-sixth-century kore which, being unfinished, must be of local workmanship.[2] The seated goddess in Berlin[3] is known to have been found at Taranto, and comes from a sanctuary, probably of Persephone, in the eastern part of the town, among the cemeteries.[4] It is certainly a local work, as is shown by comparison with other western works (especially some Lokrian pinakes), by the lack of close relation with eastern or mainland Greek schools, and by certain awkwardnesses of execution which suggest that the sculptor was not used to handling large blocks of marble. It is a majestic but rather cold figure, whose undoubted sculptural qualities suffer from too much preoccupation with the surface decoration of dress, throne, and footstool, and from the archaic traits still present in the treatment of head and face. Historically, the statue is of the greatest importance, as the most ambitious surviving work of the period in the west and one of the few cult-statues which have come down from antiquity, and as showing what a colonial sculptor was capable of. In its archaic features it agrees with all the rest that we know of early classical art in the west.

The seated goddess belongs to the decade 480–470, the period of Tarentine expansion and of the dedications at Delphi for their victories over Messapians and Peucetians.[5] Another work of about the same date, more distinguished in its treatment of

was made at Taras (K. A. Neugebauer, *Gnomon*, 1939, 421), on the ground that as it is unfinished it will have been made where it was found. This is not necessary, for the absence of the white coating on Kyrene's face and arms (see Lane, loc. cit.) is by no means such a blemish as would remove the value of the vase, and may have been due to an oversight. The likeness to other late Laconian vases indicates that the Kyrene cup is metropolitan. Such vases of colonial manufacture as can be distinguished in the sixth century are of very indifferent quality (cf. p. 261 above). Neugebauer (loc. cit.; cf. E. Kirsten, *Die Antike*, xiv, 1938, 159 ff.) holds that other vases commonly called Laconian were made at Taras, notably the black kraters found in such numbers on Italian sites. But only a few can on technical grounds be distinguished as not of Laconian origin, and it appears that local imitation was unimportant (Lane, op. cit. 186).

[1] Berlin 578; Wuilleumier, *Tarente*, 268 and pl. IV. 4.

[2] Taranto Mus.; Wuilleumier, op. cit. 269. I do not recall this work.

[3] Berlin 1761; *AD*, iii, pll. 37–44; Wuilleumier, op. cit. 269 ff. (where bibliography) and pl. III.

[4] See the history related by Signora P. Zancani Montuoro, *SMG*, 1931, 159 ff. Though its vicissitudes are here told in full detail, not all scholars are convinced of their truth; some still think that the goddess may have come from Lokroi or Poseidonia, others regard it as a forgery (e.g. C. Picard, *Manuel d'archéologie grecque: La Sculpture*, ii. 110 ff.).

[5] See above, p. 149.

the face, is the head of Athena in Boston,[1] which Ashmole suggests may be 'the work of a Tarentine sculptor trained in the Aeginetan school or imitating an Aeginetan model'. These remain at present isolated. It is not until after the middle of the fifth century that it is possible to distinguish an independent Tarentine style of sculpture, which is unrelated to the Berlin goddess and the Boston head.[2]

The other main centre of bronze-working in south Italy was Lokroi. Here, however, there is little evidence of a local school before the second half of the sixth century.[3] From that time until the fourth century there is a vigorous school, with its own style and specialities. Most of its products have been found at Lokroi itself, where bronze mirrors and vases were frequently deposited in graves. Others come from other Italian colonies, from places in the interior of south Italy (Armento, Acerenza) and a few from Sicily.[4] It produced especially mirrors, with sirens on the handles, and with other figures in open-work in square frames at the base of the handle, or unframed. These, however, belong to the classical period. The smaller number of late archaic and early classical mirrors have handles composed of single standing figures, male or female, as in the Peloponnesian mirrors which they resemble in form and to some degree in style. There are also figures which were attached to bronze vases. The common element of style in the Lokrian bronzes is a rather hard treatment of hair and features which develops with time into a summary but effective realism. The origins and nearest parallels for the style and many of the types are to be sought in the Peloponnese, especially Argos and Corinth. In the early classical period Attic influence is increasingly felt, as in the contemporary western terra-cottas. There is no close relationship to East Greek work.[5]

[1] Boston 00.307; Caskey, *Cat. Greek and Roman Sculpture*, 9 f., no. 6; Ashmole 14 and fig. 17; Wuilleumier, pl. IV. 3.

[2] Ashmole, loc. cit.; A. Rumpf, *RM*, 1923–4, 446 ff.

[3] The earlier members of Jantzen's Lokrian group (op. cit., 1 ff.) do not form a coherent whole. No. 1 has little to do with no. 5, with which Jantzen compares it. It seems not to be pure Greek, and may be Campanian. No. 4 is not provincial, but belongs to a mainland workshop (Ashmole, *Gnomon*, 1939, 426, compares it to an Attic bronze, Lamb, pl. 39a). No. 6 is probably Corinthian (cf. Payne, *Perachora*, i. 135). The other sphinx, no. 3, is not closely related, and may be Lokrian. It follows that there are too few Lokrian bronzes older than the late sixth century to allow us to express any judgement of the Lokrian style or styles earlier than that date.

[4] See lists in Jantzen, loc. cit. To his group nos. 62–75 add Crotone Mus. no. 1766, from Kroton.

[5] Cf. V. H. Poulsen, *Acta Archaeologica*, viii. 92, 99 ff., 106.

The main product of the late archaic and early classical art of Lokroi is the clay reliefs or pinakes, which are shown by their clay to have been manufactured at Lokroi, where the majority of them were found.[1] Others come from the Lokrian colonies of Medma and Hipponion,[2] one from Sicily.[3] They are rectangular plaques of 8 to 12 inches square, with holes for hanging or nailing to a wall. The rather poor clay is covered with a white slip, on which red and blue, less often green-grey and yellow, colour is applied.[4] The subjects represented include many divinities, Hermes, Aphrodite, Persephone, and Hades, and also cult-scenes in one of which the discovery of a child in a basket is illustrated, and such scenes as the charming one of a girl filling her lap with fruit picked from a tree. They are commonly related to a chthonic cult with a mystery element, such as is generally regarded as one of the most widespread and popular features of the religion of the western colonies. Those from the main find at Lokroi come from a sanctuary of Persephone,[5] the fame of whose shrine there is recorded by Livy.[6] The sanctuary lay in a deep valley between two of the three hills which form the upper part of the site of Lokroi, and was laid out anew in the middle of the fifth century, at which time the old offerings were broken and deposited in a pit.

Technically the pinakes are not of the highest quality, as the poor clay does not allow sharp modelling. But the drawing is done with freshness and an archaic love of the rendering of detail, and the interest of style and subject makes them one of the most attractive products of western colonial art. There are many points of connexion with bronze-work. Bronze vases

[1] Q. Quagliati, *Ausonia*, iii. 136 ff.; P. Orsi, *Boll. d'Arte*, iii. 406 ff., 463 ff.; *N Sc*, 1911 Suppl., 73. Full bibliography in *RE*, xiii. 1356; add P. Zancani Montuoro, *Paolo Orsi* (1935), 195 ff.; *RI AS A*, vii (1940), 205 ff. In a grave at Lokroi fragments of pinakes were found: *N Sc*, 1913 Suppl., 25. Though no moulds have been found, the suggestion that they were imported is unlikely. The traces of reworking of the moulds, as determined by detailed study of groups of pinakes from a single mould, prove that the artists were at work at Lokroi, where the clay shows that the pinakes were cast (P. Zancani Montuoro, *Paolo Orsi*, 199).

[2] Medma: *N Sc*, 1913 Suppl., 130. Hipponion, *N Sc*, 1921, 480; Vibo Valentia, Coll. Capialbi.

[3] Selinus: *M A*, xxxii, pl. 78. 6.

[4] For a chemical analysis of the colours see P. Zancani Montuoro, *Paolo Orsi*, 197.

[5] Orsi, *Boll. d'Arte*, loc. cit.; Giannelli, *Culti e Miti della Magna Grecia*, 222 ff. Livy (xxix. 18. 16) states that the sanctuary of Persephone lay outside the walls. The decisive factor in the identification is the discovery of inscriptions recording dedications to Persephone: *N Sc*, 1909, 321 ff.

[6] xxix. 18. 3.

are often shown in the pinakes in use or hanging on a wall, and there are representations of doors studded with bronze rosettes, and of bronze fittings on furniture. These should be used to supplement our knowledge of Lokrian bronze-work gained from the small bronzes themselves, which begin at about the same time as the pinakes, though their greatest development is after the middle of the fifth century. Evidence of close contact between bronze and clay workers is the unusual technique on many pinakes of stippling for dress, which would be more effective in bronze than in clay.

The general style of the pinakes has long been recognized as East Greek, but detailed comparisons have not been made to suggest to which East Greek works or schools they are related. Though different hands and tendencies may be detected, they form a single style with strongly marked local characteristics. This appears suddenly, without antecedents in Lokroi or anywhere in the western colonial area; and, as it ionizes in many details, it is likely that the men responsible for its introduction came to Lokroi from Ionia in the last decades of the sixth century. The pinakes belong to a period from c. 510 to the middle of the fifth century, thus covering two generations. The first generation has a marked East Greek impression in such details as the splendid winged horses, recalling those on Klazomenian vases, and the long pointed head which is a feature of many East Greek monuments. As the East Greek influence is not single or constant, it is likely that the Ionian element was reinforced by new immigration in the early fifth century. The second generation is more affected by the dominant Peloponnesian and Attic art of the period, and retains some strongly archaic characteristics well into the classical period. This is natural in a school cut off from its origins and remote from the great centres of art. The dominant impression of all the pinakes is, however, not their dependence on Ionia nor their slight archaism, but their strong individual quality. The artists, whatever their origin, developed a school of their own and produced a worthy independent style.

The masterpieces of this style are to be recognized in the great reliefs, the Ludovisi and Boston thrones[1] and the

[1] Ludovisi throne: Rome, Terme Museum; *AD*, ii, pll. 6–7; E. Peterson, *RM*, vii. 32 ff.; L. D. Caskey, *AJA*, 1918, 101 ff. Boston throne: Boston; *AD*, iii, pll. 7–8; F. Studniczka, *JdI*, 1911, 50 ff.; Caskey, *AJA*, 1918, 101 ff. There is a long and controversial literature about the two 'thrones' and their original purpose and place of origin. I follow B. Ashmole, *JHS*, 1922, 248 ff.

Esquiline stele.[1] The Ludovisi and Boston thrones are the two halves, in marble, of a hollow square with reliefs on the outer face, and it seems likely that they once decorated the two sides of a shallow pit in the sanctuary of Persephone at Lokroi, where the pinakes were dedicated. They were brought in ancient times to Rome, where they were found. The case for this origin rests in part on the excavations of Lokroi, in part on stylistic arguments. There are many points of comparison between the thrones and the pinakes and, more important, the effect of the style, with its slight archaisms and its emphasis on purity of line, is like that of the pinakes and most unlike the sculptural 'severe style' of contemporary works of mainland Greece. The sweet nobility of the Ludovisi throne, in particular (for the Boston half, though surely to be associated as part of the same original whole, differs in execution and bears the impress of a different artistic personality), makes it one of the finest works of Greek art.

We have few of the major works of sculpture which may stand to the small terra-cottas and bronzes of the western cities as the Ludovisi throne does to the Lokrian pinakes. Most of them fall outside the limits of the period covered by this book, as indeed the Ludovisi throne does strictly. One other large work has survived at Lokroi: the pair of akroteria in marble, representing the Dioskouroi dismounting from their horses, whose hoofs are supported by Tritons.[2] This belongs to the middle of the fifth century, and commemorates the highest point of Lokrian history, the victory of the Sagra about a hundred years earlier, when the Dioskouroi came over the sea from Sparta to aid the Lokrian arms.[3] The subject appears to be treated also in the earlier fragmentary terra-cotta akroterion from the Marafioti temple, of a youthful rider whose horse is held up by a sphinx.[4]

At Lokroi, and there only, the Ionic order of architecture was introduced in the early fifth century. The Marazá temple, the only Ionic building of so early a date in the west, was

---

[1] Rome, Conservatori, no. 5; *JHS*, 1922, pl. 11.

[2] Naples; from the Ionic temple of Marazá. *N Sc*, 1890, 248 ff.; E. Peterson, *RM*, 1890, 161 ff.; *AD*, i, pl. 52; S. Ferri, *Boll. d'Arte*, 1927, 159 ff. Ferri rejects the connexion with the battle of the Sagra in favour of a chthonic interpretation, the Dioskouroi, one of whom lives above ground for a day while the other dies, being the guides to the lower world. But is this a likely subject for an akroterion, as far towards heaven and Olympos as a man can reach?

[3] See below, p. 358 f.

[4] *N Sc*, 1911 Suppl., 42 ff.; P. Orsi, *Dedalo*, vi. 345 ff.

rebuilt *c.* 480 B.C.[1] Its earlier form is unknown, but it is likely
that it was an uncanonical building with wooden superstructure, like many early colonial temples. It was rebuilt many
times both before and after 480 (the akroteria of the Dioskouroi
were added in the middle of the fifth century), and it is not
certain at what point of time the Ionic form was introduced;
but it was certainly in the late sixth or early fifth century.
The columns are like those of the Samian Heraion, and the
Samian foot has been detected as the basis of its measurements.[2]

There is only one other Ionic temple in Italy, of later date
(fifth to fourth century B.C.), at the Lokrian colony of Hipponion.[3] But some Doric temples have Ionic elements. The
Marafioti temple, at Lokroi, has some Ionic details in the treatment of the entablature.[4] A temple of mixed forms, with
Ionic capital and Doric frieze, is shown on Lokrian pinakes.[5]
It is convincingly argued by Signora Zancani Montuoro that
this is not a fantastic construction of the artist (the most
fantastic feature, the representation of pentaglyphs instead of
triglyphs, is paralleled in the Marafioti temple) but illustrates
an actual building. Further, the building will naturally be the
shrine of Persephone in which the pinakes were dedicated, of
whose superstructure nothing has survived. A mixture of Doric
and Ionic forms is found at Poseidonia also, where the archaic
temple of Hera at the mouth of the Sele, built at about the
same time as the Marafioti temple, has an Ionic kymation.[6]
The so-called 'temple of Ceres' also has a Lesbian kymation
and perhaps other Ionic forms; an Ionic base was found in the
porch.[7] Elsewhere in south Italy an East Greek influence is
traceable in architectural details, for instance, the late sixth-
century sima from Kaulonia,[8] the fine clay head of a sphinx-

---

[1] Koldewey and Puchstein, 7; Robertson, 103, 332; *N Sc*, 1890, 248 ff. For divergent
opinions on the date see G. Säflund, *Opuscula Archaeologica*, ii (1941), 87. As the dedications
of the temples at Lokroi are unknown, they are called by the modern name of the locality
in which each is found.

[2] Dörpfeld ap. Petersen, *RM*, 1890, 182 f.   [3] *N Sc*, 1921, 476.

[4] Robertson, 103–5; *N Sc*, 1911 Suppl., 27 ff.

[5] *Ausonia*, iii. 228–9, figs. 80–1; P. Zancani Montuoro, *RIASA*, vii (1940), 205 ff.

[6] *N Sc*, 1937, 234 ff.

[7] Koldewey and Puchstein, 19, 22; Robertson, 76 ff. ('the porch columns may have been
Ionic'); F. Krauss, *RM*, 1931, 1 ff. Another western building with a mixture of Doric and
Ionic forms, belonging also to the late sixth century, is the temple at Kardaki on Corfu,
a Doric temple without frieze, with Ionic *kymation* on the architrave (Weickert, *Typen der
archaischen Architektur*, 154 ff.; cf. de La Coste-Messelière, *Au Musée de Delphes*, 33 ff.).

[8] *MA*, xxiii. 863 ff.; G. Säflund, *Opuscula Archaeologica*, ii (1941), 77 ff.

acroterion, and the lions' masks from the Passoliera temple in the same city.[1] Other buildings at Kroton, Metauron (another Lokrian colony), and Rhegion had terra-cotta revetments of Ionic form.[2]

These combinations of Doric and Ionic architectural features, the chief archaic example of which in Old Greece was the throne of Bathykles at Amyklai, were carried out on a larger scale at Lokroi and Poseidonia. The classical Doric of the Parthenon received one such Ionic addition in the frieze of the Panathenaia which surrounds cella and opisthodomus. Other experiments were not so received, but their adoption in the west shows how vigorous was the architecture of the Italian colonies in the late sixth and early fifth centuries, and makes the temples of Poseidonia one of the most interesting groups of buildings in the Greek world. In Sicily architects were at this time more conventional. The innovations of Poseidonia were followed at Selinus, alone of Sicilian cities.[3] Elsewhere the adoption of Ionic details is limited to non-architectural features. The finest example is the splendid relief with volutes on the late-sixth-century altar of the Athenaion at Syracuse.[4] Other pieces in a similar style are a relief from Akrai[5] and a pilaster from Megara Hyblaia, which will be older than the destruction of Megara c. 483.[6] There is an Ionic capital, of unknown purpose but good period, from Molinello near Leontinoi.[7] At Selinus the Apollonion (G) has Ionic *anta* capitals, which belong probably in the first half of the fifth century.[8] Ionic forms are further used for votive stelai[9] and are illustrated on coins.[10] Many of the capitals or other Ionic forms surviving in the west can be paralleled on small buildings such as the fountains illustrated on Attic black-figure vases.[11] The Ionic column had, of course, a much more widespread use as an accessory, on furniture, small objects such as mirror-handles, and other small bronzes.

[1] Säflund, op. cit. 95, fig. 15; *MA*, xxix. 426 ff., pll. 3–7.
[2] Ionic frieze (?) in the Griso-Laboccetta temple at Rhegion: N. Putortì, *Italia antichissima*, i. 27 ff. Terra-cotta volutes from an archaic temple at Metauron, *N Sc*, 1902, 129. Kroton: Säflund, op. cit. 87 f.
[3] Koldewey and Puchstein, 213.
[4] *MA*, xxv. 693 ff., pl. 23.
[5] Ibid., fig. 253.
[6] *MA*, i, pl. 2 *bis*.
[7] *N Sc*, 1902, 419, fig. 10.
[8] Koldewey and Puchstein, 122.
[9] Selinus: Koldewey and Puchstein, 84, 94; Syracuse: *MA*, xxv. 419, fig. 34. Cf. Metapontion, Borrmann, *JdI*, 1888, 276.
[10] See examples quoted by Pace, *Arte ed Artisti*, 480, n. 1.
[11] B. Dunkley, *BSA*, xxxvi. 161 ff.

A special class are the large clay sarcophagi of Gela, many of which have Ionic columns inside at the corners.[1]

The East Greek influence, which at Lokroi and elsewhere in south Italy is felt in the last quarter of the sixth century, hardly affects Sicily before the end of the century.[2] In the middle of the sixth century Sicily, and especially Syracuse, was stagnant, and it is only under the rule of the tyrants or very little before their time that there are signs of a general economic emancipation which brought artistic awakening.[3] In the early fifth century East Greek influence is strongly felt in Sicily also, and is probably to be ascribed to the settlement of Ionian artists, whether they came as members of migrant bodies or were attracted as individuals by the tyrants. This influence is not so strong as the dominant mainland influence, first Peloponnesian, later Attic. It is patchy, as might be expected if it is the personal influence of individual artists, not impersonal 'influences' which follow the import of works of art.

There are more records of Ionian immigration to Italy than to Sicily, and with this the evidence of art agrees. There is one artist's name preserved, Pythagoras of Rhegion. His artistic activity falls in the first half of the fifth century; he made statues of the Olympic victors Astylos of Kroton, Euthymos of Lokroi, and Leontiskos of Messana, of whom the first was victor in 484, the last in 452.[4] So it is likely that he came to Rhegion as a young man with the Samians invited to Sicily by the Zanklaians in 494.[5] Most of his recorded activity was in Italy or for Italiot clients, and he is commonly called a Rhegine. But he describes himself in a surviving inscription, that on the base of the monument of Euthymos, as ΠΥΘΑΓΟΡΑΣ ΣΑΜΙΟΣ.[6] None of his works has survived, nor can copies be recognized with conviction. His influence is observed in a group of terra-cottas from Lokroi and Medma.[7] It is likely that his style owed little to his Samian origin, but was formed by the common influences

---

[1] *MA*, xvii. 519 ff., figs. 362, 365 ff.; 737, fig. 558.

[2] Ionizing terra-cottas of the second half of the sixth century: Syracuse, from Megara, V. Müller, *RM*, 1923–4, 60 ff.; Gela, *MA*, xvii, pl. 52; fig. 532 and others. See also p. 288.

[3] See above, pp. 249 ff.

[4] Euseb., ed. Schoene, i. 204; *Ox. Pap.* 222. The dates of Astylos' victories are given in the Eusebian list as the 73rd, 74th, and 75th Olympiads (488, 484, 480). As *Ox. Pap.* 222 names him as victor in 480 and 476, and his three victories were in successive Olympiads (Paus. vi. 13. 1), the date given in Eusebius for his first victory must be wrong.

[5] See below, p. 388.

[6] *Olympia*, v. 247 ff.; Loewy, *Inschriften griechischer Bildhauer*, no. 23.

[7] Von Duhn, *Ausonia*, viii. 35 ff.

which were creating the classical style in the most advanced regions of Greece.

Rhegion was then certainly a centre of artistic influence in the first half of the fifth century, but chance has preserved little of this date there. Similarly Sybaris, which must have been the centre of colonial culture before its destruction in 510, and from its friendship with Miletos may be expected to have been open to East Greek influences, is archaeologically unknown.[1] The hazard of survival has decreed that the finest art of this period should come from the little city of Lokroi. Lokroi had won renown but not riches by her victory over Kroton at the Sagra (c. 540), and as late as c. 468 was much less a power than her neighbours Kroton and Rhegion. Perhaps the exiles who included the artists of the pinakes welcomed a quiet town and so charming a scene as Lokroi. For, though we must assume that Ionian artists settled elsewhere, whose works have not survived, it cannot be simply the accident of preservation which makes Lokroi so prominent in the artistic history of the time. Enough is preserved elsewhere, at Taras and in Sicily for example, to show that the East Greek influence was not equally strong everywhere. Many of the sites which show it are colonies or neighbours of Lokroi. Elsewhere it is seen in works, such as terra-cotta revetments and figurines, whose makers are not definitely men from Ionia, but may have absorbed Ionian influences as something external. Lokrian art has not indeed a wide influence before the middle of the fifth century; it is surprising that it is not more imitated. The dominant influences are those of the Peloponnese and Athens.[2] In the middle of the century, when a general western style can be distinguished with branches in many local schools in the colonies, the Lokrian style and the presumed influence of Pythagoras are only two of many elements which contribute to the formation of this style.

[1] Cf. above, p. 76, n. 1.
[2] See V. H. Poulsen, *Acta Archaeologica*, viii. 87 ff.

CHAPTER X
HIMERA, SELINUS, AKRAGAS

SOON after the middle of the seventh century the first step was taken in the Greek colonization of the west of Sicily.[1] A body of Zanklaians, with the not inconsiderable support of the exiled clan of the Myletidai from Syracuse, sailed along the north coast and occupied the site of Himera. Three oecists are named, Eukleides, Simos, and Sakon. They passed many promising sites and settled in a position which is not strongly recommended by possessing either good corn-land or a harbour. It has indeed rich mixed country and a way into the interior of the island, and the beach with a river-mouth was at that period all that was needed for shipping; but there is no obvious reason for settling at Himera rather than many other sites. The only logical reason is that it is the westernmost site outside Phoenician territory, and has, moreover, considerable natural strength. This does not necessarily mean that it was directed against the Phoenicians; there is no evidence so early as this of an anti-Phoenician policy, and no reason why Khalkidians or Syracusans should be hostile. It may be only that they wished to push as far to the west as possible, with a view not only to securing the greater part of Sicily to Greek colonists but to taking up a position for ventures farther west. Whatever the purpose of the colony, its foundation and that of Selinus were the first unwitting steps in the long warfare of Greek and Phoenician in Sicily.

Another possible reason for the placing of Himera so far to the west was to serve as a convenient port of call between Kyme or Etruria and Carthage.[2] It has been suggested that most of the Corinthian vases at Carthage were imported via Italy, and possibly in Kymaian ships;[3] they would naturally, on the voyage to Carthage, call at one of the Phoenician ports in Sicily. This traffic, which began so far as we know c. 675, became considerable in the late seventh century. If some of the ships took to calling at Himera *en route* instead of Panormos

---

[1] Thuk. vi. 5; Strabo 272. The date rests entirely on Diod. xiii. 62; precisely the same evidence is generally rejected in the case of Selinus, so it cannot be taken as exact for Himera: the two foundations may have been nearer in time, as Diodoros suggests. There is no archaeological evidence; cf. Payne, *NC*, 24.

[2] The suggestion is Blakeway's.

[3] *NC*, 188.

or Motye, that would be another reason why the foundation of Himera should ultimately poison relations between Greeks and Phoenicians. Himera was certainly interested, from the early sixth century and possibly earlier, in the trade with Spain, being the nearest Greek colony on the direct route.[1] Stesikhoros' *Geryoneis* reflects the interest of the Himeraians in Spain and in other distant Greek ventures, as well as his personal feelings. The coinage of Himera, which is one of the earliest western colonies to coin, before the middle of the sixth century,[2] is witness to the prosperity of the city. The source of silver may have been Tartessos, but the coinage continues to be copious after the breaking off of Greek relations with Tartessos (*c.* 540). Silver may then have come indirectly from Spain through Carthaginian hands. Apart from the value of direct imports from Spain and Carthage, the advantages of revictualling and refreshing ships' crews on these two important routes must have been great.

In or about the year 628[3] the Sicilian Megarians followed this example and founded a colony at Selinus, with as oecist Pamillos, a citizen of old Megara. As in the case of Himera, there is no compelling reason why they should settle there rather than elsewhere on the south coast. It has often been asked why they sailed past Akragas to settle at Selinus. It is likely, though not certain, that Akragas already had a Geloan post.[4] But in any case it does not lie in an area of plain land like most colonial cities. Its wealth lay later in vine and olive and stock-raising. Selinus, though in a less strong military position and a less varied country-side, had a good corn-raising plain, which is what the land-hungry Megarians most needed. They were crowded out of their little plain, wedged between Syracuse and Leontinoi, who prevented them from expanding into the hills behind. About 608 they were at war with the Leontines over the borders of the land,[5] and this may well have been a chronic state since their first settlement.

There was no obvious site for a city at Selinus, and many disadvantages in that chosen. Though defensible, the low hill is not a commanding position, and needed strong fortifications. There was no port and very poor shelter.[6] The marshes into

[1] See above, p. 248.
[2] Cf. Milne, *Num. Chron.* 1938, 36 ff.; Cahn, *Die Münzen der Sizilischen Stadt Naxos*, 76.
[3] For the date see below, pp. 437 ff.
[4] See pp. 137, 307 ff.   [5] Polyainos v. 47.
[6] The suggestion in Hulot–Fougères, *Sélinonte*, 154 ff., that there were deep bays at the

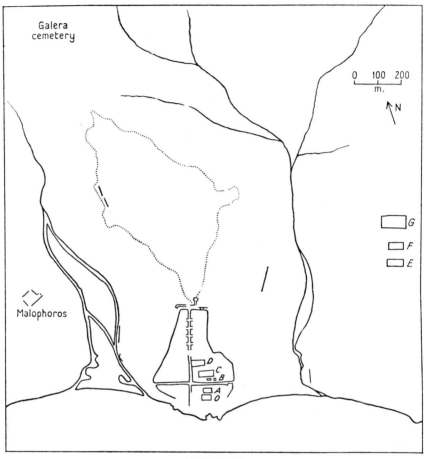

Galera
cemetery

0 100 200
m.

N

G
F
E

Malophoros

D
C
B

A
0

SELINUS

which the two rivers run made it unhealthy. In all these respects it is like a rather inferior version of Gela. The plain of Selinus, like the plain of Gela, to-day supports a town of the second rank for Sicily, but Castelvetrano, the successor of Selinus, turns its back on the sea and devotes itself entirely to agriculture. The present desolation of Megara and Selinus is an interesting commentary on Megarian blindness. But in spite of the natural disadvantages of the site, Selinus flourished greatly, chiefly through the energy and originality of the inhabitants, and largely also from its favourable position for trade with Carthage. We cannot say whether many citizens of Megara Nisaia came with Pamillos to Selinus. The north-eastern expansion in the second quarter of the seventh century should have relieved old Megara of most of her surplus population, and the obvious barriers to the expansion of Megara Hyblaia suggest that the colony was for her advantage and that she provided most of the men.[1] The forms of grave at Megara and Selinus are similar,[2] and the burial customs the same. In both places most of the graves were used several times, the period of use being often nearly a century. The cemeteries of Megara Nisaia have not been excavated, so it is not possible to extend the comparison.

Close constitutional parallels exist between Megara Nisaia and the Pontic colonies, but no such connexion is traceable between Megara and Selinus.[3] Little is known of the constitution of Selinus and nothing of that of Megara Hyblaia. The cults suggest that Selinus had greater independence than other Megarian colonies. There are many more exact parallels with Megara Nisaia at Byzantion, Khalkedon, Kallatis, and the other Megarian colonies of this area than with Selinus.[4] The principal cults of Selinus, indeed, were derived from old Megara. Apollo is the chief god of both cities.[5] In his temple at Selinus,

mouths of the two rivers is unlikely, though the remains of quays (loc. cit.) show that the sea has receded.

[1] The name or ethnic ΜΕ]ΓΑΡΕΥΣ is recorded in a Selinuntine inscription, *N Sc*, 1917, 344, n. 3.

[2] Cavallari, *Bollettino della Commissione di Antichità e Belle Arte di Sicilia*, 1872, no. 5, 11–16. Hulot–Fougères, *Sélinonte*, 162.

[3] K. Hanell, *Megarische Studien*, 149 ff.

[4] Ibid. 163.

[5] Ibid. 164; Pareti, 236 ff. Apollo was worshipped as Pythaeus at Megara, and also at Kallatis and Byzantion. Though Selinus was very closely connected with Delphi there is no evidence that Apollo was worshipped there as Pythaeus. This argument is, however, not to be pressed: Paian is the only title of Apollo known at Selinus (*IG*, xiv. 269).

the colossal temple on the eastern hill,[1] was set up the great fifth-century inscription rendering thanks to all the gods for victories granted.[2]

The cult of Malophoros is certainly derived from Megara Nisaia,[3] and is the only one which is common to the metropolis and colony and no other state. Pasikrateia, who is associated with Malophoros in her temenos outside the city to the west, may be of Sicilian origin. The name is nowhere else known as a title of Kore. Zeus Meilikhios, whose cult was at Selinus practised in the temenos of Malophoros, is attested at Megara Nisaia as an object of private worship only.[4] None of the other cults of Selinus can certainly be traced back to Megara; it must be remembered that the intermediate stage of Megara Hyblaia is completely unknown.

Other parallels between Selinus and Megara, or Selinus and other Megarian colonies, are of the most general kind.[5] But none of the Selinuntine cults can be shown to be probably derived from any other Greek state. There is no evidence that the site of Selinus was inhabited by Sikels before the foundation of the colony, and no indication that there may be native elements in the cults of the Greek city. It is probable, therefore, that most of the cults of Selinus are Megarian, common to both Megara Hyblaia and Megara Nisaia. But the precise proof which is presented in the Pontic colonies of Megara is lacking at Selinus, and it may be that the religion of Selinus was more generally panhellenic, or, in the cult of Kore, pansikeliot.

The rectangular street-plan of the acropolis of Selinus is as old as the sixth century.[6] The existing houses all belong to the reconstruction of the city after the Carthaginian sack of 409. But the exact alinement of the temples indicates that at least the two main cross-streets are as old as temple D. C is differently oriented from D. C, F, the megaron south of C, and the altar east of C are the oldest buildings on the acropolis which were left standing after the middle of the sixth century. D, the buildings facing the street west of C, and the house A to the south of C, perhaps a Propylon, are all alined to the rectangular

---

[1] See above, p. 284.   [2] *IG*, xiv. 268; Tod, *GHI*, no. 37.

[3] Hanell, 175; Paus. i. 44. 3; cf. Byzantine month Malophorios (Hanell, 190).

[4] *JHS*, 1898, 332. Cf. also at Perachora, *Perachora*, i. 7.

[5] Pareti, ch. ix; and Hanell's criticism, p. 163.

[6] *MA*, xxxiii. 109 ff.; see plans, pll. I–V. Pl. V represents most clearly the sixth-century remains. Contra, von Gerkan, *Griechische Städteanlagen*, 31, 36, who wrote before the results of Gàbrici's excavations on the acropolis were known.

plan. Older walls (I on Gàbrici's pl. III) lie underneath D, and the main north–south street cuts across some foundations to the north of the temples. These may all be of the early sixth century, and the buildings which face on the two main streets of the second half of the sixth century. There was a replanning of the acropolis area soon after the middle of the sixth century, when the south-eastern terrace was built to support the colonnade running round the outside of the open space east of temple C.[1] At the same time, probably, at least the framework of the rectangular plan was laid down. If this is correct it is the first piece of regular Greek town-planning which has survived.[2]

The architecture and art of Selinus, and particularly the evidence from the important sanctuary of Malophoros, which has been excavated with a care and thoroughness unequalled in Sicily and is rich in the remains of the archaic period, dating from the early years after the foundation of the colony, are discussed above.[3] This sanctuary shows an almost incredible architectural activity, buildings having become obsolete and having been replaced after twenty years.[4] This energy is constant throughout the history of Selinus, where half a dozen large temples were taken in hand within a century and which had the only school of sculpture known in Sicily in the sixth century, and a flourishing commerce. In these respects Selinus is at this time the most interesting of the western colonies. Politically as well as artistically and economically she forms with her neighbours Himera and Akragas a separate province from the cities of eastern Sicily. This is perhaps due to the stimulus of closer relations with another civilized people, the Phoenicians.[5]

Akragas is the only site in the west of Sicily where Bronze Age vases from the Aegean have been found.[6] It has the nearest approach to a harbour on the south coast, and though the port of the Greek city was not at Porto Empedocle but on the open beach, the shelter near at hand would be an advantage to shipping. When the Greeks first visited the vicinity is not clear. Siculan III–IV vases with traces of Greek influence

---

[1] Op. cit. 100.

[2] For traces of rectangular plan in other Sicilian towns cf. Orsi, *N Sc*, 1925, 313.

[3] pp. 276 ff., 280 ff.

[4] See *MA*, xxxii. 154 for the short life of the first megaron of Malophoros and the homogeneity of the deposits of votives.

[5] Cf. below, pp. 334 ff.   [6] *Ausonia*, i. 10, fig. 3.

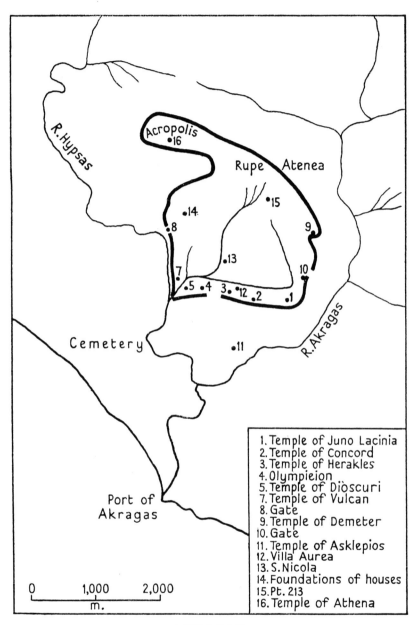

Port of
Akragas

Cemetery

R.Hypsas

Acropolis
•16

Rupe   Atenea

•15

•14

•8

•13

7
•
•5 •4   3• •12 •2   •1

9

10

R.Akragas

•11

0   1,000   2,000
m.

1. Temple of Juno Lacinia
2. Temple of Concord
3. Temple of Herakles
4. Olympieion
5. Temple of Dioscuri
7. Temple of Vulcan
8. Gate
9. Temple of Demeter
10. Gate
11. Temple of Asklepios
12. Villa Aurea
13. S. Nicola
14. Foundations of houses
15. Pt. 213
16. Temple of Athena

AKRAGAS

have been found at Naro and at Montaperto near Agrigento,[1] without Greek imports, but do not prove that their makers were in direct contact with Greeks. Protocorinthian pottery is said to have been found in the cemetery of Montelusa, between Akragas and the sea.[2] It may be doubted whether it is not Corinthian rather than Protocorinthian.

At the sanctuary below S. Biagio, Marconi records 'a first stratum of sherds of the third and fourth Siculan periods mixed with Greek Geometric sherds, especially Protocorinthian, with the usual decorative repertory of points and wavy lines'.[3] This material, or some of it, is in the vaults of Syracuse Museum. None of it was accessible to me. Only the Hellenistic deposit is illustrated by Marconi,[4] and it alone is exhibited in Agrigento Museum. To judge from the brief description, the 'Protocorinthian' might be Late Corinthian. The oldest part of the existing sanctuary building is considered to belong to the seventh century.[5] It is a long, narrow building in front of a cave from which a stream of water issues, passes through a raised channel which divides the building into two unequal parts, and flows into a series of troughs along the front of the building. The remarkable architectural features are the false vault which roofs the narrow space, which is not regular in Greek architecture, though it was very widespread in the Mediterranean in the second millennium B.C. and survived in the tholos tombs of the Sikels, of which there are roughly contemporary examples at S. Angelo Muxaro, within fifteen miles of Agrigento;[6] and the 'proto-Doric' cornice, which is the most

[1] P. Marconi, *Agrigento*, 21. Siculan III from Montaperto in the Museo Preistorico at Rome, Blakeway, *BSA*, xxxiii. 188.

[2] *Agrigento*, 22 (end of eighth and seventh centuries); *RIASA*, 1930, 55: 'Geometric and Protocorinthian pottery, of Greek importation the small vases, aryballoi, bombylioi, &c., of local manufacture those of large dimensions'—Geloan geometric amphoras (?) Marconi thinks from a settlement on the beach. None of this material is exhibited in Agrigento Museum, and Protocorinthian alabastra are such a rarity that one suspects them of being Early Corinthian.

[3] *Studi Agrigentini*, 43. His strata here are (1) Siculan III–IV and Protocorinthian, (2) Corinthian, b.f., and archaic statuettes, (3) hellenistic. In *Agrigento*, 25, he speaks of 'frammenti fittili del III e IV periodo siculo, e sopra, da molti frammenti protocorinzi e corinzi' of the eighth and seventh centuries. Siculan IV is distinguished from Siculan III chiefly by its associations with Greek pottery. It could not lie under Protocorinthian. I have heard of Early Corinthian and perhaps Transitional vases which were seen during the excavation of the site.

[4] *Studi*, fig. 9.

[5] Loc. cit.

[6] Orsi, 'La necropoli di S. Angelo Muxaro', in *Atti della R. Accademia di Palermo*, xvii. Cf. above, pp. 139 ff.

rudimentary example known. The slightly more developed cornice in the first Megaron of Malophoros at Selinus[1] belongs to the earliest years of the colony, and takes its place at the beginning of the development of Doric architecture. But this at Akragas is so simple that it can hardly be said to have stylistic elements, and may be the work of builders out of touch with the architectural ideas of the day. It is not a temple or similar rectangular building, but a spring-house, one of the compartments of which was probably full of water, and there was no access to the inside, unless there was a floor at about 4 feet above the ground. Offerings to the spring are not inconsistent with this view, which would also explain why such offerings had been made by Sikels before the Greeks. The false vault also may be a device that occurred independently to the builders to roof a narrow space rather than a borrowing from Sikel funerary architecture, which would indicate a mixing of Greeks and Sikels in the local worship.[2] On the hypothesis of extreme inexperience, as of pioneering architecture, the building is likely to be older than the foundation of the colony. The earliest buildings of Akragas, with this exception, are simple but perfectly regular, and at no time after the foundation could the city have lacked architects to apply the known principles of architecture. But it is impossible to put a date to the spring-house, and by implication to the little group of Greek pioneers who put it up.

There is said also to be Protocorinthian from the two altars in the sanctuary by the temple of the Dioscuri,[3] and Marconi carries the sanctuary back to the seventh century. None of the 'Protocorinthian' is much older than the middle of the sixth century, which is also the date of the earliest Attic. The area is not rich in pottery. The oldest terra-cottas belong to the early sixth century, and are as old as nearly anything at Selinus. There are few seventh-century terra-cottas from Selinus, but one would expect the interval of half a century between the foundations of Selinus and Akragas to be reflected in the terra-cottas. The architectural forms of the little build-

---

[1] *MA*, xxxii. 66; xxxv. 141 ff.   [2] As Marconi, *Agrigento*, 27.

[3] *Studi*, 65, figs. 22–4 (degenerate Late Corinthian kotylai; in fig. 22, some Attic b.f. of the late 6th cent.); in *Agrigento Arcaica*, 70, all the material in this sanctuary area is published together, and in Agrigento Museum it has been lumped together without distinction of exact provenience or level. It includes aryballoi, pl. XVI, no. 4, cf. Payne, *NC*, no. 1263, fig. 161; no. 5, cf. *NC*, no. 1244, fig. 160; nos. 6, 7, 8, miniature kotylai. Fig. 39, no. 1 is not Protocorinthian but Attic.

ings are also very little developed from the earliest buildings at Selinus. But the same forms were still used in the fourth century for treasuries and other little sanctuary buildings, and some of the examples at Akragas are certainly not as old as the early sixth century. The conclusion is that this sanctuary belongs to the first years of the colony of Akragas, but nothing in it is certainly older than this date. A few of the terra-cottas may have been brought there already made, or made on the spot from old moulds or in a style that had begun to go out of date.

To complete the tale, Marconi speaks of Protocorinthian from the precinct on the hill point 213,[1] and from the little temple at the Villa Aurea.[2] In both places there are only degenerate Late Corinthian kotylai. In fact I know of no Protocorinthian or Early Corinthian with a definitely attested Akragantine provenience. All that I have seen of Marconi's Protocorinthian is Late Corinthian, except some that is not Corinthian at all. The only possibility is that there is in Syracuse Museum from Marconi's excavations genuine Protocorinthian, or, more likely, Early Corinthian. In Agrigento Museum, which houses a good deal of material from unscientific excavations in the cemeteries, there is very little Corinthian, and that all Late or late in the Middle period, exactly corroborating the historically recorded date of the foundation. In private collections in Agrigento[3] I know of three Late Protocorinthian aryballoi, about a dozen Transitional aryballoi,[4] and a good deal of Early and Middle Corinthian. None of these vases is certainly from Akragas, for all the collections have been made in part elsewhere. Nothing therefore has been found which was certainly imported to Akragas before the foundation of the colony, but some Early and Middle Corinthian without assured provenience was possibly found there. In both public and private collections there is a good deal more Late Corinthian than Early or Middle.

No one supposes that Akragas was founded out of the blue

---

[1] N Sc, 1932, 408; Agrigento Arcaica, 144, 'documento cronologico, un piccolo scodellino protocorinzio'.

[2] Studi, 57. On the evidence of ground-plan and revetments this little building belongs to the second quarter of the sixth century, and the pottery agrees very well with that date.

[3] I thank Barone Giudice, Professore Giuliano, Cav. Giuffrida, and Signor De Angelis for permission to study the vases in their collections, and for information about them. In Dumont–Chaplain, ii, 181, M. Haussoullier is reported to have seen Corinthian vases from Akragas in the Museum of Termini Imerese. There are now no vases there and I have not traced them.   [4] Including NC, no. 264 (Giudice Coll.).

in the year 580 B.C. The site had been visited in Mycenaean times,[1] and Greek influence in the Siculan pottery of the neighbourhood shows that communications were resumed in the seventh century. Perhaps as early as the last quarter of the seventh century there were visitors, presumably Geloans; it may be, a small trading-post. The S. Biagio sanctuary was built probably before the foundation of the colony. This is the only evidence of Greek occupation, as distinct from trading visits. The quantity of material belonging to the period 580–550 contrasts strongly with this scanty evidence of pre-colonization settlement, which, however, is more clearly witnessed here than elsewhere, as might be expected in view of the late date.[2]

The foundation was 108 years after Gela,[3] which is c. 688. It has not yet been suggested that 108 is three generations of 36 years. The hundred years of Pindar Ol. ii. 93[4] are said by the scholiast to be a round figure for 104, and the foundation to fall in Ol. 50. The victory which Ol. ii celebrates was won in 476. 580 is probably the exact date. The scholiast's note is probably based on a system of dates like the Eusebian ones, drawn from Thukydides.

The oecists Aristonous and Pystilos were probably one Rhodian, one Geloan.[5] There is no evidence of Cretan participation, and Crete had already declined into the apathy in which she remains through the sixth and fifth centuries. Many of the colonists came from Rhodes and the neighbouring islands. Indeed Polybios calls it a Rhodian colony.[6] Among the Rhodians was Theron's ancestor Telemakhos, with a following.[7] The passage Pindar, Ol. ii. 7 ff.[8] was anciently interpreted of

---

[1] Ausonia, i. 10.

[2] Marconi's opinion (Agrigento, 27) is that Akragas was visited more than a century before the foundation, and he allows a long period of continuous occupation. The nature of the evidence on which he bases this has already been discussed.

[3] Thuk. vi. 4.

[4] τεκεῖν μή τιν' ἑκατόν γε ἐτέων πόλιν
φίλοις ἄνδρα μᾶλλον
εὐεργέταν πραπίσιν ἀφθονέστερόν τε χέρα
Θήρωνος.

[5] As at Zankle, where one oecist was from Kyme, one from Khalkis (Thuk. vi. 4).

[6] ix. 27.

[7] Schol. Ol. ii. 82d: . . . ὅθεν συλλέξας δύναμιν ἔρχεται εἰς Σικελίαν.

[8] εὐωνύμων τε πατέρων ἄωτον ὀρθόπολιν·
καμόντες οἳ πολλὰ θυμῷ
ἱερὸν ἔσχον οἴκημα ποταμοῦ, Σικελίας τ' ἔσαν
ὀφθαλμός.

the foundation of both Gela and Akragas, but the balance of opinion favoured Akragas. The phrase ἱερὸν οἴκημα ποταμοῦ is much more appropriate to Akragas[1] than to Gela, a city with which Pindar had no concern. And the encomium on Theron,[2] quoted by one of the scholiasts ad loc., is conclusive: ἐν δὲ ʹΡόδον κατᾳοίκισθεν ... ἔνθεν δ᾽ ἀφορμαθέντες ὑψηλὰν πόλιν ἀμφινέμονται: the lofty city can only be Akragas.[3]

The cults earliest attested at Akragas are Rhodian. The cult of Zeus Atabyrios was brought from Rhodes to Akragas,[4] the acropolis of Akragas was apparently called Atabyrion,[5] and the famous bull of Phalaris was derived from the bronze bulls on top of Mount Atabyrion in Rhodes.[6] The cult of Zeus Atabyrios is not known at Gela, though little is known of the cults of Gela. In Rhodes it is Kamiran, though the worship was common to all Rhodes.[7] Its importance at Akragas suggests that Kamirans as well as Lindians may have taken part in the colonization. The Athena whose temple was also on the acropolis of Akragas must be Athena Lindia, for whom frequent offerings were sent to Rhodes from Gela and Akragas. Apart from these offerings there is no evidence for her cult at Gela. The other chief worship at Akragas in archaic times, that of Demeter and Kore, would be derived from Gela. Two of the three chief cults of Akragas were thus connected with particular localities in Rhodes, and in the case of Athena Lindia the connexion was kept up by offerings sent to the mother country. This suggests that they were instituted by Rhodians from Rhodes rather than from Gela.

The year 580 is too late to expect to find Rhodian pottery at Akragas. There is a considerable import of Rhodian terracottas from that date onwards, as well as East Greek influence in the local style.[8] The sixth-century stamped pithos-rims which are a speciality of Akragas,[9] and spread in small numbers to Selinus and Motye,[10] are Rhodian in style, whereas those of Gela are derived from Crete.[11]

---

[1] Cf. *Pyth.* xii. 1–3.   [2] Fr. 105 Bowra, 119 Schroeder.

[3] The variant pedigree of Theron in Schol. *Ol.* ii. 82d, which is incomplete, brings Telemakhos to Sicily not from Rhodes, but from Thera. Telemakhos was the founder of his family, and it was not quite clear to Theron's laureates how he traced his descent back to the Theban heroes. The derivation from Thera was surely made on the strength of Theron's name.   [4] Polyb. ix. 27. 7.   [5] Cf. below, p. 316.

[6] See below, p. 320.   [7] Blinkenberg, *Lindos*, ii. 175.

[8] *Agrigento*, 174 ff.; cf. above, p. 239.   [9] *Agrigento*, 200 ff., figs. 136 ff.

[10] Selinus, Marconi, *Agrigento*, 200, 204; Motye, Whitaker, *Motya*, fig. 103.

[11] Payne, *NC*, 5 n.

It is probable that some of the citizens came from the Dorian islands and mainland cities, neighbours of Rhodes, just as Pentathlos' contemporary expedition was made up of Rhodians and Knidians. It has been thought that Phalaris came from Astypalaia, on the ground that he would not be so called in the *Letters* if it were not true.[1] This is dangerous ground. It should not be beyond the imagination of the sophist to endow him with a birthplace. And this is the only detail in the *Letters* which anyone has tried to redeem as history.

The land of Akragas is more varied and interesting than most of Sicily. Instead of the great corn-growing plain that the Greeks sought for by preference in their colonies, it is a land of hill and valley, suited for olive as well as wheat. Inland there is easy access to the undulating table-land which became one of the great granaries of the ancient world. This is the only one of the western colonies, except Leontinoi, which does not cling to the shore. In an age when the inhabitants of Old Greece were creeping down from acropolis to harbour town it is something of an anachronism. An acropolis which dominates the city is a rarity in these colonies, but this is one of the most magnificent of sites. From the sea it appears as a series of terraces, from the land as an abrupt wall. Its strength is lessened by the immense length of the circuit, and in a few points the configuration hindered the fortification instead of helping it. But it is one of the most commanding of Greek cities, and the early settlers were men of imagination to take advantage of such a site. There is no doubt that the city was planned from the first, or almost from the first, to include the whole area over which it afterwards spread. The acropolis was large and strong enough for an ordinary city, and now holds a flourishing town of 25,000 inhabitants. The area within the walls is about 900 acres (1,817 hectares), larger than any Sicilian city except Syracuse. There must from the earliest times have been conscious rivalry with the double city of Syracuse. But Syracuse could hardly exist without a mainland extension, whereas if the founders of Akragas had been less ambitious they could well have limited themselves to the acropolis.

At several points along the wall black-figure and black-glaze fragments have been found, in rocky places where they could not have to do with anything except the wall. At the Porta

---

[1] Freeman, ii. 65, 459.

Sesta were found Corinthian and black-figure sherds[1] which should date that part of the wall to about the middle of the sixth century. Even more convincing is the evidence of the temples. All the great temples along the south wall, the earliest of which was built c. 500, are exactly alined to the wall. So also is the little temple of the Villa Aurea, which belongs to the second quarter of the sixth century. There can be no doubt that the wall was already in position when these buildings were put up.[2] The methods of construction too are particularly appropriate to the sixth century. The natural line of the ground is followed faithfully, and advantage taken of every break in the rock, so that the work is less an artificial fortification than a strengthening of the natural defences. When possible the rock is cut away leaving a shelf which served as foundation for the wall, and in places along the southern edge the whole face is cut from the living rock, to a height of about 10 feet. Not all the existing work dates from the sixth century. In particular the fortifications of the gates were strengthened in the fifth century, and the massive wall at the weak point on the western side, where it crosses the valley separating the acropolis from the town, is also of that century. But it is certain that the general plan was laid down before the middle of the sixth century, and that most of the existing remains belong to that date.

Most of the earliest sanctuaries are at various points in the lower city. The great ancestral gods, Zeus and Athena, had their temples on the acropolis, but in the sixth century there were other little sanctuaries by the Olympieion,[3] by the temple of the Dioscuri,[4] and at the Villa Aurea,[5] along the southern terrace, and by S. Nicola,[6] under the temple called Vulcan's,[7] and on the hill point 213,[8] in the middle of the city; as well as the sanctuary outside the walls below S. Biagio, discussed above. These need not of course have been in the residential area, or even within the city, for at Selinus most of the temples were outside. But when it is known that all these sites were

[1] RIASA, 1930, 39.

[2] Ibid. 40 (see pp. 7–40 for these arguments at length); cf. Agrigento, 32. Schubring was already of this opinion (Akragas, 15).

[3] N Sc, 1925, 437 ff.; Agrigento, 155–6; N. Breitenstein, Acta Archaeologica, xvi. 116, fig. 2. See below, p. 325.

[4] Studi Agrigentini, iii; Agrigento Arcaica, 78–88.

[5] Studi Agrigentini, ii.

[6] Agrigento, 46; N Sc, 1926, 93 ff.

[7] Agrigento Arcaica, 123–6.

[8] N Sc, 1932, 407.

within the city walls, it is natural to suppose that they correspond somewhat to the distribution of population. The bold
southern wall was so proper a place for a line of temples that
even the earliest buildings there may have regarded nobility
of site rather than convenience of access. But those in the
middle of the city area were probably the centres of small
groups of houses.

The agora was in the lower part of the city, probably just
inside the gate (the Porta Aurea) by which the road from the
harbour entered. This was presumably its position in the sixth
century as well as later.[1] A group of sixth-century houses has
been excavated on the westernmost of the three hills that form
the central terrace.[2] The lower stories were cut from the rock,
and at the back of each house are rock-cut steps that led to the
upper story. They are not large houses, the ground floors consisting of one or two rooms, and there is nothing luxurious in
their contents. They do not lie on one of the roads leading
down to the gates, but traces of a side-road leading up to them
have been found. Foundations of other houses, and sherds
indicating habitation, have been found in many other points,
but the houses cannot be dated without excavation. On the
level ground in the south-eastern corner are the extensive
foundations of what appears to be a rich man's house. The
vast city area was never covered with houses, but in the sixth
century, as later, there appear to have been little groups of
houses over most of the area, wherever there was a spring or
fountain. There was plenty of room for public buildings and
for the immense establishments for which the rich Akragantines
became famous.

This spaciousness is something new in town-planning. When
they decided to wall the lower city the Akragantines provided
at one stroke for all conceivable growth. No other Greek city
could combine such strength with open spaces within the walls
and an uncrowded private life. It is not easy to decide whether
this plan was laid down at the foundation or is due to Phalaris.
The date of the wall and of the little sanctuary buildings cannot be determined within so narrow a period as ten years; the
sanctuary by the temple of the Dioscuri is the only one which
can confidently be ascribed to the period 580–570. But there

---

[1] Polyb. ix. 27; Cic. *Verr.* II. iv. 43, 94, 'Herculis templum est apud Agrigentinos non
longe a foro'. See *Agrigento*, 99.

[2] *RIASA*, 1930, 41–7; *Agrigento*, 41–4, figs. 17–19.

is some ground for preferring Phalaris as the originator of so striking a scheme. It was clearly a man of genius who designed the city, and the fantastic tyrant sounds more the man than the colourless oecists. The first decade was a troubled period if Pindar's phrase καμόντες οἳ πολλὰ θυμῷ is justified.[1] The Phoenicians, following up Pentathlos' defeat,[2] were making things difficult for the western colonies, perhaps also for Akragas. Phalaris had to fight several Sikan wars, and before he seized power the Sikans may have been threatening the still incompletely fortified city. Whatever the difficulties, external or internal, they were too much for the governors of the new colony, and within ten years there was a tyrant. He was not for Aristotle one of those who rose from the generalship, but one who abused a position of trust (Φάλαρις ἐκ τῶν τιμῶν).[3]

Polyainos may preserve the occasion of his seizure of power.[4] He relates that Phalaris was responsible as τελώνης for the construction of a temple of Zeus Polieus on the acropolis. With the money contributed he hired foreigners and bought slaves, accumulated materials, and persuaded the people to allow him to fence off the acropolis to prevent thefts. In other words, he formed an armed camp inside the acropolis. Then while the Thesmophoria were being celebrated he 'killed most of the men and made himself master of the women and children'—more probably seized the women who were celebrating their festival of the Thesmophoria and held them as surety for the acquiescence of the men.[5] Thus he made himself tyrant. Many of the details of this story ring true. It agrees with the topography of Akragas and with the conditions one would expect in a city only ten years founded. Polyainos' term τελώνης, though it cannot of course be pressed, agrees well with Aristotle's ἐκ τῶν τιμῶν. The political value of the building-contract for a temple is seen in the case of the Alkmaionids, and, in Sicily, of Agathokles of Syracuse.[6] The fortification of the acropolis was no doubt part of the public works on which Phalaris was engaged. There are now no traces of an acropolis wall separate from the city walls, but the depression where it would have run has been cut out and filled up since, and bears no

---

[1] *Ol.* ii. 8. See above, p. 310. But no specific difficulties in the early years of Akragas were known to the commentators; therefore they tried to explain the passage by the foundation of Gela, and Aristarkhos (ap. Schol. 29*d*) even by stasis in Rhodes which drove them out.

[2] See below, pp. 332 ff.

[3] *Pol.* 1310[b] 28.

[4] v. 1. 1.

[5] Freeman, ii. 68 n. 3.

[6] See above, p. 58

resemblance to its original form. For the most part the acropolis is defended by cliffs, and would need only a short wall to cut it off from the lower town. There could be nothing intermediate between walling the acropolis only and walling the whole area of the town, and the former is a very likely first stage. When it was done the master of the acropolis would be the master of the whole city.

The temple of Zeus Polieus has not been identified. It has been supposed that it lies under the modern cathedral of Agrigento,[1] but no traces of a temple have been found under this building.[2] The cult of Zeus Polieus is the same as that of Zeus Atabyrios, brought by the colonists from Rhodes,[3] and the Atabyrion recorded as a mountain of Sicily by Timaios[4] will be another name for the acropolis of Akragas.[5]

The scene of the Thesmophoria was perhaps the Dioscuri sanctuary in the lower town,[6] the largest sanctuary of the two goddesses in Akragas, which is sufficiently remote from the acropolis for a surprise of the kind described by Polyainos to be possible. The other story in Polyainos,[7] that Phalaris disarmed the people by holding games outside the city, shutting the gates, and setting his mercenaries to search the houses, is a colourless version of the rise-of-a-tyrant story, and the games are a doublet of the Thesmophoria held in the lower part of the town.[8]

Phalaris carried out a vigorous foreign policy. Polyainos has two tales of Sikan wars,[9] one against Teutos of Ouessa, whom he tricked by offering him his daughter's hand and sending young soldiers dressed as bridal attendants into the town; another against an unnamed town which he reduced by persuading the natives to exchange good corn for bad. We may

---

[1] Koldewey and Puchstein, 139.   [2] Marconi, *Agrigento*, 80.
[3] Polyb. ix. 27. 7. Cf. above, p. 311.
[4] Schol. *Ol.* vii. 159–60; Steph. Byz. s.v. Ἀτάβυρον . . . ἐστι καὶ Σικελίας Ἀταβύριον, ὡς Τίμαιος (fr. 3 Müller); Hesych. s.v. Ἀταβύριον.
[5] Cf. Schubring, *Historische Topographie von Akragas*, 24; Cook, *Zeus*, ii. 910.
[6] See below, p. 323.   [7] v. 1. 2.
[8] The Eusebian chronicle has two dates for Phalaris: v. Arm. 650 (652) 'Phalaris apud Acracantinos tyrannidem capessiuit' (Fotheringham, p. 167; Schoene, ii. 86); 623 (625) 'Phalaris a tyrannis euersus est' (Fotheringham, p. 171, Schoene, ii. 88); *Ol.* 52, 3 or 2 (570: 571 Jerome) 'Phalaris apud Acragantinos tyrannidem exercuit annos XVI' (Sync. 402, 15; Fotheringham, p. 179, Schoene, ii. 94). The earlier date is quite meaningless. It can by no ingenuity be used to support an earlier date for the foundation of Akragas, for it is before Eusebius' own first tyrant in Sicily, Panaitios of Leontinoi. The second date, 571–555, is supported by Suidas' date, *Ol.* 52 (572–568) and should be approximately correct.
[9] v. 1. 4; v. 1. 3 and Frontinus iii. 4. 6.

accept the fact of Sikan wars, and the names in the first story. Ouessa, or, as we should write, Vessa, is nowhere else named and there is no indication where this εὐδαιμονεστάτη καὶ μεγίστη Σικανῶν πόλις lay.

The only native places in the district which have been excavated are S. Angelo Muxaro and Mussomeli.[1] Both show signs of Greek influence and Greek imports in the sixth century, but at neither is there a break; both were Sikel (or Sikan) even after Phalaris. Both lie near the way north from Akragas to the centre of Sicily and the north coast at Himera. S. Angelo Muxaro is only fifteen miles from Akragas, and commands good corn-land. It is evident therefore that Phalaris' expansion at the expense of the Sikans was partial.

To the east the country had been penetrated by the Geloans with posts at Palma, Canicatti, Ravanusa, and perhaps Licata.[2] The Sikels at Naro had come into contact with Greeks before the foundation of Akragas. At a later date Ravanusa is apparently Akragantine, as the houses and tomb-groups of the fourth century are similar to those of Akragas.[3] It lies on the Akragantine bank of the Himeras, the natural frontier between Gela and Akragas. In 310 Greeks and Carthaginians faced each other across the Himeras, the Carthaginians at Eknomos, ὅν φασι φρούριον γεγενῆσθαι Φαλάριδος, and Agathokles in the Φαλάριον.[4] Why should Phalaris have set up two forts so close together at this point of the frontier? I suggest that Eknomos (Licata) was originally Geloan; that Phalaris attacked and took it, and fortified it against the Geloans; and threw out an advanced post across the river, possibly on the loop of land called Il Greco, surrounded on three sides by the river. Phalaris was also associated with Eknomos by its etymology, from his lawless doings, and his bull is said by Diodoros[4] to have been set up there; the etymology is bad, and the bull was certainly at Akragas. A motive for this hypothetical Geloan war of Phalaris may be found in an Akragantine claim to that part of Geloan territory which lay west of the Himeras. There were other forts of Phalaris,[5] which may have lain along this debatable frontier. This reconstruction is in the highest degree tentative, but it does satisfy all the extremely scanty evidence.

[1] See above, pp. 139 ff.   [2] See above, pp. 137 ff.
[3] Marconi, N Sc, 1928, 499 ff.; Mingazzini, MA, xxxvi. 690 ff.
[4] Diod. xix. 108.
[5] Ibid., ἕτερον τῶν Φαλάριδος γεγενημένων φρουρίων ... τὸ προσαγορευθὲν ἀπ' ἐκείνου Φαλάριον.

A 'war of independence' when the Geloans found that their new colony was likely to outstrip them is not inconceivable.

Phalaris extended Akragantine territory also to the west. He dedicated to Athena Lindia a krater with the inscription Δαίδαλος ἔδωκε ξείνιόν με Κωκάλωι.[1] This should be part of the spoils from Kokalos' capital Kamikos,[2] which is not, however, named in the Lindian Chronicle. The site of Kamikos is uncertain, but it was inland from Minoa and probably to the east of it.[3] Phalaris' success may have been only in a raid, but by 480 Kamikos is Akragantine, and it was very probably taken in his time. The discovery of a work of Daidalos at Kamikos is parallel to Antiphemos carrying off a Daidalic statue from Omphake,[4] and in both places there is the question whether the object was a work which had reached the Sikan town by intercourse with the Greeks before the foundation of the colony, or whether it was planted on the site in order to justify the claim of the Cretan colonists to Sikan territory. This is less plausible in the case of Kamikos, for the Cretan connexion was weaker at Akragas, and the story of Minos and Daidalos would give poor justification for claiming Kamikos, which had remained obstinately Sikan. Phalaris' dedication was made in Rhodes not Crete, so the case is not parallel to Theron's discovery and shipment to Crete of the bones of Minos.

Phalaris may have anticipated Theron in seeking an outlet on the north coast, though he had not conquered all the country that lay between. Phalaris is said to have been appointed στρατηγὸς αὐτοκράτωρ by the Himeraians and to have asked for a bodyguard; whereupon Stesikhoros related to the Himeraians the fable of the horse who allowed himself to be bridled and took a rider to be rid of a deer which was damaging his pasture.[5]

---

[1] Lind. Chron. xxvii (Lindos, ii. 171).
[2] Herod. vii. 170; Schol. Pind. Pyth. vi. 5; Diod. iv. 78.
[3] See BSR, xvi. 1 ff.
[4] Cf. above, p. 112.
[5] Arist. Rhet. ii. 20; Conon, Narr. 42. Pareti, 87 ff., accepts the version which names Gelon, following Wilamowitz' date for Stesikhoros of Himera. He supports it with Bergk's emendation of Philistos fr. 16, Müller:

μῦθον δὲ ὁποῖός ἐστι παρὰ Ἡροδότῳ τοῦ αὐλητοῦ, καὶ παρὰ Φιλίστῳ τοῦ ἵππου· ἐν ἑκατέρῳ ἐν τῇ πρώτῃ καὶ ἐν τῇ δευτέρᾳ.

Bergk proposed τοῦ ἵππου καὶ τῶν ⟨'Ιμεραίων· παρ'⟩ ἑκατέρῳ. The reference to Herod. is to i. 24; to Philistos, therefore, to the second book. Pareti's argument that Philistos' second book cannot have dealt with Phalaris is unsatisfactory. The first book came down after 690 (fr. 4, foundation of Maktorion; see above, p. 113); the second book included the war of Syracuse and Kamarina in 552 (fr. 8): but none of the other fragments of either book is approximately datable. Dionysios quotes fr. 8 as ἐν ἀρχῇ τῆς δευτέρας τῶν περὶ Σικελίας. But

Most of the details are impossible. The title στρατηγὸς αὐτο-κράτωρ is an anachronism, and the bodyguard simply the conventional sign of the progress to a tyranny. Phalaris cannot have been a magistrate at Himera, constitutional or otherwise. But Stesikhoros and Phalaris are contemporary, and the story in spite of its romantic form has good authority. A common Phoenician danger threatened all the western cities, and it may be that the Himeraians decided to ally themselves to Phalaris, the foremost general in Sicily, and trust their arms under his direction. It may be that Malchus' transference from Sicily to Sardinia[1] was due to a check inflicted by Phalaris.

If the story is accepted, it means that Phalaris was the first to conceive a united front against the Phoenicians, as Gelon and Dionysios did, but was not powerful enough to impose himself on the other Greeks. The romancers took this view of Phalaris, calling him τυραννεύσας Σικελίας ὅλης. His only certain operations are against the Sikans in the neighbourhood of Akragas, and some activity on the Geloan frontier. He may have warred against the Phoenicians, and meditated a coalition with Himera and Selinus. Only one scrap of evidence suggests his presence in eastern Sicily, the proverb ἀεὶ Λεοντῖνοι περὶ τοὺς κρατῆρας. οἱ γὰρ ἐν Σικελίᾳ Λεοντῖνοι περὶ τοὺς πότους ἐσχόλαζον. Φάλαρις δ' αὐτοὺς καταπολεμήσας εἰς τοὺς κρατῆρας ἔρριψεν.[2] With this may be compared Herakleides' list of his tortures: καὶ τοὺς μὲν εἰς λέβητας ζέοντας, τοὺς δὲ εἰς τοὺς κρατῆρας τοῦ πυρὸς ἀπέστελλε, τοὺς δὲ καὶ εἰς χαλκοῦν ταῦρον ἐνέβαλλε καὶ κατέκαιεν.[3] This sounds like a less artistic variant of the bull, but has been interpreted as the craters of Etna, thus providing a link with

this must not be pressed to mean that it was the first thing in the book, and it is not certain that Philistos wrote according to so rigid a chronological scheme as Pareti implies. Phalaris' attempt at Himera need have been very few years before 552. It is not absolutely certain that the quotation from Philistos comes from the second book, and far from proved that it therefore describes an event later than 552; not indeed certain that the reference is to Himera at all. Philistos is merely a tantalizing prospect, and the mangled quotation yields nothing to upset Aristotle. I find Pareti's arguments that Aristotle cannot have meant Phalaris tyrant of Akragas a little captious. στρατηγὸς αὐτοκράτωρ is not a possible title of any state in the sixth century (Scheele, *Strategos Autokrator*), and the Himeraians' invitation to an Akragantine could only have been to command their armies, not to hold a magistracy; therefore more likely after he had become tyrant than before. Aristotle's error is in using a title which had by his time taken a technical meaning of a period before it had that meaning. The variant which has Gelon's name for Phalaris' is explainable on Freeman's principle that any Sicilian tyrant may be substituted for any other. Freeman himself thinks that Phalaris has been substituted for some nameless citizen of Himera who attempted to make himself tyrant. But Aristotle is not likely to have made such a substitution.

[1] Justin xviii. 7. 1.
[2] Diogenian. *Paroem.* ii. 50.   [3] Fr. 37 Müller, *FHG*, ii. 223.

the kraters of the heavy-drinking Leontines. Phalaris provided a homoeopathic cure at the expense of a rather bad pun. But this is not the historical Phalaris but the fabulous monster.

The military activity of Phalaris can be dimly made out. His recorded home policy is simply a list of gruesome cruelties. He has a bodyguard, like any other tyrant. He had a brazen bull. This is as well attested as any piece of sixth-century Sicilian history. It is full-blown by Pindar's time. He mentions it not in any of his Akragantine odes, but as the horrible example of the bad tyrant:

> τὸν δὲ ταύρῳ χαλκέῳ καυτῆρα νηλέα νόον
> ἐχθρὰ Φάλαριν κατέχει παντᾷ φάτις.[1]

This brief reference is as damning as all the details in later writers: the door in the shoulder through which the victims were put in, the ingenious device by which their cries simulated the lowing of the bull;[2] the name of the artificer, Perilaos, who by a piece of poetic justice, the only just act which Phalaris committed,[3] was himself the first victim. The bull began as a punishment for his enemies; the sophists made it an instrument to which he fed all strangers who came to his hospitality;[4] an older generation of scholars saw in it a horrible piece of Carthaginian influence.[5] In fact, it was a direct import from Rhodes, where there were bronze bulls on the top of Mount Atabyrion which lowed when any disaster was coming to the city.[6] Phalaris was responsible for the building of the temple of Zeus Polieus or Atabyrios, and built also a bull on the Sicilian Mount Atabyrion.[7]

The common tradition was that the bull was carried off by the Carthaginians in 405, and returned to Akragas by Scipio.[8] Timaios denied this, saying that the real bull was sunk in the sea (not, as Polybios quotes him, that there never was a bull).[9]

---

[1] Pyth. i. 95–6.   [2] Diod. ix. 18.   [3] Plut. Parallela 39.

[4] Only when Phalaris had grown in stature to equal Busiris and Diomedes was this charge added (Plut. loc. cit.; Kallimakhos ap. Schol. Lykophron 717).

[5] See Freeman, ii, appx. vii, for a discussion of the older literature.

[6] Timaios ap. Schol. Pind. Ol. vii. 160c: εἰσὶ δὲ καὶ βόες χαλκοῖ ἐπὶ τῷ ὄρει τῆς Ῥόδου, οἳ ὅταν μέλλῃ τι τῇ πόλει γίνεσθαι κακὸν μυκῶνται. Small bronze bulls, statuettes and outlines cut from a sheet, were dedicated on top of Mount Atabyrion in Rhodes.

[7] Diod. xix. 108 says that the bull stood on Mount Eknomos. This is a valueless bit of etymologizing. Though it is not stated that the bull stood on Mount Atabyrion, this seems a valid deduction. Mount Atabyrion is to be identified with the acropolis of Akragas, where the temple of Zeus Atabyrios stood (see above, p. 316).

[8] Polyb. xii. 25; Diod. xiii. 90; Schol. Pind. Pyth. i. 185; Cic. Verr. ii. iv. 33, 73.

[9] Schol. Pind. loc. cit. That which was shown in the city (not in Timaios' time, for it

The balance of probability is that he is right. According to one tradition it was used for revenge on Phalaris' family and friends;[1] this may be mere poetic justice. If it was sunk in the sea, because of its close association with the tyrant, it does not follow that it had been used for the purpose to which every writer from Pindar on believed it to have been put. The evidence for this use is as good as for anything in the sixth century, but it is very difficult to believe such refinement of cruelty. It may have originated in a grim jest. Phalaris' enemies said that he and his bull portended ill to the city; he said that if that was so he would make the bull roar with their cries. A verbal jest of this kind, amplified by malevolent survivors, might be the foundation of his fame to which Pindar gives expression eighty years after his death. Whether or no there was any more to it than this, it was certainly an instrument neither of policy nor of religion. All his later reputation rests on this one assertion of his enemies, a bizarrerie so striking that it was worth while to search out and invent other stories about him, till we reach Klearkhos' statement that he ate sucking children.[2] It is not, however, worth while to sort out the grain of fact from the mountain of fancy. The only really solid fact is that after his overthrow he was thoroughly detested.

One story may be mentioned, not for any substratum of fact which it contains, but because it shows that even before Lucian and the sophists set about whitewashing so black a character there was something to be said for Phalaris. The beautiful young Akragantine Melanippos had a suit against a friend of Phalaris, and the tyrant obliged the judge to strike out the case. Melanippos persuaded his lover Khariton to join him in an attempt against Phalaris. Khariton, persuaded that fear would prevent any of his fellow citizens from joining, made his

was then in Carthage; this part of the scholion rests therefore on later authority) was said not to be the original but a statue of the river Gelas. The Gelas appears on the coins of Gela as a human-headed bull, but there is no reason why it should have a statue in Akragas. The river Akragas is not so represented, but this is the regular formula for a river-god. However, if the scholiast meant the river Akragas, why did he not say so? The bull which Polybios saw was certainly not a river-god, for it had a door in the shoulder. But, *pace* Polybios, it may have been a model made in Carthage, lest so notable a memory should perish. It certainly pointed a very useful moral for Scipio. Cf. F. W. Walbank, *CR*, 1945, 39 ff.

[1] Herakleides, fr. 37.

[2] Ap. Athen. 396*e*. His fame survived after the end of antiquity; he occurs in distinguished company in the Carolingian palace of Ingelheim, where were illustrated 'the deeds of ancient kings and heroes: Ninus, Cyrus, Phalaris, Remus, Hannibal and Alexander' (R. Hinks, *Carolingian Art*, 101).

attack single-handed. He was arrested and put to torture, but refused to name his confederates. After some pretty devotion on the part of the two friends, Phalaris pardoned them, expelling them from Sicily.[1] For this generosity Apollo gave him a respite from death. This tale, descended in some of the detail from Harmodios and Aristogeiton, in spirit a close relation of Damon and Phintias, has no relevance to the state of Akragas under Phalaris. But it shows that there was something good to relate about him.

An inconsequential fragment of Diodoros illustrates Phalaris' forebodings before his fall. Seeing a flight of doves chased by a hawk, he remarked on their cowardice, for if they turned they would easily get the better of the hawk.[2] This suggests that it was a coalition of the noble families which overthrew him. An ancestor of Theron took a prominent part in his fall. The Ambrosian scholiast on Pindar says that it was his grandfather Emmenes, the other scholiasts say Telemakhos, the founder of the family. Telemakhos must have been an old man. He came to Akragas twenty-five years earlier, taking a prominent part in the foundation. His great-grandson was born probably about 540 and he, therefore, well before the end of the seventh century.[3] It is very likely to have been a family matter in which both he and his son took part. The scholiasts are not agreed on the name of the son, giving Emmenes or Emmenides, and in another place Khalkiopeus. He may have had two names, like many of the younger Kypselids.[4]

One document of Phalaris' fall sounds more genuine than the tales of the cruel punishment of his supporters and his mother. Plutarch speaks of a law that no one should wear blue cloaks, for that was the colour of the tyrant's bodyguard.[5]

His fall was probably followed by a restored oligarchy. The schol. nov. on Pindar says that Telemakhos made himself

---

[1] Athen. 602a; Aelian VH ii. 4: μὴ μόνον τῆς Ἀκραγαντίνων πόλεως ἀλλὰ καὶ τῆς Σικελίας: Phalaris already thought of as ruling all Sicily?

[2] Diod. ix. 30.

[3] See the table on p. 484. Theron's nephew Thrasyboulos was a grown man in 490.

[4] Τηλέμαχος γάρ τις καταλύσας τὴν Φαλάριδος τυραννίδα ἐν Ἀκράγαντι, τὴν βασιλείαν ἐκτήσατο: Schol. nov. Pind. Ol. iii. 68 Boeckh, quoted by Freeman, ii. 79. Schol. Ol. iii. 68a (A): ἀπὸ Ἐμμένους τινὸς τοῦ τὴν Φαλάριδος τυραννίδα καθελόντος. ἦν δὲ ὁ Ἐμμένης Τηλεμάχου παῖς, οὗ γίνεται Αἰνησίδαμος, οὗ Θήρων, οὗ Θρασυδαῖος καὶ Φιλοκράτης. 68d (BCDEQ): Τηλεμάχου καταλύσαντος τὸν τῶν Ἀκραγαντίνων τύραννον Φάλαριν παῖς γίνεται Ἐμμενίδης, οὗ Αἰνεσίδαμος, οὗ Θήρων καὶ Ξενοκράτης· Θήρωνος δὲ Θρασυδαῖος, Ξενοκράτους δὲ Θρασύβουλος. Schol. Pyth. vi. 5a: Emmenides Theron's grandfather. Schol. Ol. ii. 82d: Khalkiopeus Theron's grandfather.

[5] Plut. Eth. 821 D.

master of the city, but if this were so the older scholia should have mentioned it. It is unlikely that the later scholiasts had access to fresh information. Herakleides names two successive tyrants: μεθ' ὃν (Phalaris) Ἀλκαμένης παρέλαβε τὰ πράγματα· καὶ μετὰ τοῦτον Ἄλκανδρος προέστη, ἀνὴρ ἐπιεικής.[1] They sound more like tyrants than constitutional magistrates, regular or extraordinary. Probably there was a gap between Phalaris and Alkamenes. If so, the oligarchy was more competent in damning its predecessor than in managing the State.

In spite of his mildness, Alkandros did not hand on his rule. There was an oligarchy again for some time before Theron. There is no contemporary parallel for this alternation of tyranny and oligarchy, within a hundred years three separate tyrannies being set up. It seems not to have affected the steady growth of the city, which was already before Theron a power in Sicilian politics, and under him soon became unquestionably the second city of Sicily.

The first century of Akragas' existence is rightly designated as 'il periodo della forza'.[2] The most striking work of this period is the wall. The first of the great temples, the so-called temple of Herakles, was built about 500.[3] Before that time the Akragantines worshipped in little buildings whose only architectural pretensions were in their painted terra-cotta revetments, and in open sanctuaries, the most important of which was one in the lower part of the town near the 'temple of the Dioscuri', probably dedicated to Demeter and Kore, whose chief feature was two large altars, one round, one square.[4] The greatest activity of this sanctuary was in the sixth century, though some of the little treasury-like buildings are probably of the fifth and fourth centuries.[5] The temple 'of Herakles' is the only one which was begun before Theron. Theron was, before the battle of Himera, connected with the building of the temple of Athena on the acropolis, and the remains under S. Maria dei Greci agree with this date.[6] All the other temples, beginning

---

[1] Herakleides Pontikos, fr. 37 (*FHG*, ii, p. 223).

[2] Marconi, *Agrigento*, 29 ff.

[3] Koldewey and Puchstein, 145 ff.; Marconi, op. cit. 51.

[4] Marconi, op. cit. 44 ff.; *Studi Agrigentini*, iii; *Agrigento Arcaica*, 17 ff. C. Picard suggests that this sanctuary was dedicated to the Dioskouroi (*RA*, cx, 1937, 247 f.). But Marconi's identification as a sanctuary of Demeter and Kore, though not proved by the finds, is more probable. The name given to the adjacent temple 'of the Dioscuri', built towards the middle of the fifth century (*Agrigento Arcaica*, 78 ff.), is, like those given to the other temples of Akragas, purely fanciful.

[5] See note on p. 324.   [6] Between 490 and 460, Marconi, *Agrigento*, 77.

from the Olympieion and the temple of Demeter (S. Biagio), are after 480.

The great achievements of Akragantine art, as of architecture, are of the fifth century, but the beginning of building in the years 510–480 corresponds to the import of some of the finest works of late archaic art. The best piece of early red-figure, and one of the few from Sicily older than 480, is the 'muletto di Dioniso'.[1] A number of moulds for the manufacture of terra-cottas has been found in Akragas.[2] The oldest are of the second half of the sixth century, proving that the industry was well established then; the pinax mould of a gorgon,[3] one of the finest of Akragantine terra-cottas, is of the late sixth century. The best of the pithos rims are of this period.[4] There is at this date at Akragas, as in most western cities, a revival of artistic endeavour under strong Ionian influence. At Akragas it reinforced the somewhat weakened traditions which the colonists had brought from Rhodes.[5]

NOTE

Marconi's publication of the small buildings in the sanctuary near the temple of the Dioscuri deserves close examination (see *Agrigento Arcaica*, 18 ff., and plan on p. 19). The extreme simplicity of their plan is not evidence of an early date; and certainly not all the fifteen *tempietti* and altars of the sanctuary were in use together in the sixth century. The material from their foundations has not been published with exact provenience, nor kept separate in Agrigento Museum. It can be used to date only the round altar (second quarter of sixth century) and Marconi's tempietto 3 (last quarter of sixth century or earlier; the 'muletto di Dioniso', *Boll. d'Arte*, xxv. 64 ff., was found in it). Tempietto 3 is above one of two pavements laid down as foundations of a temple which was never finished. The first of these pavements was alined, within five degrees, to the square altar and tempietto 1. Tempietto 3 was built with a corner across it, and a new foundation laid with slightly different orientation but over the earlier foundation. Neither of these was finished, as there are no remains of elevation. The earliest foundation, being under tempietto 3, must belong to at least the third quarter of the century, the second one perhaps to the last quarter. Finally, in the second quarter of the fifth century the temple 'of the Dioscuri' was built. The measurements are remarkably near one another: first foundation, 22·90 × 8·05 m.; second foundation, 23·45 × 10·30 m.; cella of temple, 23·75 × 8·76 m. (see *Agrigento Arcaica*, 85 ff.).

[1] *Boll. d'Arte*, xxv. 64 ff.; Beazley, *ARV*, 27, no. 2 (manner of Euthymides).
[2] Rizzo, *RM*, 1897, 253 ff.; Bovio-Marconi, *N Sc*, 1930, 73 ff.; N. Breitenstein, *Acta Archaeologica*, xvi. 137, figs. 57–9. See above, p. 265.
[3] Marconi, *Agrigento*, fig. 133.
[4] Ibid. 202, figs. 137–8.
[5] Ibid. 217. See above, p. 239.

Some of the other buildings may be approximately dated by the different levels of their foundations. Those of tempietto 2 and of altars 7 and 6 are about a foot higher than the base level on which the earliest foundations rest. I have found black-glaze sherds, which may be of the sixth century but are more likely to be of the fifth, under the foundation of the west part of the cross-wall of tempietto 2; under altar 6; sherds and a crescent of bronze under altar 7. These three structures cannot therefore be among the earliest in the sanctuary and are probably later than the sixth century. Sherds under the east end of recinct 2, to which altar 6 is alined, may have penetrated sideways under the foundations, which have been disturbed by the building of a Byzantine house on top. There are fragments of tile and plain pottery under altars 13 and 12, which are alined to the temple 'of the Dioscuri', the commencement of whose building is to be dated 480–470 (c. 480, Marconi, *Agrigento Arcaica*, 85). Altar 11, whose corner abuts on altar 12, has its foundations on rock at a lower level than those of altar 12. Nos. 12 and 13 are therefore comparatively late.

The date of a similar small building near the Olympieion is also disputed. Gàbrici, the excavator, put it in the fourth century, I think rightly (*N Sc*, 1925, 437 ff.). There was a small sixth-century building on the site, the revetments of which only were found (Marconi, *Agrigento*, 155–6; N. Breitenstein, *Acta Archaeologica*, xvi. 116 ff.). Marconi regards the existing building as the sixth-century one (*Agrigento Arcaica*, 131 ff.). It is possible that the little building was rebuilt in the fourth century with stones which had been burnt in the sack of the city in 406. It has been disturbed by the building of a house over it, partly of other burnt stones.

CHAPTER XI

GREEKS AND PHOENICIANS: PENTATHLOS AND DORIEUS

THERE was no friction that we know of between Greeks and Phoenicians over the colonization of Selinus, which was in an area in which the Phoenicians had never been interested. At this period relations are as likely to have been friendly as not. Selinus was thrust forward almost to the boundary of the Phoenician sphere, as Himera had been on the north coast. It may be that trade with the Phoenicians and Elymians was more profitable than with the Sikans, who seem to have resented the intrusion of Greeks. If the colony had been intended from its foundation as an outpost of Hellenism against the Phoenicians, it might have been situated more favourably either in the little hills a few miles east, or to the west, covering the plain. It is not very strong by nature, and not in a strategic position, though adequate for a city of traders and farmers.

But conditions were greatly changed within a short time by the effects of mere neighbourhood, by the rise of Carthage, and by the opening up of Tartessos. Kolaios' voyage was about a decade before the foundation of Selinus. Selinus was not very well situated for tapping this new source of wealth, being on the wrong coast, but must have profited from being one of the two nearest Greek ports.[1] The desire to possess a good harbour on the north coast, for better communications with Spain and Etruria, was a moving force in that century-long strife with Segesta which had begun before 580. The same considerations probably moved Pentathlos in his attempt to seize the extreme western point of Sicily, which profoundly affected Selinus' relations with her neighbours.

The withdrawal of the Phoenicians to Motye, Panormos, and Soloeis[2] may well have taken place after the coming of the Greeks, not to Sicily, but to the west of the island. It has been suggested that Thermai was a Phoenician post, evacuated when Himera threatened it from so near, and refounded 200

---

[1] There are coins of Selinus in the hoards of Tarragona (Noe, *Greek Coin-hoards²*, 278) and Mongo (op. cit. 185), which suggest that in the fifth century at least Selinus was concerned with the trade with Spain.

[2] Thuk. vi. 2. 6; cf. Freeman, i. 246.

years later after the destruction of Himera.[1] Mazara, with its Phoenician name, may have been another post, evacuated soon after the foundation of Selinus. Later it was a Selinuntine emporion.[2] No other place in Sicily except Minoa (on the evidence of its alternative name Makara) has with much likelihood been suggested as a Phoenician post. The absence on sites of eastern Sicily of anything that could be ascribed to Phoenician traders or settlers makes it unlikely that they were more than casual visitors there.[3] It is possible that the Phoenician colonies in Sicily came not from Asia but from Africa, and at no very early date. Nothing earlier than 700 has been found at Motye.[4] In that case the Phoenician colonization of the west and the Greek colonization of the east of Sicily were going on at the same time, and the foundations of Himera and Selinus upset the balance.

The withdrawal suggests a common direction, such as Carthage exercised in the sixth century but not before, so far as is known. Thukydides' mention of Carthage as the support of the Phoenicians strengthens this view, if it is not held to be an anachronism. The position of Soloeis also, an outpost of Panormos, too near for full development as an independent state, and in a strong position facing east, suggests that its importance was to guard the frontier against Himera, and that its choice as one of the three Phoenician places in the island came after the foundation of Himera.

There is no evidence of hostilities at this point, but relations were becoming strained. Imports of Protocorinthian vases to Motye are considerably more numerous than Corinthian, and there is more Early Corinthian than Middle and Late together.[5] This may be due to accident of discovery, as there are only about forty pieces in all, but development of the native pottery continues without a break. It is much more likely that there was a slackening of imports in the last quarter of the seventh

---

[1] Gàbrici, *Atti della reale accademia di archeologia, lettere, e belle arti*, Napoli, xvii (1893), 11–12.   [2] Diod. xiii. 54.

[3] See above, pp. 20 ff. A Phoenician pirate is said to have come into conflict with the founders of Gela, but on no good authority: Zenobius i. 54: ἄκουε τοῦ τὰ τέσσαρα ὦτα ἔχοντος· ἐπὶ τῶν ἀπειθούντων. Χρησμὸς γὰρ ἐδόθη Ἐντίμῳ τῷ Κρητὶ καὶ Ἀντιφήμῳ τῷ Ῥοδίῳ, φυλάξασθαι τὸν τετράωτον· ἦν δὲ οὗτος λῃστὴς Φοῖνιξ· οἱ δὲ τοῦ χρησμοῦ ἀμελήσαντες ἀπώλοντο. Cf. Pais, *St. Sic.* 235. A. B. Cook, *Zeus*, ii. 322, nn. 5–7, suggests that the image carried off from Omphake was ὁ Τετράωτος, 'later rationalised into a Phoenician freebooter'.

[4] Whitaker, *Motya*, 206 ff., 290 ff. Cf. Åkerström, *Der Geometrische Stil in Italien*, 162 ff., who gives a slightly lower date.

[5] See Whitaker, *Motya*, figs. 84–7.

century, and a further decline in the sixth. The few Corinthian vases may have been imported via Carthage. Direct trade between Selinus and Motye is not established, and would surely have brought a much greater number of Greek vases.

The first open war between Greeks and Phoenicians in Sicily of which we hear is c. 580. At that period the Rhodians made an effort to get a firm hold of the west and south of Sicily. In 580 Akragas was founded, and the whole south coast was now firmly Greek. Very little later (Ol. 50, 580–576) Knidians and some Rhodians, under the leadership of Pentathlos the Knidian, set out to found a colony at Lilybaion, the extreme western point of the island, which commands the entrance to the harbour of Motye and was then presumably unoccupied.[1] They found Selinus and Segesta at war and assisted the Selinuntines; they were themselves opposed and expelled from Lilybaion by a combination of Phoenicians and Elymians.[2] Pausanias says that they founded a city, and were expelled by the Elymians and Phoenicians; Diodoros, that being in the neighbourhood

[1] The absence of remains older than the fourth century confirms the historical tradition (Diod. xxii. 10. 4) that the Phoenicians did not found a town at Lilybaion until after the fall of Motye.

[2] I have attempted to combine the two versions of Pentathlos' attempt (Diod. v. 9; Paus. x. 11. 3), which are not actually contradictory. Neither of them is a full history of the events. Diodoros, who is the fuller, relates while speaking of the Lipari Islands what in its proper chronological place came in one of his missing books. Pausanias, who quotes Antiokhos for Pentathlos' name and no doubt takes his whole account from him, is much briefer, and has made for himself the mistake of confusing the three corners of Sicily, writing Pakhynos for Lilybaion, as he has done in v. 25. 5. He obviously does not give the full text of Antiokhos, and none of the details added in Diodoros are inconsistent. Pareti (pp. 24–7) thinks that Pausanias' account (i.e. Antiokhos) is the only true one, and that the added details in Diodoros were taken by Timaios from the history of Dorieus. The one to which he most objects, the war between Selinus and Segesta, is not exactly parallel to anything in Dorieus' attempt, in which the Selinuntines are not named.

I do not agree that Antiokhos must have named Pentathlos as the founder of Lipara, though Pausanias may have thought that he was. Pausanias has very much abbreviated Antiokhos, and Diodoros' naming of Pentathlos' successors, Gorgos, Thestor, and Epithersides, is perfectly circumstantial.

For other brief references to the foundation of Lipara see Thuk. iii. 88; Strabo 275; ps.-Skymnos 262–3.

The date, Ol. 50, is in Diodoros alone, and is most likely to be that of the foundation of Lipara, the most memorable accomplishment of the expedition. The Eusebian date is c. 628 (see below, p. 437). A double colonization is inadmissible, for Diodoros states that they found only about 500 natives (descendants of Αἴολος) on Lipara. A date c. 575 is admirably supported by the vases found in Lipari and now in the Museo Mandralisca at Cefalù. Late Corinthian is fairly plentiful, and there is nothing older except one Late Protocorinthian aryballos (no. 64, unpublished; of Johansen's Class C) which is not in itself evidence of an earlier colonization. Another sporadic object of pre-colonization date is a blue paste vase, in Oxford (1944.35), with the cartouche of Necho (c. 671–664). For the date of the foundation cf. Libertini, Le Isole Eolie, 89, 176.

of Lilybaion they assisted the Selinuntines against the Segestans, were defeated, and Pentathlos killed. The order of events
may have been: first, that they settled at Lilybaion; second,
that they took part in a joint action with the Selinuntines, and
were defeated;[1] third, that the Elymians followed up their
success by attacking the Knidians at Lilybaion, with Phoenician
help.

The alliance between Phoenicians and Elymians, vouched
for by Thuk. vi. 2. 6, was presumably a good deal older than
this. It is natural to suppose that Selinus was at war also with
the Phoenician allies of Segesta, and directed the Knidians to
settle at a place where, if they established themselves, the
Phoenician hold on the western corner would be completely
broken. Selinus advanced against the Elymians of Segesta, the
Knidians settled at Lilybaion to mask the chief of the Phoenician colonies. Selinus had commercial relations with Rhodes
in her early years, and there is a strong East Greek influence in
her terra-cottas, from which we may certainly infer the import
of Rhodian models. Possibly there were Rhodian craftsmen
settled at Selinus.[2] I suggest that the strong commercial and
artistic relations were accompanied by a political understanding between Selinus and the Rhodians of Sicily and the motherland, and that the foundation of Akragas and the expedition
of Pentathlos are part of a drive to make the west of Sicily
entirely Greek.[3]

One motive may be found in the desire to share the trade
with Tartessos. Himera and Selinus, the two nearest Greek
cities, must have found it profitable, both in direct trade and
in supplying ships sailing to and from Spain. But Selinus,
though very favourably placed for trade with Carthage, was on
the wrong side of Sicily for trade with Spain and Etruria. The
south coast is harbourless and is generally a lee shore, and the
dangers of the Straits are nothing to those of this coast. The
century-long enmity with Segesta may be put down largely to
the Selinuntine desire to possess a good port on the north coast
—the same desire which moved Theron to conquer Himera.

---

[1] It is not clear where Diodoros places this action; one would suppose near Lilybaion,
but the natural battlefield between Selinus and Segesta is farther east.

[2] Cf. Von Duhn, *Vorgesch. Jahrbuch*, i (1926), 103; *Gnomon*, 1929, 535.

[3] The Rhodians are named in Diodoros. Thuk. iii. 88 calls the Liparaians Κνιδίων
ἄποικοι. The majority of the colonists, and the leader, were Knidians, but it may be that
the Rhodians suggested the expedition to their neighbours. A Rhodian terra-cotta from
Lipari is published by Murray, *JHS*, 1886, 56; cf. Libertini, op. cit., pl. v. 1.

Lilybaion, the westernmost point of Sicily, has obvious advantages, both for trade with Spain and for tapping, peacefully or otherwise, the shipping between Etruria and Carthage. If Pentathlos had succeeded, the Greeks would have won control over the whole western Mediterranean.

The legend of Herakles' travels in the west was written down either during Pentathlos' attempt or soon after it. It was afterwards used to justify Dorieus; it may already have been used for Pentathlos. It would be possible to detach the Sicilian adventures from the main narrative, and dissociate them from Stesikhoros. But it is very unlikely that the account of the baths which the nymphs set up to refresh Herakles when he reached Himera is due to any other than the poet of Himera. One purpose of the *Geryoneis* was the glorification of the brave Greeks who were winning new lands for Greek settlement. A Sicilian appendix, claiming as Greek the lands immediately neighbouring Himera, and encouraging the Herakleid Pentathlos to win back his heritage, would be in keeping. Though the wrestling of Herakles and Eryx is never brought into relation with the expedition of Pentathlos, Diodoros goes out of his way to mention Pentathlos' Herakleid descent.

Motye and Soloeis were both included in the land of Herakles. Hekataios is evidence for the connexion of Herakles with both.[1] He composed his book in all probability during the decade 520–510, before Dorieus thought of going to Sicily, and probably took his information from Stesikhoros. Certainly he is evidence of the tendency which regarded the western end of Sicily as Herakles' possession, to be won back from the barbarians, and carries it back before the time of Dorieus. Then we think at once of the earlier Herakleid venture of Pentathlos, which was specifically to win Lilybaion and Motye. A Stesikhorean origin of the story, as a part of the *Geryoneis*, is more likely than an unknown sixth-century origin. The date of composition of the *Geryoneis* is uncertain; it may well have been before 580. The alternative is to ascribe the account of Herakles' visit to Soloeis and Motye to a Himeraian follower of Stesikhoros. In that case, it may have encouraged some unknown attempt, after Pentathlos' defeat, perhaps under Himeraian leadership, to win the western corner of the island.

---

[1] Fr. 76, Jacoby: Μοτύη· πόλις Σικελίας ἀπὸ Μοτύης γυναικὸς μηνυσάσης Ἡρακλεῖ τοὺς ἐλάσαντας τοὺς αὐτοῦ βοῦς. Ἑκαταῖος Εὐρώπη. Fr. 77: Σολοῦς· πόλις Σικελίας, ὡς Ἑκαταῖος ἐν Εὐρώπη· ἐκλήθη δὲ ἀπὸ Σολοῦντος κακοξένου, ὃν ἀνεῖλεν Ἡρακλῆς.

There was much fighting in the sixth century and the Greeks were presumably not on the defensive all the time between 580 and 510.

After their defeat and Pentathlos' death the Knidians chose themselves other leaders from his kin, who abandoned the attempt to settle in Sicily, and set off homewards round the north coast of Sicily. On the way they landed at Lipara, the largest of the Aiolian islands, which was inhabited only by a handful of the reputed descendants of Aiolos, estimated at 500. What manner of men these Aiolids were there is no knowing, but they were probably of the same stock as the Sikels who inhabited the neighbouring coasts of Italy and Sicily. The Knidians were well received and decided to stay and share the island with the natives. They founded their city on Lipara, and crossed over to the other islands to farm them.[1] At a later date they lived communistically, holding all the islands in common, applying the produce to common meals in *syssitia*, and warring against the Etruscans. This is one of the few instances in which we have any detail of the way in which the land of a colony was divided. According to Diodoros, there was a gradual progress from complete communism to a modified form. After some years of common ownership, they divided the island of Lipara, still owning the other islands in common. Later they divided the whole territory, but for twenty years only, at the end of which time it was allotted anew.

This communism was not introduced at once, but after the pressure of Etruscan raiders made it necessary to leave some of the community free to fight. Diodoros compresses all the developments of communal ownership into the period before the great naval victories of the late sixth century. If this is true it shows that the experiment was not a practical success. Thukydides has no hint of it in discussing the events of 425.

[1] Pausanias is uncertain about the manner in which the Knidians possessed themselves of Lipara: τὰς νήσους δὲ ἔσχον ἐρήμους ἔτι ἢ ἀναστήσαντες τοὺς ἐνοικοῦντας. This suggests that he is no longer directly quoting Antiokhos. His language at this point is closely reminiscent of Thuk. iii. 88: Λιπάραν μὲν κτίσαντες πόλιν ἐνταῦθα οἰκοῦσιν, ʿΙέραν δὲ καὶ Στρογγύλην καὶ Διδύμας γεωργοῦσι διαβαίνοντες ναυσὶν ἐς αὐτάς Paus.; cf. Thuk. τὰς δὲ ἄλλας ἐκ ταύτης ὁρμώμενοι γεωργοῦσι, Διδύμην καὶ Στρογγύλην καὶ ʿΙέραν. He quotes Antiokhos, explicitly only for Pentathlos' name, perhaps also in fact for the details of the attempt at Lilybaion; Thukydides, it seems, for the settlement on Lipara, leaving a little gap which he had to fill by his own imagination. Thukydides is not necessarily drawing on Antiokhos in book iii. It is an interlude, before he comes to treat in full of Sicilian affairs, and very probably he is simply repeating what he heard about the islands. His words may very well apply to his own day. On the Lipari Islands see Columba, *Porti*, 308 ff. It is possible to row from Lipari to Vulcano in one hour, to Salina (= Didyma) in two.

Perhaps the spoils won from the Etruscans were too much for the principle of common ownership.[1]

The excellent position of the Lipari Islands for raids on Etruscan ships trading with the Straits suggests that it was not accident that led the Knidians there. The Etruscans attacked the Knidians, but we may suspect that they were provoked by attacks on their shipping. The great period of the Etruscan navy was after Alalia, but they were already developing their coastal towns earlier, and probably had in their own hands the rich trade with the Sybarite ports on the Tyrrhenian Sea. Their alliance with Carthage is not known to be so old as the colonization of Lipara, and it was not till forty years later that the two powers were able to close the far west to all Greek ships except the Phokaian pentekonters. How early their attacks on the Knidians began we do not know; they may not have been earlier than the period of Alalia and joint action with Carthage.

Motye was extended during the first half of the sixth century, probably during the period after Pentathlos' repulse. The original cemetery on the island was abandoned, and the dead carried over to the mainland.[2] Perhaps the mole joining island and mainland was built when the cemetery was transferred. The causeway would aid action on the mainland. The island was also walled for the first time, the wall crossing the old cemetery.[3] This cannot be dated more accurately than in the second quarter of the sixth century. It may have been that the threat of a Greek colony at Lilybaion warned the Phoenicians to strengthen their defences. Motye seems to be at this period the chief Phoenician place in Sicily; it is to be noted that it is also the nearest to Carthage.

The Carthaginians are not mentioned in the war against Pentathlos, which was carried on by the Phoenicians of Sicily and their Elymian allies. But it seems that there was more war in the succeeding period (that of the expansion and fortification of Motye), of which the Carthaginians undertook the direction. Malchus' conquests in Sicily should belong here.[4] Justin's

---

[1] See Th. Reinach, 'Le Collectivisme des Grecs de Lipari', *Rev. ét. gr.* 1890, 86–96. Freeman (i. 591) notes the 'kind of pleased curiosity' in Thukydides' reference to the Liparians. The same quality is in all the accounts of their doings, Diodoros on their communism, Pausanias on their wars with the Etruscans under the direction of the Pythian oracle. There was something about their settlement which caught the imagination.

[2] The date cannot be precisely established. There is a single black-figure lekythos from the island cemetery (Whitaker, *Motya*, 314); the earliest pottery from the mainland cemetery of Birgi is of the third quarter of the sixth century (ibid., figs. 88, 90).

[3] Ibid. 142 ff., 208.   [4] Justin xviii. 7. 1.

chronology is vague in the extreme, but Orosius adds a note of time: 'haec temporibus Cyri Persarum regis gesta sunt'.[1] A tithe of the Sicilian spoils was carried by Malchus' son Carthalo as an offering to Melkart at Tyre. This is possibly before the capture of Tyre by Nebuchadrezzar in 573: Tyre lost a good deal of her prestige after this capture, and though relations between the Phoenicians of west and east were still kept up, Carthage came more completely to hold the position of supremacy among the western Phoenicians. If the offering was made before 573, Malchus must have been engaged in following up immediately the victory over Pentathlos and the Selinuntines, if he did not indeed win that victory.

According to Justin[2] Malchus was succeeded as commander-in-chief by Mago, and Mago by his sons Hasdrubal and Hamilcar, of whom Hasdrubal died in Sardinia, having held eleven dictatorships and four triumphs, and Hamilcar was killed at Himera. Justin's narrative is thoroughly unreliable and full of gaps. In a parallel case he calls Himilco Hamilcar's son instead of grandson.[3] But taking him at his face value, Malchus' generation is c. 580–550,[4] Mago's c. 550–520, Hamilcar's c. 520–480. Not much can be gained by considering the date of the campaigns in Sardinia, where Malchus turned his arms after his Sicilian victories, but the Phoenician advance in Sardinia appears to have begun early in the sixth century, under Carthaginian direction.

What conquests Malchus made it is impossible to say. The Carthaginian advance in Sicily of which we know was the subjection of the once independent Phoenician colonies, which would hardly be an event to celebrate with offerings sent to Tyre.[5] The Sikans bordered the Phoenicians at few points, and no expansion at the expense of their Elymian allies was possible. Perhaps the territory of Selinus was curtailed. It has been suggested that there was an attack on Akragas, to ward off which Phalaris was made general and rose to be tyrant, and also a threat to Himera, where Phalaris was appointed στρατηγὸς αὐτοκράτωρ.[6] It is not certain that the danger which drove Akragas into the arms of a tyrant came from overseas, but it

[1] iv. 6.　　　　　　　　　[2] xix. 1.　　　　　　　　　[3] Ibid.
[4] Busolt, ii. 752 n. 4, c. 570–540; Freeman, i. 297, 540, hesitatingly accepting the indication of time in Orosius. But so vague a synchronization added to an excerpt of Justin carries no conviction that there was independent evidence for it.
[5] Freeman, i. 298.
[6] Busolt, i. 422. See above, p. 318.

is probable that during his reign both Akragas and Himera were threatened by the Phoenicians.

This is perhaps the period when Selinus first found it politic to take the Carthaginian side. Apart from the military question, trade with Carthage must always have played a large part in her life. The half-century following 570 was that in which they built the first of their great temples, and the first great period of their art. The appearance of the city is not that of one subject to constant warfare and fear of invasion, but of a peaceful and prosperous community. Probably they made their peace with the Phoenicians and kept a neutrality which must in the circumstances have been favourable to Carthage, enabling her to threaten Akragas and Himera.

One war between Selinus and the Carthaginians[1] falls probably in this period 580–510, perhaps towards the end of it. The Carthaginians won a battle not far from the city, perhaps at its gates, and the Selinuntine dead were left unburied until Theron son of Miltiades undertook to bury them. The rest of the story is the ordinary one of the trick by which the tyrant rises to power, and the victorious Carthaginian army is heard of no more. It is not a valuable story, but it fits this period better than another, and it gives the name of a tyrant of Selinus. Perhaps he was the predecessor of Peithagoras, tyrant in 510, and a lukewarm patriot. A policy of peace with Carthage and building at home is no unlikely one for tyrants of Selinus.

The penetration by Greeks of the Phoenician places of Sicily went on in spite of hostile relations. The only archaic inscriptions of Motye are Greek.[2] These are the work of Greek-speaking masons and therefore were almost certainly cut for Greek or half-Greek inhabitants. In the fifth century Motye was a half-Greek town;[3] these inscriptions, which probably belong to the sixth century, show that it had already become so then.[4] Otherwise the sixth-century remains witness no extraordinary intercourse between Phoenicians and Greeks. The proportion of Greek terra-cottas, though high, is not higher than at Carthage, in Sardinia, and in Ibiza. Phoenician imitation of Greek terra-cottas and import of stamped pithos-rims,

[1] Polyainos, i. 28. 2. Freeman, ii. 81–3, places it after Pentathlos.
[2] Whitaker, *Motya*, 286 ff.; *N Sc*, 1917, 347–8.
[3] Diod. xiv. 53. 2; Whitaker, op. cit. 133 ff., 151.
[4] Cf. Beloch, *RG*, i. 309.

the most definitely Sicilian objects found at Motye, are in no case so old as the sixth century.

Segesta also was so effectively hellenized from Selinus that in the late fifth century it was indistinguishable from a Greek city. Apart from one passage (vi. 11. 7) where he insists on it, one could read the sixth book of Thukydides without becoming certain that the Segestans were not Greek. Whatever their origin, the Elymians were much more receptive than the other peoples of Sicily. The Phoenicians and Greeks were able to treat them as equals. Eryx became a thoroughly Punic town. Segesta, though its political sympathies were with the Phoenicians, became rapidly Greek. There is no sixth-century evidence,[1] but in the fifth century Segesta had *conubium* with Selinus,[2] and are the only barbarian people of Sicily known to have had rights of intermarriage with any Greek community.

The heroic honours paid by the Segestans to their dead enemy Philippos of Kroton[3] are Greek in sentiment. The obvious parallel is with the honours paid by the Caeretans, many of whom were Greek, to the Phokaians killed in the battle of Alalia.[4] The Segestans' admiration for the personal beauty of Philippos is quite Greek. Mythology which is at home in Elymian territory finds its way into Greek story. The tale of Herakles' wrestling-match against Eryx, wagering the oxen won from Geryoneus against the land of Eryx, was told by a Greek poet to support Greek claims to the land.[5] But many of the details, including the genealogy of Eryx,[6] have no bearing on Pentathlos' or Dorieus' venture, and may be of genuine local origin. A daughter of Eryx, Psophis, is said to have been brought back by Herakles to Greece and to have given her name to the Arcadian town of Psophis.[7]

[1] Taramelli speaks of pottery akin to Siculan III–IV in a grotto under the theatre of Segesta (*N Sc*, 1929, 296 ff.; cf. ibid. 1931, 399–400, Marconi). This is the only archaeological document of Segesta earlier than the temple and the coins, which begin before the middle of the fifth century (Head, *HN²*, 165).

[2] Thuk. vi. 6. 2.

[3] Herod. v. 47; cf. below, p. 351. I do not believe that Herodotos has confused Philippos son of Butakides with a native hero Byto (Ciaceri, *Culti e miti nella storia dell' antica Sicilia*, 41 ff.; see Pareti, 21, n. 2 for objections).

[4] Herod. i. 167.   [5] See above, p. 330.

[6] Diod. iv. 23.

[7] Paus. viii. 24. 2; Steph. Byz. s.v. Ψωφίς (= Hekataios fr. 6 Jacoby; but it is not clear that Hekataios recorded the alternative which made Psophis daughter of Eryx). The date of the story is uncertain, and it is likely to belong to the Hellenistic or Roman period, when the shrine of Venus Erycina became world-famous. For the legendary connexions of Elymians and Arcadia see Bérard, *Colonisation*, 375 ff.

The Elymians are an enigma. There are considerable remains of their chief city, Segesta, and their sacred place, Eryx.[1] Segesta appears thoroughly hellenized, Eryx is in most respects completely Phoenician in externals.[2] The worship of the goddess identified as Venus Erycina has its greatest extension in the Roman period; it is plausible to compare her with the Phoenician Astarte.[3]

The Elymians show on their coins more genuinely non-Greek religious material than the Sikel towns.[4] Especially interesting is the representation of the river-god Krimissos on the coins of Segesta as a dog.[5] The river-god takes the form of a dog also in the foundation-legend of Segesta,[6] and the dog occurs on the coins of the neighbouring Eryx and Panormos.[7] The importance of the dog in the cult of Hadranos, whose shrine was guarded by a thousand dogs,[8] may suggest that this representation was part of the common religious fund of pre-Greek Sicily. But it is more plausible to see Phoenician influence at Segesta. The coins of Segesta and Eryx both show the ending ꟊ I B to their place-names.[9] The meaning of the suffix is unknown, but it is apparently of Phoenician origin;[10] compare the legend transliterated *ziz* on the coins of Panormos.[11] The Elymians were commonly found on the side of the Phoenicians against the Greeks,[12] rather no doubt because the Greeks were more numerous and offensive than because of any especial affinity. They needed external support to maintain themselves; after the Carthaginian defeat at Himera, Segesta was the first city of Sicily to ally herself with Athens, so far as we know.[13]

The origin and ethnic relationships of the Elymians are thoroughly obscure. The scanty prehellenic remains of this

---

[1] It is uncertain whether there were other Elymian places than these two, named by Thukydides. See Freeman, i. 120 ff., 551 f.; Bérard, op. cit., 378 f.

[2] Most of the remains of Eryx are of Hellenistic and Roman date (see *N Sc*, 1935, 294 ff.). For the earliest finds see ibid. 308: Geometric, Corinthian, Attic b.f. sherds, not illustrated or more fully described. See also summary in *JHS*, 1936, 217 ff.

[3] Diod. iv. 83. 4; Athen. 394*f*; Aelian, *NA* iv. 2; cf. Farnell, *Cults*, ii. 641. Evans, *Palace of Minos*, iv. 960, suggests that Aphrodite of Eryx and her doves are descended from the Minoan nature-goddess; cf. *BSR*, xvi. 1 ff.

[4] For which see above, p. 177.   [5] Head, *HN²*, 165.

[6] Serv. *ad Aen.* i. 550, v. 30.   [7] Head, *HN²*, 138, 161–2.

[8] Aelian, *NA* xi. 3, 20. See above, p. 132, and for sacred dogs Evans, *Palace of Minos*, ii. 765.

[9] Head, *HN²*, 138, 164 ff.

[10] Whatmough, *Prae-Italic Dialects*, ii. 473–4.   [11] Head, *HN²*, 161.

[12] Thuk. vi. 2. 6; against Pentathlos, above, p. 329.

[13] *IG*, i². 19; see A. E. Raubitschek, *TAPA*, lxxv (1944), 10.

area are in no important way different from those of the rest of Sicily, Siculan III vases being found on a number of sites.[1] Thukydides says that the Elymians were of mixed Phokian and Trojan origin, having come west after the fall of Troy.[2] The Trojan origin was taken up by the Romans and rendered famous from its treatment in the *Aeneid*. If, as has been thought, the arrival of Aineias in the west was related by Stesikhoros,[3] it may be that he learnt it from the Elymians, who were not far distant from Himera; or that he invented it on the basis of Greek legends of Aineias' wanderings and some similarity of name in the cult or legend of the Elymians.[4] In any case, their Trojan origin is older than Thukydides, who found it in his books of reference on Sicily. It may indeed be that there is some truth in the story and that the Elymians came by sea to Sicily from the east, at some time before the Greeks. There is as yet no archaeological warrant for this, but there has been little excavation of remains of the right period in western Sicily. Toponomastical and other linguistic parallels are inconclusive.[5] The ease with which the Elymians absorbed a higher culture and assimilated themselves to Greeks or Phoenicians favours the view that they were of different origin from the other peoples of Sicily.

Much of the credit for hellenizing the Elymians must be given to the broad-mindedness of the Selinuntines. In contrast to the exclusiveness of the Greeks of eastern Sicily, who held firm to their traditions derived from Corinth, they developed equal relations with all their neighbours, Greek and barbarian. They did not lose any of their Hellenic culture in so doing. Their grave- and temple-offerings are as Greek as those of Syracuse, and none of the long list of Selinuntine personal names is other than Greek. But from their intercourse with Elymians and Phoenicians issued a broader outlook. They were the first of the Sicilian cities to produce an art which was not a reflection of the current tendencies in the Peloponnese.

[1] See above, p. 143. There are vases of Punic shape found on native sites in these areas, but these are of late date (fifth century and later).

[2] Thuk. vi. 2. 3. Hellanikos, however, brought the Elymians from Italy (F 79 B Jacoby= Dion. Hal. i. 22. 3). For a discussion of the legendary origins of the Elymians see Bérard, *Colonisation*, 368 ff.; cf. also the Φρύγες of Paus. v. 25. 6.

[3] Pais, *Storia Critica di Roma*, i. 235 ff.; Vürtheim, *Stesichoros' Fragmente und Biographie*, 34 ff. Contra, Perret, *Les Origines de la légende troyenne de Rome*, 84 ff.

[4] For the cult of Aphrodite Aineias at Eryx see Dion. Hal. i. 53; Diod. iv. 83; Farnell, *Cults*, ii. 638 ff.

[5] Bérard, op. cit. 377, 479.

This art, expressed even better in their terra-cottas than in the metopes, is, of course, derived from Peloponnesian, but has a vigour and an independence which are lacking in the late sixth century in eastern Sicily. There is no Carthaginian influence in it, nor could we well expect to find any, but there is a quality which may be traced to the effect of intercourse with a great non-Hellenic power. Their close friendship with the Etruscans may well have had a similar effect on Sybaris, though without successful excavation of Sybaris this cannot be proved. Certainly Sybaris, and to a less extent the other Italian cities, won economic independence from Greece, with which goes cultural independence, earlier than the Sicilian cities. In Sicily Selinus was, thanks to the nearness of Carthage, independent of Corinthian commercial interests earlier than the eastern cities, and was also the first city to express in its art a specifically local point of view. The other western cities were probably associated with Selinus in this independence. Selinus and Himera were the first of the western colonies to issue their own coins.[1] The fragments of Stesikhoros are otherwise all we possess of sixth-century Himera.[2] His poems are Sicily's great contribution to archaic culture, and, so far as we can judge, thoroughly Sicilian. Akragas occupies an intermediate position between the western cities, concerned chiefly with the Phoenicians, and the east, looking towards Greece. Akragas in her first century is preoccupied with internal affairs, and with her immediate neighbours, but she afterwards makes splendid contributions to Sikeliot culture.

The warfare between Greeks and Carthaginians in Sicily is only a part of a larger warfare waged during more than a century over the whole western Mediterranean. The seventh century saw the Greeks advancing, the Phoenicians retreating, but so far as we know without coming into conflict. The subjection of Tyre to the Assyrians cut Phoenician connexions with the far west, where they had probably in the eighth century, perhaps even earlier, visited the south of Spain.[3] In

[1] See above, p. 245. A. H. Lloyd, *Num. Chron.* 1935, 81 ff., points out that the earliest coins of the two cities are in a similar style, though of different weights, and concludes that their relations were friendly.

[2] There are few material remains of archaic Himera : some sixth-century vases and terra-cottas (Marconi, *Himera*, figs. 99, 100, 108 a, 111); a Panathenaic amphora of the end of the sixth century (Palermo Mus. 2561) is said to be from Himera. The site of the cemetery is well known (cf. L. Mauceri, *MA*, xviii. 421 ff.), but nothing of importance is known to have come from it.

[3] Isaiah ii. 16; xxiii. 1; perhaps Psalm lxxii. 10; Schulten, *Tartessos*, 4, 16 ff. Tyre was

c. 638 Kolaios the Samian visited Tartessos and found a virgin market,[1] which implies that the Tyrians had long ceased to come and the Carthaginians had not yet taken up their heritage. The Samians did not follow up Kolaios' success, but left it to the Phokaians, who were well received by Arganthonios, king of Tartessos. The reign of eighty years ascribed to him probably represents the period during which Tartessos was visited by the Phokaians (*c.* 620–540).[2] The Samians themselves kept up an interest in Kyrene, the colony founded by Therans at the time of Kolaios' voyage.[3] At some time or other a tribe or clan of them made their way far into the interior of Africa and settled on an oasis.[4] Kyrene lay across one line of communication between eastern and western Phoenicians; almost contemporary with its foundation was that of Selinus, which, with Himera, pushed into the Phoenician part of Sicily and obliged the Phoenicians to concentrate on their three posts in the far west of the island.

The Phokaians spread over most of the western Mediterranean, founding stations to serve on the voyage to Spain, and developing other interests. They and other Greeks had been visiting Massalia and the neighbouring coast since the eighth century, but did not settle permanently until *c.* 600. They founded a colony with the consent of the natives, one of their leaders marrying the daughter of the Gallic chief.[5] It is not stated that this was the earliest of the Phokaian colonies. Imports of Greek pottery at Olbia are nearly as old as at Massalia. Nikaia, Antipolis, and others are said to have been colonies of Massalia, but they may have been independently founded Phokaian colonies which later came under the sway of Massalia. The dates of Hemeroskopeion and Mainake on

many times besieged by the Assyrians; Schulten (op. cit. 24) suggests *c.* 700, Blakeway *c.* 669 as the date of the end of the Tyrian voyages; on the evidence of Isaiah perhaps the former is preferable.

[1] Herod. iv. 152. The date is seven years before the foundation of Kyrene, while the Theraians were still on the island of Platea. The Eusebian date *c.* 631 for Kyrene is shown to be approximately correct by the genealogy of the kings in Herodotos. A Corinthian helmet of this period has been found by the Guadelete river near Jerez de la Frontera (see Bosch-Gimpera, *CQ*, 1944, 53).

[2] Herod. i. 163; Anakreon fr. 8, ap. Strabo 151; see Schulten, *Tartessos*, 29.

[3] Herod. iv. 151–7; Euseb., p. 169 Fotheringham.

[4] Herod. iii. 26.

[5] Athen. 576*a*; Justin xliii. 3; Strabo 179; ps.-Skymnos 209–14, 600 B.C. according to Timaios; Eusebian dates are 598 (Hieronymus, ed. Fotheringham, p. 175) or 593 (Vers. Arm., ed. Schoene, ii. 92). See Jacobsthal and Neuffer, *Gallia Graeca*; Vasseur, *L'Origine de Marseille*; Clerc, *Massalia*; Blakeway, *BSA*, xxxiii. 199–200.

the Levante coast are not known, but they were probably not much later than the opening up of Tartessos.[1] It is not known what route the Phokaians used to reach Tartessos. The colonies in Gaul and Spain would be useful ports of call for coasting journeys; but a route from the Bay of Naples to Spain via Sardinia and the Balearic Isles is traced by a trail of names ending in -usa, which are particularly East Greek.[2]

Pityusa (Ibiza) is said to have received a Phoenician colony 160 years after Carthage, i.e. c. 654.[3] No such exact reliance need be placed in the date given by a Greek historian for a Phoenician colony as for a Greek; in the absence of any remains older than the sixth century, it may be doubted whether it is older than 600. Moreover, more of the earliest objects found there are Greek than Phoenician; this holds especially of the terra-cottas. Greek terra-cottas are more numerous than at Carthage and Motye, and it is possible that in the early sixth century the island was not exclusively Phoenician. Its value, to either Greeks or Phoenicians, would be as a stepping-stone to Spain. This also suggests that it did not become Phoenician until the Carthaginians set out to take up the Tyrian heritage in Spain, which was not earlier than the sixth century.

The -usa names may have been given by Phokaians, or equally well by Rhodians; the Rhodians are said to have made voyages to Spain before the first Olympiad, and to have colonized the Balearic Islands, as well as Parthenope on the Bay of Naples.[4] The early date is difficult to accept; Gela is the only well-established Rhodian colony in the west in the early colonizing period. In the last quarter of the seventh century Rhodian commerce with Sicily and the Adriatic increased. The Rhodians may at this period have made wider journeys, and founded or re-founded Rhode in Spain.[5] I have suggested that the foundation of Akragas and Pentathlos' attempt to settle at Lilybaion form a Rhodian drive to conquer the western end of Sicily. This failed, and Carthage followed up Pentathlos' repulse by sending Malchus into Sicily, where

---

[1] Strabo 156, 159; ps.-Skymnos 145 ff.; Avienus, ed. Schulten; Schulten, *Tartessos*, 26; Rhys Carpenter, *The Greeks in Spain*; P. Bosch-Gimpera, *Klio*, xxii. 350 ff.; *CQ*, 1944, 53 ff.
[2] Rhys Carpenter, op. cit. 13 ff.; Schulten, op. cit. 28.
[3] Diod. v. 16. Antonio Vives y Escudero, *La Necropoli de Ibiza*.
[4] Strabo 654.
[5] Strabo 654; ps.-Skymnos 204-6. Schulten, *RE*, i A, 954; *Tartessos*, 46, sets aside this account of a Rhodian colonization previous to the Massiliots on the ground that it is not named in Avienus. See above, p. 237.

after long warfare the position between the two races was stabilized.

The Carthaginian successes in Sicily were followed up by an advance into Sardinia. There is no evidence that either Phoenicians or Greeks had taken much interest in Sardinia before the sixth century. Malchus set out to conquer the island, but met with a serious reverse and was sent into exile. For the greater part of the sixth century it was anyone's who could take it. We possess a good deal of propaganda for a Greek Sardinia. One version of the story of Daidalos says that he abandoned Kamikos when the Cretans approached, and joined Aristaios' colony in Sardinia.[1] As well as Aristaios, the protagonist of Greek culture, Iolaos is said to have led a colony of Thespians and Athenians.[2] Some of Aineias' wanderers found their way there and joined this colony, which was destroyed by an incursion of Libyans. These stories must in their first form be at least as old as the sixth century, before the island was finally conquered by the Carthaginians. Some of them may derive from Stesikhoros. Daidalos in Sardinia is an appendix to Daidalos in Sicily, probably from a Sicilian source. The Iolaos legend has some points of contact with Stesikhoros.[3] The *Geryoneis* reflected in terms of myth the Greek expansion into Spain and over the far west in general. The Sicilian exploits of Herakles were used as justification for the attempt to conquer the western corner. Iolaos is the companion of Herakles, and the story of his colonization of Sardinia might have been intended to inspire the Greeks to follow him. Aineias is associated with Iolaos; Stesikhoros may have written of Aineias' coming to the west. It would be rash to assert that Stesikhoros had anything to do with the story, but it is likely that Pausanias' ultimate source was a Sicilian poet of the school of Stesikhoros. This is not to say that the stories originated at that period. They may go back farther, and may even have some basis in Minoan–Mycenaean contacts with Sardinia.[4] But the sixth century is a period when they would naturally arouse interest, and at any later date, when Sardinia was a Carthaginian possession and closed to the Greeks, they would not.

---

[1] Paus. x. 17. 4; cf. Solinus iv. 1 ff.

[2] Paus. x. 17. 5; Diod. iv. 29; Solinus i. 61; iv. 1–7.

[3] The mythical history of Sardinia is connected with Geryon in the person of Norax son of Erytheia daughter of Geryon, the eponym of Nora, whither he led a colony of Iberians (Paus. x. 17. 5).

[4] For Cretan traces in Spain and Sardinia see Schulten, *Tartessos*, 7, 80.

It is obvious what interest Sicilians, particularly those of the west of the island, would take in a colonization of Sardinia. Not only would they profit from trade with the island, but their own problems would become easier as the result of a formidable blow to the Phoenicians. The Greeks still had the chance of winning the western Mediterranean.

Corsica had already received a Phokaian colony at Alalia in c. 560.[1] The Phokaians may also have settled in Sardinia. The Greek name Ikhnusa[2] given to Sardinia, probably at the time of the Tartessos voyages, does not imply Greek settlement there, but Olbia, said to be the name of Iolaos' colony in the north-east near Terranova,[3] may, in fact, have been a short-lived Phokaian colony, sharing the name with the Olbia in Gaul; the name would agree with the 'greatest and richest of islands' propaganda. Diodoros names among the cities of Corsica Kalaris, a Phokaian colony, from which they were expelled by the Etruscans.[4] No such town is otherwise known in Corsica; he may have written Kalaris by mistake for Alalia, which he does not mention; or he may have misspelt and misplaced Karalis, the chief town of Sardinia, which would then have been for a short time a Phokaian colony. Some Greek pottery has been found near Tharros, and may precede the Phoenician colony.[5]

In 540, after the conquest of Ionia by Harpagos, Bias proposed at the Panionion that the Ionians should migrate in a body and found a single city in Sardinia.[6] I take this to be a proposition actually made and considered. Sardinia was not well known, and was more attractive in prospect than in fact. The error that it is the largest of the islands of the Mediterranean has been repeated in modern times, and indeed it is very nearly the same size as Sicily. Stories about its fertility were current. Pausanias says of it ἡ δὲ Σαρδὼ μέγεθος μὲν καὶ εὐδαιμονίαν ἐστὶν ὁμοία ταῖς μάλιστα ἐπαινουμέναις,[7] though he knows of its unhealthiness. The phrase about its εὐδαιμονία, conflicting with all other ancient opinion, may well be a

---

[1] Herod. i. 165–6; Thuk. i. 13.   [2] Paus. x. 17. 1; Solinus iv. 1.

[3] Paus. x. 17. 5; Diod. iv. 29.

[4] v. 13. The other city in Corsica named by Diodoros, Nikaia, said by him to be Tyrrhenian, shares its name with the Phokaian colony, now Nice. It may have been in the first place Phokaian, pace Diodoros.

[5] Clerc, Massalia, i. 90. He dates it in the first half of the sixth century. Cf. also von Duhn, Strena Helbigiana, 61 ff. (Tyrrhenian amphora from Tharros, in Sassari).

[6] Herod. i. 170.

[7] x. 17. 1; cf. iv. 23. 5 (a reminiscence of Herod. i. 170; cf. below, p. 396).

reminiscence of this period of imperfect knowledge and boundless expectations.

Histiaios and Aristagoras are both suspected of designs on Sardinia. Aristagoras is said to have thought of Sardinia as an alternative to Myrkinos as a refuge on the failure of the Ionian revolt,[1] Histiaios to have cajoled Darius with the prospect of conquering Sardinia, the greatest of the islands.[2] In neither case is it a fact for which Herodotos vouches, and we cannot be sure that Sardinia was still on the cards after 500.

The decisive stroke was played not in Sardinia but in Corsica. The Phokaians had for some time been at war with the Carthaginians.[3] They sailed prepared for war, not in cargo-boats but in pentekonters, the regular ship-of-war of those days. After their abandonment of Phokaia nearly half of them settled at Alalia, where they joined the earlier colonists. Thence they carried on indiscriminate piracy for five years. At the end of that time they were attacked by a joint fleet of Carthaginians and Etruscans, whom they defeated in a Kadmeian victory which was so severe that they were obliged to desert Alalia. They retired first to Rhegion, and then found an abiding home at Velia.[4] From that time not only settlement in Corsica but hopes in Sardinia were at an end. Corsica passed to the Etruscans, who had from now on the control of the Tyrrhenian Sea. Sardinia became definitely Carthaginian. The wars under Hasdrubal and Hamilcar,[5] which should fill the last part of the sixth century, conquered all the island except the mountainous interior, and it was firmly closed to Greeks. After the battle of Alalia they ceased to be able to sail direct to Tartessos. For a few years the Massaliots carried on coast voyages, landing this side of the Straits of Gibraltar, which were closed by the

---

[1] Herod. v. 124.   [2] Herod. v. 106; vi. 2.

[3] It does not follow from Thuk. i. 13 that this warfare began as early as 600, for the Phokaian fleet whose action he discusses is said to belong to the reign of Cyrus or Cambyses, and one would infer from his order that it was later than Polykrates. This is impossible (but see Bosch-Gimpera, *CQ*, 1944, 55–6, who refers the passage to wars of the Massaliots, not Phokaians). But Thukydides clearly regards the great days of the Phokaian fleet as coming little before the fall of the city. With this agrees the entry in the Eusebian list of thalassocracies (cf. Myres, *JHS*, 1906, 102). Thukydides may refer not to the original foundation of Massalia, but to its reinforcement when the Phokaians deserted Ionia. ἐνίκων need not mean a series of victories; it is constantly used for a single victory; e.g. Herod. i. 82; vi. 113 (thrice); vii. 44; ix. 71. 2; Thuk. i. 49. 6; 105. 2; 116. 1; iii. 108. 2; vi. 101. 4; vii. 34. 7; viii. 25. 5; Xen. *Hell.* ii. 4. 19 (the references are due to Mr. R. H. Dundas).

[4] Herod. i. 167; Antiokhos (*FHG*, i. 183) ap. Strabo 252; Timagenes (*FHG*, iii. 323) ap. Amm. Marcell. xv. 9.

[5] Justin. xix. 1.

Carthaginians; but soon the Carthaginians destroyed Tartessos so that it never arose again.[1] The Greek share of the far west dwindled to the coasts of Gaul and north-east Spain, and as the way thither lay through waters controlled by the hostile Etruscans, Massalia and the other colonies must have been largely thrown on their own resources.

The alliance between Carthage and Etruria, which Aristotle quotes as the example of treaties in general,[2] should belong to the period of Etruscan thalassocracy. Herodotos says that they acted in concert at Alalia (κοινῷ λόγῳ χρησάμενοι). After this victory there was probably a formal alliance, and a division of spheres, the Carthaginians taking Sardinia and the Etruscans Corsica. When Rome revolted, and appeared for the moment to inherit the position of Etruria, the Carthaginians made a treaty with her in 509.[3]

The Etruscans made a great effort to conquer Kyme, which would carry with it all Campania. In the year 524, we are told, they gathered a host of half a million barbarians, with 18,000 horse, and if it had not been for the portentous backward course of the rivers Volturnus and Glanis, the Kymaians would not have resisted. But fighting with one-third of their force, 4,500 foot and 600 horse, on a narrow front before the town, with swamp on one side and mountain on the other, they routed the Etruscans. Aristodemos killed the enemy general in single combat. The numbers of the Kymaians are plausible, all the other details, including the date, uncertain.[4] At the same period the Greek element was reinforced by a Samian settlement at Dikaiarkhia, in a region which had long been Greek but was threatened by the Etruscan advance.[5]

This check was followed after a decade by the movement which drove the Etruscan kings from Rome, and raised a short-lived Latin alliance to resist Etruscan attempts at reconquest. The decisive factor was the support of Kyme. A great battle was fought at Aricia, in which the Kymaians under Aristodemos bore the brunt of the fighting and routed the Etruscans.[6] Dionysios speaks also of intended naval action against the

---

[1] Schulten, *Tartessos*, 44 ff.; Bosch-Gimpera, *CQ*, 1944, 56, implies a later date (*c.* 500?) for the destruction of Tartessos, and points out that 'the last third of the sixth century seems to have been a flourishing period of commerce for the Greeks in Spain'.

[2] *Pol.* 1280ª 36: Τυρρηνοὶ καὶ Καρχηδόνιοι, καὶ πάντες οἷς ἔστι σύμβολα πρὸς ἀλλήλους.

[3] Polyb. iii. 22. The suspicions cast on this treaty are unjustified; see R. L. Beaumont, *JRS*, 1939, 74 ff.

[4] Dion. Hal. vii. 3–4.

[5] In 531, Euseb., ed. Fotheringham, 185.

[6] Livy ii. 14; Dion. Hal. vii. 5–6.

Etruscans. This victory finally cut off the Etruscans in Campania from direct connexion with Etruria, and they had to make their peace with the Greeks of Kyme and Poseidonia. The prosperity of their farthest outpost at Fratte near Salerno[1] and the quantity of Greek imports indicate that they reached a *modus vivendi*. Pompeii was either a mixed city, like Spina, or had at least a strong Hellenic element. The Doric temple of the late sixth century has curious features unparalleled elsewhere.[2]

There had already been stasis in Kyme, where Aristodemos led a democratic faction against the aristocracy, and the strain of the war brought about a revolution, which made Aristodemos tyrant. His military prowess at Kyme and Aricia made him a popular hero. As tyrant, he brought about a *rapprochement* with the Etruscans. Tarquinius Superbus spent his last years at Kyme, after his final defeat at Lake Regillus.[3] Livy calls Aristodemos the heir of the Tarquins, and relates under the year 492 that he detained Roman ships which came to Kyme to buy wheat.[4] Aristodemos, who was called by the uncomplimentary surname of Malakos, was a little-loved tyrant. Dionysios' highly coloured picture makes him seize power with the aid of his Etruscan prisoners, who became his bodyguard, prevent the citizens from having arms, exile those of the aristocracy whom he did not kill, send their children out of the city as shepherds, put an end to gymnastic and warlike exercises, and bring the children up as girls; a very thorough levelling, to which he hardly need add γῆς ἀναδασμὸν καὶ χρεῶν ἄφεσιν. The exiles gathered in Capua, and at some date after 490, according to Dionysios' chronology, captured the city and put all the house of Aristodemos to death.[5] Kyme now returned to her anti-Etruscan policy, which led to the Etruscan attack which Hieron helped to beat off in 474.

The Eleans should assuredly have taken a part in these Etruscan wars which followed their own defeat and expulsion at Alalia. But we hear in this period only of their philosophers and their εὐνομία. They had to fight against the Poseidoniates,

---

[1] *Studi Etruschi*, iii. 91 ff.

[2] Maiuri, 'Studi e ricerche sulla fortificazione di Pompei', *MA*, xxxiii; Carrington, 'The Etruscans and Pompeii' (*Antiquity*, 1932, 5 ff.); *Pompeii*, ch. ii.

[3] Livy ii. 21. 5; cf. Dion. Hal. vii. 2.

[4] ii. 34. 4: 'frumentum Cumis cum coemptum esset, naves pro bonis Tarquiniorum ab Aristodemo tyranno, qui heres erat, retentae sunt.'

[5] Dion. Hal. vii. 7–12; cf. Diod. vii. 10.

but this is quite undated; in the text of Strabo it is mentioned after the Lucanian wars. As they were conducted to Velia by a Poseidoniate, it is likely that they had at first good relations, and that the war is of later date.[1]

The Etruscan power was now at its height. Their extension north of the Apennines to Felsina and Spina[2] took place c. 530, and was part cause of the increasing Greek activity on the Italian coast of the Adriatic.[3] The southern extension into Campania began earlier, and a little before 530 they reached their farthest point, at Fratte near Salerno.[4] Though Greek settlers, especially artists and, we may believe, traders, were welcomed in most of the cities of Etruria at this period, there is reason to believe that the Etruscans kept in their own hands most of the trade from Greece. They had a commercial alliance with Sybaris, the greatest of the cities of Magna Graecia, and goods from the Sybarite port of Laos were doubtless carried in Etruscan ships. The importance of the overland route must belong to a period when the Straits of Messina were closed to those who used it, and this is true of the years from 540 onwards.[5] Rhegion was allied to the Phokaians, and assisted to establish them at Velia after the evacuation of Alalia. The Liparaians were carrying on a privateering war against the Etruscans. Access to the Straits, and any Sicilian waters, would be dangerous to the Etruscans. But this was not of the first importance to them while they had a route via Sybaris and Laos, and other cities of south Italy were anxious to develop trade by the overland route from the Ionian Sea to the Tyrrhenian; while Ionians, Corinthians, and other Greeks were coming in ever greater numbers to settle in Etruria, and while they had the Carthaginian alliance.

The position in the western Mediterranean at the end of the sixth century was that the Carthaginians had strengthened themselves in Africa, had won Sardinia and the Balearic Isles, and controlled the Phoenician remnant in Sicily. The Etruscan power by land and sea had reached its highest point. The Greeks, after eighty years' profitable intercourse with Tartessos, had been cut off from the south of Spain but had greatly strengthened their hold on the trade with the north-eastern

[1] Strabo 252; Herod. i. 167.

[2] Strabo 214; Felsina, Pellegrini, *Vasi greci delle necropoli felsinee*; Spina, *N Sc*, 1924, 279 ff.; 1927, 143 ff.; S. Aurigemma, *Il R. Museo di Spina*.

[3] Cf. R. L. Beaumont, *JHS*, 1936, 178 ff.

[4] *Studi Etruschi*, iii. 91 ff.   [5] See above, pp. 206 ff.

coast and the south of Gaul. They had lost their temporary foothold in Corsica, and their hopes of Sardinia. In Sicily the Greeks were no stronger at the end of the century than at the beginning. After their advance at Himera, Selinus, and Akragas, they were unable to complete the conquest of the west. Pentathlos failed in his main object, and the three Phoenician settlements were strong in the support of Carthage and the alliance with the Elymians. We cannot follow the vicissitudes of the struggle between Carthage and the Greek cities, in which both sides won temporary advantages, possibly including territorial conquests. But the situation was the same in general outline for Dorieus as for Pentathlos, except for the very important change that Carthage now stood firmly behind the Phoenicians in Sicily. On the Greek side, the Knidians on Lipara were carrying on piracy against the Etruscans, and perhaps against the Carthaginian allies of the Etruscans. Akragas prospered mightily, and became one of the greatest of Greek cities. But on the other side must be set the uncertain attitude of Selinus, whom economic advantage and military pressure inclined to make her peace with Carthage.

The weakness of the Greeks was, as usual, their division. The Phokaians, and with them probably other Ionians, and the Knidians of Lipara, carried on the struggle for Greek predominance against all enemies and by all means. The Khalkidian colonies gave them at least moral support. But of the cities already established and flourishing Sybaris, and to a lesser degree the other cities of Magna Graecia, found the friendship of the Etruscans profitable. Selinus, in the forefront of the struggle in Sicily, was tempted by the Carthaginian alliance. There is no indication that the cities of south-eastern Sicily, Syracuse, Gela, and Leontinoi, took any especial interest in the Greek expansion into the far west.

The time when the Greeks missed an opportunity to extend the range of their civilization in the west was after the Ionian revolt. In the half-century between the capture of Ionia by Harpagos and the suppression of the Ionian revolt there must have been tens of thousands of men who left Ionia for ever. A mass migration following the advice of Bias and the example of the Phokaians would have been defeatism; the Ionians had a mission in the Aegean as well as in the greater Greek world. But those men who did in fact leave Asia could with better direction have accomplished more than they did. Not all of them were fitted for pioneer work. Many of them brought a revivifying influence to the south Italian cities and to a less extent to Sicily. Others spread Greek art and Greek manners in Etruria, and their influence, working from within, was one of the strongest forces in the hellenizing of Italy. But there were still many men, sailors, traders, and the like, who sought a new home, and might, if they had acted together, have formed a nucleus of Greek civilization in the far west. Many of them preferred to settle singly in cities already flourishing ; some of them, like the Samians at Zankle, using treachery to win a home. One man showed that he had the spirit to fight for Hellenism against the barbarians. Dionysios of Phokaia, the leader whom the Ionians at Lade would not obey because he had only three ships, sailed to Sicily and carried on piracy, not indiscriminately, but against Carthaginians and Etruscans.[1] One would like to know more about him and where he had his base ; but he had not the men to accomplish anything constructive. Of course there was nothing like a 'crusade' of Hellenism. The enemies, Carthage and Etruria, were both peoples of a high degree of civilization. It is arguable that more might have been accomplished by peaceful intercourse than by war. From one point of view, the Liparaians and Dionysios were common pirates, who hindered Greek trade as much as Etruscan and Carthaginian. From any point of view, those Greeks who settled in Etruria rendered greater permanent services to the spread of Hellenic culture than those who attacked Etruscan shipping. But there were great areas untouched by Carthage or Etruria where the foundation of even a single Greek colony would have been of great advantage, not only by opening new markets to Greek commerce but by civilizing the impressionable barbarians. The example of Massalia and the other Phokaian colonies might have been a guide. But it took remarkable qualities to succeed as the Phokaians had done, and it is unfair to blame the other Ionians for lacking some of these qualities.

Sparta's one effort in the struggle of Greeks and Phoenicians was made when affairs had reached this state of stalemate. Dorieus, second son of Anaxandridas, discontented with his position under his brother Kleomenes, received the permission of the Spartan state to leave to found a colony. He went first to the Kinyps, on the coast of Africa between Kyrene and

[1] Herod. vi. 17.

Carthage. There he remained two years, and in the course of the third was driven out by the natives in combination with the Carthaginians. Returning to Greece, he set out a second time for Sicily, intending to colonize the land which Herakles had won from Eryx. As he passed down the Italian coast he ran into the war between Kroton and Sybaris. Herodotos could not decide on the evidence before him whether he turned aside to aid the Krotoniates. The remnant of the Sybarites said so, the Krotoniates denied it, but Herodotos, with most modern opinion, is inclined to think that he did.[1] Whether this was so or not, it must be allowed that his voyage to Sicily was at the same time as the fall of Sybaris, i.e. c. 511–510.[2] If the synchronization was false, the Krotoniates would have used this argument to prove that Dorieus did not join them in the attack on Sybaris, instead of the very weak argument that they had shown him no gratitude. This establishes the chronology of his attempt at Kinyps. As he kept his expedition together, he can have spent only a few months in Greece on his return. Therefore the two years and a bit at Kinyps were c. 514–512.

He set out on this first venture with the full consent of the Spartan state. It is most unlikely that the king's brother could have begun such an undertaking unofficially. He had to ask for his colonists, though what body he should ask at Sparta is not clear. His men were Spartan citizens, and it is contrary to Sparta's secular policy to let so many men go abroad and be lost to her. Kleomenes had recently refused to assist Maiandros to return to Samos,[3] and his consistent policy was to decline distant commitments while organizing the patriotic front within mainland Greece. This apparent weakening of the Spartan power by an undertaking which infallibly came into conflict with Carthage needs some explanation. There may have been an element of opposition, led by Dorieus, which Kleomenes feared. It is doubtful whether the direction of the colony was determined by any official party at Sparta, and very doubtful whether the anti-Carthaginian purpose of both Kinyps and Herakleia was favoured by the State. But the colony set out with official Spartan sanction.

Kinyps was one of the chief fertile areas of the Mediterranean coast still left uncolonized. Herodotos waxes eloquent about the charm of the land, χῶρον κάλλιστον, the λόφος Χαρίτων, and

---

[1] Herod. v. 42 ff.
[2] Fifty-eight years before the refoundation in 453–452; Diod. xi. 90.　　[3] Herod. iii. 148.

the three-hundredfold yield of its wonderful soil.[1] There were prophecies flying about, oracles that the Lakedaimonians would colonize the island of Phla in Lake Tritonis, that there must infallibly be a hundred Greek cities around the lake.[2] From the time of the Argonauts, Libya was held in readiness for the descendants of the Lakedaimonians. But they succeeded in winning only a part, the kingdom of Kyrene.

The settlement was undoubtedly made with the closest co-operation of the Kyrenaians. Since the growth of the Carthaginian power in Africa, and Kambyses' conquest of Egypt, their position between the two great powers needed strengthening. Dorieus was guided by men of Thera, the mother city of Kyrene, and he passed by Kyrene, where he was joined by the exile Philippos of Kroton.[3] It would be immensely to Kyrene's advantage to have a strong Greek neighbour to protect her, as the desert appeared inadequate.[4] The three-hundredfold yield and the black well-watered earth read like extracts from the prospectus calling for settlers. It is very probable therefore that Dorieus' first venture was intended against the Carthaginians. It was certainly so understood by them, for within three years they had joined with the natives to expel him. His next attempt was a definite challenge to them in a region where they had been long established but which was perhaps the weakest point of their empire. It is nowhere suggested that he was invited to Sicily by the Selinuntines or other Greeks.[5] The story of the wrestling of Herakles and Eryx, and the land waiting for the descendants of Herakles, was probably current long before Dorieus,[6] and its political implications might be recalled as well in Greece as in Sicily. Herodotos names a Boiotian, Antikhares, as the maker of the suggestion. There is no word in his or any other account of co-operation from the Sicilian Greeks. It is impossible that they should not take the greatest interest in this attempt to conquer the barbarian corner, but it is not certain that this interest was entirely favourable.

Carthaginians, Phoenicians of Sicily, and Elymians were all threatened by the attempt to settle under Mount Eryx, which

---

[1] Herod. v. 42; iv. 175, 198.

[2] Herod. iv. 178–9. These oracles cannot be *post eventum*, as the event never took place.

[3] Herod. v. 47.   [4] Herod. iii. 13.

[5] Justin xix. 1. 9 is usually emended to refer to Dorieus. I believe that the text is sound and the appeal came later. See below, p. 411.

[6] See above, pp. 330 ff.

if successful would be as serious a blow as Pentathlos' attempt might have been, and combined to expel the Greeks, killing Dorieus and three of his four commanders.[1] One of them, Philippos of Kroton, received heroic honours from the Segestans.[2] According to Diodoros, Dorieus first founded a city, Herakleia, whose rapid growth was such that the Carthaginians saw that it threatened their hegemony and destroyed it. This is usually taken to refer to the renaming of Herakleia Minoa (see below, p. 353), which, however, was not founded by Dorieus and was not, so far as is known, destroyed by the Carthaginians. It is probably to be referred to a short-lived foundation under Mount Eryx.[3] It is odd that Herodotos, who implies that Dorieus was defeated and killed almost as soon as he arrived in Sicily, does not record the foundation of Herakleia, which would have fulfilled the oracle given to him at Delphi, that he would take (αἱρήσειν) the land for which he set out. The μαρτύριον μέγιστον of the Sybarite remnant was that if he had not turned aside from his purpose and destroyed their city, εἷλε ἂν τὴν Ἐρυκίνην χώρην καὶ ἑλὼν κατέσχε. The oracle was in strictness fulfilled when he first seized the land of Eryx, for however little time he held it.[4] But the priests were not happy about this literal interpretation. They put it out that Dorieus had been very rude to them. He set off on his Libyan venture without consulting them at all, and when that failed he made up his mind without assistance, and asked the Pythia only whether he would take the land for which he was setting out. The oracle's careful dissociation from his failure suggests that in fact it had something to do with the direction of the enterprise. This was before the days when it medized. The oracles about Lake Tritonis are not Pythian, but the long myth of the clod in Pindar, *Pyth*. iv, sounds like an apologia. If Euphamos had not lost the clod given him by Eurypylos,[5] his descendants would have won the whole continent instead of Kyrene only. The Μηδείας ἔπος is not part of the Pythia's word to Battos, but

---

[1] Herod. v. 46; Diod. iv. 23. 2; Paus. iii. 16. 4. Diodoros mentions only the Carthaginians, Herodotos names Phoenicians and Segestans, Pausanias Segestans only. There is nothing contradictory here; the different accounts are supplementary.

[2] See above, p. 335.

[3] Pareti, 14 ff. Diodoros' ultimate source is probably Antiokhos, who may have mentioned details not given in Herodotos' brief narrative. See above, p. 328, for objections to Pareti's thesis that Diodoros' account of Pentathlos' expedition is padded with details which really belong to Dorieus. The similarity between the experiences of the two expeditions is easily explained by their identity of object.

[4] Pareti, 15–16.   [5] i.q. Triton., Schol. *Pyth*. iv. 57.

is enclosed in it in such a manner as to make it clear that the story is of Delphic origin. The failure of the wide plans lay on the conscience of Delphi.[1]

Dorieus failed for the reason that he had not enough men. The five leaders of the Spartans, Thessalos, Paraibatas, Keleas, Euryleon, and Dorieus, perhaps each commanded a ship. The expedition set out during the brief period of Spartan thalassocracy,[2] but Sparta can have had few ships or men for so distant an undertaking. Her subjects and allies probably provided a large part of the force. Five ships and not much over a thousand men is a not improbable figure for the fighting force of the expedition.[3] To this was added Philippos of Kroton, with his own trireme and his own men, no contemptible accession. With the Spartans were one hundred Athenians, who received the honour of a heroon at Sparta.[4]

No mention is made of Selinuntines or any other of the Sicilian Greeks. Our accounts are so brief that this is not at all conclusive. But there are grounds for believing that Selinus stood aside, that is, favoured the Carthaginian.[5] After the death of Dorieus, Euryleon gathered up the survivors, seized the Selinuntine colony of Minoa, and freed Selinus from her tyrant Peithagoras. Thereupon he made himself tyrant of Selinus, but was soon overthrown and killed on the altar of Zeus in the agora. He may have been merely self-seeking, but it is more likely that he wished to save something from the wreck and to strike a last blow for the Greek cause. His seizure of Minoa appears to have been only a first step against Selinus. Nothing is known of Peithagoras, but it is plausible to suppose that his tyranny was based on friendship with the Phoenicians:

[1] Schroeder, *Pindars Pythien*, 35; Wade-Gery and Bowra, *Pindar's Pythian Odes*, xxxvi.

[2] Myres, *JHS*, xxvi. 99.

[3] For numbers of settlers in Greek colonies see Beaumont, *JHS*, 1936, 169: 1,000 is the largest number recorded.

[4] The text of Pausanias reads Ἀθηναίων ρω. The usually accepted conjecture Ἀθηνοδώρου is meaningless. No Athenodoros is known, and the grammar Ἀθηνοδώρου τῶν . . . σταλέντων is curious. Professor Wade-Gery proposes to keep Ἀθηναίων ρ' and suggests that these Athenians were the hostages deposited in Naxos by Peisistratos (Herod. i. 64), and liberated by the Spartans when they put down the tyrant Lygdamis, during the Spartan thalassocracy of 517–515, a little before Dorieus left Sparta.

[5] A small piece of evidence in this direction is the occurrence of the name Τυρρανά at Selinus in a *defixio* of the 6th–5th century (Arangio-Ruiz and Olivieri, *Inscriptiones Graecae Siciliae et infimae Italiae ad ius pertinentes*, 160 ff.). Such a name can hardly be imagined in a city which was sympathetic with the struggle against the barbarian allies, Carthaginians and Etruscans. But, as it occurs in a *defixio*, perhaps Tyrrhana's enemy was a patriot who invoked the gods against the fifth column.

not necessarily an alliance, but a peace that would enable Selinus to reap the profit of trade with Carthage. Euryleon made an attempt to win Selinus to the patriotic cause, but on his overthrow she returned to the Carthaginian alliance to which she held in 480.

Minoa is mentioned for the first time in sixth-century history in connexion with Euryleon, and Herodotos calls it Σελινουσίων ἀποικίην. At some time in the late sixth century it was taken by Akragas, whose dedication from the spoils of Minoa to the Lindian Athena[1] comes after Amasis' linen corselet (probably a little before 540), before the offering of -lis, of uncertain date,[2] and of Artaphrenes (490). It has been supposed that it was conquered by the Akragantines before 510, and won back by Selinus also before that date.[3] But the naming in the *Lindian Chronicle* of Minoa instead of Herakleia does not prove that its conquest by the Akragantines was earlier than Euryleon's occupation; Minoa is the name used in Diodoros' account of the discovery of the bones of Minos in the eighties of the fifth century.[4] The name Herakleia does not occur earlier than 314,[5] if Diod. iv. 23 is rightly referred to a settlement under Mount Eryx. It is only an inference, though a plausible one, which associates the name Herakleia with Euryleon's occupation. But it is weakened by the fact that Herodotos has nothing to say about such a fulfilment of the oracle given to Dorieus, and by Diodoros' use of the old name in speaking of events later than Euryleon. It is possible indeed that the name was used first in the fourth century as a translation of the Phoenician name which Makara represents.[6] Certainly if Diodoros uses the old name for fifth- and fourth-century events, the Akragantines may have used it in their dedication to Athena Lindia after the time of Euryleon. This is a simpler hypothesis than that of a colony originally Selinuntine, an Akragantine capture, an unrecorded Selinuntine recapture, and another unrecorded Akragantine capture.[7] Euryleon seized Minoa as a stepping-off ground against Selinus.[8] After his overthrow, it passed again

---

[1] *Lind. Chron.* xxx (*Lindos*, ii. 175).   [2] See above, p. 94.
[3] Reinach, *Rev. épig.* i. 105.   [4] Diod. iv. 79.
[5] Ibid. xix. 71. 7. Not only in iv. 79, where the old name might be used because of the association with Minos, but in xvi. 9, 4 (of the year 357) Diodoros uses the name Minoa.
[6] Herakleides Pont. fr. 29 (*FHG*, ii. 220).
[7] Pareti, 13 ff.; Ziegler, *RE*, viii. 437, art. 'Herakleia', 28.
[8] Pareti suggests that the seizure of Minoa by Euryleon was by agreement with the Selinuntines, who wished to protect their boundary against Akragantine attacks. He points out that the Lindian inscription does not speak of the conquest of Minoa, but only of a

to the Selinuntine state. Carrying on the warfare against the Carthaginian and the Phoenicizing Greek, the Akragantines attacked the Selinuntines and took this, their easternmost post. This was probably about the end of the sixth century, soon after Euryleon's death. It was certainly before Theron, for the Lindian inscription names οἱ Ἀκραγαντῖνοι and no individual. Minoa was Akragantine in Theron's day, when he discovered the bones of Minos, and remained so until 383, when the Carthaginian boundary was advanced to the river Halykos.[1]

The chronology is of the vaguest. Accepting the year 511–510 for Dorieus' arrival in Sicily, the Herakleia under Mount Eryx had a short existence before its destruction and the death of Dorieus. Two or three years is as much as is likely.[2] Dorieus' death need not have been fresh when Gelon undertook to avenge him, probably about 489.[3] Vengeance has a long memory, especially when jogged by policy. Euryleon's seizure of Minoa may then have been c. 508–507, his death soon after, and the Akragantine capture of Minoa any time between c. 505 and 490.

victory. A partial success is less likely to be commemorated than the conquest, which we know to have happened before Theron. I disagree entirely with this view of the position of Selinus; there is no evidence that she gave help to Dorieus, and she appears to be already on the Carthaginian side in 510, in sympathy if not in act. Pareti dates the beginning of the alliance with Carthage from the time of the 'struggles with Euryleon after he had made himself tyrant, and with the Akragantines'. On this view, Euryleon was guilty of self-seeking and the Akragantines of the most wanton aggression against a state which deserved well of the Greek name. I prefer to think that Selinus was already lukewarm, if not actually unpatriotic, and that Euryleon tried to coerce her into the patriotic league, and the Akragantines exacted reprisals for her disloyalty. I agree that the Akragantine capture of Minoa was effected with the co-operation of the Spartan survivors, but would put it after the death of Euryleon.

[1] Diod. xv. 17. 5, where the town is not named.

[2] Pareti (pp. 5, 78 ff.) bases on Herod. vi. 48 an argument that Dorieus' death was not much before Kleomenes' death in 489. But Dorieus cut himself off from Sparta as soon as he left for the first time. It is unlikely that he would still be considered for the succession. From the Spartan point of view, it made little difference how long he lived in Sicily. Moreover, nothing can get over the difficulty that Herodotos says οὐ γάρ τινα πολλὸν χρόνον ἦρξε ὁ Κλεομένης, which is flagrantly untrue. Pareti's interpretation (p. 5), that he did not long survive Dorieus, is not what Herodotos says, nor would it be relevant to his moralizing.

[3] Niese, Hermes, 1907, 453–4; cf. Pareti, 11–12.

CHAPTER XII

THE SOUTH ITALIAN COLONIES

NOTHING is known about the south Italian cities or their relations with each other before the middle of the sixth century. From that date it becomes possible to construct a thin but continuous history, depending mainly on late sources but also on the coins which most of the cities begin to issue during this period. We may begin from the appearance at Agariste's wedding (*c.* 570) of Smindyrides of Sybaris and Damasos son of Amyris of Siris. Smindyrides ἐπὶ πλεῖστον δὴ χλιδῆς εἷς ἀνὴρ ἀπίκετο (ἡ δὲ Σύβαρις ἤκμαζε τοῦτον τὸν χρόνον μάλιστα).[1] The later stories about the luxury of the Sybarites and Smindyrides must have some truth in them, to justify this opinion of Herodotos; to them are added similar stories about the luxury of Siris.[2] The pioneering days were over. Sybaris' empire over the Oinotrians was no doubt already established, and her subordinate colonies founded.

In the second half of the sixth century the Akhaian colonies had a common bond in their coinage. This begins about 550.[3] The cities have each its own type, but share the fabric, a broad thin piece of silver in which the reverse type is the incuse of the obverse, and standard. The standard weight is something over 120 gr., divided into thirds. The range within which most of the coins of the archaic period fall is as follows:[4]

			gr.
Taras	.	.	118–26: sixths, 20: twelfths, 11.
Metapontion	.	.	118–26: thirds, 29–40.
Sybaris	.	.	121–7: thirds, 39–42.
Laos	.	.	120–3.
Kroton	.	.	115–24: thirds, 37–40.
Kaulonia	.	.	119–26: many light weight.
Poseidonia	.	.	112–16: halves 50–9.
Velia	.	.	112–17: halves 58–61.

These coins weigh slightly less than the staters of Corinth, which are also divided into thirds. They were for practical purposes on the Corinthian standard, the reduction of weight being due to the comparative scarcity of silver, which had to

---

[1] Herod. vi. 127. [2] Athen. 523*c–e.*

[3] See references on p. 246, n. 2.

[4] The range is less deceptive than the average, for some coins fall a long way short of making weight. There are a few coins above the limit of the range.

be imported from sources not under the control of the south Italian cities.[1]

The coins of Taras are on the same standard as those of the Akhaian cities, but only a few are of the incuse fabric. This fabric was also used by Rhegion, Zankle, and Poseidonia, which used a different standard. Poseidonia, though a colony of Sybaris, lay outside the sphere of her direct influence. The relations indicated by the common fabric are cultural, not commercial. On the other hand, we may infer that Taras, using the same standard as the other cities of south Italy, had commercial but not close cultural or political relations. There are no coins of Lokroi until the fourth century; this suggests that Lokrian economy was in the archaic period different from that of her neighbours, and that her relations with them were limited.[2]

The four cities which issued coins of the incuse fabric most freely—Sybaris, Metapontion, Kroton, and Kaulonia—were all Akhaian colonies. Many other cities used the same fabric and standard: Laos, Siris and Pyxus, and the towns whose names begin with Asi- or Ami-, and Pal- and Mol-. There is reason to regard most of these as subordinate to Sybaris.[3] Laos was certainly, Ami- probably, a colony of Sybaris. The joint coins of Siris and Pyxus have the Sybarite type of a bull, and probably belong to the period after the overthrow of Siris.[4] The independent cities, Metapontion, Kroton, and Kaulonia, probably also took their lead from Sybaris. Sybaris kept up a higher weight than the others, which suggests that she set the standard, and they often fell short because silver was expensive. Sybaris was without question the greatest of these cities.

The common fabric and standard of coinage implies a certain unity of purpose and is probably the mark of collaboration in other spheres. In the third quarter of the sixth century the Akhaian colonies were allied and sought to bring their neighbours into the alliance. Kaulonia is not heard of in the history of this period, and was perhaps politically subordinate to Kroton. Metapontion, though separated from Sybaris by the Sirite territory, had been founded by her aid and supported by her arms. Kroton joined with Sybaris and Metapontion in a successful attempt to coerce Siris. Siris was only less flourish-

[1] Cf. Perret, *Siris*, 231 ff.   [2] See above, p. 248.
[3] See above, p. 158.
[4] Cf. Perret, *Siris*, 247 ff.

ing and luxurious than Sybaris;[1] there are stories about Sirites very like the Sybarite stories. The two cities have indeed been confused, the likeness of name helping. Amyris ὁ σοφός, whom Herodotos calls a Sirite, is brought into Sybarite history.[2] The stories of the fall of the two cities are distressingly parallel. Siris perhaps ruled over the native peoples of the valleys behind, and had a connexion with Pyxus on the Tyrrhenian Sea.[3] This is inferred from their joint coins, which are later than the subjection of Siris to Sybaris but must reflect a previously existing state of affairs, for such a connexion could not grow up after Siris had passed into the Sybarite hegemony. The route to Pyxus, though much longer and less practicable than the Sybarite portages, was a possible alternative.[3] Siris was then a rival to Sybaris, but second to her in all things; less rich, less powerful, less well situated for commerce. But she was important enough to be destroyed. The most likely reason is commercial jealousy; considering how mixed the population of the Akhaian colonies, especially Sybaris, must have been, it is unlikely that there was much racial feeling.

The occasion of the attack is not recorded, nor any details of the campaign. The Sirites were defeated and the city sacked; fifty youths and the priest of Athena were torn from the statue of the goddess and slaughtered on the altar. Athena turned her eyes away, and a plague fell on the guilty Akhaians, until they set up statues of the goddess and the victims in propitiation.[4] Siris had no independent existence for a century after this, but the city was not completely destroyed. Her only coins, bearing the bull of Sybaris, indicate that she stood in the same relation to Sybaris as Laos did: and are therefore after her fall. It is likely that she continued to have a separate existence, but followed the economic and political direction of Sybaris.[5]

This stroke was to the interest of Sybaris and Metapontion.

[1] Athen. 523c: ὡς φησι Τίμαιος καὶ Ἀριστοτέλης, εἰς τρυφὴν ἐξώκειλαν οὐχ ἧσσον Συβαριτῶν.

[2] Ibid. 520a; see below, p. 362.

[3] See above, p. 153; Ponelle, Mélanges d'Archéologie et d'Histoire 1907, 275; contra, Perret, Siris, 247 ff.

[4] Justin. xx. 2; Schol. Lyk. 984.

[5] I cannot bring the foundation of Velia into relation with the capture of Siris, though the two events happened at the same period. Velia was founded in territory outside the Sybarite sphere, and its commercial relations were via the Straits, not across Italy. Poseidonia and Velia were closely connected from their foundation: Poseidonia appears at this period to have been independent of Sybaris, though she assisted in the refounding of her mother city. The weight of the Siris–Pyxus coins is not the same as that of the coins of Velia and Poseidonia, as is sometimes stated; there are too few to be certain of their regular weight.

The complement was a Krotoniate attack on Lokroi.[1] The Lokrians are said to have assisted the Sirites; which can only mean that they had made a raid across the southern frontier of Kroton, or rather of Kaulonia, while the Krotoniate army was engaged in the north. Kroton was left to deal with Lokroi without assistance from Sybaris, but even alone had overwhelming superiority. Lokroi was a small city with no rich territory, and it needed a series of miracles to save it from Kroton, a power not much less than Sybaris. One hundred and twenty thousand Krotoniates, we are incredibly told, met fifteen thousand Lokrians.[2] The only help the Lokrians received was from Rhegion, and was probably small. They had sought aid from the most powerful Greek state at the time, Sparta. The Spartans, as might be expected, were unable to send material help so far overseas, but sent the Dioskouroi, who ceremonially travelled back in the same ship as the Lokrian ambassadors. The Lokrians had other divine assistance; they outbid the Krotoniates by offering a ninth of the booty for the support of the Pythian Apollo, against a tenth. Finally, on the day of the battle the Lokrian Aias was seen to fight in their ranks, as well as the Dioskouroi in scarlet cloaks on white horses. The Lokrians in gratitude erected altars of the Dioskouroi on the spot.[3] When the Ionic temple in the city (Marazà) near the sea was rebuilt in the middle of the fifth century, it had life-size marble akroteria representing the Dioskouroi in the act of alighting from their horses, whose forelegs are supported in the hands of sea-creatures with women's busts. The sixth-century temple (Marafioti) had a terra-cotta statue of a horseman supported by a sphinx. It is not known to whom the temples were dedicated, but it is possible that the Marafioti temple, built not long after the victory of the Sagra, was in honour of the Dioskouroi, and that when nearly a century later the Lokrians rebuilt the Marazà temple (perhaps of Aphrodite, one of the chief gods of the city), they again recorded in the most solemn and beautiful way the arrival of the Dioskouroi over the sea for their deliverance.[4]

The victory was announced in Greece on the same day, during the games at Olympia according to a version disbelieved

---

[1] Paus. iii. 19. 11–13; Diod. viii. 32; Justin xx. 2–3; Strabo 261; Konon 18.

[2] These are Justin's figures; Strabo says that 10,000 Lokrians and some Rhegines met 130,000 Krotoniates.

[3] Strabo, loc. cit.   [4] See above, p. 295.

by Strabo; at Corinth, Athens, and Sparta, according to Justin (the Spartans must have been gratified to hear so promptly of the exploits of the Dioskouroi). It passed into a proverb of events happening contrary to expectation: ἀληθέστερα τῶν ἐπὶ Σάγρᾳ. With so much of the miraculous and divine about it, it is hard to find a sober fact about the victory. Indeed we know only that it happened at the river Sagra, and the Lokrians won against heavy odds. One conjecture may be made. The Sagra is not certainly identified, but was perhaps the Allaro, the largest river between Lokroi and Kaulonia, and the most natural boundary. This is a torrent with half a mile of stony bed, which would give trouble even if dry. I suggest that the Krotoniates got into difficulties advancing over it, trusting too much to their superior numbers; and that the Lokrians made good use of the cover on its south bank.

The tale of wonders is not yet ended. The Krotoniate general, variously named,[1] was wounded by Aias, and was sent by the Pythia to the island of Leuke, to be healed by the hero who had dealt the stroke. There he saw Akhilles and Helen, among others, and was sent by Helen with a message to Stesikhoros, whom she had blinded because he had composed a slighting poem about her. Stesikhoros wrote his famous Palinode, and recovered his sight. It need hardly be said that this is pure fiction, and attached loosely enough to the story of the Sagra. It is quite unjustified to infer that Stesikhoros referred to the battle.[2] If he had done so it would certainly have been quoted unequivocally.

The chronology may be inferred from Justin. The capture of Siris was followed by the battle of the Sagra; then came a period of Krotoniate decline, from which they were aroused by the arrival of Pythagoras. Pythagoras left Samos at the beginning of the tyranny of Polykrates, in 532, or perhaps a few years earlier, but did not necessarily come straight to Kroton. Justin says he lived twenty years in Kroton before he retired to Metapontion; this was just before the anti-Pythagorean revolution which came soon after the fall of Sybaris. His arrival at Kroton will therefore be soon after 530;[3] the capture of Siris and the battle of the Sagra in the previous decade at the latest.

[1] Paus. iii. 19. 12 calls him Leonymos; Konon, *Narr.* 18, Autoleon.

[2] Holm, i. 166 ff.

[3] Rostagni, *Atti d. R. Acc. di Torino,* xlix (1913–14), 376 ff.; K. von Fritz, *Pythagorean Politics in Southern Italy,* 48 ff.; Minar, *Early Pythagorean Politics,* 133 ff., put it in 529–8. This date is given by Cicero, *Rep.* ii. 15. 28; not a very good source for exact chronology.

This is a little after the date when the coinage of the Akhaian cities, which illustrates their close relations, begins. Some confirmation of the date may be found in the Lokrian appeal to Sparta. This is inconceivable before Sparta had become, at the head of the Peloponnesian League, the foremost power of Greece. This is not before the early years of Anaxandridas, that is, hardly before 550. Sparta's exchanges with Kroisos and Amasis, and her challenge to Kyros on behalf of the Ionians, belong to the decade 550–540.[1] After this she drew in her horns a little from oversea diplomacy. So this decade is the most likely time for the Lokrian appeal, and for the Sagra and the fall of Siris.[2]

By this victory Lokroi was free to develop her territory on the other side of the Italian peninsula, and a great impulse was given to her arts, in which from this period she surpasses all the Italian cities. For Kroton it was a great set-back. Kaulonia, which coins copiously in the sixth century, may have been detached from Kroton,[3] but in the absence of any literary evidence it is dangerous to argue from the coins. The Krotoniates are said to have given themselves to a life of luxury and sloth: *nulla virtutis exercitatio, nulla armorum cura fuit*.[4] From this they were roused by the teaching of Pythagoras.

There is a gap in the roll of Krotoniate victors at Olympia between 548 and 532, which may approximately represent the period of decline after the Sagra. Between 588 and 548 Krotoniate runners won the stadion six times. In 532 Milon won the first of his six successive victories, and from 508 to 480 seven of the eight victors in the stadion are Krotoniates. Milon's first victory is very near the date of Pythagoras' arrival at Kroton. The political effects of his teaching, with which alone we are here concerned, are most obscure, and much of the information about the Pythagorean clubs (ἑταιρεῖαι) belongs not to his lifetime but to the fifth century. It is clear,

---

[1] Herod. i. 69; iii. 47; i. 152.

[2] The position of the fragment Diod. viii. 32, which in the Vatican excerpts precedes Solon, implies a seventh-century date (Vogel gives the year 612). Each of the arguments given above is against a date before the middle of the sixth century. Though they are far from exact or compelling, I prefer the date which they suggest. The reason for Diodoros' date is no doubt that he went on to relate the tale of Stesikhoros and the Palinode, and put the whole account in the year of Stesikhoros' *floruit* (611, Jerome). Needless to say, no argument for the date of the battle can be drawn from this tale, even if Stesikhoros' chronology could be taken as settled.

[3] Cf. Ciaceri, *Storia della Magna Grecia*, i. 182.

[4] Justin xx. 4. 1; cf. Timaios ap. Athen. 522a.

however, that in his lifetime his followers exercised considerable influence in the affairs of Kroton, though not yet of the other south Italian cities.[1] Their direction, like that of political clubs elsewhere in Greece, was oligarchic. It is uncertain how far Pythagoras himself was concerned with politics. The portrait of him given by the Neo-Pythagoreans is of a visionary more concerned with the doctrine of metempsychosis than with contemporary affairs. But no thinker in the small society of a city-state could avoid playing some part in public affairs; Sokrates is an example. And the Pythagorean tradition, overlaid as it is with wonders and edifying anecdotes, represents him as leaving Samos because of his political activity,[2] and as advising the rejection of the Sybarite demands in 510 and the choice of war against Sybaris.[3] His political influence was, however, a secondary consequence of his teaching. The moral regeneration which he wrought was the necessary condition of Krotoniate expansion, political and otherwise. We need not believe that he was invited to address the citizens on his arrival at Kroton, or that he at once made 2,000 converts.[4] His influence was no doubt more gradually felt, as his teaching was favourable to the interests of the aristocratic rulers. There is no reason to doubt that the Pythagorean ἑταιρεῖαι did for the first half of the fifth century direct the affairs of Kroton and most of the other south Italian cities.[5] This they will have done through the existing forms of government; the part of the ἑταιρεῖαι in determining the policy of the State may be roughly compared with that of a party caucus in parliamentary government. The importance in the account of the Pythagorean society of ἑταιρεία and other terms with a political meaning, and the history of the revolts against the Pythagoreans, indicate sufficiently clearly that real power was in their hands. In what form this applies in the sixth century is uncertain, but it must be noted that the ἑταῖροι are spoken of in connexion with the events of 510.[6] Further, one of the followers of Pythagoras was the athlete Milon, general of the victorious army which defeated Sybaris.[7]

---

[1] See the recent discussion in K. von Fritz, *Pythagorean Politics in Southern Italy*; E. L. Minar, *Early Pythagorean Politics* (with bibliography).
[2] Dionysophanes ap. Porph. *Vit. Pyth.* 15.
[3] Diod. xii. 9. 4; cf. Minar, op. cit. 13 ff.
[4] Iambl. *Vit. Pyth.* 37, 30; cf. Minar, op. cit. 7 ff.
[5] von Fritz, op. cit. 94 ff.; Minar, op. cit. 15 ff.
[6] Iambl. *Vit. Pyth.* 177.   [7] Strabo 263.

Relations between Sybaris and Kroton became complicated during this period of Krotoniate recovery. At an uncertain date a demagogue Telys became tyrant of Sybaris[1] and drove into exile the oligarchic faction, who retired to Kroton. The Krotoniates, under the influence of Pythagoras, refused to give them up.[2] There was a party at Kroton which favoured submission to Sybaris. The Olympic victor Philippos, the handsomest man of his time, sought the hand of Telys' daughter, but was exiled from Kroton and, being no longer of any value to Telys, lost his bride and left Italy for Kyrene.[3] He was pretty clearly the head of a party who hoped to make a diplomatic marriage and seize power at Kroton with Telys' aid. If it was indeed he who induced Dorieus to help in the destruction of Sybaris, it may be that he hoped in that way to secure his return to Kroton and be avenged on Telys for dropping him.

Philippos was already in Kyrene when Dorieus returned from his venture at Kinyps, if he was not already associated in it. Probably, therefore, he was in exile at least three years before the fall of Sybaris. It is evident that Diodoros' account of the events that led to the war between Sybaris and Kroton is highly compressed. The Sybarite demand for the return of the exiles is represented as the *casus belli*, but their exile had probably begun many years before, from the time of Telys' assumption of power.

The Krotoniates had a strong moral case in refusing to give up suppliants. The Sybarites were agreed to have brought the wrath of the gods on themselves by their insolence and impiety. There was a curse on Sybaris, since in the foundation of the colony the Akhaians had expelled their Troizenean companions.[4] This had done them little visible harm in two centuries, but was now reinforced by a series of portents. They were warned by the Pythian oracle not to honour mortal men above the gods, and threatened, when they should do so, with war and civil strife. This oracle was given to the sage Amyris.[5] He was, Herodotos says, a Sirite,[6] and the question arises whether he was transferred to Sybaris as the greater city or the oracle was originally related of Siris and transferred to Sybaris. The oracle was fulfilled when a whipped slave took

---

[1] For the popular nature of Telys' tyranny (like that of Peisistratos at Athens) cf. Gilbert, *Griechische Staatsalterthümer*, ii. 243 ('ohne Zweifel an der Spitze des Demos').

[2] Diod. xii. 9.

[3] Herod. v. 47.

[4] Arist. *Pol.* 1303ᵃ 30.

[5] Athen. 520a.

[6] Herod. vi. 127. 1.

sanctuary, and his master went on whipping.[1] Another impiety was the proposal to hold games at the same time as the Olympia, with rich money prizes.[2] These are, however, remoter causes of the anger of the gods. The immediate cause, one of the greatest impieties of which Greeks were capable, was that they killed thirty envoys from Kroton, who had come perhaps bearing the refusal to surrender the Sybarite exiles. Soon after this all their leaders saw the same dream: Hera advanced into the middle of the agora and spewed bile, and a stream of blood opened in her temple.[3] A similar scene had already taken place in Siris, and was to happen again in Sybaris before its fall. The confusion over the nature of the impiety and the sign of divine wrath suggests that the account of the fall of Sybaris current in antiquity was largely historical romance. Already two generations after the event Herodotos could not convince himself of the truth on a single important and comparatively simple point: whether Dorieus assisted the Krotoniates.[4] All the details due to later authorities must therefore be taken with reserve.

The Sybarite army was reckoned at 300,000, a figure which is also given as that of the whole citizen population.[5] The Krotoniates had only 100,000 men, but were strong in a just cause, a well-exercised army, and a valiant leader. This was the athlete Milon, now a man of about forty, dressed as Herakles with lion-skin and club, and his Olympic wreaths. His bodily strength, we are told, had much to do with the victory.[6] They had the support of the seer Kallias the Iamid, who deserted Telys because the omens were unfavourable; he and his descendants long enjoyed his reward at Kroton. They had probably also the more tangible assistance of Dorieus and his band on their way to Sicily.[7] Dorieus had no very large expedition; the single ship brought by the exile Philippos of Kroton was no contemptible addition to it, and the total was perhaps five ships and about a thousand men.[8] This gives a better notion of the size of the forces engaged than the inflated figures already quoted.

---

[1] Athen. 520b.

[2] Herakleides Pontikos ap. Athen. 522a. According to Athenaios (522c) Timaios said that it was the Krotoniates.

[3] Phylarkhos ap. Athen. 521d–e.   [4] Herod. v. 44–5.

[5] Strabo 263; Diod. x. 23; xii. 9. 5 (in § 2 of the same chapter Diodoros gives this figure as the number of citizens).   [6] Diod. xii. 9.

[7] Herod. v. 44–5. See above, p. 349.   [8] See above, p. 352.

The campaign was decided by a single battle, which took place perhaps on the borders of the two states, near the coast.[1] Apart from the record of Milon's prowess, one detail of the fighting is preserved. The Sybarite cavalry had been corrupted by teaching their horses to dance to the flute. The Krotoniates had flute-players in uniform in their army, who threw the opposing horse into confusion. This has the sober authority of Aristotle.[2]

The victory was complete. The Krotoniates gave no quarter, and pressing on took and sacked the city. Apparently it stood a short siege first; Strabo gives the figure seventy days, which may be that of the whole campaign or of a siege.[3] Then it was thoroughly laid waste. The river Krathis was diverted from its course to flow over the city. A temple was built to Athena Krathia in the dry bed, it was said by Dorieus.[4] This suggests that the diversion was an important military operation, and that it was thus that the Krotoniates took the city. The last scene was the overthrow of Telys and slaughter of his adherents, in the temple of Hera. Again the goddess turned her face away and a stream of blood flowed.[5] The action is most striking in this context, most effective after the murder of the Krotoniate envoys; it may, however, originally belong not to Sybaris at all but to Siris.

This was the end of the greatest Greek city of Italy, which never rose again to significant existence, but left a name which has continued to this day. Its fall was a shock to the Greek world; the whole body of the Milesians went into mourning.[6] In the luxuriant fever-stricken forest near the mouth of the Crati, perhaps 20 feet under one of its abandoned stony beds, still lies what the Krotoniates left after its sack; a harvest of archaic Greek art which has always excited the hopes of scholars. Perhaps some day the wealth and skill needed for its discovery will be united, to produce the richest and most valuable reward which a Greek archaeologist can imagine.

The date is given by Diodoros as 511–510, fifty-eight years before the refoundation in 453–452.[7] It is stated most

---

[1] Iamblikhos, *Vit. Pyth.* 260, speaks of a battle on the river Traeis.
[2] Ap. Athen. 520c–d. See also Aelian, *NA* xvi. 23.
[3] Loc. cit. ἀφῃρέθησαν ὑπὸ Κροτωνιατῶν ἐν ἡμέραις ἑβδομήκοντα.
[4] Herod. v. 45. 1.
[5] Herakleides Pontikos ap. Athen. 521e–f.
[6] Herod. vi. 21.
[7] Diod. xi. 90.

emphatically that the city was completely destroyed.[1] But it is unlikely that there was not some habitation at or near the site. Herodotos says that the survivors retired to the Sybarite colonies Laos and Skidros τῆς πόλιος ἀπεστερημένοι.[2] Sybaris was a large city. Though we do not believe that its army was 300,000 strong[3] or accept the figure 300,000 for its citizens,[4] it is likely both from the extent and fertility of the country which it ruled and from its importance that it was the largest of colonial cities at the time of its destruction, with a population, including the country-side, of perhaps some 500,000.[5] However heavy was the loss of life in battle and sack, the remnants are likely to have been more numerous than can have found refuge in Laos and Skidros.[6] Laos, from its geographical position, can have been only a small place, as its immediate surroundings are poor country.[7] The site of Skidros is not known, but it is to be sought on the barren west coast.[8] As it never coined and is not further heard of in history, it was presumably insignificant.

It is likely that other Sybarites went to Poseidonia, whose citizens assisted in the refoundation of their mother city in 453 B.C.[9] Others may have occupied the site near Rossano which later became Sybaris on the Traeis. This was certainly in occupation in the second quarter of the fifth century, for some good bronzes of that date have been found there.[10] But in default of more extensive excavations we cannot do more than guess at the political condition of the inhabitants of this site at this period.

The main reason for believing that there was a city of Sybaris between 510 and 453 is the existence of coins with the tripod of Kroton on the obverse, the Sybarite bull and the letters VM on the reverse.[11] These are dated after the fall of Sybaris, just before or soon after 500. They are in place in a series of 'alliance' coins in all of which Kroton is the dominant

---

[1] Diod. xii. 10: τὴν πόλιν διήρπασαν καὶ παντελῶς ἔρημον ἐποίησαν; Strabo vi. 263: ἐλόντες τὴν πόλιν ἐπήγαγον τὸν ποταμὸν καὶ κατέκλυσαν, the subject in each case being the Krotoniates. Herodotos uses simply the word ἐλεῖν or a derivative (v. 44–5; vi. 21), but his reference to the dry bed of the Krathis implies the story of the diversion of the river.

[2] vi. 21.   [3] Diod. x. 23; xii. 9. 5; Strabo 263.
[4] Diod. xii. 9. 2.   [5] See above, p. 77.
[6] Cf. Ciaceri, *Storia della Magna Grecia*, ii. 300.
[7] For the site of Laos see E. Galli, *SMG*, 1929, 151 ff.
[8] See above, p. 204.   [9] Head, *HN²*, 84–5.
[10] *Boll. d'Arte*, 1919–20, 95 ff.
[11] *BM Cat. Italy*, p. 357; Head, *HN²*, 95.

member.[1] It follows that some remnant of the Sybarite state was left as a subject ally of Kroton. This was presumably on or near the site of the city, not among those Sybarites who fled to Laos and Skidros. In 476 Hieron received an appeal from the Sybarites for help against Kroton;[2] these were probably not at Laos and Skidros, which are not named, but at Sybaris.[3]

This Sybaris, though it appears to have had still some limited political existence, was subject to Kroton and in some sense part of the Krotoniate state. It is said in the late Pythagorean writers that the land of Sybaris was divided among the Krotoniates, and dissatisfaction at the manner of the division led to a democratic movement against the Pythagoreans.[4] Kylon, the leader of this movement, is called ὁ Συβαριτῶν ἔξαρχος,[5] and was perhaps the Krotoniate governor of the city of Sybaris.

Kylon had personal grounds for opposition to Pythagoras, as his application for admission to the Pythagorean society had been rejected.[6] The Kylonian movement may be interpreted as due to a combination of democratic elements discontented with the concentration of privilege in the hands of the rulers and some of those rulers who were opposed to the activity of the Pythagorean clubs.[7] Pythagoras himself retired from Kroton to Metapontion, where he ended his days.[8] This was twenty years after his arrival at Kroton, and soon after 510.[9] His followers also were temporarily expelled.

This revolt against the Pythagoreans is confused in the Pythagorean tradition with the great revolt of some fifty years later, when the members were attacked in the house of Milon and many of them burnt to death. The details related of the earlier revolt are unreliable.[10] Though fighting between the

---

[1] U. Kahrstedt, Hermes, liii. 180 ff. The fact that the Sybarite type is in a subordinate position prevents these coins from being dated before 510.

[2] Schol. Pind. Ol. ii. 29; Diod. xi. 48.   [3] So Kahrstedt, loc. cit.

[4] Iambl. Vit. Pyth. 255.   [5] Ibid. 74.

[6] Ibid. 248 ff.; Diod. x. 11. 1.   [7] See Minar, op. cit. 53 ff.

[8] Arist. fr. 191; Iambl. Vit. Pyth. 249; Porph. Vit. Pyth. 57.

[9] Justin xx. 4. 17. Taking 529–528 as the date of Pythagoras' arrival at Kroton, Minar (op. cit. 134) gives 509–508 as the year of his expulsion and the Kylonian revolt. But this is too soon after the successful war against Sybaris, as the support of the people for Kylon was due to dissatisfaction at the division of the conquered land (Iambl. Vit. Pyth. 255; Minar, op. cit. 53 ff.) which should have taken more than a year or two to come to a head. Justin's chronology does not necessarily command much respect, but it is all that we have, and in any case the year of Pythagoras' arrival at Kroton is not known, further than that it was not far from the year of Polykrates' seizure of power at Samos; cf. above, p. 359.

[10] Cf. von Fritz, op. cit. 86 ff.

Pythagoreans and the followers of Kylon is recorded,[1] and it appears that the former were eclipsed and driven out of Kroton, this was only a temporary reverse. For the greater part of the first half of the fifth century they appear to have had control of the affairs of Kroton.

At some time during this period Kroton fell under the rule of a tyrant named Kleinias, who is said to have armed slaves and exiles and conquered many cities.[2] His rule, however, must have been short, as neither he nor Kylon interfered seriously with the development of Kroton which was guided by the Pythagoreans. Though Pythagoras himself died at Metapontion of starvation, being shut up in the temple of the Muses,[3] his followers extended their influence not only in Kroton but in most of the other south Italian cities, including Metapontion and, at a later date, Rhegion and Taras, which did not form part of the Krotoniate empire.

Though she did not inherit the whole empire of Sybaris, Kroton was now unquestionably the first power in south Italy for a generation. To this period belong the 'alliance' coins in which the type or initial letters of one of Kroton's neighbours appears on the reverse.[4] Coins with the tripod of Kroton on the obverse, the bull of Sybaris in incuse on the reverse, are found in the Cittanuova hoard, which is held to have been buried before 494.[5] The helmet of Temesa similarly appears on coins of Kroton, but these are no longer of the incuse fabric, but have both sides in relief.[6] Coins of Kroton, with the tripod on both sides, have the letters TE on one or other side, which may refer to Temesa or Terina. Kaulonia and a number of unidentified places are similarly associated with Kroton by having the first letters of their names set on the reverse of coins of Kroton.[7] This practice was adopted also on the colonial

---

[1] Iambl. *Vit. Pyth.* 261.

[2] Dion. Hal. xx. 7. Dated by Minar, op. cit. 71 ff., *c.* 494, on account of the reference in the following passage to Anaxilas' seizure of power at Rhegion in that year. This presses the words of Dionysios too far. There is no other evidence of date, or any other reference to Kleinias.

[3] Porph. *Vit. Pyth.* 57; Diog. Laert. viii. 40. Other foolish stories were told about the death of Pythagoras.

[4] Babelon, II. i. 1453 ff.; Head, *HN²*, 95–6; U. Kahrstedt, *Hermes*, liii. 180 ff.

[5] F. von Duhn, *Zeitschrift für Numismatik*, vii, 1880, 380 ff.

[6] One of these was found in the Curinga hoard, buried *c.* 480 (*N Sc*, 1916, 186 f.; Noe, *Bibliography of Greek Coin Hoards²*, 85). Some time after 480 Temesa was conquered for Lokroi by Euthymos (Strabo 255) and it issues no more coins.

[7] These include ME (identified by Kahrstedt, loc. cit. 184, and others with Medma, rather than Metapontion), OP (the Portus Orestis of Pliny, *NH* iii. 73, near Medma ; a very

coinage of Corinth, issued at this period for Anaktorion, Leu-
kas, and Ambrakia.[1] It may be inferred that Kroton exercised
at least as much control over these subordinate towns as
Corinth did over her north-western colonies. Sybaris and
Temesa are the only two places whose types are used in these
alliance coins together with that of Kroton,[2] and they may be
regarded as having *iniquum foedus* with Kroton. Kaulonia and
the unidentified places will have had an especial Krotoniate
coinage minted for their use, as a measure of decentralization
of the large Krotoniate territory of which they formed part.
Kaulonia, however, had monetary independence for most of
her existence, but there was apparently a short gap between
the archaic incuse coins and those of the classical period. It
may be conjectured that early in the fifth century she changed
allegiance from Lokroi to Kroton.[3] The coinage of Terina
begins *c.* 480,[4] and it may be that at this time, which is approximately when the Sybarites rose against her, Kroton had to
make concessions to her southward dependencies, which henceforth were allowed to issue their own coins. Between 510 and
480, however, Kroton ruled a solid block of territory between
Metapontion and Lokroi, and the independence of both these
small cities must have been insecure. Metapontion perhaps
entered into the alliance with Taras in which she stands
throughout the second half of the fifth century. Behind Lokroi
stood the growing power of Rhegion.

The only other independent Greek states at this time were
the Sybarite colonies on the west coast (Laos, Skidros and
Poseidonia), Velia, and the distant Kyme, maintaining itself
precariously against the Etruscans.[5] Of Rhegion we know
little before 494, when Anaxilas seized power, and most of her
relations were with Sicily rather than Italy; Anaxilas' affairs
will be narrated in connexion with Zankle and the Sicilian

---

doubtful identification), Δ A (Dankle; if so, to be dated after 460, when the old name was
restored for a short time, as it is impossible to place the coins before or during the tyranny
of Anaxilas of Rhegion; but see S. W. Grose, *Num. Chron.* 1915, 188 f.), I M (Himera?), Ϙ, I A,
and Υ Λ I. Von Fritz (op. cit. 82 ff.) suggests that Δ A and others of the unidentified letters
may be the beginning of the names of magistrates, not of allied or subject towns. The
Corinthian parallel supports the other hypothesis. The chronology of these issues and the
conclusions drawn by Kahrstedt, op. cit., as to the growth and decline of Krotoniate power
are uncertain.

[1] Head, *HN²*, 406 f.; Ravel, *The "Colts" of Ambracia.*

[2] The 'alliance' coins of Kroton and Pandosia are doubtful, and are therefore not discussed here.   [3] See above, p. 360.

[4] Head, *HN²*, 112; K. Regling, *Terina*, 32.   [5] Cf. above, pp. 344 ff.

tyrants.[1] She aided her neighbour Lokroi against Kroton at the battle of the Sagra. This is all that we know of the relations of the two cities earlier than *c.* 476, when Anaxilas attacked Lokroi and was restrained by Hieron.[2] The close artistic relations of the two cities in the early fifth century[3] suggest that they were ordinarily on good terms.

In the late seventies Rhegion occupied Pyxus,[4] in the area of the west coast where the Sybarite remnant maintained itself, and also was allied with Taras.[5] Taras also was expanding in the early fifth century at the expense of her barbarian neighbours.[6] Little is known of her internal development, but she was certainly oligarchically governed. She still had a king in the late sixth century.[7] The great defeat by the Iapygians, in which her Rhegine allies were involved, brought about a change to democracy.[8] But it did not interfere for long with the steady extension of Tarentine power over her neighbours, both Greek and Italian.

The influence of Kroton did not then extend so far as Taras and Rhegion. She was, however, the greatest power in south Italy for a long period. The record of this has been rather obscured, as most of the extant works which treat of her history at this period are concerned only with the Pythagoreans and have very little historical sense. If we had Timaios' work other than in citations, there would no doubt be a different tale. For Timaios, power corrupted and caused $\tau\rho\upsilon\phi\acute{\eta}$; so naturally Kroton, like Sybaris and Siris, fell into luxury. But he can find nothing worse to censure than that the magistrates wore purple robes, a golden crown, and white shoes.[9]

This, the greatest period of Kroton's history, is marked by her wide rule over the Italian cities to which the proverb $\mu\acute{\alpha}\tau\alpha\iota\alpha$ $\tau\acute{\alpha}\lambda\lambda\alpha$ $\pi\alpha\rho\grave{\alpha}$ $K\rho\acute{o}\tau\omega\nu\alpha$ $\tau\mathring{\alpha}\sigma\tau\epsilon\alpha$[10] may refer; and by her brilliant athletic successes and flourishing medical school. As already stated, Krotoniate athletes won the stadion at Olympia seven times in the eight contests between 508 and 480, and it was probably at one of these races that the seven Krotoniate

---

[1] See below, pp. 387 ff.

[2] Pind. *Pyth.* ii. 18 and Schol.; Schol. *Pyth.* i. 99. Giannelli, *La Magna Grecia da Pitagora a Pirro*, 43 ff., supposes the Rhegine support for Lokroi at the Sagra to be a reversal of a common state of enmity between the two cities. But there is no evidence for this rather than the contrary view; see above, p. 169.

[3] See above, pp. 292 ff.

[4] Strabo 253.

[5] Herod. vii. 170; Diod. xi. 52.

[6] See above, p. 149 f.

[7] Herod. iii. 136.

[8] Arist. *Pol.* 1303[a] 3 ff.

[9] Timaios ap. Athen. 522a.

[10] Schol. Theocr. iv. 33b.

B b

runners filled the first seven places, giving rise to a proverb.[1] Kroton is said to have started a rival to the Olympic Games, offering big money prizes,[2] but the story is better attested of Sybaris. The medical school may have had its origin in the training of athletes; it is associated also with the Pythagoreans.[3] We know its two most eminent practitioners, the society doctor Demokedes and the scientist Alkmaion. Demokedes spent most of his life in the east, first at Aigina, where he was paid a talent a year from public funds, then at Athens, where his fee rose to a hundred minas, and then in Samos, where he was one of Polykrates' household. When Polykrates was captured and put to death by the Persians, Demokedes was carried up to Susa, and found his way into Darius' favour by curing Queen Atossa of a tumour. He was sent by Darius to escort a party of Persians to spy out the coasts of Greece, and ran away from them at Taras, returning to his native Kroton, where he married Milon's daughter and, secure in the shadow of that great name, defied the Great King.[4] We know none of the vicissitudes of Alkmaion's life, but something of his scientific activity. He was a man of both practical and theoretical ability, a student of anatomy and physiology who was one of the first to practise vivisection and made discoveries about the nerves, the eye, and the human semen.[5] He also gave a philosophic content to his view that disease was due to the disturbance of the equilibrium of the four elements in the body. Some of his practical discoveries may be related to the opportunities for observation given in the palaestra and to the advance in knowledge of the rendering of anatomy made by the sculptor Pythagoras;[6] his speculative side to the Ionian philosophers and Pythagoras. He is said to have been a younger contemporary of Pythagoras,[7] and his activity will like that of Demokedes belong to the late sixth century.

The south Italian cities are famed for many of the leaders of

---

[1] Strabo 202; Eustath. ad Dion. Per. 369. [2] Athen. 522c.
[3] Aelian, VH ix. 22; Iambl. Vit. Pyth. 264. The name Demokedes is given in Iamblikhos as that of one of the followers of Pythagoras. The name may be that of the great physician (cf. von Fritz, op. cit. 61; Minar, op. cit. 61), for almost every known name in the history of Magna Graecia is pressed into service by Iamblikhos to fill out his roll of Pythagoreans. But it would be very rash to believe that Demokedes the physician in fact played the part in resisting the Kylonian conspiracy stated by Iamblikhos (Vit. Pyth. 257, 261).
[4] Herod. iii. 129–37.
[5] Diels, Vorsokratiker, i⁵. 210 ff.; Waechtler, De Alcmaeone Crotoniata (Leipzig, 1896); A. Olivieri, Neapolis, i. 241 ff.; Ciaceri, Storia della Magna Grecia, ii. 70 ff.
[6] Pliny, NH xxxiv. 59. [7] Arist. Metaph. 986ᵃ 22.

Greek thought and culture at this vital period, the latter part of the sixth and early fifth centuries. Some were born in Italy, others were immigrants from Ionia who spent most of their active life in the west. Pythagoras and Xenophanes and Pythagoras the sculptor are the most illustrious of the latter; of the native born, Parmenides of Elea, the doctors of Kroton, the poet Ibykos of Rhegion, the Lokrian musicians, followers of Xenokritos. Without going so far as a patriotic Italian historian who contrasts the splendour of Magna Graecia with the backwardness of mainland Greece,[1] we must recognize that the Italian cities were at this time in material culture worthy to stand beside Athens and Corinth, and played a leading part in the development of Greek thought. There is a striking contrast with Sicily, where the comparable names belong to an older (Stesikhoros) or a younger generation (the Sicilian comic poets and Empedokles). The splendid life of the courts of the Sicilian tyrants throws up the darkness which preceded them.

The same is true of the political development of the two areas. The first, unsuccessful, attempt at democracy in Sicily was c. 490, at Syracuse. There had already been democratic ideas at Sybaris a generation earlier, and Kroton appears to have had a democracy in the last decade of the sixth century, after the first expulsion of the Pythagoreans. In other less praiseworthy respects Sybaris and Kroton were in advance of the Sicilians. Hippokrates set about building up an empire over Greeks and barbarians after 498; he was preceded by the Sybarites by over thirty years. The first of the Sicilian cities to suffer destruction at the hand of Greeks was Megara in c. 483; in Italy the melancholy tale had already begun at Siris some fifty years earlier.

The Italian cities appear to have been more developed politically than the Sicilian. The constitution of all of them was aristocratic or oligarchical, but the Italians seem to have been more progressive. Two social and political tendencies might be expected to show themselves in the colonies, according to their attitude to the institutions of their mother city: radicalism and conservatism. Whatever the sentiments of their founders, the Sicilian cities developed into a rather narrow political conservatism with few important ideas or innovations. It is otherwise in Italy. The Akhaian cities made some steps

[1] Ciaceri, op. cit. ii. 184 ff.

towards federalism, and in their coinage at least were joined by most of the other Italian cities. The government by Pythagorean clubs had in it elements of a genuine aristocracy of merit. Unfortunately, neither of these experiments was successful. The league of Akhaian cities was dominated by first Sybaris then Kroton, the Pythagoreans were expelled from Kroton and other cities by party strife. The hellenization of Sicily was more abidingly successful than that of south Italy,[1] because the Italiots never succeeded in combining to resist the pressure of Italian tribes from the north. But the Italiots first had a splendid life and made a real, though now obscure, contribution to civilization.

In the history of the south Italian colonies, scanty as it is, there is a strong element of fancy, almost of myth. The tales about Sybarite luxury, though fanciful, are caused in an ordinary enough way by gossip and moralizing. The wrath of the gods preceding the destruction of Sybaris, the aversion of Athena and the miraculous flow of blood before the destruction of Siris, are striking but not unusual examples of the heightening of the record of human folly by divine intervention. A more remarkable case is the battle of the Sagra, in which the lesser Aias, or the Dioskouroi, fought in the Lokrian ranks. The result of the battle, like that of Mykale, was announced in Sparta on the day of the battle. The numbers of the Krotoniate army are fabulous, and its defeat was beyond the power of human arms. On such a story that of Stesikhoros' Palinode has been grafted. The parallel between the battle of the Sagra and the battle of Lake Regillus is so remarkable that it is hardly doubtful that the details of the latter are copied from the former. It is likely that other of the great events with which early Roman history is crammed are taken from Greek historians' accounts of the history of Magna Graecia.[2] Some, like Tarquin's cutting off the heads of the tallest poppies, come from Greece; more, and the more marvellous, seem at home in Italy. Many similar marvels occur in the history of the Italian colonies, fragmentary though it is. The fight of Euthymos and the Hero at Temesa[3] is more like a page of *Beowulf*, even in the abbreviated form in which we have it, than a sober record of

---

[1] See p. 191.

[2] This was first suggested by Pais; cf. *Ancient Italy*, 233 ff.; *Storia di Roma*, i. 35 ff.; but Pais emphasizes the Sicilian rather than the Italiot elements in early Roman history.

[3] Strabo 255.

fifth-century history. The appearance of Aristeas at Metapontion, told by Herodotos,[1] is pure romance. The story of Pythagoras in Italy is almost all embroidery, not of an anecdotal character as many Greek biographies are, but consistently marvellous. Most of it is not contemporary, and it may be that its lines were fixed by his followers of the fourth century or even later. But it is equally likely that marvellous stories were put about by his immediate school, and that he himself had an element of the Aimée Semple Macpherson which appealed to the Italiots.

In a word, scarcely an event in early south Italian history is not tinged with a romantic or miraculous colour. The difficulty which it presented to write a straightforward narrative of any event may be judged by Herodotos' uncertainty whether Dorieus took part in the destruction of Sybaris. This twist is not characteristic of Antiokhos of Syracuse or any other historian, western or not, whose style we can recognize. There is not much of it in Sicilian history, and the chief example there is in the person of Empedokles, who could be regarded as one of the Pythagoreans. It may therefore be due to Pythagorean historians, who dealt with the events from the destruction of Siris to their own dispersal, whose works provide the ultimate source of Justin's miserable abridgement and were also available for the first historians of early Rome.

The end of our period contains the first recorded relations of Sicily and the south Italian cities, in the intervention of Hieron of Syracuse in favour of the Sybarites and Lokroi. Perhaps Hieron had been preceded by Gelon in these relations.[2] This is the beginning of a policy which bore fruit effectively nearly a century later, when Dionysios used Lokroi, wedged between more powerful neighbours and in need of support, as a springboard against the Italian cities.

At the same time we have the first evidence of Athenian intervention, which was to play so fatal a part in the affairs, not of the west, but of Greece. Athenian vases had long conquered all Italian markets, but there is no reason to suppose

---

[1] Herod. iv. 15.

[2] Gelon had a country seat at Ἀμαλθείας κέρας near Hipponion (Duris ap. Athen. 542a). And the Krotoniate Astylos, victor at Olympia in 480 and 476 (Ox. Pap. ccxxii), had himself proclaimed as a Syracusan (Paus. vi. 13. 1: Pausanias says persuaded by Hieron, but the dates of Astylos' victories indicate that in the first instance it must have been by Gelon). This is thin stuff on which to build a theory of Gelon's intervention in Italian affairs. Cf. Ciaceri, *Storia della Magna Grecia*, ii. 311 ff.

that in the sixth or early fifth centuries they were brought by Athenian merchants.[1] The first Athenian to show a political interest in Italy was Themistokles. He is said to have suggested in 480 that the Athenians should migrate to Siris, which is described as ἡμετέρη ἐκ παλαιοῦ ἔτι,[2] presumably as being an Ionian (Kolophonian) colony.[3] The suggestion is often regarded as unhistorical, and thought to have grown up after the time of the colonization of Thuria. The very fact that the Athenians did *not* colonize Siris is a strong argument for believing that the suggestion belongs to 480, not to 443 or later. Two sites in south Italy were deserted at the time. Surely it would have been more natural to suggest that Sybaris should be recolonized, rather than Siris; and if the suggestion was never made by Themistokles, but was put into his mouth at the time of the foundation of Thuria, it would be against all reason to name Siris, with which the Athenians had nothing to do, and not Sybaris, whose site they did in fact colonize. One possibility remains, that Siris is written by mistake for Sybaris. This confusion is common enough in later authors, and many stories belonging originally to Siris are transferred to the better-known Sybaris,[4] but the mistake is unlikely to happen in the reverse order, and Herodotos knew the country and is near enough to the time to avoid such a mistake.

The plan of a mass migration of the Athenians may well have been impossible. But Herodotos does not say that Themistokles proposed it in the Athenian assembly; only that he used the possibility as a threat to Eurybiades. Many Ionians had recently migrated to the west after the fall of Miletos,[5] and Bias had earlier proposed that all the Ionians should migrate to Sardinia.[6]

Themistokles' interest in Italy is also shown in the names Sybaris and Italia given to his daughters.[7] If the names are historical,[8] they will probably have been given during the eighties (Themistokles was thirty at the time of his archonship in 493–492).[9] If not, Sybaris will probably be a mistake for Siris, and the reference will be to the suggested migration there.[10] This is possible; but the reference would be obscure, and it may be that the names are real (whether as given names

---

[1] See above, pp. 241 ff.
[2] Herod. viii. 62.
[3] See above, p. 34.
[4] See above, pp. 357, 362.
[5] Herod. vi. 17. 22 ff. Cf. pp. 348, 386 ff.
[6] Id. i. 170.
[7] Plut. *Them.* 32.
[8] As Busolt, *GG* iii. 519, n. 0.
[9] Cf. Wade-Gery, *BSA*, xxxvii. 263, n. 1.
[10] Beloch, *Hermes*, xxix, 1894, 604.

or as nicknames preserved in an anecdote) and that Themistokles' interest extended to Sybaris also.

The year 480, in which Themistokles' suggestion about Siris
was made, is that in which forces from the western colonies
first fought in the wars of Old Greece. Gelon, though invited
to assist against the Persians, was prevented by the unwillingness of the Spartans and Athenians to serve under him, or rather
by the war against the Carthaginians which he had on his
hands.[1] But one colonial took part with his own ship at the
battle of Salamis, Phayllos of Kroton, the Pythian victor
and holder of the long-jump record.[2] He was joined by those
Krotoniates who happened to be in Greece, whether as visitors
or exiles,[3] and thanks to them, though the name of the
Krotoniates was absent from the Serpent Column at Delphi,[4]
Alexander sent to Kroton a part of the spoils of Asia.[5]

[1] See below, pp. 421 ff.
[2] Herod. viii. 47; Paus. x. 9. 2. For Phayllos cf. p. 85.
[3] As suggested by Blakesley ap. Macan in Herod. loc. cit.
[4] Tod, *GHI*, no. 19.
[5] Plut. *Alex.* 34.

CHAPTER XIII
HIPPOKRATES

THE sixth century so far as can be judged is a period of political quietude, except at Selinus and Akragas, where there are tyrannies either continued or alternating with short periods of oligarchy. There is some information about political movements in the seventh century, none at all in the sixth. This is sufficiently remarkable to make it likely that it is not simply due to defect of our sources, but reflects an actual contrast. At Lokroi, Katane and Rhegion the lawgivers preserved the aristocracy. At Syracuse and Gela it survived stasis, and at Gela secession. No tyranny after that of Panaitios is known of in eastern Sicily or in south Italy before the late sixth century. The date of Agathokles' unsuccessful attempt at tyranny at Syracuse is uncertain; the fact is indeed not securely established.[1] The tyrannies of Selinus and Akragas were forced on them by external circumstances, the constant pressure of native peoples and Phoenicians. Elsewhere, the oligarchies survived till the late sixth century, and the crop of tyrants[2] comes at a period when such things had almost disappeared from Greece. All those of whose government we can form a clear idea were conservative in feeling, except Phalaris of Akragas[3] and the demagogue Telys of Sybaris.[4]

Politically the colonies were as conservative as they were economically and artistically. In all these respects south Italy was a good deal ahead of Sicily. Just as Sybaris is the first state to break away from the traditional colonial economics, as Lokroi is the first town we know to have produced a vigorous independent art, so democracy appears at Sybaris earlier than in Sicily. It was never a sturdy growth in the colonies, in spite of Timaios' bias in favour of the Syracusan democracy of the fifth century, which has transmitted itself to modern historians. In the archaic period, before the migrations and mixing of population which began in the late sixth century, it did not raise its head. The exact nature of the oligarchies preserved

[1] See above, p. 58.
[2] Justin iv. 2. 3: 'singulae civitates in tyrannorum imperium concesserunt, quorum nulla terra feracior fuit.'
[3] Phalaris' unpopularity with his conservative successors (Pind. *Pyth.* i. 95–6) implies that he was a radical; but not therefore of democratic sympathies.
[4] See pp. 362, 371 above.

until this period is uncertain. In some cities settlers who came after the first colonists may have been admitted to citizenship; this is especially likely of the south Italian cities whose origin was uncertain and mixed. But this liberality seems not to have continued, for the impression we form of the colonial oligarchies is that they were closed circles of landowners ruling by right of descent.

An accumulation of changes brought all the oligarchies to the end of their usefulness. The economic conditions of colonial life changed radically in the second half of the century, with the weakening of the ties which bound all the west to Corinth and the adoption of coinage. The dedications at Olympia and Delphi, and the remains of temples and cemeteries on Sicilian sites, bear witness to growing wealth. Already a fresh stream of colonists was beginning to pour in, especially from disturbed lands in Ionia and the islands, and expected a share of wealth and privilege. The unprivileged class in the cities was beginning to grow conscious of itself. The great days of the colonial aristocracies were passing. In the more advanced cities of Sybaris and Kroton they had already given way before 510. In Sicily every one of them fell within the next quarter of a century.

The break begins at Gela, where Kleandros set up a tyranny in or about the year 505, overthrowing the oligarchy.[1] The occasion of his rise was perhaps connected with Euryleon's attempt at tyranny at Selinus, the date of which should be c. 505. Gela, Akragas and Selinus form in the sixth century a group more affected by East Greek commercial contacts than Syracuse.[2] Gela was still, so far as can be judged, nearer to Syracuse, socially and politically, than to Selinus, but Gela and Akragas may both have been interested in Dorieus' success. After Euryleon's defeat and Selinus' definite phoenicism, Gela and Akragas inherited Dorieus' war. Akragas took Minoa, which had been Euryleon's starting-point against Selinus.[3] Gelon carried on, certainly with the acquiescence, probably with the support, of Akragas, the war to avenge Dorieus.[4] It is likely that this alliance goes back to the time when Euryleon was living, if not to the time when Dorieus landed in Sicily.

[1] Arist. *Pol.* 1316[a] 37, states that Kleandros was preceded by an oligarchy.
[2] See above, pp. 235 ff.
[3] After Euryleon's death, rather than in concert with Euryleon (as Pareti, 81). See above, p. 353.
[4] See below, pp. 411 ff.

Kleandros' father, Pantares, is very probably the Pantares, son of Menekrates, who won a chariot victory at Olympia, probably in 512 or 508.[1] He is the first Sicilian known to have taken a team across to the great games, a predecessor of the princes and their dependants, and therefore probably the chief man of Gela. After a rule of seven years Kleandros was slain by a Geloan named Sabyllos. Whether Sabyllos acted from personal motives or for the public good, the effect was to substitute one tyrant for another. Hippokrates, Kleandros' brother, who succeeded, was an able and vigorous man, the first Sicilian, after Phalaris, of whose character and actions we can form any conception. He was probably a youngish man, for he left two sons under age in 491; Pantares, his presumed father, was still active not long before the end of the sixth century. He was the first man to make a hegemony over the whole of Sicily a possibility. A series of tireless campaigns over all the east of Sicily made the tyrant of Gela without question the first man in the island. He took up the question of the Sikels and proposed to carry out by force the hellenization which was being slowly effected by peaceful trading. Like many Sicilian tyrants after him, he seems to have had a complete lack of morality and practised a policy of bare force.

His first action must have been to ensure his position in Gela. His brother had been assassinated, and it is implied in a fragment of Timaios that there was some difficulty before his rule was acknowledged.[2] Gelon stood by him and was rewarded with advancement. It appears that Gelon was already popular with his fellow citizens, and that his support was especially valuable for that reason. The reference is vague, but it is likely that there was some popular feeling against Hippokrates which Gelon helped to quell.[3]

[1] *Olympia*, v. 241 ff.; Roehl 512a. The date rests on the following argument. Kleosthenes of Epidamnos, victor in 516, was the first winner of the chariot race to dedicate a statue (Paus. vi. 10. 8). Dittenberger and Purgold say (*Olympia*, v. 241) of Pantares' dedication: 'Die Platte war zum Einlassen in die Basis einer Statue bestimmt.' If this is so, his victory was after 516, and if he was Kleandros' father, it was probably before 505 when Kleandros became tyrant.

[2] Schol. *Nem.* ix. 95 (Müller, fr. 85). Cf. Macan on Herod. vii. 154: ἀναλαμβάνει generally of resuming a broken succession.

[3] Freeman, ii. 123, 496, first called attention to the Pindar scholiast. He suggests also that a reference to the same event has fallen out of Herod. vii. 154, ἔχοντος δὲ Ἱπποκράτεος τὴν τυραννίδα ὁ Γέλων ... πολλῶν μετ' ἄλλων καὶ Αἰνησιδήμου τοῦ Παταίκου †ὃς† ἦν δορυφόρος Ἱπποκράτεος. There may be a short lacuna after Παταίκου, as Macan reads, or Stein's υἱέος may be right. I think that Γέλων is the subject of ἦν. The sense obtained by reading ὃς ἦν, qualifying Αἰνησιδήμου, with a lacuna after Ἱπποκράτεος (Freeman, following Bekker),

The Geloan territory did not yet include all the land that could be seen from the walls of Gela. At Monte Bubbonia, and possibly other places on the northern rim of hills, there were still independent or semi-independent Sikels. When the ruler of Gela determined to expand from a second-rate city to a great power, they were the first to fall. Hippokrates' campaigns north of the Heraian hills against the Khalkidians could not have been carried out until he had control of the passes. His absences in the north of Sicily would have been dangerous if he had left an independent neighbour within marching distance of Gela. The 'palace' of M. Bubbonia was burnt about the end of the sixth century, and there are no traces of later habitation on the site.[1] The temple of S. Mauro was burnt about the same period, and the site abandoned.[2] These two fires may be unrelated, and may have both been accidental, but it looks very much as if they were connected. S. Mauro, the Geloan advanced post, had no defences, and the Sikels of M. Bubbonia seem to have lived at peace with the Greeks. But when once the Geloans made a forward move, M. Bubbonia had to go, and S. Mauro became untenable. The burning of the two places at about the same time may be due to reprisals taken by one race on the other. As the Sikels had nothing to gain by disturbing the peace, the order of events may be this: that Hippokrates began a move to bring in all the independent Sikels neighbouring Geloan territory, and sacked M. Bubbonia in the course of his activities; the Sikels retaliated on the undefended Geloans of S. Mauro, who had to withdraw, and whose town was burnt. This was the only success the Sikels gained, for the way over into the plain of Leontinoi, which passed by S. Mauro, was always open to Hippokrates.

Caltagirone was down to this period probably still held by independent Sikels.[3] The small settlement of Geloans at S. Luigi was for purposes of trade, not defence, and the Geloan frontier seems not to have been held in force in the sixth century. What became of the Sikels of Caltagirone is not known. But a small Sikel town at Piano dei Casazzi, about eight miles

would be more naturally expressed by an apposition, δορυφόρου Ἱπποκράτεος ἐόντος. If I am right, nothing of importance has fallen out, at most a short note about Ainesidemos.

[1] See above, p. 121.

[2] *MA*, xx. 846. Orsi suggests that it was conquered by Duketios, but nothing on the site comes below the very beginning of the fifth century. The fire which destroyed the palace is completely unrelated to this supposed sack. See above, p. 119.

[3] So Pais, *Ancient Italy*, 134. See above, pp. 113 ff.

north of the pass, or twelve from S. Mauro, became a Greek military post. The Sikel cemetery has been entirely despoiled. The Greek cemetery of the fifth century, like that of S. Luigi at Caltagirone, produced poor material mainly but not entirely Greek. The narrow hill-top (about 5 acres) was fortified with an isodomic wall and square towers. This post was intended to hold down the country either after Hippokrates' Sikel War or (as Orsi thinks) after the war with Duketios. The brief excavation did not give results sufficiently definite to determine the point.[1]

These Sikel conquests may have been made before Hippokrates. Nothing is known of Kleandros' policy or achievements, and it is possible that he began the expanding movement; it is not likely to go back to the oligarchy, for it marks a complete change of policy such as is likely to be initiated by a tyrant. Such a change fits very well with what is known of Hippokrates, and the archaeological evidence, though it cannot give an exact date, suggests that the sack of M. Bubbonia, the abandonment of S. Mauro, and the fortification of Piano dei Casazzi are not earlier than the beginning of the fifth century. They may indeed be later; but M. Bubbonia, at least, must have been in Hippokrates' hands before he felt free to act north of the Heraian hills. Having secured his communications, he then attacked the Khalkidian cities which had become his neighbours.

It is generally taken that the list of his campaigns in Herod. vii. 154 is arranged chronologically. Herodotos names sieges of Kallipolis and Naxos, Zankle and Leontinoi, and wars against Syracusans and barbarians. The only event for which there is good evidence of date is the affair of the Samians at Zankle, which I try to show below belongs entirely to the year 493. It is by no means certain that this is the siege of Herod. vii. 154, but if it is not, the siege is in an earlier year. Zankle cannot have come into Hippokrates' power till Naxos at least was conquered. Such evidence as there is favours a date 492–491 for the attack on Syracuse and refounding of Kamarina. So Naxos, Zankle, Syracuse are in chronological order. Kallipolis goes with Naxos. This leaves open only the siege of Leontinoi, which one may perhaps assume to be in its true place. The assumption is the only one which allows any order to be introduced into Hippokrates' campaigns; this does

[1] *N Sc*, 1907, 488–9.

not, of course, justify its use as the basis of a reconstruction, but it is perhaps worth while attempting a reconstruction, bearing in mind that it stands on an unprovable assumption.[1]

Briefly, I suggest the following scheme. As soon as Hippokrates was sure of his position in Gela, he attacked the Sikels on the northern fringe of the Geloan plain and made himself master of the passes to the Khalkidian territory. This may have brought him into collision with Leontinoi. He did not directly attack Leontinoi, but moved against the weaker Khalkidian states to the north, received their submission, and then laid siege to Leontinoi. At Zankle and Leontinoi at least he set up his officers as tyrants. He then planned a drive against the northern Sikels, and was probably behind the proposed colony of Kale Akte, but the machinations of Anaxilas compelled him to give up this part of his programme. Having settled the affairs of Zankle, his next move was against Syracuse, where the Gamoroi no longer had the confidence of the people. He defeated them in battle and laid siege to the city, but was obliged to come to terms, accepting the territory of Kamarina which he refounded. Finally he campaigned once more against the Sikels of Mount Etna, where he met his death at Hybla.

---

[1] The grouping of the six enterprises in pairs,

πολιορκέοντος . . . Καλλιπολίτας τε καὶ Ναξίους
καὶ Ζαγκλαίους τε καὶ Λεοντίνους
καὶ πρὸς Συρηκοσίους τε καὶ τῶν βαρβάρων συχνούς . . .

is, I think, entirely literary, though Macan makes it into three wars. Zankle and Leontinoi do not easily go together, and all the Sikels attacked were not 'subjects' of Syracuse. This artifice of style is slightly in favour of Pareti's suggestion (p. 43) that the names are arranged in order of relative importance. Pareti, in spite of his doubts, admits the chronological order as the basis of discussion, though he does not build on it so strongly as I have done: see pp. 33 and 43: 'Se non ammettessimo *a priori* che Erodoto abbia disposti i fatti di Ippocrate cui partecipò Gelone, per ordine cronologico; dappoichè nulla di sicuro indica che Erodoto intendesse di seguire quel sistema, più che, ad esempio, il criterio dell' importanza relativa. Chi nutrisse dubbi di questo genere e pensasse, ad es. per motivi geografici ed analogici colle imprese di Gelone, che la presa di Camarina e il tentativo su Siracusa non siano tra gli ultimi, ma piuttosto tra i primi fatti di Ippocrate . . .' (footnote: 'Io sono lontano dal sostenere questa tesi, ma certo essa sarebbe savorita [*read* favorita] da qualche elemento; non irrefutabile [*sic: read* non refutabile?] per altro'). But the geographical reasons for attacking your neighbour first are outweighed when the more distant foe was by far the weaker. It is at least as likely that Hippokrates waited till he controlled the rest of eastern Sicily before attacking Syracuse as that, failing at Syracuse, he turned against the Khalkidians. The moment of his attack on Syracuse was probably determined by the internal affairs of that city. Nor does a date at the beginning of Hippokrates' career make it easier to understand why he submitted to the arbitration of Corinth and Korkyra. Complications to the north were more probable when it was already Hippokrates' to lose than before he had touched it, for there is no reason to suppose that the Leontines would assist the Syracusans against Gela.

With the object of bringing the whole of the Khalkidian land into his power, Hippokrates' first operations were against the weaker but more distant cities, in order to encircle Leontinoi. The situation of Kallipolis is unknown, but it was a colony of Naxos,¹ and probably in the region of Etna. Kallipolis and Naxos might be expected to fall in the same campaign, and it is likely that at this time Zankle came within Hippokrates' orbit. Herodotos' words πολιορκία and δουλοσύνη do not apply very well to the dealings of Hippokrates with the Samians, or to the earlier state of Zankle under Skythes. But seeing that we have a fuller account of the later affair, in which no siege is recorded, it is likely that the siege was the occasion when Zankle entered the Geloan alliance. The alternative is to suppose an inexactitude in Herodotos' use of terms.² Since Skythes was an alien and a new-comer to Zankle, being in all probability a Koan and the father of Kadmos,³ he is more likely to have been placed in the tyranny by Hippokrates than to have received it in any other manner, and the way in which Hippokrates treated him as responsible to himself for the loss of the city supports this view. Though called βασιλεύς Skythes is clearly the inferior partner in an unequal alliance.⁴

If the conquest of Leontinoi came after Naxos and Zankle had already been brought into Hippokrates' empire, it is hard to see why Leontinoi did not interfere, or cut his communications, unless it had already been silenced by a preliminary campaign. A *casus belli* with Leontinoi can be imagined in a quarrel over boundaries, since Gela and Leontinoi had become neighbours in the Heraian hills. But it is difficult to see what quarrel Hippokrates could have had with Kallipolis and Naxos unless as allies of Leontinoi. If Herodotos' order is to be taken chronologically, therefore, we may infer that Hippokrates' expansion north of the Heraian hills began with a campaign

---

¹ Strabo 272; ps.-Skymnos 283 ff. Mascali, on the north-eastern slope of Etna opposite Naxos, is plausibly suggested by Giuliano (*Riv. St. Ant.* xi. 256). Freeman's view (i. 380) that it was on the coast between Naxos and Zankle is unlikely. It would have been difficult to support a large population on this coast before the lemon was introduced.

² Dodd, *JHS*, 1908, 57: Macan, *Herod. VII–IX*, I. i. 214. Of Hippokrates' operations against the Samians Herodotos says only σὺν τῇ στρατιῇ ἧκε βοηθέων, which is far from a siege.

³ See below, p. 384.

⁴ The difficulty of reconciling σύμμαχος in vi. 23 and δουλοσύνη in vii. 154 is lessened by the fact that in the earlier passage Herodotos is following a source favourable to Skythes. He calls Skythes βασιλεύς, a title to which it is extremely unlikely that he was entitled, and to speak of his overlord as his ally is a similar compliment. See Macan ad locc.

against Leontinoi followed by the conquest singly of the northern Khalkidian cities, which cut off Leontinoi from support by her kinsmen.

It is not known how Katane was treated. If it were taken by force, it should have been mentioned by Herodotos. But it cannot have held out against Hippokrates when the larger Khalkidian cities fell, nor could he have attacked the Sikels behind the city until he was sure of it. Probably it surrendered to him on his Naxos campaign.[1]

The way in which Naxos and Kallipolis were secured is not known. The coinage of Leontinoi continues, but the type is assimilated to that of Gela, and the unit changes to the Attic standard. The mint of Naxos was closed.[2] At Leontinoi it appears that one of Hippokrates' officers was set up as tyrant. The identification of Ainesidemos tyrant of Leontinoi with the member of Hippokrates' bodyguard is highly probable. He was, after Gelon, the most distinguished of Hippokrates' officers, and therefore entrusted with the government of Hippokrates' most important conquest. The rival of Gelon named in Arist. *Rhet.* i. 12 is the same man.[3] Pausanias is perhaps right in distinguishing from the tyrant the Ainesidemos of Leontinoi who made the offering of a colossal statue of Zeus at Olympia, for the statue bore the names of two other Leontines who would not easily be associated with a tyrant.[4] It is possible that Hippokrates' officer was a prominent Leontine who entered the service of the tyrant of Gela and was made tyrant of his own city, but the view that he was Akragantine is more plausible. He cannot have been Theron's father. He is called ὁ Παταίκου, to distinguish him from his namesake, who was son of Khalkiopeus or Emmenides (the two names may both be genuine). Theron's ancestry farther back than the crossing to Sicily was uncertain, but surely there was no doubt about his grandfather's name. In any case Theron's father was too old to take service with Hippokrates. His grandson Thrasyboulos was a young man in 490, and he must if still alive in the nineties

---

[1] I do not attach great weight to the argument (Pareti, 44) that only those feats of Hippokrates in which Gelon distinguished himself are mentioned in vii. 154. As Hippokrates' master of the horse and right-hand man, Gelon would naturally have been with him on his big campaigns, and I think that in fact Herodotos has given a brief summary of the whole of Hippokrates' military activity.

[2] Cahn, *Die Münzen der Sizilischen Stadt Naxos*, 35 ff.

[3] See below, p. 410.

[4] Paus. v. 22. 7.

have been an old man past active service.[1] The Ainesidemos in Hippokrates' service may well have been of Emmenid family. It is a rare name and apart from those who are under consideration here there are no western bearers of it.[2] Certainly Gela and Akragas must have been on good terms, as they were later under Gelon and Theron. All Hippokrates' activity was to the north and east, and it was safe for him to leave his western frontier undefended. Inykon, where he later kept Skythes in custody,[3] was in the western part of his empire, towards Akragas.[4] Ainesidemos son of Pataikos may have been the link between the tyrants of Gela and the family which was already the leading one of Akragas.

Skythes' position at Zankle was probably the same as Ainesidemos' at Leontinoi. The subordinate tyrant was the regular means used by these Sicilian tyrants to control a large empire. Glaukos of Karystos was set up at Kamarina by either Hippokrates or Gelon.[5] When he removed to Syracuse Gelon left Hieron in charge of Gela. Theron ruled Himera through his son. No system of governing a large area occurred to these tyrants except an aggregate of cities bound by personal relations to the ruler.

There are too many things in common between the career of Skythes of Zankle and Kadmos son of Skythes for them not to be father and son. Skythes was in Hippokrates' service, Kadmos in Gelon's. Both ruled at Zankle. Skythes was in high favour with the Persian king, Kadmos was an acceptable go-between if Gelon should need to make his peace with Persia. Kadmos was associated with those Samians whom Skythes invited to Sicily. With the agreement of name, and the δικαιο-σύνη which both exhibited, this goes beyond coincidence, and makes it extremely unlikely that Skythes of Zankle was a different man from Skythes, father of Kadmos.[6] The family history is quite comprehensible. Skythes hands over to his son the tyranny of Kos, perhaps during the years when the Ionian revolt was going well. Coming to Sicily, he entered Hippo-

---

[1] See the genealogical table on p. 484.

[2] Freeman, ii. 105; *RE*, i. 1022.   [3] See below, p. 393.

[4] This is an inference from its occurrence as a variant for Kamikos in the story of Daidalos in Sicily. See *BSR*, xvi. 1 ff.

[5] See below, p. 416.

[6] Pareti (pp. 75–7) puts the case for the identification of the two Skythes very well. See also Macan, *Herod. VII–IX*, I. i. 227–8, and *IV–VI*, vol. i. 287. Freeman (ii. 109, n. 3) expects Herodotos to supply cross-references, which is more than he was in the habit of doing.

krates' service, and with his support was made tyrant of Zankle. This was the occasion on which he obtained from Darius permission to go to Sicily, laying down his post of tyrant in the Persian interest. Herodotos does not state that he returned to Sicily after his flight from Inykon.

Skythes cannot then have been accurately called βασιλεύς. An alien is much more likely to have become monarch of Zankle through the good graces of his ally the tyrant of Gela than of the free will of the Zanklaians. But even if Skythes was a Zanklaian, a regular kingship is inconceivable.[1] It seems to me impossible to differentiate Herodotos' use of βασιλεύς, μούναρχος, and τύραννος,[2] and distinguish Skythes, who is called βασιλεύς and μούναρχος (twice), from Anaxilas and Hippokrates who are both τύραννος. μούναρχος is a colourless word, equated with τύραννος in vii. 154. Telys of Sybaris is called βασιλεύς and τύραννος in the same chapter (v. 44). Here the difference rests on the difference of source; but Telys was certainly no more rightly called βασιλεύς than the Sicilian tyrants, having risen ἐκ δημαγωγοῦ. The only possible West Greek king properly so titled is Aristophilides of Taras.[3] In this Spartan colony a limited kingship on the Spartan model is possible. All the other instances are inexact, and derive from personal intercourse. They illustrate the weakness of the democratic feeling in the west and the authoritarian tendency evident also in the Pythagorean reverence for the Master. The tyrants were ready to be called βασιλεύς, as a mark of honour rather than a title, and they found flatterers. Pindar in the same ode addresses Hieron as βασιλεύς (*Pyth.* iii. 70) and calls him τύραννον (l. 85). The use of τύραννος in this particularly affectionate ode shows that Hieron did not regard it as a reproach, though βασιλεύς was more complimentary. None of the earlier Sicilian tyrants had a regular constitutional position, except perhaps Deinomenes at Aitna, and it was difficult to know what to call them politely. Apart from the frequent use of the title βασιλεύς by Pindar and Bakkhylides, Herodotos makes the Athenian envoy address Gelon ὦ βασιλεῦ Συρηκοσίων.[4] When he follows the Sybarite remnant in calling their tyrant βασιλεύς, and Skythes' friends in calling him βασιλεύς, he employs this complimentary use a stage farther removed.

---

[1] Macan ad. loc. regards it as indicating only that Herodotos' source was friendly to Skythes.
[2] Freeman, ii. 434–5.   [3] Herod. iii. 136.   [4] vii. 161. 1; cf. the fisherman to Polykrates, ὦ βασιλεῦ, iii. 42; and see Powell, *Lexicon to Herodotus*, s.v. βασιλεύς, 2 c.

As a result of his intervention at Zankle Hippokrates came into conflict with Rhegion across the straits. Since the foundation of Rhegion, in which the Zanklaians co-operated, the relations between the two cities had always been close. Their earliest coinage is closely connected.[1] Zankle is the only Sicilian city to issue coins with the reverse type that of the obverse incuse, like those of the Italian cities. The weight agrees with the standard of Himera and Naxos, a stater of about 88 grains.[2] The first coins of Zankle are:

> Babelon, nos. 2200–1; Evans, *Num. Chron.* 1896, 101, nos. 1–2; Dodd B1:[3] port and dolphin, reverse same type incuse, weight 88 gr.
> *BM. Cat. Sicily*, 99, nos. 1–8; Babelon, nos. 2202–5; Evans, loc. cit., nos. 3–5; Dodd B2:[3] same type obverse, reverse scallop-shell in incuse noughts-and-crosses board pattern, weight 88 gr.
> Babelon, no. 2209; Dodd B2*a*: same types, weight 116 gr., which is approximately the weight of the Akhaian coins of Magna Graecia, but cannot be brought into relation with any standard current in Sicily.[4]

The earliest coins of Rhegion (Babelon, no. 2187; Dodd A1) with human-headed bull, reverse same type incuse, weight 87 gr., agree in weight and fabric with those of Zankle. They share the incuse fabric with the Akhaian cities, the standard with Himera and Naxos, thus forming a united group intermediate between Magna Graecia and Sicily. There are many fewer sixth-century coins of Rhegion than of Zankle, and none corresponding to the scallop-shell reverses. The dating of these earliest coins is very uncertain, but it is agreed that they are before 510. The scallop-shell reverses are later than the incuse sickles and should be of the period immediately before the arrival of the Samians. The change of fabric suggests that at the end of the sixth or beginning of the fifth century Zankle loosened her Italian ties and strengthened those with the other

---

[1] C. H. Dodd, *JHS*, 1908, 56 ff., and Pareti, 50–8, discuss *ex proposito* the historical bearings of the early coinage of Zankle-Messana and Rhegion.

[2] See above, p. 246.

[3] Evans, loc. cit., describes a hoard, buried probably at the time of the Samian invasion, including drachmae of both these types, the latter, 'comparatively fresh from the mint', forming the bulk of the hoard. Pre-Hippokratean coins of Naxos, as *BM Cat. Sicily*, p. 118, nos. 1–3, form the rest of the hoard.

[4] It has been interpreted as a didrachm on the Attic standard, but is a good deal too light; *c.* 131 gr. would be the normal weight for such a coin. Another coin with the same types (Head, *HN*2, 152; Ward, *Greek Coins and their Parent Cities*, pl. IV, no. 202) weighs 146·3 gr., too heavy for an Attic didrachm, and agreeing with no conceivable standard. It is difficult to argue from the weights of isolated examples such as these, for not only coins a long way light of standard but also coins a good deal heavier than the average are found in more complete series. The anomalies do not justify the view that the change to the Attic standard took place before the introduction of the Samian types.

Khalkidian cities of Sicily. The change is in the first place artistic, and the standard remains the same. It indicates perhaps a political difference, with the adoption of the Sicilian idea in place of the Italian, and would make no difference to commerce. But the experiments with coins of different standard (they cannot be called other than experiments, as they are too few to determine what the standard really is) imply that economically as well as politically Zankle was leaning away from Rhegion, perhaps towards the Phokaians and Velia. But neither without the other had complete control of the Straits. Zankle had the harbour, into which the natural set of the currents brings ships southward bound, and where ships northward bound would wait for a favourable current to carry them through. But Rhegion commanded the approach to Zankle, and the position of the acropolis appears to have been chosen for the view through the Straits. In the sixth century the two states were so much in harmony that those powers which had not their friendship sought other routes by which their goods might reach the markets of Etruria. About the end of the century this union seems to have weakened, and it may be that this circumstance allowed Hippokrates to extend his power over Zankle. In the interval between Hippokrates' first intervention and the arrival of the Samians, Anaxilas son of Kretines became tyrant of Rhegion;[1] this was in 494 or 493.[2] He was a member of the aristocracy of Messenian families which ruled Rhegion.[3] Possibly the events at Zankle by discrediting the oligarchy helped him to seize power. He at once set about strengthening his position by an attempt to win Zankle,[4] his negotiations with the Samians being his earliest known activity. The cause of the quarrel lay in the Zanklaians' entering Hippokrates' alliance, which threatened Rhegion's economic existence. The land of Rhegion, a narrow shelf between the sea and Aspromonte, was of little value for agricul-

---

[1] Herod. vii. 165.

[2] His death is placed by Diod. xi. 48 in 476–475, after eighteen years' rule. It is not quite certain that all the western events related by Diodoros under that year belong to 476–475 rather than the year before or after, and not certain whether the reckoning is inclusive or exclusive. But allowing a year's margin, Anaxilas was newly in power when the Samians reached Italy early in 493.

[3] Thuk. vi. 4. 6; Herakleides Pontikos fr. 25 (*FHG*, ii. 219); Paus. iv. 23. 6 (with a pedigree faked by Rhianos or some other pro-Messenian source; cf. Pareti, 72, n. 3; Kroymann, *Sparta und Messenien*, 35 f., 45 ff.; see below, p. 396, n. 3).

[4] I do not agree with Pareti (p. 34) that the phrase τότε ἐὼν διάφορος τοῖσι Ζαγκλαίοισι implies that he had warred with Zankle before the Samians came on the scene.

ture before the orange was introduced, and Rhegion depended more than the other western colonies on the sea and the friendship of Zankle which was necessary in order to control the Straits. The presence of the Samians offered Anaxilas an excellent opportunity of strengthening his position in Rhegion by winning Zankle to his alliance. Far from thinking, therefore, that he must have been some little time in power when the Samians arrived, and that if he became tyrant only in 494–493 they cannot have seized Zankle so early as 493, I think that it is reasonable to suppose that he had been tyrant only a few months when he sent the Samians to Zankle, and that his quarrel with that city was inherited from the oligarchy.

The suggestion that the Samians assisted Anaxilas to establish himself in Rhegion is completely unsupported by the literary evidence and the numismatic evidence does not demand it.[1] The next coins after the incuse reverse types at Rhegion have lion's head facing obverse, calf's head l. reverse. These are an adaptation of the current Samian type, lion's mask facing and bull's head (*BM Cat. Ionia*, p. 351, nos. 19 ff.). Some (*BM Cat. Italy*, nos. 1–2; Babelon, nos. 2188–9; Dodd A2) weigh *c.* 88 gr., agreeing with the earlier coins of Rhegion. Others (*BM Cat.*, nos. 3–4; Babelon, nos. 2190–1; Dodd A3) weigh *c.* 272 gr., being tetradrachms on the Attic–Euboic standard. The corresponding coins of Messana (*BM Cat. Sicily*, p. 100, no. 10; Babelon, no. 2210; Dodd B3) are all tetradrachms, and all have the legend MESSENION. It looks at first sight as if the coins of Rhegion with Samian types are older than those of Zankle-Messana with the same types, in which case the Samians came to Rhegion earlier than to Zankle. But it must be borne in mind that the change of type is a matter primarily artistic and only inferentially commercial or political. It is certain that there were Samian artists in charge of the coinage of both Rhegion and Messana, but by no means certain in what relation they stood to the Samians who intended to colonize Kale Akte. Other Ionian artists came west individually or in small groups at this period and a little earlier, and many of them settled at Lokroi and Rhegion. One Samian who settled permanently at Rhegion was the sculptor Pythagoras, the dates of whose recorded activity fit the hypothesis that he came with the Samians in 494–493 as a young man.[2] The

---

[1] Dodd, 72.
[2] Cf. above, p. 298.

artists who were responsible for the coins may have detached themselves from the main body and settled in Rhegion, at Anaxilas' invitation.[1] To commemorate his alliance he adopted a new design founded on the Samian types but differing in details. The change of standard, or more accurately the change of unit, keeping the same standard, should not be ascribed to the Samians,[2] for the earliest coins with the Samian types are of the old weight. In any case the Samian standard was of *c.* 202 gr., not *c.* 270 which is the weight of the new coins. Though the 90-gr. drachma was easily convertible with the 270-gr. coin current in the rest of Sicily, all the cities whose unit had been the drachma ceased to coin or adopted the new unit about this period, Leontinoi after its conquest by Hippokrates,[3] Himera at the conquest by Theron. Samians or no Samians, Rhegion could not alone maintain the old standard. These types were introduced to Zankle with the change of name to Messana, that is, when Anaxilas finally made himself master of the city. The congruity of type between Messana and Rhegion, both using the same adaptation of the Samian type, shows that when these coins were issued the two cities were united. That is to say, the Samian types at Messana are Samian only at second hand, and their introduction is due not to the Samian settlers but to the Rhegines who had adopted the Samian type. This explains why there are no coins of Samian type with the legend of Zankle or on the 90-gr. standard. Only by dissociating the Samian coiners from a too close association with their compatriots who seized Zankle is it possible to reconcile the numismatic evidence with the literary. This separation of art and politics makes fewer demands on probability than Dodd's rewriting of history. The coins then are not the clue to the complicated tangle of the literary evidence concerning the Samians at Zankle, but form another closely allied problem. Though the beginning of the Samian types at Rhegion is connected with Anaxilas' reception of the exiles, their continuance is not bound up with the movements of the main body, and their appearance at Messana a little later is not the direct consequence of the seizure of the city by the Samians.

This is the conclusion to which Pareti comes,[4] and I quote

[1] As Dodd, 73, n. 82.   [2] Cf. Pareti, 35, n. 1.
[3] Cf. above, p. 383.
[4] p. 58.

his summary, which may be clearer than my own presentation of the argument:

I. From the beginning of coinage to the arrival of the Samians.
Rhegion, Babelon, 2187.
Zankle, ,, 2200–8.
,, 2209 after the alliance with Hippokrates (see above for doubts whether this coin is in fact on the Attic standard).

II. From the arrival of the Samians to the capture of Zankle by Anaxilas (c. 486).[1]
Zankle, Babelon, 2191–2 (see below).
Rhegion, Babelon, 2188–9.
'a Regio si adotta dai vicini Sami, con cui si è in buoni rapporti, e forse anche per l'affluenza di Sami in città, un tipo simile al samio . . .'

III. Anaxilas ruler of Rhegion and Messana.
'Anassilao prende Zancle, la ripopola e le dà il nome di Messene, che compare nelle monete, il cui tipo viene ricalcato sulle precedenti imitazioni regine del tipo samio, ma la cui valuta si conserva attico-euboica (2210–2212); e per uniformare in tutto le monete, anche a Regio si continua il tipo samio modificato, ma si adotta la valuta attico-euboica (2190).'
After Anaxilas' Olympic victory, the mule-chariot and hare, at Rhegion (2193–9) and Messana (2213–15 bis).

The only full account of the affair of the Samians at Zankle is Herodotos', from which the order of events and the chronology are to be derived. He says that immediately after the battle of Lade they determined to sail westward (μετὰ τὴν ναυμαχίην αὐτίκα βουλευομένοισι). The battle of Lade was fought early in 494.[2] The capture of Miletos was in the same year. As soon as the traitorous Samian fleet returned, and before Aiakes arrived to take up his kingdom, οἵ τι ἔχοντες determined to leave Samos. Aiakes might be expected at any time after Lade. He was restored, with the aid of a Phoenician fleet, μετὰ τὴν ναυμαχίην, apparently before Miletos fell. Those of the Milesians who joined the Samians were a few who escaped when their fellow citizens were carried off to the Persian Gulf. For neither Samians nor Milesians was it safe to stay long after the capture of Miletos. In the autumn of 494, then, they sailed west. It has been inferred from the presence of coins of Athens and Akanthos as well as of Samos in a hoard buried at Messina

---

[1] His date c. 486 is bound up with his view that Hippokrates' death was c. 486. If Hippokrates died in 491–490, a date c. 490–489 is rather more probable, and agrees with the presence of the Messenians inferred to have left the Peloponnese at that time.

[2] Grundy, The Great Persian War, 121 ff.

probably in 494–493[1] that they called at Athens on their way. It is unnecessary to take them to Akanthos as well, for these coins could be picked up in Athens.[2] They were not wandering homeless over the Mediterranean, but had a definite invitation from the Zanklaians. Their arrival at Lokroi would be in the winter or early spring, 494–493. While they were waiting for directions from Skythes Anaxilas got into touch with them.

The invitation was probably sent before the battle of Lade, when the affairs of the Ionians began to go wrong. A number of cities, including Ephesos, had made their peace before Lade,[3] and many of the others were convinced that the game was up. After the defeat, when it was every man for himself, a general invitation to the Ionians would be impossible. If time is allowed for 'the notice of the defeat to reach Zankle, the deliberations of the Zanklaians, the sending of the invitation to Asia, the preparations of the Samians and Milesians for departure',[4] the fugitives would have been arrested and kept in slavery in Samos or Persia. After the autumn of 494 it would not have been safe for them in the east. Communications between east and west must have been good for the Sicilians to have such accurate knowledge of the state of the Ionians.

The view that it was Dionysios of Phokaia who suggested the Pan-Ionian colony on the north coast of Sicily is impossible.[5] Dionysios sailed straight from Lade to the Phoenician coast, and thence to the western Mediterranean. His arrival would be late in 494. The Samians, although they left later than he and were not equipped for action, will have arrived at the most a few months later.

The invitation was probably transmitted by Skythes through his son Kadmos. Kadmos laid down the tyranny of Kos δεινοῦ ἐπιόντος οὐδενός. That is to say, it was not the course of events at home that moved him, but the brighter prospects in Sicily. He was one of those tyrants who depended on Persian support, and at the end of the Ionian revolt his rule should have been more secure than ever. In 480 he was a good man to send to

[1] Noe, *Bibliography of Greek Coin Hoards*[2], 181, no. 685.

[2] Coins of Akanthos as well as other cities of north Greece and the islands are found in the famous silversmith's hoard of Taranto, buried soon after 510 (Babelon, *Revue Numismatique*, 1912, 1 ff.; Noe, op. cit. 275) and also in later hoards found at Caltagirone and Mazzarino in Sicily (Noe, ibid. 61, 177), where they are the only coins from east of the Adriatic except those of Athens.

[3] Grundy, loc. cit.

[4] Pareti, 34, n. 3. The defeat of which he is thinking is the fall of Miletos.

[5] Holm, i. 198; Freeman, ii. 109. For Dionysios cf. above, p. 348.

medizing Delphi, to make Gelon's peace with Xerxes if need
be. Probably he was charged to bring the colonists to Kale
Akte. Whether he actually came with them depends on the
reading in Herod. vii. 164, μετά or παρά. The two readings have
about equal authority, and the only point open is how soon
Kadmos became associated with the Samians. If μετά is read,
it does not follow that he accompanied them. He may have
preceded them, as Pareti suggests, thus avoiding the difficulty
of understanding what he was doing when the Samians
abandoned their voyage to Kale Akte and seized Zankle. παρά
cannot mean 'at the expense of the Samians', as it is clear that
he was not Anaxilas' man, assisting to expel the Samians. Even
reading παρά he 'might still be of their company and even their
leader'. Whichever is read, Kadmos' period is certainly from
the establishment of the Samians until the city came finally
into Anaxilas' hands. In 480 he was at Gelon's side, so he must
have been expelled when the city was definitely won for
Anaxilas' anti-patriotic alliance.[1]

Hippokrates may have been at the back of the Kale Akte
colony,[2] which as well as reinforcing the Greek element on the
north coast, otherwise empty from Mylai to Himera, would
suit his purposes very well as a Greek post in the west of his
empire, in the rear of the Sikels whom he was later to attack.
Kale Akte is not the most promising site on the north coast for
a colony. In spite of its 'prospectus' name, it has no port, but
a shingle beach. It is in a comparatively poor region, the best
land being farther to the west. It was later colonized by
Duketios, but was never an important place, even in the Roman
period when the north coast ports were the nearest from which
to ship corn to Rome. Its chief advantage was the great forest
whose remains survive in the Bosco di Caronia.[3] For a colony
intended to carry on a naval war against Carthage and Etruria,
this would weigh heavily. Cefalù is the best port on this part
of the coast, and would very effectively have reinforced Himera,
but it was in Sikel hands.

[1] Macan, *Herod. VII–IX*, I. i. 230, puts the alternatives very clearly, and the view to
which he inclines is that which I adopt. 'Was Kadmos himself the leader of those very
Samians who seized Zankle, in the absence of Skythes? Had the invitation to Kale Akte
been addressed by Skythes to his son in Kos, or in Samos, or wherever his address for the
time being was? ... In that case (reading μετὰ) Kadmos appears as the leader of that very
band of Samians which seized Zankle in the absence of his father Skythes ....'

[2] So Hackforth, *CAH*, iv. 367

[3] In Smyth's time (before 1821) it still covered an area of fifty square miles (*Sicily and
its Adjacent Islands*, 96).

While awaiting the arrival of the Samians the Zanklaians
were attacking a Sikel town, presumably to gain territory for
the new colony. Hippokrates was not with them, but he was
accessible, and the speed with which he reached Zankle suggests that he was already in the north of Sicily about some
other Sikel campaign. This was early in the spring of 493. The
Samians had not yet moved from Lokroi, where perhaps they
wintered, when Anaxilas got into touch with them. At his
suggestion they seized Zankle. Skythes and the Zanklaians at
once abandoned their Sikel campaign and advanced against the
city. They sent a message to Hippokrates, who soon arrived
at Zankle. The Samians were masters of the situation. They
must have been in considerable force, as they had proposed to
form a colony of themselves. They had ships, and it is unlikely
that Hippokrates had a fleet which could cope with them and
Anaxilas together. Zankle was not a difficult place to hold,
given command of the sea. Hippokrates withdrew from the
awkward situation by abandoning his Zanklaian allies and buy-
ing off the Samians. He agreed to share the movable possessions and slaves of the Zanklaians, to his own profit as well as
that of the Samians. An example was made of Skythes, who
was held responsible for losing the city, and with his brother
Pythogenes was imprisoned in the Sikan town of Inykon. He
soon escaped from Inykon to Himera, where he took ship and
travelled to Darius' court.[1] He was greatly honoured by Darius
as the one faithful Greek who returned to Persia after he had
been permitted to visit Sicily, and lived there full of years and
riches. Hippokrates was probably willing enough to see him
out of Sicily.[2] In Sicily he was discredited. At Susa he might
be a link in case of need between the tyrant of Gela and the
Persian king, as Gelon proposed to use Kadmos in the event
of Persian victory in 480.

Three hundred leaders of the Zanklaians were handed over
to the Samians to slaughter, which they did not do. These
three hundred were probably the leaders of the oligarchical
party, which would naturally be hostile to Hippokrates, and
had presumably been in power before Skythes became tyrant.
They would have a good deal in common with the Samian

---

[1] Aelian, *VH* viii. 17, copies Herodotos' account in vi. 24 with the curious confusion of
ὁ Ἰνυκῖνος ὁ τῶν Ζαγκλαίων μόναρχος. He contrasts Skythes' 'justice' with Demokedes'
conduct. Skythes did not return to Sicily after his flight from Inykon; see above, p. 385.

[2] Macan, *Herod. VII–IX*, I. i. 230.

oligarchs, who probably admitted them to citizenship. There was still an old Zanklaian element in the citizen body of Messana, which revived the old name and coin types for a short period after the fall of the Rhegine tyranny. Among the descendants of these Zanklaians who remained citizens of their city were the athletes Leontiskos and Symmakhos, the only victors from Messana known to Pausanias, both of whom were said to be of the old Zanklaian stock.[1]

It is uncertain whether Kadmos was already at Zankle and Hippokrates was obliged to recognize his position, or whether Hippokrates succeeded in imposing him on the Samians as his nominee. In either case he must have kept the confidence of Hippokrates, as he did of Gelon after him. It is to be noticed that he is not spoken of as tyrant of Zankle.[2] If he had laid down the tyranny of Kos to take up one in Zankle, it would have hurt his reputation for δικαιοσύνη in Herodotos' eyes. Herodotos speaks of him as an equal of the Samians. Probably he remained as Hippokrates' representative and leader of the anti-Anaxilas party, without exercising supreme power. When Anaxilas got control of the city he did not immediately expel the Samians, but it is probable that Kadmos left then to take refuge with Gelon. Kadmos must have been a masterly diplomat. His position as tyrant of Kos during the Ionian revolt must have been difficult, *pace* Herodotos.[3] But he laid down his pro-Persian tyranny on such terms that he was in 480 an envoy who would be acceptable to the Persian king. If he was responsible for bringing the Samians to Sicily, he was unable to prevent them from listening to Anaxilas and seizing Zankle. But Hippokrates' wrath fell on his father Skythes, and Kadmos was left in Zankle to represent Hippokrates' interests. We should like to be more certain about the career of a man who was able to fish in such troubled waters and bring out an apparently quite undeserved reputation for justice.[4]

---

[1] Paus. vi. 2. 10. Leontiskos won the wrestling in 456 and 452, and had a statue by Pythagoras of Rhegion (*Ox. Pap.* ccxxii; Paus. vi. 4. 4; Pliny, *NH* xxxiv. 59). Symmakhos won the stadion in 428 and 424 (Diod. xii. 49, 65).

[2] ἔσχε τε καὶ κατοίκησε πόλιν Ζάγκλην. ἔσχε 'seized' (though if παρά is read, Macan points out that in the phrase σχεῖν παρά τινος the verb may mean little more than τυχεῖν), κατοίκησε 'lived in'.   [3] See Macan's note on εὖ βεβηκυῖαν.

[4] It is doubtful whether Pindar wrote a poem for Kadmos. *Vit. Pind. Ambr.* reads καὶ γὰρ Σιμωνίδης τὴν ἐν Σαλαμῖνι ναυμαχίαν γέγραφε καὶ Πίνδαρος μέμνηται τῆς Κάδμου βασιλείας (fr. 285 Bowra, 272 Schroeder). Κάδμου is probably a false reading (so Bowra). Schroeder's attempt to find a reference in Suidas s.v. Σιμωνίδης· καὶ γέγραπται αὐτῷ Δωρίδι διαλέκτῳ ἡ Καμβύσου καὶ Δαρείου βασιλεία by reading Κάδμου for Καμβύσου is improbable.

The immediate result of the whole business was that outwardly Hippokrates and Anaxilas stood in the same position as before with regard to Zankle, but Hippokrates' position was in reality weaker. Anaxilas was on the spot, Hippokrates at a considerable distance and tied up with many other interests. The Samians were uncertain allies who could be trusted to play off one tyrant against another. Their preservation of the κορυφαῖοι of the Zanklaians was a direct blow to Hippokrates almost before he had finished the negotiations. The Kale Akte scheme was abandoned and Greek interests in the Tyrrhenian Sea left to the piratical operations of the Liparaians and Dionysios of Phokaia. The abandonment of Kale Akte must have greatly encouraged the Etruscan raiders, whose pressure forced Anaxilas to fortify Skyllaion to protect the Straits.[1] The only gainers from a proceeding in which all parties except the unfortunate Zanklaians behaved with a typical neglect of all moral principles were the Samians, who betrayed their hosts and painlessly became possessed of a very fine city. The leaders of the Zanklaian oligarchy appear not to have lost, but the main citizen body was the first in Sicily to suffer the fate of enslavement which befell most of the smaller cities of Sicily at the hand of one or another tyrant.

All the events at Zankle which concern Hippokrates should fall in the year 493. They are those of a single season, beginning with Skythes' campaign against the Sikels, before the Samians had moved from Lokroi to take up their part. Their seizure of Zankle, the attempt to dislodge them (if indeed there were any hostilities), and Hippokrates' diplomatic activity are not very lengthy operations. The negotiations and the dispositions for the security of Zankle, which might take longer than the military operations, may have spread into the following winter. I think it not only possible but very probable that they were completed in the winter of 493–492.[2]

Aristotle's reference to the Samians is practically a one-line summary of Herodotos: *Pol.* 1303ᵃ 35, Ζαγκλαῖοι δὲ Σαμίους ὑποδεξάμενοι ἐξέπεσον αὐτοί. So also Thuk. vi. 4. 5, ὕστερον δ' αὐτοὶ μὲν ὑπὸ Σαμίων καὶ ἄλλων Ἰώνων ἐκπίπτουσιν, οἳ Μήδους φεύγοντες προσέβαλον Σικελίᾳ. For the sequel, short of which

---

[1] Strabo 257. The date is uncertain.

[2] Pareti allows too long both for the journey west and for the events at Zankle when he calculates that 'non si possa supporre che Ippocrate fosse libero da queste imprese prima del corso del 492, o forse del 491' (p. 35).

Herodotos stops, Thukydides is the chief authority: τοὺς δὲ Σαμίους Ἀναξίλας Ῥηγίνων τύραννος οὐ πολλῷ ὕστερον ἐκβαλὼν καὶ τὴν πόλιν αὐτὸς ξυμμείκτων ἀνθρώπων οἰκίσας Μεσσήνην ἀπὸ τῆς ἑαυτοῦ τὸ ἀρχαῖον πατρίδος ἀντωνόμασεν. The most probable date for this seizure is after Hippokrates' death, while Gelon was occupied with the revolt of Gela. The ξύμμεικτοι ἄνθρωποι who were introduced probably included some Messenians who left their country after the abortive helot rising brought about by Kleomenes in 490–489.[1] This is an additional reason, besides devotion to the land of his ancestors, to induce Anaxilas to rename the city.

Pausanias probably contains a reference to the arrival of Messenians at Zankle by invitation of Anaxilas, carried back by his source from the period soon after 490 to the end of the Second Messenian War.[2] Elements in the story, including the suggested colonization of Sardinia, are derived from the westward movement of the Samians and Milesians. But the core: Ἀναξίλας διεβίβασεν ἐς Σικελίαν αὐτούς. . . . τότε δὲ τοὺς Ζαγκλαίους ὅ τε Ἀναξίλας ναυσὶν ἀνταναγομένους ἐνίκησε καὶ οἱ Μεσσήνιοι μάχῃ πεζῇ: is at variance with Herodotos' account of the seizure of Zankle by the Samians, and may contain the details of the action by which Anaxilas expelled the Samians. The advice of Anaxilas to the Messenians to kill the Zanklaians, and the refusal of the Messenian leaders to do so, are taken from the dealings of Hippokrates with the Samians; the result is that the two parties held the city in common. In conclusion Pausanias relates that this is the occasion of the change of name, which occurred in fact when Anaxilas conquered the city. A further argument that the central part of the story at any rate describes the events after 490 is that Pausanias knows that there was a Samian element in Zankle; he makes one of the oecists, Krataimenes, a Samian.[3]

[1] Plato, *Laws* 692d, 698e; for mention of a Third and Fourth Messenian War see Strabo 362. Cf. Pareti, 70 f. [2] Paus. iv. 23. 5 ff.

[3] See Pareti, 72 ff. Freeman, ii. 486, suggests that Rhianos took his story from a fifth-century Messenian settlement at Zankle, but dates it after the fall of Ithome. Messenians may have come then to Zankle-Messana, but the change of name, and so presumably the chief Messenian influx, was earlier. It may seem hazardous to attempt to extract any history from the romance narrated in Pausanias, which has as its foundation the passages of Herodotos and Thukydides dealing with Zankle–Messana and Rhegion (cf. Pareti, loc. cit.; Kroymann, *Sparta und Messenien*, 33 ff.), and the naval and land battles may have been invented by the romancer. This is Kroymann's conclusion, loc. cit.; cf. Niese, *RE*, i. 2083. Whether Pausanias' source for the Anaxilas episode is Rhianos, as is commonly supposed, or some later writer of Messenian history, as Kroymann shows good reason to believe, is unimportant to the historian.

Thukydides says that Anaxilas expelled the Samians. On the other hand, it is held that the coins of Samian type with the legend MESSENION show that the Samians continued to inhabit the city for some time after the change of name. These coins are apparently later than those of corresponding type at Rhegion. Their introduction at Zankle should coincide with Anaxilas' conquest. The types are at Zankle Samian only at first remove, and directly taken from Rhegion. They are to be connected less closely with the Samian settlers at Zankle than with the Samian coiners whom Anaxilas invited to Rhegion. If the types are thought of in the first place as Rhegine, and as Samian only by descent,[1] it is not inconceivable that their introduction might coincide with the expulsion of the Samians from Zankle, though it is a little topsy-turvy. The introduction of the 'Samian' types happens at the same time as the change of name.[2] The occasion of this is certainly Anaxilas' capture of the city. Herodotos throws no light on the date of the change of name. His reference in connexion with Kadmos, vii. 164, ἔσχε τε καὶ κατοίκησε πόλιν Ζάγκλην τὴν ἐς Μεσσήνην μεταβαλοῦσαν τὸ οὔνομα, is timeless. If he wished to say that the change happened at the same time as the seizure, he would have used the present participle μεταβάλλουσαν; if he thought that it was earlier, he would have used the perfect μεταβεβληκυῖαν. Another indication that he did not connect the change of name with the Samians is that throughout vi. 23 he uses the name Zankle.

The Ionic form of the name is earlier than the Doric. This does not prove that the Samians continued in occupation. There was a remnant of the old Zanklaians, and others of the ξύμμεικτοι ἄνθρωποι may have been Ionians. Though Anaxilas was of Messenian origin, the bulk of the population of Rhegion was Khalkidian. Messana became a city of mixed speech, in which the Dorian in the course of time outweighed the Ionian. Meanwhile, the men who made the coins were Samians, who would prefer to use their own dialect. But this does not mean that the mass of the population for whose use the coins were struck was Samian.

It is very doubtful whether the Attic standard was introduced at Zankle earlier than at Rhegion. Leaving aside the coins of the old Zanklaian type and irregular weight, there

---

[1] Pareti, 54: 'Quando Anassilao prese Zancle, il nuovo tipo modificato si sarebbe da Regio esteso a quest' ultima città.'   [2] Pareti, 66–7; Dodd, 58; Freeman, ii. 486 ff.

are the coins, Babelon, 2191–2; Dodd, C1–2; of Samian type, lion's scalp facing, reverse samaina, which are held to have been struck by the Samians at Zankle.[1] These coins are of the same types as Babelon, nos. 463–4, on the Samian standard (c. 202 gr.), one of which (*BM Cat. Ionia*, no. 30) has the letters ΣΑ on the reverse. The latter coins are certainly Samian. The coins of Attic weight, without inscription (one of them has A on the reverse, probably a mint-mark), are found only in the Messina hoard and in Egypt.[2] As extremely few western coins of such early date are found in the eastern Mediterranean, it is likely that they were struck in Samos and carried by the Samians to Zankle.[3] There is no reason to be disturbed by the failure to find any coins which may be ascribed to the Samians at Zankle before Anaxilas took the city. They held it for only four or five years.

Anaxilas won a victory with a team of mules at Olympia, perhaps in 480.[4] He celebrated it magnificently with a great banquet, Simonides wrote an ode beginning χαίρετ' ἀελλοπόδων θύγατρες ἵππων,[5] and the mule-car appeared on the coins of both Rhegion and Messana.[6] The reverse was a running hare. Anaxilas is stated to have introduced the hare into Sicily, clearly by a misunderstanding of a canting reference to this coin type. The mules and hare coins have both MESSENION and MESSANION. Head thinks that the change of spelling coincided with the expulsion of the Samian element some time before 476.[7] It is possible, however, that the change indicates

[1] Babelon, loc. cit.; Pareti, 54 ff.

[2] Dodd, 70; Noe, *Bibliography of Greek Coin Hoards*[2], 94; *ZfN*, xxxvii, 1927, 103.

[3] So Dodd, 69, following von Sallet.

[4] The precise date is not recorded, and the mule-race is not included among the Olympic victories listed in *Ox. Pap.* ccxxii, which covers part of the period in question. That it was late in Anaxilas' life might perhaps be inferred from Athen. 3e, who states that Anaxilas' son Leophron celebrated the victory; but this causes further difficulties, for Anaxilas was succeeded not by his son but by his servant Mikythos as guardian for his sons. Leophron may have gone in person to Olympia to represent his father, as Thrasyboulos represented his father Xenokrates at Delphi (Pind., *Pyth.* vi), and may have died before his father. I therefore prefer 480 to 476 as date for this victory. The coins favour a late rather than an early date.

[5] Fr. 7 Bergk; Arist. *Rhet.* iii. 2. 14: καὶ ὁ Σιμωνίδης, ὅτε μὲν ἐδίδου μισθὸν ὀλίγον αὐτῷ ὁ νικήσας τοῖς ὀρεῦσιν, οὐκ ἤθελε ποιεῖν ὡς δυσχεραίνων εἰς ἡμιόνους ποιεῖν, ἐπεὶ δ' ἱκανὸν ἔδωκεν, ἐποίησε· χαίρετ' ἀελλοπόδων θύγατρες ἵππων· καίτοι καὶ τῶν ὄνων θύγατερες ἦσαν. Herakleides fr. 25: καὶ νικήσας Ὀλύμπια ἡμιόνοις, εἱστίασε τοὺς Ἕλληνας· καί τις αὐτὸν ἐπέσκωψεν εἰπών· οὗτος τί ἂν ἐποίει νικήσας ἵπποις; ἐποίησε δὲ καὶ ἐπινίκιον Σιμωνίδης· χαίρετ' κτλ.

[6] *BM Cat. Italy*, p. 373, no. 3; Babelon, 2193–4; Dodd, A4: *BM Cat. Sicily*, p. 100, nos. 11–19; Babelon, 2213–15; Dodd, B4–5. Sometimes with Nike crowning the charioteer; cf. Nike on the coins of Gelon.

[7] *HN*[2], 153.

no violent move but a gradual strengthening of the Dorian element against the Ionian. The MESSANION coins are probably not earlier than *c.* 460, and it may be that more Messenians came then, after the fall of Ithome. Their arrival, and the MESSANION coins, would then be after the short period in which the old name and types were revived by the Zanklaian remnant after the fall of the tyrants.

As soon as he was free of complications in the north, Hippokrates turned against Syracuse, the only city of eastern Sicily which had escaped servitude. Syracuse was unquestionably the first city of Sicily, but its internal condition gave hope that it would not offer a whole-hearted resistance, and Hippokrates' trained army of citizens and mercenaries might expect to be a match for more numerous Syracusan forces.

On the march from Gela to Syracuse lay Kamarina, which had so far recovered from her destruction of 552 as to be materially flourishing.[1] Since her defeat in the war of independence she was more tightly bound to Syracuse than before, and Hippokrates would have to deal with her before he was free to march against Syracuse. A garbled quotation of Timaios in the scholiasts to *Ol.* v. 19 appears to refer to a destruction by Hippokrates, previous to the refounding after the battle of Heloros.[2]

The Syracusans made a stand at the river Heloros, where they were defeated in battle. A young Geloan, Khromios son of Hagesidamos, who afterwards became Gelon's brother-in-law, won his spurs in the battle. Pindar describes the scene:[3]

βαθυκρήμνοισι δ' ἀμφ' ἀκταῖς Ἑλώρου,
ἔνθ' Ἀρέας πόρον ἄνθρωποι καλέοισι, δέδορκεν
παιδὶ τοῦθ' Ἁγησιδάμου φέγγος ἐν ἁλικίᾳ πρώτᾳ.

The site of the battle is debated. Though Pindar's epithet is so vivid, he need never have visited it.[4] Freeman puts it inland, where the stream issues from the hills.[5] In that case Hippokrates was taking the direct route to Syracuse, disregarding the town of Heloron. The lower course of the river is through a two-mile wide valley, Ovid's Heloria Tempe,[6] in

---

[1] See above, p. 106.   [2] Pareti, 38 ff. See note on pp. 407 ff.   [3] *Nem.* ix. 40.
[4] There is nothing to show whether 'Péas or 'Apéas is the correct form. Schröder reads one, Bowra the other. The scholiasts (95a–c Drachmann) do not know how to spell it or where it is; one (95c) puts it at the Straits of Messina; another (95b) suggests, as I do above, ἡ δὲ μάχη ἐν στερρῷ χωρίῳ τῷ ˙Ελωρι· ὁ δὲ αἰγιαλὸς καλεῖται Ἀρείας πόρος.
[5] ii. 116. Giuliano (*Riv. st. ant.* xii. 86) is bold enough to find the root of 'Péas surviving in the Monte di Renna, on the left bank of the river Heloros and some six miles from the town.   [6] *Fasti*, iv. 477.

which it stagnates. There is a bar, through which it hardly reaches the sea, and low sandy cliffs on top of which is the town. Perhaps Hippokrates left the road to mask Heloron, and attacked across the mouth of the river.[1]

After the victory Hippokrates marched on Syracuse and encamped at the Olympieion. It is related that he found the priest and other Syracusans carrying off the gold offerings, including the golden cloak of Zeus. He rebuked them as temple-robbers, and himself refrained from touching the offerings, with one eye on the gratitude of the god and one on the effect of his restraint on the Syracusans. Diodoros' rhetoric covers a suggestion that all was not well in Syracuse and that Hippokrates hoped that dissension inside would work in his favour: ἅμα δε νομίζων διαβάλλειν τοὺς προεστῶτας τῶν ἐν Συρακούσαις πραγμάτων πρὸς τὰ πλήθη διὰ τὸ δοκεῖν αὐτοὺς πλεονεκτικῶς, ἀλλ' οὐ δημοτικῶς οὐδ' ἴσως ἄρχειν.[2] The προεστῶτες are probably the Gamoroi, whose oligarchy was soon to fall. The passage has been taken to imply that the democratic revolution had already taken place, for no one would expect the γαμόροι to govern δημοτικῶς.[3] But this interpretation is too literal, considering that we have not even the original words of Diodoros.

Hüttl's view that the democracy began c. 520, when the first coins of Syracuse were issued, is impossible. Thirty-five years, or rather forty-five, since the beginning of the Syracusan coinage dates about c. 530,[4] is an impossibly long time for the Gamoroi to wait at Kasmenai for a deliverer. There is nothing democratic about the issuing of coins, which began in nearly all the cities of Sicily and south Italy in the sixth century, without a democratic revolution in any. Syracuse was, even under the Gamoroi, the commercial centre of Sicily, and the introduction

[1] The scholiasts on Pindar add nothing to our knowledge of the campaigns although they quote Timaios as an authority (95a). Didymos said that there was no other contemporary battle of Heloros ὅτι μὴ σὺν Ἱπποκράτει τοῦ Γέλωνος πρὸς Συρακουσίους. One scholion makes it a victory of Gelon over the Carthaginians (93a, ἐνίκησε γὰρ ἐνταῦθα Καρχηδονίους συμμαχῶν Γέλωνι τῷ τυράννῳ τῷ Ἱπποκράτους διαδόχῳ). The column of the Pizzuta, north-west of the town, is to be connected with the battle of 413, in spite of the difficulty that it is two and a half miles from the Assinaros, rather than with this battle. Orsi suggests that it is a memorial of the Heloros, only to reject the suggestion (N Sc, 1899, 243–4). Neither side would commemorate the battle of the Heloros. Hippokrates would not have time to build so solid a monument, and the Syracusans, in whose possession the site remained, would not build a memorial of their defeat. Gelon would be the last man to commemorate the war between Syracusans and Geloans.   [2] Diod. x. 28.

[3] Hüttl, 54–5; he thinks that τοὺς προεστῶτας τῶν ἐν Συρακούσαις πραγμάτων is a reminiscence of the unofficial title προστάται τοῦ δήμου.

[4] Boehringer, Die Münzen von Syrakus, 6, 91.

of coinage did not mark a change of policy. Boehringer stresses the aristocratic type of the quadriga, and concludes 'aus dem Mangel an Kleingeld in dieser Zeit können wir wohl schliessen, dass am Ende des sechsten Jahrhunderts in Syrakus noch grösstenteils Ackerwirtschaft herrschte und dass die Gamoren Selbstversorger waren'.[1]

Hippokrates apparently did not attack the city. Herodotos' change of language, πολιορκέοντος γὰρ ʿΙπποκράτεος Καλλιπολίτας κτλ. . . . καὶ πρὸς Συρηκοσίους, implies that the battle of the Heloros was not followed by a siege. Hippokrates was waiting for the people of Syracuse to break out against their rulers, and when this did not happen he accepted the mediation[2] of Corinth and Korkyra. Perhaps the siege of so large a city, as it was even before Gelon increased it, was beyond his power. Of all the armies which lay before Syracuse, none succeeded in taking it before Marcellus. Both the natural strength and the greater man-power of Syracuse made it a very different matter from the other sieges in which Hippokrates had been successful. If he could not take it by assault, he had no hope of reducing it without a powerful fleet. It was probably inability to proceed which obliged him to accept the mediation of Corinth and Korkyra. There were reasons of sentiment to bring Corinth and Korkyra to the aid of Syracuse, and probably a number of citizens of each lived there. The relations of Syracuse and Corinth had always been very close, and Corinthian trade with Sicily was closely bound up with Syracuse, and might suffer a shock if Syracuse fell into enemy hands. Korkyra must have had a profitable share of this trade. Corinth and Korkyra were of the four great naval powers of Greece the two which were interested in the west, and acting together could control the traffic between Greece and Italy. None of the colonial powers had any fleet to speak of, until Hippokrates began to build up a navy. At Gela he would not be formidable, but if he established himself at Syracuse and built up a great fleet, as Gelon did afterwards, the Corinthian naval control of the Ionian Sea, and with it their commercial control, might be brought to an end.

It is hard to see why Hippokrates should recognize the mediation of Corinth and Korkyra. I can think of no way in which they could enforce their will on him, except by the

---

[1] Ibid. 75.

[2] Mediation rather than arbitration: Tod, *Greek International Arbitration*, 65; Macan, *Herod. VII–IX*, I. i. 214.

threat of naval action against his new-built fleet. With the improvement in design and the growth of fleets which was taking place such action would not be inconceivable. But probably Hippokrates needed no such threat, as Syracuse was too strong for him to take by force. He was waiting for dis-affection inside to play into his hands. This did not happen in 492, but seven years later civil strife made Gelon master of Syracuse.

The terms of settlement were that Hippokrates should receive the land of Kamarina as ransom for the Syracusan prisoners he had taken.[1] He became the oecist of a refounded Kamarina. The population was probably not changed. The score of names in a *defixio* datable probably to this period of Kamarina's existence[2] have almost all Doric forms; Arkhias should be a Syracusan and other names are also met with at Syracuse. So probably most of Hippokrates' settlers were Syracusan by descent. In contrast, another *defixio* later than the Geloan refounding of 461 has some strange names in it, and some of the names have ethnics which show that the population was drawn from many sources.[3]

The dealings with the Samians are over in 493. The Heloros campaign belongs to 492, the negotiations with the Corinthians and Korkyraians and the re-establishment of Kamarina filling the rest of that season and the following winter. This leaves 491 and possibly the early part of 490 for a campaign or cam-paigns against the Sikels, to which belong the capture of Ergetion with the aid of Kamarinaian soldiers and the attack on Hybla. In 491-490, according to the received chronology, Hippokrates died while attacking Hybla. If it is granted that the affairs of the Samians fill 493 and that the siege of Leon-tinoi is earlier, all the events of Hippokrates' life may be fitted in before 491-490. Even if the order of operations in Herod. vii. 154 is not chronological, the dates of the events of 493-491 are established, for the attack on Kamarina which preceded Heloros is κατὰ τὴν τοῦ Δαρείου διάβασιν, i.e. c. 490, and therefore unlikely to be before 493. As Ergetion and Hybla are in any case after the refounding of Kamarina, there is very little play for the events of 492 and 491.[4]

---

[1] Herod. vii. 154; Thuk. vi. 5. 3.

[2] Ribezzo, *RIGI*, viii. 82 ff.; Pace, *Camarina*, 161, no. 12; cf. ibid. 38. Pace is too positive in saying that it 'mostra con il suo elenco di nome coll' etnico, che il fondo della popolazione era ancora unitario e siracusano', for no ethnics are given.

[3] Ribezzo, loc. cit.; Pace, op. cit. 162, no. 13.   [4] See Note on pp. 407-9.

After his half-success against Syracuse Hippokrates returned to the north, and spent his last year in a Sikel campaign. He had Sikel mercenaries in his army, many of them drawn from Ergetion. These men were attracted to his standards by liberality with the spoils, presumably won from other Sikel towns in the neighbourhood. Hippokrates did not trust to the goodwill of the Ergetines, but seized their city while they were absent, and set the Greek part of his army to attack them.[1] Polyainos' picturesque story has many phrases which sound authentic, including the detail ἐπεὶ δὲ ἀπεφράχθησαν πρὸς ταῖς ῥαχίαις τῶν κυμάτων, which suggests that his source was more explicit on the topography. The site of Ergetion is not known, except that Polyainos' story places it above the Laistrygonian plain, and within a night-march of the sea. This might be either in the neighbourhood of Leontinoi or to the west or north of the plain, but an independent Sikel town of the importance of Ergetion is more likely to have been among the group on the slopes of Etna.[2]

The attack on Ergetion was after the restoration of Kamarina, for Hippokrates had Kamarinaians as well as Geloans in his army. It must therefore be in 491. The attack on Hybla in which he died was either in the same campaign or possibly early in the season of 490. It is uncertain which of the Hyblas it was.[3] The Greek quarter of the Heraian Hybla appears not to have been inhabited later than the early fifth century,[4] and it may be that this is because the occupants were expelled when Hippokrates began his drive against the independent Sikels. This Hybla, the most southerly place still held by free Sikels, was completely surrounded by Greeks. It is unlikely to have been of sufficient importance to draw a separate campaign from Hippokrates. He marched past it on his Syracuse campaign and if it offered any trouble he might have dealt with it

[1] Polyainos v. 6.

[2] Freeman, i. 153, calls it 'a place of many spellings and small renown'. The lack of references is the consequence of its destruction by Hippokrates. It was clearly a place of importance before this, supplying a large contingent of mercenaries, and its capture called for a guileful lack of honesty on Hippokrates' part. Freeman, following Fazello, i. 432, 447, places it near Aidone, but this is too far from the sea. The coins sometimes ascribed to Ergetion, following Pais, *Ancient Italy*, ch. x (cf. Pareti, 59–60), belong to an unknown south Italian city.

[3] Freeman, ii. 121, states without reason given that it was the Heraian Hybla. Pareti, p. 43, leaves it open: p. 340, is very doubtful about the 'politica etnea' of Hippokrates and the tyrants of Syracuse, and by implication favours the Heraian. I follow Ciaceri, *Studi Storici*, ii. 170 ff.

[4] See above, p. 108.

then, or left it to his allies of Kamarina. Hybla Geleatis on the slopes of Etna is more likely to have been Hippokrates' objective. If so, Ergetion and Hybla may have been part of the same campaign, a move to subjugate all the Sikels of Etna. Other conquests may be inferred to have preceded Ergetion, both from Herodotos' phrase τῶν βαρβάρων συχνούς and Polyainos' account of the partition of spoils to the Ergetine mercenaries. The Sikels of this area were the strongest and in many ways the most advanced of their race,[1] and having conquered the Greek cities Hippokrates wished to round off his empire. The attack on the northern Sikels may reasonably be some time after the conquest of the Greeks of that region.

Hippokrates' main strength lay in the cavalry, commanded by Gelon, his best general and right-hand man. The plains of Gela were among the best horse-breeding areas in Sicily. Pantares is the first Sicilian known to have competed with a chariot at Olympia.[2] Gelon, Hieron, and Polyzalos all won competing as Geloans. It is a curious fact that Geloan hoplites are never heard of, whereas the cavalry is mentioned occasionally.[3] As well as his citizen forces, and in his last campaign those of Kamarina, he had Sikel mercenaries. Seven years of continuous warfare, aggressive wars waged for foreign conquest, would be a great strain on a citizen army, and Hippokrates may have begun the system which Gelon followed of building up a large personal army of Greek and barbarian mercenaries. If he treated other conquered peoples as he did the Zanklaians, confiscating their property and selling them as slaves, he would not lack for ready money. It may be inferred that he also began to build a fleet. Thuk. i. 14 ὀλίγον τε πρὸ τῶν Μηδικῶν καὶ τοῦ Δαρείου θανάτου . . . τριήρεις περί τε Σικελίαν τοῖς τυράννοις ἐς πλῆθος ἐγένοντο καὶ Κερκυραίοις is probably to be taken as exact, not approximate, in its chronology. The only tyrants in the period immediately before 490 were Hippokrates and Anaxilas. Hippokrates' position at Zankle vis-à-vis the Samians and Anaxilas was made much more difficult by his inability to act by sea as by land, and if he meant to hold Zankle against Anaxilas he needed to control the Straits. This may well have been the occasion on which the two tyrants set out to build up a great fleet. Gela was completely unsuited for

[1] See above, pp. 129 ff.
[2] The first colonial is Kleosthenes of Epidamnos (Paus. vi. 10. 6).
[3] Thuk. vi. 67. 2; vii. 33. i; cf. Ziegler, RE, vii. 953.

a naval base, and there was no even passable harbour in the Geloan territory. The open beach served well enough for merchant shipping, but there was no shelter from the prevalent on-shore breeze, and for a good part of the year the beach could be used only with difficulty. With the development of shipbuilding, increased use of the trireme, and improvement of tactics necessitating perfect sailing-condition, a good harbour with docks became a necessity. Polykrates' constructed harbour, protected by the famous mole, became a model; Polykrates was the first new-style thalassocrat, the first whom Herodotos recognized.[1] In the Greek part of Sicily there were two first-class natural harbours, Syracuse and Messana. Hippokrates and Anaxilas clashed over the latter, Hippokrates attempted to secure the former. I have suggested that the intervention of Corinth and Korkyra in favour of Syracuse was partly brought about by apprehension as to what Hippokrates might do with his new fleet if he controlled Syracuse. There is no indication how far Hippokrates' fleet progressed towards the round figure of two hundred which Gelon had at his disposal, but sixty ships is a common figure for Thukydides' other great sea-powers. Hippokrates and Anaxilas may have built up to something like this figure.[2]

Nothing is known of Hippokrates' home policy, but it may be inferred that it was oppressive. After his death the Geloans revolted against the tyranny and there was civil war. Hippokrates was nothing but a soldier, and his subjects were tired of war. The only unmilitary action which has been ascribed to him is the enlargement of the Treasury of the Geloans at Olympia. The porch of this building was added in the early fifth century,[3] and a plausible hypothesis is that it was done by Hippokrates from the spoils of his victories.[4] In seven years of continuous warfare he accomplished a good deal, and made the tyrant of Gela indisputably the first man in all Sicily, but he left much undone. He failed to win complete control over

---

[1] iii. 122.

[2] The Phokaians had 60 ships at Alalia, the Samians 60 at Lade; other East Greek fleets were a little larger. Polykrates' fleet was 100 pentekonters and at least 40 triremes. In 480 Korkyra manned 60 ships, the largest fleet after the Athenians (Herod. vii. 168), whose figure in 490–489 is 70 (vi. 132), and with the 20 ships bought from the Corinthians (to replace 20 ships sent to aid the Ionian revolt in 498, see Macan ad loc.) they had 70 against the Aiginetans (vi. 89).

[3] *Olympia*, ii. 56. For material of *c.* 500 from the Treasury of the Geloans, and a suggestion that the building was repaired about that date, see above, p. 272, n. 1.

[4] L. Giuliano, *Riv. st. ant.* xi. 259; cf. L. Dyer, *JHS*, 1905, 297.

Zankle, and after his death it fell to his most formidable rival. He defeated the Syracusans, but left their conquest to his successor. His Sikel schemes, though far-reaching, were incompletely carried out. On the whole, the northern Sikels preserved their independence. Of the southern Sikels, Morgantina and Menai, at the least, were independent half a century later. The only lasting results of his Sikel campaigns were in the neighbourhood of Gela, where the end of Monte Bubbonia, the beginning of the fortified post of Piano dei Casazzi, and on the other side the end of S. Mauro and of the Greek post at Hybla Heraia, are witness to the great change in the relations of Greeks and Sikels. This change from the peaceful relations of the sixth century led ultimately to the national movement of Duketios, who may have been a boy when Hippokrates first began to attack his countrymen.[1] Hippokrates had no hostility to the Sikels as barbarians, for he used them as mercenaries. They fell simply in his grandiose schemes of empire over Sikels and Sikeliots alike.

Hippokrates began the ruin of the Khalkidian cities, which was prosecuted more effectively by Gelon and Hieron. On moral grounds he appears to have been a worthy predecessor of Dionysios and Agathokles, a worshipper of power for power's sake. Nothing is known of the causes of war with either Sikels or Greeks, but Hippokrates is clearly the aggressor in most cases, and his hand was against every man. His double-dealing at Zankle and his invitation to the Samians to slaughter the leaders of the Zanklaians are as callous pieces of treachery as any in the history of Sicily. The boundless schemes of conquest, the indifference to the fate of whole populations, the widespread destruction which laid many Greek cities waste and roused a dangerous Sikel war, all have their origin with him.

---

[1] One of the schemes mooted in Hippokrates' time, the colonization of Kale Akte, was left for Duketios to accomplish as a mixed enterprise of Greeks and Sikels.

NOTE TO PAGE 402

Schol. *Ol.* v. 19:

<table>
<tr><td align="center">a (A)</td><td align="center">b (CDEHQ)</td></tr>
</table>

νέοικον ἕδραν εἶπε τὴν Καμάριναν ὁ
    Πίνδαρος.
σαφηνίζει Τίμαιος ἐν τῇ δεκάτῃ.
εἰσὶ δὲ οὗτοι οἱ Καμαριναῖοι . . .
ὑπὸ τοῦ Γελω. τυράννου ἀνηρέθησαν·
5 εἶτα ὑπὸ Γελω. συνῳκίσθησαν
ἐπὶ τῆς . . . ᾿Ολυμπιάδος.

    [νου ἀνηρέθη·
᾿Ιπποκράτης ὑπὸ τοῦ τῶν Γελώων τυράν-
εἶτα ὑπὸ Γελω. συνῳκίσθη ἡ Καμάρινα
κατὰ τὴν †μβ′ ᾿Ολυμπιάδα,
ὡς φησι Τίμαιος·
διὸ καὶ νέοικον ἕδραν εἶπε τὴν πόλιν.

ἡ δὲ ἅλωσις ἐγένετο κατὰ τὴν
    Δαρείου τοῦ Πέρσου διάβασιν.

ἡ δὲ ἅλωσις αὐτῆς ἐγένετο κατὰ τὴν
    Δαρείου τοῦ ῾Υστάσπου στρατείαν.

3. οἱ in lac. suppl. Boeckh.
4. ἀπὸ scr.: corr. Boeckh. Γέλωνος Drachmann, Γελώων Pareti.
5. Γελώων Drachmann, cf. *b.*

4. τῶν om. C. Γελώνων E.
5. Γέλωνος scr.: Γελώων Wesseling appro-
   bantibus omnibus.
6. κβ′ E.

b 4. post ᾿Ιπποκράτης fort. lac. statuenda Drachmann. ὑπὸ ᾿Ιπποκράτους
Pareti. 'Il prof. Vitelli supporrebbe che in origine vi fosse solo ὑπὸ τοῦ ecc.,
e che in seguito una glossa marginale ''Ιπποκρατ', identificante il tiranno in
questione, sia passata nel testo, al nominativo', Pareti, 40, n. 1.

The number of the Olympiad is absent in one version, corrupt in the other.
Boeckh read οθ′ (461–460) in both cases, referring to the final rebuilding of
461–460 (Diod. xi. 76). This is the occasion to which the νέοικον ἕδραν in fact
refers, and the most natural one to be mentioned. But Boeckh's correction
throws over completely the manuscript reading of *b.* In the two variants
μβ′ and κβ′ the β′ is common: both are impossible figures (532–528 and
572–568). Horn reads πβ′ (452–448), the date of Psaumis' chariot victory
(452: *Ox. Pap.* ccxxii; so also Schol. Pind. *Ol.* iv, inscr., *Ol.* v, inscr. *b*). It is
not impossible that the Scholiasts substituted this date for that of the slightly
previous foundation, as *Ol.* v celebrates both foundation and victory (not the
chariot victory, but a mule victory won perhaps at the previous Olympiad
(456) (Schroeder, *Pindar,* 506); but the Scholiasts took it that it was the
chariot victory).

Pareti (p. 40) reads οβ′ (492–488) and refers to the reconstruction by
Hippokrates. But not even a Scholiast should speak of this as a reconstruction by 'the Geloans' in contrast to the previous destruction by a tyrant of
the Geloans. Considering also that this restoration was a short-lived affair,
and that of 461 is the permanent settlement, which is commemorated in the
Ode, I find it most natural that it is the one to which the Scholiasts refer.
There are difficulties in both Boeckh's and Horn's supplement of the figure,
but either is preferable to Pareti's, which introduces new difficulties and gives
a less probable result.

A gives a reference to the tenth book of Timaios. This book included the
battle of the Heloros (fr. 85 Müller = Schol. Pind. *Nem.* ix. 95). The settlement after Himera came in the fourteenth book (fr. 89 Müller = Schol. Pind.
Pyth. ii. 2). It follows that some part of the scholion refers to events nearly

contemporary with the Heloros. This would be the destruction. But it is
not certain that the whole scholion comes from the tenth book, and the
destruction and reconstruction would probably be in different passages of
Timaios. For this reason Pareti's argument that the reconstruction of 461
would be mentioned in a book much later than the tenth is not valid.

The question of the destruction is more important than that of the reconstruction, because the latter must be one of two known rebuildings, and the
only question is on which of the two the Scholiasts have picked. If I am
inclined, in opposition to Pareti, to prefer the later and better-known reconstruction, I agree with him that the destruction is probably not that of 484–483.
The reading Γελω. may be expanded into either Γέλωνος or Γελώων, and there
is only historical probability to guide. In l. 5, speaking of the reconstruction,
b reads Γέλωνος, but as Gelon did not rebuild Kamarina this must be emended
to Γελώων. In l. 4, speaking of the destruction, b reads Γελώων, and this is
therefore to be preferred in the parallel passage of a; Gelon when he destroyed
Kamarina was tyrant not of the Geloans but of the Syracusans. For the
reading in b 4 I favour Vitelli's suggestion, quoted by Pareti, rather than
Pareti's own. The addition of the name Hippokrates is the only important
point in which a and b differ, and that is more likely to have been added as a
gloss than to have been omitted by the Ambrosian Scholiast. On the other
hand, more than the simple relative may have fallen out of A after οἱ Καμαριναῖοι. It is not certain then that the naming of Hippokrates has more
authority than an attempt to identify the tyrant of Gela. But in any case,
the reference is to a destruction 'about the time of Dareios' expedition'. This
does not agree with the destruction at the hands of Gelon, which was nearer
the time of Xerxes' expedition. The reference to the tenth book of Timaios
makes it probable, though not absolutely certain, that the event is earlier
than 484; though again it is not absolutely certain that it was the destruction
of which Timaios spoke in book x. The balance of probability, however, is in
favour of Pareti's view that the destruction was executed by Hippokrates
c. 491–490.

I do not, however, agree with Pareti in tying this destruction explicitly to
the year 491–490, rather than 492. I do not think that the phrase κατὰ τὴν
Δαρείου τοῦ Πέρσου διάβασιν is capable of such precision. This is the central
point of his objections to the traditional chronology of Hippokrates. If he
is right in insisting on 491–490, it is clear that the rest of Hippokrates' reign,
the attack on Syracuse, the refounding of Kamarina, the conquest of Ergetion,
and his death at Hybla, cannot come before 491–490. But the date need be no
more than an approximation, and we have not the words of Timaios but a
confused selection from him, so that a variation of one or two years is quite
reasonable. Whether Pareti is right or not in thinking that the scholiasts
speak of a reconstruction in 492–488 makes no difference. That date is accepted
in any case for the refounding under Hippokrates. It is a little disingenuous
to take the lower limit of the Olympiad and date the activities of Hippokrates
with regard to Kamarina and Syracuse to 491–490 to summer 488 (p. 42).

The third scholion, quoting Philistos, 19c (ACDEHQ) Φίλιστος ἐν γ΄ φησὶν
ὅτι Γέλων Καμάριναν κατέσκαψεν· Ἱπποκράτης δὲ πολεμήσας Συρακουσίοις καὶ
πολλοὺς αἰχμαλώτους λαβὼν ὑπὲρ τοῦ τούτους ἀποδοῦναι ἔλαβε τὴν Καμάριναν καὶ
συνῴκισεν αὐτήν· ὁ γοῦν Πίνδαρος συνῳκισμένην οἶδε τὴν Καμάριναν, is most easily
explained by transposition, assuming that the Scholiast refers to the well-

known destruction by Gelon and the refounding by Hippokrates, and has mistakenly put the former before the latter. Pareti (pp. 38–9) explains it as an act of Gelon as Hippokrates' general, at the beginning of the campaign against Syracuse. But I do not believe that this act of Gelon's, serving under Hippokrates and in his presence, would be ascribed to him instead of Hippokrates, or that any one would refer to it in words which would apply as well to his later action as tyrant of Syracuse. The argument that in his third book Philistos would be treating events earlier than 484 is false. It is difficult to be certain of the limits of Philistos' single books, but fr. 23 of book v appears to refer to the Syracusan expedition of 453 against Aithalia (Diod. xi. 88). The naming of Therma in fr. 20 of book iii ($\Theta\acute{\epsilon}\rho\mu\alpha$, $\chi\omega\rho\acute{\iota}o\nu$ $\Sigma\iota\kappa\epsilon\lambda\acute{\iota}\alpha s$· $\Phi\acute{\iota}\lambda\iota\sigma\tau os$ $\tau\rho\acute{\iota}\tau\wp$) is perhaps in connexion with the Himera campaign. Pareti is completely unjustified in saying that 'della distruzione del 484 o 483 Filisto doveva parlare non nel 3°, ma nel 5° o 6° libro' (p. 39, n. 1).

CHAPTER XIV

GELON

ON Hippokrates' death there was confusion and civil war in Gela. His sons Eukleides and Kleandros were apparently too young to govern, and Gelon was left as their guardian. The Geloans broke into open rebellion. Gelon fought a battle on behalf of his wards, defeated the rebels, and then threw over the boys and set himself up as tyrant.[1] He was supported, presumably, by Hippokrates' mercenaries against the citizen forces. Before accusing him of ingratitude to his old master's sons we should know whether it was possible to rule in their name. Neither Kleandros nor Hippokrates seems to have been popular, whereas Gelon was a likeable man, milder than Hippokrates, to whom his popularity had been of service. His military reputation was very high, and it may be that the Geloan people would accept him though they rebelled against Hippokrates' sons.

Ainesidemos also had designs on Gela. He sent Gelon a present of κοττάβια for forestalling him in an enslavement, which is more likely to be that of Gela than any minor triumph.[2] This Ainesidemos will be Gelon's fellow officer, to be identified as the tyrant of Leontinoi set up by Hippokrates;[3] he was the only man important enough to think of forestalling Gelon. The jocular tone of his message well befits old comrades in arms.

The date of Gelon's accession is 491–490. Pausanias says that Gelon's chariot dedicated at Olympia for his victory in 488 must be dedicated by another Geloan of the same name and father, for Gelon had become tyrant of Syracuse in 491–490. But he became ruler of Syracuse in 485; Pausanias has therefore confused the beginning of his rule at Gela with the beginning at Syracuse.[4] The date 491–490 is confirmed by Dionysios of Halikarnassos.[5]

---

[1] Herod. vii. 155.   [2] *Rhet.* i. 12. 30.

[3] See above, p. 383.   [4] vi. 9. Cf. Busolt, ii². 780 n.; Freeman, ii. 124.

[5] vii. 1. Dionysios does not himself fall into the error of saying that Gelon became tyrant of Syracuse in 491–490. Plutarch (*Vit. Cor.* 16), following the same source, does; but Dionysios just keeps clear of saying so, and must be given the benefit of the doubt (*contra* Pareti, 48). The sending of corn from Sicily to Rome is a doublet of the dispatch in 433 (Livy iv. 25. 4) or 410 (Livy iv. 52. 6). Some Roman historian said that it was sent in 491 (also Livy ii. 34. 3, without naming Gelon); the same or another said that it was sent by Dionysios. We are

The difficulty is frequently raised, what occupied Gelon at Gela from 491–490 to 485.[1] Herodotos goes straight from his seizure of power at Gela to his reception at Syracuse: μετὰ δὲ τοῦτο τὸ εὕρημα. . . . In the first place, 491–490 represents not the final establishment of his power at Gela, but Hippokrates' death, at which Gelon was left as guardian of his sons and master of his army. Hippokrates' death must have been late in 491, if it was not early in 490. If we could press Dionysios' words νεωστὶ τὴν Ἱπποκράτους . . . τυραννίδα παρειληφώς, we might believe that the rebellion of the Geloans was regarded as an incident interrupting Gelon's tyranny, which began on Hippokrates' death. This is in any case probable. Gelon's first year or so, then, was occupied in securing his position in Gela. He must also have had to consolidate the empire so rapidly won by Hippokrates.

Zankle fell away to Anaxilas. Provision had to be made for the security of the other Greek cities, and for the holding down of the Sikels. The Geloans were probably war-weary and needed a breathing-space. This unspectacular organization may have taken some time. Hippokrates had raised Gela to a great power and bequeathed to his successor the foundations of an empire over half Sicily, but he had not had time to organize his conquests, and left many enterprises half-completed.

The one concrete action which may be ascribed to Gelon's Geloan period is the war to avenge Doreius and free the Emporia.[2] Dorieus' death was not too distant in the early eighties to serve as the occasion of a Carthaginian war. The war may perhaps be accurately dated from Justin xix. 1. 9, in which the words *ad Leonidam fratrem regis Spartanorum* are usually emended *ad Leonidae fratrem*, &c., and referred to Dorieus' expedition. But it is odd to call Dorieus Leonidas' brother or to refer to Leonidas at all. Good sense can be made of the passage without emendation, if it is taken of an un-successful appeal to the Spartans by Gelon. The death of Kleomenes was probably in 489; down to that time Leonidas was 'the brother of the king of Sparta'; but while Kleomenes was engaged in private intrigue against the Spartan state,

not concerned with the credibility of early Roman history. The relevant fact is that Dionysios of Halikarnassos, or his source, found 491–490 as the date of Gelon's accession, and said that if corn was sent, then it was sent not by Dionysios but by him. The error of calling Gelon Hippokrates' brother does not affect the date.

[1] Pareti, 44 ff. For a discussion of Pareti's arguments see below, pp. 432 ff.
[2] Herod. vii. 158; Justin xix. 1. 9; iv. 2. 6.

Leonidas would be the proper man to appeal to. The war to avenge Dorieus would belong then to 489, after Gelon was established at Gela, before Leonidas became king of Sparta.[1]

The second object of the war was to free the Emporia. This term has a special geographical limitation to the part of Africa nearest Sicily.[2] A campaign in Africa, with the new fleet built by Hippokrates, was a possibility. The liberation of the Emporia was represented by Gelon as a source of profit to the Greeks of Hellas. An opening for trade in Africa would be of much more value to their commerce than any success in Sicily, as trade with Carthage in Greek goods was probably carried on at this time through the Etruscans as intermediaries.[3] Gelon's first objective, however, must have been the part of Sicily in Carthaginian hands. For a war in Africa he needed a stronger fleet than he had, and probably one reason for his transference to Syracuse was that there was no harbour at Gela for warships. τὰ ἐμπόρια συνελευθεροῦν is presented only as an intention, not as a campaign actually carried out. The war went on for some time, but Gelon's plans to make a descent on Africa did not get beyond paper. The successes which he claims must have been in Sicily, presumably in driving the Phoenicians out of territory occupied by them after Dorieus' defeat.

The warfare of which Justin speaks as preceding the battle of Himera was in Sicily. Its course, *diu et varia victoria*, is that of all Justin's Carthaginian wars. But, if he is to be trusted, he implies that Theron as well as Gelon took part, *cum tyrannis* referring not only to the Himera campaign but to the earlier warfare. Theron may have been tyrant of Akragas in 489. His seizure of the tyranny is usually dated to 488, his death after sixteen years' rule being recorded by Diodoros under the year 472–471;[4] the excerpt from the tenth book which records his rise comes after Heloros, and before Kimon's payment of Miltiades' fine, i.e. before 489.[5] Either his death was dated a

---

[1] There is no reason to think that Gelon is taking to himself the credit of a war which he waged as Hippokrates' officer (Freeman, ii. 99. 479; Macan, *Herodotus VII–IX*, I. i. 221). Hippokrates' reign is full enough of known events. Similarly Gelon's Syracusan rule is busy enough, and the period of his rule at Gela is the natural time to put this war, even without the support of Justin. So Niese in *RE*, vii. 1008; *Hermes*, xlii. 453–4.

[2] Polyb. i. 82. 6, τῶν καλουμένων Ἐμπορίων; Livy xxix. 25. 12. Arist. *Pol.* 1259ᵃ 25 may have the same special sense; cf. Bosch-Gimpera, *CQ*, 1944, 56–7.

[3] Cf. Payne, *NC*, 188.   [4] xi. 53. 1.

[5] x. 28. 3; *exc. de virt. et vit.* p. 254 V, 558 W: ὅτι Θήρων ὁ Ἀκραγαντῖνος γένει καὶ πλούτῳ καὶ τῇ πρὸς τὸ πλῆθος φιλανθρωπίᾳ πολὺ προεῖχεν οὐ μόνον τῶν πολιτῶν, ἀλλὰ καὶ πάντων τῶν Σικελιωτῶν.

year too late, or his seizure of power too soon, or sixteen years is not quite accurate. As Diodoros has no Sicilian affairs under 473–472, and has under 472–471 Theron's death, Thrasydaios' rule at Akragas, his war with Hieron, and his expulsion, good measure for a single year, it is possible that Theron's death actually happened in the previous year, and that his rule lasted from 490–489 to 473–472.

In 490, when his brother Xenokrates won the chariot race at Delphi, he was not yet tyrant, but his shadow had begun to fall over Akragas.[1] It was a family victory; *Pyth.* vi. 15, πατρὶ τεῷ, Θρασύβουλε, κοινάν τε γενεᾷ . . . νίκαν; and in l. 5 the Emmenids are named before Akragas and Xenokrates. Theron is not named, but his splendour is a model for Thrasyboulos:

vv. 44–6   τῶν νῦν δὲ καὶ Θρασύβουλος
               πατρῴαν μάλιστα πρὸς στάθμαν ἔβα,
               πάτρῳ τ' ἐπερχόμενος ἀγλαΐαν ἅπασαν.

The glory of this victory may have had some part in winning favour for Theron's attempt at the tyranny. Polyainos has a story of the seizure of power,[2] but it is a doublet of Phalaris' rise, without any verisimilitude of detail. He says that Theron was responsible for the building of the temple of Athena, an unknown son Gorgos being the titular contractor, and diverted the money to pay his bodyguard. As Theron was one of the richest men of his time, this is unlikely.[3] The temple of Athena, whose columns exist under S. Maria dei Greci, belongs to the early fifth century and was one of the many temples built under Theron.[4]

Perhaps Theron's discovery and dispatch to Crete of the bones of Minos[5] was part of the attempt to win support from Old Greece for the war to avenge Doreius. The story of Minos in Sicily comes oddly into Herodotos' account of the determination of the Cretans to refrain from joining the Greeks against Xerxes.[6] It would be more in place in answer to an appeal from Sicily, and it may be that the response was suggested by such an appeal, and attached to the more important call to arms in 481. Crete was one mother country of both Akragas and Gela, and an appeal backed by the sentiment contained in the restoration of Minos' relics would be very natural. The date may be any time before 480. If it had been after 480, Diodoros

---

[1] Cf. Wade-Gery and Bowra, *Pindar's Pythian Odes*, 14 ff.   [2] vi. 51.
[3] Freeman, ii. 145–6, rejects the story.   [4] Marconi, *Agrigento*, 77 ff.
[5] Diod. iv. 79.   [6] Herod. vii. 170.

would have mentioned it in its proper place in the books which survive. Gelon's first Carthaginian War may have lasted some years, and the absence of other known activity during his rule at Gela suggests that it did. Theron probably took part as tyrant of Akragas at least in its later stages. At no time could Gelon have made war on the Carthaginians in Sicily without the consent, and probably also the support, of Akragas.

The friendly relations and good understanding between the two cities which existed in the time of Hippokrates were strengthened by Gelon and Theron. Gelon married Damareta daughter of Theron, and Theron married Polyzalos' daughter.[1] This system of dynastic marriages was probably built up soon after Theron became tyrant.

At Syracuse in the meantime the civil strife which Hippokrates had expected to aid him worked after his departure, and the Gamoroi, finally discredited no doubt by the defeat at the Heloros, were expelled by the demos and the Killyrioi. The Killyrioi were given some share in the government.[2] The first democracy in Sicily was set up by this unnatural coalition, but did not prosper. A disputed excerpt from Diodoros may describe the conditions: ὁ γὰρ τοῖς πολλοῖς κατὰ τῶν πολιτῶν φθόνος τὸν ἔμπροσθεν χρόνον ἐγκρυπτόμενος, ἐπειδὴ καιρὸν ἔλαβεν, ἄθρους ἐξερράγη. διὰ δὲ τὴν φιλοτιμίαν τοὺς δούλους ἠλευθέρωσαν, μᾶλλον βουλόμενοι τοῖς οἰκέταις μεταδοῦναι τῆς ἐλευθερίας ἢ τοῖς ἐλευθέροις τῆς πολιτείας.[3] The contrast of οἱ πολλοί and οἱ πολῖται is that between the citizen body and the oligarchy who alone possessed the πολιτεία, that of ὁ δῆμος and οἱ γαμόροι. If the passage should refer to Syracuse, it shows that the Gamoroi, despairing of keeping their position after their defeat by Hippokrates, freed the serfs, who deserted them and threw in their lot with the demos. The date of x. 26 is between 494–493 (x. 25, Artaphrenes' settlement of Ionia) and 490 (x. 27, Marathon), and the passage would well suit the conditions after Heloros.

Some support for the date c. 491 for the fall of the Gamoroi may be derived from Dion. Hal. vi. 62. Appius Claudius,

---

[1] Schol. Pind. *Ol.* ii inscr. ἐκήδευσε (ὁ Θήρων) δὲ Γέλωνι τῷ τυράννῳ, δοὺς αὐτῷ τὴν θυγατέρα Δημαρέτην . . . καὶ αὐτὸς δὲ ὁ Θήρων τὴν Πολυζήλου τοῦ ἀδελφοῦ Ἱέρωνος (θυγατέρα) ἔγημε, καθά φησι Τίμαιος. Cf. Schol. *Ol.* ii. 29.

[2] Photius s. Κιλλικύριοι: ἐν Συρακούσαις τινὲς ἐκλήθησαν, οἱ ἀντὶ τῶν γεωμόρων μέρος καταλαβόντες τοῦ πολιτεύματος. Cf. Gilbert, *Griechische Staatsalterthümer,* ii. 249. For the Killyrioi see above, p. 111.

[3] x. 26. The suggestion that this passage refers to Syracuse was made by Mr. A. Andrewes.

opposing the concessions to the plebs proposed by Menenius Agrippa, quoted the recent fate of the Gamoroi as a warning. The parallel cannot be pressed, but it is possible that Dionysios or his source found the expulsion of the Gamoroi dated to 492–491, and so threw in the reference.

The democracy did not take over all the territory of Syracuse, for the Gamoroi maintained themselves at Kasmenai. Possibly to their brief rule there belongs an inscription on a bronze tablet, found near Akrai and now in New York.[1] The exact place of finding is unknown, but the most likely place near Akrai for a piece of bronze to turn up in the twenties of this century is Monte Casale.[2] The date of the inscription is the early fifth century and it names the Gamoroi; the context is uncertain, and there may always have been in the small towns of Syracusan territory bodies called Gamoroi, perhaps with judicial functions.[3] But it is at least as likely, bearing in mind the coincidence of date, that the Gamoroi named are the governing body of the Syracusan state.

The new democracy lost no time in getting into difficulties, and was drifting into anarchy[4] when the Gamoroi appealed to Gelon. The democracy was in no condition to resist, and surrendered itself and the city to Gelon. The Gamoroi came back, but presumably their serfs remained free and kept some of the privileges of citizenship.

Gelon transferred from Gela to Syracuse. This was in 485, for Gelon had a seven years' rule at Syracuse.[5] Syracuse was the greatest city of Sicily and had possibilities which Gela had not. It was more nearly central in his empire than Gela. It was on the east coast, which looked to Italy and Greece, instead of the south coast of treacherous currents and the African Sea. Gela could not be more than a prosperous agricultural state; Syracuse was the commercial centre of Sicily. What probably weighed more with Gelon than any other factor was its port. He had already something of a fleet, but it was impossible to base a great fleet on Gela, and Syracuse was one of the best

---

[1] *Bull. Metr. Mus.* 1925, 269. I thank Mrs. V. Wade-Gery for information about this inscription.

[2] Cf. p. 102, where I suggest, partly on the basis of this argument, that the town at Monte Casale was Kasmenai.

[3] Such as the Gamoroi exercised at Syracuse in condemning Agathokles (see above, p. 58).

[4] Arist. *Pol.* 1302[b] 25: διὰ καταφρόνησιν δὲ καὶ στασιάζουσι καὶ ἐπιτίθενται . . . ἐν ταῖς δημοκρατίαις οἱ εὔποροι καταφρονήσαντες τῆς ἀταξίας καὶ ἀναρχίας, οἷον . . . ἐν Συρακούσαις πρὸ τῆς Γέλωνος τυραννίδος.

[5] Arist. *Pol.* 1315[b] 36; Diod. xi. 38. Eusebius, ed. Fotheringham, p. 190, gives 487.

ports in the Mediterranean. He knew that he would have to fight with Carthage and Anaxilas, probably by sea as well as land. Perhaps he had been hindered in his first Carthaginian war by deficiencies in his fleet, which would be very useful in directly attacking the Carthaginian possessions and in cutting off supplies. At Syracuse he built up a naval power the equal of any Greek state.

He carried out a synoecism at Syracuse, the parallel to which is not as much the synoecism of Attica and other single Greek states as the grant of Roman citizenship among the peoples of Italy. More than half of the dwellers (ἀστῶν, not πολιτῶν) of Gela were brought to Syracuse and made citizens. The re-founded Kamarina was destroyed, and the inhabitants brought to Syracuse. The occasion was the revolt of Kamarina against Glaukos of Karystos, the boxer, who had been set up as governor by Gelon. Glaukos, the farmer's boy who straightened a ploughshare with his fist for a hammer,[1] was a rough-and-ready governor for a new city. His death is said to have been due to Gelon's machinations.[2] Considering his treatment of the Megarians, it is possible that Gelon rid himself of Glaukos, and put the Kamarinaians at his mercy, by using *agents provocateurs* to set them in revolt.

One of the Kamarinaians transferred to Syracuse was perhaps Praxiteles son of Krinis, a native of Mantineia. He was a man of substance, who made an important dedication at Olympia on which he describes himself as Συρακόσιος . . . καὶ Καμαριναῖος.[3] The double nationality and Arcadian origin may be most easily explained if he was, like other Arcadians, a mercenary leader in the service of the tyrants. He may have been established in Kamarina by Hippokrates, or have been one of the subordinates of Glaukos, in either case transferred to Syracuse by Gelon.

The enlargement of Syracuse by the forced migration of Geloans and Kamarinaians, and the wealthy men of Megara and Euboia, took place probably in the year or two years after Gelon's transference to Syracuse, at the same time as Theron's seizure of Himera. The years 483–482 to 480 are then left for the preparations against the Carthaginians. Megara at least

[1] Paus. vi. 10. 1; Philostratos 20.

[2] Schol. Aeschin. *in Ctes.* 190: κατασταθεὶς ὑπὸ Γέλωνος ἐν Καμαρίνῃ καταψηφισαμένων τῶν Καμαριναίων θάνατον ἀνῃρέθη. Bekker, *Anecd. Gr.* i. 232: ἀπέθανε δὲ ἐξ ἐπιβουλῆς Γέλωνος τοῦ Συρακουσίου τυράννου.

[3] *Olympia*, v, pp. 389 ff.; Hicks, *Greek Historical Inscriptions*, no. 15; Pace, *Camarina*, 41.

cost Gelon a campaign and a siege.[1] The Megarian oligarchs were responsible for the war; in spite of the disparity of forces, it was they who provoked Gelon. Gelon won the support of the Megarian populace by inviting them to settle in Syracuse and giving them money through their leader, so that they disobeyed their magistrates. But in the sequel the oligarchs were unexpectedly rewarded with Syracusan citizenship; the demos, which had no part in the war, was sold into slavery, on condition that they should be taken out of Sicily.[2] Gelon had no use for a host of poor citizens, the population of Syracuse being already swollen with the Kamarinaians and Geloans. What he needed was the land of Megara, to round off his empire. The land became Syracusan, with its possessors, and Megara is never again heard of as a city. In 415 the site was deserted.[3]

An inscription at Olympia[4] tells of Megarian exiles received at Selinus, more probably from Megara Hyblaia than from Megara Nisaia. The date is early in the fifth century, probably little before the fall of Megara. The conditions of the reception of the exiles, and arrangements about their possessions, were registered at Olympia, but are too ill preserved to give much information about the circumstances of the exiles or the constitution of Selinus. It is not even certain that the exiles were not from Megara Nisaia, but more probably they were from Megara Hyblaia. In that case the reference is to stasis slightly preceding the fall of the city and giving Gelon his opportunity. It appears from Herodotos that the πάχεις and the δῆμος were not at unity. Perhaps a party within the oligarchy was driven out before the remainder of it declared war on Gelon. It is not possible that the inscription should refer to exiles who had escaped being sold after Gelon took the city, for it is implied that the exodus from Megara is continuing ([τ]οὶ δὲ πρόσθε ἔφευγον τῶν γραμάτων . . .) and that Megara still exists and return is possible. But it is likely that some Megarians escaped at the fall of the town, and they would naturally go to Selinus both

---

[1] Herod. vii. 156; Thuk. vi. 4; vi. 94; Polyainos i. 27. 3. I have used Polyainos' story to supplement Herodotos and Thukydides; it is surprising that he should preserve such a piece of secret history, but he often has a good Sicilian source, and his naming of the Megarian leader Diognetos (presumably a general) is circumstantial.

[2] Freeman, i. 389, wrongly supposes the demos of Megara was not Greek; there is no reason apart from this episode to suppose that they were not pure bred.

[3] Thuk. vi. 49. 4: Μέγαρα . . . ἃ ἦν ἐρῆμα.

[4] Olympia, v, no. 22.

because it was their colony and because it was the city of Sicily farthest from Gelon's reach.

Though some of the poems in the book of Theognis are probably western,[1] I do not think that it is possible to draw any conclusions about the politics of Megara Hyblaia. The most urgent poems are certainly related to Old Greece, and either fall in ll. 1–254, which are agreed to be by Theognis of Old Megara, or in single poems such as ll. 667–82, 757–8, 945–8, which, on internal evidence, were composed east of the Ionian Sea. The central portion of the book, ll. 255–656, which has the best claim to be western, contains more gnomic and less intensely personal poetry. It may have been put together from a number of sources, not necessarily western. The πόλις of ll. 541–2, for instance, may be Megara Hyblaia, or Syracuse, or perhaps not a city of Sicily. There is no real information about it in the lines.

The ἐλέγεια εἰς τοὺς σωθέντας τῶν Συρακουσίων ἐν τῇ πολιορκίᾳ, recorded by Suidas as a work of Theognis, may have been a poem on the Megarians who received Syracusan citizenship.[2] The common view that it commemorated Hippokrates' withdrawal from before Syracuse[3] disregards Herodotos' differentiation of the attack on Syracuse from the πολιορκία of Naxos, &c.,[4] and the inappositeness of the partitive when all the Syracusans were saved except those who fell at the Heloros. No other appropriate siege of Syracuse is known and, if it is safe to believe that Suidas preserves anything like the title of the poem, it may well have been on those Megarians who became Syracusans after the siege of Megara.

Euboia was treated in the same way as Megara, and disappears completely from history. What became of Leontinoi, Katane, and Naxos is not clear, as they are not mentioned under Gelon. It remained for Hieron to uproot their populations, so probably they kept under Gelon the position they had under Hippokrates.

It was clear in the late 'eighties that the time for a decisive conflict with the Phoenicians and Etruscans was approaching. Gelon and Theron in alliance had built up a strong league which included most of Greek Sicily. But their power had the

---

[1] Wade-Gery, in *Greek Poetry and Life*, 75–7.

[2] Suidas s.v. Θέογνις. See Harrison, *Studies in Theognis*, 295–7; he reads ὑπὸ τῶν Συρακουσίων.

[3] Pareti, 92 ff.

[4] See above, p. 401.

result of hardening the opposition and driving all powers independent of them into the arms of Carthage. Anaxilas, holding the third great power of Sicily, was from the time of his seizure of the tyranny of Rhegion in direct conflict with the tyrants of Gela. He succeeded in winning Zankle from the Geloan alliance, but he had not the resources which Gelon controlled. When Gelon won Syracuse and built up his fleet of 200 ships, Anaxilas could not but feel threatened. Either then or earlier, as a counter to the alliance of Gelon and Theron, he married Kydippe daughter of Terillos of Himera.[1] Terillos was a Carthaginian ally, having ξεινίη with Hamilcar. Anaxilas was drawn into the alliance of Carthage, the only power which could support him against Gelon.

Selinus moved from Carthaginian friendship to Carthaginian alliance, as the only means of holding off Akragas. Meanwhile Gelon brought into his alliance the south-eastern cities, Syracuse and Megara, which had been indifferent. In the treatment of the Megarians, men of her mother city, Selinus had another cause for hating the tyrants of the patriotic alliance. It is likely that some exiles were received at Selinus, and helped to stiffen her policy. Indeed, there were many Sicilians who must have regarded a war to liberate barbarian Sicily as a mockery while they themselves were enslaved to the tyrant of another city. But Gelon and Theron were able to present the war as a holy war, and steadily made their preparations. Since his removal to Syracuse, Gelon was building up his fleet until it became one of the two greatest Greek fleets. The figure of 200 triremes in Herod. vii. 158 is a paper strength, but it may be taken that his fleet was about the equal of the new Athenian fleet, and far superior to any other Greek fleet. There may be this added point to the unwillingness of the Athenian envoy at Syracuse to allow Gelon the command of the fleet. The other figures, 20,000 hoplites, 2,000 horse, 2,000 bowmen, and 2,000 slingers, may represent without undue exaggeration the whole force which Gelon could command. The high proportion of horse, which had been Hippokrates' strength and was an arm capable of more development on the wide plains of Sicily than in Greece, is important. It is uncertain how many of the men were mercenaries, but about 10,000 were admitted by Gelon to citizenship.[2] The mercenary and the citizen forces may have been about equal, and the light-armed doubtless included Sikel sub-

[1] Herod. vii. 165.   [2] Diod. xi. 72.

jects. Diodoros' figure of 50,000 foot and 5,000 horse under Gelon's own command at Himera is hardly reliable.[1]

Gelon's preparations for war included a large issue of coinage. In the seven years of his reign the mint of Syracuse used over 200 pairs of dies.[2] For his first issue in 485 he borrowed dies and personnel to inaugurate his coinage at Syracuse,[3] and new issues follow every few months. There is no evidence of the source of his silver. His wife Damarata is said to have given her ornaments to be made into coin.[4] One of Plutarch's anecdotes about Gelon says that he raised a war loan from the citizens of Syracuse.[5] This is in Plutarch one of the many stories of Gelon's just dealings with the people, like that of the assembly in which he laid down his ἀρχή.[6] It may be accepted that Gelon had to find money from every possible source to pay his troops. His copious coinage shows that his finance was successful.

The occasion of the war came when Theron expelled Terillos from Himera and attached it to his own empire.[7] Terillos appealed to the Carthaginians and especially his friend Hamilcar the suffete to restore him, and was warmly supported by his son-in-law Anaxilas, who gave his own children to Hamilcar as hostages. The Carthaginians are said to have spent three

---

[1] xi. 21.

[2] Boehringer, *Die Münzen von Syrakus*, 75.

[3] Ibid. 79 f.

[4] Hesykh. s.v. Δημαρέτιον. νόμισμα ἐν Σικελίᾳ ὑπὸ Γέλωνος κοπέν, ἐπιδούσης αὐτῷ Δημαρέτης εἰς αὐτὸν τὸν κόσμον. The Damareteion was struck from the Carthaginian indemnity after Himera (see below, p. 426), and the occasion on which Damareta sacrificed her jewellery must have been before the war.

[5] Plut. *Apophth. Gel.* 3: αἰτῶν δὲ χρήματα τοὺς πολίτας, ἐπεὶ ἐθορύβησαν, αἰτεῖν εἶπεν, ὡς ἀποδώσων, καὶ ἀπέδωκε μετὰ τὸν πόλεμον.

[6] See below, p. 427.

[7] Marconi makes the suggestion (*N Sc*, 1930, 555 ff.) that the fort of Castronovo, which commands the pass on the road from Akragas to Himera, was built when Himera first came under the sway of Akragas. It was certainly built for the purpose of guarding the pass, but probably at a later date than the early fifth century. The walls, of two periods, one marking an extension and one an elaboration of the defence of the gate, are the chief remains. The pottery, almost entirely black-glaze fragments, is not sufficient to give a date. Mr. D. F. Allen, who has made a special study of the Greek walls of Sicily and Italy, is of the opinion that Castronovo is of the fourth or third century. On the route from Akragas to Panormos and Himera see Pace, *ACSA*, i. 438. It is suggested by Mingazzini (*MA*, xxxvi. 665) that exiles from Himera, descendants of the founder, were received by the Akragantines and settled at the small Greek town of Ravanusa (see above, p. 138). This is acutely argued from an archaic inscription found at Ravanusa (loc. cit., fig. 23) recording Mylos son of Sakon and Sakon son of Mylos. The name Sakon is otherwise known as that of a founder of Himera (Thuk. vi. 5. 1), and this may be a descendant; the name Mylos recalls the Myletidai, who joined in the colonization of Himera. If Mingazzini is right, these will be oligarchic exiles driven out of Himera by Terillos.

years in preparations.[1] This would put Terillos' expulsion in 483 or possibly the year before. Gelon finished his round-up in eastern Sicily in 483 or 482, and could devote the next years to military and naval preparations.

In 481 the Greeks in council sent an appeal to Gelon to assist the alliance against the Persians. The details of the negotiations are obviously unhistorical, set speeches in which the Spartan and Athenian envoys rudely reject Gelon's mildly preferred claims to command at least a part of the combined forces.[2] There is a strong vein of comedy running through the speeches of Syagros and the unnamed Athenian, and Freeman may be right in thinking that Herodotos' source was a comedy in the style of Epikharmos ridiculing the pretensions of the mother country.[3] But some points are worthy of close attention. A summary of the forces of Gelon is included. The offer to feed the Greek army is important. Whether it was made or not, it was what the Greeks most needed and what they were most likely to get from Gelon. When the Carthaginians were already preparing to invade Sicily, it was impossible that the Greeks should expect military support from Gelon, or that he should think for one moment of giving it. It was uncritical patriotism which asserted that Gelon was preparing to send aid to the Greeks when he was surprised by the Carthaginian invasion. Herodotos gives it as what λέγεται . . . ὑπὸ τῶν ἐν Σικελίῃ οἰκημένων; in Diodoros it has become matter of history.

Diodoros' account of the embassy, in the summary we have of it, differs in no point from Herodotos.[4] Polybios turns it completely round, making Gelon send an embassy to the Greek assembly at Corinth.[5] It is unlikely that Polybios or his source had authority for this, for the details of Gelon's offer are as in Herodotos. He probably followed Ephoros, who toned down the Sicilian bias in Herodotos. He makes the Greeks return a πραγματικώτατον ἀπόκριμα, in his patriotic opinion, to Gelon's offer, which contrasts with the rudeness of· the answer in Herodotos, and reduces the psychological improbability by saying that Gelon's offer was a spontaneous one, not· made in answer to a request from the Greeks.[6] But he adds nothing to our knowledge of the facts. Polybios takes this occasion to protest against Timaios' bias in favour of Sicily and Syracuse.

---

[1] Diod. xi. 1. 5.
[2] Herod. vii. 157–64; Diod. x. 33–4, xi. 1; 26. 4.
[3] ii. 178, 418, 515.
[4] x. 33.
[5] Polyb. xii. 26b.
[6] See Pareti, 127 ff.

But this bias is present already in Herodotos, though he provides the means of distinguishing what the Sicilians said from the truth.[1] It is implied already in Pindar's phrase Ἑλλάδ' ἐξέλκων βαρείας δουλίας.[2] It has coloured all the evidence on which we have to form our opinion of Gelon.

What Gelon did was to send Kadmos, that just man, to Delphi with a large sum of money, καραδοκήσοντα τὴν μάχην τῇ πεσέεται. By this Herodotos means the war with the Persians. If they were successful, Kadmos was to make submission on behalf of Gelon. It has been suggested that Gelon's intention was to have something to fall back on if he was defeated in Sicily. It is quite impossible to determine what motive or combination of motives he had, but in support of Herodotos is the medism of Delphi, which would make it a good go-between if Gelon found it necessary to make a nominal submission.

Herodotos regards the Carthaginian invasion as coming out of the blue. It was mere accident that it coincided with the Persian invasion, and that Himera was fought on the same day as Salamis. Aristotle used the synchronization as an example of unmeaning coincidence.[3] Other historians were not certain whether Himera was fought on the same day as Thermopylai or Salamis,[4] but agreed that the two battles happened at exactly the same time. Holm's suggestion that Himera was fought in the year before the Persian invasion is therefore not happy.

Herodotos did not see the victory of Himera as more than an incident which prevented Gelon from sending men to help the Greeks. But from details in his narrative, notably the synchronization and the importance attached to the embassy, it appears that the Sicilians already saw it in its proper light as a conclusive victory over the barbarians. Pindar couples it with Salamis and Plataiai.[5] But it was left for later historians, not Sicilian only, to make capital of this double front against barbarism. There are many versions, all derived from Ephoros, which emphatically deny that the synchronization was coincidence, and assert that there was a Persian–Carthaginian understanding.[6] The simplest form is that Xerxes sent an

---

[1] Cf. Grundy, *The Great Persian War*, 575, distinguishing the Greek from the Sicilian sources of Herodotos for the account of the embassy and of Himera.

[2] *Pyth.* i. 75. [3] Herod. vii. 166; Arist. *Poet.* 1459ᵃ 25.

[4] Thermopylai: Diod. xi. 24. 1. [5] *Pyth.* i. 75–80.

[6] Justin xix. 1. 10; Diod. xi. 1. 4 and cf. xi. 20. 1; Schol. *Pyth.* i. 146a (in two versions). Justin carries the embassy back to the reign of Darius, and confuses with it the interference

embassy to the Carthaginians, and it was agreed that they should invade Sicily in great force at the same time as he invaded Greece. This is not in itself impossible, for though Persia had not, even since the conquest of Kyrene, come into direct relations with Carthage, her Phoenician subjects could have carried her messages. On the other hand, though Herodotos' silence is not in itself conclusive, Aristotle denies any causal connexion.[1] The story of a formal embassy may be rejected and, indeed, the Ephorean reconstruction is too neat not to be artificial: embassy from the Greeks to Gelon, embassy from the Persians to Carthage; Gelon ready to help the Greeks, Persians and Carthaginians ready to help one another after they had defeated their own enemies; a splendid opening for panhellenic rhetoric. But the Persians were interested in the western Greeks, as Demokedes' voyages with Persian officers to collect information for the king shows.[2] The Greek embassy to Gelon tried to persuade him that he was threatened as well as they, and that the Persians would come to Sicily if they were successful in Greece.[3] This may have been a reasonable expectation; if Gelon's motive in sending Kadmos to Delphi was indeed to buy off the Persians, he may have believed it. So the known fact of the Carthaginian preparations for an invasion of Sicily, following a warfare which had gone on since Dorieus, fitted well with Xerxes' plans. The 'understanding' between Persians and Carthaginians can be no more than this, that the two powers which had long been preparing to invade Greek lands chose to do it in the same season. This prevented either western or mainland Greeks from helping the other, if they had been so minded, and may have been no accident.

The Carthaginian invasion[4] was led by Hamilcar, son of Mago, who had commanded in Sardinia,[5] by a Syracusan

with Carthaginian religion which other secondary authorities assign to Gelon as part of the terms after Himera (Plutarch, *Apophth. Gel.* 1; Schol. Pind. *Pyth.* ii. 2). The scholiast to Pindar quotes Ephoros, saying that Pindar read of the embassy in his Ephoros: εἰκὸς δὲ ταῖς Ἐφόρου ἱστορίαις ἐντυχόντα τὸν Πίνδαρον, ἐξηκολουθηκέναι αὐτὸν αὐτῷ. ἱστορεῖ γὰρ Ἔφορος κτλ.

[1] Pareti (127 ff.) believes that Aristotle intended directly to contradict Ephoros.
[2] Herod. iii. 136.   [3] Herod. vii. 157.
[4] The main ancient account of the campaign and battle of Himera is in Diodoros xi. 20 ff. Herodotos is concerned only with the fate of Hamilcar (vii. 166–7). The foundation of the topography has been laid by L. Mauceri (*MA*, xviii. 385 ff.), who may be followed for the campaign of 480, though for the siege of 409 he allows too great an extension of the city since 480. Pareti gives an admirable account (pp. 113 ff.) which I follow.
[5] Justin xix. 1. Cf. above, p. 333. Herod. vii. 165 gives his father's name as Hanno, but the text may be corrupt; cf. Macan, ad loc.

mother.[1] Its strength is given by Herodotos as 300,000, including Libyans, Iberians, Sardinians, and Corsicans; modern opinion allows a tenth of that figure.[2] Diodoros adds 200 ships of war[3] as well as 3,000 transports. This is a figure equal to the paper strength of Gelon's fleet. Theron probably had few ships, nor were any of the other combatants, except Anaxilas, naval powers. Hamilcar lost the transports with his cavalry and chariots in a storm (as Pareti points out, these were added to his forces by Timaios, and had to be got rid of somehow; in fact, he relied on his Greek allies for cavalry, as will be seen below) but with his main force sailed safely into Panormos harbour.

From Panormos he marched on Himera, under Terillos' guidance, and established a camp to the west of the town, with his ships drawn up on the beach. The town stood on a low hill about a mile from the sea, on the west bank of the river Himeras (Fiume Grande). Its port was at the mouth of the river, where there was perhaps a suburb. To the west and south are other low hills stretching to the Fiume Torto, across which the imposing mass of Monte San Calogero rises to 4,000 feet.[4] On one of these hills Hamilcar had his army encamped. He made a demonstration against Himera, and Theron, who was in command there, sent off at once to Gelon for support. Gelon led up from Syracuse an army of 50,000 foot and 5,000 horse—the figures, though smaller than those given for the Carthaginians, are still unreliable. He encamped outside the city to the south, and his cavalry won an immediate success over the Carthaginian foragers. Letters from Hamilcar to his Selinuntine allies appointing a rendezvous for their cavalry fell into Gelon's hands. Gelon sent out his cavalry to ride to Hamilcar's naval camp, as had been arranged for the Selinuntines. They did so, were received by the Carthaginian outposts, and surprised Hamilcar as he was sacrificing. He was killed or, according to a Carthaginian story recorded by Herodotos,[5]

---

[1] Herod. vii. 166. 1.   [2] Herod. vii. 165; Diod. xi. 20. 2; Pareti, 147.

[3] xi. 1. 5; πλείους τῶν διακοσίων, xi. 20. 2. The manuscript reading in the latter passage is δισχιλίων, retained by Pareti (p. 140) as representing Timaios' inflated figure.

[4] See map in Pareti, map 1.

[5] This story states that Hamilcar threw himself into the flames when after a long day's action he saw his troops give way. It is thus in complete contradiction with Diodoros' account, according to which Hamilcar's death preceded the main action. But it should be noted that Herodotos, while relating the Carthaginian story, does not vouch for its truth; secondly, that he does not place Hamilcar's death in the land as opposed to the naval camp (as Pareti, 152; Macan, ad loc.), as he speaks of only one camp.

threw himself into the flames as a sacrifice. The ships were set on fire. As this success was signalled to him, Gelon attacked the main Carthaginian camp, and Theron and the Himeraians sallied out of the town.[1] The victory was complete, the Carthaginian fleet was burnt, and there was no way of escape for the survivors. Twenty ships are said to have escaped burning and picked up stragglers, but were wrecked on the way home, so that a boatload of men only came safe to Carthage to tell of the defeat. Some men fled to a strong hill in the neighbourhood, but were compelled to surrender owing to lack of water. Large numbers of prisoners were taken, others were picked up wandering about the country-side, especially in the territory of Akragas.

Nothing is heard of any naval action by Gelon, though two minor sources speak in general terms of a Greek naval victory.[2] The Carthaginian fleet was drawn up on the beach at Himera and waited quietly to be burnt. When he sailed into Panormos harbour Hamilcar said that the war was as good as over.[3] His fear may have been not only of the storm which miraculously destroyed his cavalry and chariots without harming the infantry, but also of the Greek fleet. An attack while he was in heavy order and encumbered with transports might have cut him off before he landed in Sicily. Probably the chief of Selinus' services to him was that the allies could not use the ports of Selinus and Mazara to wait for the Carthaginian fleet. This may have been another reason, in addition to Terillos' guidance, why the Carthaginians came to the north side of the island, instead of to Selinus. If Hamilcar had landed at Selinus and advanced against Akragas he would have had a stronger city to attack, and would also have been exposed to annoyance from the sea.

Gelon marched his forces overland to Himera, and nothing is heard of his fleet during the campaign. Nor is anything heard of Anaxilas, for all his zeal in Terillos' cause. It is tempting to think that Anaxilas' and Gelon's fleet neutralized one another. Anaxilas could hold the Straits with many fewer than 200 ships.

I suggest tentatively that Khromios was Gelon's admiral. He had won his spurs under Hippokrates at the Heloros, and had married a sister of Gelon. He was a man of war, and spent

---

[1] No mention of Theron's action is made by Diodoros. It is inferred by Pareti (156 ff.) on the basis of general probability and of Polyaen. i. 28.

[2] Schol. Pind. *Pyth*. i. 146*a*; Paus. vi. 19. 7.   [3] Diod. xi. 20. 2.

his life παρὰ πεζοβόαις ἵπποις τε ναῶν τ' ἐν μάχαις.[1] But there is no mention of his service at Himera. After the naming of the Heloros, Pindar continues,

τὰ δ' ἄλλαις ἀμέραις
πολλὰ μὲν ἐν κονίᾳ χέρσῳ, τὰ δὲ γείτονι πόντῳ φάσομαι.[2]

No naval action of Gelon or Hieron is known except Kyme, but there must have been others, and it is most improbable that there was not some action in 480. If it was not against the Carthaginians but against Anaxilas, that would explain why the historians do not mention it, and why Anaxilas' part in the Himera campaign is not mentioned.

Hagesias the Iamid also took part in some naval action:

ἀκίνδυνοι δ' ἀρεταὶ
οὔτε παρ' ἀνδράσιν οὔτ' ἐν ναυσὶ κοίλαις τίμαι.[3]

Compare also the nautical metaphors at the end of the ode.[4] He was above all a soldier, ἀμφότερον μάντιν τ' ἀγαθὸν καὶ δουρὶ μάρνασθαι, so the reference is more likely to be naval than commercial. Either in 480 or at some other date he served at sea.

The single battle of Himera was decisive. The Carthaginians, in fear that Gelon would make a descent on Africa, sent ambassadors to ask for peace. This was granted on very moderate terms—the payment of an indemnity of 2,000 talents and construction of two temples in which the terms of the treaty were to be recorded.[5] It is added that Gelon with his customary humanity obliged the Carthaginians to give up human sacrifice.[6] To the payment of 2,000 talents the Carthaginians added a crown of gold of the value of a hundred talents, a present to Gelon's wife Damareta, who had aided with her counsel the petition of the ambassadors for peace. From this money was struck the famous Damareteion, the commemorative decadrachm or, as the Sicilians called it, fifty-litre piece,[7] one of the most splendid of Greek coins. With it is associated the copious and beautiful issues of the mints of Syracuse and Leontinoi after 480.[8]

After the battle, Diodoros says, Gelon came unarmed into the armed assembly of the Syracusan people to give an account

---

[1] Pind. *Nem.* ix. 34. [2] ll. 42–3.
[3] *Ol.* vi. 9–10. [4] ll. 100 ff.
[5] Diod. xi. 26. 2. [6] Schol. Pind. *Pyth.* ii. 2; Plut. *Apophth. Gel.* 1.
[7] See above, p. 190. [8] Boehringer, *Die Münzen von Syrakus*, 36 ff.

of his actions, and was hailed as εὐεργέτης, σωτήρ, and βασιλεύς.[1]
The association of the two first terms shows that, even if
Diodoros' language is exact, βασιλεύς is to be regarded only as
an honorific appellation, not as a constitutional title. But it is
most improbable that Diodoros preserves anything like the
terms of a resolution; the most that can be said is that he may
truly represent the state of feeling in Syracuse at the time.
Aelian gives the same story, in two halves; the central part of
it is that Gelon offered to lay down his ἀρχή, and that a statue
of him unarmed was set up in the temple of Hera.[2] The statue
may be historical, and may have in a later generation helped
to give the story form. Polyainos is yet more definite. Gelon
was elected στρατηγὸς αὐτοκράτωρ for the war against the Carthaginians; after Himera he gave an account of his office in the
assembly, invited the δῆμος to elect another such general, was
re-elected, and so from στρατηγός became tyrant.[3] Finally,
Diodoros says that the precedent for Dionysios' position of
στρατηγὸς αὐτοκράτωρ was Gelon's command at Himera, under
that title.[4] On these passages has been founded a view of Gelon
as a constitutional monarch, with the title of στρατηγὸς αὐτοκράτωρ before Himera, of βασιλεύς after, conferred by Syracusan
assemblies.

There is no good evidence that either Gelon or Hieron had
any constitutional position at Syracuse. In his dedication from
the spoils of Himera, where he might be expected to use a title
of honour if he had one, Gelon calls himself simply Γέλων ὁ
Δεινομέν[εος] . . . Συραφόσιος.[5] Hieron also makes a dedication
in his own name and the Syracusans' in the terms Ἱάρων ὁ
Δεινομένεος καὶ τοὶ Συρακόσιοι.[6] Polyzalos is the only one of
the Deinomenids to call himself officially βασιλεύς and he was
obliged to retract.[7]

Herodotos' usage of terms, as noticed above,[8] is not always
exact; but he never calls Gelon anything but tyrant, though
he puts the address ὦ βασιλεῦ Συρακοσίων into the mouth of the
Athenian spokesman.[9] Diodoros seldom gives Gelon or Hieron
a title, but in xi. 38. 7 he uses ἐβασίλευσεν, ἐβασίλευσε of both
Gelon and Hieron; the verb may, however, be used generally,
and need not imply a specific title of βασιλεύς.

---

[1] xi. 26.   [2] VH vi. 11; xiii. 37.
[3] i. 27. 1.   [4] xiii. 94.
[5] Tod, GHI, no. 17.   [6] Tod, no. 22.
[7] Wade-Gery, JHS, 1933, 101 ff.   [8] See p. 385.
[9] Herod. vii. 161. 1; cf. 156. 3; 163. 1; Thuk. vi. 4; vi. 94.

It is clear that none of the tyrants of Syracuse was officially or semi-officially called βασιλεύς or στρατηγὸς αὐτοκράτωρ. The title of στρατηγὸς αὐτοκράτωρ, and its implications, must have been assumed by Dionysios and applied in his time to Gelon. The position of first man in a democratic state, and the title of στρατηγός by which he went, were both evolved at Athens in the course of the fifth century; στρατηγὸς αὐτοκράτωρ could have no meaning in Gelon's time and circumstances.[1] The position which he held in the Himera campaign could be untechnically so described, but it is unlikely that it was specially conferred and certain that it had no political implications. Gelon's army was his own, not that of the Syracusan people; he ruled Syracuse by right of conquest. Both the Gamoroi and the demos had submitted themselves to him, the latter in war. He may have had some position as an informal διαλλάκτης or αἰσυμνήτης, but this was not the origin of his power, nor did he need it as justification.

The later historians regarded Gelon's rule as a Golden Age. His πραότης and his clemency to defeated enemies and to all his neighbours are the qualities which Diodoros praises.[2] He grew old in his kingship and was held in high honour. It was a time of peace and plenty; like a later tyrant, he led out his people to 'the battle of the grain'.[3] The memory of his good rule preserved the power of his house to Hieron and Thrasyboulos, and his fame was kept alive by contrast with later tyrants of Syracuse, first Hieron and Thrasyboulos, then Dionysios; the point is well made by Plutarch, καὶ μὴν σὺ τυραννεῖς διὰ Γέλωνα πιστευθείς, διὰ σὲ δὲ οὐδεὶς ἕτερος πιστευθήσεται.[4] There were wonderful scenes at his death. Though he had directed that his funeral should keep within the Syracusan law which forbade costly funerals, the Syracusan crowd followed his corpse to his wife's property at the Nine Towers, and built a magnificent tomb. It was destroyed by the Carthaginians in the course of the war with Agathokles, but nothing could destroy his immortal fame.

This reputation rests almost entirely, so far as we know, on his victory at Himera. He had the good fortune to die within two years of it, before more recent events clouded the memory. If he had been judged on his treatment of Megara and Euboia,

---

[1] See Scheele, *Strategos Autokrator.*
[2] xi. 23, 38, 67; xiii. 36; cf. Aelian, *VH* xiii. 37.
[3] Plut. *Apophth. Gel.* 2. [4] *Dion.* 5.

his fame would have been less bright. But he seems to have been genuinely popular, and apart from hardships inflicted in war or policy, after the example of Hippokrates, he may have had a gentler side to his nature. His character is not so well known as Hieron's, because no poet celebrated his victories and won his friendship. But he had a shrewd wit, and as well as silly stories about his childhood and his dog[1] there are anecdotes with a more genuine ring. Some of his sayings in Herodotos may come from his own mouth, δῆμον εἶναι συνοίκημα ἀχαριτώτατον, and perhaps οὕτω δὴ Γέλωνος μνῆστις. He was said to be ἀμουσότατος,[2] to point the contrast with Hieron. Plutarch tells the story of the dinner-party at which all the other guests played the lyre as it was brought round, but he called for his horse and leapt on it in the dining-room.[3] That is to say, he was a soldier, and his accomplishments a soldier's. He began his career in Hippokrates' service, and after twenty years' assiduous campaigning was probably the foremost general of his day; but we have hardly the slightest details of his battles. Certainly he had a military power second to no Greek state.

The victory of Himera was splendidly commemorated both in Sicily and outside it. Apart from the two temples which the Carthaginians were bound by the peace treaty to build (whether these were to be in Sicily or Carthage),[4] Gelon built from the spoils temples of Demeter and Kore in Neapolis, the quarter of Syracuse built to house his new settlers.[5] Another temple was built at Himera, in the port-suburb. Its foundations have been excavated and have yielded a fine series of marble lion's-head spouts, now in Palermo Museum.[6] It was begun soon after 480 and finished in the decade 470–460.[7] It is not known to whom the temple was dedicated—perhaps to Zeus Eleutherios, whom Pindar names in the opening line of an ode for Ergoteles of Himera.[8] Most of the great temples of Akragas which line the steep seaward scarp of the south side of the city, including

---

[1] Diod. x. 29 = Tzetzes iv. 266; Aelian, *VH* i. 13; *HA* vi. 62; Philistos fr. 44 Müller, ap. Pliny, *NH* viii. 40. 144.

[2] Aelian, *VH* iv. 15.   [3] *Apophthegmata Gelonis*, 4.

[4] Freeman, ii. 210, thinks in Carthage; Holm, Busolt (*Gr. Ges.* ii. 795, n. 4), Pareti and others, one at Carthage, one at Syracuse (Pareti, 164). See n. 7 for another suggestion.

[5] Diod. xi. 26. 7; cf. Cic. *Verr.* II. iv. 53. 119.   [6] Marconi, *Himera*.

[7] Ibid. 53. On pp. 164 ff. Marconi suggests that this is one of the two temples built at the expense of the Carthaginians, and was on the site of the naval camp where the fate of the battle was decided with Hamilcar's death. For reasons why the naval camp cannot have been so far east see Pareti, 143, n. 2.

[8] *Ol.* xii. 1.

the colossal Olympieion with its bold innovations of plan and its gigantic human figures reinforcing its pilasters,[1] were built in the period following Himera, and it is likely that some of them commemorate the victory; but there is no direct evidence.

Many of the spoils were nailed up in the temples of Himera, others carried back to Syracuse and sent to the sanctuaries of Greece, Olympia, and Delphi. Those at Olympia are recorded by Pausanias (a statue of Zeus and three linen corslets, in a treasury called the Treasury of the Carthaginians)[2] but are not otherwise known. The offerings at Delphi consisted of four round bases, each supporting a golden Nike and tripod, with the epigram ascribed to Simonides:[3]

φημὶ Γελῶν᾽, Ἱέρωνα, Πολύζηλον, Θρασύβουλον,
παῖδας Δεινομένευς τοὺς τρίποδας θέμεναι,
βάρβαρα νικήσαντας ἔθνη, πολλὴν δὲ παρασχεῖν
σύμμαχον Ἕλλησιν χεῖρ᾽ ἐς ἐλευθερίην.

Each base had a separate dedicatory inscription. Part of those of Gelon and Hieron have survived; that of Gelon reads:

Γέλων ὁ Δεινομέν[εος] | ἀνέθηκε τὠπόλλωνι | Συραφόσιος.
τὸν τρίποδα : καὶ τὴν : Νίκην : εἰργάσατο : Βίων Διοδώρου υἱὸς Μιλήσιος.[4]

The golden tripods are described by Bakkhylides in speaking of Hieron's glory:[5]

λάμπει δ᾽ ὑπὸ μαρμαρυγαῖς ὁ χρυσὸς
ὑψιδαιδάλτων τριπόδων σταθέντων
πάροιθε ναοῦ, τόθι μέγιστον ἄλσος
Φοίβου παρὰ Κασταλίας ῥεέθροις
Δελφοὶ διέπουσι.

Such was the glory of Himera. It is surprising that nothing is heard of any attempt by Gelon and Theron to follow up their victory and drive the Phoenicians out from the west of Sicily. The Akragantines won a victory over Motye, from the spoils

---

[1] Diod. xiii. 82; Robertson, 122 ff.; Pace, *MA*, xxviii. 173 ff.; Marconi, *Boll. d'Arte*, vi (1926), 33 ff.; *RIASA*, i (1929), 185 ff.

[2] vi. 19. 7.

[3] Schol. Pind. *Pyth.* i. 152b (Simon. fr. 141 Bergk); *Anth. Pal.* vi. 214 and Suidas s.v. Δαρετίου have a slightly different version introducing the couplet:

ἐξ ἑκατὸν λιτρῶν καὶ πεντήκοντα ταλάντων
δαρετίου χρυσοῦ, τᾶς δεκάτας δεκάταν.

[4] Tod, *GHI*, no. 17; Diod. xi. 26. 7; Theopomp. ap. Athen. 231f (fr. 189 Grenfell and Hunt). There is a considerable modern literature (see Tod, loc. cit.; Pareti, 173 ff.; Pace, *ACSA*, iii. 725 ff.), and questions of the recorded weights of the tripods and the gold of Damareta (read Δαμαρετείου for Δαρετίου) are very complicated. [5] Bakkh. iii. 17 ff.

of which they dedicated at Olympia a group of bronze boys, the work of Kalamis.[1] Kalamis belongs to the generation after the Persian Wars (his only dated work is the monument of Hieron's Olympic victory, dedicated after Hieron's death in 467–466 by his son),[2] so this Akragantine victory probably belongs to the years after Himera. At this period Motye puts the eagle and crab of Akragas on her coins, with the legend sometimes in Greek, sometimes in Punic, characters.[3] So also does Eryx.[4]

Selinus and Rhegion abandoned the Carthaginian alliance. Selinus is not heard of until the 'fifties, when she was, it appears, at war with Egesta.[5] Her great temples show that she, as well as Akragas and Syracuse, shared the general well-being which followed the return of peace. Anaxilas of Rhegion accepted the Syracusan direction and was admitted to the circle of tyrants bound together by dynastic marriages by the marriage of his daughter to Hieron.[6] The Attic standard of weight was now introduced into the coinage of Rhegion, under Syracusan influence.[7] It was most probably in 480 that Anaxilas' team of mules was victorious at Olympia.[8] The strength of his hold on Rhegion and Messana was unaffected by his backing the wrong side at Himera, and when he died in 476 his tyranny was preserved for his sons by his servant Mikythos.[9]

The Carthaginians themselves were by no means completely knocked out, for a few years later Pindar speaks of a fresh invasion as something to be feared and hardly avoided.[10] But for seventy years Sicily had rest from the scourge of Carthaginian invasion, until the Athenians had shown the Carthaginians the way to the walls of Syracuse. In this, as in other respects, Himera marks the end of an epoch. The most splendid period of Sicilian history was at hand, when the poets of Greece thronged Hieron's court, the magnificent temples whose ruins still adorn the site of Akragas were built, the Sicilian cities issued some of the finest coins ever struck. Though wars, internal and external, do not cease, the generation after Himera is one of peace and prosperity and the triumphs which ennoble it are those of art and literature. As

---

[1] Paus. v. 25. 5.   [2] Paus. vi. 12. 1.
[3] Head, *HN²*, 158. For the hellenization of Motye see above, p. 334.
[4] Head, *HN²*, 138.
[5] Diod. xi. 86, 2; *IG* xiv. 268; cf. Freeman, ii. 338 ff., 549 ff.
[6] Schol. Pind. *Pyth.* i. 112.   [7] So Mr. E. S. G. Robinson.
[8] Cf. above, p. 398.   [9] Diod. xi. 48. 2.   [10] *Nem.* ix. 28 f.

in Greece the Persian Wars mark the end of archaism and are succeeded by the full glory of the Athens of Kimon and Perikles, so in Sicily the battle of Himera is the last stage of the growing up of the colonies. As the British colonies found their nationhood at Anzac and their full independence in the years which followed, so it is not too fanciful to take Himera as the sign that the Sicilian colonies were now the equal of the cities of Greece. Already they had cast off most of their economic and cultural dependence on Old Greece which is the mark of their archaic period. Now they proved themselves the saviours of western Hellenism as Athens was of eastern. The Deinomenids boasted rightly in their epigram at Delphi of the friendly hand their victory over the barbarians extended to the free Greeks. Pindar said the same thing in even fewer words: 'Ελλάδ' ἐξέλκων βαρείας δουλίας.[1]

CHRONOLOGICAL NOTE

The following alternative chronology has been proposed by Pareti (ch. ii) and is accepted by Hackforth in *CAH*, iv, ch. xi.

c. 499–492	Kleandros.
c. 492–485	Hippokrates.
(492–491)	Samians at Zankle.
491–490	Capture of Kamarina: attack on Syracuse.
486–485	Death of Hippokrates.
485 second half	Gelon tyrant of Gela.
484 first half	Gelon takes Syracuse.
484–483	Transplantation of Kamarinaians.
483–482 or 482–481	Undertakings against Megara and Euboia.
480–479	Battle of Himera.

This table, except the first four entries (i.e. from the death of Hippokrates downwards), is set out by Pareti on p. 46. He does not vouch for the earlier dates on the table within a year, but the dates which I have put down are those which he states in the text to be most plausible. He uses two sets of arguments in maintaining this chronology: that the known acts of Hippokrates cannot be confined to the years before 491, the traditional date of Gelon's succession, and that the dating of Gelon's succession to that year is invalid.

To take the latter point first: Pareti (pp. 46–9) explains the date 491–490 as a confusion of the capture of Syracuse by Gelon tyrant of Gela (484) with the war against the Syracusans which led to the siege of Syracuse by Gelon, still Hippokrates' hipparch, which he dates to 491–490. But he fails to prove that Pausanias and Dionysios have the same source (see above, p. 410). In favour of the date 485–484 for Gelon's seizure of power at *Gela*, his first argument (pp. 30–1) is that Diodoros (xi. 38) speaks of his death in 478–477 after a seven years' rule, which should include his Geloan period as well as his Syracusan:

[1] *Pyth.* i. 75.

for he says of Gelon only ἐβασίλευσεν, of Hieron ἐβασίλευσε τῶν Συρακοσίων. The truth is that the chronographers neglected the Geloan period, and began Gelon's rule with his transference to Syracuse. Aristotle gives only the length of the tyranny at Syracuse, overlooking Gelon's rule at Gela and the rule of Kleandros and Hippokrates whom he succeeded. Eusebius gives a date for Gelon's seizure of Syracuse, but none for any event connected with the Geloan tyranny. The early historians of Sicily all had a Syracusan outlook, and Gelon's capture of Syracuse was a more important epoch than his tyranny at Gela.

Gelon's rule at Syracuse is agreed to belong, within a year, to 485–478. It was seven years and a few months, according to Aristotle (Pol. 1315ᵇ 34), whose phrase ἡ περὶ Ἱέρωνα καὶ Γέλωνα περὶ Συρακούσας (sc. τυραννίς) excludes the Geloan period. Diodoros' ἑπταετῆ χρόνον is the same figure. However much the Geloan period be minimized (Pareti speaks of 'una decina di mesi'), an exact figure of seven years plus some months for the Syracusan period and a rough seven years for the combined rule at Gela and Syracuse cannot both be right. On Pareti's reckoning, Diodoros should have written eight for seven. It is a possible approximation, but it is more likely that his source spoke only of the seven years' Syracusan period. The evidence for Gelon's beginning at Gela in 491–490 is not irrefragable; but the case for 485–484 is, in itself, weak. It could be upheld only if it were proved that Hippokrates cannot have died so early as 491. It would be tempting to allow a little more time for the events which follow the refounding of Kamarina; but I have endeavoured above to show that the acts of Hippokrates may be fitted into the years 498–491, and think that Herodotos has recorded all his most important campaigns (see above, p. 402 f). Pareti demands too long for the affair of the Samians, and insists that the attack on Leontinoi came after this affair, assuming that the order of Herod. vii. 154 is chronological. I think it far more probable that the Samian affair was over in 493, and that the siege of Leontinoi comes after Zankle entered Hippokrates' alliance and before the arrival of the Samians, the πολιορκία of vii. 154 not being part of the events of vi. 23–4. I am also unconvinced by the arguments by which Pareti draws out the resettlement of Kamarina towards 488 (cf. note on pp. 407 ff.). These are negative arguments only, showing that the traditional view is tenable. There is also a strong argument against Pareti's chronology in the Samian affair, which is the best dated of Hippokrates' actions. I think that this can hardly be earlier or later than 493. The Samians and Milesians could not stay in the Aegean after the autumn of 494, and I find it unreasonable to suppose that they lingered on the way west or in Italy instead of pressing on to what was to be their permanent home. But Hippokrates was already the ally of the Zanklaians, and overlord of their tyranny. According to Pareti's chronology, he had newly succeeded his brother in 493. Indeed, a strict interpretation would place his succession in 492 (so Hackforth, 365), and would therefore have to put the arrival of the Samians later than 493. Even if Hippokrates' years are stretched to nine, the enterprise at Zankle must be regarded as one of his earliest exploits. But it must be preceded by the alliance with Skythes, and the capture of Naxos and Kallipolis. Even if the siege of Zankle is part of the dealings with the Samians, which I doubt, Hippokrates must have become a power in the north of Sicily before Zankle submitted to his alliance. Before he could move so far north as Naxos and Zankle, he must have controlled the road that led thither; he can hardly have campaigned so far north in his first year. If the dealings with the Samians belong to the year 493, and are preceded by the fall of Naxos and at least one year's activities nearer home, 496–495 is the earliest possible year for Hippokrates' accession. If he died in 486–485, this is stretching Herodotos' seven years more than they will bear. Pareti does not tie himself down to a year for any event in Hippokrates' life, but Hackforth, adopting his chronology, produces an impossible result: 492, Hippokrates' succession (p. 365); 491, Heloros (p. 369); 492 covering the conquest of Naxos, Kallipolis, Zankle, Leontinoi, and all the affairs of the Samians from the dispatch of the invitation to Kale Akte to the establishment of Kadmos: truly an *annus mirabilis*, even for so active a man as Hippokrates. Pareti's greater caution says 'si debba credere che degli scrittori antichi fissero per lui [Gelone] il 485/4–478/7; per Ippocrate il 492–485; per Cleandro il 499–492'. Allowing a year or two's play for the round number of seven 'non siamo certi che Ippocrate salisse al potere nel 492 più che nel 493, o magari nel 494; e Cleandro nel 499, più che nel 500 o nel 498' (pp. 31–2). Even accepting 494, and allowing the affairs of Zankle to draw on to 492 or 491, it is crowded measure for the early part of his reign. If I have made out my case for dating the arrival of the Samians to 493, it is impossible that Hippokrates began to rule so late as 494.

If Herodotos vii. 154 is not in chronological order, Pareti's whole argument falls to the ground. None of Hippokrates' dealings with Syracuse and Kamarina are proved to be later than 491. As all his other activities, with the exception of the attack on Ergetion in which he used Kamarinaian troops, and the attack on Hybla in which he died, might come anywhere before or after the Zankle and Syracuse campaigns, there is nothing to speak in favour of 493–486 rather than 498–491, and, on the other side, there is the extreme improbability that the Zankle affair was his first foreign undertaking.

Pareti's answer is (p. 49): 'tutta l'azione databile di Ippocrate è posteriore al 494–3'. Footnote: 'Se anche si crede, contro la nostra opinione, che Ippocrate *conquistasse* Zancle prima dell' arrivo dei Sami (493 o seguenti), non ci sarebbe motivo di risalire oltre il 494. — Così pure, anche ponendo gli assedi di Callipoli e di Nasso, secondo la successione erodotea, prima di quello di Zancle, non si risale oltre il 494, perchè si vide che l'assedio di Ippocrate ai Sami, occupatori di Zancle, è al più presto del 492 circa.' But 493 is not the upper limit only, but the very probable date of the affair of the Samians; so that 495 is the latest year possible for Hippokrates' accession. If, as I think, the 'siege' of Zankle was earlier than the affair of the Samians, his accession must have been still earlier than 495.

No one has cut the knot by ascribing part of the northern expansion, including the alliance with Zankle, to Kleandros. Kleandros is only a name, and it may be that some of the Sikel warfare which I have ascribed to Hippokrates' earliest years was in fact carried on by Kleandros. But it was certainly Hippokrates who advanced Geloan arms to Zankle and Naxos, and until a Geloan army appeared in the Khalkidian region there was no reason why Zankle should submit to the Geloan alliance.

APPENDIX I

THE CHRONOLOGY OF THE WESTERN COLONIES

THE foundation-dates of the western colonies, with which are closely connected two other problems, the chronology of Protocorinthian and other contemporary vase-fabrics, and the date of the earliest Greek intercourse with Etruria, have been much debated in recent years. The fundamental treatment is still that of Schweitzer in *AM*, 1918, 1 ff., and Johansen in *Les Vases sicyoniens*; the chronology of Protocorinthian and Corinthian has been further discussed by Payne in *Necrocorinthia*, 21 ff., and *Protokorinthische Vasenmalerei*; also important on the archaeological side of the argument are the works on Protoattic by J. M. Cook, *BSA*, xxxv. 165 ff., and R. S. Young, *Late Geometric Graves and a Seventh-century Well in the Agora*, and *AJA*, 1942, 23 ff. The foundation of the western colonies is treated by Pareti, *Studi Siciliani*, 310 ff.; Pace, *Arte e Civiltà della Sicilia Antica*, i. 169 ff.; J. Bérard, *La Colonisation grecque de l'Italie méridionale et de la Sicile*; and the chronological problems of the period in general by Burn, *JHS*, 1935, 130 ff. On the Etruscan side are Karo, *AM*, 1920, 106 ff.; Randall-MacIver, *Villanovans and Early Etruscans*, esp. 155 ff., and *The Iron Age in Italy*, 160 ff.; Schachermayr, *Etruskische Frühgeschichte*, 187 ff.; Sundwall, *Villanovastudien*, 62 ff., and *Zur Vorgeschichte Etruriens*, esp. 170, 189 ff.; Blakeway, *BSA*, xxxiii. 170 ff., and *JRS*, 1935, 129 ff.; Åkerström, *Studien über die etruskischen Gräber*, esp. 39 ff., and *Der geometrische Stil in Italien*, passim; Dohan, *Italic Tomb-groups*; to name only full-length studies of the problem. Finally, an able study by Byvanck, *Mnemosyne*, iv. 181 ff., followed by Åkerström's second work just mentioned, surveys the whole field of early Greek imports to the west and compels a close examination of all the evidence, literary and archaeological.

I. THE THUKYDIDEAN DATES

The primary source for the chronology both relative and absolute of the western colonies is in the early chapters of Thukydides vi. He gives a series of dates relative to the foundation of Syracuse, which may be made absolute by means of three links, one supplied by Thukydides himself, two from other sources.

1. Thukydides dates the destruction of Megara 245 years after its foundation. It was destroyed by Gelon between 485 and 480:[1] 483–482 is the most probable date. This puts the foundation of Megara in or about 728–727. Thukydides does not state how much later Megara was than Leontinoi, but regards them as about contemporary. Leontinoi was founded in the fifth year after Syracuse. This gives a date for Syracuse a little before 732–731.

[1] Herod. vii. 156. Cf. above, p. 416 f.

2. Kamarina is placed by Thukydides 135 years after Syracuse. The date of Kamarina, as given by a combination of Schol. Pind. *Ol.* v. 16 and pseudo-Skymnos 294–6, is 598–597; the date of Syracuse is therefore 733–732.

3. Pindar in *Ol.* ii. 93 says that Akragas had been founded a hundred years at the time of the victory which he is celebrating, in 476–475. The scholiast gives the date of the foundation as 580–579. Akragas is 108 years after Gela, which is 45 years after Syracuse. This gives 733–732 for Syracuse.

The exact agreement of these figures gives for the Sicilian colonies the dates in the first column of the following table.[1] A variation of a year or two in some of the dates is possible.

Sicilian Colonies

	Thuk.	Eusebius		Other authorities	Remarks
		Vers. Arm.	Jerome		
Naxos . .	734	736	741		
Syracuse .	733	734	736	788? Mar. Par. ep. 31.	
Zankle . .	..	..	756		
Leontinoi .	729				
Katane . .	729	734	736		
Megara . .	728				
(Khersonesos)	..	716	717		
Gela . .	688	690	690		
Enna . .	..	..	..	663 Steph. Byz.	Mistake for Akrai?
Akrai . .	c. 663				
Himera .	..	..	..	649 Diod. xiii. 62.	
Kasmenai .	c. 643				
Selinus . .	628	..	650	651 Diod. xiii. 59.	
Kamarina .	c. 598	598	600	600–596 Schol. Pind. *Ol.* v. 16; ps.-Skymn. 296.	
Akragas .	580	..	..	580 Pind. *Ol.* ii. 93+Schol.	
Lipara . .	..	627	630	580–576 Diod. v. 9.	

We must now ask whether these dates are consistent with themselves, with other chronological evidence, and with such relevant dates as may be drawn from archaeological evidence. First, let us take other chronological evidence. The dates in Pindar and his scholiast have been shown to agree exactly with Thukydides. The other main series of dates is that given in the Eusebian *Chronica*, which is set out in the second and third columns of the table; together with certain dates in Diodoros drawn from the same tradition. The Eusebian dates for the original colonies, from Naxos to Gela, agree within a very few years with those drawn from Thukydides, so that there is no doubt that they are derived either from him or from his source. Considering the number of times they must

---

[1] This agrees with the table of Thukydidean dates in Pareti, *Studi Siciliani*, 313.

have been copied, each time with the possibility of error, this is remarkable. Syracuse and Gela, and also, of the later colonies, Kamarina, are placed within two years of the Thukydidean dates. So is Naxos, in one version of Eusebius; Jerome, however, places it a few years earlier. The discrepancies are:

(1) the dating of Katane in the same year as Syracuse, and the omission of Leontinoi and Megara;

(2) the date of Selinus.

The first may be due to a lacuna in the list at some stage intermediate between Thukydides and Eusebius, in which mention of Leontinoi and note of the interval of time after Syracuse have fallen out.

The second is more serious, inasmuch as the Eusebian date for Selinus is supported by Diodoros, who says that Selinus was founded 242 years before its destruction in 409–408, i.e. in 651–650. Where we should expect Selinus from the Thukydidean list, Eusebius has instead Lipara, which was in fact colonized shortly after 580. This suggests that the chronographer used by Diodoros and Eusebius took his dates from a list from which he omitted Himera, so that the date of Himera became attached to Selinus, that of Selinus to Lipara.[1]

	Original	Eusebius	
649–648	Himera	Selinus	650
628–627	Selinus	Lipara	627
580–579	Lipara	..	..
580–579	Akragas	..	..

This involves certain difficulties; why is Kamarina, for instance, not on the hypothetical list? If the date of Himera was given in an early chronographer, why is it not in Thukydides? Perhaps because there was no date for Zankle, so that he cannot date Himera with relation to its mother city as he does all other secondary foundations. The figure in Diodoros xiii. 62 of 240 years at its fall is generally taken to be the era of the city. It may be the same figure as the 242 years for Selinus, both destroyed in the same year. This would mean that the Eusebian error was already present in Diodoros, and that the latter either mistakenly wrote the Himera figure for the Selinus figure, or calculated from a foundation list in which Selinus had already been put down to the year to which Himera really belonged. In spite of these difficulties I offer this suggestion not because I am convinced ·of its truth but because it is one's duty to find some explanation of a variant so well supported as the Eusebius–Diodoros date.

To accept the date c. 650 involves even more serious difficulties of an archaeological nature. Payne says (NC, 23–4): 'The archaeological evidence speaks strongly for the later date. There is scarcely a trace of the Protocorinthian industry among the finds from Selinus. . . . The

---

[1] For displacement of items in Eusebian lists see Fotheringham, JHS, 1907, 82.

overwhelming majority of the vases and fragments are Corinthian.'
The foundation of Selinus, and the beginning of the Corinthian style, is
one of the central dates of seventh-century archaeology; Selinus dates
the Corinthian style, and not vice versa. But the alternative to Payne's
date 625–600 for Early Corinthian is to lower it into the sixth century;
no one would raise it to 650, with the implication that the Protocorinthian style was already abandoned by then. So Thukydides' date is
very strongly, though indirectly, supported by the finds from Selinus.
The mass of Early Corinthian vases, and the fact that the earliest are
all of the same period, make it almost certain that that period was not
far removed from the foundation.

The suggestion has recently been made (K. M. T. Atkinson, *BSR*, xiv.
115 ff.) that 650 represents, probably not very accurately, the first
settlement at Selinus, 628 the formal colonization. The arguments in
support of this are vitiated by Mrs. Atkinson's dating the graves at
Selinus with which she is specifically concerned in the Early instead of
the Late Corinthian period; and in view of the complete absence of Late
Protocorinthian material at Selinus and its neighbourhood it is unlikely
that there was any such settlement as there was at Akragas (see above,
p. 310). I discuss her paper at more length elsewhere (*BSR*, xvi. 1 ff.), and
need only say here that the archaeological evidence is definitely against
any form of a double foundation. The variant 650 is practically put out
of court by the archaeological evidence, and I think its origin is to be
sought in a corruption of the literary tradition; though the solution
offered above may not be the exact one.

To return to the recorded dates, we have a consistent chronology,
found in Thukydides, Eusebius (with two variants), the scholiast on
Pindar, and (for Kamarina) pseudo-Skymnos. Over most of these dates
these different sources agree within a few years. It is, of course, not
possible to use Eusebius and the other later sources as independent
confirmation of the Thukydidean chronology, but their close agreement
with Thukydides is of value in indicating that the system which we first
meet in his work was, on the whole, accurately preserved until late
antiquity. Who first worked out this chronological system is uncertain.
It is commonly supposed that Thukydides drew his early Sicilian
material from Antiokhos of Syracuse. It is not, however, certain that
Antiokhos gave dates.[1] Hellanikos referred to the foundation of Naxos
in the second book of his *Priestesses of Hera*;[2] so presumably he dated
it and related its date to his general system of Greek chronology. It is
therefore suggested that he, not Antiokhos, was Thukydides' immediate
source.[3] Whoever first drew it up, the chief authority of this system is
derived from its acceptance by Thukydides. He, who elsewhere is
sceptical about early Greek history, thought it reliable enough to present
it in full detail.

---

[1] Cf. Dion. Hal. i. 22. 5.   [2] F 82 Jacoby.   [3] Jacoby, *FGH*, i. 456 f.

II. THE ITALIAN COLONIES

Are there other remains of this chronological system? We should expect to find them in Eusebius, who has so far followed the Thukydidean dates fairly faithfully. There are other Sicilian dates in Eusebius, for Zankle and Khersonesos (which is generally identified with Mylai). That for Zankle, 756, cannot be reconciled with Thukydides, as it is earlier than the date for Naxos which is described by him as the oldest Sicilian colony. It is further discussed below. For Mylai, there is no other evidence.

There are also in Eusebius a number of dates for the Italian colonies, for which Thukydides did not give dates. These are set out, with dates given by other authorities, in the following table:

Italian Colonies

	Eusebius		Other authorities	Remarks
	Vers. Arm.	*Jerome*		
Kyme . . .	1051			
Metapontion . .	773			
Pandosia . . .	773			
Sybaris . . .	708	709	720 ps.-Skymn. 256–60	
Kroton . . .	708	709	710 Dion. Hal. ii. 361	
Taras . . .	. .	706		
Lokroi . . .	673	678		
Rhegion . .				
Siris . . .				
Kaulonia . .				
Poseidonia . .				

Can these dates be derived from the same source as the Thukydidean dates for the Sicilian colonies? There is a certain presumption that, as Eusebius' dates for the Sicilian colonies are derived from Thukydides or his source, and on the whole reproduce that source accurately, his dates for the Italian colonies will come from the same source. The margin of error will in that case be at least as great as in the Sicilian dates; that is, some dates may be quite in error, and even those which are substantially correct may vary by five years or a little more from their original.[1] The upper dates, for Kyme, Metapontion, and Pandosia, cannot, as transmitted, come from such a source nor, as will be seen, can any *fides* be attached to them. For Sybaris, Kroton, Taras, and Lokroi there is no immediate difficulty in reconciling the Eusebian dates with the Thukydidean–Eusebian dates for Sicily.

The Eusebian date for Kroton is confirmed by Dionysios of Halikar-

---

[1] This is partly due to the fact that in the extant manuscripts one entry often extends over several lines, and as each line commonly has a new year, the probability of a small error being introduced in copying is high. See further below, p. 442; and cf. Fotheringham, *JHS*, 1907, 85.

nassos, who gives the year 710–709.[1] For Sybaris there is an alternative date in pseudo-Skymnos, who places its foundation 210 years before its destruction, that is, in 720.[2] Other evidence on the order of foundation of the colonies is given by Antiokhos, as cited by Strabo. This is to the effect that Sybaris was already founded when the founder of Kroton set out,[3] and that Metapontion was founded on the initiative of the Sybarites, at a time when Taras had been founded but Siris not yet.[4] Antiokhos therefore placed the colonies in the order Sybaris, Kroton, Metapontion, Siris, with Taras coming before Metapontion, though whether before or after Sybaris and Kroton we cannot say.

There is further evidence, of an indefinite kind, in the order in which Diodoros dealt with the colonies in his eighth book. After the foundation of Kroton follow some stories about Sybaris, related on the occasion of its foundation; after that, the foundation of Taras, then Gela, the Khalkidian settlement at Rhegion; this is followed by a fragment which appears to refer to the code of Zaleukos at Lokroi[5] (the Eusebian date for Zaleukos is 662, only a few years after the foundation of the colony).

Setting all these sources side by side, we get the following order:

Eusebius	Antiokhos	Diodoros
(Kyme)	Kyme	
(Metapontion)		
{Sybaris	Sybaris	Kroton
{Kroton	Kroton	Sybaris
Taras	Taras	Taras
	Metapontion	
	Siris	
		(Rhegion)
Lokroi		Lokroi

Sybaris, Kroton, and Taras are the only three included in all lists. Diodoros appears to agree with Eusebius, for he may well have placed Kroton and Sybaris in the same year, as the excerpts from him give some of the history of Sybaris immediately after the foundation of Kroton and before that of Taras. His mention of Gela also agrees with the place of Gela in the Eusebian list. Also, he placed Sybaris after Syracuse.[6] The only point in Diodoros to which we shall have to recur is the fragment about Rhegion (viii. 23. 2), which follows the foundation of Gela.

The Eusebian dates do not agree so easily with Antiokhos, and the following discrepancies appear:

[1] ii. 59. 3. [2] vv. 256–60.
[3] Strabo vi. 262. [4] Id. vi. 264.
[5] Excerpts in Vatican codex, Diod. viii. 17–23, ed. Vogel.
[6] This is the result of comparing Diod. viii. 18, 19 with viii. 10 (both fragments from the excerpta de virtutibus et vitiis).

(1) The high date for Metapontion, which Antiokhos says was founded after Sybaris.

(2) The synchronization of Sybaris and Kroton, whereas Antiokhos places Sybaris before Kroton, and pseudo-Skymnos also gives an early date for Sybaris.

On the first point, Eusebius' date is unacceptable; an attempt has been made above to find an explanation for it.[1] The second point is less serious, because the period at issue is short. Antiokhos' account of the foundation of Kroton implies that Sybaris was not yet very firmly settled, as the founder of Kroton thought at first of either reinforcing his compatriots at Sybaris or driving them out. An interval of ten or twelve years (accepting the dates 720 for Sybaris, 710 or 708 for Kroton) suits his account quite well, though the dates must be taken as representing his chronology only approximately. The Eusebian variant which makes Sybaris and Kroton contemporary may be due to a careless reading of Antiokhos or a work derived from him.

The Eusebian date for Taras is confirmed, and an approximate date for Rhegion may be obtained, from the history of the First Messenian War. Rhegion was said by Antiokhos to have been founded on the invitation of the Zanklaians by Khalkidians to whom were joined some Messenians who fled from their country in the course of the First Messenian War;[2] and Taras was founded after the war by the bastard breed of Spartans who had grown up during the war, and were deprived of citizenship after the end of it.[3] The First Messenian War is dated by Eusebius 746–726 or 744–724; the Partheniai were supposed to have been born in the tenth year of the war, and exiled on reaching the age of thirty; this gives the date 706 for Taras. A slightly later date for the First Messenian War, c. 736–716, may be obtained from the Olympic victor-lists.[4] It is not clear from Strabo's words whether Antiokhos said that the Messenians left their country for Rhegion at the beginning of the war or when it had been going on for some time. So the date for Rhegion may have been anywhere between 746 and the early 'twenties. But, for Eusebius as for Antiokhos, Naxos was the oldest colony in Sicily, and therefore older than Zankle, whose citizens helped to found Rhegion; on this line of argument, Rhegion cannot be older than c. 730. So we may assume that it was given a date in the 'twenties.

The Diodoran variant which implies a seventh-century date for Rhegion will be due to attaching its foundation to the Second Messenian War instead of the First. This is a point on which there was considerable uncertainty, as the issue was confused by the fifth-century settlement by Messenians at Zankle-Messana.[5]

---

[1] See pp. 33 ff.
[2] Strabo 257.
[3] See above, p. 29.
[4] Wade-Gery, *CAH*, iii. 537.
[5] See above, p. 396.

We have now the following list for the Italian colonies, with such dates as are offered by various sources already considered:

Rhegion	.	.	.	c. 730–720
Sybaris	.	.	.	720 or 708
Kroton	.	.	.	710–708
Taras	.	.	.	706
Metapontion	.	.	?
Siris	.	.	.	?
Lokroi	.	.	.	678 or 673.

These dates may be taken as representing a single tradition, less good than the tradition for the Sicilian colonies because the chain of transmission is longer and less reliable. But though the dates cannot be pressed closely, they may be regarded as standing within about ten years of an original fifth-century list of dates. It is simplest to believe that this was drawn up by the same author as Thukydides' source for his Sicilian dates. The only difficulty (and it is a considerable one) in fitting the Italian to the Sicilian dates and treating them as part of a single system lies in the synchronization of Syracuse and Kroton, which has the authority of Antiokhos. This is discussed in the next section. I believe the difficulty to be not insoluble, and hold that the Sicilian and the Italian dates may be accepted as part of a coherent system.

III. VARIANT DATES: AN ALTERNATIVE SYSTEM?

A number of data may be drawn from Ephoros which do not fit into this chronological scheme. He said that Naxos and Megara were the first of the Sicilian colonies, founded in the tenth generation after the Trojan Wars.[1] Syracuse was almost contemporary with Naxos and Megara, and exactly contemporary with Kroton and Korkyra;[2] Lokroi a little later than Kroton and Syracuse.[3] The order given in pseudo-Skymnos, following Ephoros, for the Sicilian colonies is (omitting secondary foundations):

Naxos
Megara
Syracuse
Leontinoi
Zankle
Katane
Himera.

This differs from Thukydides' order in placing Megara at the top, and in giving a (relative) date for Zankle, which Thukydides recorded but did not date.

Do these variants from Thukydides imply that Ephoros presented an

[1] Ps.-Skymn. 272; Strabo 267 (where δεκάτῃ is supplied from ps.-Skymn.).
[2] Strabo 269.   [3] Id. 259.

alternative chronology? Let us examine them one by one, bearing in mind the discrepancies already noted in drawing up the Thukydides–Eusebius scheme.

1. *The absolute date.* The tenth generation after Troy is, at best, an uncertain epoch. It is doubtful whether Ephoros had clearer views about the date of the fall of Troy than we. Possibly he reckoned upwards from a relatively well-established date for the earliest colonies, not downward from an epoch otherwise fixed. So attempts to extract an absolute Ephorean date for Naxos by a calculation of generations are unlikely to succeed.[1]

The tenth generation recurs in the Parian Marble, where Arkhias, founder of Syracuse, is said to be eleventh from Herakles, i.e. ten generations after the Trojan War.[2] Unfortunately the date for the foundation of Syracuse is missing from the Parian Marble.[3]

For what it is worth, Timaios dated Syracuse in 734, 600 years after the fall of Troy, which he dated in 1334.[4]

2. *The precedence of Megara over Syracuse.* We have here to do with a point which raises a difficulty in Thukydides' narrative, taken in itself. The wanderings of the Megarians before they finally settled at Megara Hyblaia, including their joint occupation with the Khalkidians of Leontinoi, would be expected to occupy more than the year or two years allowed to them. The archaeological evidence also, to anticipate, suggests that Megara was founded more than a few years later than Syracuse, and therefore than Naxos and Leontinoi. A possible explana-

---

[1] Pareti (p. 316) says *c.* 790, and accepts this date for Naxos; Burn (*JHS*, 1935, 137), by a different calculation, gets *c.* 784 for the tenth generation after Troy. Schweitzer's attempt (op. cit. 25) to get an Ephorean date 736 for Naxos, reading ιγ´ γενέᾳ in the corrupt passage of Strabo 267, is unsound.

[2] Accepting Jacoby's interchange of Arkhias for Pheidon, which seems to me, though not to all scholars, compelling. The Parian Marble says that Pheidon of Argos is eleventh from Herakles, and Arkhias tenth from Temenos, first Herakleid king of Argos; but Arkhias can hardly be of Temenid descent, *pace* Lenschau (*RE*, Suppl. iv. 1013). The synchronization of Arkhias and Pheidon in Plut. *Am. Narr.* 772 is not chronologically helpful. Though Pheidon's action appears to belong to the seventh century, ancient views on his date differed widely, the commonest being in the middle of the eighth century. This agrees well enough with the traditional date for Syracuse, but the date of Pheidon is too uncertain to be useful.

[3] It is generally given as 757–756, but Jacoby points out (*F Gr Hist*, ii D. 685) that this is not well founded. The *MP* dates the foundation of Syracuse in the twenty-first year of the Athenian archon Aiskhylos; according to Eusebius (p. 148, ed. Fotheringham) the first Olympiad fell in the second year of Aiskhylos, and the combination gives the date 757–756. But the *MP* does not use Olympiads (its first fixed date is not Ol. 1 but 683–682, the beginning of yearly archons) and reduced its dates differently. Jacoby (loc. cit.) suggests the *MP* dated the foundation of Syracuse in 788–787; so also Schweitzer, 23. This date agrees with that given by Pareti and Burn for the tenth generation after the Trojan War, but is not sufficiently well established to support that date. The attempt by Beloch (*Gr. Ges.* i. 2². 224), followed by Pareti (p. 317) and Byvanck (p. 197), to derive the supposed date 757–756 in the Parian Marble from Philistos, on the ground that Philistos, contrary to his usual custom, named the Olympic victor of the year 756 (*FHG*, i, fr. 6), is ill founded.

[4] Schol. Ap. Rhod. iv. 1216; cf. Schweitzer, 26.

tion is that the age of Megara was reckoned not from the permanent establishment of the Megarians but from the year of their first arrival in Sicily. Alternatively, the period of wandering may have been before, not after, the given date 728 (245 years before the destruction of the city). In that case, their arrival in Sicily might be at about the time of the foundation of Naxos. This receives some confirmation by the story in Strabo, whose origin I cannot determine, that Arkhias on his way to Syracuse picked up at Lokroi some Dorians who had come so far with the Megarians.[1] It leaves the difficulty that the period of joint settlement with the Leontines, which I consider to have been fairly long,[2] and the settlement at Thapsos must fit into a single year after the foundation of Leontinoi. Some such reasoning may underlie Ephoros' statement that Naxos and Megara were contemporary. He may therefore at this point have been correcting Thukydides on a point of detail, whether rightly or wrongly, not abandoning Thukydides' chronology and setting up an alternative.

3. *The synchronization of Syracuse and Kroton.* This may be explained thus. The dates of the Sicilian colonies are all related to Syracuse, not necessarily because of the local pride of Antiokhos of Syracuse, but because Syracuse was indisputably the greatest of them. Similarly Kroton was in the time of Antiokhos and the other early historians the chief of the Italian colonies. So the two were brought into relation by means of a joint Delphic oracle to their founders.[3] The terms of the oracle promising wealth to the Syracusans, health to the Krotoniates, are applicable to the late sixth century, when Kroton's medical school became famous, or the fifth. It is not in itself impossible that Delphi should be consulted in the eighth century about the site of a colony. But this oracle has a rather mythical ring; a story which brings both Myskellos and Arkhias to Delphi at the same time on the same errand cannot be accepted literally.[4] It is a story with a moral, of a type which commonly disregards chronology. It does not necessarily imply that there was a historian who dated the foundation of Syracuse and Kroton in the same year; it may have been invented to carry back to the foundation of the colonies the contrast of their state in the fifth century. Synchronizations of this sort, centring on an anecdote, are the weakest basis for chronological arguments; an example is the synchronization of Solon and Kroisos.

Syracuse and Korkyra are said to have been founded in the same year, as well as Syracuse and Kroton.[5] The Eusebian date for Korkyra is 708, the same as for Kroton. This might be thought to imply an alternative date of *c.* 708 for Syracuse; an alternative explanation is that Korkyra and Kroton, not Korkyra and Syracuse or Syracuse and Kroton, were

[1] Strabo 270.   [2] See above, p. 45.
[3] Strabo 269; Suidas s.v. Ἀρχίας; Schol. Ar. *Knights* 1091.
[4] Cf. Parke, *A History of the Delphic Oracle*, 71–2.
[5] Strabo 269; Plut. *QG* 11; Schol. Ap. Rhod. iv. 1212; Plut. *Am. Narr.* 772.

associated by some historian, and that Syracuse has crept in because it was the greatest of the colonies; alternatively, and perhaps most likely, that somewhere in the long chain of transmission of the Eusebian dates someone slipped a line and wrote Korkyra against the date which in fact belonged to Kroton instead of against the date of Syracuse.

4. *The date of Lokroi.* This is said by Strabo to have been a little later than Kroton and Syracuse, which perhaps implies the synchronization of these two colonies, perhaps names them as the greatest colonies of Italy and Sicily. Though not a very definite note of time, it does not agree too well with the Eusebian date according to which Lokroi is among the latest of the primary colonies. The archaeological evidence, however, agrees with Eusebius, as will be seen: there was, however, a long period of intercourse with the native inhabitants of Lokroi before the Greek colony was founded, and it is very probable that some Greeks were settled there as early as the foundation of Syracuse. This might explain how, in another passage of Strabo, Arkhias is said to have found Greeks at Zephyrion when he put in on his way to Syracuse.

5. *The date of Zankle.* Thukydides has no date for Zankle, or for its colony Himera. But Diodoros gives a date for Himera, Eusebius a date for Zankle, and pseudo-Skymnos a relative date for Zankle. The Eusebian date for Zankle is corrupt: under the year 756 the Armenian version has the entry 'In Italia Calicum et Liconia conditae sunt' with the v. l. 'in Sicilia silinus et gangle . . .'.[1] No meaning can be attached to so early a date for Selinus and I cannot interpret the two names given as Italian cities. Zankle, which appears as 'gangle', should not be so old as 756, or it, not Naxos, would be described as the oldest colony in Sicily. It is possible that Kyme, the mother state of Zankle, was the colony dated in or about that year, and that its name lurks behind these corrupt entries.[2]

Thukydides gives no mark of time for Zankle; yet its era should have been preserved, for the oecists were known and were honoured annually.[3] All authorities agree on the primacy of Naxos among the Sicilian colonies. So the placing of Zankle by pseudo-Skymnos after Naxos and with Leontinoi and Katane is natural and need not imply an exact date.

The date of Himera, found only in Diodoros, is likely to be derived from the era of the city; it is presented in the form that the city had existed for 240 years at the time of its destruction in 409. It is not necessarily related to the date of its mother city Zankle. Thukydides

---

[1] Ed. Schoene, ii. 80.

[2] Professor Wade-Gery has suggested to me that the date 757 for Kyrene (one of many variants) should read Kyme. The two possibilities are not exclusive. The date *c.* 1050 for Kyme is manifestly wrong. It may belong to the Aiolic Kyme, as suggested by Schweitzer (32–3), quoting Rühl, *Fleckeisens Jahrbücher*, 1888, 342 ff., and Pareti (322–3); or to Myrina; one version reads *Myrena condita* for the vulgate *Mycena in Italia condita uel Cumae*. The last two words are not found in all manuscripts (see Fotheringham, 115), and may have been added by a learned commentator who knew that Kyme was the oldest Greek colony in the west.　　　　　[3] Kallim. in *Ox. Pap.* xvii, no. 2080.

presumably did not give a date for it because he could not relate it to Zankle.

So far we have found no evidence that Ephoros presented an alternative chronological system to Thukydides. It is not certain that he presented any dates at all, beyond the 'ten generations after the Trojan War' which does not necessarily imply a firm date. The variants from the Thukydidean chronology may be explained as due to a series of mistakes and mistransmissions, carelessnesses about chronology, and perhaps corrections or supplements to Thukydides, or rather, to his source.

The dates in Eusebius and elsewhere which vary from the Thukydidean chronology are combined by Burn (*JHS*, 1935, 136 ff.) into a single alternative 'long' chronology. This does not carry so much conviction as the 'long' chronologies recognized for the northern and eastern colonies and for other dates in eighth- and seventh-century history which can be checked by synchronisms with the eastern empires. Burn insists that the relative dates worked out by the chronographers are approximately correct, though their absolute rendering is too high. But this criterion cannot be applied to the 'long' chronology of the western colonies:

	'Long'	Accepted	
Naxos	c. 784	735	
Metapontion	773	after 700	
Syracuse	757	734	
Selinus	650	629	
Lipara	629–628	580	(Burn, p. 137, gives 588, which is presumably a misprint).

There is no rhyme or reason in the 'long' chronology; it is likely that it is not a system but a number of unrelated mistakes and miscalculations. I do not regard it as proven that there was any alternative systematic chronology to that given in Thukydides and followed, in the main, by Eusebius. Burn allows that the traditional chronology of the western colonies is in a different case from that of the eastern and northern colonies. I should like to stress the difference more than he does, and emphasize the reliability of the dating of the western colonies, over which he wavers.

It may be convenient to recapitulate:

	Accepted	Variant
Kyme	?? 756	1051
Naxos	734	(c. 784)[1]
Syracuse	733	(788)[1] or (757),[1] 708 (*temp.* Kroton)
Leontinoi	729	
Katane	729	734–3

[1] These dates are doubtful modern reconstructions. The same may, of course, be said of those dates in the 'accepted' column preceded by queries.

		Accepted	Variant
Megara	. .	728	734 (temp. Naxos)
Zankle	. .	(?? c. 730)[1]	756
Rhegion	. .	(? 730–720)[1]	
Sybaris	. .	720	708
Kroton	. .	c. 708	
Taras	. .	c. 706	
Poseidonia	.	(? c. 700)[1]	
Metapontion	.	(? 690–680)[1]	773
Gela .	. .	688	
Siris .	. .	(? 680–670)[1]	
Lokroi	. .	c. 673	Earlier?
Kaulonia	.	(?? c. 675–650)[1]	
Akrai	. .	663	
Himera	. .	649	
Kasmenai .	.	643	
Selinus	. .	628	650
Kamarina .	.	598	
Akragas	. .	580	
Lipara	. .	580–576	627

IV. GENEALOGIES OR WRITTEN RECORDS?

The literary tradition of the chronology of the colonies, though full of corruptions and variants, appears to have been single, and the variants do not establish a complete system.[2] It is argued that this tradition is substantially reliable, and that if it could be established in full in the form in which it was known to Thukydides it could be depended on for fairly exact dates. The variants may be explained as in the main due to one of two causes: either to slips in transmission, and especially slips of the kind by which one entry has fallen out of a list by the time of Diodoros and Eusebius, and the date of the next higher entry attached to a given colony (Katane, Selinus, Lipara); or to unhistorical synchronizations. The synchronization in the form of an anecdote is of all types of historical material that which has least regard for chronology (cf. Solon and Kroisos). The 'anecdotal' synchronizations which cause most trouble are those which associate Syracuse and Kroton, Sybaris and Kroton, the greatest of the colonies in the late sixth and fifth centuries, which is probably the date at which the anecdotes about their founders gained currency.[3] It must not be overlooked that the Thukydidean dates depend on the synchronization of Syracuse and Naxos, Megara

[1] These dates, not given by ancient sources, are added here for convenience and completeness.

[2] Schweitzer concludes (p. 27) 'dass wir einer geschlossenen, einheitlichen Überlieferung gegenüberstehen', and the historians had a good date for Syracuse, and reach up from this to the Fall of Troy, varying in their calculation of the higher date, and not vice versa.

[3] Schweitzer rightly points out that the existence of foundation legends attaching to the person of the founder in no wise impugns the historicity of the fact and date of the foundation (p. 29, n. 1).

and Leontinoi, and Ephoros' on the variant Megara and Naxos. These are in somewhat different case because they are not 'anecdotal' and because of the comparative obscurity of their subjects at all periods at which we know anything of their history; why should anyone bother to invent stories about a third-rate place like Megara?

We must now discuss a more serious objection to the historical validity of the accepted chronology, that which reduces it to a system built up on the slippery ground of a calculation of generations. It is said that the 245 years of Megara's existence, by which Thukydides' early dates are attached to a secure base in the fifth century, are 7 generations of 35 years; that the 210 years of Sybaris' existence, according to pseudo-Skymnos, are 6 generations of 35 years; the 70 years between Syracuse and Akrai 2 generations of 35 years.[1]

This argument, which looks plausible when confined to certain selected dates, breaks down when applied to all Thukydides' dates. The foundation of Akragas in or about 580, implied already in Pindar, is questioned by no one; it is said to be 108 years after Gela. 108 is an uncomfortably knobbly figure to explain away; it is by no means round; if it is 3 generations of 36 years, why should one suppose that the Geloans habitually married a year later than other Sicilians? 108 is such a precise figure that it must be accepted as a fact; then the foundation of Gela in or about 688 is assured. We are now very near the eighth century, and it becomes very difficult to lower the dates of Naxos and Syracuse very much, as is the tendency of the generationists; impossible to bring Syracuse down by half a century, as Beloch proposes. And Syracuse is said to be 45 years before Gela. This is no number of generations, nor easily divisible by any magic figure; the simplest course is to suppose it to be correct. This gives c. 733 for the foundation of Syracuse, which is so near the date arrived at by a calculation upwards from the destruction of Megara as to give reason to believe that that calculation is based on something more exact than a number of generations. Again, the foundation of Kamarina in one of the years 600–598 is not questioned; it belongs in a period in which the sceptics allow that there were written records; the 46 years of its existence before its first destruction must derive from such a record, not from calculation or guess. Kamarina was founded about 135 years after Syracuse. It is true that Thukydides does not vouch for the exactness of his figure, saying ἔτεσιν ἐγγύτατα πέντε καὶ τριάκοντα καὶ ἑκατὸν μετὰ Συρακουσῶν

---

[1] A generation of 35 years is recognized by Schweitzer (p. 19) in the lists of Athenian archons on which the Parian Marble is based. It is not otherwise common in Greek chronography. It is the only possible calculation with which one has to deal here. Of an 'Eratosthenic' 40-year generation no trace can be recognized in the west, unless in the 'long' dates discussed by Burn. Many dates might be regarded as derived from a calculation of three generations to 100 years; particularly the 200 years (approximately) of Sybaris, on the Eusebian date, and the 100 years between Megara and Selinus. But the 245 years of Megara's existence cannot be explained thus. This is the vital figure in the Thukydidean chronology, and the generationists must therefore postulate a generation of 35 years.

κτίσιν. But there should be an error of a year or two at most. 135 is not a number of generations, though if there had been much uncertainty about it, it might easily have been given as a round figure of 140. By this means also we get *c.* 733 for Syracuse, a date arrived at by two sets of calculations neither of which is open to suspicion that it is founded on generations.

It remains possible that the figures in Thukydides and later writers agree so well because they are arrived at by simple subtraction: that having got figures for the foundation of each city by means of a calculation of generations, Thukydides or his source proceeded to relate them to a fixed point; and that the figures 108, 135, and others just discussed have no independent validity; that they are all related by subtraction to the foundation of Syracuse, which in turn is made absolute by the 245 = 7 generations figure for Megara. It is true that later writers such as pseudo-Skymnos will have taken their figures from a ready-made list, not examining the annals of each state separately; for instance, pseudo-Skymnos' 46 years of life for Kamarina is no doubt obtained by subtracting one given date from another, not from independent records. But I cannot agree that this list was compiled in this way in the first place. Let us see how it could be compiled:

Megara was destroyed after 7 generations: $7 \times 35 = 245$: this gives the foundation of Megara.

Naxos, Syracuse, Leontinoi, Katane are related to the foundation of Megara by means of synchronizations implicit in the traditions of their foundations.

So far, so good. Now the lower range. The dates for Kamarina and Akragas may be allowed to have been preserved reasonably accurately into the fifth century. Kamarina is related to Syracuse by subtraction. Akrai is 2 generations = 70 years after Syracuse. Kasmenai is 20 years later, not a generation-figure but a round number, so let it pass. Selinus is put 100 years after Megara, a round figure. We are left with a hard core of obstinate figures. Akragas is 108 years after Gela. Three generations of 36 years is hard to swallow; why does Thukydides set it down, unless he had good evidence for it? Of course, it might have gone wrong in transmission, as many of Thukydides' figures have; but that possibility appears to be ruled out by the fact that the date for Syracuse reached through Akragas and Gela agrees with that reached by other routes. Then Gela is 45 years after Syracuse. This is not a generation-figure; if it was reached by subtraction, it implies that there was an independently reached date for Gela; and we have seen that the date for Gela reached through Akragas does not yield to generation treatment. Whichever way we approach it, the date for Gela is a nut which the generationists cannot crack. And it is already on the threshold of the eighth century; if there was a date for Gela not reached by calculation of generations, why not also Syracuse and Naxos?

I do not believe that Thukydides would have given in such detail a

G g

series of dates founded on calculation of generations. It seems that he gives the dates of Akrai, Kasmenai, and Kamarina to the nearest five years only, with the note ἐγγύς, ἐγγύτατα, as we might say *circa*. It is not unlikely that there would be some slight uncertainty about the year of the foundation of a secondary colony, or rather about which point in an occupation which may have taken a few years to complete was to be regarded as the moment of the foundation. To take a modern parallel: it is written in the text-books of Australian history that Melbourne was founded in 1837; the centenary was celebrated 100 years from the first occupation of the site in 1835; the existence of the town was first officially recognized, and the name given, in 1838. If then the foundation is generally placed in 1837, the year of the first regular occupation, the existence of variants does not justify the throwing of doubts on the authenticity of the date, still less on those of other Australian cities. To return to Syracuse and Kamarina. The fact that Thukydides is careful to qualify the figures of the intervals between Syracuse and her secondary colonies implies that where he uses no such qualification he was reasonably certain of the exactness of his figures. In a historian so sceptical about early Greek history, and so much concerned elsewhere to minimize its importance and some of its chronology, we may be sure that where he gives precise figures for events 300 years before his time they had been recorded in a way which he considered reliable.

To sum up: Thukydides gives seven long intervals, two of which only can possibly be reduced to generations; another, the 100 years of Selinus, might be a round figure;[1] but the 45 years between Syracuse and Gela, the 108 between Gela and Akragas, the 135 between Syracuse and Kamarina, sound obstinately factual. Moreover, the notes of time which relate Naxos and Syracuse, Leontinoi and Syracuse, sound exact; the more so because he does not give such precise notes for Katane and Megara.

There is no *a priori* reason why the colonies should not have had written records of their foundations. The date at which the alphabet came into use in Greece is not agreed on all sides, but the latest date assigned to it is in the last quarter of the eighth century; I think that this date is too late and that the earliest extant Greek inscriptions are as old as the middle of the eighth century.[2] It is plausibly suggested that one of the earliest uses of alphabetic writing was to keep lists of eponymous archons or priests.[3] But to keep an exact record of their

[1] It is, of course, explained as three generations; but why should generations of Selinuntines be calculated differently from generations of Megarians?

[2] Carpenter dates the beginning of alphabetic writing in Greece *c.* 720 (*AJA*, 1933, 8 ff.; 1938, 58 ff.); R. S. Young doubts whether any extant Greek inscriptions are older than 700 (*AJA*, 1940, 1 ff.; 1942, 124–5). It would take too long here to review the evidence on which I would prefer to date them *c.* 750. Fortunately it is not necessary for the present purpose, as on the lowest dating writing reached Greece within the generation of the foundation of the colonies and would therefore be available for keeping records *ab initio*, or at least within the lifetime of the original colonists.   [3] Holland, *AJA*, 1941, 356.

age it was not even necessary for the colonies to keep written lists of magistrates; it would be sufficient to cut a notch on a board once a year on the anniversary of the foundation, and to be able to count, or to drive a *clavus annalis* into a wall, as Livy says was done at Volsinii and Rome.[1] It is likely that records would begin to be kept earlier in the colonies than in mainland Greece, because they had a definite point from which to begin, whereas the cities of Greece, and Ionia too, were founded at a period too early for such a record to be kept and had not so early as the eighth century any crisis in their history to serve as a starting-point.[2]

It would be rather surprising indeed if the colonists had not sufficient interest to keep a skeleton history and some record of their age. And when we have in Thukydides a set of figures which would naturally be derived from these records, whose exactitude implies that they were taken from records or from some equally reliable source, and which cannot be satisfactorily explained on any other hypothesis, it is reasonable to suppose that records, accessible to the historians, were kept which gave the era of the individual colonies. The dates which have come down to us, though derived from these records, are by no means accurate in every case. Thukydides' figures have sometimes been transmitted wrongly in manuscript, and may have been in the sixth book; a range of a couple of years for most dates is possible, owing to his method of presenting his figures. For those dates, including those of all the Italian colonies, which are not recorded by Thukydides, a wider range is probable. Eusebius' figures may in any case be five years or more out, though he has substantially preserved the tradition; and in some cases he has made a palpable mistake. However, he appears in the main to derive from the same tradition as Thukydides. There are gaps; we have no date for Zankle, for Metapontion, or for Siris. But we can recover their relative positions, and may be reasonably certain of the relative order of the foundations. As for absolute dates, those which depend on Thukydides may be taken as accurate within five years, those taken from other sources within a wider range, but still as fairly close approximations. This is better than we can do for most eighth- and seventh-century dates in Greek history, which is, I think, what we should expect. The foundations of the colonies are important events

---

[1] Livy vii. 3. 5–8; cf. Festus ap. Paul. Diac. ed. Lindsay, 49; see K. Hanell, 'Sulla questione del Clavus annalis' (*Bullettino Comunale*, lviii, 1930, 163 ff.).

[2] The other side to this argument from probability is put by Burn, *JHS*, 1935, 143. Some colonies will have lived a 'frontier life' in their early days; the piratical Zankle, for instance; more important, the Milesian trading-posts in the Black Sea (for Olbia, see ·Burn, pp. 134–5); others, and among them most of the Sicilian colonies, I suppose to have lived from the first the full life of a *polis*. For the early days of Syracuse see above, pp. 48 ff. Schweitzer also regards the dates for the foundation of the colonies as based on reckonings *ab urbe condita*. For the contrast between the specific dates for the western colonies in Thukydides and his, for the most part, timeless references to early Greek history cf. Pearson, *The Local Historians of Attica*, 40.

and, to the colonials themselves, far more striking than any date in the history of a longer-established state could be. The colonies have their beginning, not in the mists of the dark ages, but in the full activity of history.[1] So it should not be surprising if the rudimentary beginnings of chronicles should be made in the colonies.

V. THE ARCHAEOLOGICAL EVIDENCE

There is one line of argument which I have not yet touched, the archaeological. As regards absolute dates, no reasoning based on archaeological premisses can affect a chronology firmly based on other evidence. Artefacts may be arranged by style and typological development in a series the members of which are securely dated relatively to one another, but absolute dates can be established only by contexts which themselves supply such date; which can be given only by a literary or epigraphic record. In the last resort, all absolute dates depend on some written source.[2] Now the chronology of Protocorinthian vase-painting is established absolutely by reference to two historical events, the foundation of Syracuse and the foundation of Selinus; relative dates are made absolute by working forward and back from these two events, with checks wherever possible from other approximately datable associations. The chronology of other vase-fabrics, and all Greek archaeological dates of the eighth and seventh centuries, are founded on comparisons and associations with Protocorinthian. The date of the foundation of Syracuse is therefore, archaeologically, a fixed point, not to be overthrown by any reasoning from grounds of Greek archaeology alone. It may indeed come to be questioned if a more secure eighth-century anchor is produced, in the shape of a dated document or event with which vases are associated in such a way that their contemporaneity cannot be doubted. Research in the Near East may at any time produce such an anchor. At present, the absolute chronology of Protocorinthian vase-painting, and with it of other Greek art of the period, is as secure as the chronology of the colonies, on which it depends. I shall discuss the chronology of Protocorinthian in another place. It is enough here to remark that Payne has, implicitly in *Protokorinthische Vasenmalerei*, explicitly in *Perachora*, i. 31, found no ground in it for questioning the traditional chronology of the Sicilian colonies.

Some eight of the western colonies have thus far produced material relevant to the present discussion. Most of this comes from graves. Kyme has yielded graves, the contents of which may be contrasted with Greek vases in the prehellenic graves, whose site within the walls of the Greek city shows that they are earlier than its foundation. From

[1] It is evident from the first book of Thukydides that this antithesis is not due only to the state of our knowledge. The earliest events of Greek history recorded in Herodotos which are assignable to a definite period are, also, of the late eighth and seventh centuries. This is the period when writing first became common in Greece.

[2] Cf. Burn, *JHS*, 1935, 134–5.

Syracuse there are graves, temple deposit, and other scattered material from the city area. Gela also has produced both graves and temple deposit. At Megara there are graves only; at Taras graves, details of whose excavation have not been put on record; at Lokroi graves and, as at Kyme, a contrast with Greek vases in prehellenic graves. At Selinus there are both graves and temple deposit. Lastly, Poseidonia has recently yielded a copious temple deposit. There are serious gaps. None of the Achaean colonies of Italy has been productive, though there is a little material from a temple deposit recently excavated at Metapontion. The Khalkidian colonies in Sicily are also archaeologically unknown. A Sikel village on the site of Leontinoi, with Greek vases of about the time of the foundation of the Greek colony, has been excavated, but the cemeteries of Greek Leontinoi have not been found. There is some sporadic early material from Zankle, but not enough to base an argument on.

It may be asked whether we are right to assume that the oldest graves found on each site belong to the period of the foundation of the colony. This point is discussed by Byvanck (op. cit. 224–5), who concludes that about twenty-five years will have elapsed between the foundation and the earliest graves. He is not, however, right in doubting that there will have been burials in the first years after the foundation. Though all the colonists were young and strong, the young and strong die, in battle or childbed, by disease or accident; also, a high proportion of burials in most archaic Greek cemeteries are those of children. Figures from the history of a modern colony show that the death-rate in early years when most of the population belongs to low age-groups is at least as high as the average. The figures are those for Sydney during the first twenty years of its existence.[1]

Period	Population	Deaths	Death-rate per 1,000 per annum
26 Jan. 1788–Oct. 1789 .	1,030	72	41
31 July 1798–31 July 1799	c. 4,000	67	17
30 Sept. 1800–31 Dec. 1801	5,975	96	13
1802	5,975	155	25
1803	—	57	9·5
Sept. 1800–Aug. 1805 .	c. 6,000	468	13

To-day's death-rate in Australia is about 10 per 1,000.

The number of first settlers at Syracuse, or any other Greek colony earlier than the fifth century, is not known. Presumably they were numbered in hundreds rather than thousands, but they will still, on the analogy of Sydney, have had a steady death-roll which in twenty-five years could hardly fail to reach half the original number of settlers. This assumes a death-rate of 20 per thousand, which is low for ancient

[1] Compiled for me from the original records by my father, Thomas Dunbabin.

Greece.[1] In other words, if the original citizen population of Syracuse is put as low as 200, in the first quarter-century of its existence there will have been a hundred Greek graves, excluding the nameless graves of slaves, serfs, and Sikels. One hundred is a minimum, not a probable, figure, for the figure for the original population is chosen as a minimum, and the death-rate is on the low side. The number will have gone on growing with the growth of population.

The difficulty which Byvanck felt in assuming the oldest objects from the graves to be coeval with the foundation may persist in spite of this argument. Though there must have been graves belonging to the earliest years of each colony, it does not follow that these have been found. At Syracuse some 500 graves have been excavated, belonging in the main to the first 100 or 150 years of the city's existence; at Megara, over 1,000, covering the whole 245 years of the city's existence; at Gela, many hundreds, covering a rather longer period; at Taras, we do not know how many. These are but a small fraction of the many thousands of burials which must have been made at each city. Let us take Megara, where less guess-work is needed than elsewhere, as the subject of a rough calculation. Orsi estimates on the basis of the area of the town and its suburbs (61 hectares = 30 acres within the walls) that it could contain a population of 18,000 to 20,000.[2] For an average population from the foundation to the destruction, let us halve this figure. Then, on a death-rate of 20 per thousand, there will have been some 49,000 deaths in the 245 years of the city's existence. Halve this figure again, if you will, to avoid any possibility that it is exaggerated: the thousand-odd graves discovered at Megara are still a small fraction of all the burials which took place during its existence. Many of these will have been burials in bare earth, without funeral offerings. Even so, the number of graves discovered is but a small fraction of those which will have contained the vases and other small objects in which we are interested. They may be an even selection of all the number, or they may have lacunas of long periods, all the graves belonging to which have disappeared. A lacuna of twenty-five years in the middle of the series would be noticed, because we should observe that vases of a given style and stage of development were missing. If the lacuna came at the beginning we should not have the means of detecting it. It is unlikely, however, that the earliest graves of Kyme, Syracuse, Megara, Gela, Taras, Lokroi, Selinus should all be missing. This could hardly be caused by coincidence or the accident of discovery, but would require some special factor which is not present to our knowledge. It is likely there-fore that we have some graves belonging to the first quarter-century of some or most, if not all, of these colonies. And this, it seems to me, is what we have, on Johansen's chronology. The agreement between the

---

[1] Gomme assumes a death-rate of 20 per thousand for Athens (*Population of Athens*, 79). For comparable modern figures cf. ibid. 76–7.

[2] *MA*, i. 742.

traditional order of foundation of the colonies and the order in which they are placed according to the oldest objects found in their cemeteries indicates, either that we have some objects which belong to the oldest period of the existence of each colony, or that in every case the oldest objects are missing. The latter hypothesis, possible if we were dealing with two or three sites only, becomes highly unlikely in the case of seven; for we can formulate no general rule according to which the objects belonging to the first quarter-century of a city's existence should disappear. We cannot argue with Byvanck that no one died and was buried during the first twenty-five years of a colony's existence. We must therefore in most cases have some of the oldest objects used at each colony.

We have, too, the exception which should prove this rule. At Megara, nothing has been found which is, on the received chronology, older than 700. As Johansen says: 'A en juger par le contenu des nécropoles, on supposerait plutôt l'intervalle entre Syracuse et Mégara Hyblaea plus grand et l'intervalle entre cette dernière colonie et Géla plus petit' (p. 182).[1] That is to say, the graves of the first thirty years of Megara's existence appear not to have been found, whereas we have some of the earliest of Syracuse and Gela.

The most that can be established by this line of argument is that few among the finds from any site will belong to the earliest years of its existence, and in some cases the first twenty-five years or even longer of a site's occupation will be unrepresented in its discovered graves. The number of graves concerned is in any case small. At Syracuse some six graves belong, on Johansen's chronology, to the period 735–690. The case is not capable of mathematical precision, but the proportion to the number of burials which must have taken place is of the same order as the proportion of graves discovered to total burials estimated for Megara, that is, under 5 per cent.

A not unrelated question is, how old might a vase or bronze be when deposited in a grave? This question applies also to temple deposits. Temene will have been set aside for the gods from the day of the foundation of a colony, and offerings will have been made at once, before temples were necessarily built. The objects need not have been new when dedicated—many of the first offerings will have been brought with them from the mother country by the colonists—so theoretically some of the offerings made in a colonial sanctuary may be older than the colony itself. This may explain why some vases of types slightly older than those found in the earliest graves come from the temple

[1] Cf. also Orsi, *N Sc*, 1895, 132 n.: 'In the thousand tombs explored in the cemetery of Megara are found none of these vases, and none of the little pot-bellied lekythoi, Protocorinthian geometric, which means either that the foundation of Megara, contrary to the historical tradition, should be put about a quarter of a century after that of Syracuse, or that the most ancient part of the Megarian cemetery is not yet found, which is unlikely after the very extensive excavations carried out there.'

deposits of the Athenaion at Syracuse and of Gela. The available evidence, however, indicated that the vast majority of objects were dedicated or placed in a grave while new (disregarding a life of a few years only, for a decade is the shortest period with which we are concerned).

It would be a tedious and unprofitable business to tabulate and form statistics of all datable Greek grave-groups, but most archaeologists are agreed that objects found in the same grave are for practical purposes contemporary; and this may be confirmed by looking through any series of grave-groups of the late sixth and fifth centuries, in whose chronology there is little that is debatable. Moreover, it appears from their condition that many vases were new when deposited in the grave; this is particularly true of vases of common types and decoration, such as the aryballoi, oinochoai, and kotylai on which the chronology of the Protocorinthian vase-fabric, and thus the question we are at present discussing, depends. The need for caution is illustrated by a number of grave-groups in which vases, which on grounds of style and typology would be dated as much as twenty-five years apart, are found in the same grave. Without going outside the small number of graves at present under discussion, we can point to Syracuse 219, which contains the oldest aryballos from Syracuse (*NC*, pl. 1. 1) together with one a whole stage of development later (*NC*, pl. 1. 2); Megara 499, which contains the oldest aryballoi from Megara together with others of later date; Phaleron 11, where aryballoi which may spread over as much as twenty-five years are found together; an extreme example is Rhitsona 99, where among a mass of aryballoi which would appear to have been bought especially for the funeral is one which may be as much as 150 years earlier.[1] It may be remembered in parenthesis that the typological development is always over-simplified; that a number of closely related stages of development may be current at the same moment of time, in more or less advanced workshops.[2] The validity of the typological method for chronology is not thereby impugned; the example of our own industrial design in the last hundred years may show that, in spite of the multiplicity of concurrent tendencies, a majority of products may be securely dated on the ground of elements in their design and decoration.

A venture to date any object to a decade in the eighth century is bold in the extreme, and the small and simple vases and bronzes with which we are concerned can in no case be dated closer than a conventional quarter-century. The possibility therefore that some of them may have been a quarter of a century old or even more when they were buried in graves does not seriously limit our inquiry, as in any case we could scarcely hope for a closer dating than this interval of time will allow.

[1] See the remarks in Ure, *Aryballoi and Figurines from Rhitsona*, 19–20.
[2] Compare Payne's remarks on the development of the cup in Corinthian Geometric, *Perachora*, i. 55 ff.

Furthermore, it should be noticed that this amount of upward play tends to counteract the time-lag suggested by Byvanck and already discussed in the dating of the earliest graves in the western colonies. If the oldest of these graves may be later than the foundation of the colonies by a quarter of a century or so, to grant Byvanck's case in full on this point, then the vases in those graves may be anything up to a quarter of a century older than the moment of the interment. The two cancel out and we have the equation that the date of the oldest objects found in the graves should be approximately the date of the foundation of the city, that is to say, should be of the same quarter-century. Closer than this we cannot hope to get on archaeological evidence alone.

Two associations need to be inquired into more closely: Syracuse and Selinus. For they are the two fixed points by which the chronology of Protocorinthian pottery is tied down, the first providing a date for the beginning of the orientalizing style, the second for the end of the Protocorinthian and the beginning of the Corinthian style. Let us take the lower date first.

Archaeologically Selinus is distinguished from the other colonies under consideration by the quantity of material which it has produced and the fact that most of this comes from a temple deposit. The sanctuary of Malophoros has produced a great deal of Early Corinthian pottery, and only isolated pieces of Late Protocorinthian and Transitional. It appears therefore to have begun to accumulate dedications when the Early Corinthian style was well established. On the other hand, it is shown by the intensive building activity in it in the period before the building of the great temples of Selinus to have been much favoured in the early years of the colony.[1] So it is a fair deduction that the temenos was set aside and began to receive dedications at the period of the foundation. The equation that Early Corinthian begins at about the date of the foundation of Selinus is therefore established with a fair degree of accuracy. The earliest vases from the cemeteries are also Early Corinthian but belong to the latter part of the period.[2] The oldest vases from the graves appear to be about fifteen years later than the oldest vases from the sanctuary. This interval is not of great importance for our present inquiry and may be due to incomplete exploration of the cemeteries. It should, however, be borne in mind when we are discussing other sites whose material is entirely from graves.

At Syracuse also there is relatively abundant early material from both graves and temple site, as well as other sporadic pieces from the city area.[3] As at Selinus, the oldest material from the city appears to be slightly older than the earliest vases from the graves.[4] The interpretation of this fact is not easy because the stratification in the lowest levels

[1] Cf. Gàbrici, *MA*, xxxii. 123 ff.; Payne, *NC*, 22 ff., 339.
[2] A different view is expressed by K. M. T. Atkinson, *BSR*, xiv. 130 ff.; see my remarks in *BSR*, xvi. 1 ff.
[3] For the latter see above, p. 51.   [4] Cf. Blakeway, *BSA*, xxxiii. 180 f.

of the Athenaion site, which has produced most of this early material, is confused. In the lowest strata Greek geometric sherds were found mixed with the remains of the Sikel predecessor of Syracuse, and Orsi, who excavated the site, was uncertain whether to treat them as pre-colonization imports or as intrusions of colonization date into the Siculan strata.[1] In places the Siculan sherds were clearly separated from the earliest Greek, but it does not appear from the publication whether any Greek sherds were found in the uncontaminated Siculan deposits. It seems likely on stylistic grounds, as well as on general probability, that the Sikel site imported Greek vases some of which are preserved: but the case is not proved stratigraphically. The issue is not a wide one chronologically, for the sherds in question are little earlier than the oldest vases from the cemeteries and from elsewhere within the bounds of the Greek city.[2]

One individual aryballos from the Fusco cemetery appears to be among the oldest found in the west and indeed among the oldest Corinthian vases of the shape known.[3] But the grave in which it was found is not the earliest Syracusan grave, for it contained four other aryballoi, one of which is of considerably later date.[4] As the date of the grave is that of the latest object in it, we are left with the theoretical possibility that the very early aryballos may be older than the foundation of Syracuse. This is another warning against pressing too closely the correspondence of archaeological and historical dates. In such a connexion, the important archaeological date is that of the oldest considerable body of contemporary material, not that of the oldest object, taken in isolation; and the application of archaeological dates to historical events gains in validity with the bulk of the material available. Fortunately, for the vital events, the foundation of Syracuse and Selinus, we have a great deal of material, derived from different sorts of site, both cemetery and temple.

The first result of the study of the archaeological evidence is to confirm the *relative* chronology of the colonies. This is best observed by following the development of a single form, the aryballos, which is found in most graves. The sequence is set out by Johansen, and there is nothing to add to his discussion, as no important new finds have been made since he wrote.[5]

The tradition that Kyme is the oldest of the western colonies is borne out by its remains; a stage in the development of the aryballos which is richly represented here has only a single example at Syracuse, and that in a grave with another of considerably later date (that discussed immediately above). Syracuse, Megara, Gela, Lokroi, Selinus follow in that order, which agrees with the order given in Eusebius; Taras is more

---

[1] *MA*, xxv. 373 ff.   [2] See above, p. 13.
[3] *NC*, pl. 1. 1 = *PV*, pl. 5. 1; *N Sc*, 1895, 138, fig. 15.
[4] *NC*, pl. 1. 2 = *PV*, pl. 5. 3; *N Sc*, 1895, 137, fig. 14; Johansen, *VS*, pl. 14. 1.
[5] See especially Johansen, 179 ff.

recent than Syracuse and probably than Megara, but older than Gela; Zankle is shown to be early, though it has not produced enough material to say how early. On the archaeological evidence alone, one cannot determine the interval between the colonies, for the reasons given above.

This close agreement of the archaeological and literary evidence for the order of founding of the colonies is a strong argument for the substantial accuracy of the historical tradition. This is further supported by the archaeological confirmation of such important details as the Greek settlement on Ischia which preceded Kyme,[1] the temporary occupation by the Megarians of Thapsos,[2] the existence of Sikel settlements on Ortygia, at Leontinoi, at Lokroi—all sites where the presence of Sikels is mentioned by early sources, whereas in the case of most colonies the natives are not mentioned. On occasion the archaeologist can intervene on points which are debatable in the historical tradition. Thus the remains of Selinus offer a decisive argument for the Thukydidean against the Eusebian date for its foundation; otherwise we should have to believe that the Protocorinthian style came to an end well before 650, which is contradicted by all that we know on other grounds of the development of the style.

In the next section we shall examine an attempt to lower the beginning of the Protocorinthian style, and with it the foundation of Syracuse, to a date near 700. On the evidence of the western colonies as presented in Schweitzer and Johansen we cannot say that the traditional date of 733 is preferable to a lower date. We can say only that the earliest preserved remains from Syracuse are older than those from any other western colony except Kyme. This is not incompatible with a lower range of dates for the earliest Sicilian colonies (of which Syracuse and Megara alone have produced remains belonging to that period). But though the confirmation of the relative chronology of the colonies cannot be used as proof of their absolute dating, it offers presumption that this is approximately correct. For if the dates in Thukydides were derived from genealogies, they would be in the same confusion as most seventh- and indeed sixth-century chronology of the Greek mainland, synchronizations would be vague or lacking, the order of events would be uncertain at many points, and the archaeological evidence would provide, not a few minor points of variance from the tradition, but a series of *cruces*. The close agreement of the two kinds of evidence suggests strongly that the traditional chronology is accurate, even in the case of dates separated by only a few years. It is hard to see how this degree of accuracy could have been obtained if Thukydides and his contemporaries had only a number of generations (and those, from the nature of colonial politics, not of kings or rulers, but of private individuals) on which to form a chronological framework. It is still open to believe that while the tradition is historically accurate the absolute

---

[1] Büchner, *BPI*, 1936–7, 65 ff.
[2] See above, p. 19.

dates are not; that the history of the colonization period was preserved substantially accurately for three centuries, but that in providing absolute figures the fifth-century historians had recourse to a calculation which might or might not be historically correct. I feel great doubt whether so much accurate historical knowledge as is involved in placing in the right order all those colonies for which we have an archaeological check could be preserved without a chronological framework; the tradition would then be less consistent with itself and with the archaeological evidence. I therefore conclude that the archaeological argument offers indirect but strong support for the view that the fifth-century historians had reliable historical material to work on and that their chronology has absolute as well as relative validity.

VI. AN ALTERNATIVE ARCHAEOLOGICAL CHRONOLOGY

Some scholars have drawn different conclusions from the archaeological evidence in that, while agreeing that it confirms the relative order of events, they find in it arguments to overthrow the absolute chronology. This is a very large problem, involving the chronology of Protocorinthian vase-painting and other Greek fabrics of the eighth and seventh centuries, and of the earliest Greek finds in Etruria. It cannot be dealt with in full here, but must be discussed at some length in its bearing on the western dates.

There has been much work recently on Greek vase-fabrics of the eighth and seventh centuries and there is a general tendency to lower all dates round 700. This is clearest in the case of Protoattic, which has been exhaustively studied by J. M. Cook and R. S. Young; and the Cretan, Cycladic, and Cypriot fabrics are also affected. The chronology of Protoattic, and to a certain extent of Cretan and Cycladic, is based on that of Protocorinthian. On the basis of the development of Protoattic vase-painting, Cook proposes to bring down the date of some early Protocorinthian vases, placing the transition from the globular to the ovoid aryballos about 700.[1] As Cook himself says, 'there is in Protoattic nothing that points to an absolute dating',[2] which is founded on the Protocorinthian series. It seems illogical to argue back from the relative chronology of the Protoattic series to the Protocorinthian. But the argument may be well founded, even if not compelling in abstract logic; it may lead to a re-examination of the bases of Protocorinthian chronology which will result in a lower dating.

Many students have felt a difficulty in the eighth-century part of Johansen's chronology, which is generally now subject to a downward revision. Payne's dates in *Protokorinthische Vasenmalerei* are appreciably lower, though Payne did not abandon the basis of Johansen's chronology and the close association of its beginnings with the foundation dates of

---

[1] *BSA*, xxxv. 203.   [2] Ibid. 200.

the colonies.[1] Weinberg's publication of the vases from Corinth adopts dates which are substantially lower than Payne's, and for the earliest grave at Kyme he adopts Byvanck's date of 725 B.C.[2] The reasons which induce a lower dating are twofold: comparison of Protocorinthian vases with those of other fabrics at the same stage of development, which are on internal grounds assigned to a lower absolute date; and a vacuum in the second half of the eighth century, where Early Protocorinthian (globular aryballoi) fills an unduly long period, whereas one would expect this to be a time of rapid development.

This is not the place to discuss at length the chronology of Protocorinthian and its relations to other fabrics. We may, however, discuss briefly other evidence not derived from the foundation dates of the colonies, and then turn to the question how, if Johansen's dating for Protocorinthian must be lowered, this affects the chronology of the colonies, which is so closely associated with that of Protocorinthian.

The first place in which to look for an absolute dating is in the Egyptian scarabs and other objects found in Greek graves or on stratified sites. These need to be used with caution because not every scarab is accurately datable. In the first line come scarabs or other objects inscribed with a royal name and therefore to be treated as exactly dated historical documents. Very few of these came to Greece or Italy in the period under discussion. Secondly, those scarabs which can be dated on grounds of shape and style are valuable because they belong to a country whose history is fuller and more exact than that of Greece. But not every egyptianizing object is of Egyptian manufacture; many are of Asiatic or even Greek origin. And many of the Egyptian or egyptianizing objects found in Greece are dated, not on their own merits, but on their Greek context. The Third Intermediate Period is a very obscure one in Egyptian archaeology, and as most of the objects in Greece of this and the Saite period are in poor preservation and without inscriptions, they are often less rather than more securely dated than the Greek objects with which they are associated. In particular, many of the types common in the Saite period are now thought to have been current also under the preceding Ethiopian dynasty.[3] With these precautionary remarks, and with apologies for embarking on a specialist subject in which I am entirely dependent on the views of others, let us examine the Greek contexts of the Egyptian objects of the XXVth and XXVIth dynasties.

The most important graves containing datable Egyptian objects are the Bokkhoris tomb at Tarquinia, the Isis grave at Eleusis, Amathus grave 9, and an unpublished tomb at Knossos. The Egyptian objects

---

[1] Cf. above, p. 452. [2] *Corinth VII*, i. 39; cf. *AJA*, 1941, 35.
[3] Cf. Scharff, *Gnomon*, 1931, 537 (review of Pendlebury, *Aegyptiaca*): 'Die Datierung 26 Dyn. . . . die so bezeichneten Skarabäen brauchen keineswegs nur aus den Regierungen der Psammetiche zu stammen, sondern können etwas älter (bis etwa 800 v. Chr.) oder auch wesentlich jünger sein.'

found on stratified sites at Ajia Irini in Cyprus and at Perachora are also important.

Bokkhoris and his vase have been put into place recently by Mrs. Dohan, with the help of a brace of Egyptologists.[1] Bokkhoris is dated by Professor Gunn, 718–712, within two or three years. But, as the vase illustrating his triumph found at Tarquinia is not an original Egyptian work but a Phoenician imitation, it was not necessarily made during his lifetime. Further, it is uncertain how long after its manufacture the vase was placed in the grave. Byvanck says reasonably that its good condition shows that it was not long in use, and suggests that the interval was not more than the lifetime of the original owner.[2] This introduces many doubtful elements into the argument, which may be assessed differently by different students; the only safe conclusion is that the vase was made not before *c.* 715, which is therefore a *terminus post quem* for the grave.[3] From this Mrs. Dohan passes to an attempt to date the grave by means of the other objects found in it. That is, the Bokkhoris vase is only valuable as providing a general check on a chronology arrived at by other means. The Italian imitations of Proto-corinthian vases found in the grave could not be placed before the seventh century, and not at its very beginning. Therefore the accepted chronology for these vases is in agreement with the *terminus* provided by the Bokkhoris vase.

In the tomb of Isis at Eleusis a scarab of Men-Kheper-Ra of the XVIIIth dynasty (not XXIst dynasty, as stated by Pendlebury, *Aegyptiaca*, 80, no. 161; see G. A. W[ainwright], *JHS*, 1932, 126) and other scarabs of the Third Intermediate Period were found. The former scarab gives a *terminus post quem* which is of only formal nature; the others are not precisely dated by a royal name, but are themselves to be dated on grounds of type and style. It may be that von Bissing's date in the second half of the eighth century[4] is right, but it cannot be taken as agreed by Egyptologists. Nor is the dating of the Attic vases in the grave agreed; R. S. Young dates the grave shortly before 700 B.C.,[5] Kahane in the second half of the ninth century[6] (the latter date is certainly too early). This celebrated grave can therefore contribute little in the present discussion.

Three scarabs were found at Knossos in a polychrome tripod-pithos (no. 8 in tomb II of the 1933 excavations).[7] One of these is perhaps of the Ethiopian king Shabataka, 700–689, according to Shorter;[8] the other two are reissues of Amenhotep III, and may belong to the XXVth

---

[1] *Italic Tomb-Groups*, 106 ff.   [2] Op. cit. 182–3.

[3] Åkerström also (*Der Geometrische Stil in Italien*, 77) denies any especial value for chronology to the Bokkhoris tomb.

[4] *'Εφ. 'Αρχ.* 1898, 120. Von Bissing's date is based on the technique and style of the scarab of Men-Kheper-Ra.   [5] *Late Geometric Graves*, 234 ff.

[6] *AJA*, 1940, 482.   [7] Mentioned *JHS*, 1933, 290.

[8] Communicated to me by J. K. Brock, to whose kindness also I owe the statements quoted below. The conclusions *outside* the quotation-marks are mine, not Brock's.

or XXVIth dynasty.[1] They date the pithos in which they are found *after* 700, perhaps as late as 650. 'A slightly earlier burial in the same tomb (no. 11)—i.e., next to and rather lower than no. 8—included a Protocorinthian kotyle of the type Johansen pl. xvii, 3 and 4; shape roughly between the two; ht. 11·4 cm., mostly red varnish. There were fragments of another near no. 8.'

These data fit well enough with the agreed dating of Protocorinthian; the kotyle would normally be dated in the second quarter of the seventh century. They involve a lowering of the dating of Cretan early orientalizing vases, and a certain loss of primacy for Crete; on the basis of the scarabs, Brock reasons that 'the polychrome style cannot have started much before 700 . . . the Protocorinthian early orientalizing style must have preceded Cretan polychrome and be contemporary with early orientalising in Crete, i.e., last quarter of eighth century. Johansen's dating of *aryballes pansus* would be too early by a quarter of a century.' The final criticism is implied in Payne's chronology in *Protokorinthische Vasenmalerei* and is generally upheld.

Amathus 9 is well dated to the Saite period by its scarabs. The vases from this grave are assigned by the excavators to the Cypriote Archaic II period; they included two Late Geometric 'Rhodian' cups and what looks like a Corinthian kotyle or an East Greek imitation thereof (9. 19; *SCE*, ii, pl. xv, fifth row from top, sixth from l.). This is, to judge from a photograph, of a type not current before the middle of the seventh century. There are also Cypriot aryballoi of a type common in Crete (cf. *BSA*, xxix. 256).

A number of deposits were made in the grave and not all the objects in it are therefore as late as the scarabs. It must be allowed, however, that the Cypriote vases appear to cover no very long period of time; it is therefore likely that the two 'Rhodian' cups belong to the seventh century and may come well down it. This is not inconsistent with what is known of the late survival of the geometric style in East Greece, however surprising that phenomenon may be on geographical grounds. A seventh-century date for the Cypriote aryballoi involves a lower dating than envisaged by Payne for the Cretan vases which show the influence of this Cypriote style. This agrees with the lower date for Cretan orientalizing proposed by Brock. It has only a vague and indirect effect on the dating of Protocorinthian, by means of the Cretan influence in Early Protocorinthian.

The three scarabs from period 3 at Ajia Irini are dated by the experts to the eighth or early seventh century.[2] These scarabs, as pointed out

---

[1] For commemorative scarabs in Ethiopian graves of the XXVth dynasty cf. F. Ll. Griffith, *LAAA*, x. 110 ff.

[2] 'Scarabs admitting an exact date are almost entirely missing' at Ajia Irini. The only exception, no. 2718, is of Psamtek I (*SCE*, ii. 819). This was found in a stratum of period 6, and is therefore not of great chronological value, as no one would doubt that period 6 is later than the seventh century.

by the Swedish excavators (*SCE*, ii. 818 ff.), give a *terminus post quem*, but what is the terminus? Strictly, it is *c.* 745, the beginning of the Ethiopian dynasty; the scarabs may belong to any time from that date till the early seventh century, the vases associated with them to that period or later. The excavators, if I have understood them correctly, have taken the *lower* bracket as the *terminus post quem*, and conclude that period 3 as a whole belongs to the seventh century. But not all the pottery in this period is necessarily later than the scarabs; the most that can be concluded in strict logic is that the end of the period is later than *c.* 700, the date of the scarabs. Period 4 extends after 663, as it contains XXVIth dynasty scarabs, but does not necessarily begin after 663. The considerable number of XXVth dynasty scarabs[1] suggests that these were not very old when they were deposited at Ajia Irini, and may be contemporary with some of the pottery of that period; which is therefore not all later than 663. The excavators rightly point out that the scarabs of earlier date present are of less value for dating, and that the latest scarabs in each level provide the most reliable material; but this caution can be over-driven. The scarabs, strictly speaking, provide only a *terminus post quem*, and their long life makes them of uncertain value as contemporary evidence. Agreed; but in estimating the period of a given stratum of occupation all the material in it is relevant, and we should not confine ourselves to the latest objects.

The end of Cypro-Geometric III and beginning of Cypro-Archaic I fall within period 3. This may therefore be placed *c.* 700, which is a mean date; the evidence of the scarabs would not formally contradict an even higher date. This has no direct bearing on Protocorinthian chronology, but it is possible to get an indirect line through comparing the development of other late geometric and early orientalizing fabrics with Cypriot, and through tracing Cypriot influence, particularly in Crete. The results of this inquiry will not upset the accepted chronology of Protocorinthian, if the transition between Cypriot Geometric and Archaic is placed *c.* 700.

The evidence from Perachora is twofold. In the geometric deposit of Hera Akraia, the latest vases of which are contemporary with the oldest found in the western colonies, were found three scarabs assigned by Pendlebury to the XXVIth dynasty.[2] This, like the presence at Sparta of scarabs assigned by Pendlebury to the XXVIth dynasty with geometric and Laconian I pottery, presents a serious difficulty. It cannot be resolved in either case by assuming that the scarabs are intrusive in the geometric strata. Either the scarabs are earlier than the XXVIth dynasty, or the late Corinthian and Laconian geometric styles, instead

[1] Of a total of 141 scarabs in level 4, 12 are New Kingdom or older, 3 are dated 1000–800, 7 are Ethiopian, 30 Saite, 12 uncertain, perhaps pre-Saite, and the rest undatable. I follow Pieper's dates given in Appendix II to *SCE*, ii, as he has attempted to date more scarabs than Newberry in Appendix I.

[2] *Perachora*, i. 76–7.

of ending in the third quarter of the eighth century, must come down a hundred years later. In *Perachora*, i. 76–7, Pendlebury and I stated the two sides of the case. In view of the bad condition of the Perachora, and also the Sparta, scarabs, I prefer to ask the Egyptologists to reconsider whether these scarabs cannot belong to an earlier period.

In the temenos of Hera Limenia at Perachora a large number of Egyptian objects were stratified in association with Protocorinthian and Corinthian sherds, that is, in Greek seventh-century contexts. Most of these are of the XXVIth dynasty but there are also a number belonging to the XXVth dynasty, including two with the royal name Menkara, dated by Pendlebury to the end of the eighth century. One of these comes from the lowest levels of the temenos, with Protocorinthian and Corinthian pottery. This causes no difficulty for Payne's Protocorinthian chronology.

To sum up, the only Egyptian associations which cause difficulty for the accepted chronology of Protocorinthian are the ill-preserved scarabs from the geometric deposit at Perachora. The other evidence of Tarquinia, Knossos, Hera Limenia at Perachora and Cyprus sorts well enough, but owing to the unprecise nature of many of the associations and the difficulty of getting exact dates for the Egyptian objects little is gained. It may seem unscientific to accept the evidence of these sites and reject that of Perachora and Sparta. The alternative is the radical one of reducing all our Greek dates by a hundred years. There are those to whom this will appeal. But I feel that before throwing over a consistent and coherent Greek chronology we need more firmly rooted evidence than that of the Perachora scarabs.

Other fabrics, especially Cypriote and Cretan, are more affected by the Egyptian evidence than Protocorinthian. Through them it may be possible to get a closer dating for the early stages of Protocorinthian and Protoattic. But as far as I can see this will not entail lowering the accepted dates to such a point that the new chronology reacts on the traditional dates for the colonies.

The Cypriote evidence is only partly published, and further discussion is promised in the fourth volume of the *Swedish Cyprus Expedition*.[1] Daniels also finds reason in Cypriote associations with both east and west to propose a new low chronology. Only a summary of his paper has been published,[2] and it is therefore not possible now to discuss his arguments. It appears that his chronology will agree with R. S. Young's Protoattic chronology; that is based on Payne's dating of Protocorinthian, and though it tends to shade those dates downwards, does not call for any serious modification of them. It may be taken therefore that there is no new evidence at present available to compel a revision of Payne's chronology. This was Payne's conclusion ten years ago,

---

[1] Cf. Furumark, *Op. Arch.* iii. 260, n. 7.
[2] *AJA*, 1939, 300; cf. his review of R. S. Young's *Late Geometric Graves* in *AJA*, 1940, 159–61.

H h

when he wrote 'that the dating of the Sicilian foundations is correct seems to me sufficiently certain, and I shall therefore assume throughout that the latest period of the geometric style, the style represented in the earliest Syracusan graves, is the third quarter of the eighth century',[1] and this appears still to apply.

Payne's chronology is indeed appreciably lower than Johansen's, but the latter's is not very precise and I infer from the manner of his discussion of absolute chronology that he would not wish to insist too closely on the date c. 725 for the transition from the globular to the ovoid aryballos. This date, given in his table on p. 185, is not demanded by his arguments on the preceding pages, where he repeatedly puts the transition 'towards the end of the eighth century' or 'at the end of the eighth century', and assigns the majority of ovoid aryballoi to the seventh century. It does not do violence to his arguments to prefer a date c. 700 for the transition, and to place most of his subgeometric style in the seventh century. This modification (cf. Payne's chronological table, *Protokorinthische Vasenmalerei*, 20) does not involve the rejection of the traditional dates for the colonies. Indeed, it fits some of them better (e.g. Gela, where the earliest vases are intermediate between the globular and ovoid aryballoi).

VII. ÅKERSTRÖM'S CHRONOLOGY

One radical rehandling of the whole question remains to be considered. Åkerström in his *Der Geometrische Stil in Italien* proposes a dating for the earliest Greek vases from the colonies which, if acceptable, would entail reducing their foundation dates by about half a century. The main part of Åkerström's book is concerned with the geometric vases found in Etruria, and his principal arguments are drawn from Etruria. We are more directly concerned here with the geometric vases found in Sicily; but the two problems are indissolubly connected.

Åkerström takes his stand for his *Sicilian* chronology on Finocchito, and on the following points:

(i) comparison of the oinochoai and other vases with metope-decoration with geometric and sub-geometric examples found in Greece;

(ii) comparison of the general contents (especially fibulas) of Finocchito with Syracuse;

(iii) comparison of vases, fibulas, and other bronze objects with Etruscan finds.

The latter series of comparisons can be held over until Etruscan chronology is itself better settled; they will help rather to date a series of Etruscan graves over which there has been much uncertainty. The comparison of Finocchito with Syracuse leads to the conclusion, already stated by Johansen and Blakeway, that there is a long overlap but

[1] *Perachora*, i. 31 n.

Finocchito begins sensibly earlier. We are brought back to the date of Syracuse and of Protocorinthian pottery, and Åkerström attempts to bring both down to *c*. 675. His main arguments again are based on Etruscan comparisons, his subsidiary arguments on the uncertain nature of the *absolute* date for the foundation of Syracuse and on the dating of sub-geometric pottery at Athens and elsewhere. To take the latter argument first: the chronology of Attic sub-geometric and Protoattic vases is based on associations with Protocorinthian. If the dating of Protocorinthian is to be reduced as radically as Åkerström wishes, the dates of Protoattic must come down too, and then the circular argument must begin all over again. I have attempted to show above that there is no reason either in the development of other contemporary Greek fabrics or in eastern synchronizations to lower Protocorinthian chronology so steeply. So Åkerström's case must stand or fall on the arguments he adduces from Etruria.

The relative chronology of the orientalizing period in Etruria is now fairly well agreed, and the long series of rich graves makes it possible to establish their order with precision. On the other hand, the circumstances in which the graves were excavated make many individual associations untrustworthy.[1] The absolute chronology is less firmly based, though it is commonly given with great confidence. The Bokkhoris grave has now lost much of its value for dating, as it can provide only a *terminus post quem*, not a firm date. The great seventh-century graves are dated by the Protocorinthian vases found in them, as there are fewer grounds on which to put absolute dates to any of the other classes of orientalizing objects which they contain (though relative dates can be given, and these objects, and the grave-groups which contain them, placed in order, with a considerable degree of accuracy). As Etruscan chronology is thus based on Protocorinthian, there is a vicious circle in finding in it arguments for lowering the dates of Protocorinthian.

The central point for Åkerström's Etruscan dating is Bisenzio. The Greek geometric pottery there, as he rightly points out, belongs to the Late Geometric style and is among the earliest Greek pottery in the west. On p. 68 he argues from the likeness of a shield at Bisenzio to others at Marsiliana and Palestrina, found in graves with orientalizing objects, and therefore dates the Bisenzio grave to the seventh century. It seems to me that more evidence is required before bringing down the dating of the geometric vases so sharply. If Bisenzio grave X belonged to the seventh century, it should have had other orientalizing objects in it. The existence of one single point of contact between two complexes so different as the Bisenzio grave-groups and the *Circolo degli Avori* at Marsiliana does not justify regarding them as contemporary or nearly so. In general, bronzes are of less value for dating than pottery, because their chronology is less surely established and because individual

[1] Cf. Åkerström, 75 ff., on the Warrior grave at Tarquinia, which is shown not to be a single grave-group and thereby loses its value as a chronological landmark.

pieces may have had a long life. The shields at Praeneste and Marsiliana, found in very different contexts from the similar one at Bisenzio, may have been old when deposited in the graves. They do not in themselves demand a seventh-century dating.

On Åkerström's own chronology the Greek parallels for the geometric vases at Bisenzio belong to the eighth century (p. 88). He is compelled to assume an intermediate stage, which has disappeared, between the Greek models and the imitations at Bisenzio. But this accords ill with his view that these vases are from the hand of Greek potters resident in Etruria (pp. 62 ff.), who should themselves represent the intermediate stage between Greek model and Italian imitation. He frequently dates vases found in Italy too low *vis-à-vis* Greek parallels by failing to distinguish Greek imports from local geometric vases. He is inclined to regard most of the geometric vases found in Italy and Sicily as of local manufacture, though he recognizes the existence of Greek potters on Italian soil. The distinction, on grounds of fabric, is not difficult, and I believe that there are many more imports than Åkerström allows.[1] The distinction is very important, because we need to know whether Greek craftsmen were active in Sicily and Italy working primarily for the barbarian market. For chronological purposes, it should be less important, as the existence on Italian soil of imitations of Greek vases implies the existence there of Greek models, or else of Greek potters, and in either case the imitations will be dated not much later than the classes of vase which they imitate. Åkerström, however, gives chronological significance to the distinction, for in deriving Sicilian geometric, for example, from the Greek sub-geometric style whose beginnings he puts in the period 725–700 he concludes that the Sicilian vases cannot be earlier than 700. But if many of them are imported from Greece, there is no reason to lower their dates below 700 (accepting for the moment Åkerström's dates for sub-geometric in Greece). Similarly in Etruria he dates to 700–675 vases whose parallels in Greece are dated by him 750–700. We are not here concerned with those easily recognizable cases in which Greek elements survived in a local style long after they had gone out of date in Greece, but with vases of which it is not easy to say whether they were manufactured in Greece or Italy. Therefore they should be dated not substantially later than their parallels in Greece.

Åkerström's main argument, if I do not misrepresent him, is that too long a period must not be allowed between the earliest geometric vases in Etruria and the securely datable seventh-century graves, both on the ground of the development of the geometric style, and also because similar bronzes and jewellery are found with both. Therefore, preserving the temporal relation of these geometric vases to Protocorinthian, the

---

[1] In his reluctance to distinguish Greek import, Greek manufacture in Italy, and local imitation Åkerström is retrogressive, as compared with Blakeway; for though Blakeway may on occasion have put individual vases into the wrong class, he was surely right to attempt a complete classification on grounds of fabric.

dates of Protocorinthian must be lowered. But in that case the dates of the seventh-century graves, in which Protocorinthian vases are found, will also come down. Alternatively, the development of Protocorinthian must be ignored and geometric vases dated only a few years earlier than developed Middle Protocorinthian. Åkerström remarks that it is surprising that Protocorinthian should appear in Sicily so much earlier than in Etruria, and finds in this another argument to lower the date of the earliest Protocorinthian from Syracuse to 675 (pp. 32 ff.). This does not solve his difficulty. For there is a class of Protocorinthian vases— the whole period of the globular aryballoi—which is unrepresented, or, rather, poorly represented, in Etruria. By lowering the dates one can shorten the interval between Syracuse and the Regolini–Galassi tomb (for Protocorinthian only becomes common in Etruria from this time onwards), but the interval is still present, being in the nature of the finds and not in the chronological system of this or that modern archaeologist. The answer is given by Blakeway, though Åkerström's dislike for Blakeway's high chronology has deflected him from a sufficiently close study of his matter: that at the period of the colonizations Corinth was only one among a number of Greek states trading with the west, and except in the neighbourhood of her own colony Syracuse was not the chief; whereas in the course of the early seventh century she achieved a monopoly. At the time when the earliest Protocorinthian vases were imported to Syracuse and Kyme, other Greek wares were more common in Etruria (cf., for example, the Warrior grave at Tarquinia).

Åkerström throws out in a couple of pages his revolutionary dating for Protocorinthian; it is not unfair to say that he has not considered the consequences, not only for Greek but also for Etruscan seventh-century chronology. That it involves the Greek archaeologist in immediate difficulties and does not accord with his accepted ideas is no reason for rejecting it out of hand; far less, that it involves the rejection of Thukydides' dates for the western colonies. But it is a fair criticism to require a more solid basis for such a new dating than is provided by Etruscan chronology, which is closely bound up with Greek chronology and is, to say the least, no more firmly established. From the east, and only from the east, can we get absolutely firm associations which may provide for Greek archaeology a more accurate chronology than is obtained from the traditional dates for the western colonies.

This brief discussion does not do justice to the many merits of Åkerström's book, which reduces to order the geometric and sub-geometric vases found in Italy and Sicily and for the first time deals systematically with the bronzes and other small finds associated with them. On *relative* chronology I have little reason to differ from him; he agrees that south Etruria was open to Greek influence before Sicily, and that colonization was preceded by a short period of trade.[1] This after all is of more impor-

---

[1] The other recent exponent of a low chronology, Byvanck, also allows pre-colonization imports (op. cit. 200).

tance than absolute chronology, affecting as it does our whole judgement on the nature of western colonization. Åkerström's radical lowering of dates involves difficulties in the middle of the seventh century,
assuming far too rapid a development for early orientalizing art. But
within the period under discussion he is consistent, and the question
whether certain geometric or sub-geometric vases were made before or
after 700 is less important than the question whether or not they are
older than the oldest finds from the Greek colonies.

VIII. CONCLUSIONS

My conclusions are:

i. There existed in antiquity a single chronological system for the
foundation-dates of the western colonies. This is preserved in Thukydides for the Sicilian colonies and followed in the main by Eusebius for
the Sicilian and some Italian colonies. Variants in Ephoros, in Eusebius,
and in other sources are due to faulty transmission or unchronological
anecdote.

ii. Attempts to show that this chronology was drawn up in the fifth
century from a calculation of generations break down on the Thukydidean figures for Gela and Akragas, which cannot be satisfactorily thus
explained.

iii. There is no reason why the colonies should not from their foundation have kept written or other records, and in a number of cases the
era of a colony appears to have been preserved.

iv. The archaeological evidence strongly confirms the relative order
of the colonies according to the historical tradition. The oldest vases
from seven colonies, which may be taken as belonging approximately
to the period shortly after their foundation, are on grounds of style and
shape to be ranged in the same order as given in Eusebius for the
colonies. This supports though it does not prove the absolute validity
of the foundation dates.

v. The absolute chronology of Protocorinthian vase-painting and of
other Greek fabrics of the same period is based on the absolute dates of
the western colonies. This chronology is not inconsistent with Egyptian
material and attempts to establish a lower chronology are not cogent.

This is not the last word on the subject. The conclusions are not all
equally solid. It is established that the accepted tradition of the foundation of the colonies, found in Thukydides and Antiokhos and in the
main followed by later sources, contains a great deal that is historical
and substantially accurate. I do not find that the inconsistencies within
this tradition are of such a nature as to cast doubt on its reliability. The
relative order of the foundations may be taken as established, with a few
doubtful points, and the chronological relation between the Protocorinthian pottery found in the colonies and the foundation dates is also firm.

Thus, it can no longer be questioned that trade preceded colonization and that the earliest colonies were also the most distant. In converting this firm relative chronology into absolute dates there is inevitably an element of uncertainty. I have attempted to show that the traditional dates may be derived from reliable written records, and that such records are likely to have been kept in the colonies; and that they are within a certain narrow range accurate. It is still possible that more reliable chronological data for Greek eighth- and seventh-century archaeology (though hardly directly for history) will be obtained in the Near East, and that the now accepted chronology, based on the foundation dates of the colonies, will be confirmed or modified. Until such evidence is forthcoming, I believe that the accepted chronology is substantially reliable, and that the foundation dates for the colonies are accurate not only relatively (which cannot be questioned) but also absolutely.

RHODIAN AND EAST GREEK IMPORTS[1]

A. RHODIAN

Gela

1–5. Bitalemi.	*MA*, xvii, figs. 407–8.	Five fragments of plates. Fig. 408 is possibly of the first half of the seventh century, the others all late in the century.
6. ,,	Ibid., fig. 406.	Flask.
7. ,,	Ibid., fig. 414.	Cup fragment; cf. Price, *JHS*, 1924, 187, fig. 10.
8. ,,	Ibid., figs. 454–6.	Kamiran B oinochoe.
9. Borgo 374.	Ibid., fig. 128.	Plate. With Transitional Corinthian.
10. ,, 132.	Ibid., figs. 57–8.	Fragments of large vase. With unfigured Corinthian, probably Early.
11. Sporadic.	Ibid., fig. 188.	Dinos, in Palermo.
12. ,,	Ibid., fig. 186.	Bird-bowl.
13. ,,	Ibid., fig. 187.	Dinos fragment with goose.
14. ,,	Ibid., figs. 185 and 185 *bis*.	Plate fragments.
15–16. Tempio arcaico.	Unpublished.[2]	Two geometric fragments, one with tongues in metope, one with herring-bone. Bright-red clay, imperfectly baked, and remaining red inside; in section exactly like no. 37 below.
17. ,,	,,	Plate, lion's paw r., above exergue line.
18–21. ,,	,,	Four fragments of plates, one of third quarter of seventh century, others of last quarter or early sixth.
22–4. ,,	,,	Three small fragments of large vases, with volutes.

[1] The dating of these vases given here and above in Chapter VIII does not always agree with the systems of chronology recently proposed. In particular, I am unable to follow Rumpf's classification in *JdI*, 1933, 55 ff., where many of these vases are cited. I am unfortunately unable to illustrate the vases in question, desirable as this is. I hope to do this at a later date, and to draw the conclusions for the general chronology of Rhodian vase-painting to be obtained from their associations in Sicilian graves. This evidence has until now been completely neglected.

[2] This deposit is mentioned *MA*, xix. 89; *N Sc*, 1907, 38 f.

25. Tempio arcaico.	Unpublished.	Fragment of oinochoe (?), lion and goat facing; third quarter of seventh century.

This is all the painted pottery at Gela. Most of it belongs to the last quarter of the seventh century. Four pieces (nos. 1, 12, 15, 16) are possibly before the middle of the century, a few more are of the third quarter, mainly towards its end. Some pieces may belong to the early sixth century.

Syracuse

26. Piazza d'Armi.		*N Sc*, 1925, 319.	Bird-bowl. Context eighth–early seventh century; see above, p. 51.
27–9. Athenaion.		*MA*, xxv, fig. 82.	Bird-bowl and fragments of two others. From Cortile Arcivescovado, in stratum with Protocorinthian but no Corinthian.
30.	,,	Ibid., fig. 113.	Rhodian, cf. Payne, *JHS*, 1926, 211, n. 32. *c.* 700?
31–2.	,,	Ibid., fig. 110, l., lower (same date?) and third piece from l., lower.	
33.	,,	Ibid., fig. 117, left.	*c.* 650?
34.	,,	Ibid., fig. 118.	Bird-bowl.
35.	,,	Ibid., fig. 114.	Fragment of plate.
36.	,,	Ibid., pl. XII, fig. 119.	Oinochoe, Kamiran B; incision on animals.
37.	,,	Ibid., fig. 120.	Oinochoe.
38–44.	,,	Ibid., fig. 115 (except piece to l., lower).	
45.	,,	Ibid., fig. 121, right.	
46.	,,	Ibid., fig. 117, top right.	
47.	,,	..	Fragments of plates not illustrated, about half a dozen.
48. Piazza S. Giuseppe.		*N Sc*, 1925, 317, figs. 70–1.	Dinos.
49.	,,	Ibid., fig. 72.	Fragment of lip of another dinos, perhaps not Rhodian but of an allied East Greek fabric.
50. Uncertain.		Johansen, *VS*, 176, figs. 122–3.	Berlin 3360. Rhodian (?) imitation of ovoid aryballos. Third quarter of seventh century.

51–2. Fusco 200.	*N Sc*, 1895, 131.	Two black kylikes with white bands (cf. Price, *JHS*, 1924, 189).
53. „ 29.	*N Sc*, 1893, 458, fig.	Cf. Rumpf, *JdI*, 1933, 62, n. o, 'Verwilderte Stücke'. With Late Protocorinthian (Johansen, *VS*, 105; Payne, *NC*, 26).
54. Ex-Spagna 72.	*N Sc*, 1925, 202, fig. 37.	Bird-bowl. With Late Protocorinthian—Transitional.
55. Fusco.	*Ann. dell' Inst.* 1877, pl. CD. 5.	Bird-bowl. This or another bird-bowl wrongly exhibited in Syracuse Mus. as from grave Fusco 341.
56. Ex-Spagna 1.	*N Sc*, 1925, 182, fig. 5 *bis*.	Plate. Grave a little before 600.
57. „ 113.	Ibid. 297, fig. 47.	Dish. With Late Corinthian kotylai, probably of middle of sixth century.
58. „ sporadic.	Ibid. 306, fig. 62.	Two fragments, (*a*) running goats; (*b*) three small pieces of meander.

Other sites

59. Megara 820.	*N Sc*, 1893, 464, n.; *MA*, xxv. 538.	Bottle.[1] With Late Corinthian.
60. Ossini (Militello).	*RM*, 1909, 83, fig. 16.	Plate.
61–73. Selinus.	*MA*, xxxii. 308, pll. 81, 82, 83. 2 and 5; 84. 1 and 2; 89. 3 and 6.	About as much again is not illustrated.

Italy

74–7. Rhegion.	*N Sc*, 1914, 209, figs. 1–2.	Bird-bowl and three fragments of Kamiran B.

No other south Italian site has produced Rhodian. Dr. Randall-MacIver's statement (*Greek Cities*, 77) that there is Rhodian painted pottery at Taranto is false.

For Rhodian from Rome (Comitium) see *N Sc*, 1900, 332, fig. 35; Ryberg, *An Archaeological Record of Rome*, 8. Cf. *MA*, iv. 273, fig. 131, from Narce.

B. OTHER EAST GREEK

Chiot

Selinus.	*MA*, xxxii, pl. 83. 4.	Another fragment unillustrated. Price, *East Greek Pottery*, 16, speaks of 'Naukratite' at Syracuse. See below.

---

[1] For the shape, unique in Rhodian and borrowed from Corinthian models, see K. Friis Johansen, *Act. Arch.* xiii, 1942, 29.

An uncertain fabric

Syracuse, Athenaion.	*MA*, xxv, fig. 117, lower.	Fragment in Syracuse Museum labelled Naukratite. One other fragment.
Gela, Tempio arcaico.		Fragment with goats.

These four fragments belong to an easily distinguishable fabric, with light-brown clay, white slip (which on the sherd labelled Naukratite has flaked) and very neat, clear drawing in a paint which varies from a light to a dark brown. The slip is like that on Naukratite (Chiot), which has caused some of these fragments to be called Naukratite. The drawing is more like early Samian orientalizing. I like to think of these pieces as Milesian.

Fikellura (cf. R. M. Cook, *BSA*, xxxiv. 1 ff.)

Syracuse, ex-Spagna 36.	*N Sc*, 1925, 192, fig. 20; Cook, p. 47, Y 7.	Amphoriskos. With two Ionic krateriskoi and Late Corinthian.
Ceglie di Bari.		Oinochoe, in Taranto Museum. Early fifth century? (Dr. Drago was kind enough to call my attention to this vase.)

Uncertain

Syracuse, Fusco 65.	*N Sc*, 1893, 463; *CVA Siracusa*, i, pl. 3. 3; *BCH*, 1936, pll. 15–16.	Amphora. Late Rhodian, or imitation thereof? Cf. Orsi, *N Sc*, 1893, 464, n.
,, ,, 19.	*N Sc*, 1893, 454; *CVA Siracusa*, i, pl. 3. 2; *BCH*, 1936, pl. 14. 1.	Krater.
Gela, Borgo 476.	*MA*, xvii, fig. 155.	Bottle. Pale clay, dull surface, and matt purplish paint.
Syracuse, Agora.	*N Sc*, 1891, 391–2.	Fragment of large vase with rosette in metope; another with small concentric circles. With Protocorinthian kotylai and Late Protocorinthian pyxis.
Gela, sporadic.	*MA*, xix. 95, fig. 1.	Patera. Perhaps local imitation of Cycladic.
Syracuse, Fusco 378.	*N Sc*, 1895, 159, fig. 45; *CVA Siracusa* i, pl. 3. 1; *BCH*, 1936, pl. 14. 2.	Krater. Cycladic? From an eighth–seventh-century grave, with Early Protocorinthian.

Melian

Selinus.	*MA*, xxxii, pll. 69–71.	Signed amphora.

C. PLAIN POTTERY

See Orsi, *MA*, xvii. 676; Kinch, *Vroulia*, 40, n. 1, on similarity of amphora shapes.

Amphora. Gela, Borgo 372.   *MA*, xvii, fig. 127. Cf. Ialysos V (*Ann*. vi–vii. 265).

Hydria.   ,,   ,,   160.   Ibid., fig. 72. Cf. Ialysos XIV (*Ann*. vi–vii. 268).

Askos.   ,,   ,,   157.   Ibid., fig. 69.

,,   ,,   ,,   181.   Ibid., fig. 80 (with Transitional Corinthian).

,,   ,, La Paglia 1.   Ibid., fig. 166 (with Early Corinthian; several burials).

Rumpf, *JdI*, 1933, 76. Cf. *Délos*, x, nos. 83 ff., pl. 16; xvii, pl. 47, no. 43, &c.

Olpe.   ,,   Bitalemi.   Ibid. 667, fig. 488. Cf. Ialysos XVIII. 2 (*Ann*. vi–vii. 270, fig. 170); Ialysos XXV. 4 (ibid. 281); Kamiros CXLIV (*Clara Rhodos*, iv, fig. 302); Lindos 2565, pl. 123; Samos, *AM*, 1929, 31, fig. 23. 4.

Jug, unglazed, banded.   Ibid., fig. 486. Cf. Kamiros VI. 12 (*Clara Rhodos*, iv. 62, fig. 34); Vroulia, pl. 26. 14; &c.

,,   ,,   ,,   Ibid., fig. 487. 1. Shape derived from a jug like ibid., fig. 486.

Oinochoe, banded. Gela, Borgo 153.   Ibid., fig. 67. Cf. Samos, Boehlau, pl. 8. 15.

Oinochoe, banded. Gela, Borgo 81.   Ibid., fig. 34 (with a Middle Corinthian kothon). Shape derived from a pot like Ialysos XXIII. 8 (*Ann*. vi–vii, fig. 178).

Stamnos, wavy line. Gela, Borgo 459.   Ibid., fig. 151. Cf. Ialysos CLXXXIX Jacopi (*Clara Rhodos*, iii. 198, pl. 3); Kamiros C. 2 (*Clara Rhodos*, iv. 199, fig. 213).

Cups. Syracuse, ex-Spagna 1.   *N Sc*, 1925, 182, fig. 6. Rhodian, cf. Payne, *NC*, 310; Price, *JHS*, 1924, 182.

Similar cups are common at Megara and Gela (e.g. La Paglia 1, Borgo 124, *MA*, xvii, fig. 46).

Lekythos. Gela, Borgo 60.

,,   ,,   ,,   76.   *MA*, xvii, fig. 30.

,,   ,, Bitalemi.   Ibid., figs. 504–5.

Cf. Ialysos LIII (*Ann*. vi–vii. 306, fig. 203) Kamiros CCV. 5 (*Clara Rhodos*, iv. 359, fig. 399).

,,   ;, Borgo 164.   Ibid., fig. 73.

,,   ,, La Paglia 1.   Ibid., fig. 168.   } Cf. Kamiros CCV. 4 (ibid.).

,,   ,, Borgo 86.   Ibid., fig. 37 (inscription on neck).

,,   ,,   ,, 285.   Ibid., fig. 105.

,,   ,, Lauricella 14.   (Third quarter of sixth century.)

Cf. Ialysos I. 6 (*Ann*. vi–vii. 261, fig. 162) for shape and inscr. For shape, Samos, Boehlau, pl. 7. 8. For inscr. Kamiros CLX (*Clara Rhodos*, iv. 282). This kind of lekythos especially favoured for graffito on neck.

See *MA* xvii. 246 on this shape (so-called Samian lekythos). This is a common East Greek shape, not essentially different from one current in the Early Iron Age at Lachish.

Lekythos. Gela, Bitalemi.	Ibid., fig. 503. ⎤
,, Syracuse, ex-Spagna 94.	⎟ Cf. Kamiros CLXXV. 2 (*Clara*
,, Syracuse, ex-Spagna 151.	⎬ *Rhodos*, iv. 305, fig. 340) ; Samos, Boehlau, pl. 7. 3. ⎦
Loop ∞ on neck of hydria Borgo 160 above.	Cf. amphoras Gela, Bitalemi, *MA*, xvii, figs. 483, 484, and on Ialysos XXV. 1 (*Ann.* vi–vii. 281, fig. 180) ; Ialysos XXXVI (ibid. 290, fig. 186) ; Kamiros LXXII. 3 (*Clara Rhodos*, iv. 170, fig. 174) : trade-mark of a Rhodian workshop?
Olpe. Gela, Borgo 157.	*MA*, xvii, fig. 69. Pinkish clay, like the clay of the plain pottery found in Rhodes. The hydria, Gela, Bitalemi, ibid., fig. 398, and amphora, ibid., fig. 480, are of similar clay. Cf. Ialysos, *Ann.* vi–vii, fig. 183 ; Kamiros XCVIII. 1 (*Clara Rhodos*, iv, fig. 211) ; &c.

This list is by no means complete. I have chosen only representatives of common types, and examples from Rhodes might be multiplied many times.

D. IONIAN RED-GROUND VASES

(Price, *Classification*, IIA)

Krateriskos. Gela, Borgo 203.	Payne, *NC*, 323, s. no. 1327, with Late Corinthian.
Krateriskos. Gela, Borgo 262.	Ibid., s. no. 1332, with Late Corinthian ; 'several burials, none much earlier than 550 B.C.'
Krateriskoi. Syracuse, ex-Spagna 30 and 36.	
Krateriskos. Akragas.	Copenhagen, private coll.; Breitenstein, *Acta Archaeologica*, xvi. 143, fig. 65.
,, Gela, in Palermo Museum, unpublished. Lydian shape, larger than usual.	
Also at Megara.	
Amphora. Gela, Borgo 342.	Cf. Kamiros CIX. 14 (*Clara Rhodos*, iv. 220), grave of *c.* 520.
Cup. Gela, Bitalemi.	*MA*, xvii, fig. 501.
Kylix, reserved band. Gela, Bitalemi.	Ibid. 642, fig. 461. Cf., for example, Ialysos LIII. 6 Jacopi (*Clara Rhodos*, iii. 89, pl. 1), with Early–Middle Corinthian ; Boehlau, pl. 8.
Kylix. Syracuse, ex-Spagna 13.	
Kylix. Syracuse, ex-Spagna 104.	
Kylix. Syracuse, ex-Spagna 113.	

Kylix. Akragas. Copenhagen, private coll.; Breitenstein, op. cit. 143.

Amphoriskos. Syracuse, Fusco 498 *bis*.

Amphoriskos. Syracuse, ex-Spagna 30.

Plate, moulded edge. Gela, Bitalemi. *MA*, xvii, fig. 494. Cf. ibid., fig. 466.

Plate, Gela, Bitalemi. Ibid., figs. 495, 499.

,, b.f. design. Gela, Bitalemi. Ibid., fig. 496.

Dish with foot, Gela, Bitalemi. Ibid., fig. 500. Cf. Boehlau, pl. 8. 3.

Kylikes, b.f. Syracuse, Fusco 3. *N Sc*, 1891, 406. These are the only figured vases of this class found in Sicily.

I have omitted all but a few of the black-glazed kylikes with reserved band, which are especially common on native sites (from near Taranto, in Taranto Museum and in Bari, e.g. Gervasio, *Bronzi e Vasi*, pl. XIII. 4, 6, 8, from Noicattaro in the Heraian hills, e.g. Orsi, *RM*, 1898, 337, fig. 52) because I am not confident that most of them are not Attic. There is, however, certainly more of this unimportant East Greek pottery from these areas than here recorded.

E. TERRA-COTTAS

Rhodian figurine alabastra

1. As Maximova, *Les Vases plastiques*, fig. 63.
   Selinus. Not illustrated in *MA*, xxxii.
   Gela. Sporadic: *MA*, xvii. 265, fig. 201.
   Sicily. *CVA Scheurleer*, pl. 9. 1.

   Janiform.
   Selinus. *MA*, xxxii, pl. 38. 5.
   Eryx (?). Albizzati, *Antike Plastik*, 1 ff.; *Bull. Metr. Mus.* 1930, 242 ff.; cf. Webster, *Ant. Journ.* 1936, 141.

2. As Maximova, op. cit., fig. 64, (cf. Winter, *Typen*, 41, no. 2).
   Gela, Borgo 64. *MA*, xvii. 52, fig. 25.
   ,, Bitalemi. Ibid. 705, fig. 528.
   Selinus. *MA*, xxxii. 210 ff., pl. 38. Cf. *N Sc*, 1894, 208.
   ,, grave 24 (1889). With Late Corinthian vases.
   Akragas. *Agrigento Arcaica*, pl. 15. 9, figs. 33–4.
   Syracuse, Achradina. *N Sc*, 1893, 128.
   ,, Fusco 275. *N Sc*, 1895, 144. With Late Corinthian pyxis. Cf. Mingazzini, *Vasi Castellani*, 99.

   Orsi says (loc. cit., n. 1) 'codesti alabastra sono rarissimi a Siracusa (un solo esemplare da oltre 500 sep.) ed a Megara (uno solo da circa 1000 sep.), mentre sono frequentissimi a Selinunte'. Cf. *MA*, xvii. 265, n. 1, for the contrast with Gela; *MA*, xxv. 745, for the rarity of East Greek terra-cottas at the Athenaion of Syracuse.

Syracuse, ex-Spagna 146, unpublished. Two figurine alabastra, two Samo-Milesian seated figures, with Corinthian kotyle as *NC*, fig. 150.

Megara 16.   *MA*, i. 805.

Lokroi.   *CVA Scheurleer*, pl. 9. 3; Buschor, *Alt-Samische Standbilder*, fig. 121. Ibid., p. 34, Buschor regards this and fig. 122, from Rhodes, as 'vielleicht echtsamische'. Webster, *Ant. Journ.* 1936, 140 (see pl. 24. 2), calls it Rhodian, I believe rightly, and puts it in its place in a long series.

Western Sicily.   *Bull. Metr. Mus.* 1935, 178.

Sicily.   Berlin 1299.

I observed only one figurine-alabastron at Taranto, no. 2278.

3. *Seated statuettes with polos*

Gela, Bitalemi.   *MA*, xvii. 710, fig. 535.

   ,,   Tempio arcaico.

Syracuse, ex-Spagna 146. (See above.)

   ,,   Athenaion.   *MA*, xxv. 565.

Megara.   *MA*, i, pl. 7. 3.

Selinus.   *MA*, xxxii, pl. 39. 1–3, 5, 8, 9, 10.

   ,,   (probably).   *Bull. Metr. Mus.* 1934, 126; 1935, 178.

One only at Taras, from a grave of *c.* 580–570.

4. *Masks*

Selinus.   *MA*, xxxii, pl. 39. 6; 40. 1, 6, 9; see ibid. 218.

Akragas.   *Agrigento*, 174.

Syracuse, Athenaion.   *MA*, xxv, fig. 152.

Megara.   *MA*, i. 935 (mostly local copies); Pace, *Arte ed Artisti*, 524, figs. 32–3.

5. *Various*

   Male figures:

Selinus.   *MA*, xxxii, pl. 41. 2, 4, 6, 8, 9.

   Sirens:

Gela, Borgo 60.   *MA*, xvii. 50, fig. 23. ⎤

   ,,   Bitalemi.   Ibid., figs. 544–5.   ⎥ Cf., for example, Ialysos

Syracuse.   Kekule, fig. 63.   ⎬   XXXVI. 29 (*Ann.* vi–

Selinus.   *MA*, xxxii, pl. 38. 6. ⎦   vii, fig. 194).

   Attenuated bird-vases:

Gela, Borgo 165.   *MA*, xvii, fig. 74. ⎤ Cf. Ialysos XXXVI. 30–41

   ,,   Bitalemi.   Ibid., fig. 543.   ⎬ (ibid., fig. 195); Boehlau, ⎦   pl. 6. 7.

   Bird protecting chickens under wing:

Gela, Bitalemi.   Ibid., fig. 546. ⎤

Kamarina.   *MA*, xvii. 716. ⎦ Cf. Ialysos LXXIII (ibid. 326).

These lists offer only a representative collection of types, and from the very great number available I have quoted only the best published examples, or those which for distribution or chronology have especial value.

ATTIC VASES IN SICILY AND SOUTH ITALY, 600–530 B.C.

(For earlier imports see p. 240)

Syracuse

7th cent.	Amphora, SOS.	N Sc, 1895, 131, fig. 9; cf. Dohan, Italic Tomb-Groups, 101.
600–550.	Kotylai, Swan group.	Ann.d.Ist. 1877, pl. CD. 4; Beazley, Hesperia, 1944, 55 and CVA Oxford, ii. 103.
	Siana cup, C group.	Syracuse 6028. Metr. Mus. Stud. v. 108, no. 41.
	BP cup, Siana-like stem.	N Sc, 1893, 460; JHS, 1932, 191.
550–525.	Droop cup.	N Sc, 1893, 466; Ure, JHS, 1932, 60, no. 29.
	Three Cassel cups.	JHS, 1932, 192; one, N Sc, 1891, 404.

Megara

600–550.	Lidded lekane, Swan group.	Syracuse 3025. Hesperia, 1944, 56.
	Comast cup, KY painter.	MA, xix. 96, fig. 5; NC, 194, no. 18; Hesperia, 1944, 48, no. 14.
	Amphoriskos, SOS.	Beazley, Raccolta Guglielmi, 51.
	Similar, plain.	Syracuse 7623. Ibid.

Akrai

580–570.	Comast cup, Palazzolo painter.	Benndorf, Gr. und Sic. VB, pl. 43. 1; NC, 194, no. 19; Hesperia, 1944, 49, no. 1.
	Siana cup (C group?).	Palazzolo 2574 (J. D. Beazley).

Monte Casale

575–550.	Siana cup, C group.	Syracuse 49271. Metr. Mus. Stud. v. 108, no. 30.

Licodia

575–550.	Siana cup, after C group.	Syracuse 29617. Haspels, ABL, 35.

Gela

600–550.	SOS amphora.	MA, xvii. 210, fig. 165. Associated material is of first half of sixth century.
	Lidded lekane, Swan group.	Hesperia, 1944, 56.
	Comast cup, manner of KX painter.	MA. xix. 96, fig. 4; NC, 194, no. 9; Hesperia, 1944, 46, no. 2.
	Cup with lid.	Leipzig. JdI, 1896, 178, no. 5; 1903, 132, no. 12, fig. 6 and pl. 9; MA, xvii. 431, fig. 309; Rumpf, Sakonides, no. 38.
	Fragments (of krater?).	MA, xvii, figs. 189–90.

Gela

600–550 (cont.).	Siana cup, C group.	Syracuse 25418. *MA*, xix. 96, fig. 7; *Metr. Mus. Stud.* v. 104, no. 17.
	Krater, Sakonides group.	Oxford 190. *CVA*, ii, pl. 12. 1–4; Rumpf, *Sakonides*, no. 95.
550–525.	Lip-cup, Hermogenes.	Boston 95. 17. *JHS*, 1932, 170, figs. 1–2.
	Lip-cup, Tleson.	Syracuse 43985. *JHS*, 1932, 182.
	Droop cups.	Ure, *JHS*, 1932, 60, no. 36; *MA*, xvii, fig. 459. Syracuse 20442. Ure, op. cit., no. 66, fig. 4.

Akragas

600–550.	Jug, Swan group.	Copenhagen, private coll.; Breitenstein, *Acta Archaeologica*, xvi. 145, fig. 67.
550–525.	Droop cup.	Copenhagen, private coll.; ibid. 146, fig. 68.

Ravanusa

575–550.	Siana cup, late.	*MA*, xxxvi. 669, figs. 26–7.

Selinus

600–550.	Amphoriskos, SOS.	Beazley, *Raccolta Guglielmi*, 51.
	Similar, plain (nine).	Ibid.
	Pyxis-lid, Swan group.	*Hesperia*, 1944, 55.
	Lekane lid, Swan group.	Ibid. 56.
	Siana cups, C group.	*Metr. Mus. Stud.* v. 112, fig. 24, nos. 21, 70, 73.
	,, Heidelberg group.	*JHS*, 1931, 280 ff., nos. 7, 9, 16–21; *MA*, xxxii, pl. 91. 8–9.
	Lid, Sakonides group.	*MA*, xxxii, pl. 93. 4; Rumpf, *Sakonides*, no. 42.
550–525.	Lip-cup, love-name Theognis.	Gàbrici, *Atti R. Acc. Palermo*, xv, figs. 1 and 10; *JHS*, 1932, pl. 6. 2.
	Droop cups.	Ure, *JHS*, 1932, 61, nos. 54–5.

Motye

580–570.	Comast cup, KY painter.	*NC*, 194, no. 5, pl. 51. 4; *Hesperia*, 1944, 47, no. 11.

Taras

600–575.	Horse-head amphora.	Cf. *JHS*, 1929, 254.
	Another similar.	
	Olpe.	*NC*, 193; cf. *JHS*, 1929, 254.
	Lekythos of tall Deianeira shape, black.	Haspels, *ABL*, 4, no. 5.
	Flat-bottomed aryballos of Corinthian shape.	Haspels, *ABL* 3, n. 2.
	Neck-amphora, painter of Dresden lekane.	*NC*, 201; *Hesperia*, 1944, 44, no. 2.

I i

Taras

600–575 (*cont.*).	Amphoriskos, SOS.	Beazley, *Raccolta Guglielmi*, 51.
	Similar, plain.	Ibid.
	Comast cups, Falmouth painter.	*NC*, 194, nos. 15 and 16; *Hesperia*, 1944, 48, nos. 1 and 2.
	Comast cup, KX painter.	New York 22.139.22. *NC*, pl. 51. 6; *Hesperia*, 1944, 46, no. 17.
575–550.	Siana cups, C group.	*Metr. Mus. Stud.* v. 93 ff., nos. 6, 20, 22, 24, 31, 32, 34, 35, 36, 39, 40.
	,,　　C Heidelberg group.	*JHS*, 1931, 275 ff., nos. 10, 22, 25, perhaps no. 2 (figs. 21–4).
	Siana cup, fragment in manner of KX painter.	*Hesperia*, 1944, 46, no. 6.
	Siana cup, uncertain.	Taranto 5844. *Metr. Mus. Stud.* v. 111.
	Hydria (Herakles and Nereus).	Haspels, *ABL*, 8, 35 n. 2.
	Amphora, Lydos.	*JHS*, 1931, 284; Rumpf, *Sakonides*, pl. 25.
550–525.	16 Droop cups (two signed by Antidoros).	Ure, *JHS*, 1932, 57–71.
	Lip-cups and band-cups very frequent.	Ure, 'Αρχ. 'Εφ. 1915, 114 ff.; *AJA*, 1941, 474, figs. 27–30.

Leporano

575–550.	Cup signed by Sakonides.	*N Sc*, 1903, 33 ff.; Rumpf, *Sakonides*, no. 16.
	Amphoriskos.	Villa Giulia 11692. Beazley, *Raccolta Guglielmi*, 51.

Lokroi

600–575.	Hydria, Polos painter.	Naples. *Hesperia*, 1944, 52, no. 22.

Rhegion

600–550.	Kotylai, Swan group, two. Pyxides, Swan group, two. Lekane lid, Swan group.	} *Hesperia*, 1944, 55–6.

Kyme

600–550.	Lekane, Kerameikos painter.	*MA*, xxii. 475, fig. 178; *Hesperia*, 1944, 43, no. 6.
	Amphora, SOS.	*MA*, xiii. 262, fig. 42; Dohan, *Italic Tomb-Groups*, 101.
	Pyxis-lid.	*MA*, xxii, pl. 57.

Siana cups and vases of later period are common.

THE DEINOMENIDS

1. Deinomenes
2. Telines
3. Molossos
4. Deinomenes

Damareta = 5. Gelon   (1) dau. of   = 6. Hieron = (2) dau. of Xenokrates   (1) ? = 7. Polyzalos = (2) Demareta   8. Thrasyboulos
Nikokles of   (3) dau. of Anaxilas
Syracuse

13. Dau. = Theron

9. Dau. = Aristonous   10. Dau. = Khromios

11. Son   12. Deinomenes

1. Deinomenes from Telos, founder of the family, confused in *Lind. Chron.* xxviii and Schol. Pind. *Pyth.* ii. 27*b* with Deinomenes father of Gelon. Came to Gela *c.* 688.

2. Herod. vii. 153. Probably seventh century; son or grandson of 1.

3, 4. *Lind. Chron.* xxviii. Deinomenes' offering is after Phalaris', before Amasis'; therefore *c.* 560–540. Molossos should be third or fourth in descent from Deinomenes 1.

5–10. Gelon's generation; Theron married 13, *c.* 485, so Polyzalos was born at latest *c.* 525, Gelon *c.* 530. 9 and 10 were married *c.* 490.

11. Gelon's son, born *c.* 484, a young man in 466–465.

12. Hieron's son, born *c.* 490, approaching years of discretion in 475.

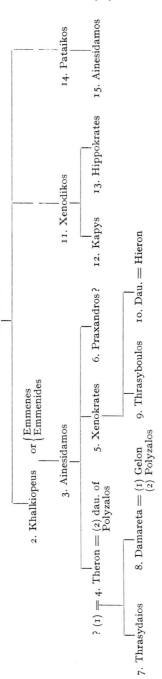

THE EMMENIDS

1. Telemakhos

2. Khalkiopeus or (Emmenes / Emmenides)

3. Ainesidamos   5. Xenokrates   6. Praxandros?   11. Xenodikos

? (1) = 4. Theron = (2) dau. of Polyzalos

7. Thrasydaios   8. Damareta = (1) Gelon / (2) Polyzalos   9. Thrasyboulos   10. Dau. = Hieron

12. Kapys   13. Hippokrates

14. Pataikos   15. Ainesidamos

1. Telemakhos or Emmenes (A only) overthrew Phalaris 555: perhaps Telemakhos as an old man (at his prime 580; foundation of Akragas) and Emmenes or Khalkiopeus as virtual head of the family. See above, p. 322.

9. Thrasyboulos a young man in 490, born c. 510.

7–10. The generation Thrasydaios, Damareta, Thrasyboulos was older than the children of Gelon and Hieron, and took a part in public affairs. Theron and Xenokrates were therefore perhaps ten years older than Gelon and Hieron. Theron's father cannot have been born much later than c. 560.

11–13. Schol. Pind. Ol. ii. 173. Presumably Kapys and Hippokrates were cousins of Theron, Xenodikos a grandson of Telemakhos.

14–15. See Arist. Rhet. i. 12. The connexion is doubtful.

CHRONOLOGICAL TABLES

1. FOUNDATION DATES

Kyme	. . .	.? 757–756
Naxos	. . .	734
Syracuse	. .	733
Zankle	. . .	? *c.* 730
Leontinoi	. .	729
Katane	. . .	729
Megara	. . .	728
Rhegion	. . .	.?730–720
Sybaris	. . .	720
Mylai	. . .	716
Kroton	. . .	*c.* 708
Taras	. . .	*c.* 706
Poseidonia	. .	? *c.* 700

Metapontion	. .	? 690–680
Gela	. . .	688
Siris	. . .	? 680–670
Lokroi	. . .	*c.* 673
Kaulonia	. .	.? *c.* 675–650
Akrai	. . .	663
Himera	. .	649
Kasmenai	. .	643
Selinus	. .	628
Kamarina	. .	598
Akragas	. .	580
Lipara	. .	580–576
Velia	. . .	*c.* 535

2. GREEKS AND PHOENICIANS

	Greeks in Sicily	Carthaginians in Sicily	Carthaginians in Far West	Greeks in Far West	
648	Himera	..	..	Kolaios	638
				Kyrene	631
628	Selinus	..	..	..	
				Phokaian voyages to Spain: Mainake, Hemeroskopeion, Olbia, Massalia	600
580	Akragas	..	..	..	
580	Pentathlos	..	..	..	
		Malchus' conquests in Sicily	..	..	
571–555	Phalaris	..	..	Alalia	560
			Malchus transferred to Sardinia		
		(Mago)	..	Bias' proposed colony	*c.* 550
				Phokaians' withdrawal from Corsica	*c.* 540
					535
			Hasdrubal and Hamilcar	..	
	War of Liparaians and Etruscans	..	Hasdrubal killed in Sardinia	..	
510	Dorieus	..	..	..	
			Carthage–Rome Treaty	..	509
510–505(?)	Euryleon at Herakleia Minoa	..	..	Spain closed to Greeks	
				Histiaios and Aristagoras still think of Sardinia	500
c. 490	War to avenge Doreius. Appeal to Leonidas	..	Embassy of Darius. *diu varia victoria cum tyrannis dimicatum*	..	
480	Himera	..	..	..	

3. SOUTH ITALIAN COLONIES

Beginning of coinage	. .	*c.* 550?
Destruction of Siris .	. .	*c.* 540?
Battle of Sagra	. . .	*c.* 540
Foundation of Velia .	. .	*c.* 535

Sybarite predominance	. .	*c.* 540–510	⎧ Alliance coins; Siris–Pyxus ⎪ coins? Tarentine coins of ⎨ Akhaian type and stan- ⎪ dard. ⎩
Pythagoras' arrival at Kroton .		*c.* 530	
Pythagoras' ascendancy at Kroton		*c.* 525	
Krotoniate athletic successes .		532–480	
Destruction of Sybaris .	. .	510	
Anti-Pythagorean movement .		*c.* 505	
Krotoniate empire .	. .	*c.* 510–460	Alliance coins of Kroton and Sybaris, &c.
Tyranny of Kleinias at Kroton .		before 494	
Anaxilas tyrant of Rhegion .		*c.* 494–476	

4. SICILIAN TYRANNIES

505/4–498/7.	Kleandros.
498–497.	Hippokrates' accession.
	Securing of Gela.
(496.)	Sack of M. Bubbonia; Sikel retaliation on S. Mauro.
	? Campaign against Leontinoi, on north side of Heraian hills.
(495.)	Siege of Kallipolis; of Naxos; Zankle allies herself with Hippokrates.
(494.)	Siege of Leontinoi.
494–493.	Anaxilas tyrant of Rhegion.
493.	Projected colony of Kale Akte; Skythes' Sikel campaign.
	Samians at Zankle; siege of Zankle; terms with Samians.
492.	Heloros.
	Intervention of Corinth and Korkyra.
492–491.	Settlement of Kamarina.
491.	Ergetion.
491–490.	Hybla. Death of Hippokrates.
	Gelon guardian of Hippokrates' sons.
	Revolt at Gela. Gelon tyrant.
490 or 489.	War to avenge Dorieus. Appeal to Leonidas.
488 (or earlier).	Theron tyrant of Akragas.
488.	Gelon's Olympic victory.
485–484.	Gelon removes to Syracuse.
484–483.	Depopulation of Kamarina.
484 or 483.	Theron seizes Himera.
483–482.	Destruction of Megara and Euboia.
483–480.	Preparations of Carthaginians.
480.	Himera.
478.	Gelon's death; Hieron at Syracuse, Polyzalos at Gela.

SELECT BIBLIOGRAPHY

THE publication of J. Bérard's *Bibliographie topographique des principales cités grecques de l'Italie méridionale et de la Sicile dans l'antiquité* (Paris, 1941) makes any attempt at a full bibliography unnecessary. The following bibliography has two parts:

(i) a short list of the books of which I have made most use. These are frequently quoted by author's name only, or by author and short title.

(ii) short bibliographies of small Greek and Italian settlements in Sicily and south Italy. These make no claim to completeness but give the main references required for Chapters III and IV.

I. PRINCIPAL WORKS CITED

Å. Åkerström, *Der Geometrische Stil in Italien* (Lund, 1943).

V. Arangio Ruiz and A. Olivieri, *Inscriptiones Graecae Siciliae et infimae Italiae ad ius pertinentes* (Milan, 1925).

B. Ashmole, *Late Archaic and Early Classical Greek Sculpture in Sicily and South Italy* (*Proceedings of the British Academy*, xx, 1934).

K. J. Beloch, *Griechische Geschichte*, ed. 2.

J. Bérard, *La colonisation grecque de l'Italie méridionale et de la Sicile* (Paris, 1941).

—— *Bibliographie topographique des principales cités grecques de l'Italie méridionale et de la Sicile* (Paris, 1941).

A. A. Blakeway, 'Prolegomena to the Study of Greek Commerce with Italy, Sicily, and France in the Eighth and Seventh Centuries B.C.', *BSA*, xxxiii. 170 ff. (1935).

C. Blinkenberg, *Fibules grecques et orientales* (Copenhagen, 1926).

—— *La Chronique du temple lindien* (Copenhagen, 1912); and in *Lindos*, ii (Berlin and Copenhagen, 1941).

E. Boehringer, *Die Münzen von Syrakus* (Berlin, 1929).

A. W. Byvanck, *de Magnae Graeciae Historia Antiquissima* (Hague, 1912).

—— 'Untersuchungen zur Chronologie der Funde in Italien aus dem VIII. und VII. vorchristlichen Jahrhundert', *Mnemosyne*, 3rd series, iv, 1937, 181 ff.

H. A. Cahn, *Die Münzen der sizilischen Stadt Naxos* (Basle, 1944).

F. S. Cavallari and A. Holm, *Topografia di Siracusa* (Palermo, 1883); trans. B. Lupus, *Die Stadt Syrakus im Alterthum* (Strasburg, 1887).

E. Ciaceri, *Culti e Miti nella Storia dell' antica Sicilia* (Catania, 1911).

—— *Storia della Magna Grecia* (Milan, vol. i, ed. 2, 1928; ii–iii, 1927, 1932).

G. M. Columba, *I Porti della Sicilia antica.*

W. Darsow, *Sizilische Dachterrakotten* (Berlin, 1938).

F. von Duhn, *Italische Gräberkunde* (Heidelberg, vol. i, 1924; ii, ed. F. Messerschmidt, 1939).

K. Fabricius, *Das antike Syrakus* (*Klio*, Beiheft xxviii, 1932).

E. A. Freeman, *History of Sicily* (4 vols., Oxford, 1891–4).

E. Gàbrici, *Cuma* (*MA*, xxii, 1913).

—— *Il santuario della Malophoros a Selinunte* (*MA*, xxxii, 1927).

—— 'Acropoli di Selinunte', *MA*, xxxiii, 1929, 61 ff.

—— 'Per la storia dell' architettura dorica in Sicilia', *MA*, xxxv, 1933, 137 ff.

M. Gervasio, *Bronzi arcaici e Ceramica geometrica nel Museo Nazionale di Bari* (Bari, 1921).

G. Giannelli, *Culti e Miti della Magna Grecia* (Florence, 1924).

—— *La Magna Grecia da Pitagora a Pirro* (Milan, 1928).

R. Hackforth, 'Carthage and Sicily', *CAH*, iv. 347 ff. (1926).

B. V. Head, *Historia Numorum*, ed. 2 (Oxford, 1911).

A. Holm, *Geschichte Siciliens* (3 vols., Leipzig, 1870–98).

W. Hüttl, *Verfassungsgeschichte von Syrakus* (Prague, 1929).

J. Hulot and G. Fougères, *Sélinonte* (Paris, 1910).

U. Jantzen, *Bronzewerkstätten in Grossgriechenland und Sizilien* (*JdI*, Ergänzungsheft xiii, 1937).

K. Friis Johansen, *Les vases sicyoniens* (Paris and Copenhagen, 1923).

R. Koldewey and O. Puchstein, *Die griechischen Tempel in Unteritalien und Sizilien* (Berlin, 1899).

E. Langlotz, *Zur Zeitbestimmung der strengrotfigurigen Vasenmalerei und der gleichzeitigen Plastik* (Leipzig, 1920).

F. Lenormant, *La Grande-Grèce* (3 vols., Paris, 1881–4).

—— *A travers l'Apulie et la Lucanie* (2 vols., Paris, 1883).

G. Libertini, *Le Isole Eolie* (Florence, 1921).

—— *Il Regio Museo Archeologico di Siracusa* (*Le Guide dei Musei Italiani*, Rome, 1929).

P. Marconi, *Agrigento* (Florence, 1929).

—— 'Studi Agrigentini', *RIASA*, i, 1929, 29 ff., 185 ff., 293 ff.; 'Agrigento', ibid. ii, 1930, 7 ff.

—— *Himera* (Rome, 1931).

—— *Agrigento Arcaica* (Rome, 1933).

M. Mayer, *Apulien vor und während der Hellenisirung* (Leipzig, 1914).

—— 'Metapontum', *RE*, xv, 1326 ff. (1932).

F. Messerschmidt, see F. von Duhn.

S. P. Noe, *A Bibliography of Greek Coin Hoards*, ed. 2 (*Numismatic Notes and Monographs*, no. 78, New York, 1937).

W. Oldfather, 'Lokroi', *RE*, xiii. 1289 ff. (1927).

P. Orsi and F. S. Cavallari, 'Megara Hyblaea', *MA*, i, 1890, 689 ff.

P. Orsi, 'Le necropoli di Licodia Eubea ed i vasi geometrici del quarto periodo Siculo', *RM*, xiii, 1898, 305 ff.

—— 'Camarina', *MA*, ix, 1899, 201 ff.

P. Orsi, 'Siculi e Greci in Leontinoi', *RM*, xv, 1900, 62 ff.

—— 'Camarina. Scavi del 1899 e 1903', *MA*, xiv, 1903, 757 ff.

—— 'Siculi e Greci a Caltagirone', *N Sc*, 1904, 65 ff.

—— *Gela* (*MA*, xvii, 1906).

—— 'Anathemata di una città sicula-greca a Terravecchia di Grammichele', *MA*, xviii, 1907, 121 ff.

—— 'Sepolcri di transizione dalla civiltà Sicula alla Greca', *RM*, xxiv, 1909, 59 ff.

—— 'Di una anonima città siculo-greca a Monte S. Mauro presso Caltagirone', *MA*, xx, 1910, 729 ff.

—— 'Rapporto preliminare sulla quinta campagna di scavi nelle Calabrie durante l'anno 1910', *N Sc*, 1911 Suppl.

—— 'Scavi di Calabria nel 1911', *N Sc*, 1912 Suppl.; 'nel 1913', *N Sc*, 1913 Suppl.

—— 'Caulonia', *MA*, xxiii, 1914, 685 ff.

—— 'Rosarno: Campagna del 1914', *N Sc*, 1917, 37 ff.

—— 'Locri Epizefirii: Campagne di scavo nella necropoli Lucifero negli anni 1914 e 1915', ibid. 101 ff.

—— 'Gli scavi intorno a l'Athenaion di Siracusa', *MA*, xxv, 1918, 353 ff.

—— 'Caulonia. II Memoria', *MA*, xxix, 1923, 409 ff.

—— 'Nuova necropoli greca dei secoli vii–vi a Siracusa', *N Sc*, 1925, 176 ff., 296 ff.

—— 'Le necropoli preelleniche calabresi di Torre Galli e di Canale, Ianchina, Patariti', *MA*, xxxi, 1926, 5 ff.

—— *Templum Apollinis Alaei* (Rome, 1933).

    See also bibliography of P. Orsi in *Paolo Orsi* (Rome, 1935), 353 ff. Most of the articles from *MA*, *N Sc*, and *BPI* quoted in the text without author's name are by Orsi.

B. Pace, 'Arte ed Artisti della Sicilia Antica', *Mem.Acc.Linc.* 1917, 471 ff.

—— *Camarina* (Catania, 1927).

—— *Arte e Civiltà della Sicilia Antica* (vols. i–iii, Milan, Genoa, Rome, and Naples, 1935, 1938, 1946).

E. Pais, *Storia della Sicilia e della Magna Grecia*, vol. i (Turin, 1894).

—— *Ancient Italy* (Chicago, 1908).

L. Pareti, *Studi Siciliani ed Italioti* (Florence, 1914).

H. Payne, *Necrocorinthia* (Oxford, 1931).

—— *Protokorinthische Vasenmalerei* (Berlin, 1933).

T. E. Peet, *The Stone and Bronze Ages in Italy* (Oxford, 1909).

J. Perret, *Siris* (Paris, 1941).

Q. Quagliati, *Il Museo Nazionale di Taranto* (*Itinerari dei Musei e Monumenti d'Italia*, Rome, 1932).

D. Randall-MacIver, *Greek Cities in Italy and Sicily* (Oxford, 1931).

G. M. A. Richter, *The Sculpture and Sculptors of the Greeks* (New Haven, 1929).

D. S. Robertson, *A Handbook of Greek and Roman Architecture*, ed. 2 (Cambridge, 1943).

A. Rumpf, *Chalkidische Vasen* (Berlin and Leipzig, 1927).

W. Smyth, *Sicily and its Adjacent Islands* (1824).

P. N. Ure, *The Origin of Tyranny* (Cambridge, 1922).

—— *Sixth and Fifth Century Pottery from Rhitsona* (Oxford, 1927).

—— *Aryballoi and Figurines from Rhitsona* (Cambridge, 1934).

E. D. van Buren, *Archaic Fictile Revetments in Sicily and Magna Graecia* (London, 1923). References by author's name only are to this book.

—— *Greek Fictile Revetments in the Archaic Period* (London, 1926).

C. Weickert, *Typen der archaischen Architektur in Griechenland und Kleinasien* (Augsburg, 1929).

J. Whatmough, *The Prae-Italic Dialects of Italy*, vol. ii (London, 1933).

—— *The Foundations of Roman Italy* (London, 1937).

J. Whitaker, *Motya* (London, 1921).

E. Wiken, *Die Kunde der Hellenen von dem Lande und den Völkern der Appeninenhalbinsel bis 300 v. Chr.* (Lund, 1937).

P. Wuilleumier, *Tarente* (Paris, 1939).

P. Zancani Montuoro and U. Zanotti-Bianco, 'Heraion alla Foce del Sele', *N Sc*, 1937, 207 ff.

IIA. SMALL TOWNS IN SICILY

Adernò. *N Sc*, 1909, 387–8; 1912, 414 ff.; 1915, 227 ff.; *BPI*, xxxv, 1910, 43. P. Russo, *Adernò* (Catania, 1911); Libertini, *Guida*, 33, fig. 4; Darsow, *Sizilische Dachterrakotten*, 12. Inscriptions, *N Sc*, 1912, loc. cit.; F. Ribezzo, *Neapolis*, i. 372 ff.; *RIGI*, vii. 225 ff. (unreliable); Whatmough, *Prae-Italic Dialects*, ii. 441; *IG*, xiv, p. 135; Freeman, i. 183 ff. P. 132.

Agyrion = S. Filippo d'Agirò. Diod. xvi. 83; *IG*, xiv, p. 138; Freeman, i. 155, 182.

Aitna. *See* Inessa.

Akrillai. Perhaps Chiaramonte Gulfi. P. 102.

Alimena. *N Sc*, 1928, 510 n. Information from Dr. P. Marconi and Mr. D. F. Allen. P. 137.

Ariaiton. P. 113.

Brikinniai = Scordia. P. 121.

Burgio. *N Sc*, 1905, 427 ff. P. 103.

Buscemi. *BPI*, 1898, 164; *N Sc*, 1899, 452. P. 100.

Caltagirone. Molino del Vento, *N Sc*, 1879, 27.
    Bersaglio, *BPI*, 1928, 82 ff.
    Montagna, *N Sc*, 1904, 65 ff.
    S. Luigi, *N Sc*, 1904, 132 ff.; 1905, 440–1; also 1901, 345–6; 1903, 431–3; *RM*, 1898, 344; *BPI*, 1905, 18 ff.; G. Libertini, *MA*, xxviii. 101 ff. Some material of second half of sixth century in Syracuse Museum, other in Liceo, Caltagirone.
    Perticone, *Antichità della Greca Gela Mediterranea, oggi Caltagirone* (Catania, 1857). Some of P.'s collection now in Liceo, Caltagirone. Amore, *La necropoli sicula della Rocca presso Caltagirone* (Caltagirone, 1898). P. 113.

Caltanisetta. *N Sc*, 1879, 231; 1880, 502; 1881, 250; 1884, 444 ff.; *ASS*, N.S. vii, 120 ff.; Freeman, i. 122; Landolina, *Osservazioni sul sito delle antiche città di Nisa e Petelia* (Palermo, 1845); Bertolo, *Caltanisetta e suoi dintorni* (Caltanisetta, 1877). P. 139.

Canicatti. *N Sc*, 1879, 231. P. 139.

Castellaccio (HIMERA). *N Sc*, 1936, 462 ff. (I. B. Marconi); L. Mauceri, *Sopra una acropoli pelasgica esistente nei dintorni di Termini Imerese* (1896). P. 142.

Castelluccio. *N Sc*, 1891, 348 ff.; *BPI*, 1892, 13–14. P. 98.

Castronovo. *N Sc*, 1930, 555 ff.; 1879, 235. Pace, *ACSA*, i. 55. P. 420.

Cefalù (KEPHALOIDION). *N Sc*, 1929, 273 ff.; *CIL*, x, p. 767; *IG*, xiv, p. 60; Freeman, i. 139 ff. P. 142.

Centorbi, CENTURIPE. *See* KENTORIPA.

Chiaramonte Gulfi. *N Sc*, 1898, 38; *BPI*, 1898, 164; Pace, *Camarina*, 116–18; Malfi, *Ricerche sulle antichità di Gulfi* (Caltagirone, 1889, with Appendix, 1891) and *Cenni storici sulla città di Chiaramonte Gulfi*. Collection made by Barone Malfi di San Giovanni, now in Syracuse Museum.

   Perhaps AKRILLAI; see p. 102.

Cocolonazzo di Mola. *N Sc*, 1919, 360 ff. P. 45.

Comisò. *N Sc*, 1912, 368; 1915, 214; 1937, 456 ff. (P. E. Arias); Pace, *Camarina*, 32, 119 ff.; *ACSA*, i. 183. P. 103.

Contessa Entellina (ENTELLA). P. 143.

DAEDALIUM = Palma di Montechiaro(?). P. 138.

Dessueri. *MA*, xxi. 349 ff.; *N Sc*, 1936, 368 ff. (P. E. Arias). P. 112.

ECHETLA. *See* Grammichele. P. 122.

EKNOMOS = Licata. P. 139.

ENGYON. Near Nicosia (?). P. 137.

ENNA. *N Sc*, 1931, 373 ff.; 1915, 232. *CIL*, x, p. 736; Freeman, i. 170 ff. P. 136.

ENTELLA = Contessa Entellina. P. 143.

ERGETION. Freeman, i. 153; ii. 120; Pais, *Ancient Italy*, ch. x. P. 403.

ERYKE. Pais, *Ancient Italy*, ch. ix. P. 125.

ERYX. *N Sc*, 1935, 294 ff. (Gàbrici); 1881, 70; 1882, 361; 1883, 254 ff.

EUBOIA. P. 128.

Favara. *N Sc*, 1898, 462. P. 125.

Finocchito. *BPI*, 1894, 23 ff.; 1897, 157 ff.; *N Sc*, 1896, 242; 1897, 69; 1900, 210. Blakeway, *BSA*, xxxiii. 189 ff.; Åkerström, 17 ff. P. 97.

GALARIA. Perhaps San Mauro. Pais, *Ancient Italy*, 142. P. 116.

Gangi. P. 137.

Giarratana. *N Sc*, 1898, 37; 1892, 324 n. 2; *BPI*, 1900, 267; Peet, 465.

Grammichele. *MA*, vii. 201 ff.; xviii. 121 ff.; *BPI*, 1900, 276 ff.; 1905, 96 ff.; *N Sc*, 1920, 336–7 (accounts in earlier years of *N Sc* resumed in *MA*); van Buren, *AFR*, 21.

   Perhaps ECHETLA. P. 122.

HADRANON = Adernò. P. 132.
HELORON. *N Sc*, 1899, 241 ff.; Freeman, ii. 17 ff.; Aelian, *NA*, xii. 30. P. 102.
HYBLA HERAIA = Ragusa. P. 107.
HYBLA MAIOR = Melilli. P. 19.
HYBLA MINOR = Paternò. P. 130.

INA = Vindicari. P. 103.
INESSA = S. Maria di Licodia. P. 130.
Ispica. *N Sc*, 1905, 431 ff.; *IG*, xiv, p. 40; Freeman, ii. 26. P. 109.

KALLIPOLIS (perhaps Mascali). P. 382.
KASMENAI. Pp. 102, 103.
KENTORIPA. G. Libertini, *Centuripe* (1926); Orsi, *RM*, 1909, 90 ff.; *N Sc*, 1907, 491 ff.; *IG*, xiv, p. 136; *CIL*, x, p. 719; Freeman, i. 156 ff.; Ansaldi, *I monumenti dell' antica Centuripe* (1851). Mammano Collection, made at Centuripe, now in Syracuse Museum (Libertini, op. cit. 101); some late-sixth-century material in Palermo. P. 133.

Licata = EKNOMOS (later PHINTIAS). P. 139.
Licodia. *RM*, 1898, 305 ff.; 1909, 59 ff.; cf. 1899, 172 ff.; *N Sc*, 1897, 327; 1902, 219 ff.; 1903, 435 f.; 1905, 441 ff.; 1909, 386; *IG*, xiv. 254. MORGANTINA (?). P. 126.

Magazzinazzi. *N Sc*, 1912, 363. P. 109.
MAKTORION. Freeman, i. 409; Pais, *Ancient Italy*, 138. P. 113.
Mazzarino. *N Sc*, 1912, 454. P. 113.
Melilli = HYBLA. *BPI*, 1891, 53 ff.; Freeman, i. 388. P. 19.
MENAI = Mineo. P. 125.
Mendolito. *See* Adernò.
Militello. *See* Ossini. P. 122.
Milocca. P. 143.
Mineo = MENAI. *N Sc*, 1899, 70; 1901, 346; 1903, 436 ff.; 1905, 438; 1909, 383 ff.; 1920, 337; *BPI*, 1900, 275, 284. Freeman, i. 152; ii. 361; Schubring, 'Die Landschaft des Menas und Erykes nebst Leontinoi' (*Zeitschr. d. Gesellschaft für Erdkunde*, ix. 365 ff.). P. 125.
Mistretta = AMESTRATOS. Pace, *ACSA*, ii. 115, fig. 108. P. 142.
Modica. *N Sc*, 1915, 212 ff.; 1896, 243; 1905, 430; 1907, 485; 1912, 366 (Roman); *BPI*, 1900, 166 ff.; Freeman, i. 150; Peet, 465; *IG*, xiv, p. 40. P. 109.
Molinello. *N Sc*, 1902, 411 ff.; 631 ff.
Monte Bubbonia. *N Sc*, 1905, 447 ff.; 1907, 497 f.; *MA*, xx. 744; van Buren, *AFR*, 44–5. P. 119.
Monte Casale. Perhaps KASMENAI. P. 100.
Monte Iudica. *N Sc*, 1907, 489. P. 122.
MORGANTINA. Perhaps Licodia. P. 125.
MOTYE. J. S. Whitaker, *Motya* (London, 1921). Cf. B. Pace, *N Sc*, 1915, 431 ff.; 1917, 347 f.; *AJA*, 1934, 490, fig. 15.
Mussomeli. E. Gàbrici, 'Polizello' (*Atti R. Acc. Palermo*, xiv, 1925); *Ripostoglio di bronzo della Sicilia* (Palermo, 1925); *N Sc*, 1881, 68. P. 140.

Naro. P. 139.

NEETON = Noto. P. 103.

Nicosia. *N Sc*, 1899, 71. P. 137.

Niscemi. *BPI*, 1927, 43 ff. P. 113.

Noto. *N Sc*, 1897, 69 ff.; also 1891, 348; 1894, 152; 1896, 212; 1933, 197; *BPI*, 1889, 217 f.; *RM*, 1898, 338; *IG*, xiv, p. 38.
   NEETON. P. 103.

OMPHAKE. Pp. 112, 116.

Ossini. *RM*, 1909, 73 ff.; *N Sc*, 1903, 440; 1904, 374; Blakeway, *BSA*, xxxiii. 189; Johansen, *VS*, 89. P. 122.

Palma di Montechiaro. *MA*, xxxvii. 585 ff. (G. Caputo); *BPI*, 1928, 45 ff.
   DAEDALIUM (?). P. 138.

Pantalica. *MA*, ix. 33 ff.; xxi. 301 ff.; *BPI*, 1889, 162 ff.; *N Sc*, 1895, 268, 326; G. Säflund, *Studi Etruschi*, xii. 45 ff.; Åkerström, 15. P. 95.

Partanna. P. 143.

Paternò. *RM*, 1909, 84 ff.; *N Sc*, 1903, 441; 1909, 386; 1915, 226; *CIL*, x, no. 7013; Freeman, i. 160, 512 ff.; Blakeway, *BSA*, xxxiii. 188; van Buren, *AFR*, 25.
   HYBLA. P. 129.

Patti. P. 142.

Pergusa. *RM*, 1898, 345 f. P. 136.

PIAKOS. Perhaps S. Maria li Plachi. P. 135.

Piano dei Casazzi. *N Sc*, 1907, 488 ff. Pp. 126, 379.

Ragusa. *N Sc*, 1892, 321 ff.; 1897, 278 ff.; 1899, 402 ff.; 1912, 363; *RM*, 1898, 338 f.; Freeman, i. 162.
   HYBLA HERAIA. P. 107.

Randazzo. G. E. Rizzo, *RM*, 1900, 237 ff.; *Antichità Greche dell' Etna* (Adernò, 1905); *N Sc*, 1907, 495 ff. Material in Museo Vagliasindi, Randazzo, and in Palermo Museum. Gàbrici, *Atti R. Acc. Palermo*, serie 3, xi. 10, pl. ii. 4.
   Possibly TISSA. P. 134.

Ràvanusa. *MA*, xxxvi. 621 ff. (P. Mingazzini); *N Sc*, 1928, 499 ff.; 1930, 411 ff. Other early-fifth-century material, lekythos Palermo 996, Haspels, *ABL*, pl. 19. 5; bronze mirror-handle, Jantzen, pl. 22. 91. P. 138.

Salemi. P. 143.

Sambuca. P. 143.

S. Angelo Muxaro. P. Orsi, 'La Necropoli di S. Angelo Muxaro' (*Atti R.Acc. Palermo*, xvii, 1932). P. 139.

S. Cataldo. *BPI*, 1927, 50 ff. P. 126.

San Mauro. *MA*, xx. 729 ff.; *N Sc*, 1879, 27 f., 52 f., 82; 1904, 373; 1915, 225 f.; *BPI*, 1927, 38 ff.; Pais, *Ancient Italy*, ch. xii; van Buren, *AFR*, 49 ff. Pp. 115, 128.

S. Margherita Belice. *N Sc*, 1931, 400.

S. Maria di Licodia. *N Sc*, 1903, 442; *CIL*, x, p. 719; *IG*, xiv. 573; Freeman, i. 148; ii. 322; van Buren, *AFR*, 25.
   Probably AITNA-INESSA. P. 130.

S. Maria di Niscemi. *N Sc*, 1900, 248.

Scicli. *RM*, 1898, 339 f.; *N Sc*, 1886, 467. Freeman, ii. 27. P. 103.

Scifazzo. *RM*, 1898, 328 ff. P. 127.

Scordia. *N Sc*, 1899, 276 f.; *BPI*, 1928, 79 ff.; Libertini, *Guida*, 62, fig. 13; Orsi, 'Insigne scoperta a m. Casale presso Scordia' (*Aretusa*, 1 June 1922). P. 121.

SEGESTA. *N Sc*, 1929, 295 ff. P. 143.

Serra Orlando. *N Sc*, 1884, 350; 1909, 66; 1912, 449 ff.; 1915, 233 f.; *Riv.st. ant.* v. 52 ff.; Arangio-Ruiz and Olivieri, 128 f. P. 136.

Spaccaforno. *BPI*, 1897, 119; *N Sc*, 1905, 427; Freeman, ii. 25. P. 103.

TISSA. Freeman, i. 156. P. 135.

Tremenzano. *BPI*, 1892, 84 ff.; *N Sc*, 1891, 353 f. P. 98.

TRINAKIA (f. l. in Diod. xii. 29). Pais, *Ancient Italy*, ch. xi. P. 135.

Troina. P. 137.

Vassalagi. *N Sc*, 1881, 69, 174; 1905, 449 ff. P. 139.

Vicari. P. 143.

Vittoria. P. 104; also *N Sc*, 1891, 347 (Roman).

Vizzini. *BPI*, 1888, 167 ff.; *RM*, 1898, 343; *N Sc*, 1902, 213 ff.; Pais, *Ancient Italy*, 136. P. 128.

XUTHIA. Perhaps Sortino. P. 128.

IIB. SMALL TOWNS IN SOUTH ITALY

Acerenza. P. 151.

AMINAIA. P. 158.

Anzi. *N Sc*, 1900, 34; Lacava, *Metaponto*, 28. P. 150.

ARINTHE (Rende?). P. 156.

Armento. *N Sc*, 1901, 266. P. 151.

ARTEMISION. P. 156.

Atena Lucana. *N Sc*, 1901, 498 ff.; 1926, 252 ff. Lenormant, *A travers l'Apulie et la Lucanie*, ii. 86; Lacava, *Istoria di Atena*. P. 154.

Banzi. *N Sc*, 1932, 395; 1936, 428 ff.

Belvedere di Spinello. P. 161.

BLANDA. Livy xxiv. 20. Wrongly placed at Tortora by Lacava, *Blanda, Lao e Tebe Lucana* (Napoli, 1891); Pliny, *NH* iii. 72, places it on the Bruttian coast south of Laos, but this is in irreconcilable conflict with Livy, who names it with a number of Lucanian towns all in the northern part of their territory.

BRENTESION = Brindisi. *N Sc*, 1923, 207 f., and see Index to *N Sc*, 1876–1930, for unimportant references. Johansen, *VS*, 89.

BRYSTAKIA (Umbriatico). P. 156.

Cariati. *N Sc*, 1900, 604. Lenormant, *GG*, i. 372, identifies as KHONE. P. 160.

Ceglie Messapica. P. 148.

Cirella = KERILLOI. P. 155.

Cossa (Cassano). P. 156.
Croccia Cognato. P. 150.
Curinga. *N Sc*, 1916, 186. P. 162.
Cutro = KYTERION. P. 156.

DRYS. P. 156.

ERIMON. P. 156.

Faggiano. P. 147.
Ferrandina. *N Sc*, 1900, 38; 1935, 383 ff.
Francavilla Marittima. *N Sc*, 1879, 155; 1936, 77 ff. P. 157.

Gallichio. *N Sc*, 1901, 269. P. 153.
Gravina. *N Sc*, 1901, 217 ff. P. 151.
Gravinola. P. 147.
Grottole. *N Sc*, 1901, 263 f. P. 150.
GRUMENTUM. Lacava, *Metaponto*, 91. P. 151.

IXIAS. P. 156.

KERILLOI = Cirella. P. 155.
KHONE. P. 159.
KYTERION (Cutro). P. 156.

Laino. E. Galli, *SMG*, 1929, 155 ff.; *N Sc*, 1931, 655 ff. (N. Catanuto). Galli quotes a manuscript *Reflessioni sull' antica Tebe Lucana* (1856) by L. Grimaldi, and Lucio Cappelli's *Annali Civili del Regno di Napoli* (1855). Excavations were then made on behalf of the Cappelli family and some of the material is still preserved in their collection at Morano; other in Reggio Antiquarium. See also Lenormant, *GG*, i. 259 n. P. 205.
LAMETINOI. P. 162.
Leporano. *N Sc*, 1903, 33 ff. (cf. *JHS*, 1932, 188 f.). Johansen, *VS*, 101, no. 70 = Payne, *NC*, no. 13. Most of the material is unpublished. P. 147.
LEUKOPETRA. P. 170.

MAKALLA. P. 159.
MALANIOS. P. 156.
Malvito. P. 157.
Massafra. P. 147.
Matera. *N Sc*, 1897, 203 ff.; 1900, 345; 1925, 257 ff.; 1930, 552 ff.; 1935, 107 ff., 380 ff.; 1936, 84 ff. P. 151.
MENEKINE (Mendicino?). P. 156.
METAURON. *N Sc*, 1902, 126 ff.; van Buren, *AFR*, 43 f.; *MA*, xxix. 459; *Bull. Metr. Mus.* 1925, 14 ff.; Strabo 256. P. 168.
Mileto. *N Sc*, 1921, 485 ff.; 1939, 141 ff. (Roman).
Monteiasi. P. 147.
Montescaglioso. P. 151.

Nicotera. S. Ferri, *N Sc*, 1928, 479; P. Orsi, *SMG*, 1926–7, 31 ff. See also Bérard, *Bibliographie*, 65, s.v. Medma. P. 167.

NINAIA (perhaps S. Donato di Ninea). P. 156.

Nocera Terinese. *N Sc*, 1916, 335 ff.

Oliveto Citra. *N Sc*, 1930, 229 ff.

Oppido Mamertino. P. 167.

PATYKOS. P. 156.

PETELIA (Strongoli). *N Sc*, 1880, 68 ff., 163 f., 501 f.; 1881, 67 f., 97, 197, 331 f.; 1886, 171 f.; 1894, 18 ff.; 1926, 445; 1939, 147 f. P. 161.

Pietrapaola. *N Sc*, 1900, 605; 1901, 27. P. 160.

Pisticci. *N Sc*, 1887, 332; 1902, 312 ff.; 1903, 262 ff.; 1904, 196 ff.; 1935, 389; Lenormant, *A travers l'Apulie et la Lucanie*, i. 336; FR, iii. 160. P. 150.

Pomarico Vecchio. *N Sc*, 1926, 331. P. 150.

PYXIS. P. 156.

Rossano. P. Orsi, *Boll. d'Arte*, 1919, 95 ff.; *N Sc*, 1934, 459 ff. (N. Catanuto). P. 157.

Sala Consilina. *N Sc*, 1896, 171 ff., 383; 1897, 163 ff.; *BPI*, 1899, 42 ff.; *CVA Paris, Petit Palais*, pll. 1–5, pp. 1–5. P. 154.

S. Agata all' Esaro. *IG*, xiv. 643. P. 157.

S. Arcangelo. *N Sc*, 1932, 377. P. 153.

S. Giorgio sotto Taranto. *N Sc*, 1879, 348. P. 147.

S. Lorenzo del Vallo. *Boll. d'Arte*, xxix, 1935, 228 ff. (G. Pesce). P. 157.

S. Marco Roggiano. *N Sc*, 1897, 357; *Boll. d'Arte*, xxix, 1935, 231 ff. (G. Pesce).

S. Mauro Forte. *N Sc*, 1882, 119; 1884, 379 ff.; 1892, 209; 1893, 53, 338; 1895, 399; 1901, 264; *IG*, xiv. 652. P. 151.

S. Stefano di Rogliano. *N Sc*, 1932, 383.

Serrarossa. *Boll. d'Arte*, xxviii, 1935, 516 ff. (G. Pesce).

SESTION. P. 156.

SIBERINE (S. Severina). P. 156.

SKIDROS. Pp. 155, 204.

SKYLLAION. P. 170.

SKYLLETION. P. 162.

Tarsia. *N Sc*, 1879, 77; 1880, 162. P. 157.

Tiriolo. *N Sc*, 1881, 172 ff.; 1882, 390; 1883, 249; 1898, 174 ff.; 1926, 329; 1927, 336 ff. Pais, *Ricerche Storiche*, ii. 63; 'Ancora sulla posizione di Terina' (*Historia*, vi. 388 ff.).

Torre Galli. *MA*, xxxi. 5 ff. Pp. 165 ff.

Tortora. *SMG*, 1929, 192; *N Sc*, 1921, 467 (Orsi); *N Sc*, 1891, 137; 1897, 176 (G. Patroni). Lacava, *Blanda, Lao e Tebe Lucana* (Napoli, 1891). P. 206.

Tropea. *N Sc*, 1927, 334; 1932, 384 ff.

Verzino. *N Sc*, 1897, 356. P. 161.

INDEX

See also list of sites on pp. 490–6

K k